# MODERN SPORTING RIFLE CARTRIDGES
## By Wayne Van Zwoll

D1616569

## STOEGER PUBLISHING COMPANY

**TITLE:** Modern Sporting Rifle Cartridges
**EDITOR:** William S. Jarrett
**COVER ART DESIGN:** Ray Wells
**BOOK DESIGN AND LAYOUT:** Lesley A. Notorangelo/DSS
**PROJECT MANAGER:** Dominick S. Sorrentino
**ELECTRONIC IMAGING:** Lesley A. Notorangelo/DSS

Published by Stoeger Publishing Company
5 Mansard Court
Wayne, New Jersey 07470

ISBN: 0-88317-213-5
Library of Congress Catalog Card No.: 98-061494
Manufactured in the United States of America

Distributed to the book trade and to the sporting goods trade by Stoeger Industries, 5 Mansard Court, Wayne, New Jersey 07470

In Canada, distributed to the book trade and to the sporting goods trade by Stoeger Canada, Ltd., 1801 Wentworth Street, Unit 16, Whitby, Ontario L1N 8R6.

# ACKNOWLEDGEMENTS

Many people and companies contributed to this book. The people listed here--and others not included--have my sincere thanks. I've learned much from all of them and value many as friends. The companies on this roster have not only shared their expertise and data but have actively promoted and defended the shooting sports. They've earned our patronage.

| | |
|---|---|
| Don and Norma Allen | Accurate Arms |
| Art Alphin | A-Square Company, Inc. |
| Linda Blackburn | Alliant Techsystems |
| Adam Braverman | Arnold Arms |
| Randy and Coni Brooks | Barnes Bullets, Inc. |
| John Champion | Black Hills Ammunition, Inc. |
| Paul Coil | Dakota Arms, Inc. |
| Chub Eastman | Federal Cartridge Co. |
| D'Arcy Echols | Hodgdon Powder Co. |
| Doug Engh | Hornady Manufacturing Co. |
| Mike Fine | Lazzeroni Arms Co. |
| Chris Hodgdon | Nosler, Inc. |
| Jeff and Kristi Hoffman | PMC Ammunition |
| Allan Jones | Remington Arms Co. |
| Mike Jordan | Sierra Bullets |
| Mike Larsen | Speer/CCI (Blount) |
| John Lazzeroni | Swift Bullet Co. |
| Marty Liggins | Winchester Ammunition |
| Larry McGhee | Wolfe Publishing Co. |
| Tom McGovern | |
| Bob Nosler | |
| Dick Quesenberry | |
| Lee Reed | |
| Dave Scovill | |
| Tom Shepherd | |

# ABOUT THE AUTHOR

**W**ayne van Zwoll has been writing about firearms and big game hunting for nearly 25 years. More than 300 of his articles have appeared in nearly every major shooting and outdoors publication. His previous book, **America's Great Gun Makers** (Stoeger, 1992) exemplifies the great attention to detail and accuracy evident in **Modern Sporting Rifle Cartridges**. Wayne has also authored two books on big game hunting: **Mastering Mule Deer** and **Elk Rifles, Cartridges and Hunting Tactics**. His columns (on handloading, optics and big game rifles and cartridges) appear regularly in **Rifle, Rifle Shooter, Bugle** and **Mule Deer**. He is also a contributing editor at **Field & Stream** and **American Hunter** and writes regularly for **Shooter's Bible**.

Wayne now divides his time between Utah, where he is at work on a doctorate at Utah State University, and his adopted home state of Washington. He has served as editor of **Kansas Wildlife** and as one of the first field directors for the Rocky Mountain Elk Foundation. His hunts have taken him to Canada, Alaska, Mexico and Africa, but he enjoys most the high country and forests of the coastal and intermountain West. When he's not staring at a computer screen, Wayne is apt to be at the range testing new loads, or hiking the hills in search of big elk or mule deer.

# INTRODUCTION

This book is intended as a reference work for seasoned shooters and as a beginner's guide. It may be the first to combine descriptions of modern rifle cartridges with published load data from all major sources and comprehensive ballistics tables for ammunition manufactured in the U.S. It will hopefully prove a launchpad for anyone eager to know more about sporting rifle cartridges and ballistics. No one book can hold the wealth of information available concerning the history, development and performance of rifle cartridges. This book not only distills what I've considered the most useful and intriguing facts from many sources, it offers a list of other books that can add even more detail by topic.

This is not a reloading manual. Though it provides data that indicates the potential of popular commercial and wildcat cartridges in addition to basic instruction on handloading procedure, wise shooters will also consult the manuals published by Accurate Arms, A-Square, Barnes, Hodgdon, Hornady, Nosler, Speer and Sierra for more complete listings of charge weights and bullet types. All loads published here are safe *maximums* as determined by the tester. Test conditions vary, as do rifle barrels. The standard procedure when loading for a new cartridge is to start at 10 percent below listed maximum charge weights and work gradually toward higher performance. NEITHER STOEGER PUBLISHING COMPANY NOR I CAN BE RESPONSIBLE FOR ANY INJURIES OR MECHANICAL PROBLEMS CAUSED BY HANDLOADING, EVEN WITH THE LOADS LISTED IN THIS BOOK.

As with any publication that includes partial lists, this one cannot claim to be a complete work. The cartridges featured are modern (smokeless) rifle cartridges intended for sporting use. Such blackpowder favorites as the .38-55 and .45-70, which survived the 1890s transition to smokeless propellant and were chambered well into the 20th century, have all earned their place. Blackpowder cartridges that withered shortly after smokeless entered the market--the .32-32 Remington and .50-95 Winchester among them--were not included. Few decisions were that easy, however. The .32-20 was developed in 1882 for Winchester's Model 73 rifle, subsequently appeared in a host of other rifles, and is still factory loaded. But its utility as a hunting cartridge remains limited. The .312 bullet is not standard for any other rifle round and is now regarded primarily as a revolver cartridge. Arguments could be made in support of the .32-40 and .40-65, both of which plugged along into the 1930s. Sadly, space constraints forced the drawing of sometimes fine and almost arbitrary lines. How many people does the reader know who own .32-40s or who shoot deer with a .40-65?

Lumping cartridges into categories is likewise difficult. The .338-06 is considered a wildcat by most shooters; yet it's been classified as a factory-loaded round ever since A-Square first offered it commercially. Today, it can be found under the common factory loadings. Since this book is primarily addressed to American shooters, it includes mainly cartridges designed in the U.S. So the 6.5x55, which is a military round, may look out of place next to the 6.5 Remington Magnum. And yet American deer hunters have used 6.5x55 Swedish Mausers since the first surplus rifles came over. Likewise, Norma has been loading sporting ammunition for it, and now the 6.5x55 is both factory-chambered and produced commercially by U.S. firms. The same holds true for the 7x57 and, save for commercial production, the 8x57. Charles Newton's .22 Savage High Power, on the other hand, is as red-white-and-blue as they come; but it's been long dead in the U.S. and can be imported only by Norma as the 5.6x52R. The 9.3x62 is also found in the Norma section, although it is now loaded in the U.S. by A-Square as well. A-Square properly has its own section for cartridges developed in-house and others like the .375 JRS that was adopted for commercial production solely by the company. Popular cartridges that have been recently chambered in American rifles, the .308 Norma Magnum among them, appear throughout this book with American factory cartridges, though most (or all) of the ammunition is imported.

The list of big-bore African cartridges could have been tacked onto the A-Square list, too, because it's the only U.S. company still producing those traditional British and old wildcat favorites. With well-deserved plaudits to Art Alphin of A-Square for making them available to the shooting public, however, they have been kept separate from the rounds born at A-Square. Two British cartridges *not* currently loaded in or imported to the U.S. have been included, mainly because they have played such an important role in African hunting, and because rifles for them are still quite plentiful.

Some cartridges appear to be missing altogether. The .44 Remington Magnum, for example, was developed mainly for use in revolvers, whereas this book is about rifle cartridges. Granted, the .44 has been chambered in rifles, but its potential does not lie there and it cannot compete against cartridges designed for long barrels. The same can be said of the .256 and .357 Magnums. The .221 Fireball was tough to leave out because it performs so well in rifles. Suffice it to say that round will do in a pistol about what the .222 Remington will do in a

rifle with the same powders (*not* the same charges) and bullets. Dropping the .30 Carbine was easier because it is a military round with no practical sporting application. The same goes for the 7.62x39. Military cartridges with a place in the field or at the target range earned a spot provided they were made available to American shooters.

Choosing wildcats for inclusion was perhaps the toughest job of all, because there are so many of them--and they are so *useful.* A cynic could argue that *no* wildcats are necessary, and that so many rifle cartridges are commercially loaded there's ballistic redundancy at every turn. But to most serious shooters precise matching of cartridge to application has always seemed worth a new design. The lure of higher performance levels, moreover, affects shooters just as it does automobile buffs who tear apart a perfectly good engine in order to install a different camshaft. Cartridges for the wildcat list were chosen on the basis of popularity and longevity as well as their utility. Some not featured are indeed excellent rounds; but perhaps they resemble too closely a factory round or another wildcat with a richer history.

The ballistics tables in the rear section of this book are included for reference and comparison. Because new factory loads are introduced every year, while others are dropped, these lists will change. But with some exceptions, data for each load stays essentially the same year to year. Tables for bullets only are taken from my previous book, "*Elk Rifles, Cartridges and Hunting Tactics,*" and can be used to determine the downrange performance of wildcat rounds, along with those factory-loaded cartridges that don't register on a chronograph what company charts claim they should. All one needs to know are the bullet's ballistic coefficient and velocity.

*Wayne Van Zwoll, August 1998*

The numbers and words used to describe ammunition can confuse even veteran shooters. Some terms make sense; others seem like nonsense. Cartridge nomenclature dates back to early muzzle-loading times, before anyone had cartridges. Like rifle ammunition, shotshells are named according to bore size. Gauge is an ancient measure of bore diameter: the number indicating the number of bore-size lead balls that weigh a pound. The bigger the bore, the smaller the gauge. Balls that fit a 16-gauge shotgun bore weigh an ounce apiece; those that fit a 20-gauge weigh less because the bore is smaller in diameter; hence more small balls are required to equal one pound. An exception is the .410, which is actually a caliber designation (.410-inch bore diameter). A .410 is 67 1/2 gauge. Sometimes we substitute "bore" for "gauge" when referring to a shotgun, as in "a 12-bore double."

Common shotgun gauges are 10, 12, 16, 20 and 28. During the 19th century, "punt guns" (really cannons mounted in small boats) of 4 gauge and even larger were used to kill waterfowl for market. Early African explorers shot 8-bore muskets, launching 1250 grain bullets at 1500 feet per second and generating three tons of muzzle energy.

Powder charge also appears on shotshell labels. Charge is given in "drams equivalent," a reference to early times when the propellant was black powder. A dram is a unit of weight; 16 drams equal one ounce. When smokeless powder appeared at the turn of the century--a type known as "bulk powder"--it could be loaded in place of black powder "bulk for bulk" (not by weight). "Dense" smokeless powders that came later took up much less space in the shell, so neither charge bulk nor weight matched that of blackpowder loads. A "3 1/4 dram equivalent" charge says nothing about the smokeless fuel in a modern shotshell, except that ballistically the load approximates the performance of a 3 1/4-dram blackpowder charge.

The other numbers on a shell box labeled--specifically, "1 1/8" and "6"--refer to shot weight (1 1/8 ounces) and size (#6). Lead birdshot ranges in size from number 12 ("dust shot") to BB. A #12 pellet is just .05 inch in diameter, while a BB is .18. (This is not the same as a steel .177 air rifle BB.) Buckshot in sizes 4, 3, 2, 1, 0, 00, and 000 range from .24 to .36 inch. One ounce of #9 birdshot contains 585 pellets, while an ounce of 00 buck has only 8. Since steel shot became mandatory for waterfowl, several new shot sizes have appeared (or been resurrected), from 7 to F. These were developed to duplicate the performance of lead pellets commonly used for ducks and geese.

Labels on boxes of rifle and handgun cartridges usually specify bore diameter and parent (originator), as well as the name of the manufacturer. Thus, ".270 Winchester ammunition produced by Remington," or ".257 Roberts cartridges by Federal." This is important to know because a box of .300 Winchester Magnum rounds was not always the same as a box of "Winchester .300 Magnums." For some time after its debut in 1925, the .300 Holland and Holland Magnum was the only commercial .300 magnum around, so "Winchester" on the box meant only that the .300 H&H cartridges inside were manufactured by Winchester. In 1944 Roy Weatherby came up with a different .300 magnum, and Winchester introduced still another in 1963.

Incidentally, the term "magnum" simply means that the cartridge generates extra-high energy or velocity. But some magnums are not as potent as others with the same bore diameter. And some rounds not called magnums (though they may come from magnum cases) outperform cartridges bearing a magnum label--for example, the 7mm STW (which stands for "Shooting Times Westerner") vs. the 7mm Remington Magnum. "Belted magnum" refers to the belt in front of the extractor groove found on cartridges derived from the .300 H&H or .378 Weatherby case. Almost all magnum rifle cartridges have been fashioned from the .300 Holland, which itself came from the

.375 H&H around 1912. The belt is a headspacing device and, like the "high brass" on heavy-load shotshells, has nothing to do essentially with structural reinforcement. A belt is a "stop" similar to the shoulder, case mouth and rim (*flange*, in British parlance) on other rounds. It prevents the case from entering the chamber too far and then separating under pressure when fired.

Magnum handgun rounds like the .357 and .44 magnums are much smaller than the .300 H&H and are not belted. Magnum shotshells may be longer than standard shells, or they may simply contain a heavier charge of shot. Standard-length magnum shotshells commonly produce *lower* velocity than non-magnums, but additional shot means denser patterns. The British equivalent to "magnum" is "Nitro Express," which brings to mind nitroglycerine, an explosive used in some gunpowders, while also evoking the image of a fast-moving train. The term applies mainly to rifle cartridges designed for thick-skinned African game. ("Black Powder Express" predated it in the late 1800s). Dual numbers on British cartridges, by the way, signify parent cartridge and bore in that order; i.e., *reverse* order from American custom. Thus, a .577/.500 uses a .500 bullet.

The numbers that designate caliber can be confusing because in rifle and handgun bores there exist two diameters: one for the bore and one for the grooves cut as rifling to spin the bullet. The bore diameter (measured across the lands between grooves) is less than the groove diameter, and either number could be used as "caliber." The .250 Savage and .257 Roberts, for example, have bullets of the same diameter: .257 inch. That's groove diameter. But both .250 and .257 rifle bores have a .250 land diameter. The .270 Winchester measures .277 across the grooves; .300s are .308 across the grooves, as are the .308 Winchester and .308 Norma Magnum. Centerfire .22s--from the .222 Remington to the .225 Winchester--use the same .224 bullets. Bullets for the .303 British mike .311, for the .338 Winchester and .340 Weatherby Magnums .338, and for the .350 Remington and .358 Norma Magnums .358. The .243 Winchester, .375 H&H Magnum and .458 Winchester Magnum are named for their bullet, or groove, diameters.

What about such two-digit designations as .22 Hornet, .30 Carbine and .35 Remington? These numbers simply indicate bore diameter in hundredths, not thousandths of an inch. By adding a zero, you'll often emerge with the name of a similar cartridge and a close approximation of the bullet diameter; for example, the .220 Swift (.224), .300 Savage (.308) and .350 Remington Magnum (.358). Sometimes this rule doesn't hold, witness the .38 Special, which uses the same .357 bullet as the .357 Magnum. *Two* two-digit numbers usually indicate the cartridge is an old one, with the second pair indicating the number of grains of black powder in the original load. The .30-30, for example, was charged with 30 grains (weight) of black powder before being loaded with smokeless, with 437 grains equaling one ounce. Some old cartridges wear a third set of numbers, designating bullet weight in grains, as in .45-70-405, a standard designation for the official U.S. Army cartridge from 1873 to 1892.

The best-known exception to the paired double-digit tradition is the .30-06. A 30-caliber cartridge adopted by the U.S. Army for its new Springfield rifle in 1906, it replaced the .30-03 and has since spawned several "wildcat" (not commercially manufactured) rounds like the .338-06, which is the .30-06 case "necked up" to .33 caliber. Some wildcats, such as the .25-06, have gone commercial. The .270 Winchester and .280 Remington derive from the '06, as does the .35 Whelen, named after Colonel Townsend Whelen, a firearms authority during the 1920s.

Other old cases have produced modern cartridges. The 7x57, circa 1892, was revamped in the 1930s to create the .257 Roberts and, later, the 6mm Remington. The .308 Winchester case fathered the .243 and .358. Remington's 7mm-08 is also a .308 derivative. The 7-30 Waters is a .30-30 case necked to .284. The .250-3000 Savage, developed by Charles Newton for Savage around 1913, featured an 87-grain bullet that travelled at an advertised speed of 3,000 feet per second. The company wanted that velocity, which was considered very high at the time, in the cartridge name. Necked to 22 caliber, it became the wildcat .22-250, which Remington began producing commercially in 1965.

The earliest of many .22 rimfire cartridges was probably the .22 BB ("bulleted breeching") Cap, designed in 1845 for what were then known as "parlor" or "saloon" (salon) rifles. Because the priming ensured enough thrust for indoor target shooting, this round initially held no powder. In the 1880s the CB (conical bullet) Cap appeared, loaded with 1 1/2 grains of black powder. In Europe, bores are measured in millimeters, not hundredths of an inch. Some American rounds have also been labeled in this manner. The 6mm Remington uses a .243 bullet, the 6.5 Remington Magnum a .264 bullet. The various 7mms fire .284 bullets, and the 8mm Remington Magnum uses a .323 bullet. European cartridge designations also include case length in millime-

ters; thus, the 7x57 Mauser has a 7mm groove diameter and a case that's 57mm long. The .308 Winchester cartridge is known in military circles as the 7.62x51 NATO. As noted there's usually a good reason why a cartridge carries a certain name, but you may have to dig into history and use some imagination to find it!

Velocities are rounded to the nearest 10 fps (case capacities to the nearest grain at the case mouth). Case capacities vary with brass thickness, which varies, in turn by maker. They *in no way* indicate appropriate powder charges but are listed simply to show relative volume. Most of the case volumes are supplied by the Barnes Bullets Reloading Manual. Operating pressures shown are largely from the reloading manual published by Accurate Arms. Pressures in pounds per square inch (PSI) do not equate to copper units of pressure (CUP). Both have been used by the industry to indicate maximum breech pressures.

# NOTES ON DATA AND REFERENCES

The loading data used throughout this volume is with the permission of the publishers. It is **not** to be construed as a recommendation. All data listed represents near-maximum pressure levels in each test firearm. Because bore and chamber dimensions vary, and because bullets of different design (but the same weight) can produce substantially different pressures, initial handloads should be conservative--from 5 to 10 percent below listed maximums. The more ambitious charges were chosen for this book merely to show the potential of each cartridge in comparison with that of other cartridges. In researching this book, startling differences in published maximum charge weights surfaced. Before handloading, gun owners should consult several manuals, not just one. Test conditions and powder lots, case volumes, bullet styles and rifles vary, with old manuals typically listing stouter loads than those found in current editions. High pressures are not only dangerous; they reduce case life, impose additional strain on rifles and seldom yield the best accuracy.

The name of the company responsible for each load that has been excerpted from a manual appears throughout this book after the listing. Thus, loads from "Wildcat Cartridges" (Wolfe Publishing) are accompanied by the name of the chapter author and the page number in "WC." A lower-case "cw" indicates "Cartridges of the World" by Frank Barnes. Anyone interested in cartridges or handloading is well served by both books and as many loading manuals as he can accumulate. Handloading, like any hobby, is more fun when you know what you're about. Even if you shoot factory ammunition, learning how cartridges are assembled and what options can best serve your purposes will make any rifle more effective and hunting more satisfying. Learning what influences a bullet's flight and terminal performance, and how that bullet can be made to do your bidding, offers a huge advantage. Success in shooting, as in almost everything, hinges mainly on what you know, not on what you own.

# TABLE OF CONTENTS

# PART 1

## CARTRIDGE HISTORY

# THE DAYS OF WHITE SMOKE

Most people think of ammunition as cartridges, though by dictionary definition anything shot or otherwise hurled from a weapon qualifies. People who know little about shooting say "bullets" when they mean cartridges, as if what streaks through the air toward the target does so of its own volition. A bullet is no more self-sufficient than an arrow. A firearm differs from a bow in that, since it has no power to kick the projectile forward, it needs help. The propellant that moves bullets was not always called gunpowder, which came along before any guns existed. It had to. Just as internal combustion engines followed the discovery of petroleum fuels, so firearms followed the development of propellants.

A compound known as "Chinese snow" first appeared in fireworks a couple of centuries before Roger Bacon, an English friar and philosopher, described it in 1249. Berthold Schwarz later experimented with the substance as a propellant, and by 1314 crude firearms began popping up in England. Edward II used guns as weapons during his invasion of Scotland in 1327. The first gunpowder contained about 41 percent saltpeter, with equal proportions of charcoal and sulphur. In 1338, French chemists changed the composition to 50-25-25. Shooters subsequently tried various formulas to find the best mix for specific tasks. By 1871, the English had settled on a combination of 75 percent saltpeter, 15 percent charcoal and 10

percent sulphur. That remained the standard composition of black powder until the development of guncotton in 1846.

American powder manufacture antedated gun manufacture. A powder mill at Milton, Massachusetts, near Boston, was probably the first. By the beginning of the Revolution, colonists had amassed, by manufacture or capture, 40 tons of black powder. Half went to nearby Cambridge, where it was wasted before George Washington took control of the Revolutionary Army. By the end of 1775 the colonists had no powder left. Scrambling to arm themselves, they built new mills and by war's end had accumulated 1,000 tons. By 1800 American powder mills were producing 750 tons annually.

Igniting black powder was easy out in the open air. Igniting it in a chamber that bottled the violence, then used that violence to accelerate a ball, was not so easy. The first guns were simply heavy pipes, which the Swiss called *culverins.* One person held the tube, while another applied a priming charge, then lit it with a smoldering stick or rope. Such weapons were clumsy, undependable and inaccurate. They were also popular, largely because the noise and smoke they generated could easily unnerve an enemy armed with pointed sticks.

Culverins were eventually lightened so that one man could load and fire them unassisted. The heavy barrels were hard to steady by hand, so

Modern muzzleloaders similar to this Thompson/Center caplock bring back the mystique of frontier times and add challenge to the hunt.

the barrel, embodying in one piece what would later become the hammer and trigger. The serpentine or cock that held the match was later made stationary, enabling the wick to keep smoldering on top of the barrel. The shooter eased the serpentine into the wick until the match caught fire. He then moved the mechanism to the side and lowered the match to the touch-hole. A spring was added later to keep the match away from the touch-hole, and a trigger was adapted from crossbows to provide more control.

The name "matchlock" applies to several guns of this type, perhaps the best known being the Spanish *arquebus*. Arquebusiers carried extra wicks that were kept smoldering in perforated metal boxes on their belts, but even the best of these weapons proved unreliable. During the battle of Kuisyingen in 1636, one soldier managed only seven shots during a period of eight hours. Two years later at Wittenmergen, the rate of fire doubled to seven shots in four hours. Eliminating the wick as an ignition source became the priority of 16th-century German gun designers, who came up with the "monk's gun." A spring-loaded jaw on its barrel held a piece of pyrite (flint) against a serrated bar. To fire, the shooter pulled a ring at the rear of the bar, then scooted it across the pyrite to produce sparks. The sparks fell in a pan containing a trail of fine gunpowder that led into the touch-hole and the main charge.

A more sophisticated (and costly) rendition of this design, called the *wheel lock*, appeared around 1515 in Nuremberg. It featured a spring-loaded sprocket wound with a spanner wrench and latched under tension. Releasing the wheel with a trigger sent it into a spin against pyrite, sparks showering into the pan. Wheel locks were less affected by wet weather than were match locks. They also provided quicker ignition and were faster and less cumbersome, enabling these early

shooters commonly used mechanical rests. A forked brace adapted from 14th-century artillery showed up often. The *petronel*, a hand cannon held against the breast for firing, could be steadied with a forked stick angled to the ground or even to the saddle of a mounted warrior. A stationary cannon, whose muzzle was aimed at an enemy camp or a mass of men, could be fired without regard to timing because gun and target had a fixed relationship. Soldiers with hand cannons needed quick, efficient ignition that was instantly controllable in order to hit moving targets. Without a partner, or *gougat*, separate ignition devices couldn't work. Enter the "lock" or firing mechanism.

The first lock was simply a crude lever by which a smoldering wick was lowered to a touch-hole in

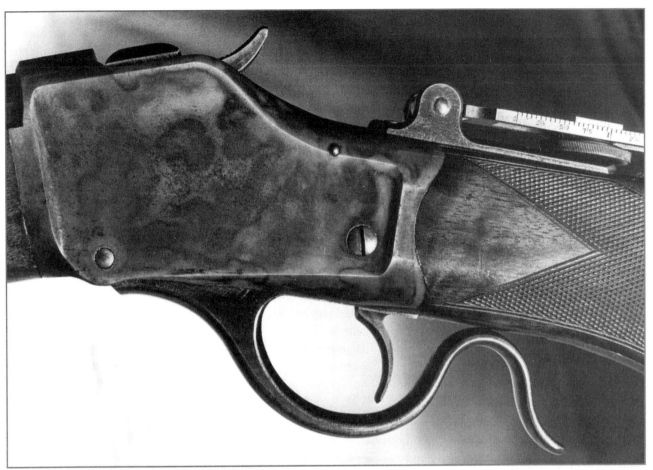

This Winchester Model 1885, or "High Wall", came from John Browning's bench. It was the first of dozens of Browning designs bought and marketed by Winchester.

guns to be used conveniently by cavalry.

The next major step in ignition came when the roles of pyrite and steel were reversed. Later known as flintlocks, guns of this type featured a spring-loaded cock that held a piece of flint and swung in an arc when released. The flint struck a pan cover or hammer, knocking it back to expose the primed pan. The cock eventually became known as the hammer, or frizzen. Flint locks were less expensive to build than were wheel locks, and the later ones more reliable.

A common weakness among all these guns was exposed priming. Moisture could render a flint lock as useless as a match lock with a cold wick. Weak sparks failed to ignite even dry priming; and if the priming did indeed "catch," the flame often

failed to finish its trip to the main charge, yielding only a "flash in the pan." Generating a spark *inside* the gun no doubt seemed an impossible dream to early inventors; but it all became possible with the discovery of fulminates. Chemists found during the early 1700s that fulminic acid (an isomer of cyanic acid) produced shock-sensitive salts. Percussion between metal surfaces would occasionally ignite black powder and some nitro compounds, but never as predictably nor as violently as fulminates, which released all their energy instantly. In 1774 the chief physician to Louis XV reported on the explosiveness of fulminate of mercury, but more than a decade passed before Antoine Fourcroy and Nicolas Louis Vauquelin followed up with more experiments.

French chemist Claude Louis Berthollet found that substituting chlorate of potash for saltpeter in gunpowder made it highly unstable. Combining fulminates of mercury with saltpeter produced a shock-sensitive but more predictable explosive. Called "Howard's powder" (after Englishman E.C. Howard, who discovered it in 1799), this mixture caught the attention of Scotch clergyman Alexander John Forsythe, who became in 1806 the first man on record to generate a spark in the combustion chamber of a gun. A few years later, Swiss gunmaker Johannes Pauly designed a breech-loading percussion gun utilizing a cartridge with a paper ignition cap on its base. When the trigger was pulled, a needle was released, piercing the cap and detonating the fulminate. The Lefauchex needle gun soon followed.

Suddenly, it seemed, everyone knew that this internal spark would make existing firearms obsolete. New ammunition and the guns to fire it were developed simultaneously by legions of inventors who rushed to boost the speed and reliability of ignition. In 1818 Joseph Manton, an Englishman, built a gun with a spring-loaded catch that held a tiny tube of fulminate against the side of the barrel and over the touch-hole. A hammer strike detonated the fulminate, and breech pressure blew the tube off to the side. In 1821 the London firm of Westley Richards designed a percussion gun that used various fulminate primers. The pan cover, having been forced open flintlock-style by the falling hammer, exposed a cup of fulminate. The sharp nose of the hammer pierced the cup, sending sparks through the touch-hole. Two years later, American physician Dr. Samuel Guthrie found a way to make fulminate pellets, which proved much more convenient than loose fulminate or paper caps.

Though many people have claimed credit for inventing the copper percussion cap, most historians attribute its birth to a sea captain named Joshua Shaw of Philadelphia. Denied a patent in 1814 for

"Sabots" are sleeves that fall away from an encapsulated bullet during flight. They have become popular for shotgun slugs and muzzleloading bullets. The jacketed pistol bullets shown are paired with plastic sleeves offering better ballistic form and longer reach than most lead bullets.

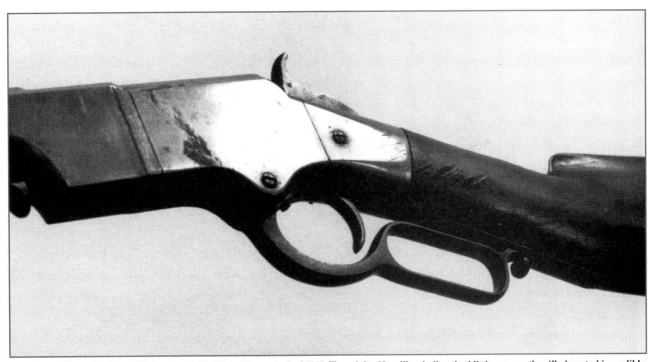

The Henry rifle evolved from Walter Hunt's "Volitional Repeater" of 1848. Though its 44-caliber bullets had little energy, the rifle boasted incredible firepower for its day. To Confederates in the Civil War, the Henry was "that damned Yankee rifle you loaded on Sunday and fired all week."

a steel cap because he was British-born and not yet a U.S. citizen, Shaw kept on working. His disposable pewter cap was followed by one made of copper. The hollow nipple appeared shortly after and eventually became standard on all percussion guns. It featured a tunnel that caught sparks at their origin and transmitted them directly to the chamber without need for a priming charge. Between 1812 and 1825 the U.S. patent office issued 72 patents for new percussion caps, only a few of which proved out. Some fragmented under breech pressure, endangering the shooter, while others failed to ignite the main charge because they lacked enough priming mix--or because they contained so much that the ball started down the bore before the powder could generate a slower, more powerful thrust.

Oddly enough, percussion rifles and shotguns did not catch on at first. Flintlocks had improved greatly, while fulminates, being chemical, were still viewed with suspicion by many people. Moreover, early caps often proved unstable or inconsistent; and governments, which were traditionally wary of new things, resisted replacing pyrite with primers. Percussion guns were said to kick harder but deliver less punch downrange. Colonel Hawker, a British firearms authority, qualified his praise of percussion ignition this way: "For killing single shots at wildfowl rapidly flying, and particularly by night, there is not a question in favour of the detonating system, as its trifling inferiority to the flint gun is tenfold repaid by the wonderful accuracy it gives in so readily obeying the eye. But in firing a heavy charge among a large flock of birds the flint has the decided advantage."

Indeed, accidents involving percussion caps got plenty of press. When British munitions engineer Charles Eley was blown up at his factory by priming compound in 1828, percussion ignition took another beating. Such events may also have stalled the evolution of breech-loading guns. Loading a gun from the rear, however, had several obvious advantages: it was quicker and required less movement that might spook game or alert an enemy. There was no need for a ramrod or the muscle to force a ball against the resistance of rifling. A shooter couldn't deform a ball by loading a gun from the rear, and the barrel could be easily cleaned or cleared.

Hunters and soldiers had longed from early times to feed their guns from behind; in fact, breechloaders have deep roots in history. An arquebus discovered in the Tower of London has a hinged breech block, the owner's engraved initials and a date of 1537. A German gun of the same era had a removable thimble that, after being filled with powder, was then inserted and held in place with a cotter pin. A 17th-century French musket featured a cylindrical breech plug that dropped when the trigger guard was turned. After inserting the charge and raising the block, a shooter was ready to fire.

The most famous example of this type, designed in 1776 by British Major Patrick Ferguson, had a threaded breech plug that retracted as the trigger guard was rotated, much as one might loosen a screw. A charge was inserted in the barrel through an open breech plug hole and the plug spun back into place. The Theiss breechloader, introduced in 1804, had a sliding block that was activated by a button located in front of the trigger guard. The block was *raised* for loading, lowered to close the breech. This mechanism, a flint lock, leaked lots of gas. Captain John Harris Hall of Maine designed one of the first successful breechloaders in this country that employed the same principle, with hammer, pan and frizzen riding on a movable block.

Hinged-barrel guns--mostly flintlocks--date to the 16th century, though a few wheellocks have been found. Some hinges permitted the barrel to move sideways, others vertically. Many had fixed chambers that were loaded from the front, their barrels pivoting well forward of the action.

Several European inventors pioneered in fashioning useful breechloaders for cartridges. The first cartridges were made of paper. They had no priming, of course, and the guns were still loaded from the muzzle. Shooters had to bite off the cartridge base before loading so as to expose the powder charge. The case burned to ashes upon firing. Replacing pyrite with the percussion cap did away with this process because the cap's more powerful spark was able to penetrate thin paper.

One of the first inventors to put a primer in a cartridge was Johann Nikolaus von Dreyse. The bullet in his paper cartridge carried a pellet of fulminate on its base. After penetrating the paper cartridge from the rear, a long striker lanced through the charge, pinching the pellet against the bullet. About 300,000 of von Dreyse's "needle guns," were built for the Prussian army between 1835 and 1865.

Eliminating gas leaks in breechloaders, with their weak or perforated bases, proved a major problem for early designers. Gilbert Smith devised a rubber hull that protruded slightly from a chambered round while still allowing the action to close. It failed as a gas seal and was rejected by the British ordnance people in 1838. Two years later, the French inventor Lepage tried to use a metallic primer in a combustible case, but the primers proved too hard to remove after firing. A fellow Parisian named Houllier later replaced the paper case with a metal one and inserted a priming pellet. When the hammer struck an external pin, the primer ignited. More importantly, the case, having been expanded by the burning powder, gripped the chamber wall tightly, thereby reducing gas leaks. This design, patented in 1847, was adapted to Lefaucheux's hinged-barrel gun. Crude as it was, the Lefaucheux proved that Houllier's cartridge design had merit.

"In-line" muzzleloaders combine modern design with an early ignition system. Topped with scopes, they're as effective as cartridge rifles at woods ranges.

Westley-Richards then developed its "capping" breechloader with its fixed barrel and a standing breech that pivoted up to give access to the chamber. Despite its use of paper cartridges, there were no leaks because, upon lowering the block, a "bolt" wedged itself between barrel and breech. The capping breechloader could be converted to a muzzleloader by inserting a metal plug and two wads. The British adopted this gun as a cavalry arm in 1861 and kept it in service in South Africa until the turn of the century.

Changes in propellants influenced changes in rifle and cartridge design. Nitroglycerine, discovered in 1846 by Ascanio Subrero in Italy, promised higher performance but also higher breech pressures. "Nitro" is a colorless liquid comprising nitric and sulphuric acids plus glycerin. Unlike gunpowder, it is not a blend of fuels and oxidants; rather it is an unstable, oxygen-rich chemical compound. It can rearrange itself instantly into more stable gases. All it needs is a little prompting-- a jolt, but not necessarily a flame. As nitro-glycerine ages it can become more unstable and more dangerous.

In 1863 Swedish chemist Emmanuel Nobel and his son Alfred (of Nobel Prize fame) figured out how to store this touchy substance in cans, making it easier to handle but no less hazardous. Several shipments blew up, as did the Nobel factory in Germany. Alfred later discovered that soaking the porous earth *Kieselguhr* with nitro made the chemical less sensitive. This process led to the manufacture of dynamite, which Nobel patented in 1875. Dynamite in its original form is now rarely used, but the term has become a generic name for more effective, more manageable explosives.

While ballisticians and miners were contemplating the potential of nitroglycerin, Swiss chemist Christian Schoenbein discovered that a mixture of nitric and sulfuric acids applied to cotton formed a compound that burned so fast as to consume a cotton patch without setting fire to a pile of black powder placed on top of it. Schoenbein obtained an English patent to cover his work and then sold the operating procedure to Austria. Shortly thereafter, John Hall and Sons built a guncotton plant in Faversham, England, which promptly blew up, as did most of the other guncotton plants that followed. The substance had little use as a propellant because it burned too fast, almost detonating; but as an explosive designed to tear other things apart it worked very well.

Unlike guncotton and nitroglycerin, which can release gases in a wave action as high as 21,000 feet per second, gunpowder is not a "high explosive."

This Thompson/Center caplock muzzleloader produces the same target-obscuring cloud of smoke as its predecessors.

It's a propellant designed to burn at a pace that allows a bullet to accelerate. Gunpowder is not shock sensitive; when ignited in open air it will burn, but not violently. Torched in tight confines, its gases will expand at a rate determined by the composition of the powder (and its coatings) and by the shape and size of the granules.

Chlorate powders, pioneered by Berthollet in the 1780s, had great energy. But when a French powder plant at Essons blew up in 1788, the chemist concluded that potassium chlorate was too sensitive for use as a propellant. Combined with other compounds, though, it was later put to harness. During the 1850s J.J. Pohl developed a substance called "white powder," comprising 49 percent potassium chlorate, 28 percent yellow

prussiate of potash and 23 percent sulfur. Although a second-rate propellant, it proved valuable to the Confederacy during the Civil War when black powder became unavailable. Wartime backyard powder mills turned out propellants of varying colors, shapes and potencies. Some formulas were sold through the mail by con artists who baited innocents with claims that ammunition could be fashioned from coffee, sugar and alum combined with potassium chlorate and a lead ball.

In 1869 German immigrant Carl Dittmar built a small plant to make "Dualin," a sawdust-like material treated with nitroglycerin. A year later, Dittmar introduced his "New Sporting Powder." By 1878 he had done well enough to start up a mill in Binghampton, New York. Unfortunately, the mill blew up a few years later, taking part of Binghampton with it. When Dittmar's health failed, he sold what was left of the firm. One of his foremen, Milton Lindsey, wound up at the King Powder Company, where he teamed up with G.M. Peters to develop "King's Semi-Smokeless Powder," which they patented in 1899. Dupont's "Lesmoke" appeared a short time later, with roughly the same components and proportions: 60 percent saltpeter, 20 percent wood cellulose, 12 percent charcoal and 8 percent sulfur. These and a handful of other semi-smokeless powders preceded the appearance of smokeless propellants shortly before the turn of the century. "Lesmoke" in particular proved a fine powder for .22 rimfires. Fouling remained a problem, but the residue didn't harden as it did with black powder. "Lesmoke" was apparently more hazardous to produce than smokeless, however, and was discontinued in 1947.

The first successful smokeless powder is generally credited to French engineer Paul Vielle, whose single-base "Poudre B" comprised ethyl alcohol and celluloid. A decade before Vielle's achievement,

"Scheutzen" rifles are traditionally single-shot, dropping-block guns built for offhand target shooting with lead bullets.

however, Austrian chemist Frederick Volkmann patented some new cellulose-based powders. Unfortunately, Austrian patents were not acknowledged world-wide, and in 1875 the Austrian government started enforcing its monopoly on domestic powder supplies. Volkmann's plant closed, but the proven attributes of his powder--transparent smoke, less barrel residue, more power, safer handling--indicated that he was close to producing what we know as smokeless.

In 1887 Alfred Nobel increased the proportion of nitrocellulose in his blasting gelatin and found he could use the new compound as a propellant. A year later, he patented "Ballistite," a double-base powder (containing both nitrocellulose and nitroglycerin) that was quite similar to a new

powder developed at the same time by Hiram Maxim, of machinegun fame. About this time the British War Office, searching for a more effective rifle powder, came up with "Cordite." This propellant was at one stage in its manufacture a paste that could be squeezed through a die, forming spaghetti-like cords. The early mix, containing 58 percent nitroglycerine and 37 percent guncotton, was later changed to 30 percent nitroglycerine and 65 percent guncotton (the rest was mineral jelly and acetone).

Because they contained nitrated lignin, many early smokeless powders were lumpy and fuzzy in appearance. Densities varied, so handloaders needed their wits about them. "Bulk" powders could be substituted--bulk for bulk--for black powder. "Dense" or gelatin powders could not be safely measured by bulk, because their energy-per-volume ratios were higher. The shooting industry responded by marking shotgun loads in "drams equivalent;" i.e., the smokeless powder performed the same as black-powder shotshells when loaded with a marked number of drams.

The first military rifle designed for smokeless powder was France's 8mm Lebel in 1886. Other countries quickly followed--England with its .303 British in 1888 and Switzerland with the 7.5x55 Schmidt-Rubin a year later. By the mid-1890s most armies were equipped with small-bore bolt rifles firing smokeless cartridges. The new propellant boosted bullet speed by one-third without revealing a rifleman's position with white clouds of spent saltpeter. Velocities increased, too. The only problem was pressure--each gun had to contain all that invisible muscle and do so safely. This was hardly a new problem; in fact, it dated four decades back, to the birthing days of the self-contained cartridge. Firearm design, then as always, remained a slave to the ammunition makers.

# CARTRIDGE CASES AND INVISIBLE SMOKE

By the mid-18th century, gunmakers on both sides of the Atlantic were scrambling to keep pace with changes in ammunition. The race to design powerful, reliable self-contained cartridges that lent themselves to mass manufacture heated up. Stakes were high, matching the demand by sportsmen and ordnance people alike. In Europe, guns with pivoting barrels became popular. Some shotguns and rifles were built with eccentric hinge pins so the barrels moved forward a bit before dropping. The metallic case that everyone was talking about could not by itself ensure control of high-pressure gas. A weak mechanism or imperfectly fitting parts could still permit leaks, especially in the event of case rupture. As propellants improved, pressures were bound to rise, defying all but the tightest, strongest actions.

Out on the American frontier, Christian Sharps had figured out a way to combine breechloading with the strength of a plugged-breech muzzleloader. Ironically, his dropping-block rifle sold at least as well in England as it did in the U.S. Sharps' 52-caliber boasted linen cartridges and Maynard primers that advanced on a paper roll to an external nipple. This priming method derived from Maynard's 1851 cartridge design featuring a metallic case with a hole in its flat base to admit primer spark. Though his tape primers lasted only four years, they resurfaced in modified form during the 20th-century as fodder for millions of toy cap pistols.

Noted handgunner Hal Swiggett shot this Texas whitetail with a scoped Thompson/Center Contender. Chambered for the .30-30, .35 Remington and other similar cartridges, this single-shot pistol has become a favorite among hunters.

Some inventors who tried to package powder charges in a bullet's hollow base turned to caseless ammunition. Stephen Taylor won a patent in 1847 for one such bullet whose perforated end cap admitted sparks from an outside primer. A year later Walter Hunt designed a similar bullet, with a base cap of cork and perforations sealed by thin paper. He called this his "rocket ball" ammunition, fired by primers advanced mechanically from a pill box on the rifle. Hunt's repeater, with an ingenious under-barrel magazine, was later revamped to become the famous Henry rifle (and, later, the Winchester 66).

In 1854 Horace Smith and Dan Wesson perfected a metallic case for the Hunt bullet. It looked like a rimfire case, but priming mix was smeared across the entire head inside, and a disk anvil inserted. A strike anywhere on the head ignited the priming. The cartridge, though promising, proved difficult to make, whereupon Smith, Wesson and B. Tyler Henry redesigned the Hunt rocket ball. It consisted of a glass cup with a primer pellet resting on an iron anvil and a cork base wad that held the propellant in place. The first charge-- a modest dose of fulminate--was later supplanted by 6 1/2 grains of black powder. Walter Hunt had assumed succeeding shots would clear cork residue out of the barrel, but Smith and his co-workers found that too much of it remained, impairing rifle function. In response they installed a copper base cap, which was later changed to brass.

Smith and Wesson achieved lasting fame as gun designers, of course, but arguably their biggest contribution was the .22 Short rimfire cartridge, introduced in 1858. No other cartridge can claim the longevity of this useful round. Not only has it outlived its contemporaries by many decades, but it remains a big seller. Today, it is made almost the same as before the Civil War, albeit much more efficiently and to closer tolerances. The rimfire

The Marlin 336, descendant of the Marlin 1893, is still popular with deer hunters in eastern woods.

case Smith and Wesson pioneered began life as a disc punched from a sheet of thin metal. The disk was drawn into a cup until a rim was "bumped" into the closed end. The rim did not pinch closed at the base, however, but enfolded a small groove filled with fulminate of mercury. When the striker hit the perimeter of the base, it first dented the rim, then crushed and detonated the priming compound. The advantage of the brass case over a hollow-based bullet with an internal primer became obvious: it could hold more propellant. The bullet could also be any shape or weight desired.

About this time, other brass cases came along, though none proved so brilliant in conception. The conical case engineered by Major Ambrose

Burnside of Civil War fame was tapered to the rear. Moreover, it had to be loaded into the front of the chamber--back end first! An external cap provided the ignition. E.H. Martin received a patent for a rimfire case in 1869, but his rim, unlike Smith and Wesson's, had no room in the fold for priming. His "double-folded" case, patented in 1870, evolved into a balloon-head case with a center pocket for a metallic primer. As it turned out, drawn brass, which was just becoming available then, had no weakening folds or creases. Eventually the balloon case became, along with drawn brass, the semi-balloon and then the modern solid-head case (which is strongest because the web between primer pocket and extractor groove is so thick).

That early Martin cartridge fashioned at Springfield Armory is generally recognized as the first successful centerfire round developed in the U.S. It featured a 50-caliber bullet and a bar anvil, which was simply a tinned iron strut inserted at the mouth and crimped into position against the case head. The striker pinched the priming compound between case head and bar. About this time the Snider "coiled" cartridge appeared in England, complete with a base of brass and steel, a body of layered brass foil, and paper. The layers were wound around a mandrel during case manufacture, then shellacked and glued to form a cylinder. The inside was coated with shellac to ward off the corrosive effects of black powder. The Snider was adopted by British Ordnance in 1867 but lost its place in military circles four years later to the .577-450 Martini-Henry. This round, with its case made of thin brass, was also formed on a mandrel.

In folded-head cartridges the central primer cup provides its own anvil. Since drawn-brass, solid head cases have no anvil, primer cups were manufactured (beginning in 1880) with anvils and cases with central flash holes. Boxer primers

Beginning in the late 1800s, the .44-40 was a popular black-powder cartridge chambered in both rifles and revolvers.

(named after Edward Boxer, a British military officer) now in common use derive from these 19th-century percussion caps, which are available in two sizes for rifle cartridges (two for handguns). Large and small rifle primers are of the same depth and diameter as large and small pistol primers, respectively, but the primer pellets differ. A large rifle primer weighs 5.4 grains and carries .6 grain of priming compound.

By the turn of the century, European cartridge designers were following their own path, opting to incorporate the anvil in the case while punching two flash holes on its perimeter. The Berdan primer (named after Hyram Berdan, an American military officer) had no anvil, hence there was more room for priming compound; also, its flame went straight through the holes rather than scooting around the anvil and its braces. The Boxer primer was popular among handloaders because they could pop the old primer out during sizing in a die with a decapping pin. Berdan primers must be pried out with a special hook or forced free with hydraulic pressure.

The first Boxer primers ignited black powder easily but sometimes failed to fire smokeless. When more fulminate was added to the priming mix, cases began to crack. Blame fell on the propellant, but the culprit was really mercury residue from the primer. This residue, which was largely absorbed by the fouling from black powder, accumulated in harmful concentrations in the wake of clean-burning smokeless. It attacked the zinc in the case walls, causing them to split.

The first successful non-mercuric primer for smokeless loads was the military H-48, developed in 1898 for the .30-40 Krag. The main detonating component was potassium chlorate, whose corrosive salts did not damage the case but could ruin the bore. Scrupulous cleaning with hot water and ammonia, followed by oiling, kept rifling sharp and shiny; but even short-term neglect left rifles with pitted bores. In 1901 the German Company Rheinische-Westphalische Sprengstoff (RWS) announced a new primer that used rust-resistant barium nitrate and picric acid instead of potassium chlorate. By 1911 the Swiss had developed a non-corrosive primer while the Germans were producing rimfire ammunition that featured *Rostfrei* (rust-free) priming. *Rostfrei* contained neither potassium chlorate nor ground glass, the common element used to generate friction when the striker hit.

The solution proved imperfect, though, because barium oxide formed as a residue, scouring the barrel as aggressively as had the glass that was abandoned by the U.S. military before World War I (when the H-48 primer was replaced by the FH-42). Primer production during wartime overloaded drying houses in the U.S., causing misfires when sulfuric acid formed in the priming mix. The FH-42 gave ground to the Winchester 35-NF primer (later known as the FA-No. 70), which remained in military service through World War II.

Non-corrosive priming first arrived in the U.S. in 1927 as Remington's "Kleanbore." Winchester followed with its "Staynless," Peters with "Rustless," all containing mercury fulminate. It would fall to German chemists to remove both potassium chlorate and mercury fulminate from primers. Again, Remington took the lead with the first U.S. version of a non-corrosive, non-mercuric primer. The main ingredient--lead tri-nitro-resorcinate, or lead styphnate--comprised up to 45

Popular and versatile .30 magnums, are, left to right: .308 Norma, .300 Winchester, .300 Weatherby, .300 H&H.

percent of the priming mix and remains an important component in small arms primers.

During the 1940s, Roy Weatherby reformed .300 Holland and Holland cases to fashion a line of ammunition whose assets included high velocity and flat trajectory. These big, broad-shouldered rounds required the extra-slow-burning powders just then becoming available. But large charges of such propellants proved hard to ignite with standard primers. More priming compound was not the answer, because it might well shatter powder directly in front of the flash hole, causing erratic pressures and performance. Dick Speer and Victor Jasaitis, a chemist at Speer Cartridge Works,

Five-shot groups like this, using British-made Eley .22 rimfire match cartridges, have helped the author win two state prone championships.

came up with a better idea: the addition of boron and aluminum to the lead styphnate mixture. This enabled primers to burn *longer*, resulting in more heat and more complete ignition before primer fade. This first successful magnum primer was just what Weatherby needed; indeed, it remains in the company's product line in Lewiston, Idaho.

Shotshell manufacture was plagued with the same primer problems visited on the production of rifle and pistol cartridges. And it came by the same salvation, albeit with a shotshell cup assembly that is quite different. Here a deep battery cup holds the anvil while a smaller cup contains the detonating material. As with rifle primers, a foil cover protects the pellet. The primer pocket of a shotshell has no bottom; hence, there's no flash hole (which is in the battery cup). Made of thin, folded brass, the shotshell head is reinforced with a dense paper base wad or a thick section of hull plastic. The battery cup seals the deep hole in the base wad.

Primer manufacture for both rifles and shotguns remains much the same as it was when World W II began. True, today's equipment is more sophisticated, and safety precautions are better understood and enforced. But huge batches of primer cups are still punched and drawn from sheet metal and indexed on large perforated metal tables. A second perforated plate is smeared with wet, dough-like priming compound and laid with precision on top of the first. That way, little dabs in the holes can be punched down into the open-faced cups; or the cups can be filled by brushing the compound across the face of the table. Then the thin foil disc (or a shellacked paper cover) is applied, followed by anvils punched from another metal sheet. The mix is stable when wet, but extremely hazardous to work with when dry.

These U.S. military cartridges--from left: .30-40 Krag, .30-06 Springfield, 7.62 NATO (.308 Winchester) and 5.56mm (.223)-- represent 100 years of development.

## THE ERA OF SMOKELESS POWDERS BEGINS

Most of the companies established in the 1890s to manufacture smokeless did not long survive. Fierce competition, the hazardous nature of the process and imperfect product all combined to undermine the young industry. Fortunately, because powder manufacture called for expensive, specialized machinery, many of the businesses that failed managed to sell their equipment to larger, profitable powder makers. Then in 1890 Samuel Rodgers, an English physician practicing in San Francisco, formed the United States Powder Company to produce his own ammonium nitrate propellant. That same year he merged his business with the Giant Powder Company. Three years later, Rodgers' "Gold Dust Powder" comprised 55 percent ammonium picrate, 25 percent sodium or potassium nitrate and 20 percent ammonium

bichromate. This foul-smelling shotgun powder also fell by the wayside when an explosion destroyed the Giant Powder Company plant in 1898.

When The Leonard Powder Company of Tennessee, maker of "Ruby N" and "Ruby J" powders, folded in 1894, it was succeeded by the American Smokeless Powder Company. This New Jersey firm produced propellants under government contract until it was taken over in 1898 by a creditor, Laflin & Rand, which had once sought U.S. rights to Ballistite. The manufacture of Ballistite later came under the control of DuPont, which contracted that job out to Laflin & Rand. The famous "Lightning," "Sharpshooter," "Unique" and "L&R Smokeless" powders were Laflin & Rand developments.

In 1903 the American E.C. & Schultz Powder Company sold to DuPont, then became part of Hercules when DuPont was split by court order in 1912. These and other corporate restructurings were caused mainly by under-capitalization. Ambitious entrepreneurs who saw the huge profit potential in smokeless propellants either failed to procure government contracts or mistakenly assumed that private sales would lift these young firms off the ground. As with rifles, one military contract could herald salvation; but rejection boded ill.

Just before the turn of the century "Peyton Powder" (produced by the California Powder Works) began fueling .30-40 Krag ammunition for the U.S. military. This was a double-base powder with a small amount of ammonium picrate. Laflin & Rand also manufactured a double-base powder for the Krag: the "W-A". Its 30 percent nitroglycerin produced high burn temperatures and erosive tendencies. Meanwhile, the U.S. Navy, whose interest in single-base powders had been growing since 1897, began doing business with DuPont and California Powder Works. Their

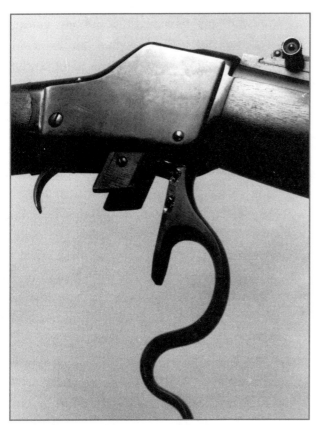
The Winchester High Wall boasts a strong dropping-block action developed by John Browning and bought by Winchester in the early 1880s.

nitrocellulose powders were somewhat like Cordite in form; i.e., guncotton was dissolved in ether and alcohol to form a colloid. Pressed into thin, hollow strands, the colloid was then chopped into short tubes. "Government Pyro" became one of the first of these powders to see military use (in Springfield's .30-06). DuPont later fueled that cartridge with 1147 and 1185 powders, while IMR (Improved Military Rifle) 4895 became the powder of choice for the .30-06M2. It is still among the best choices for handloaders who seek maximum velocity and accuracy from middle-weight bullets in the .30-06.

DuPont continued to dominate the powder industry after Hercules began its own operation in New Jersey, where it manufactured dynamite and up to a ton of small arms powder daily. By the onset of World War I, Hercules had started up a new plant in New Jersey, producing nitro-cellulose and several popular powders, including Bullseye, Infallible and HiVel. But it was DuPont that got the big war contracts. Two new plants were built in Old Hickory, Tennessee, and in Nitro (really), West Virginia. Their combined capacity grew to 1.5 million pounds per day. After the war, DuPont *bought* the town of Old Hickory, where it established a rayon factory. But the powder magazines were still there. One day in August, 1924, they caught fire. In an instant, more than 100 buildings and 50 million pounds of powder vanished.

Hercules also manufactured Cordite powder for the British government, producing up to 12,000 pounds a day and, during wartime, a total of more than 46 million pounds. In addition, it produced 3 million pounds of small arms propellants and 54 million pounds of cannon powder. Consider that, prior to 1914, Hercules had made no artillery powder and only token amounts of small arms powder for sportsmen.

Plagued by copper residue that fouled cannon bores, U.S. munitions experts took a tip from the French and added tin to their propellants. Soon rifle powders got the same treatment. DuPont's No. 17 became No. 17½ with a dose of 4 percent tin, and No. 15 became No. 15½. Tin levels were halved when dark rings started showing up in the bores of National Match rifles, a result of the tin cooling off near the muzzle.

Powder manufacture has changed little since World War I, though automation has made it easier and safer. Black powder still comprises sulfur, charcoal and saltpeter, ground fine and mixed at 3 percent moisture. The powder "meal" is then pressed into cakes, which are fed through a granulating machine where toothed cylinders chop them up. Screening segregates the particles by size; then they're polished in revolving wooden barrels.

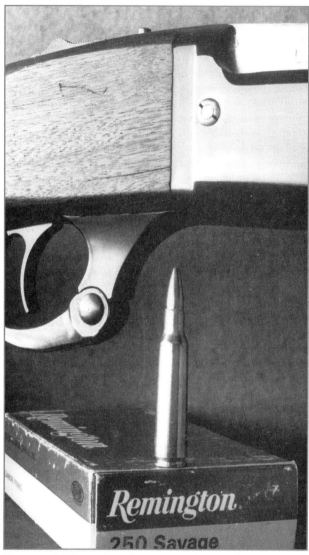

Because of high manufacturing costs, the future of Savage's Model 99 rifle looks bleak. The .250 cartridge was developed by Charles Newton for Savage before World War I.

Black powder is labeled as to its coarseness in decreasing order of size: A-1, Fg, Ffg, FFFg, FFFFg and FFFFFg. Bigger grains generally burn slowest and work best when pushing heavy balls or bullets. Extremely fine black powder is suitable only for priming charges.

Smokeless powders start as nitrocellulose (vegetable fiber soaked in nitric and sulfuric acids). The industry name "Pyrocellulose" referred to artillery powders during World War I. Guncotton is a special kind of nitrocellulose, with a slightly higher nitrogen content (13.2 percent compared to a standard 12.6) and lower solubility in ether-alcohol solution. Like other forms of nitrocellulose used in powder production, it derives from short crude-cotton fibers or "linters," which are first boiled in caustic soda to remove oils.

Water formed by nitric acid during the nitration process is absorbed by the sulfuric acid, thereby preventing decomposition by hydrolysis, A centrifuge then strips excess acid. Following a rinse, the linters are boiled for 48 hours to remove all traces of acid. Next the cotton is beaten to a pulp and boiled again--five more times--while agitators fluff it (remember, acid residue can cause spontaneous combustion). The nitrocellulose is washed in solvent, then heated to evaporate the solvent. Only hard grains of powder--and water--remain.

"Cooking" the solvent off with heat applied to a wet solution is less dangerous than the old air-dry method. Ether is used to dissolve the fibers in nitrocellulose marked for single-base powders, acetone for double-base. Nitroglycerin is then added to form the double-base powder. At this stage, the powder is really a soup, as unstable as it will ever be. More mixing turns the soup to a plastic jelly, which is squeezed through dies (extruded) to form slender tubes of precise dimensions. Rollers run these "noodles" through a plate, where a whirling knife shears them off in measured increments.

Because the sections or grains of single-base powders still contain ether, they are transferred to a warm solvent recovery room and then "water-dried" (soaked in water) for about two weeks. Wet single-base and freshly sheared double-base grains of powder are air-dried and sieved, then polished in drums and coated with graphite. The tumbling process smooths edges that might produce heat if allowed to scrape against other grains, while the graphite further reduces friction. Gunpowder's

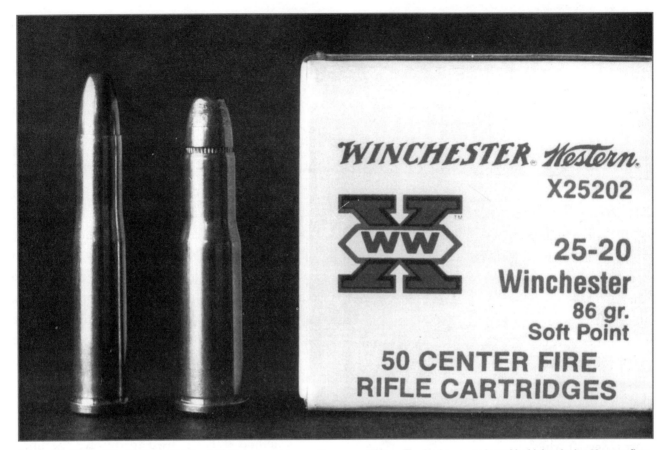

Prior to World War II the .22 Hornet (left) and .25-20 were popular small game cartridges. They've been supplanted by high-velocity .22 centerfires.

slate-gray color, incidentally, derives from that graphite coating. Uncoated powder is yellow.

The tube shape of extruded powders mitigates the "burn down" effect that reduces gas production as the grains shrink in size. Perforated sections burn from both the inside and outside. The burning rate of a powder is partly determined by the ratio of inside diameter to outside diameter, partly by grain size and wall thickness, and partly by deterrents that can be added to powders to impede quick consumption.

Ball powder manufacture differs from the production of extruded powders, though the raw materials are essentially the same. Nitrocellulose intended for ball powders goes through a hammer mill that reduces it to a pumice. Blended with water and pumped in slurry form into a still, the nitrocellulose combines with chalk that's been

added to counteract the nitric acids. Ethyl acetate dissolves the nitrocellulose, producing a lacquer that is broken into small particles by heat and agitation. The lacquer is then pressed through plates much like extruded powders and chopped to pieces by whirling knives. Tumbling and heating leave the grains round.

When using grains that are of proper size and roundness, the ethyl acetate is distilled off and salt is added to draw out any retained water. In a slurry of fresh water, the powder rushes through sizing screens. A heated still adds nitroglycerin to boost potency. Coatings of burning deterrents come next, smoothing the pressure curve by controlling burn rate. A centrifuge removes excess water. The grains are tumbled in graphite, then sized again. And with that, the powder process is complete. Next comes the bullet itself.

# HOW THE BULLET EVOLVED

**M**odern bullets and shot differ as much from their forebears as ball powders differ from the "Chinese snow" in medieval fireworks. A hand cannon dating to 1388 used a third of an ounce of powder to launch a half-pound iron arrow! Bores were commonly tapered so they could accept projectiles of various shapes and sizes. Iron balls wrought such devastation that they were outlawed in central Europe. Accuracy figured less than noise and smoke in deciding some battles, and the short ranges at which soldiers fought made a bore full of rocks supremely effective. Even after 17-horse teams were drawing great bronze culverins about the battlefront, however, hand-to-hand combat continued to spill most of the blood.

Lead became popular with shooters as early as the 15th century, its high density giving it long range and increased penetration. Lead's low melting point assured easy molding to various bore sizes. More important, its softness at normal temperatures enabled riflemen to size it tight to a rifled bore, yet still load it from the muzzle with

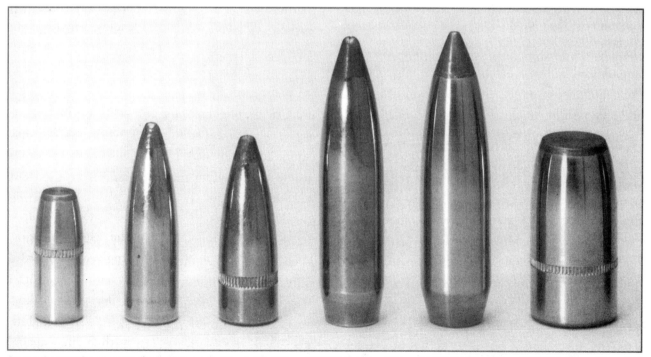

Among the 1900 Speer centerfire bullets are (left to right): .257-gr. 75 FFSP Hot-Cor; .284-gr. 120 SP Hot Cor; .311-gr. 125 SP Hot Cor; .338-gr. 225 BTSP; .375-gr. 270 BTSP; .458-gr. 350 FPSP Hot Cor.

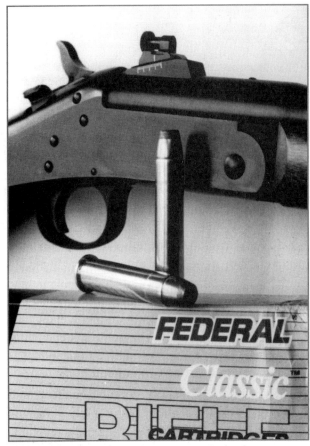

This Harrington & Richardson single-shot (with Williams receiver sight) uses the potent .45-70, a military cartridge adopted by the U.S. Army in 1873.

competed in rifle matches at Leipzig in 1498 and in Zurich six years later presumably used lead balls or bullets. They had no alternative.

When the Pilgrims came to America, lead proved valuable in their 75-caliber muskets and in trades with the local Indians. By 1700 the French-style flintlock had become the standard arm in Europe. It spawned the *jaeger* (hunter) rifle later adapted to the American frontier in the form of the famous Kentucky rifle. An 18th century *jaeger* had a bore of 60 to 77 caliber, but the pioneers stretched their supplies of precious lead by reducing bore size to .50, .45, even .40, (a pound of lead yields 70 40-caliber balls, but will produce only 15 balls of 70 caliber). America's militia and frontier fighters were quick to figure out that a patched ball was easier to load than one sized to fit the grooves. Linen patches or thin wafers of animal hide, greased with bear fat or saliva and pressed into the rifling, imparted spin to the ball and swept out powder fouling. Although the patched ball was common in Europe, mercenaries and conscripts armed with *jaeger* rifles insisted on hammering down groove-size balls. The extra effort this took not only slowed their rate of fire, it drew attention to their position.

Undersizing balls for use with a patch made sense then, and it still does. A 50-caliber rifle may shoot accurately with a ball sized to .500, but after a few shots fouling makes loading from the front all but impossible. A .490 ball with a tight-fitting patch generally performs almost as well as tighter balls in a clean bore—and it may well outperform them after a few shots. Greased patches are no substitute for cleaning solvent, which neutralizes the corrosive action of black powder. But undersize balls allow for more shooting with less swabbing, even with the relatively clean-burning Pyrodex, a modern black powder substitute.

Around 1835, percussion ignition began to

ease. A lead ball in a patch already engraved with the rifling tended to seal the powder gas behind it and spin readily to the twist of the lands. Later, lubricated lead bullets without patches were sized to groove diameter and fired with great accuracy.

Hollow-based lead bullets obturated (expanded) under the pressure of gas from the rear to "take" the rifling. As bullet speeds increased, alloys were used to harden the lead, followed by gas checks (metal heels on bullet bases). The leading of bores, once deemed inevitable as bullet velocities exceeded 2,000 feet per second, were eliminated with the advent of jacketed bullets. Lead of the proper hardness made rifles possible; softer or harder materials would simply not have conformed to the lands at acceptable pressure levels. Shooters who replace flint. About the same time, the short, heavy, big-bore Plains rifle was edging out the graceful Kentucky west of the Appalachians. It was then that conical bullets started gaining popularity. At first, target shooters found the conical "picket" ball difficult to load and quite sensitive to loading technique. But when Alvin Clark invented the false muzzle in 1840, riflemen were finally able to start a conical bullet square with the barrel proper. Paper-patched picket bullets and false muzzles halved group sizes and soon dominated at competitive shoots. On the frontier, though, patched balls still reigned; in fact, many pioneers chose smoothbore guns because they were so much faster than rifles to load and slower to foul.

A conical bullet in a smoothbore gun holds its velocity better than a ball because it has a higher sectional density (essentially, a ratio of weight to bore diameter). But its speed will be wasted if it doesn't hit where it's aimed. A bullet shot from a smooth bore is likely to tumble and stray off course. Once it tumbles, it loses the advantage of its sectional density because part of the time it's flying with its side to the front. Rifling prevents tumbling by stabilizing the bullet in flight, like a football thrown by a quarterback. The more perfect the rotation of the football, the further and straighter it flies. Similarly, a spinning top will remain upright until its rate of rotation drops low enough to destabilize it.

Early on, bullets were hard to load from the muzzles of rifled bores. Patches didn't work with bullets because of their long bearing surfaces, which also increased friction and ramrod resistance.

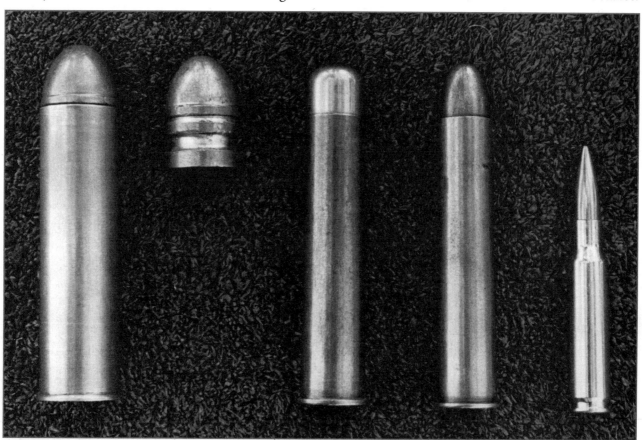

The .308 Winchester looks tiny next to mammoth rounds like the 8-bore cartridge (left), the .600 and .577 Nitro Express. Still, it outperforms many larger cases in terms of accuracy, versatility and reach. Recoil is milder too!

Henri Gustave Delvigne of France attacked this problem in 1826 with a new chamber design whose sharp corners arrested and upset undersize balls and bullets as they were rammed home. However, expanded to groove diameter in front of the powder, they were also deformed. This deformation probably had a greater effect on bullets, which could be tipped in the ramming process, than on balls. Bullets not launched in line with the bore predictably turned in poor accuracy.

In 1834, Captain Bernier, a British "Brunswicker," designed a two-groove rifled bore and a ball with a belt that fit in the grooves. Unfortunately, the ball had to be oriented each time; still, pushing it home was easy enough and accuracy proved acceptable. Soon after, English gunmaker William Greener developed an oval ball with one flat end. A tapered hole extending from the flat end to the center of the ball held a metal peg whose round head conformed to the shape of the ball. Either end could be placed in the muzzle first. Upon firing, the tapered peg drove into the undersized ball, expanding it to fit the grooves. Other British gunmakers of this era experimented with out-of-round bores that could spin a bullet without engraving it. These innovations didn't pass muster in military trials either, because the balls had to be perfectly sized and oriented exactly. French inventors, meanwhile, experimented with sabots—wood or metal sleeves that carried bullets down the bore, then released them and fell away beyond the muzzle.

The most promising future for front-loading conical bullets seemed to lie in a redesign of the bullet base. Delvigne, having figured that powder gas could expand a hollow-base bullet sufficiently to fit the grooves, developed one in 1841. Colonel Brunswick of England followed the same track with a metal skirt soldered to the base of a ball; but his projectiles, like the others, often tipped in

John Nosler developed his split-core Partition bullet in the late 1940s to ensure deeper penetration in big game.

flight. British General John Jacobs abandoned the hollow bullet base for a four-finned bullet mated to four-groove rifling. After failing to win any government contract for his design, Jacobs invented a heavy conical bullet for long-range shooting and a 32-bore double rifle that fired an exploding bullet.

That big Jacobs rifle may have impressed Sir Samuel Baker, an African explorer and elephant hunter, but he chose instead a 4-bore Gibbs with standard rifling. Its 36-inch barrel had two grooves, pitched one turn in 36 inches. As was customary in that day, the grooves were broad and the lands narrow to facilitate loading. (Barrels built for patched balls had broad lands and narrow grooves to give more support to the undersize ball.) Baker's rifle heaved out a 4-ounce conical bullet with 16 drams of powder--hardly a load for recoil-sensitive shooters!

In 1847 Captain Claude-Etienne Minie of France fashioned a bullet with an iron cup in its hollow base. Powder gas drove the cup forward, expanding the bullet into the rifling's grooves. Expansion was sometimes so violent, however, that the bullets were cut in two, leaving a ring of lead in the bore. Minie (pronounced meenáy) modified his design and tested it against balls shot from smoothbore muskets. At 100 yards the musketeers hit a 6x20-foot target 149 times out of 200 shots; but riflemen using the Minie bullet scored 189 hits. At 400 yards the difference was startling: 9 hits from the muskets, 105 from the rifles. The riflemen also hit twice as often at 300 yards as the smoothbore shooters did at 200. Later Minie marketed a new conical bullet to the British military for which he received 20,000 pounds, a generous sums in those days. William Greener protested the award and was given 1,000 pounds for first pointing out the expansion idea.

Minie's bullet, lubricated with mutton fat or beeswax, became issue ammunition for the Union Army's Enfields during the American Civil War. At first a wooden plug was placed in the hollow base of the bullet to prompt expansion, but this proved unnecessary. Bullet and powder were carried in separate paper pouches crimped together by folding. To load, a soldier would tear the tail of the powder pouch with his teeth, opening both pouches. He then dumped the powder in and used the paper bullet pouch as patching.

Walter Hunt's "rocket balls," which he developed in 1849 for his repeating rifle, were also Minie balls, but with a powder charge inside. That same rifle, redesigned for rimfire cartridges, became known as the "Henry." In Confederate camps it was referred to as "that damn Yankee rifle you loaded on Sunday and fired all week."

Until well into the 20th century, progress in the development of small arms ammunition was measured mostly on the battlefield. Eager to find more effective ammunition for its troops, the British government enlisted in 1854 the services of Joseph Whitworth, a brilliant technician who postulated that poor accuracy was less a function of loose tolerances than of barrel design. This notion ran counter to popular thinking at that time, but British Ordnance Chief Viscount

Hardinage was willing to let Whitworth test his theory, even to the extent of building an elaborate 500-yard enclosed range where Whitworth was able to experiment with various rifling types and rates of twist.

The standard rate of twist in military rifles then was one complete rotation in 78 inches of forward travel, or 1-78. The best all-around twist for short bullets, Whitworth found, was 1-20. Skeptics thought the sharp spin would retard these bullets, but a hexagonal bullet of Whitworth's own design gave more than twice the penetration of a standard ball from a slow-twist barrel. In subsequent tests that small-bore hexagonal bullet flew flat and accurately, producing a mean 500-yard deviation of 4 1/2 inches (compared to 27 inches for competing

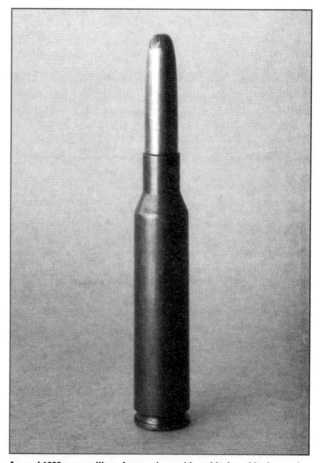

Around 1900 many military forces changed from big-bore black-powder cartridges to bottle-necked smokeless rounds like this 6.5x55 Swedish.

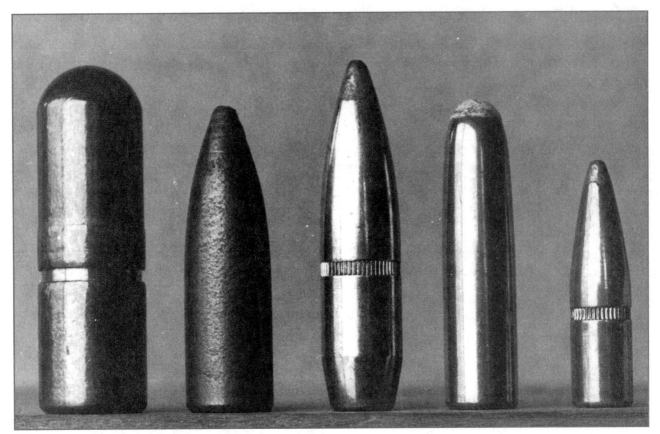

Popular hunting bullet designs (left to right): A-Square solid (full-jacket) for dangerous thick-skinned game; Barnes flat-base softpoint spitzer; Hornady boat-tail softpoint spitzer; Herter roundnose soft point; and Hornady flat-base softpoint "Spire Point." The cannelures locate and receive the crimp that holds the bullet more securely. Crimping is required with cartridges delivering heavy recoil that could unseat bullets in the magazine.

bullets). Hexagonal bullets proved expensive to manufacture and slow to load; but still, Whitworth's efforts gave other designers plenty of ideas to work with. William Greener, for example, began experimenting with narrow-land rifling pitched 1-30--a quick twist for that day--and managed to stabilize small-bore (.40 to .52) bullets out to 2,000 yards. In 1856 gunmaker James Purdey built two rifles featuring Greener-style barrels. He called them "Express Train" rifles because of their great power (the word "Express" was later applied to many potent British cartridges).

Breechloading rifles eliminated the need to design an accurate front-loading bullet. Indeed, bullets loaded from the rear could be made harder and longer and cast to full groove diameter. Hard bullets could be stabilized with shallower grooves and thus driven faster. Sharper rifling pitch could be used, even with rifling that varied in pitch and depth from breech to muzzle. Sometime after 1879, Sir Alfred George Greenhill devised a formula to determine proper rifling pitch, whereupon bullets made of naked lead were relegated to handguns. The high velocities possible with smokeless powder fouled rifle bores with lead stripped by the lands during passage. Harder bullet alloys helped to a certain extent, as did paper patching. But jacketed bullets proved the only sensible solution when speeds exceeding 2,000 feet per second were in demand.

The first commercial bullet jackets were made of steel, with a coating of cupro-nickel. Having proved satisfactory in the .30-40 Krag, they failed at the higher velocities of the .30-06 because of metal fouling. Tiny lumps of jacket adhered to the relatively cool steel near a rifle's muzzle, tearing at the jackets of other bullets. Shooters fought the fouling with "ammonia dope," a witch's brew that included half an ounce of ammonia bicarbonate, an ounce of ammonia sulfate, 6 ounces ammonia water and 4 ounces tap water. Poured into a plugged barrel and allowed to "work" for 20 minutes, the solution was then flushed out with hot water. Drying and oiling followed. Spills on exposed metal parts, if not attended, could cause pitting.

"Mobilubricant," tested by the Army before World War I, reduced metal fouling but also boosted breech pressures in the .30-06 from 51,000 to around 58,000 psi. Coating the entire cartridge sent pressures as high as 70,000, a problem that was exacerbated by the use of tin in jacket alloys. Like French artillerymen, American soldiers found that tin helped prevent copper stripping in the bore. But tin plate could also "cold solder" itself to the case neck. A lubricated case gave the neck no room to expand, while it increased back-thrust on the bolt. Add a bullet that got stuck tight in the neck and pressures would go through the roof. In one example a bullet recovered at a military range still had the case neck clamped fast. The prohibition of Mobilubricant and tin plating on service ammunition soon followed.

A safer method to avoid metal fouling was to incorporate tin in the bullet jacket. The cupro-nickel wrap on the steel-jacketed Krag bullet of 1893 had been 60 percent copper and 40 percent nickel. In 1902 cupro-nickel replaced steel as the main jacket material. Gilding metal (90 percent copper, 10 percent zinc) was thought to be too soft for the high-speed 150-grain bullet in .30-06

The Nosler Partition bullet is especially useful in big game cartridges whose high muzzle velocities can shred ordinary bullets in heavy bone and muscle. The .30-30, for which these Partitions were developed, is a mild-mannered round commonly used on light-boned game like whitetail deer.

service ammunition; but when tin plating proved hazardous, the Western Cartridge Company announced a new jacket with 90 percent copper, 8 percent zinc and 2 percent tin. Called Lubaloy, it worked so well even with the most ambitious .30-06 loads that in 1922 the honor of providing ammunition at the Palma Match was awarded to Western for 180-grain Lubaloy-coated bullets. That year, experiments at Frankfort Arsenal showed that gilding metal could stand up to high velocities. It remains (without tin) the jacket material of choice for most hunting and target bullets. Most bullet makers now favor jackets comprising 95 percent copper and 5 percent zinc. Barnes and several other makers who specialize in deep-penetrating big game bullets now employ thick jackets of "pure" copper to reduce fragmentation.

Jackets are formed by two methods: by "cup and draw" and by impact extrusion. Drawn jackets begin as wafers punched from sheet metal. Formed or drawn over a series of dies, the cups become progressively deeper and are eventually trimmed to length and stuffed with lead. The bullet is then shaped and finished off at the nose. Jackets formed

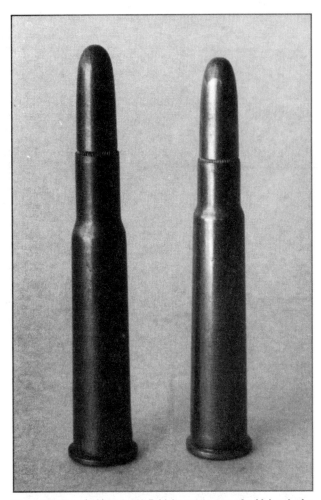

The .30-40 Krag (left) and .303 British were among the high-velocity small-bore cartridges adopted as service cartridges during the transition from black to smokeless powders during the 1890s.

by the impact extrusion method begin as sections of metal rods that are annealed and fed into a punch press that slams them into cup shape with 60 tons of force. Nosler's Partition bullets, with their cavities fore and aft, must be punched twice.

With the exception of the Barnes X-bullet, which is made from solid copper alloy stock, expanding big game bullets, military small arms bullets and target bullets contain lead cores. Most "full patch" big-bore bullets designed not to expand are also of lead-core design. Exceptions include A-Square's one-piece Monolithic solid and Speer's African Grand Slam, with its tungsten core. Lead cores commonly consist of 97$\frac{1}{2}$ percent lead

and 2$\frac{1}{2}$ percent antimony (for hardness). Six percent is about the limit for bullets. Sierra uses three proportions of antimony in its cores, depending on application: 1$\frac{1}{2}$, 3 and 6 percent. Bullets built to open quickly at low velocities work best without antimony. Some big game bullets, like the traditional Barnes softpoints, have unalloyed lead cores and depend on thick, ductile jackets to control and contain expansion.

Jackets are generally formed around cores in a die. Cannelures, which have gradually disappeared on rifle bullets, serve mainly as crimping grooves. They've been retained on bullets for heavy-recoiling rounds like the .458 Winchester (to prevent bullet creep in the magazine) and on pistol bullets (where crimping helps keep short, shallow-seated bullets in place and reinforces feeding). In the halcyon days of the lever-action, crimped cartridges resisted bullet setback in tubular magazines; in fact, crimping is still a good idea for use with the more powerful rifles of this type (neck tension alone, though, is adequate to secure .30-30-class bullets).

Hornady, Winchester and a few other makers routinely crimp bullets. Most cannelures are rolled on, but Nosler cuts the crimp in its 210-grain .338 bullet. It's become popular in some circles to use bullets coated with molybdenum disulfide. This black substance reduces friction in the bore and in the air, presumably boosting velocity without increasing pressure. Winchester's Fail Safe big game bullet wears such a coating, bonding it to the jacket with a wax. Kits that allow handloaders to "moly-coat" their own bullets have recently become available.

To guarantee a high level of accuracy, jacket and core dimensions must be held to tight tolerances. Sierra, renowned for its match-winning target bullets, keeps jacket thickness within .0003 inch of "spec" and limits bullet weight variation to .3 grain. Test lots of 168-grain 30-caliber match bullets that don't shoot into .250 inch at 100 yards can send the entire batch back into Sierra's production line. Demands on hunting bullets are less stringent, at least in terms of dimensional uniformity. Still, bullets for varmint shooting at long range must be very accurate. And they must do what a target bullet shouldn't do: *expand*. A bullet that simply passes through a creature may not fatally wound it. The larger the animal, the more critical the bullet's terminal performance. In hunting small game, bullets must shed their energy quickly; hence, they're made with thin jackets that rupture easily on contact with light-boned, thin-skinned animals like prairie dogs. Once it begins to open, a varmint bullet must release its energy before exiting. A bullet that continues to travel some distance after exit is wasting its energy.

Fragmentation inside an animal will result more often in instant kills, even when the bullets miss vitals. Hollowpoint bullets with lightweight jackets are popular with varmint hunters because they open with devastating suddenness.

In the designing of big game bullets, the guiding lights remain rate of expansion and weight retention. Jacket shape, thickness--plus the bond between jacket and core--figure heavily in ensuring controlled (rather than explosive) expansion. Deep penetration through heavy bones and muscles may be necessary to bring the bullet into the vitals. Hunters can ill afford to waste energy on large surface wounds or to lose bullet weight to early fragmentation. Mechanical locks like Nosler's partition and the internal jacket ring in Remington's Core-Lokt bullets keep at least part of the bullet intact during

The big nose cavities in these Nosler pistol bullets ensure quick expansion at low impact velocities.

Wilhelm Brenneke, the brilliant firearms designer, developed these fine cartridges. The Cone Point is for light-skinned game; the TUG is for tougher animals requiring deep bullet penetration.

the first inch of penetration; and high velocity also increases the tendency of bullets to blow apart on impact. The trick is to design hunting bullets are designed to hold together when driven fast into an elk's shoulder at close range but still open reliably when threading a deer's rib cage at long range after velocity has dropped off.

Long, pointed bullet noses, which obviously cleave the air more easily than do blunt noses, are standard on bullets designed for long-range shooting. A high ballistic coefficient--essentially a mathematical description of the bullet's ability to retain velocity--depends on streamlined shape and high sectional density. A tapered heel or "boattail" further reduces friction during flight and is popular with many target shooters. Because this design incorporates an additional fold in the jacket, it provides another area where manufacturing flaws may arise. Boattail bullets shoot flatter than flat-base bullets at long yardage, but the difference is negligible at the ranges most big game animals are shot.

Blunt noses have a few advantages over the pointed or spitzer shape. For one thing, they carry a lot of weight in a short package; and they can be stacked end to end in a tubular magazine without fear that, upon recoil, a bullet nose will detonate the primer that rests on it. Blunt noses do not necessarily cleave brush better than pointed noses. Blunt bullets may have a better record in this regard, but that's largely because they *look* beefy. Blunt bullets in some traditional deer cartridges also have high sectional densities that reduce deflection. Given the sharp spin needed to stabilize them, long blunt bullets seem to perform as well as any in thickets. The 160-grain 6.5x55, the 215-grain .303 British and the 220-grain .30-06 all make sense for brush--not because they are blunt but because they have higher sectional densities than pointed bullets of the same length. ●

penetration. Trophy Bonded bullets (now loaded by Federal) employ a chemical bond that all but eliminates separation of jacket and core; they also yield very high terminal weights. Bullets designed for deep penetration usually cost a good deal more than standard softnose bullets or even super-accurate target bullets. But the cost of a box of expensive bullets is still a small part of the cost of a big game hunt; moreover, hunters seldom need more than 3-minute accuracy to kill an animal. Reliable bullet expansion and deep penetration, on the other hand, can be crucial in the shooting of elk, moose, bears and other big-boned, heavily muscled game. Most expansion here occurs during

# BARRELS AND RIFLING

Among the first European guns were 14th-century Italian bombards whose tapered bores accommodated projectiles of various sizes. Shooters poured in some powder, then dropped a rock in the muzzle. Sometimes it would lodge halfway down; sometimes it would drop all the way to the powder. No matter. The powder of that time seldom generated too much pressure; in fact, its components often separated out during loading or when a gun was being bounced around on the battlefield.

About the same time in other parts of Europe hand cannons were propelling iron arrows (with feathers) weighing half a pound. The charge of l/3-ounce crude gunpowder limited shots to javelin range. In l4l3, Mahomet II used heavier projectiles during the siege of Constantinople. One of his cannons, which had a bore diameter of four feet, fired a stone weighing 600 pounds! Soon even uglier projectiles were devised. Iron cannon shot the size of walnuts proved so deadly that German states outlawed their use. Still, ignition was unreliable, and powder chambers were commonly a third the diameter of the bore. Iron shot had limited range, spreading from boreline as soon as it left the muzzle and quickly losing its velocity. Single balls flew farther but were inaccurate because they couldn't be made to fit the bore tightly. In fact, arrows proved more accurate than these early examples of ammunition.

A great advance came with the use of lead projectiles. Lead melted at relatively low temperatures and could be easily molded into shot of various sizes. Because it was soft, it would also yield to the bore on firing, keeping breech pressures in check while obturating to seal the bore and prevent blow-by of powder gas. Lead was also denser than iron, so it held its elevation and energy to greater distances.

By the early 16th century, special target matches with rifles were held in Liepzig and Zurich. Before the advent of lead balls, which could be squashed into the grooves, rifling had been impractical. A bore-size iron ball would actually skid its way down the lands; without obturation, a patch could neither guarantee spin nor seal powder gas. It was imposible to load iron balls of groove diameter from the muzzle; and if they were loaded from the breech they would stick in the throat upon firing, causing the gun to burst.

Jaegers, as noted, had 24- to 30-inch barrels of 60 to 77 caliber, rifled with seven to nine slow-twist grooves. Most featured double-set triggers. Practiced marksmen could hit, offhand, 3½-foot targets at 250 yards. American colonists not only learned to respect the King's elite Jaeger units, they used these guns as models when building their own rifles. The "Kentucky rifle," which originated in Pennsylvania, even improved upon the jaeger. Its smaller bore (40 to 50 caliber) saved lead; and

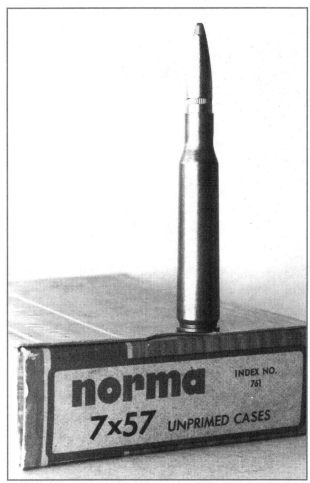

The 7x57 (7mm Mauser), which dates to 1892, was among the first smokeless military rounds.

its longer barrel produced more energy from burning powder and increased the sight radius. Hinged patchbox covers replaced the sliding lids of the jaegers, and trimmer stocks reduced weight.

One reason the Americans routed the British was the Redcoats used tight-fitting rifle balls. These had to be rammed hard down the bore-- a slow, difficult process. The colonists loaded their Kentucky rifles quickly and quietly with patched balls that, ironically, had been used in Europe for a couple of centuries before Lexington and Concord. As mentioned in the preceding chapter, black-powder fouling complicated loading for all 18th-century riflemen. After a few shots the buildup would resist balls that were only slightly undersize. Muzzleloading rifles called for truly loose-fitting balls of pure lead that slid down a fouled bore but would deform easily upon firing to seal powder gas. The barrels built for these projectiles commonly had broad lands and narrow grooves. This arrangement best supported the ball as it was rammed home. Later, when breech loading became practical, the lands were made narrow and the grooves wider to reduce friction on tight bullets.

America's oldest gun company got its start in 1816, when 23-year-old Eliphalet Remington II decided to build his own rifle from scratch. Making a good barrel was the hard part. At his father's forge in upstate New York, he heated an iron rod and hammered it until it was half an inch square in cross-section. Then he wound the rod about an iron mandrel just slightly smaller than his chosen bore size of 45 caliber. He heated the barrel white and sprinkled it with borax and sand. Holding one end in a pair of tongs, he pounded the other on the stone floor to seat the coils, then let the barrel cool before hammering out the curves. After grounding and filing eight flats to make the barrel octagonal, Remington had the bore rifled by a local machinist.

About 1840 Alvin Clark invented the false muzzle, which enabled a shooter to start a conical (parallel-sided) bullet down a barrel squarely. Paper-patched bullets soon dominated target matches. The widening accuracy gap between rifled barrels and smoothbores spurred inventors to develop a bullet that could be loaded from the front but that would take the rifling on its way out. Some of their solutions derived from earlier ways to make ball loading easier. A Spanish officer had, in 1725, developed a ball shaped to fit the rifling. A century later Captain Berner of the British Brunswickers borrowed the idea to build a rifle with two narrow spiral grooves and a ball with an integral belt to fit them. Slightly undersize and used with a patch, the ball slid home easily but was slow to start because it first had to be oriented.

Meanwhile, Delvigne was developing a hollow-based bullet later made famous by Claude Etienne Minie (see also chapter 3) featuring an iron cup in its hollow base. About that time John Jacobs of England developed a four-groove barrel and a bullet with matching fins. Called the "Lancaster," its spiraled oval bore required bullets to be perfectly sized and oriented.

Only a few of these ideas and innovations managed to survive the advent of metallic cartridges loaded from the breech. By the time of the Civil War, it was clear that bore designs were free to evolve without the constraints imposed by front loading. Among the stringent tests aimed at developing more accurate rifle barrels were those conducted by British army technician Joseph Whitworth (see also chapter 3). After determining the best rifling to be hexagonal, he made bullets to fit. Conical bullets, he discovered, also shot well and didn't require a sharp rifling twist (the standard rate of spin in Whitworth's day was one turn in 78 inches). Whitworth submitted one of his hexagonally-bored sharp-twist rifles to British Ordnance for tests. Allaying fears that a steep rifling pitch would retard the bullet, his rifle drove

its bullet through 15 inches of elm, while an issue Enfield firing an identical powder charge mustered only 6 inches of penetration. More tests at Hythe, England in 1857 proved Whitworth's rifle to be much more accurate than the Enfield. But in a decision strangely like its rejection of patched balls a century earlier, British Ordnance told Whitworth his gun was not suitable for military service. The hexagonal bullets were too expensive to make, the military insisted, and the bore wore out quickly. Besides, the rifle's ignition mechanism was faulty.

About this time, bullet-makers started using harder alloys. Breech-loaded bullets didn't have to be forced through the rifling by hand and, when sized to fit the grooves, didn't need to expand a great deal on firing to seal powder gas. Rifling in turn could be made with shallower grooves. That meant more velocity with equal pressures but no loss in accuracy because hard alloys didn't strip easily. Groove depth and pitch could even be varied within a barrel. Soon William Ellis Metford, a Britisher, began promoting wide, shallow grooves. Like the grooves in the barrels of most hunting rifles today, his were cut to a uniform depth of .004 inch. By steepening the pitch from breech to muzzle, the bullet was given a sharp final spin without boosting pressures. This gradual "gain

Weatherby's Vanguard, an inexpensive Japanese-built alternative to the Weatherby Mark V, is no longer produced. Weatherby has since introduced a smaller version of the Mark V for standard cartridges.

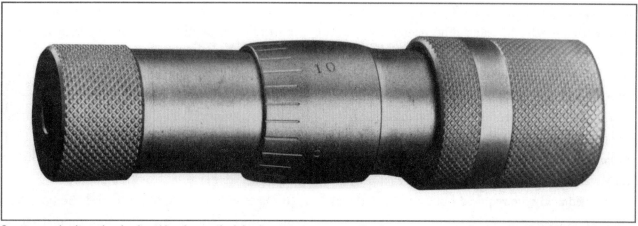

One way to check seating depth and headspace--both important measurements affecting accuracy and pressure--is with an RCBS micrometer.

twist" gave Metford's bullet one complete turn in a 34-inch barrel while imparting a l-in-l7 rotation at the muzzle. He also developed "segmented" rifling, by which the lands and grooves were shaped to appear in cross-section as segments of a circle. If you eliminated the corners at the bottom of each groove, he reasoned, you'd have less powder fouling. Some gunmakers in Metford's time cut "progressive" rifling, which changed in depth along the barrel's length. The Enfield rifle had three grooves tapering from .0l0 inch at the breech to .005 at the muzzle. Martini-Henry barrels had seven grooves ranging from .009 to .007, with a gain twist steepening from l-in-72 to l-in-22.

By the late l9th century most gunmakers had concluded that variations in twist and groove depth were unnecessary. Metford's wide, shallow grooves, when uniformly cut, afforded the best accuracy. About the time of World War I, Charles Newton devised "ratchet" rifling, with the lands sloping off to one side so each had only one shoulder. Newton reasoned that since a spinning bullet pressed on only one side of each land, the off-shoulder was unnecessary. This design, tested earlier in England, gave good accuracy but had no particular advantage over Metford rifling.

As black powder gave way to smokeless, bullets and barrels got rougher treatment. Velocities in excess of 2000 fps stripped even hard-alloy lead bullets, deforming the bullet and caking the barrel so subsequent shots flew wide of the mark. Jacketing each bullet with a thin shell of harder metal allowed the lands to grip the lead core but prevented contact between core and barrel. When jacketed bullets were seated atop compressed charges of blackpowder and were fired down bores with sharp-edged lands, fouling increased. Groove corners trapped powder residue that hardened despite the use of bullet lubricant; and powder flames were allowed to race around the bullets, which in turn failed to obturate readily the way traditional lead projectiles did.

The British .303 Lee-Metford rifle, featuring rounded lands that didn't foul easily failed when hot-burning smokeless powder replaced black. The erosive actions of hot powder gas and high-speed bullets soon ate away the mild steel barrels, and the rounded lands lost their feeble grip on the bullets. Barrelmakers revived traditional rifling, with three, four or five sharp-cut grooves equal in width to the lands between them. This pattern is still widely used on modern revolver barrels intended for lead bullets.

The .30-06 and other high-pressure, high-velocity rifle rounds that appeared just before World War II prompted the development of tougher barrel material. Soft carbon steels gave way to "ordnance" steel, used in the Springfield l903 rifle and for years in sporting rifles by Remington and other makers. Winchester had its "nickel" steel, which was more difficult to machine than ordnance steel but also more erosion-resistant. Neither of these alloys could long withstand the bullet traffic from cartridges like the .220 Swift, however; so Winchester pioneered the use of the now popular chrome-molybdenum steel. The only other material commonly used now is stainless steel, which is tougher to machine because it doesn't cut as cleanly. It costs more too, and it can't be blued in the traditional manner. Some shooters claim stainless steel resists erosion better than chrome-moly, but most barrelmakers insist this isn't so. The main advantage of stainless is that it won't rust, an important asset to hunters who have lately converted to the "all-weather" rifle.

Rifling in most elk guns follows the Enfield pattern used in the l903 Springfield and l9l7 Enfield rifles. The Springfields had four- and (later) two-groove rifling, the Enfields five grooves. What determines rifling type is the cross-sectional shape of the rifling, not the groove number. Broad, square-cut grooves with parallel shoulders characterize the Enfield type. Groove depth in 30-caliber rifles is usually .004, so a .308 bullet must be engraved to that depth by the lands in a .300 bore

with .308 groove diameter. Boots Obermeyer, a premier barrelmaker, has modified the Enfield rifling form to produce what's commonly called the "5R". Here, the sides of the lands form an angle of 55 degrees with a line tangent to the bore. The base of each land is wider than its top, and no groove corner is square. It's a marriage of Enfield rifling and the polygonal rifling now used by Heckler & Koch; i.e., lands and grooves with different radii but no distinguishable shoulders.

Barrels on modern centerfire rifles usually have four or six grooves, though Shilen, Apex and a few others favor eight. Ruger 77 rifles in .458 have eight-groove barrels. Barrelmaker H.M. Pope developed an eight-groove rifling after the design of George Schalck, whose target barrels were among the best available around the turn of the century. Pope adopted a left-hand gain twist with broad grooves that increased slightly in depth from breech to muzzle. The groove radius was three times bore radius, and each groove was just deep enough in its midsection to exceed bore diameter. This design enabled the grooves as well as the lands to align the bullet. The Metford rifling commonly in use today features wide groove bottoms with the same radius as the bullet, plus flat-topped, square-shouldered lands. Groove numbers have varied since World War I, when U.S. soldiers toted two-groove Springfields. Now most rifle and pistol

Leupold's 36x target scope on a heavy-barreled Winchester Model 70 target rifle helps produce tiny groups.

**H-S Precision's take-down rifle features a fluted barrel, bipod and Leupold tactical scope. Accuracy is typically half-minute.**

barrels have four to six grooves. There's no magic number for top accuracy.

The correct rate of rifling pitch depends mainly on the length and speed of the bullet. Long bullets require a faster pitch than short ones and slow bullets spin quicker than fast ones. Even round balls benefit from rifling, which prevents precession, a forward "rolling" action. In 1879 British ballistician Sir Alfred George Greenhill came up with a formula to determine proper spin for all bullets with a specific gravity of 10.9. The specific gravity of pure lead is 11.4, so most jacketed bullets qualify. The Greenhill formula, first published in the "British Textbook of Small Arms, 1929," states: *Required twist in all calibers equals 150 divided by the length of the bullet in calibers.* Thus a 180-grain .308 bullet an inch and a quarter long should read 150/4=37.5. Since

"37.5" is in calibers, it must be converted to inches by multiplying 37.5 by .308. or slightly more than 11 inches. Most 30-caliber barrels are rifled 1-10 or 1-12, so according to the formula they are pitched right for that bullet. A perfect mathematical match is not necessary, and the ideal rate of twist varies according to bullet shape and velocity. Round-nose bullets are easier to stabilize than spitzers because their center of gravity is closer to the bullet's center. Barrels made for long bullets usually handle short ones better than barrels made for short bullets can shoot long ones. It's a good idea, therefore, to choose a rifling twist for the heaviest spitzer bullet one plans to use.

Rifling can be pitched left or right. Most American guns, such as the '03 Springfield, have right-hand twist. Enfields have a left-hand twist, because when they were built Winchester,

Remington and Eddystone were all set up to manufacture Pattern 14 .303 Enfield rifles for the British. Colt handguns also have a left-hand twist. There is no difference in accuracy potential, though at long range right-hand rifling will cause a bullet to drift right, while left-hand rifling prompts a drift left, much the way a curve ball thrown by a pitcher reacts.

The narrow lands on typical four- or six-groove barrels occupy roughly one quarter of a bore's circumference, which is plenty for jacketed bullets. Two-groove Springfield barrels have broad lands that subtend more than half the bore circumference. Rumored to boost pressures with jacketed bullets, they handle cast bullets well because their fat lands hold the bullet nose in close alignment. Rifling can be cut, scraped, ironed or hammered into a bore. Cutting is the oldest method and is still used by those who pride themselves on making first-rate barrels. They commonly use a hook that cuts one groove while the barrel is pulled slowly through the bore under a heavy bath of pressurized oil. Each pass removes an onion-skin slice of steel before the barrel is indexed for the next groove. Multiple passes make this a slow job; indeed, during World War II it was deemed too slow. Armories replaced single hook cutters and less aggressive single scrapers with broaches -- long rods with multiple cutters arranged in steps of increasing depth. This speeded up production, but the broaches were expensive and shattered easily. Rifle barrels today are seldom broached, though Ruger and other handguns feature broached rifling.

Cutting grooves leaves minute imperfections or tool marks in the metal. Some barrelmakers lap, or polish, newly rifled bores to remove as many of these marks as possible. This process also opens up any "tight spots," making bore dimensions as uniform as possible from breech to muzzle. A good lapping job leaves a mirror finish, which most shooters appreciate. Some top barrelmakers, though, claim that a good job does not need to be finished with lapping paste. Like glass bedding, lapping is sometimes used to cover poor workmanship. A few barrelmakers also think bores can be too smooth, increasing bullet contact and friction and driving up pressures. "It doesn't matter if you lap or not," says Bill Wiseman, who manufactures McMillan barrels (which are lapped). "What matters is how careful you are." Wiseman maintains a lap will not correct shoddy work, but it can shave .0002 of roughness from the bore.

Many big gun firms now use a tungsten carbide button to "iron" or press rifling into the bore. No metal is removed, so the resulting bore surface is

The BOSS device on the muzzle of Browning's A-Bolt rifle is a counterweight used to "tune" barrel vibrations and improve accuracy with any given load.

This Weatherby Mark V Lazermark rifle is equipped with a Weatherby 3-9x44 Supreme scope on a Buehler mount.

very smooth. The operation is quick and, once the expensive machine is paid for, economical. Nearly all .22 rifles and most factory-built centerfires now wear button-rifled barrels. Some makers of premium-grade barrels also prefer carbide buttons to cutters. Buttons show a greater advantage as the groove number increases; companies that offer six- or eight-groove barrels overwhelmingly prefer buttons. Marlin's Micro-Groove rifling, which originally featured 16 grooves (but now has 12), is ironed in with a button. Another rifling technique is hammer forging. Pioneered in this country by Roy Weatherby, it remains practical only in large arms plants. The machines are huge, with great rollers that knead or hammer a barrel blank around a hard mandrel fashioned with the rifling in reverse. Done well, hammer forging leaves a bright, slick bore surface.

All barrelmakers use gauges to ensure dimensional uniformity. Two terms often bandied about but less often understood are "star gauge" and "air gauge." The former was developed in 1905 for measuring land and groove diameters in military rifles. Star-gauged Springfields had a reputation for accuracy matching that of the best contemporary sporting guns. An air gauge, on the other hand, utilizes the pressure of compressed air to "feel out" variations in bore dimensions. Air gauging doesn't make a barrel good--it simply weeds out those that aren't. Barrels that are carefully fashioned with top-drawer stock and tooling don't need air-gauging,

according to Bill Wiseman, who employs a metal plug to check bore dimensions. An air gauge can register diameter changes down to .00005, closer than necessary for even target barrels, whose breech-to-muzzle variations rarely exceed .0002. Bores on most hunting rifles are allowed .0005 tolerance. A target-grade barrel costs more because it is held to closer tolerances. It also offers a smaller selection of bore diameters (commonly .224, .243, .284, and .308).

Barrel weight has nothing to do with grade. Target-weight barrels are big in diameter--#5 and heavier by industry charts. Hunting-weight barrels are designated #1, 2, 3, and 4. Most factory sporting rifles now feature barrels with a #3 contour. Light barrels can be as reliable in first-round placement as heavy barrels, but they "walk" sooner when heated by subsequent shots. A light barrel can be stiff if it's short, but short barrels reduce a bullet's acceleration time. Small bores that channel big charges of slow-burning powder mandate longer barrels than do big bores with small charges of fast fuel. Velocity falls off as inches are lopped from the barrel. How much depends on cartridge and barrel length. Shortening a .35 Whelen barrel from 26 to 24 inches barely changes bullet speed, but cutting a .264 Winchester Magnum barrel from 24 to 22 inches will cripple the cartridge.

Keeping barrels stiff for good accuracy and long enough for reasonable velocities from magnum cases has been a problem for gunmakers offering lightweight guns for elk hunters. A recent innovation--the fluted barrel--was used for years on the target circuits, but not in the field. Assuming equal quality, concentricity, length, weight and bore, there's no inherent difference in first-round accuracy between fluted and un-fluted barrels. But fluted barrels, because they dissipate heat more evenly than round or octagonal barrels, enjoy a slight edge during extended periods of firing.

Since accuracy is a barrel's primary function, each barrel is "stress-relieved" during manufacture by heat treating, which relaxes the tremendous tensions built up in the steel by deep-hole drilling and rifling. Shooting generates heat that forces a barrel that hasn't been stress-relieved into all sorts of contortions. Cryogenic stress relieving--a process that subjects a barrel to very low temperatures under controlled conditions--has become a hot topic among shooters, some of whom have claimed dramatic results. Another factor affecting accuracy is the shape and condition of the muzzle. Rifle barrels are "crowned" on a lathe to ensure muzzles that are square with the bore, and also to protect the bore margin from damage. Some muzzles are deeply recessed; others have almost no recess to shield the rifling. The least little chip or unevenness in the barrel mouth can cause gas to escape prematurely, pushing the bullet off course or causing it to shudder on exit.

Muzzle brakes do not affect accuracy adversely if they are bored out to form a decompression chamber for escaping gas. The bullet must not touch the brake. The best brakes have holes symmetrically arrayed to vent the gas uniformly so the pressure cloud around the bullet has no strong or weak areas. Slits in the barrel roof are not as benign as a bored-out muzzle brake, because they work while the bullet is still being driven and directed. One barrelmaker swears these slits have no appreciable effect on flat-base bullets, but they can tip boat-tails. The reason: as the heel of a bullet passes the slits, gas is released from that side, with no gas bleeding from the opposing side. This pressure differential can push the bullet tail up. If true, this is of little consequence to hunters, many of whom use ported barrels and claim fine accuracy.

The other end of the barrel also affects accuracy. Chambering of factory barrels is done to SAAMI (Sporting Arms and Ammunition Manufacturers' Institute) specifications. Custom barrels can have chambers cut to the shooter's whim. Some riflemen chamber for a standard cartridge but cut the throat long or short to match a particular bullet. Tight chambers have a following among benchrest shooters, who turn case necks to fit a piston snug in the barrel. But they're bad medicine in hunting rifles that may be required to digest cartridges of various dimensions. An overly tight chamber

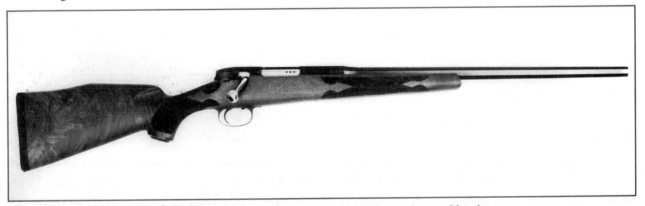

Wichita Arms produces small numbers of highly accurate rifles and pistols for hunters and competitive shooters.

When zeroing a big game rifle, this hunter pads the forend with a sandbag; his right arm should support the butt on another sandbag for a steadier hold.

impedes release of the bullet, driving up pressures. There may also be trouble getting off a quick second shot if the next cartridge comes up dirty. A chamber usually gets hogged out with a roughing reamer and completed with a finishing reamer. It may then be polished with a burnishing reamer and lapped. Barrels made late in a reamer's life can have smaller chambers than those made earlier. Oversize chambers impair accuracy because they fail to align the bullet properly with the bore.

No matter how straight or precise a barrel is made, it will be inaccurate if it's not mated squarely to the receiver, or if the bolt face or locking lugs bear unevenly. These concerns get special attention from gunsmiths whose clients insist on accurate rifles. Barrels are put on tight with wrenches that look more like tools for dismembering bulldozers. But some shooters complain that tight barrels are

not only unnecessary; they're inconvenient. These riflemen own "switch-barrel" guns with one conventional stock and one receiver but several barrels. It's an old idea, one that's been used for years to make shotguns more versatile.

Some bolt rifles are designed for easy barrel changing. (Among the most adaptable is Savage's reliable Model 110, which has a removable bolt face that can be changed from standard to Magnum cartridges and back to standard.) Each barrel must be headspaced to the parent action and its threads must be cut precisely and polished so the barrel can be screwed on by hand. The barrel channel needs to be relieved a few inches forward of the chamber so barrels can be changed without disassembling the rifle. As for prices, barrels vary a great deal. Competition-class blanks can run $300, but one large U.S. gunmaker pays less than $15 each for barrels it puts on hunting rifles.

# IMPORTANT TIPS AND TECHNIQUES ON HANDLOADING

Handloading properly starts with the cartridge case. More than merely an envelope designed to hold the bullet and primer in place and contain powder, the case locates the bullet in the bore, seals the chamber during firing, and bottles pressures that routinely run to 55,000 psi for many cartridges. It is made of brass (70 percent copper, 30 percent zinc) and is sometimes nickel-plated. Its dimensions are held to close manufacturing tolerances to ensure proper head-space (distance from bolt face to forward bearing surface of the case) and a snug primer fit. When the trigger is pulled and hot powder gas irons the brass against barrel steel, the case walls take on the shape of the chamber. The case must be hard enough to spring back from the chamber walls after firing, but not so hard that it cracks.

Case preparation for handloading affects cartridge reliability, accuracy, case life and even safety. Beyond that, priming, powder charging and bullet seating determine the effectiveness of the cartridge, transforming a brass hull into a tiny package of explosive power. The following pages explain some of the important things to keep in mind when preparing and handloading cartridge cases.

## CASE CLEANING AND INSPECTION

Wipe fired cases clean as they are boxed after firing, making sure there's no debris inside. Any grit sticking to the outside of a hull can scratch sizing dies and rifle chambers. Caked dirt inside alters case volume and pressure and can impede ignition. Tumbling cases in a device like the Vibra-Tek with walnut-shell media will leave them bright. Steel wool is too abrasive. Avoid using chemicals unless they're formulated for case polishing (like the RCBS Liquid Case Cleaner).

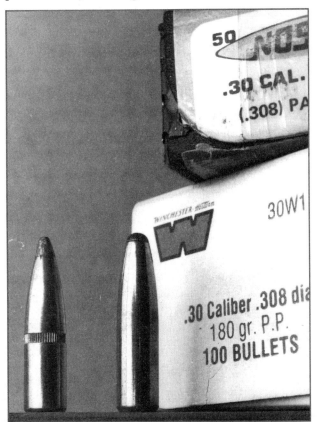

An ordinary softnose bullet like the 180-grain Winchester Power Point (left) is a good all-around deer bullet. Nosler's 200-grain Partition would be a better choice for elk, where deep penetration is required.

A case neck is turned to ensure uniform thickness—a routine operation for bench-rest shooters.

An acid wash must be weak to prevent etching. The cheapest alternative is a bath of boiling, soapy water. Dry washed cases in the sun or in an oven set for very low heat. Cases must be kept clean and dry, so wipe them thoroughly before storage.

Inspect each case as it's placed in a block for resizing. Look for hairline cracks, especially in the neck. A circumferential white line ahead of the belt on magnums means the case is weak at that point and may separate. Cases that headspace on a belt develop this line when they are full-length-sized and fired in large chambers. The front part of the case flows forward while the back end is held by the belt. The line is a stretch mark of thinning brass. Discard cases that show it and prevent its occurrence by neck sizing belted cases to be re-used in the same rifle. Signs of stretching ahead of the belt, rim or extractor groove are no cause for alarm--all cases stretch somewhat--unless they're sharp in contrast and appear crystalline. Cases are typically .005 shorter than the chamber to allow for variation in case dimensions and ensure easy bolt closure under field conditions. An extractor that holds the case tight to the bolt face on firing will, theoretically, prolong case life by eliminating the rearward motion of the case head as the case body expands to fit the chamber (extractor claws must have clearance too).

Gas-operated autoloaders with heavy breech bolts--the M1 Garand, for example--can exacerbate the problem of case stretching. The bolt slams home hard enough to shorten the case, which is punched out to chamber dimensions immediately upon firing. Some shooters claim a rear-locking bolt can stretch five times as much as a front-locking one, adding that stretch to the case. Throw away corroded brass, unless the cases are hard to replace and the corrosion is light. Tumbling can remove corrosion's ugly appearance, but pitting weakens the case. Check tumbled cases for chips of polishing media in flash holes, and measure overall length with a dial caliper or case length gauge. When jammed into the rear of the throat, a case that's too long will pinch the bullet and raise pressures. To allow for stretch, trim cases .01 short of standard length. An exception is the straight-walled variety that headspace on the mouth; these must be kept as close as possible to specified length. Rotary case trimmers ensure square, uniform mouths but leave burrs that must be taken off with a beveling/chamfering tool. Chamfering may also be necessary on new unprimed cases. It prevents bullet scarring during seating while ensuring more uniform neck tension.

Primer pockets of fired cases should be cleaned with a primer pocket tool so there's no grunge to keep primers from seating easily or making full contact with the floor of the pocket. Level each floor with a pocket deepening tool. When hit by the striker, primers seated tight against brass don't move, so all the striker's energy is used to detonate the priming mix. Primers that do not contact the pocket floor can require 50 percent more force from the striker for reliable ignition. [Note: Primers that protrude can impede bolt closure.]

Cases should be kept separate by make and weight. Volumes vary among brands because some cases are thicker than others, but there's no rule that applies across the many different case designs. The relationship between Winchester and Remington brass, for example, may not be the same (it may even be reversed) from one cartridge

A strong "O" press has the leverage and power for use on any sporting cartridge. Its large access area makes handgun cartridge reloading fast and easy.

type to another. Case weight, or brass thickness, can also vary by as much as 12 grains between lots from the same manufacturer. When case capacity is not the same from one cartridge to the next, poor accuracy and erratic pressures will result.

Keeping case weights within three to six grains of each other, depending on case size, needn't cause worry about extreme spreads in pressure or velocity, or about substandard accuracy. In fact, big game hunters could argue that they needn't bother weighing cases at all. But it can help when shooting for smaller groups. One hunter I know routinely punches less than 3/4-minute clusters from his factory-barreled .264 Model 70 because he dutifully follows bench procedures in handloading. Tight groups boost confidence and performance in the woods as well as on the target range.

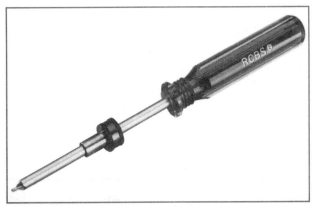

One way to gain uniformity in ammunition is to deburr flash-holes and make them all the same size.

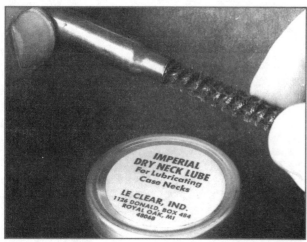

A case neck is lubricated prior to resizing. One poke with a bristle brush lightly lubed will ease passage of the expander button and prolong case life.

It's also wise to isolate cases with off-center flash-holes, keeping them for shooting practice. Cases with flash holes far from center are best discarded, because they can break decapping pins. Uniform flash-holes enhance accuracy, so it's a good idea to run a flash-hole reamer into each case. The reamer will also deburr the inside of the web where the manufacturer's punch came through. Do not attempt to remove brass from pocket walls. Pocket diameter is critical for tight primer fit. High breech pressure expands pockets.

## SIZING

Full-length sizing is not necessary for repeat firings in the same rifle. Hunters are often advised to full-length size to ensure reliable feeding afield, but this is not necessary for bolt-action rifles. Mechanisms with limited camming power--and certainly self-loaders--are best kept on a diet of full-length-sized (undersized) cases. Neck sizing for bolt guns prolongs case life because the brass is not rendered brittle by repeated compressions following expansion.

To full-length size, turn the die down in the press until it meets the shellholder (when the ram is all the way up). Lock the die in place. using the fingers only on lock rings. It's quicker than setting a screw and easier on the rings than when a tool is used to snug them. Adjust the decapping pin so it protrudes about .20 below the face of the shell holder. Lubricate the case by rolling it on a clean pad saturated with case lube, not ordinary oil, making sure to wipe off excess lube.

Next, put a small bead of lube on the inside of the case mouth by pressing it into the pad; or, using a bullet-diameter nylon brush, apply a thin film of lube inside the neck. That will prevent the expander ball from pulling too hard on the neck and stretching it. The expander ball should not squeak. Too little lubricant outside can cause a case to stick in the die, while too much dents cases. Excess lube inside can run into the powder chamber and affect ignition (substituting powdered graphite or Imperial case wax for liquid lube eliminates this problem). Lubricant left in the neck influences neck tension. Wipe cases free of lube after resizing a batch, using a bore swab or Q-tip inside the neck. Neck sizing can be done in a full-length die by leaving a gap about the thickness of a nickel between die and shellholder at the top of the ram stroke. The case body will still need lubricant, however.

Incidentally, neck expansion of straight-walled cases, such as the .45-70, does not take place in the sizing die. Another expander die must be screwed into the press until the die body touches the shell holder. The expander plug is then backed out and a case inserted into the die. Next, the expander is plugged into the die until it touches the case mouth, increaseing the contact a quarter turn at a time until the case mouth is adequately belled. Case mouths commonly split if there's too much flare.

Uniform neck tension is crucial to accuracy. A firm grip also ensures that bullets in rifles that recoil sharply will not creep out of their cases in the magazine. Neck tension hinges on the bullet's diameter and that of the sizing die neck and expander ball, plus case neck wall thickness and resiliency. Dies are made to squeeze necks down far enough so that the thinnest new brass will move. The expander ball--typically .001 smaller than the bullet--brings each neck back for a snug friction fit around the bullet.

Most chambers cut for factory ammunition provide .005 clearance around the neck. An under-size chamber neck (or thick brass) can impede bullet release, raising breech pressures. Necks that are out of round start the bullet off-axis with the bore, impairing accuracy. Multiple firings also add more brass in the neck as the case "flows" forward under gas pressure. Turning case necks, either with a power tool or by hand, shaves brass from thick spots on the outside of the neck, reducing it to uniform thickness and ensuring concentricity. Case neck turning can be done before or after sizing. A neck reamer removes brass from inside the neck and must be used before sizing, else too much material will be removed, leaving the neck so thin it may not grip the bullet firmly.

Rifles designed for competitive shooting typically include "minimum chambers" that accept only neck-turned cases. Neither turning nor reaming is necessary for hunting ammunition unless cases are being necked down (e.g., .250 to

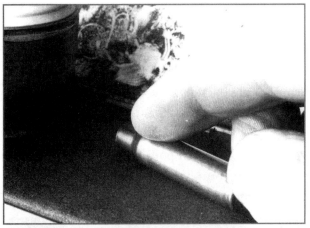

Rolling the case on a lubricated pad prevents the hull from sticking in the die, then separating when the press handle is operated.

.22-250, .308 to .243). As neck diameter shrinks, the neck wall normally gets thicker relative to the inside diameter. Neck reaming thins the brass while getting rid of any internal ledge that may have formed at the junction of neck and shoulder.

## PRIMING

Some handloaders prefer hand priming tools for primer seating because they allow a better feel than do highly leveraged press handles. Detecting loose primer pockets is important because it advises when loads are too hot or brass is "tired." It's wise to set aside cases that admit primers without noticeable friction and either discard them or load them one more time (lightly) for practice shooting. Loose pockets can cause blown primers. Even worse, a primer blown without the protection of shooting glasses can result in serious eye injury.

While hand priming tools work quite well, a little time spent priming with a press can reveal even slight differences in friction as the primer is seated. Working the handle gently (with the fingers, not the palm), then giving it a sharp tap also helps ensure a properly aligned primer. Primers should be seated .004 below flush with the case head, with the anvil legs solidly contacting the bottom of the primer pocket. Protruding primers may indicate a buildup of residue in the pocket or dimensional problems. Primers not seated flush can be driven forward by the striker, cushioning the blow and causing unreliable ignition. A protruding primer can even prevent chambering or detonate prematurely when the bolt is slammed forward violently. Those who use military cases must deal with crimped-in primers. The crimp can be removed with a deburring tool or a primer pocket swager.

Two important reminders about primers: They must be kept clean and dry to guarantee reliable ignition, and they must be kept in compartmen-talized boxes when in storage. A common mistake

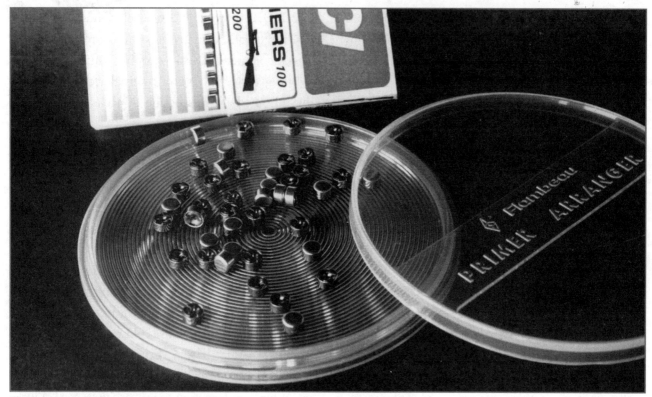

This primer tray features small concentric ridges that orient the primers for easy pickup.

among beginning handloaders is to work on a primer with sweaty fingers or greasy hands. It's smart to keep a clean, dry rag on the bench so hands can be wiped free periodically of any oils, solvents or moisture. And when inserting a primer in a charging cup it should be lifted gently by its sides, making sure to keep the finger away from the open mouth. In addition to speeding the handloading operation, an automatic primer feed protects primers. A tray that orients primers properly when given a few gentle shakes is a handy accessory. The importance of keeping primers separated in a cool place can hardly be overstated. Accidental detonation of a single primer can cause serious injury to eyes or skin; and the detonation of a large number of primers is like a bomb explosion. Indeed, the most hazardous place to work in a munitions plant is in the priming room, where wet compound is smeared like putty into empty primer cups. The compound is kept moist while precautions are taken to protect the area from concussions or sparks. Once the compound has dried it becomes extremely sensitive to shock. Priming rooms are shielded from the rest of the manufacturing activities by thick walls, one side of which is made weaker so that any explosion will be channeled where it can do the least harm. At one large ammunition facility some years ago, a worker walked from one building to another with a plastic pail full of disposable primers. Suddenly, he had a heart attack and fell. The primers detonated, leaving little of the worker to identify.

## CHARGING

Filling a case with powder may appear routine. Simply weigh out a charge on a scale and funnel it carefully into a case--or flip the handle of a powder measure. Provided you pay attention, nothing much can go wrong. Double-charging a case is possible, though, when loading fast-burning powders that take up little space in a big hull. Mixing powders or loading the wrong powder is possible when several canisters lie within easy reach. Before starting, be sure to clear the bench of everything that isn't needed to charge cases. Only one can of powder should be kept on the bench. Blocks with charged and empty cases should be separated so one can't be mistaken for the other. It's not a good idea to watch television or talk on the telephone while at the bench. Powder measures, tricklers and small containers used for sifting powder into a funnel must all be cleaned thoroughly whenever propellants are changed. Should one powder be contaminated with another, discard the mix. A clean cloth comes in handy for wiping powder residue from funnels, hoppers and drop tubes. In general, cleanliness produces better handloads and a safer workplace.

It's smart to consult several loading manuals--not just one--when working up a load for any cartridge. Data differ among manuals from one manufacturer to the next because bore and chamber dimensions among test rifles differ, as does the thickness of case brass. Working conditions vary, even from one shooting tunnel to the next. One good way to come up with a reasonable load is to average the top and starting charges from several different sources. Common sense dictates that you should *never* start at the top. Most manuals recommend reducing initial charges 10 percent below listed maximums when loading for a new cartridge or rifle. When dealing with charges of 10 to 30 grains, work up *no more than* half a grain at a time. With weights of 30 to 70 grains, do so one grain at a time. You can jump grain and a half with charges between 70 and 110 grains. There's no need to load large batches when testing for safety only. Three rounds per scale setting will indicate when cases can be extracted easily or show excessive head expansion after firing.

Powder scales must be zeroed for each use, and powder meters should be reset for different powder types. A specified charge of ball powder occupies less volume than the same weight using stick powder. The density of individual powders *within* those categories varies too. When charging from a powder measure, allow sufficient time for all the powder to fall. Experienced handloaders advise against metering maximum loads, but meters can be used with a scale for speed loading while maintaining safety. Simply set the meter half a grain below the charge weight, throw the metered charge into the scale pan, then add the last fraction of a grain with a powder trickler.

Large charges of slow-burning powders often fill the case to a point above the juncture of neck and shoulder, in which case the seated bullet must compress the propellant. To minimize crushing of

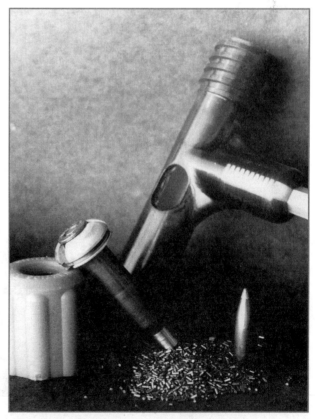

Striking an inertia bullet puller on a hard surface dislodges the bullet, which falls into the tool's hollow head along with the powder.

powder grains and potential case bulges (or bullet creep) after loading, the powder should be introduced to the case slowly. Tip the funnel so the powder grains spiral down--they'll pack tighter that way. A six-inch drop tube can be used to increase drop speed and sifting of the powder. Tipping the case and tapping it lightly on the bench as it's rotated will also help settle the powder. It's best to avoid compressed charges with boattail bullets for a couple of reasons: Boattail bullets are longer than flat-base bullets of the same weight and nose shape; they must therefore be seated deeper to stay within a given overall length. Also, when a boattail bullet enters the powder charge some powder may become wedged in the angle beween bullet and case neck, occasionally causing the case to bulge.

Once a block of cases has been charged, make a habit of inspecting everything visually. With most rifle cases, this merely means a quick glance to note that the powder levels look the same. Any that seem high or low should be weighed again.

## Bullet Seating

Bullet seating dies should be adjusted to clear the shellholder at the top of its stroke by about the thickness of a nickel. When seating a new bullet, the seating stem should extend outward almost all the way before inserting a charged, full-length-sized case and bullet. Then, with the bullet positioned loosely atop the case in the die, screw in the seating stem until it touches the bullet nose. Next, lift the ram handle, pulling the case down a fraction of an inch (a "fraction" meaning as little as .15 for smallbore cartridges) or enough to seat the bullet but not quite as deep as it will be when finished. Screw the seating stem in until it makes contact again with the bullet, then lower the press handle to complete the seating.

The Alliant Powder Company (formerly Hercules) offers a full line of propellants, including RL-15, a great choice for cartridges like the .35 Whelen. The slower RL-19 and RL-22 excel in the .270, .280 and popular belted magnums.

The next step is to insert the cartridge in the rifle chamber, closing the action *gently*. If it fails to close easily on the loaded round, the bullet is seated too far out and is in contact with the rifling. Lower the seating stem one turn, run the cartridge into the die again, and test it once more in the rifle chamber. Repeat that sequence until the bolt barely closes on the loaded round, then turn the seating stem one more revolution. The idea is to seat the bullet about $1/10$ inch off the lands so it can break free and start moving before it overcomes the initial thrust of the lands' engraving. A bullet that touches the lands offers tremendous inertia to the expanding powder gases, and they in turn must then simultaneously overcome neck friction and resistance caused by the lands. The resulting pressure curve is steep and may, at its peak, exceed acceptable limits. Bullets touching the lands can pose a problem even when they're not fired. Slight differences in case length or seating depth may cause a bullet to be gripped by the lands upon chambering. Extracting that loaded round could leave the shooter with an empty case on the bolt face, a bullet in the barrel, and a magazine full of powder!

In many rifles a bullet seated one-tenth off the lands can make overall cartridge length too great for the magazine. If the first loaded round won't fit, set it aside and load a fresh round in similar fashion, turning the seating stem down carefully until the magazine accepts the cartridge. Don't be satisfied with a good fit at the top station. All cartridges must feed from the bottom, which in some magazines imposes a slightly greater restriction on cartridge length.

In cases where magazine and throat allow extremely shallow seating (when using, for example, very light bullets for the caliber) it may prove advisable to seat bullets deeper to ensure adequate neck tension. The rule of thumb among most shooters is to allow one caliber (actually, bore

Most bullets for .22 centerfires measure .224 in diameter, but a few don't. The .227 bullet is for Savage's .22 High Power, the .223 for the .22 Hornet, and .222 for the .22 Remington Jet (a pistol cartridge).

diameter equivalent) of bullet contact. Thus, a .257 Roberts bullet should contact the neck at least one quarter-inch of its length. This may not prove critical on the target range or when single-loading varmint cartridges; but for big game rifles, where cartridges in the magazine are shaken by recoil, banged against saddles, dropped on the ground or crammed into duffle bags or glove boxes, snug bullet fit is important. Changing bullet types, by the way, can alter proper seating stem adjustment because the *ogive* (the curve of the bullet nose from parallel sides to tip) can vary from one type to the next, even when weights are equal. Always check seating depth against rifle chamber and magazine when switching bullets.

As for tube-fed lever action rifles, overall length is set by crimp grooves on the kind of blunt bullets such rifles require. These bullets should be seated so the crimp groove is even with the case mouth. Crimping is advisable for rifles with tubular magazines where the spring exerts constant pressure on bullet noses. It's also wise to crimp cartridges for autoloading rifles and any big-bore magazine rifle that generates heavy recoil. Crimping generally does not enhance accuracy, so most riflemen will avoid it. But any bullet to be crimped must have a crimping groove; otherwise, the case mouth will deform the bullet jacket.

Most seating dies can be set to crimp. Setting the die is merely a matter of seating a bullet to the cannelure, then backing the seating stem out a few turns. Loosen the lock ring on the die body and, with the ram still up and the cartridge remaining in the die, screw the die down until it contacts the case mouth. Lower the ram slightly and give the die another half turn in. When the ram is raised, the case mouth will press against the crimping shoulder in the die and fold it into the crimping groove.

## BOXING THEM UP

Every handloader has at some time found unlabeled cartridges in a box or shooting block. They are useless except for offhand practice because no data can be gleaned from them. Until proven, they must be considered substandard hunting or target loads. To avoid such embarrassment, it's best to label all boxes of handloads immediately. It's also smart when developing loads to label each cartridge with an indelible marker-- an especially good idea when one block is filled with several loads, or when one plans to shoot at the range from the block, rather than boxing them first. Blocks can tip over and spill cartridges; unless they're labeled individually, spilled cartridges can scuttle the tests. Cartridges should also be stored in a cool, dry place. Breech pressures can climb when rounds are left in a hot car for several hours. When loading, keep in mind the conditions under which shooting will occur. Hunting loads for late-season elk in the Rockies may not be what you need for gemsbok in Namibia during the warm months.

We all know handloaders who spend a lot of time fussing over their cartridges. Their benches are clean

With an Oehler 33 chronograph, an electric eye records passage of a bullet over each skyscreen. Given a known distance between screens, velocity can be calculated. Without such instruments, hand-loading become a guessing game.

enough for orthopedic surgery, and their tools gleam like a dentist's. They treat primers as if they were jewels, and there's never a stray grain of powder. Their cartridge box labels are even commercially printed. Such perfectionists may enjoy no advantages over a handloader who uses a 10-year old factory round fished from a dusty glove box while flailing away at some whitetails in a cedar swamp. But tiny groups on the range validate great care in handloading. A perfectly formed cartridge case is a first step in boosting confidence and developing loads that nip into one ragged hole. Equal attention to other handloading operations wrings top-level performance from both product and shooter.

# CHOOSING AND USING GAME BULLETS

In the day of muzzle-loading muskets and rifles, choosing a ball was easy: it had only to fit the bore! Conical bullets complicated things because, while lead balls of the same diameter weighed the same, bullet weights varied with bullet lengths. After the Civil War most hunters preferred bullets to patched balls because the former "carried up" better at long range and penetrated better at all ranges. The ratio of bullet weight to diameter--or "sectional density"--was highest with long bullets. But long bullets were heavy and generated lots of friction as they spun down the bore; hence they couldn't be driven as fast as shorter, lighter bullets.

Buffalo hunters must have argued the same way they do now about proper bullet weight and velocity. Sharps' catalogs of the late 1870s, for example, listed bullet weights of 293 to 550 grains for the .45-70. When smokeless rounds supplanted black-powder cartridges in military service a couple of decades later, ordnance officers opted in favor of heavy bullets for the bore: 162 grains in 6.5x52 Carcano, 173 grains in 7x57 Mauser, and 215 grains in .303 (.311) British. These long, blunt bullets poked along at less than 2,300 fps, which was slow by modern standards. They were streaks of lightning, however, compared to their predecessors.

Germany's 7.9x57 cartridge, designed for the Gewehr 88 (Model 1888 infantry rifle) came along two years after the French had made the first official move to smokeless powder with their 8mm Lebel. Like the military rounds that followed it, the 7.9x57 used a heavy roundnose bullet. In 1898 the modified Mannlicher action of the 1888 rifle was replaced by a new, much stronger mechanism: Paul Mauser's Model 1898. The cartridge remained unaltered until 1905, when German engineers substituted a lighter bullet at higher velocity. They changed bore diameter from .318 to .323 (8mm) and replaced the blunt 226-grain bullet with a sharp-pointed 154-grain spitzer. Muzzle velocity jumped from 2,090 to 2,880 fps.

American ordnance officers, who'd settled on a 220-grain roundnose bullet at 2,300 fps in the 1903 Springfield cartridge, were startled by Germany's switch to a lighter bullet. Almost immediately the U.S. ordered up a new cartridge. Its case was .07 inches shorter than the 1903's, but otherwise identical. The big change came with a new 150-grain bullet loaded to 2,700 fps. This racy cartridge, which became known as the .30-06, worked well during World War I but was changed in 1926, launching a 172-grain boattail bullet at 2,640 fps. This sleek missile provided a higher ballistic coefficient, thus greater energy and flatter trajectory at long range. Mostly, though, it benefitted machine-gunners. In 1940 the Army reinstated the 150-grain flat-base bullet, mainly because the Garand rifle didn't function as well with those long boattails.

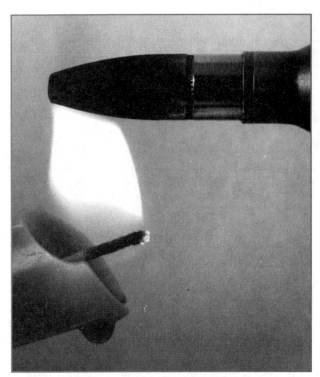

Smoking a bullet before chambering helps determine proper seating depth by showing clearly where the lands start. The followup: keep seating deeper .1 inch at a time until the land marks vanish, then turn the seating stem in another .05 to .1.

The evolution of military bullets around the turn of the century affected big game hunters because sporting ammunition had always borrowed heavily from military engineering. No smallbore smokeless rounds existed for hunters until soldiers had proven them. The first softnose bullets were long and blunt, just like the full-jacketed bullets that scarred the battlefields of France. Hunters got speedy spitzers only after the world's armies had used them against each other.

The first thing bullets had to face when pushed by smokeless powder was heat, both from the high-energy fuel and from increased friction in the bore. When driven at speeds much over 1,200 fps, pure lead would melt into the rifling. Alloying lead with up to 10 percent tin increased hardness, reducing leading and boosting allowable bullet speed. An alloy of 90 percent lead, 5 percent tin and 5 percent antimony could stand even more

heat, but velocities still had to be kept under 1,500 fps for acceptable accuracy.

By 1900 English shooters were using gas checks to protect bullet bases from powder gas. Introduced in the U.S. five years later, gas checks were brass or copper cups crimped onto the bullet from the rear. Half-jackets were similar but extended most of the way up the bullet's sides, preventing its lead core from touching the rifling. Gas checks allow lead bullets 2,000 fps without compromising accuracy. Half-jackets are good for 2,200 fps or so. Higher speeds require full jackets.

The first bullet jackets came along in the 1890s. They were of steel, coated with cupro-nickel. Though they kept bullet cores from melting and leading bores at .30-40 Krag velocities, they produced metal fouling in .30-06 barrels. Plating the bullets with tin seemed to help, but that practice was dropped when shooters found that, over time, tin "cold-soldered" to case mouths. Incorporating tin in the jacket proved a better idea. Western Cartridge Company soon announced its "Lubaloy" bullet containing a jacket of 90 percent copper, 8 percent zinc and 2 percent tin. Tin was later deemed unnecessary as a jacket component and was all but abandoned. Now most bullet jackets are of gilding metal, commonly 95 percent copper, 5 percent zinc. Nosler's Partition bullets originally had a 90-10 jacket composition.

The core of a jacketed bullet is mainly lead. Some cores are advertised as pure lead, but even the purest have traces of copper, zinc, nickel, aluminum and arsenic. Most cores contain a little antimony--about 2.5 percent--to make them harder. A little antimony makes a big difference, with 6 percent about the maximum. Sierra offers three degrees of hardness in its rifle bullets, with antimony proportions of 1.5, 3 and 6 percent. A hard core stands heat better but it fragments more readily on impact. An unalloyed lead core acts like dough when mushrooming; it holds together well but deforms so easily that heavy jackets are required to control expansion.

Bullet cores are generally cut from lead wire or extruded from bar stock to the proper diameter, then annealed to prevent dimensional changes during forming. They're inserted as cold plugs into the gilding metal cups that eventually become their jackets. A pass through a die squeezes core and jacket together and shapes the bullet. A cannelure (crimping groove) may be added to bullets for crimped factory loads or cartridges of heavy recoil.

Bonding the jacket to the core has a lot to do with how the bullet will behave when it hits an animal. Big game like elk have bones and muscles that will stop or shred a fragile bullet. The best bullets for elk expand without fragmenting. As a result, they can drive deep, then open up to plow a wide wound channel. Peters' Inner-Belted and its

The small hollowpoint (left), built to open fast with light resistance, is relatively short because sectional density matters less than speed. For big game in the woods, the long softnose (right) offers high sectional density and more weight for deep penetration.

successor, the Remington Core-Lokt, were among the first bullets whose very names challenged cores to stick with their jackets during expansion. Trophy-Bonded, Bonded Core, Plains-Bond and other bullets now lay claims to inseparable unions between jacket and core. Few companies who make these bullets let the public know about it. Corbin, the well-known manufacturer of bullet-making equipment for hobbyists, points out that anyone can make chemically-bonded bullets, along with partitioned bullets and those made with several telescoping jackets. Corbin's swaging machinery has helped launch more than 200 bullet businesses, which may explain why many more brands of big game bullets are advertised compared to a decade ago.

The first jacketed softpoint bullets were round-nosed, with lots of lead exposed in front. They were made to open readily because their great weight limited velocity to between 2,000 and 2,400 fps. When Charles Newton developed his line of powerful sporting cartridges shortly before World War I, he designed his own bullets to extend effective range and withstand higher impact velocities. Newton found traditional roundnose bullets went to pieces when driven into heavy game at velocities exceeding 2,700 fps. Spitzer bullets proved unreliable, sometimes sailing through an animal without opening. At other times they would rupture, then fragment. Finally, Newton designed a pointed bullet with a wire nose insert to help prevent magazine damage and control expansion. His bullets also featured paper insulation placed between jacket and core to keep cores from melting due to barrel friction. Newton uncovered evidence of core melt by drilling a hole in some bullet jackets and firing through white cardboard at 20 feet. The result was a smear of melted lead on the cardboard. Then, after wrapping cores in thin paper,

High-velocity impact can tear a bullet core from its jacket (right). The intact heel on the Nosler Partition (left) ensures a longer wound channel.

he repeated the test and found no smears.

Other bullet-makers went to equally great lengths to court big game hunters. Winchester's early Precision Point had a cone of jacket material covering the bullet tip and inserted at three points under the jacket proper. Three windows of lead exposed at the juncture of cone and jacket initiated expansion. Not to be outdone, Peters developed the Protected Point. A cone point capped a flat-topped lead core whose front third was wrapped in a "driving band" under the jacket. On impact, the front of the bullet pushed back as it expanded, forcing the driving band down and thus controlling the core's expansion. A Protected Point bullet, however, required three hours and 51 separate operations to make. Winchester later brought out a similar but less expensive bullet without the driving band. It became the Silvertip.

Remington's answer to bullet deformation was the Bronze Point, essentially a hollowpoint with a peg in the hole. The front half of the peg was a bronze cone forming the bullet tip. Impact forced the peg back into the bullet core, causing it to mushroom. Remington's recent best-seller, the Core-Lokt, is a modern inner-belted bullet that works well against elk, moose and bears.

Hollowpoint bullets are commonly thought suitable only for light game, mainly because

softnose bullets have become almost standard issue for big game hunters. The behavior of hollowpoint bullets depends on the dimensions of the cavity and the design and materials of jacket and core. Before World War II the Western Tool and Copper Works made a hollowpoint with a tiny cavity that proved effective on elk-size animals, even when driven by such cartridges as the .30 Newton and .300 H&H Magnum. DWM offered a "strong-jacket" bullet with a long, narrow nose cavity lined with copper tubing. Unalloyed copper jackets have helped Idaho's Bitterroot Bullet Company establish a reputation among elk hunters. Jackets as thick as .060 in .338 bullets, plus a nose cavity to start expansion, make Bitterroots long for their weight. They require deep seating and a wary eye for signs of high pressures.

When velocities began to climb after World War II, bullet failures in game increased. One moose hunter was dismayed when his bullet came apart on impact. He went home and studied the German H-Mantle, which featured a dam of jacket material separating the core into two parts. When the front end mushroomed, the dam stopped expansion, allowing the rear section to remain intact on penetration. He decided to make

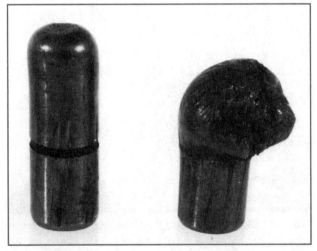

The fired Hornady full-jacketed solid (left) is only slightly bulged at the nose, while the bullet at right fared less well.

Jensen bullets, designed to penetrate, boast sleek form along with a polycarbonate tip.

a few more bullets like that, and thus did John Nosler's project begin and grow over time into a commercial business. The first jackets for his Partition bullets were machined from tube stock, leaving a distinctive frosted exterior finish and shiny belt. When the company began making jackets by impact extrusion, the result was smooth, bright exteriors. At first, shooters didn't appreciate the near-perfect interiors of the new jackets. The first Noslers also had a tiny hole in the dividing wall, that was seldom centered. The new bullets have no hole and are predictably more accurate.

Dual-core design was not new even in John Nosler's youth. Besides the H-Mantle, RWS has for many years sold TIG (Torpedo Ideal) and TUG (Torpedo Universal) bullets of this persuasion. The tail section of a TIG has a funnel-shaped mouth that accepts the coned butt of the front section. Impact starts expansion at this juncture as well as at the bullet nose. The rear core opens slowest because it's hardest. TUG bullets are similar, but the juncture is reversed. That is, the rear section fits into a cavity in the front section. On impact, the bullet nose gets battered from both ends, opening quickly. Under heavy resistance it

may even break apart; but then the rear section continues on as a solid slug. RWS still makes H-Mantle bullets and distributes them in the U.S. Swift bullets also feature a partition, and the company now supplies bullets to Remington for its "Safari" ammunition.

Hornady does not offer a partitioned bullet but claims its "Interlock" jacket band bites into the core soundly enough to prevent separation of jacket and core. The cannelures on most Hornady bullets help too. Sierra's "Pro-Hunter" flat-base and "Game King" boattail bullets have tapered jackets whose heavy bases limit expansion to the front part of the core. Speer took a different path

One of the best big game bullets for the .35 Whelen and .358 Norma Magnum is the 250-grain Nosler Partition. The right-hand bullet has been seated on a compressed charge. Note the impression of the powder grains on the bullet's heel.

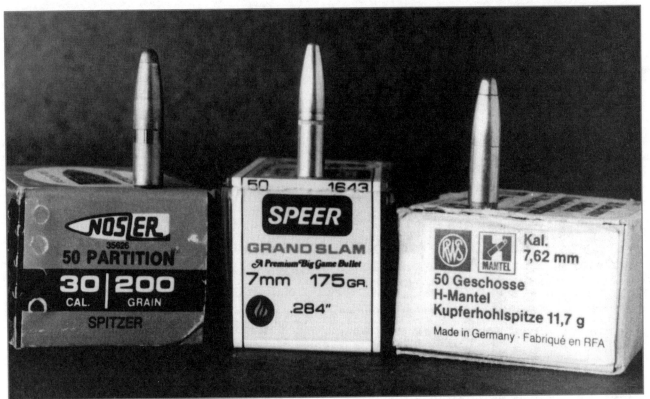

Long heavy bullets with internal devices to impede breakup are best for game the size of elk. The H-Mantle at right is the German equivalent of our Nosler Partition.

as well, providing its Grand Slam bullet with a two-part core but no divider. The rear section is harder than the front. The Grand Slam's jacket is tapered and softer at the nose than at the base. To help hold the core in place, a heel fold and swaged inner ring have been added.

The Partition's popularity, among other reasons, prompted experimenters like Jack Carter to challenge Nosler for the U.S. hunter's dollar. In 1985 Carter introduced the Trophy Bonded Bear Claw bullet, with its solid rear shank and lead core chemically bonded to the jacket for increased weight retention. Trophy-Bonded bullets (now loaded and also manufactured by Federal) wear jackets of pure copper rod that's annealed in stages to make it harder at the base than at the nose. Each tapered jacket is so thick at the base that it accounts for up to two-thirds of the bullet's diameter there. While most bullets from Carter's

Texas firm have a sleek profile, the front end of the jacket is the front end of the bullet. The core ends abruptly, with no exposed lead point. These bullets retain a high proportion of their weight even in heavy game. Two 200-grain bullets recovered from moose weighed 194.6 and 198.7 grains. These and other bullets designed to penetrate thick muscle and blast through bones have become known as "controlled expansion" bullets--a misnomer, really, because engineers control the upset of every softnose bullet, from frangible .22 missiles to the tough .458 bullets made for shooting Cape buffalo.

Swift bullets employ the Nosler and H-Mantle design but with a thicker jacket fused to the forward core to minimize lead loss. Winchester developed its own Fail Safe bullet for tough game. A lead heel core complements a hollow-point nose of solid jacket material. Speer's Grand Slam incor-

These Speer African Grand Slam bullets are (left to right): .338-275 solid; .375-300 solid; .416-400 soft point; .416-400 solid; .458-500 soft point; .458-500 solid.

porates a soft nose and harder core alloy in the rear. Partitions were used for years by Weatherby, but they are now made by Federal (augmenting the Trophy Bonded bullets in the company's Premium line). Remington offers Swift bullets in Safari Grade ammunition, and Speer loads the Grand Slam in its Nitrex cartridges.

Widely acclaimed among bullets built to drive deep, the Barnes X has no core. Its solid copper alloy body features a hollow point that initiates upset. Like the Winchester Fail Safe, the X-bullet (which comes loaded in PMC ammunition) excels at penetration. A-Square is also well known for its bullets and ammunition, mainly among the safari set. Its "Dead Tough" softnose has performed well on lions and buffalo. The Hawk bullet, created by Bob Fulton, is an ordinary-looking softnose with a ductile jacket that resists fragmentation. Fulton says its ogive has as much to do with ballistic

coefficient as the tip itself, and that the round-nosed bullets he developed fly as flat as spitzers at normal ranges. His and other small enterprises offer bullet weights to order, with small quantities available by mail for test purposes.

The first step in selecting a controlled-expansion bullet is to answer the question: Do I really need one? For many applications ordinary softpoints may be adequate or even better. Deer hunters loading a cartridge like the .270 seldom benefit from a special bullet. Sierra's softnose and hollowpoint bullets, Nosler's Ballistic Tip, Winchester's Power Point, Federal's Hi-Shok, Remington's Core-Lokt, the Speer and Hornady softpoints, all work fine. The Nosler Partition designed for the .30-30 has limited use because most 30-30s go to whitetail camps. Light-framed animals and moderate bullet speeds don't warrant special devices to limit upset. Also, controlled-expansion bullets are not, on average, as accurate as alternative designs.

For elk, moose or big bears, or quartering shots at whitetails up close with fast, lightweight bullets, a controlled-expansion design becomes useful. The next question is: What kind of wound channel is best? Some hunters seek only to punch a hole in the off side no matter what the angle, but most would rather find a bullet balled up under the far-side skin, its energy delivered entirely in the animal. Bullets that always exit typically plow a narrower channel than those that stay inside. The reason: broad noses develop more drag. The Nosler Partition, Winchester Fail Safe and Barnes XY Swift, Trophy Bonded and Hawk bullets are apt to penetrate deeper than usually open broader, shorter cavities.

Retained weight is another consideration, but it's not as important as some shooters think. Lead and jacket shrapnel causes damage, even when it no longer contributes to the bullet's kinetic energy. Partitions recovered from elk commonly weigh only about half what they do before firing--but they kill. Trophy Bonded and Fail Safe bullets, which often retain more than 90 percent of their mass, cannot kill any deader. Bullet shape affects trajectory and can pose seating problems. A rocket-like nose can make a heavy bullet too long for a short throat or magazine. Round or flat noses can benefit short-necked rounds like the .300 Winchester. Tapered heels (boattails) are a poor match for stout internal construction. But long shots should be the exception when the quarry is big and tough enough to call for controlled-expansion design. Once velocity has dropped enough to give boattail bullets an advantage, it has passed the point where expansion tends to be explosive.

Bullet weight matters because heavy bullets have higher sectional density, which helps penetration. Weight influences accuracy and seating

Left to right: .257 Winchester Silvertip, .284 Nosler Ballistic Tip, 375 Barnes softnose. The Ballistic Tip opens most violently while the Barnes drives deepest. Terminal performance depends on impact velocity as well as on bullet design and weight.

depth, too. Because controlled-expansion bullets are by definition more effective penetrators than ordinary softpoints, you're wise to consider dropping a notch in bullet weight to boost velocity (which also contributes to tissue destruction). A 165-grain Trophy Bonded bullet I recovered retained 92 percent of its original weight after traveling 32 inches through the bone and muscle of a bear. A 180-grain bullet of standard construction would likely have lost more weight and stopped sooner.

While expensive bullets are usually worth their price, even the best occasionally fail; under many circumstances, an ordinary bullet will drop an animal just as fast. One elk may fall at 100 yards to a single handloaded Winchester Power-Point, while another might take three good hits with expensive heavy-game bullets. Custom-made bullets should be checked for uniformity and to make sure they're the proper size. Full-power handloads can cause problems with oversize bullets. While jackets are typically soft in controlled-expansion bullets, their composition or bearing surface may set up more friction in the bore than do ordinary bullets. It's best to start loading conservatily with custom bullets, even if some of those expensive jewels are spent at sub-par velocities.

Trajectories of all bullets are determined by ballistic coefficient and starting velocity. A bullet, after all, has no brain. The rifling grabs a bullet violently as it exits the muzzle spinning at a rate of 3000 rotations per second, or 18,000 rpm. It hurtles downrange like a piece of shrapnel on a course determined by the bore. Bullets react to gravity predictably; but because gravity works only perpendicular to the earth's center, shots taken uphill and downhill don't show the same rate of drop as those fired horizontally, i.e., they don't drop at the same rate over a given distance of bullet travel. A 350-yard shot across a flat field allows gravity its tightest grip on a bullet; but a 350-yard shot at a 45-degree angle, up or down, requires a lower hold. For example, a .270 Winchester puts a 150-grain spitzer about 12 inches low at 350 yards, given a 200-yard zero. That means a top-of-the-back hold will hit an elk high in the lungs. Suppose the bull is standing the same distance away but on a ridge or in a canyon. The shot angle must then be changed to 45 degrees from horizontal, while the hold should be dead on. The reason: the bullet may be travelling the same distance, but gravity's effect is limited to the horizontal component of that distance: roughly 250 yards. The bullet will hit three inches low, not 12.

Imagine a triangle with the hypotenuse (long side) representing the flight path of the bullet. One leg is perpendicular to the ground (from the target, a vertical line up or down). The other leg, which extends horizontally from the shooter's position, meets it at a right angle. That second leg represents the horizontal component of the shot. When shot distance and angle are known, the following multipliers make the calculations easy.

| SHOT ANGLE, (UP OR DOWN) IN DEGREES | DIVIDE RANGE BY: |
| --- | --- |
| 0-5 | 1.00 |
| 10 | 1.02 |
| 15 | 1.04 |
| 20 | 1.06 |
| 25 | 1.10 |
| 30 | 1.15 |
| 35 | 1.22 |
| 40 | 1.31 |
| 45 | 1.41 |

Winchester's Fail Safe bullet has a lead core in the rear section only. The front looks much like the Barnes X-Bullet in cross-section.

When gravity is pulling a bullet to earth, wind will tug it to the side. It may also cause vertical displacement. Wind results when air pressure is drained from one area to another. Think of it as a turbulence in the air through which a bullet drills its way to the target. There is always pressure, but often no discernible wind. When zeroed for a no-wind condition, however, any wind at all will move a bullet from the point of aim. In hot, humid conditions, and close to the ground, wind can also move the image of a target by nudging the mirage that boils up. When vertical shimmering takes a decided slant, that means the wind has picked up and the bullet will not go where it's aimed. Apparent displacement of the target makes the shot even worse. Competitive shooters who haven't learned to read mirage don't often win.

A head wind makes little difference to a bullet that's cooking along at 50 times the speed of a gale. Drag caused by air friction--wind or no wind--can exceed 56 times the force of gravity. On a target range, a shooter armed with an accurate rifle will find that head winds cause a bullet to hit high, while tail winds drive it low--quite the opposite of what he might expect. On the other hand, winds from front and back will change the velocity of a bullet hardly at all. But they can deflect it. The reason: a bullet isn't launched parallel to the ground; it adopts a nose-up attitude, enabling it to stay close to line of bore for a reasonable distance. Unlike an arrow with its heavy point, the bullet keeps this nose-up angle throughout its flight. Wind from the front slides underneath the nose, bearing more heavily on the underside of the bullet than on its top. As a tail wind bears down on the top side of the bullet, the point of impact is lowered. Obviously, a 20-mph wind can't catch a bullet scooting along at 3,000 fps. But when a rifle is zeroed with no wind, it is fired through a motionless sea of air. Any changes in air pressure will affect the bullet's path.

The wind to watch is the side wind, because it acts on a bullet whose relative velocity is zero. How far a side wind shoves a bullet depends on its speed, of course, but also on the shape, weight and ballistic coefficient of the bullet. Fast bullets spend less time aloft than slow ones, so the wind has less time to work on them. Lag (the velocity lost between muzzle and target) also figures in. Bullets with less lag, or slower deceleration, are less affected by wind. That explains partly why competitive smallbore riflemen don't use high-speed ammunition. Standard-velocity .22 match cartridges have less drag than do high-velocity rounds. The speed and direction of bullet rotation affect shot displacement as well. Given a right-hand rifling twist, a nine-o'clock wind does not push bullets to three o'clock, but to four o'clock. And a three-o'clock wind shoves them up to ten o'clock. Most hunters won't appreciate this without careful shooting at paper targets at long range.

Heavy bullets are less affected by wind than are light ones. A bullet is most effective in flight when it's shaped like a rocket: long, thin, and pointed. The greater the weight or smaller the bullet diameter, the higher its secional density. A bullet with high sectional density not only penetrates game effectively, it slips through air handily as well. Ballistic coefficient (C) is a marriage of secional density and shape. A sleek bullet with high sectional density has a high C value. Conversely, low secional density or a flat bullet nose reduces C and the bullet's ability to battle wind.

The wind's effect on any rifle bullet can be calculated with a simple formula: D=RW/C, where D is deflection in minutes of angle, R is range in hundreds of yards, and W is wind speed

Impala, like whitetails, are light-boned animals that call for quick-opening bullets.

in miles per hour. C is a constant for a given bullet at known velocity. For most big game bullets with pointed noses, this constant is about 10. So a 180-grain spitzer booted from a .300 Winchester through a 15-mph crosswind toward an elk 300 yards away produces these numbers: D=3(15)/10. That's 4.5 minutes of angle, or 13.5 inches. Holding one foot into the wind should be close enough. Disregard the wind, though, and either a miss or a cripple will result. Another, more precise (but impractical for hunters) way to figure drift is D=W(T-Tv), where D is deflection in feet, W is wind speed in feet per second, T is time of flight, and Tv is time of flight in a vacuum.

Estimating wind speed, like estimating range, takes practice. Since wind can't be seen, we must learn to judge by feel and by watching how wind moves grasses, leaves and limbs. It's wise to disregard the clouds; even the tops of tall conifers indicate much more wind than normally affects a bullet near the ground. A sensitive anemometer helps in learning how to gauge wind speed. Watch the light vegetation nod, swing and flutter, then take a reading. It's like using a rangefinder for judging distance.

Winds of less than 5 mph can feel strong if the day has been dead-still. Most of the time they can be ignored, but not at long range, when the bullet cuts directly crosswind. Then a light breeze can indeed displace a shot enough to be a problem. A 5-mph wind makes grass nod and dislodges thistledown, whereas a 10-mph wind blows leaves and unfurls flags. Those same flags will start flapping at 15 mph and straighten out when the wind hits 20. Beyond that, unless an animal is very close or the wind is almost parallel to the sightline, it's best not to shoot.

No matter the wind speed, pickups and letoffs are deadly. So are variations in wind speed and direction over distance. During rifle competition, mid-range wind flags may blow in a direction opposite from those placed closer to the targets. Sometimes one will sag while another snaps furiously in a gust. "Doping" these differences on a range is hard enough; but in the mountains, where cliffs and canyons exaggerate thermal flows and trees, and where rocks boost wind speeds as they funnel air across prevailing currents, the task is even tougher. The stronger the wind and the longer the range, the greater the effect these strange buffetings will have on a bullet.

Reading mirage is one way to tell what the wind is doing downrange. When there's no wind, mirage boils straight up from the ground, like steam from hot soup. A breeze makes mirage lean and gives it a more purposeful, less bubbly appearance. When the undulations in mirage disappear, or when they flatten out parallel to the ground, the wind is strong enough to make a difference. Cold weather cancels mirage, which occurs when the earth warms adjacent air too fast for cool air above to absorb it.

Shooters don't like to hold off for wind. Indeed, many animals have been missed because the shooter held too high. Etched in every rifleman's mind are innumerable charts showing the parabolic sag of bullets in flight; but nowhere do we note any literature showing a bullet swinging wide in a sideways arc. It happens when the wind blows. Most riflemen don't shoot very well in wind because they take great pains not to practice when it's blowing. Wind makes groups bigger, it blows dust about the range, and it grabs the target off the frame. In fact, it runs a close second to heavy rain as a pest. If your range has covered firing points, it's worse. But just as there's only one way to learn how to ride a bicycle, there's only one way to learn how to shoot in the wind.

# PART 2

## SPORTING RIFLE CARTRIDGES: DESCRIPTIONS & LOADS

# CHAPTER 7 SEVEN

# MODERN AMERICAN-MADE CARTRIDGES

**T**he other day someone told me about a remarkable new cartridge. "It's a .300 by Remington," he whispered. "It will fill the gap between the .300 Weatherby Magnum and the .30-378. And it has no belt."

His conspiratorial tone told me this fellow was so immersed in firearms that an objective analysis of the industry's products was impossible. If there's a gap between the .300 Weatherby and the .30-378, it isn't a very big one. Game that falls to one will fall to the other. A velocity difference of 200 fps is peanuts when the trajectories of both are flat enough for point-blank hits at 300, with more than a ton of striking energy at 400.

The recent move away from belted cases shows how much American shooters dote on detail. They can afford to. Nowhere else in the world do we have such a wide range of choices in sporting ammunition; nowhere else is there a tooling industry prepared to serve all the needs of hand-loaders and wildcatters. Since World War II, especially, U.S. shooters have been served up new rounds almost faster than their credit cards can digest them. Most have been useful but unnecessary—mostly cartridges that mimic others already on the charts.

A few of these cartridges have been big hits: Remington's 7mm Magnum in 1962 and the .300 Winchester Magnum a year later. The .243 has been hugely popular since its introduction in 1955, and demand for the .30-378 has far exceeded Weatherby's expectations.

As the number of offerings has risen, however, the probability of any round matching the popularity of the .30-06 or .270 has diminished.

Most of the current American sporting cartridges are included in this chapter. A sophisticated market will decide which are the most useful. Designers do, after all, heed trends too.

 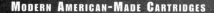

# .17 REMINGTON

A latecomer in a series of 17-caliber rounds that began around 1944, when P.O. Ackley necked down the improved .218 Bee, the .17 Remington emerged as the first factory-loaded .17. It hit the retail market in 1971, the same year Remington chambered it for the Model 700 bolt rifle. It remains the only commercial .17, not that commercial rifles haven't been chambered for .17 wildcats. The first was probably Harrington and Richardson's Sako-based rifle offered in .17-.223 in 1968. Kimber once manufactured bolt rifles in .17 Ackley Hornet and .17 Mach IV, a round developed by Ackley on the .221 Fireball case during the 1960s. It was dubbed the Mach IV by Vern O'Brien, who also built rifles for it on Sako actions and chambered it in Remington's XP-100 pistols.

As interest in .17s increased, barrel-makers learned how to finish the tiny bores more effectively, thus preventing the metal fouling that plagued early experimenters. Harder jackets found on more recent bullets have also helped in that regard. The .17 Remington came along late enough to benefit from built-up demand and technical improvements, but to date it has not set sales records. Similar to the .17-223 developed in 1965, it has a slightly longer neck but the shoulder angle is the same. Like other .17s, the Remington offers searing speed with hardly any recoil. The report is relatively mild, too, but it nevertheless is a sensitive cartridge. An additional half-grain propellant can boost velocity 100 fps along with an attendant rise in pressure. Bores still foul relatively fast, and cleaning requires a special rod. The 25-grain bullets do not battle wind effectively, due to low ballistic coefficients.

| Bullet Weight (grains) | Maximum Loads (grains, type of powder) | Top Velocity (fps) And Data Source |
|---|---|---|
| 25 | 24.0 IMR 4064 | 4100 (Speer) |
| 25 | 25.2 IMR 4320 | 4100 (Hornady) |
| 25 | 27.0 AA 2700 | 4080 (Accurate) |
| 25 | 23.0 2495 BR | 4060 (Accurate) |
| 25 | 22.8 N135 | 4040 (VihtaVuori) |
| 25 | 27.7 Win 760 | 4000 (Hornady) |
| 25 | 24.5 IMR 4895 | 4000 (Hornady) |
| 25 | 22.5 IMR 3031 | 3980 (Speer) |

**CASE CAPACITY** (grains water)
**26**

**CASE TRIM LENGTH**
**1.78"**

**STANDARD OPERATING PRESSURE**
**52,000 CUP**

**STANDARD RIFLING TWIST**
**1-IN-9"**

.378 9.60mm  .376 9.55mm  23°  .356 9.04mm  .199 5.05mm  .172 4.37mm  .260 6.60mm  1.351 (34.31mm)  1.796 (45.62mm)

*Cartridge Illustrations courtesy of Wolfe Publishing Company*

uring the 1920s a group of gun enthusiasts at Springfield Armory began experimenting with a high-velocity .22 cartridge designed to replace the .22 Winchester Center Fire (WCF), which Winchester had introduced in 1885 for its single-shot rifles. Captain G.L. Wotkyns, along with Colonel Townsend Whelen and others, came up with the .22 Hornet, which Winchester adopted around 1930. It was the first small-bore, high-velocity cartridge marketed in the U.S. specifically for small game shooting at a distance. Whereas the .22 WCF (of similar dimensions but discontinued in 1935) could kick a 45-grain bullet out at 1500 fps, the Hornet propelled that same bullet at nearly 2700. Savage chambered the Hornet in its Model 23-D bolt rifle in 1932, and that same year Winchester tooled up to offer it in its Model 54s. Stevens' "Walnut Hill" single-shots showed up in .22 Hornet a year later.

Relatively few rifles have included the Hornet among their chamberings, but they--including the Winchester 70 and Kimber 82--have overall been accurate rifles. The cartridge quickly gained a stellar reputation for accuracy out to 200 yards. It won't compete with bigger .22s in the wind, because it is slower and because most Hornet rifles offer a twist too slow for bullets heavier than 50 grains. The .22 Hornet benefitted early on from the development of Hercules 2400 powder, and it is still best served by a small group of similar propellants. Hornet bullets, incidentally, were initially .223 in diameter, but the .224 dimension--which is standard for other .22 centerfires--is now the rule for Hornets as well. Because a hit with the .22 Hornet creates a smaller wound cavity than do strikes with heavier, faster .22 bullets, this cartridge has become a favorite among those who prefer to hunt turkeys and other edible small game considered too tough for rimfires.

The .460 Weatherby has long been one of the most powerful commercial sporting cartridges in the world, dwarfing the .22 Hornet, albeit a more pleasant cartridge to shoot.

Small game and "varmint" cartridges from left: .22 Hornet, .218 Bee, .222 Remington, .223 Remington, .22-250, .225 Winchester, .243 Winchester, 6mm (or .244) Remington.

| Bullet Weight (grains) | Maximum Loads (grains, type of powder) | Top Velocity (fps) And Data Source | Case Capacity (grains water) |
|---|---|---|---|
| 40 | 11.0 H110 | 2850 (Hodgdon) | **13** |
| 40 | 11.0 2400 | 2800 (Sierra) | **Case Trim Length** |
| 40 | 14.0 1680 | 2790 (Accurate) | **1.39"** |
| 45 | 10.0 2400 | 2740 (Nosler) | **Standard Operating Pressure** |
| 45 | 12.6 Win 680 | 2700 (Hornady) | **43,000 CUP** |
| 50 | 11.5 IMR 4227 | 2650 (Nosler) | **Standard Rifling Twist** |
| 53 | 11.6 IMR 4227 | 2600 (Sierra) | **1-in-16"** |
| 55 | 12.2 IMR 4198 | 2400 (Sierra) | |

5° 38'

.350
8.89mm

.298
7.57mm

.276
7.01mm

.243
6.17mm

.224
5.689mm

.065 (1.65mm)

.825 (20.95mm)

.323
8.20mm

1.403 (35.64mm)

1.723 (43.76mm)

*Cartridge Illustrations courtesy of Wolfe Publishing Company*

# .218 BEE

ased on Winchester's .25-20 case, the .218 Bee has considerably more powder capacity than the .22 Hornet. It can drive a 45-grain bullet about 200 fps faster and push 50-grain bullets quick enough to ensure stability with the standard 1-in-16 pitch found in Bee barrels. Given the Hornet's warm reception, the Bee was doubtless expected to become an instant hit--but that didn't happen. Shooters who had the money to buy new rifles around 1938 didn't want a high-speed round in Winchester's lever-action rifle. The short life of Savage's .22 High Power (bullet diameter .228) testified to that. Winchester .92's were beautifully built but could not accommodate a top-mounted scope or yield the accuracy of a Model 54 bolt gun in .22 Hornet. The .92's tubular magazine, moreover, dictated that only blunt bullets be used.

After World War II Winchester chambered the .218 Bee in its Model 43, but the rifle lacked the charisma and performance of the Model 70. In 1950 Remington trotted out the .222, a cartridge that easily outraced the Bee while shooting one-hole groups. For a time Sako and Krico chambered rifles in .218 Bee, and Ruger has offered it in the dropping-block Number One. A fine cartridge for marmots and even coyotes out to 200 yards, it stayed in the Hornet's shadow until it was eclipsed by more powerful and versatile centerfire .22s. Oddly, what should have been the most immediate threat to the Bee--the .219 Zipper--preceded it by a year. A necked-down .25-35, it had much more case capacity than the Bee and could drive the Hornet bullets at 3600 fps. But it also suffered from the blunt-bullet curse. And when the .220 Swift was unveiled in Winchester's scope-friendly Model 70, the Zipper was dropped (along with the Model 64 following World War II). Marlin offered it in its lever-action 336 until 1961; but like the Bee, it has become a cartridge of the past.

| Bullet Weight (grains) | Maximum Loads (grains, type of powder) | Top Velocity (fps) And Data Source | Case Capacity (grains water) |
|---|---|---|---|
| 40 | 12.2 2400 | 3000 (Hornady) | **16** |
| 40 | 15.0 1680 | 2800 (Accurate) | |
| 45 | 16.0 RL-7 | 2830 (Nosler) | **Case Trim Length** |
| 45 | 13.0 IMR 4227 | 2800 (Sierra) | **1.34"** |
| 45 | 11.4 H110 | 2800 (Hodgdon) | **Standard Operating Pressure** |
| 50 | 18.1 BL-C(2) | 2700 (Hornady) | **40,000 CUP** |
| 50 | 11.5 2400 | 2690 (Nosler) | **Standard Rifling Twist** |
| 53 | 15.0 IMR 4198 | 2600 (Sierra) | **1-in-16"** |

*Cartridge Illustrations courtesy of Wolfe Publishing Company*

# .222 REMINGTON

Shortly after it was introduced in 1950 the .222 Remington began building a reputation for accuracy among benchrest shooters. It became the premier .22 round in that game and stayed on top of the competition until the mid-1970s, when it was eclipsed by the .22 PPC (developed by Ferris Pindell and Lou Palmisano). Unlike many centerfire .22s, the .222 Remington did not derive from any other case; it is an original, designed for small rifle primers that match its modest case capacity. Its long neck helps align the bullet with the axis of the case. With a muzzle velocity of 3200 fps, a 50-grain bullet from the "triple deuce" easily outruns the .218 Bee and leaves the Hornet far behind. It has a smaller powder chamber than the .219 Zipper (based on the .25-35 Winchester), but its rimless design and minimum taper make it more suitable for bolt

A fine varmint round to 300 yards, the "triple deuce" held sway as a premier benchrest cartridge in the game's early days.

| Bullet Weight (grains) | Maximum Loads (grains, type of powder) | Top Velocity (fps) And Data Source |
|---|---|---|
| 40 | 26.0 IMR 4320 | 3500 (Speer) |
| 45 | 20.5 H4198 | 3450 (Hodgdon) |
| 45 | 27.0 AA 2230 | 3450 (Accurate) |
| 50 | 21.5 RL-7 | 3300 (Sierra) |
| 50 | 24.0 BL-C(2) | 3210 (Hodgdon) |
| 52 | 26.8 Win 748 | 3200 (Sierra) |
| 55 | 22.0 H322 | 3120 (Nosler) |
| 60 | 22.6 N133 | 2930 (VihtaVuori) |

**Case Capacity** (grains water)
**26**

**Case Trim Length**
**1.69"**

**Standard Operating Pressure**
**50,000 PSI**

**Standard Rifling Twist**
**1-in-14"**

23°

.378 / 9.60mm
.376 / 9.55mm
.357 / 9.07mm
.253 / 6.42mm
.2245 / 5.702mm

1.264 (32.10mm)
.313 / 7.95mm
1.700 (43.18mm)
2.130 (54.10mm)

*Cartridge Illustrations courtesy of Wolfe Publishing Company*

rifles. Despite a 13-year head start on the .222, the Zipper floundered largely because it had no bolt-action home. The Winchester 64 and Marlin 336 lever rifles never tapped the Zipper's potential. In the Remington 722 (and later 700 and 40x), the .222 produced stellar performance. It was also chambered briefly in Remington's 760 pump rifle and Savage Model 24 over/under guns. Modern single shot and bolt action rifles make it a useful long range varmint cartridge out to 250 yards. The .222 can push 55-grain bullets to within 100 fps of the .223 Remington, but the latter has a great advantage at market because it is a military round, giving shooters plenty of cheap cases and ammunition. With the .22 PPC commanding the bench and the .223 increasingly popular among hunters, the .222 Remington has probably seen its best days.

# .223 REMINGTON

Although the .223 Remington was announced as the official U.S. Army infantry round in 1964, its development actually began in 1957, a year before the advent of the .222 Remington Magnum. Both the .223 and .222 Magnum share the shoulder angle and head dimensions of the .222 Remington, which was introduced in 1950; and both are longer (the .223 by .06). The .223 has a much shorter neck than the .222, however, and about 15 percent more case capacity. It received its military baptism in the M-16, where it also became known as the 5.56mm Ball Cartridge M193, eventually replacing the 7.62mm NATO round for most military applications. The M16A2 service rifle was given a 1-in-7 twist to stabilize the sleek 60- to 70-grain

| Bullet Weight (grains) | Maximum Loads (grains, type of powder) | Top Velocity (fps) And Data Source |
|---|---|---|
| 45 | 28.0 H335 | 3650 (Speer) |
| 50 | 26.2 N133 | 3400 (VihtaVuori) |
| 53 | 25.5 IMR 3031 | 3400 (Hornady) |
| 55 | 27.5 BL-C(2) | 3310 (Hodgdon) |
| 55 | 23.0 H4198 | 3220 (A-Square) |
| 60 | 26.2 IMR 4320 | 3100 (Sierra) |
| 68 | 24.5 RL-15 | 3030 (Nosler) |
| 70 | 25.0 IMR 4064 | 3010 (Speer) |

**CASE CAPACITY** (grains water)
**30**

**CASE TRIM LENGTH**
**1.75"**

**STANDARD OPERATING PRESSURE**
**52,000 CUP**

**STANDARD RIFLING TWIST**
**1-IN-12"**

.378 9.60mm
.376 9.55mm
23°
.354 8.99mm
.253 6.43mm
.2245 5.702mm
.203 5.16mm
1.438 (36.53mm)
1.760 (44.70mm)
2.260 (57.40mm)

*Cartridge Illustrations courtesy of Wolfe Publishing Company*

bullets that yield better downrange performance. The lightly constructed spitzers, with a turnover rate exceeding 300,000 rpm, may cause premature jacket rupture. Original military and commercial .223 rifles wore barrels with a 1-in-14 twist that now preclude the use of extra-long spitzers. They perform well with the 50- to 55-grain bullets most popular for small game hunting.

A variety of powders perform well in the .223, which has been offered in a wide assortment of rifles. Fast-burning stick powders work best in the AR-15 and M16 models. Powders slower than IMR 4320 or RL-15 can move the pressure curve forward enough to cause problems at the gas port. Ball powders leave residue that can clog the gas system. Though the .223 Remington never challenged the .222 at bench matches, it and the M16 have proven remarkably accurate in the service-rifle category on the National Match course. Varmint hunters have made it one of the best-selling sporting cartridges.

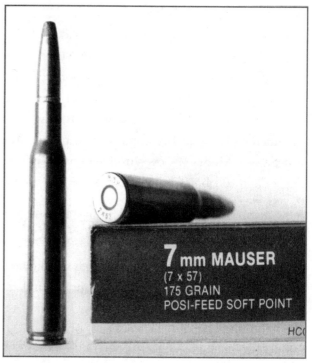

Hansen Cartridge Company manufactures softpoint loads for several military cartridges and some of the more popular modern sporting rounds.

# .222 REMINGTON MAGNUM

The .222 Remington Magnum is essentially a long .222 Remington, complete with identical head dimensions and shoulder angle. Head-to-neck length is about .2 longer, and overall the case has .15-inch on the .222. That translates to a 20 percent gain in powder capacity and a velocity boost of slightly more than 5 percent. The .222 Magnum was developed in the 1950s as a military cartridge in a collaborative effort between Remington and Springfield Arsenal. Failing approval, it showed up as a sporting round in 1958 in Remington's 722 bolt rifle (the Model 700 chambered it later as well). When the .223 Remington appeared in 1964, the .222 Magnum was doomed. It lost ground right away to the new military round, which is roughly .1 shorter but otherwise almost identical in case dimensions.

The .223 gives comparable ballistic performance and, because of its military status, has become vastly more popular. Unlike the .222, which is eight years its senior, the .222 Magnum never became the darling of the benchrest crowd. It is decidedly superior on the hunt, though, handling wind-bucking 55- and 60-grain bullets with ease. Like the .222, it is well served with frangible 50- and 55-grain spitzers. A few European rifles, including the Steyr-Mannlicher, have been chambered in .222 Remington Magnum, but there's little hope for a comeback in the U.S. Rifles bored for this cartridge will accept .223 ammunition. And because both rounds headspace on the shoulder, case rupture is the logical result when a .223 round is fired in a .222 Magnum chamber. It's best to keep 223 ammunition far from .222 Magnum rifles.

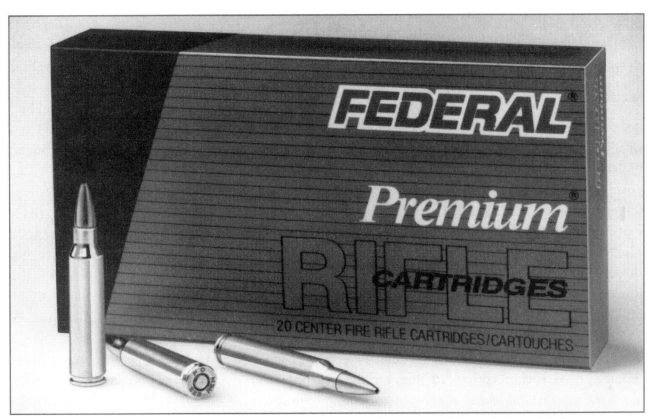

Federal's Premium line includes the .223 Remington Match load with a Sierra Matchking 69-grain hollow point boat-tail bullet.

| BULLET WEIGHT (grains) | MAXIMUM LOADS (grains, type of powder) | TOP VELOCITY (fps) AND DATA SOURCE |
|---|---|---|
| 45 | 29.3 AA 2460 | 3580 (Accurate) |
| 45 | 26.2 IMR 3031 | 3500 (Sierra) |
| 50 | 28.2 AA 2230 | 3460 (Accurate) |
| 52 | 26.0 IMR 4895 | 3370 (Nosler) |
| 55 | 22.5 IMR 4198 | 3300 (Sierra) |
| 55 | 26.0 H33 | 3290 (Hodgdon) |
| 60 | 26.0 N133 | 3160 (VihtaVuori) |
| 70 | 26.5 IMR 4064 | 3130 (Speer) |

**CASE CAPACITY** (grains water)
**31**

**CASE TRIM LENGTH**
**1.84"**

**STANDARD OPERATING PRESSURE**
**50,000 CUP**

**STANDARD RIFLING TWIST**
**1-IN-14"**

.378 9,60mm
.376 9,55mm
23°
.357 9,07mm
.253 6,48mm
.224 5,69mm
.264 6,71mm
1.464 (37,19mm)
1.850 (46,99mm)
2.280 (57,91mm)

*Cartridge Illustrations courtesy of Wolfe Publishing Company*

# .22 AND 6mm PPC

Sometime during the early 1970s, benchrest shooter Lou Palmisano decided that, as good as the .222 Remington was, it didn't have quite the right shape to shoot the smallest groups possible with available match bullets. His search for a case with a short powder column led him to an obscure target round, the .220 Russian. He and gunsmith Ferris Pindell then reduced the case taper to 10 degrees and steepened the shoulder angle to 30 degrees. After several preliminary tests, they contracted with Sako of Finland to manufacture these cases with a small primer pocket and a .066 (instead of a normal .081) flash-hole. In 1975 the two shooters tried their favorite cartridge on the benchrest circuit. Palmisano proceeded to win the 100-yard heavy varmint title at the Super Shoot, while Ferris Pindell snared the "Unlimited Grand Aggregate" crown at the National Bench Rest Shooters Association's annual championship.

Other victories followed, as did a new 6mm cartridge on the same case. The 6mm PPC is slightly shorter than its .22 forebear, though its head dimensions and base-to-shoulder length (and angle) are the same. Despite a growing demand for these cases and cartridges, Sako waited 12 years before manufacturing .22 and 6mm PPC ammunition commercially. Both cartridges work well in varmint rifles; but since factory cartridges feature only target bullets, handloading is useful. Also, because bench shooters typically use lightweight (60- to 75-grain) bullets in the 6mm PPC, barrels built for that purpose are commonly given a 1-in-14 twist, which is too slow to stabilize heavier bullets properly. Hunters who prefer this cartridge are better off with a 1-in-12 twist, which works well for bullets as heavy as 90 grains. Most rifles chambered for the PPCs are custom-built, with tight chambers that require shooters to turn case necks. Sako has marketed rifles in 6mm PPC, and Ruger offers a target model in both PPC chamberings.

Ruger's heavy barrel M77 Mark II Target model features a stainless steel action, floor plate and trigger guard. It is one of few rifles available in .22 PPC and 6m PPC.

| BULLET WEIGHT (grains) | MAXIMUM LOADS (grains, type of powder) | TOP VELOCITY (fps) AND DATA SOURCE |
|---|---|---|
| 45 | 26.5 AA 2015BR | 3590 (Accurate) |
| 45 | 28.0 AA 2495BR | 3580 (Accurate) |
| 50 | 29.0 AA 2520 | 3470 (Accurate) |
| 50 | 26.0 H322 | 3390 (Hodgdon) |
| 52 | 29.0 RL-12 | 3360 (Hodgdon) |
| 55 | 25.0 AA 2015BR | 3280 (Accurate) |
| 55 | 28.5 Win 748 | 3250 (Hodgdon) |
| 60 | 26.0 H335 | 3110 (Hodgdon) |
| 75 | 29.0 BL-C(2) | 3170 (Speer) |
| 80 | 28.5 H322 | 3100 (Speer) |
| 85 | 25.5 IMR 4198 | 3070 (Speer) |
| 90 | 29.0 H335 | 3030 (Speer) |

**CASE CAPACITY**
(grains water)
**33**

**CASE TRIM LENGTH**
**1.49"**

**STANDARD
OPERATING PRESSURE
50,000 CUP**

**STANDARD RIFLING TWIST**
**1-IN-14" (.22)**
**1-IN-12 (6mm)**

.22

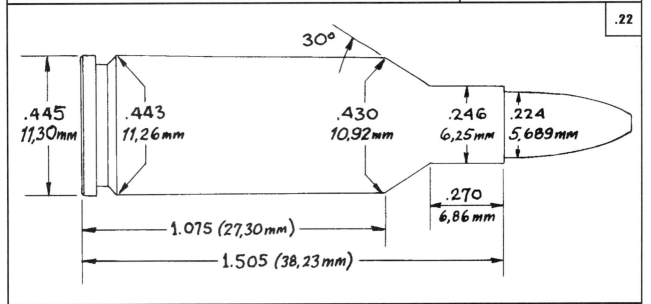

6mm PPC

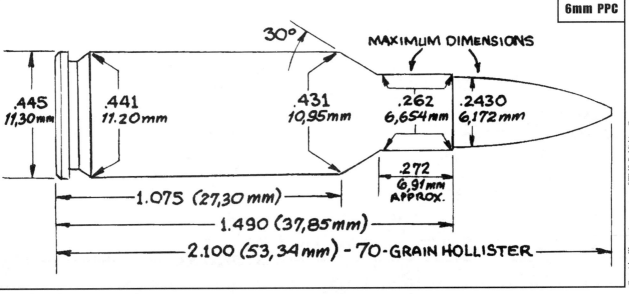

*Cartridge Illustrations courtesy of Wolfe Publishing Company*

# .224 WEATHERBY MAGNUM

oy Weatherby's first stab at marketing a .22 centerfire came in the late 1940s, when he introduced the .220 Weatherby Rocket. An improved .220 Swift, the Rocket had little to offer savvy shooters, who knew the Swift already had a cavernous case for the .22 bore. More powder simply translated into less efficiency and, in many cases, faster throat erosion. For most hunters who wanted to clip prairie dogs beyond 300 steps, the .22-250 was quite satisfactory. Roy Weatherby developed the .228 Weatherby Magnum—a .300 H&H case necked down, then in 1963, came up with the smaller .224 Weatherby Magnum. It featured a belted case with radiused shoulders and a capacity similar to the .225 Winchester. Ballistically, it didn't quite match the .22-250, but it came so close that comparisons were mostly academic. The case now resembles a scaled-

down 7mm Weatherby Magnum—an attractive and efficient design. At 1.920 inches, the hull is slightly shorter than that of a .308 Winchester (2.015), which seems irrelevant unless a rifle is built for it—which is exactly what Roy Weatherby did. The Varmintmaster (the name is sometimes used to indicate the round as well as the rifle) is a scaled-down Mark V, beautifully suited to the .224.

When Remington began loading .22-250 cartridges, Weatherby offered that round in its little rifle as well. The .22-250 case measures not quite .01 less than the .224 case. With the .224 Weatherby pushing 50-grain bullets at 3700 fps or more, there's little reason to load bullets that are any lighter. Recently Weatherby unveiled a new lightweight Mark V-style action for .308-length cartridges, because the Varmintmaster was built a tad short for that round.

| Bullet Weight (grains) | Maximum Loads (grains, type of powder) | Top Velocity (fps) and Data Source | Case Capacity (grains water) |
|---|---|---|---|
| 40 | 28.5 IMR 4198 | 4100 (Sierra) | **38** |
| 45 | 32.0 IMR 3031 | 4000 (Sierra) | **Case Trim Length** |
| 50 | 35.6 Win 748 | 3900 (Hornady) | **1.91"** |
| 50 | 33.6 N201 | 3900 (Hornady) | **Standard Operating Pressure** |
| 55 | 32.7 IMR 4064 | 3700 (Sierra) | **56,000 PSI** |
| 55 | 38.6 Win 760 | 3700 (Hornady) | **Standard Rifling Twist** |
| 60 | 32.4 IMR 4895 | 3600 (Hornady) | **1-in-14"** |
| 63 | 32.0 IMR 4320 | 3500 (Sierra) | |

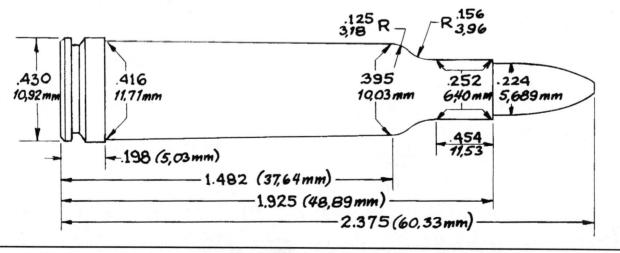

*Cartridge Illustrations courtesy of Wolfe Publishing Company*

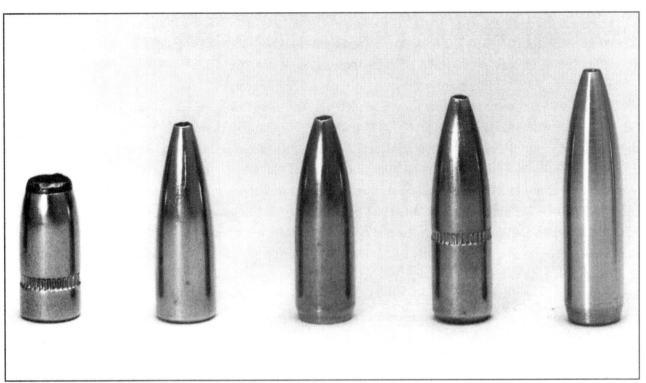

This group of Speer .22 caliber bullets are (left to right): .224 46 grain FPSP w/cann; .224 50 grain HP "TNT"; .224 52 grain BTHP match; 224 62 grain HP w/cann; .224 46 grain BTHP match.

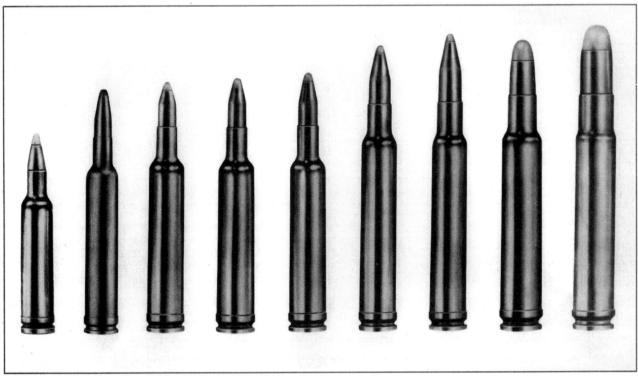

Weatherby's .224 (far left) is substantially shorter than the other Weatherby rounds available in the 1980s, from left: .240, .257, .270, 7mm, .300, .340, .378, .460.

# .225 WINCHESTER

In early summer of 1964 Winchester announced a replacement for its ailing .220 Swift, which had been chambered in the Model 70 since the rifle's debut in 1937. There was nothing wrong with the Swift, but the wildcat .22-250 had provided surprisingly strong competition. Weatherby's new .224 Magnum, introduced in 1963, likely claimed a few buyers; but Winchester's own .243 no doubt hurt the Swift the most. Along with the 6mm Remington it had chewed deeply into the .22 centerfire. The "sixes" were dual-purpose cartridges, capable of killing deer and pronghorns as well as woodchucks, prairie dogs and coyotes. With 75- to 90-grain bullets they bucked the wind well and shot as flat as the hot .22s, but with little additional recoil.

It may be, too, that Winchester had learned about Remington's imminent release of a commercial load for the .22-250. Whatever the reason, the .225 appeared the same year Winchester dropped the .220 Swift. Oddly, the 225 features a semi-rimmed case that headspaces on the shoulder like a rimless round. A rim, while ill adapted to bolt rifles, is an asset in single-shots. Maybe Winchester wanted to evoke images of the old .219 Zipper or the .219 Donaldson Wasp. The Wasp still had a fan club among benchresters in the early 1960s; indeed, by some accounts the .225 evolved as a sort of improved Wasp. With a case capacity rivaling the .22-250's, it launches 50-grain bullets at 3700 fps and 55-grain spitzers at 3600. The first .225 factory loads also had a reputation for fine accuracy. When Remington announced factory loads for the .22-250 in 1965, however, any optimism for the future of the .225 disappeared.

| BULLET WEIGHT (grains) | MAXIMUM LOADS (grains, type of powder) | TOP VELOCITY (fps) AND DATA SOURCE |
|---|---|---|
| 45 | 35.0 BL-C(2) | 3890 (Hodgdon) |
| 50 | 32.7 IMR 3031 | 3800 (Hornady) |
| 52 | 34.0 IMR 4064 | 3650 (Nosler) |
| 55 | 35.6 Win 748 | 3600 (Hornady) |
| 55 | 38.0 H414 | 3600 (Hodgdon) |
| 60 | 32.0 AA 2460 | 3400 (Accurate) |
| 60 | 32.5 H335 | 3400 (Hodgdon) |
| 70 | 39.0 N205 | 3250 (Speer) |

**CASE CAPACITY** (grains water)
**40**

**CASE TRIM LENGTH**
**1.92"**

**STANDARD OPERATING PRESSURE**
**50,000 CUP**

**STANDARD RIFLING TWIST**
**1-IN-14"**

Cartridge Illustrations courtesy of Wolfe Publishing Company

# .22-250 REMINGTON

harles Newton, creator of the .250 Savage in 1912, may have been the first to neck that cartridge down to .228. During the 1930s several shooters are credited with fashioning .22-250s, including Jerry Gebby's "Varminter" and J. Bushnell Smith's custom handloads for shooters who wanted a .22-250 but didn't load their own rounds. Before the .222 came along, the .22-250 had no competition among hunters; but when the "triple deuce" appeared its exceptional accuracy appealed to the benchrest people. In the field, however, the .22-250 held sway, combining fine accuracy with high velocity. The Varminter outpaced the .222 by 500 fps with 50-grain bullets, and it came within 100 fps of matching the great .220 Swift, which Winchester first chambered in 1935 for its Model 54. Since then, the .22-250 has enjoyed a favorable press and a solid reputation among small game shooters who seek precision beyond 300 yards.

Remington began commercial production of .22-250 ammunition in 1965, with Winchester following two years later. Since then many rifles have been chambered in .22-250, its tremendous popularity eclipsing that of the Swift and all other .22 centerfires save the .223. Its long tenure as a wildcat continues to puzzle many shooters who remain convinced the cartridge could have enjoyed stardom following World War II if factories had loaded it.

Unlike the .222 and .223, the .22-250 takes a large rifle primer. It belongs to a class of long-range .22s that include the .224 Weatherby, .225 Winchester and, of course, the Swift. All are capable of launching 55-grain bullets at over 3500 fps, so there's no need for bullets lighter than 50 grains. With 60-grain bullets crowding 3400, they can all take deer and pronghorns quite handily. Interestingly, the muzzle energy of a 60-grain bullet from a .22-250 exceeds that of a 117-grain bullet from a .25-35.

| BULLET WEIGHT (grains) | MAXIMUM LOADS (grains, type of powder) | TOP VELOCITY (fps) AND DATA SOURCE |
|---|---|---|
| 40 | 37.0 H4895 | 4060 (Hodgdon) |
| 45 | 40.3 H380 | 4000 (Sierra) |
| 50 | 41.9 Win 760 | 3900 (Hornady) |
| 52 | 34.0 IMR 4895 | 3800 (Nosler) |
| 55 | 36.5 IMR 4064 | 3690 (Speer) |
| 55 | 35.5 IMR 4320 | 3690 (Nosler) |
| 55 | 38.0 RL-15 | 3650 (A-Squre) |
| 60 | 36.0 AA 2520 | 3510 (Accurate) |
| 70 | 38.0 H4831 | 3190 (Hodgdon) |

**CASE CAPACITY** (grains water)
**44**

**CASE TRIM LENGTH**
**1.92"**

**STANDARD OPERATING PRESSURE**
**65,000 PSI**

**STANDARD RIFLING TWIST**
**1-IN-14"**

*Cartridge Illustrations courtesy of Wolfe Publishing Company*

A mong the wildcat cartridges developed in the 1920s and 1930s, one of the favorites was Charles Newton's .250 Savage. After Captain Grosvenor Wotkyns had necked it down to a .250, he turned to Winchester for commercial sanction of his cartridge. Winchester abandoned the .250 case, however, in favor of the stout 6mm Lee Navy, also a rimless design but with greater capacity. To make the .22/6mm Lee fit a standard .30-06 bolt face, Winchester engineers increased the basal diameter (the rim) from .445 to .473 without changing the body. The resulting semi-rimmed case fed acceptably from common staggered box magazines. In 1935 Winchester announced its new round as the .220 Swift, chambering it in the Model 54 bolt rifle. While rifling twist initially was 1-in-16, later rifles gave the bullets a faster 1-in-14 spin. In 1937, the Swift cartridge was among the charter chamberings in Winchester's Model 70.

At its debut, the .220 Swift boasted higher velocity than any other commercial cartridge--and it still can. The original load, a 48-grain bullet at an advertised 4110 fps, gets little use now. Most shooters recognize the ballistic advantages of 55-grain spitzers at slightly reduced speed. Winchester was forced from the outset to use a heavier bullet jacket than that found on .22 bullets of the day, such as the .22 Hornet. The Swift, while not a benchrest round, can show fine accuracy. The Hodgdon Powder Company notes that in Remington's 40x rifle the .220 Swift has produced 25-shot aggregates measuring less than .270, and that tests of 3000 full-power loads yielded a five-shot average of .344. The Swift has long been said to have an appetite for barrel throats. While speed boosts friction and accelerates throat erosion, copper fouling can ruin accuracy faster than erosion. Modern solvents lengthen the life of barrels chambered for fast steppers like the Swift.

| Bullet Weight (grains) | Maximum Loads (grains, type of powder) | Top Velocity (fps) and Data Source |
|---|---|---|
| 40 | 46.0 H414 | 4210 (Hodgdon) |
| 45 | 38.3 IMR 3031 | 4200 (Sierra) |
| 50 | 45.0 AA 2700 | 4040 (Accurate) |
| 50 | 39.0 RL-12 | 3990 (Nosler) |
| 52 | 39.0 IMR 4064 | 4000 (Sierra) |
| 55 | 37.0 RL-15 | 3980 (Nosler) |
| 60 | 36.0 IMR 4320 | 3710 (Nosler) |
| 60 | 40.9 IMR 4350 | 3700 (Hornady) |
| 70 | 42.0 N205 | 3320 (Speer) |

**Case Capacity** (grains water)
**47**

**Case Trim Length**
**2.20"**

**Standard Operating Pressure**
**54,000 CUP**

**Standard Rifling Twist**
**1-in-14"**

21°

.473 12.01 mm
.445 11.30 mm
.402 10.21mm
.260 6.60mm
.2245 5.725 mm
.300 7.62 mm

1.723 - (43.76mm)
2.205 - (56.00mm)
HOLLOW-POINT BULLETS: 2.560 (65.02 mm)
POINTED BULLETS: 2.680 (68.07mm)

Cartridge Illustrations courtesy of Wolfe Publishing Company

# 6mm BR AND .22 (AND 7mm BR) REMINGTON

When Jim Stekl of Remington designed the 6mm BR Remington in the 1970s, he doubtless had in mind competing with the new 6mm PPC (see p. 96). The creators of the 6mm (Dr. Lou Palmisano and Ferris Pindel) had based their cartridge on the squat .220 Russian case, reducing its taper and steepening its shoulder. They surmised that a short powder column and 100 percent loading density would combine to give better accuracy. The 1975 shooting season proved them right. But while Jim Stekl was fashioning the Remington BR case, Sako had not yet loaded .22 PPC or 6mm PPC ammunition commercially. The BR case is less than .02 longer than the 6mm PPC's and, in like manner, employs a small rifle primer.

Both 6mms were designed to drive lightweight (60 to 75 grains) target bullets with relatively fast powder (Hodgdon's H322 is a top choice

for either round). The Remington cartridge has one advantage over the PPC: Its head diameter is .473, the same as a .308's, so any short-action bolt rifle can be rebarreled to 6mm BR without undergoing bolt face alteration. The same applies for the .22 and 7mm BR that have evolved from the same case. At this writing Remington catalogs only the 6mm and 7mm BR as loaded ammunition, with 100- and 140-grain bullets respectively. The .22 BR, which can poke its bullets downrange at almost the same speed as the .22-250, would make a fine--but perhaps superfluous--addition to Remington's list of .22 varmint cartridges. The only Remington rifles chambered for the BRs are 40x target models assembled in the company's Custom Shop at Ilion (NY). Despite the 40x's enviable reputation for accuracy, the BR cartridges have not caught up with the PPCs among the benchrest crowd.

| BULLET WEIGHT (grains) | MAXIMUM LOADS (grains, type of powder) | TOP VELOCITY (fps) AND DATA SOURCE | CASE CAPACITY (grains water) |
|---|---|---|---|
| 60 | 33.5 AA 2230 | 3420 (Accurate) | 36 |
| 60 | 32.0 H335 | 3410 (Hodgdon) | |
| 70 | 35.0 BL-C(2) | 3290 (Hodgdon) | CASE |
| 70 | 33.0 AA 2460 | 3280 (Accurate) | TRIM LENGTH |
| 80 | 30.0 H4895 | 3100 (Hodgdon) | 1.50" |
| 80 | 30.0 AA 2495BR | 3080 (Accurate) | |
| 90 | 28.0 IMR 4320 | 2850 (Hodgdon) | STANDARD |
| 100 | 28.5 AA 2520 | 2680 (Accurate) | OPERATING PRESSURE |
| 45 | 32.5 H4895 | 3770 (Hodgdon) | 52,000 CUP |
| 50 | 35.5 BL-C(2) | 3650 (Hodgdon) | |
| 52 | 31.5 H335 | 3590 (Hodgdon) | STANDARD |
| 55 | 31.5 IMR 4064 | 3510 (Hodgdon) | RIFLING TWIST |
| 120 | 32.0 AA 2520 | 2400 (Accurate) | 1-IN-12 (6mm) |
| 139 | 31.0 AA 2460 | 2250 (Accurate) | 1-IN-14 (.22) |
| 150 | 27.5 AA 2015BR | 2140 (Accurate) | 1-IN-10 (7mm) |
| 168 | 28.5 AA 2495BR | 1980 (Accurate) | |

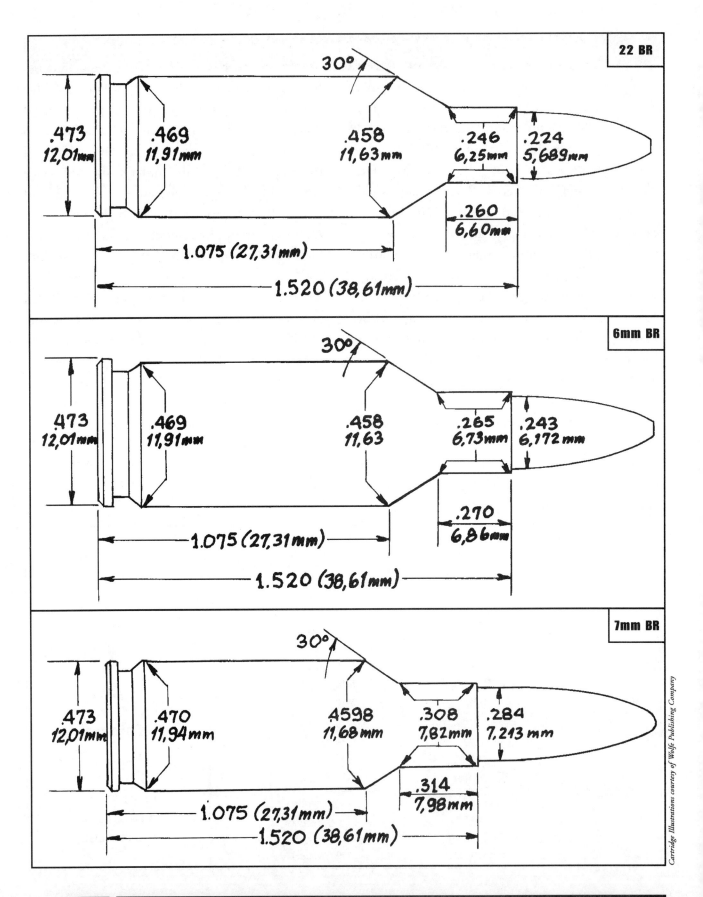

22 BR

.473
12,01mm

.469
11,91mm

30°

.458
11,63mm

.246
6,25mm

.224
5,689mm

.260
6,60mm

1.075 (27,31mm)

1.520 (38,61mm)

6mm BR

473
12,01mm

.469
11,91mm

30°

.458
11,63

.265
6,73mm

.243
6,172 mm

.270
6,86mm

1.075 (27,31mm)

1.520 (38,61mm)

7mm BR

.473
12,01mm

.470
11,94mm

30°

.4598
11,68mm

.308
7,82mm

.284
7,243 mm

.314
7,98mm

1.075 (27,31mm)

1.520 (38,61mm)

Cartridge Illustrations courtesy of Wolfe Publishing Company

# .243 WINCHESTER

Winchester's .243, a necked-down .308, was introduced in 1955 for the company's Model 70 bolt rifle and 88 lever-action. It was the result of wildcatting experiments by Warren Page, shooting editor of *Field & Stream.* Unlike the .308 and earlier .30-06, which became popular among sportsmen (partly because of their utility and availability), the .243 had no military endorsement. It has survived on its own merits afield. Indeed, it has become one of the most successful of post-war cartridges, rivaling the 7mm Remington Magnum in its distribution and use.

But this is not the first 6mm. That distinction belongs to the 6mm Lee Navy, which was developed in 1895 for the Navy and Marine Corps. It saw limited service, was never embraced by sportsmen and died an obscure death in 1935. Holland and Holland's .240 Belted Rimless Nitro Express (with a flanged double-rifle version) appeared in the early 1920s, as did the Vickers .242 Rimless Nitro Express and the .246 Purdey. No other 6mms turned up stateside until the .243 Winchester--along with its competition, the .244 Remington--hit the U.S. market. The .244 derives from a .257 Roberts hull and offers a bit more powder capacity than the .243. Winchester's cartridge pulled away from the .244 reportedly because rifles chambered in .243 had a sharper twist that stabilized heavier bullets more effectively than did the .244's 1-in-12 spin. There may be more myth to this than fact; nevertheless the story circulated widely. When Remington renamed its luckless child the "6mm Remington" in 1963, the rifling pitch had already been changed to 1-in-9. The 6mm subsequently became modestly successful, but the .243 continues to outsell it handily.

| Bullet Weight (grains) | Maximum Loads (grains, type of powder) | Top Velocity (fps) And Data Source |
|---|---|---|
| 60 | 41.0 IMR 4895 | 3700 (Sierra) |
| 70 | 43.2 RL-15 | 3660 (A-Square) |
| 70 | 47.0 IMR 4350 | 3610 (Nosler) |
| 75 | 47.0 H414 | 3530 (Hodgdon) |
| 80 | 50.0 N205 | 3370 (Speer) |
| 85 | 39.0 IMR 4064 | 3300 (A-Square) |
| 90 | 43.0 Win 760 | 3220 (Barnes) |
| 90 | 47.1 H450 | 3200 (Sierra) |
| 95 | 45.5 AA 3100 | 3190 (Nosler) |
| 100 | 46.0 H4831 | 3070 (Hodgdon) |
| 105 | 42.0 IMR 4350 | 3020 (Speer) |
| 115 | 43.0 RL-19 | 2950 (Barnes) |

**Case Capacity** (grains water)
**53**

**Case Trim Length**
**2.04"**

**Standard Operating Pressure**
**52,000 CUP**

**Standard Rifling Twist**
**1-in-10"**

.473 12,01mm | .471 11,96 mm | .454 11,53mm | .276 7,01mm | .2435 6,185mm | .240 6,10mm | 20° | 1.560 (39,62mm) | 2.045 (51,94mm) | 2.710 (68,83mm)

*Cartridge Illustrations courtesy of Wolfe Publishing Company*

# .244 (6mm) REMINGTON

Among the most vocal advocates of the 6mm bore during the early 1950s was Warren Page . He and Fred Huntington of RCBS developed 6mm bullets along with the cartridges to shoot them. Their first wildcat, based on the new T65 experimental case, became the .243 Winchester (see also p 83). Next came a 6mm/.257 Roberts, or the "Page Super Pooper," with a 28-degree shoulder and .351 neck. Winchester and Remington adopted these cartridges, respectively and with some alterations, in 1955. Remington then softened the shoulder angle to 26 degrees, still a bit steeper than on the .257 Roberts case. Winchester offered 80- and 100-grain bullets, while Remington developed loads for 75- and 90-grain bullets. Most shooters considering a new 6mm wanted 100-grain bullets for deer and lighter bullets for varmints. They were put off by reports that the Remington barrels, rifled 1-in-12, failed to stabilize heavy bullets as well as the 1-in-10 Winchester bores. So they chose the .243.

Though fine accuracy is possible with 100-grain bullets in .244 barrels, word on the street was they'd tumble. Winchester's other advantage early on was its Model 70, a much more attractive rifle than Remington's 722. Around 1958 Remington quietly began changing the twist in its Model 722 rifles to 1-in-9; and in 1963 the company renamed its ailing .244 the 6mm Remington. Despite these developments, and the 1962 debut of the Model 700 rifle, the .243 stayed well ahead of the 6mm Remington in sales. Handloaded for short-action rifles, the two perform about the same. Bullets must be seated deep in the 6mm to clear magazines designed exclusively for the .308 family of cartridges. In longer actions, or single-shots with no throat restrictions, the 6mm Remington remains the clear winner.

| BULLET WEIGHT (grains) | MAXIMUM LOADS (grains, type of powder) | TOP VELOCITY (fps) AND DATA SOURCE |
|---|---|---|
| 60 | 42.0 BL-C(2) | 3750 (Hodgdon) |
| 70 | 43.0 IMR 4064 | 3640 (A-Square) |
| 70 | 48.9 IMR 4350 | 3600 (Hornady) |
| 80 | 48.0 AA 2700 | 3420 (Accurate) |
| 85 | 45.0 IMR 4350 | 3290 (Nosler) |
| 87 | 50.0 RL-22 | 3220 (A-Square) |
| 90 | 43.5 H414 | 3200 (Sierra) |
| 95 | 49.0 IMR 7828 | 3140 (Nosler) |
| 100 | 51.0 H1000 | 3110 (Hodgdon) |
| 100 | 43.0 Win 760 | 3100 (Barnes) |
| 105 | 45.0 IMR 4831 | 3050 (Speer) |
| 115 | 44.0 RL-22 | 2980 (Barnes) |

**CASE CAPACITY** (grains water)
**55**

**CASE TRIM LENGTH**
**2.22"**

**STANDARD OPERATING PRESSURE**
**65,000 PSI**

**STANDARD RIFLING TWIST**
**1-IN-9"**

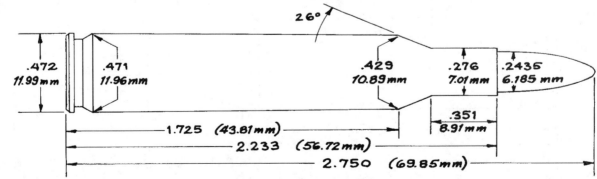

*Cartridge Illustrations courtesy of Wolfe Publishing Company*

The only belted 6mm now available--and the last Weatherby cartridge designed while Roy Weatherby was alive--the .240 Weatherby Magnum dates back to 1968. It looks like the .240 Belted Rimless Nitro Express (or .240 Apex) designed by Holland and Holland around 1923. Both hold about as much powder as the .30-06; but Holland's loading for the .240 Nitro Express is far less ambitious than Norma's factory load for the .240 Weatherby. Indeed, the .240 can boot its 100-grain bullet downrange at 3300 fps and will exceed 3700 with a 70-grain bullet. It features the radiused shoulder characteristic of the Weatherby cartridge line, plus the .473 head diameter of the .30-06.

While this would be an easy round to adapt to any .30-06-length action, it has been available commercially only in Weatherby's Mark V. The .240 Weatherby offers a bit more reach than the .243 or 6mm Remington, but its bore diameter limits bullet weight. Deer and pronghorn on the prairies are fair game, and the .240 performs well in the mountains on bighorns and goats (it is not an elk cartridge). The .25-06 and .270 offer about the same case capacity, but they can handle heavier bullets and push light ones as fast as this Weatherby round. And because they're not proprietary cartridges and need not be imported, they're also less costly. The .240 has never been one of Weatherby's most popular big game rounds, though it is the most pleasant to shoot and capable of fine accuracy. Its road might be smoother were it not for a crowded field of excellent light-recoiling, long-range deer rounds.

| Bullet Weight (grains) | Maximum Loads (grains, type of powder) | Top Velocity (fps) And Data Source |
|---|---|---|
| 70 | 53.0 H414 | 3750 (Nosler) |
| 75 | 53.0 IMR 4350 | 3670 (Speer) |
| 80 | 52.0 Win 760 | 3600 (Hornady) |
| 85 | 52.5 IMR 4831 | 3510 (Barnes) |
| 87 | 54.9 H450 | 3500 (Hornady) |
| 90 | 55.0 H4831 | 3390 (Hodgdon) |
| 95 | 53.5 IMR 7828 | 3260 (Nosler) |
| 100 | 53.0 H4831 | 3200 (Hodgdon) |
| 105 | 49.0 H450 | 3130 (Speer) |
| 115 | 49.0 RL-22 | 3090 (Barnes) |

**Case Capacity** (grains water)
**63**

**Case Trim Length**
**2.49"**

**Standard Operating Pressure**
**67,000 PSI**

**Standard Rifling Twist**
**1-in-10"**

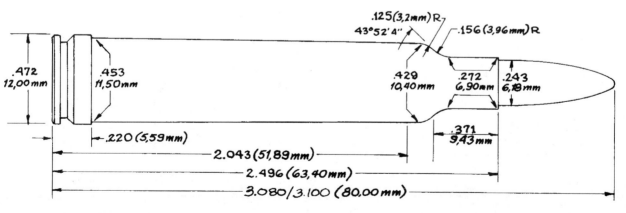

Cartridge Illustrations courtesy of Wolfe Publishing Company

# .250 SAVAGE

The .250 Savage, which appeared in 1912, was the brainchild of Charles Newton. An attorney by training, Newton spent his productive life designing rifles and cartridges that did not sell. Most had merit, and some indicated a genius at work. He conceived the .250 as a big game round launching a 100-grain bullet at about 2700 fps, but Savage management decided instead to load an 87-grain bullet at 3000 fps, which was a very high speed at the time. The cartridge went on the market as the .250-3000 and was an instant hit. Hunters used it not only on deer but on game as big as moose and tigers.

A light-recoiling, flat-shooting round, the .250 remains an excellent choice for deer and pronghorns. Competition from the .243 may have reduced its popularity but not its utility. Developed for the Savage Model 99, the .250 has since been chambered in bolt rifles. At 1.91 inches, the case is about .1 shorter than a .308's and, since the head size is the same (.473), the cartridge fits any rifle built to accept the .308 or its derivatives. Magazine and case constraints limit the performance of bullets heavier than 100 grains. The standard 1-14 twist of .250 Savage rifles is also a trifle slow to stabilize long 115- to 120-grain bullets at the velocities dictated by the case capacity. The .250 Savage has produced few wildcat offspring, but the .22-250 ranks among the most commercially successful of all wildcats ever conceived. The 6mm International, which also derives from the .250 Savage, has never been commercially adopted, probably because it would face withering competition from the more potent .243 Winchester.

| BULLET WEIGHT (grains) | MAXIMUM LOADS (grains, type of powder) | TOP VELOCITY (fps) AND DATA SOURCE |
|---|---|---|
| 60 | 36.0 H322 | 3650 (Hodgdon) |
| 75 | 35.4 IMR 3031 | 3400 (Sierra) |
| 85 | 36.0 Win 748 | 3140 (Barnes) |
| 87 | 36.5 IMR 4064 | 3110 (Speer) |
| 90 | 34.0 RL-15 | 3070 (Barnes) |
| 100 | 35.0 H4895 | 2950 (Nosler) |
| 115 | 37.0 Win 760 | 2780 (Barnes) |
| 117 | 37.0 H414 | 2720 (Hodgdon) |
| 120 | 36.0 H380 | 2700 (Sierra) |
| 125 | 36.0 H414 | 2650 (Barnes) |

**CASE CAPACITY** (grains water)
**46**

**CASE TRIM LENGTH**
**1.90"**

**STANDARD OPERATING PRESSURE**
**45,000 CUP**

**STANDARD RIFLING TWIST**
**1-IN-10"**

*Cartridge Illustrations courtesy of Wolfe Publishing Company*

# .257 ROBERTS

T he .25-06 had already been developed and the .250 Savage was more than a decade old when Ned Roberts, presumably in collusion with Townsend Whelen, A.O. Niedner and others, necked down the 7x57 Mauser case to 25 caliber. The Mauser's case capacity was midway between the .250's and the .25-06's. Given iron sights, the .250 could do everything hunters expected from a .25. The .25-06 lacked powders slow enough to test it. The .257 Roberts trundled along as a wildcat for some time. Remington began loading it commercially in 1934, but only after restoring the 7x57's 20-degree shoulder angle (which Ned Roberts had jettisoned for a more gradual 15-degree slope). To the custom rifles made by Griffin & Howe and the Niedner Rifle Company, Remington added the 30S. Winchester chambered the round in its Model 70 and Remington featured it in the 722 and slide-action 760. Like

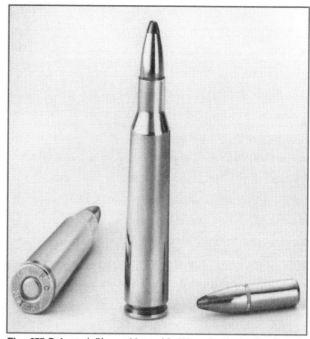

The .257 Roberts (+P) cartridge with 120-grain Nosler Partition is part of Federal's line of Premium brand centerfires.

| BULLET WEIGHT (grains) | MAXIMUM LOADS (grains, type of powder) | TOP VELOCITY (fps) AND DATA SOURCE |
|---|---|---|
| 60 | 38.0 H335 | 3890 (Hodgdon) |
| 75 | 44.2 H4895 | 3500 (Hornady) |
| 87 | 44.5 RL-1 | 3320 (A-Square) |
| 87 | 42.9 IMR 4064 | 3300 (Sierra) |
| 90 | 47.0 IMR 4350 | 3180 (Barnes) |
| 100 | 42.5 RL-15 | 3120 (A-Square) |
| 100 | 43.5 IMR 4350 | 3110 (Nosler) |
| 115 | 49.0 IMR 7828 | 2890 (Barnes) |
| 117 | 44.6 H4831 | 2800 (Hornady) |
| 125 | 44.0 RL-19 | 2700 (Barnes) |
| 125 | 42.0 H414 | 2680 (Hodgdon) |

**CASE CAPACITY** (grains water)
**55**

**CASE TRIM LENGTH**
**2.22"**

**STANDARD OPERATING PRESSURE**
**54,000 PSI**

**STANDARD RIFLING TWIST**
**1-IN-10"**

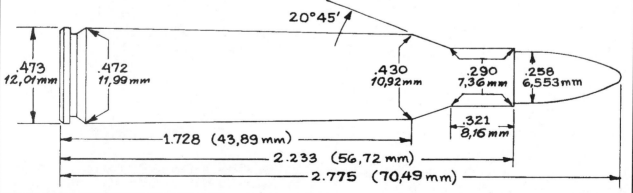

20°45'

.473 12,01 mm  .472 11,99 mm  .430 10,92 mm  .290 7,36 mm  .258 6,553 mm

.321 8,16 mm

1.728 (43,89 mm)
2.233 (56,72 mm)
2.775 (70,49 mm)

*Cartridge Illustrations courtesy of Wolfe Publishing Company*

Remington, Winchester began loading .257 ammunition with round-nose bullets. Ned Roberts apparently thought they gave better accuracy than spitzers, which they can when rifling twist is a bit slow. But twist can be steepened, and given the vertical magazines of .257 Roberts rifles there's no reason to relinquish the extra reach afforded by pointed bullets.

Since its inception this cartridge has been underloaded, partly because it has been crammed into short actions where bullets must be seated deep. In a Mauser built for the 57mm case, or in a .30-06-length action, the .257 Roberts can be loaded to launch 120-grain bullets at 2800 fps, handily beating out the .250 Savage as a big game round. For some time now Winchester and Federal have sold +P Roberts ammunition featuring thicker cases and operating under a 50,000 CUP pressure cap. All in all, this is a versatile .25, one that's proven adequate for deer hunting and ranking not far behind the .25-06 in velocity.

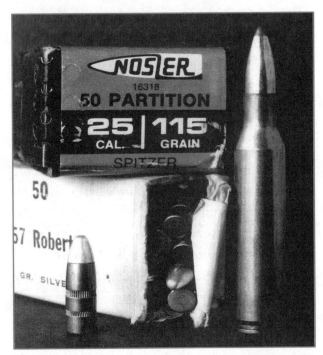

The .257 Roberts' performance can be improved substantially with handloading. Nosler's 115-grain Partition ranks high among the top .25 bullets for heavy game.

## .25-06 REMINGTON

An early derivative of the .30-06, the wildcat .25-06 was developed by A.O. Niedner shortly after World War II. Subsequently many versions of the cartridge appeared, some with sharper shoulders. When Remington finally offered commercially loaded .25-06 ammunition in 1969, it featured the original 17 1/2-degree shoulder. The early wildcats were all handicapped by the lack of propellants slow enough to yield high velocity without spiking pressures in that big case with the small mouth. When Hodgdon introduced its H4831 powder in the late 1940s, the .25-06 and many other large-capacity racehorse cartridges got a boost. In fact, it's a mystery of sorts that the major arms companies waited another two decades to produce .25-06 ammunition and chamber rifles for it. Now almost every firm that makes a bolt-action rifle for the .30-06 lists the .25-06 as well.

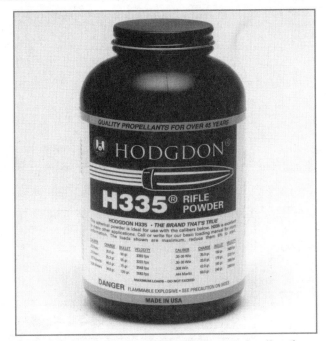

Hodgdon's H335 is a medium-fast powder in a complete line of propellants that includes such all-time favorites as 4895, 4350 and 4831.

While the 25-06 was initially intended as a super varmint round, most shooters now consider it a long-range deer cartridge. Booting 100-grain bullets out at over 3200 fps and 117-grain spitzers at nearly 3100 has no equals among rimless kin. Predictably, the 25-06 performs best in long barrels. Its deadliness against woodchucks and prairie dogs is unquestioned, but several cartridges--from the .22-250 to the 6mm Remington--almost match its effect with less noise and recoil. For big game, the .25-06 is clearly superior to any 6mm. A 110-grain bullet for the .25-06 would be a fine choice for deer at extreme range--except that nobody makes one. The weight gap between l00- and 117-grain .25 bullets is substantial, given the bore size. While flight paths for both are taut as banjo strings and pack more than enough energy to kill big deer, the ideal bullet for Niedner's pet cartridge is yet to come.

Proven as a deer killer, the .243 Winchester is a dual-purpose round, ideal for long-shooting at rodents with bullets like these 70 grain Hornadys.

| BULLET WEIGHT (grains) | MAXIMUM LOADS (grains, type of powder) | TOP VELOCITY (fps) AND DATA SOURCE |
|---|---|---|
| 75 | 57.0 4350 | 3690 (Accurate) |
| 85 | 57.3 RL-19 | 3510 (A-Square) |
| 87 | 62.0 N165 | 3410 (VihtaVuori) |
| 90 | 57.9 H450 | 3400 (Sierra) |
| 90 | 51.0 Win 760 | 3370 (Barnes) |
| 100 | 47.0 IMR 4064 | 3270 (Speer) |
| 115 | 54.0 IMR 7828 | 3060 (Barnes) |
| 117 | 52.0 H4831 | 3080 (Hodgdon) |
| 117 | 54.0 RL-22 | 3060 (A-Square) |
| 120 | 49.0 IMR 4350 | 3080 (Nosler) |
| 125 | 51.0 RL-19 | 2960 (Barnes) |
| 125 | 56.0 H1000 | 2890 (Hodgdon) |

**CASE CAPACITY**
(grains water)
**65**

**CASE TRIM LENGTH**
**2.48"**

**STANDARD OPERATING PRESSURE**
**63,000 PSI**

**STANDARD RIFLING TWIST**
**1-IN-10"**

Cartridge dimensions:

17°30'

.473 / 12,01
.470 / 11,94
.441 / 11,20
.291 / 7,39
.290 / 7,37
.2575 / 6,541
.308 / 7,82

1.948 (49,48)
2.494 (63,35)
3,250 (82,55)

*Cartridge Illustrations courtesy of Wolfe Publishing Company*

# .257 WEATHERBY MAGNUM

**D**eveloped in 1944 as one of Weatherby first belted magnums, the .257 has the look of a greyhound. Perhaps more than any other Weatherby cartridge, it showcases the "high speed at any cost" doctrine of its designer. But shooters who own .257s speak highly of its accuracy as well. What is sacrificed are efficiency, shooting comfort and barrel life. Noise and muzzle blast can be discomfiting; and a 26-inch barrel is necessary to coax published velocities from its huge case. There's little sense in loading bullets of less than 100 grains for this round, which can clock 3300 fps with a 117-grain spitzer.

Despite a prodigious payload, the .257 Weatherby gets few accolades as an elk round. The slender bullets must expand a great deal to open a lethal wound channel through the lungs. Fragmentation becomes worrisome because starting weight is half that of a .338 bullet. The .257 Magnum's high speed also complicates upset. Jackets that allow progressive expansion in soft tissue can shatter when driven fast into heavy bone, while those built to withstand high-velocity impact against solid media may not open at all when punched between ribs far from the rifle. Roy Weatherby once killed a Cape buffalo with his .257 Magnum, but even his disciples may consider that application of high velocity a stunt.

| Bullet Weight (grains) | Maximum Loads (grains, type of powder) | Top Velocity (fps) and Data Source |
|---|---|---|
| 75 | 70.5 IMR 4350 | 4000 (Sierra) |
| 85 | 75.0 RL-22 | 3750 (A-Square) |
| 87 | 72.0 H4831 | 3710 (Hodgdon) |
| 90 | 73.6 H450 | 3700 (Sierra) |
| 100 | 64.0 IMR 4350 | 3530 (Nosler) |
| 100 | 69.0 RL-19 | 3470 (Barnes) |
| 115 | 68.0 IMR 7828 | 3300 (Barnes) |
| 117 | 69.0 H4831 | 3300 (A-Square) |
| 117 | 70.0 RL-22 | 3270 (Hodgdon) |
| 120 | 66.0 AA 3100 | 3210 (Accurate) |
| 125 | 77.0 H1000 | 3180 (Hodgdon) |
| 125 | 76.0 AA 8700 | 3150 (Barnes) |

**Case Capacity**
(grains water)
**86**

**Case Trim Length**
**2.54"**

**Standard Operating Pressure**
**63,000 PSI**

**Standard Rifling Twist**
**1-in-12"**

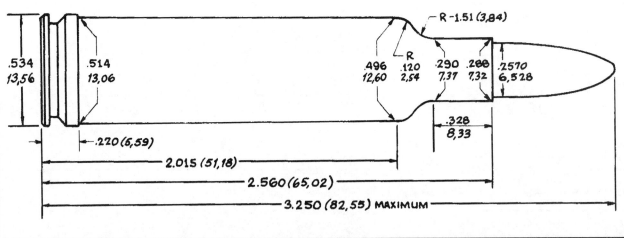

*Cartridge Illustrations courtesy of Wolfe Publishing Company*

The 6.5x55 "Swede" first appeared in the 1894 Mauser, which was used by the Swedish army. It was later chambered in the Mauser Models 96 and 38 along with Norway's Krag-Jorgensen. One of several 6.5mm military rounds developed around the turn of the century, the 6.5 x 55 Mauser remains the most popular among sportsmen. Surplus Swedish carbines imported during the 1950s sold for less than $50. They showed excellent workmanship and became the core of many a light-weight custom rifle--despite a long striker throw, cock-on-closing bolt and no safety lug. American armsmakers ignored the 6.5x55 until 1994, when Remington finally chambered it in the Model 700 Classic. Only recently has American-mode ammunition become available.

Norma has loaded 6.5x55 cartridges for years, including 139-grain spitzers at 2800 fps and 156-grain round-nose bullets at 2500. These speeds are nearly 200 fps ahead of velocities listed for military rounds using the same bullet weights in the long-barreled Model 96. (Pressures in the 94 and 96 Mausers should be kept below 45,000 CUP). At .480, the case head is slightly larger than that of a .30-06. Loaded 6.5x55 cartridges are a tad too long for short actions built for the .308. These nettlesome design differences may have something to do with the lack of commercial acceptance in the U.S. of the 6.5x55. But Remington's success with the 7-08 and the recent introduction of its .260 indicate that at least one company foresees a market for cartridges matching the Swede's performance. The 6.5x55 remains popular for game as big as moose in Europe; and with long 156-grain bullets it can deliver enough punch and penetration to take elk at modest ranges. A better whitetail round is hard to find.

The 6.5x55 Swede, which dates to the 1890s, is by some accounts an ideal deer cartridge, though few sporting rifles are chambered for it.

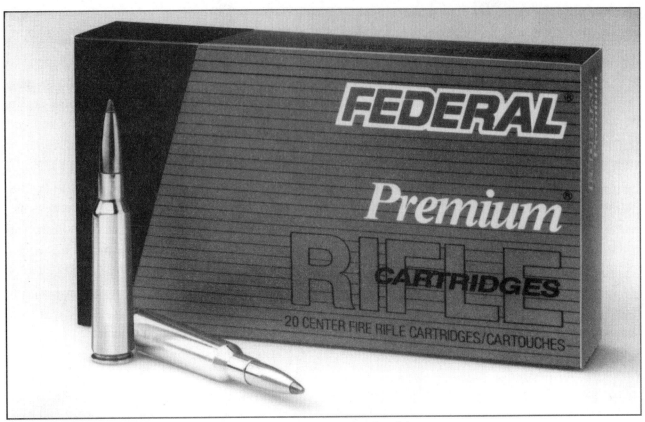

Federal's Premium line includes a 140-grain Nosler Partition bullet for the 6.5x55 Swedish.

| BULLET WEIGHT (grains) | MAXIMUM LOADS (grains, type of powder) | TOP VELOCITY (fps) AND DATA SOURCE | CASE CAPACITY (grains water) |
|---|---|---|---|
| 77 | 42.4 N133 | 3380 (VihtaVuori) | **55** |
| 87 | 48.0 IMR 4064 | 3220 (Speer) | |
| 100 | 51.0 N160 | 3020 (VihtaVuori) | **CASE TRIM LENGTH** |
| 120 | 50.0 H450 | 2950 (Hodgdon) | **2.16"** |
| 120 | 51.0 RL-22 | 2910 (A-Square) | |
| 129 | 45.0 H414 | 2870 (Hodgdon) | **STANDARD OPERATING PRESSURE** |
| 140 | 44.0 Win 760 | 2790 (Barnes) | **46,000 CUP** |
| 140 | 46.5 RL-22 | 2740 (Nosler) | |
| 160 | 44.0 IMR 4831 | 2450 (A-Square) | **STANDARD RIFLING TWIST** |
| 160 | 44.5 H4831 | 2400 (Hornady) | **1-IN-8" (TO 1-IN-9")** |

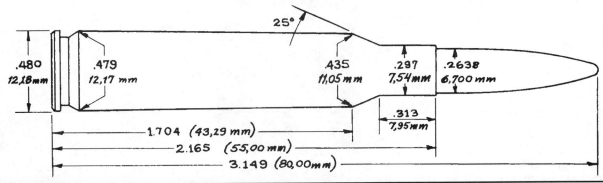

*Cartridge Illustrations courtesy of Wolfe Publishing Company*

# 6.5mm REMINGTON MAGNUM

In 1965 Remington introduced a short-action carbine with a dogleg bolt handle, 18-inch barrel and magnum (.532) bolt face. No commercial belted cartridges were available that could fit in the stubby Model 600 action, but Remington took care of that with a new round called the .350 Remington Magnum. A year later it announced the 6.5 Remington Magnum, a necked-down .350 with the same 2.170 case length and powder capacity equal to that of the .30-06. Probably because neither cartridge--especially the 6.5--performed well in the 18-inch barrel, it was replaced in 1968 by a 20-inch tube, whereupon the carbine was renamed the Model 660.

Still, the change failed to boost sales. Many shooters had, from the outset, deemed the 600-series actions downright ugly; moreover, barrels with ventilated ribs seemed odd indeed. And so Remington stopped building these rifles in 1971, chambering its 700 and 40XB rifles for the 6.5 Magnum (Ruger built a few 77s for this round too). In long barrels it shows ballistic promise; but short actions mandate deep bullet seating, which limits case capacity and velocity. Factory loads featuring 100- and 120-grain bullets prove that the 6.5 Remington is quite versatile, though it cannot claim superiority over the .25-06. Shooters who handload 140-grain bullets merely match what can be done with a .270. In any event this round is no challenge to Winchester's .264 Magnum. The Winchester case has the same head dimensions and shoulder angle (25 degrees), but it is .33 inches longer. The .264 drives 140-grain bullets as fast as the 6.5 Remington Magnum accelerates 120s; and in the 600-series carbine velocities sag about 150 fps. Remington kept loading ammunition for this hapless child long after it was orphaned, but eventually even the Ilion (NY) plant discontinued manufacture of its short belted 6.5mm.

| BULLET WEIGHT (grains) | MAXIMUM LOADS (grains, type of powder) | TOP VELOCITY (fps) AND DATA SOURCE | CASE CAPACITY (grains water) |
|---|---|---|---|
| | | | **69** |
| 77 | 58.0 H380 | 3830 (Hodgdon) | |
| 85 | 63.0 4350 | 3790 (Accurate) | **CASE TRIM LENGTH** |
| 100 | 56.0 H414 | 3470 (Hodgdon) | **2.16"** |
| 120 | 57.0 IMR 4831 | 3220 (Speer) | |
| 129 | 60.0 AA 3100 | 3110 (Accurate) | **STANDARD OPERATING PRESSURE** |
| 130 | 57.0 H4831 | 3090 (Barnes) | **65,000 CUP** |
| 140 | 56.0 RL-22 | 3040 (Barnes) | |
| 140 | 53.1 IMR 4350 | 3000 (Hornady) | **STANDARD RIFLING TWIST** |
| 160 | 54.5 H4831 | 2800 (Hornady) | **1-IN-9"** |
| 165 | 52.0 RL-22 | 2810 (Barnes) | |

*Cartridge Illustrations courtesy of Wolfe Publishing Company*

# .264 WINCHESTER MAGNUM

In 1956 Winchester announced its .458 Magnum, the first in a series of cartridges based on the .300 H&H case but shortened to fit .30-06-length actions. Two years later the company introduced the .264 and .338 Magnums in Winchester Model 70s, dubbed "Westerner" and "Alaskan" respectively. Rifles in the new .264 didn't become available until 1959. Loaded with 100- and 140-grain bullets at the factory, and given the Westerner's 26-inch barrel, the .264 should have fulfilled its mission as the ultimate cartridge for open-country shooting of varmints and big game as tough as elk. But its vaunted ballistic performance failed to ignite interest at the gun counter. When Winchester offered it in the Model 70 Featherweight, velocities dropped well below the already optimistic catalog projections of 3700 and 3200 fps. For deer and an

From left: .338 Winchester Magnum, .264 Winchester Magnum, 7mm Remington Magnum, .300 Winchester Magnum. Introduced between 1958 and 1963, all cartridges shown are "short" magnums made to fit .30-06-length actions.

| Bullet Weight (grains) | Maximum Loads (grains, type of powder) | Top Velocity (fps) And Data Source | Case Capacity (grains water) |
|---|---|---|---|
| 85 | 67.1 N160 | 3770 (VihtaVuori) | **82** |
| 100 | 59.9 IMR 4320 | 3600 (Hornady) | |
| 100 | 72.0 RL-22 | 3600 (A-Square) | **Case Trim Length** |
| 120 | 66.0 H450 | 3420 (Barnes) | **2.49"** |
| 120 | 65.0 H4831 | 3370 (Hodgdon) | |
| 125 | 77.0 AA 8700 | 3140 (Accurate) | **Standard Operating Pressure** |
| 140 | 63.0 IMR 7828 | 3100 (A-Square) | **64,000 PSI** |
| 140 | 74.0 H870 | 3090 (Nosler) | |
| 150 | 66.0 H1000 | 2920 (Hodgdon) | **Standard Rifling Twist** |
| 160 | 63.5 H450 | 2900 (Hornady) | **1-in-9"** |
| 165 | 57.0 IMR 7828 | 2900 (Barnes) | |

25°

.532 13.51mm .513 13.03 .490 12.45mm .299 7.59mm .298 7.57mm .264 6.706mm

.254 6.45mm

.220 (5.59mm)

2.040 (51.82mm)

2.500 (63.50mm)

3.340 (84.84mm)

*Cartridge Illustrations courtesy of Wolfe Publishing Company*

occasional prairie dog, the .25-06 and .270 served nicely, with less noise and recoil than the .264 Magnum. Their barrels don't burn out as fast. Then in 1962 Remington brought out its new Model 700 rifle and a 7mm Remington Magnum cartridge, which was cleverly advertised not as a plains cartridge, but as a long-range big game round. As the story went, hunters could expect magnum performance with .30-06 recoil. With bullets as heavy as 175 grains, the new belted 7mm excelled as an elk rifle. The endorsement of elk guide Les Bowman, plus a favorable press,

lent momentum to the rush for Model 700s in 7mm Remington Magnum. And so the .264 languished. It is still loaded by Winchester and Remington, but 140-grain bullets appear in the charts at only 3030 fps, barely equaling the .270. The .264 is clearly underrated. It can be safely stoked to beat original factory claims for the 140-grain bullet, whose high sectional density gives it an edge over the 140-grain 7mm bullet. In fact, it can beat the 400-yard energy of a factory-loaded 160-grain 7mm Magnum spitzer with less drop.

# .270 WINCHESTER

Since its introduction in Winchester's Model 54 bolt rifle in 1925, the .270 cartridge has enjoyed favorable press and strong loyalty among hunters. A .30-06 funneled down, and with a slightly longer neck, the .270 is an uncomplicated cartridge that has traditionally been loaded to high

performance levels at the factory. Handloaders have found it easy to work with, though the practice of carding off a loose caseload of H4831 and seating a 130-grain bullet is like adding oil to an engine without checking the dipstick. Jack O'Connor was the .270's biggest champion, and with his endorsement,

| Bullet Weight (grains) | Maximum Loads (grains, type of powder) | Top Velocity (fps) And Data Source |
|---|---|---|
| 90 | 54.4 H380 | 3500 (Sierra) |
| 100 | 61.0 IMR 4350 | 3470 (Speer) |
| 110 | 63.4 Norma MRP | 3300 (Hornady) |
| 120 | 51.0 IMR 4320 | 3180 (Barnes) |
| 130 | 61.0 RL-22 | 3100 (A-Square) |
| 130 | 54.5 H414 | 3060 (Nosler) |
| 140 | 59.0 AA 3100 | 3030 (Barnes) |
| 140 | 57.9 H4831 | 3000 (Sierra) |
| 150 | 52.5 Win 760 | 2940 (Barnes) |
| 150 | 52.0 H4350 | 2870 (Hodgdon) |
| 160 | 54.0 IMR 4831 | 2810 (Nosler) |
| 170 | 56.0 H450 | 2700 (Speer) |

**Case Capacity** (grains water) **67**

**Case Trim Length** **2.53"**

**Standard Operating Pressure** **52,000 CUP**

**Standard Rifling Twist** **1-in-10"**

*Cartridge Illustrations courtesy of Wolfe Publishing Company*

17°30'

.473 / 12,01 .470 / 11,94 .441 / 11,20 .310 / 7,87 .308 / 7,82 .278 / 7,061

.384 / 9,76

1.948 (49,48)
2.540 (64,52)
3.340 (84,84)

plus chambering in Winchester's Model 70, the .270 could hardly fail. Accurate and flat-shooting with bullets that are just the right weight for deer-size game, the .270 combines high velocity with light recoil. In fact, shortly after it appeared a few hunters thought it shot too fast, destroying too much meat. If they had a legitimate gripe, it was probably due to the light construction of some early bullets. Nonetheless, Winchester responded with a 150-grain load at 2675 fps, which nobody bought. Since then, most hunters have favored a 130-grain spitzer at about 3050 fps, though some advocate 150-grain bullets at 2850 for elk. Recently several 140-grain, top-quality game bullets have appeared. While many shooters consider the .270 marginal for elk, it has consistently appeared in surveys among the five most popular elk rounds. It has also been chambered in almost as many rifles as the .30-06, performing better in 24-inch barrels than in 22-inch tubes.

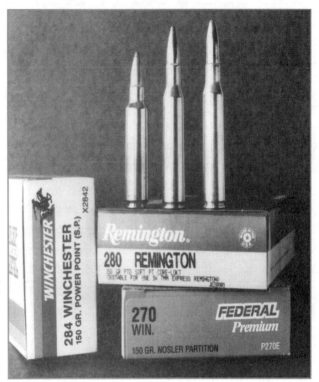

Three top deer cartridges, from left: .284 Winchester, .270 Winchester, .280 Remington.

# .270 WEATHERBY MAGNUM

Probably among the least heralded of Weatherby's line of belted magnums, this .270 was actually its first member. Developed in 1943, shortly after Roy Weatherby's experiments with an improved .220 Swift (called the Rocket), the .270 Magnum was designed to work in standard-length actions. The .257 and 7mm Weatherby Magnums have the same case length (2.579), plus the radiused shoulder junctures. It also shares a minimum-taper body featuring a powder chamber as big as that of the parent of this series: the .300 H&H. By the time Weatherby brought his .270 Magnum to market, the .270 Winchester had already become a huge success. Maybe that's what prompted Weatherby's initial effort. Indeed, these two are still the only commercial centerfire rounds featuring .277-diameter bullets. The .270 Weatherby can boot a bullet out the muzzle

faster by nearly 300 fps than a .270 Winchester.

While bullets of 90, 100 and 110 grains are available for long range coyote shooters, the .270 Weatherby is essentially a big game cartridge. Like the .264 Winchester Magnum, it makes more noise and kicks harder than a .25-06. A 100-grain .257 bullet retains its velocity and energy better downrange than a .264 or .277 bullet of the same weight, so differences in muzzle velocity decrease with distance. The magnums offer a slightly flatter trajectory, but these disparities are largely academic. For big game the .270 Weatherby offers much more than the .25-06 and .270 Winchester. Given a bullet of the proper design, it can kill cleanly any game that a 7mm magnum can. The availability of bullets heavier than 160 grains gives the 7mms a bit more appeal, but these heavy bullets extract a steep price in velocity.

| BULLET WEIGHT (grains) | MAXIMUM LOADS (grains, type of powder) | TOP VELOCITY (fps) AND DATA SOURCE |
|---|---|---|
| 90 | 76.3 IMR 4831 | 3800 (Sierra) |
| 100 | 78.0 H450 | 3690 (Hodgdon) |
| 110 | 69.0 IMR 4350 | 3530 (Accurate) |
| 120 | 72.5 IMR 7828 | 3330 (Barnes) |
| 130 | 72.5 AA 3100 | 3340 (Accurate) |
| 140 | 74.0 RL-22 | 3280 (A-Square) |
| 140 | 62.0 IMR 4320 | 3250 (Sierra) |
| 150 | 88.0 AA 8700 | 3160 (Accurate) |
| 150 | 71.5 H4831 | 3130 (A-Square) |
| 160 | 73.0 IMR 7828 | 3100 (Nosler) |
| 180 | 74.5 AA 8700 | 2750 (Barnes) |
| 180 | 62.5 H4831 | 2740 (Barnes) |

**CASE CAPACITY**
(grains water)
**85**

**CASE TRIM LENGTH**
**2.54"**

**STANDARD OPERATING PRESSURE**
**71,000 PSI**

**STANDARD RIFLING TWIST**
**1-IN-10"**

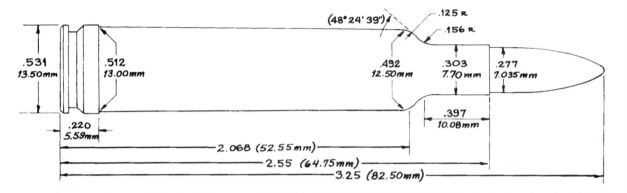

*Cartridge Illustrations courtesy of Wolfe Publishing Company*

# 7-30 WATERS

In 1976 ballistician Ken Waters began working on a high-velocity alternative to the .30-30 in lever-action carbines. The tube-fed Winchester 94s and Marlin 336s, considered traditional deer rifles in Waters' northeast woodlands, placed daunting constraints on working pressures and mandated the use of flat-nose bullets. By 1982, he had designed a new cartridge that launched a 139-grain 7mm bullet at 2600 fps without straining rifle actions. Based on the .30-30 case, it had a shorter neck and more powder capacity. With U.S. Repeating Arms having assumed manufacture of all Winchester rifles, Water's 7mm/.30-30 round was slated for chambering in the Model 94 the following year. But before it could be announced, Federal Cartridge Company developed a new load: a 120-grain bullet at 2700 fps. Reducing bullet weight offered higher velocity at lower pressure but still gave deer hunters plenty of lead for sure kills.

In 1984 Winchester's 94XTR Angle Eject was chambered in 7-30 Waters. The cartridge has since been offered in other rifles, as well as in handguns (such as Thompson/Center's Contender) designed for hunting and metallic silhouette shooting. Single-shot mechanisms allow the use of pointed bullets, which reduce the rate of bullet deceleration. That means flatter trajectories and more energy down-range. Bullet makers also offer a huge selection of pointed 7mm bullets but only a few with flat noses. Nosler developed a 120-grain Partition for the original Federal load, and Hornady now manufactures a 139-grain alternative. The 7-30 Waters works best with powders a bit slower than those most useful in the .30-30.

| Bullet Weight (grains) | Maximum Loads (grains, type of powder) | Top Velocity (fps) and Data Source |
|---|---|---|
| 120 | 41.0 H380 | 2740 (Hodgdon) |
| 120 | 37.0 AA 2520 | 2730 (Accurate) |
| 120 | 36.5 Win 748 | 2700 (Nosler) |
| 139 | 34.0 AA 2230 | 2540 (Accurate) |
| 139 | 35.5 2495 BR | 2510 (Accurate) |
| 140 | 38.0 H414 | 2520 (Nosler) |
| 154 | 33.0 BL-C(2) | 2320 (Hodgdon) |
| 154 | 37.0 H4350 | 2310 (Hodgdon) |

**Case Capacity** (grains water)
**44**

**Case Trim Length**
**2.03"**

**Standard Operating Pressure**
**40,000 CUP**

**Standard Rifling Twist**
**1-in-9.5"**

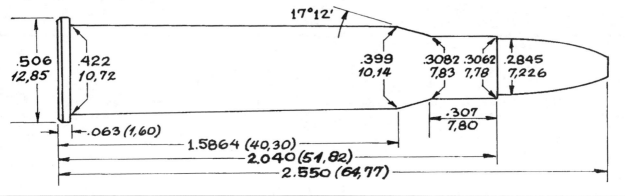

*Cartridge Illustrations courtesy of Wolfe Publishing Company*

# 7X57 MAUSER

One of the oldest cartridges still popular for big game hunting, the 7x57 (or 7mm Mauser) dates to 1892. Developed by Paul Mauser as a military round, it was quickly adopted by the Spanish government for Model 92 Mauser bolt rifles, and a year later it was chambered in a new rifle that became known as the Spanish Mauser. That rifle subsequently went to Mexico and several South American countries. It saw service against U.S. troops in the Spanish-American War. The 7x57 appeared as a hunting cartridge in Remington's Rolling Block rifle around the turn of the century and later in such landmark bolt rifles as the Remington 30S and Winchester's 54 and 70 models. Relegated to the shadow of the .270 Winchester in the U.S. after 1925, it remained popular among custom rifle enthusiasts who favored Mauser 98 actions. The English gunmaker, John Rigby and Company,

adopted it as the .275 Rigby. Jack O'Connor used it and wrote about it, as did several other important gun scribes. The 7x57 cartridge is, however, best suited to deer-size game, with 139- to 160-grain bullets at velocities of 2600 to 2800 fps. The availability of heavy 7mm bullets--to 195 grains--is less a boon to the 7x57 than to rounds of greater case capacity. For light game at a distance, 120-grain spitzers moving 3000 fps excel. The dimensions of the 7x57 make it too long for U.S. sporting rifles designed for the .308, and in .30-06-length mechanisms there's no reason to choose it in favor of the more potent .270 or .280. Still, the 7x57 has made a comeback in the last two decades. In fact, it may be as popular among sportsmen now as it has ever been. Ruger and Winchester have chambered rifles for it, and it has become known as a classic "sheep rifle" chambering among custom riflesmiths.

The "+P" designates a more ambitious load than was initially prescribed for the .257 Roberts. It and the 7x57 Mauser have been chronically underloaded and do not approach pressure ceilings for modern sporting rifles.

| Bullet Weight (grains) | Maximum Loads (grains, type of powder) | Top Velocity (fps) And Data Source | Case Capacity (grains water) 56 |
|---|---|---|---|
| 100 | 53.0 H380 | 3210 (Hodgdon) | |
| 120 | 54.0 IMR 4831 | 3010 (A-Square) | Case Trim Length 2.23" |
| 120 | 44.3 IMR 4064 | 3000 (Sierra) | |
| 130 | 52.0 Win 760 | 2950 Hodgdon) | Standard Operating Pressure 46,000 CUP |
| 140 | 49.0 IMR 4350 | 2820 (Nosler) | |
| 145 | 50.0 IMR 4350 | 2760 (Speer) | Standard Rifling Twist |
| 150 | 48.5 RL-19 | 2770 (Barnes) | 1-in-8.75" |
| 154 | 49.5 Win 760 | 2700 (Hornady) | (also slower, to 1-in-10") |
| 160 | 49.9 H4831 | 2600 (Sierra) | |
| 175 | 50.0 IMR 7828 | 2510 (Hodgdon) | |

*Cartridge Illustrations courtesy of Wolfe Publishing Company*

**S**oon after the .308 Winchester cartridge became available in 1952, wildcatters pounced on it, necking it up and down and changing its shoulder angle. The .243 and .358 Winchester were given commercial sanction in 1955, but a 7mm-08 didn't appear in ammunition catalogs until 1980, when Remington introduced the round for its Model 700 and 788 rifles. After the 788 faded, this cartridge made the list of chamberings in Remington's Model Seven. Despite the company's initial claim that it is the first modern 7mm cartridge designed for short actions, the 7-08 was actually 17 years behind the .284 Winchester. The .284 has more case capacity but is only .135 longer and can be loaded to fit the same actions. Initially capped with a 140-grain bullet at 2860 fps, the 7-08 is now also offered by Remington with a 120-grain spitzer at 3000 and a 154-grain at 2715. It has become a favorite of metallic silhouette shooters because the 140-grain

bullet is more efficient than a .308 150-grain at extended range. The 7-08 also recoils softly, which endears it not only to target shooters but to hunters of slight build. Not surprisingly, it has become popular as a lady's big game round.

While the Model 1700's standard barrel lengths give the 7mm-08 a velocity boost over the Model Seven's short tube, the Seven sells well in 7-08. As a replacement for lever-action carbines in whitetail country, this handy bolt gun offers better accuracy, flatter trajectory and more power with about the same recoil. Like the slightly larger 7x57, the 7-08 is effective for elk hunting at modest ranges when loaded with 150- to 160-grain bullets (the case is really too small to handle 175-grain bullets). Unlike the 7x57, the 7-08 has been chambered from the start in strong actions and has been loaded to relatively high working pressures. That ezplains why the charts often show this cartridge to be more ambitious than the 7x57.

| BULLET WEIGHT (grains) | MAXIMUM LOADS (grains, type of powder) | TOP VELOCITY (fps) AND DATA SOURCE |
|---|---|---|
| 100 | 49.4 N150 | 3220 (VihtaVuori) |
| 120 | 45.5 IMR 4895 | 3110 (A-Squre) |
| 120 | 44.0 RL-12 | 3080 (Nosler) |
| 130 | 49.0 H414 | 2890 (Hodgdon) |
| 140 | 43.0 RL-1 | 2850 (A-Square) |
| 140 | 44.3 IMR 4320 | 2800 (Sierra) |
| 150 | 46.5 4350 | 2730 (Accurate) |
| 150 | 44.0 H414 | 2710 (Barnes) |
| 160 | 46.0 IMR 4831 | 2680 (Nosler) |
| 168 | 43.5 Win 760 | 2600 (Sierra) |
| 175 | 47.2 Norma MRP | 2500 (Sierra) |
| 175 | 44.0 RL-19 | 2460 (Barnes) |

**CASE CAPACITY**
*(grains water)*
**52**

**CASE TRIM LENGTH**
**2.03"**

**STANDARD OPERATING PRESSURE**
**52,000 CUP**

**STANDARD RIFLING TWIST**
**1-IN-9.25"**

20°

.473 / 12.01 mm
.470 / 11.94 mm
.454 / 11.53 mm
.315 / 8.00 mm
.2845 / 7.226 mm
.284 / 7.21 mm
1.56 (39.62 mm)
2.035 (51.69 mm)
2.800 (71.12 mm) MAX.

*Cartridge Illustrations courtesy of Wolfe Publishing Company*

# .284 WINCHESTER

**W**inchester introduced its .284 in 1963, along with its Models 88 and 100 lever-action and self-loading rifles. Like the .30-06 and .308, the .284 has a .473 head; but the body diameter is similar to that of a belted magnum. Overall length is just .135 longer than a .308, which makes it suitable for the 88 and 100 mechanisms. Winchester's idea was to offer a short-action big game round with the ballistic performance of a .270 Winchester or .280 Remington--and it succeeded. There are no significant differences among the case capacities or velocities of these three cartridges when loaded with bullets of the same weight. But Model 88 and 100 Winchester rifles did not sell particularly

well and were eventually dropped. With them went Winchester's interest in the .284, although the firm still offers a 150-grain factory load. Savage chambered the round for a time in its 99 lever-action, and Ruger made a run of Model 77 bolt guns in .284. Wildcatters have given the .284 a great deal of attention, necking it up and down to every standard bore diameter. Among the most popular are the 6mm/.284, which closely matches the .240 Weatherby in performance, and the 6.5/.284, a round that has recently proven itself in long-range center-fire competition. The .30/.284 gives .30-06 performance in a compact rifle, and the .35/.284 can match the .35 Whelen.

| Bullet Weight (grains) | Maximum Loads (grains, type of powder) | Top Velocity (fps) And Data Source | | Case Capacity (grains water) |
|---|---|---|---|---|
| 100 | 51.2 IMR 4064 | 3200 (Sierra) | | **65** |
| 120 | 63.0 RL-19 | 3180 (A-Squre) | | |
| 120 | 52.9 H380 | 3100 (Hornady) | | **Case Trim Length** |
| 130 | 59.0 IMR 4831 | 3040 (Speer) | | **2.16"** |
| 139 | 50.1 H4895 | 3000 (Hornady) | | |
| 140 | 53.5 H414 | 2970 (Barnes) | | **Standard Operating Pressure** |
| 140 | 60.0 RL-19 | 2970 (A-Square) | | **56,000 CUP** |
| 145 | 56.0 IMR 4350 | 2940 (Speer) | | |
| 154 | 59.1 H450 | 2900 (Hornady) | | **Standard Rifling Twist** |
| 160 | 54.0 IMR 4350 | 2810 (Speer) | | **1-in-10"** |
| 168 | 57.2 H4831 | 2700 (Sierra) | | |
| 175 | 50.0 IMR 7828 | 2590 (Barnes) | | |

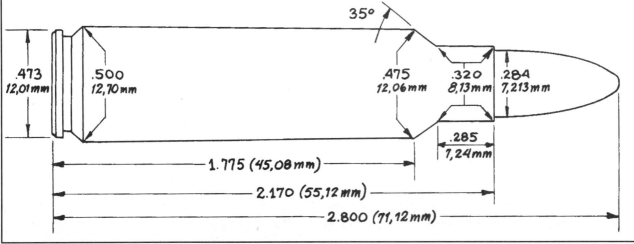

*Cartridge Illustrations courtesy of Wolfe Publishing Company*

The one factor that most often throttles .284 performance is seating depth. Deep seating mandated by short throats or magazines robs powder space and bullet velocity. Melvin Forbes considered that when building his trim bolt rifle under the banner of Ultra Light Arms. The Model 20 is a mid-length action perfectly suited to the .284 as well as to Europe's 6.5x55 and 7x57 rounds. In fact, the .284 has been chambered more often in ULA Model 20 rifles than all .308-class cartridges combined!

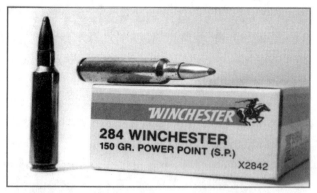

The .284 Winchester, with its rebated rim, is unusual. Its fatter case fits in a short rifle action but holds about as much powder as the .30-06.

# .280 REMINGTON

Announced in 1957 as a chambering in Remington's 740 self-loading rifle, the .280 is essentially a 7mm/.30-06. Wildcatters long ago produced the same cartridge; and in 1917 the great German designer, Wilhelm Brenneke, designed a round nearly identical to the .280. The 7x64 Brenneke has a slightly smaller rim but looks and performs the same. Development of the .280 still made a lot of sense, though, given the availability of .30-06 brass and the dimensions of common American rifle actions. The .270's huge popularity no doubt encouraged Remington. In 1957 no new 7mm cartridge had appeared since Weatherby's 7mm Magnum in 1944 and the 7x61 Sharpe & Hart in 1953. Neither had

| BULLET WEIGHT (grains) | MAXIMUM LOADS (grains, type of powder) | TOP VELOCITY (fps) AND DATA SOURCE |
|---|---|---|
| 100 | 54.0 BL-C(2) | 3370 (Hodgdon) |
| 120 | 50.0 RL-15 | 3240 (Nosler) |
| 120 | 50.0 H4895 | 3180 (A-Square) |
| 130 | 57.0 IMR 4350 | 3110 (Speer) |
| 140 | 56.0 IMR 4831 | 3070 (Nosler) |
| 140 | 60.0 H4831 | 3030 (A-Square) |
| 150 | 56.0 RL-22 | 2980 (Nosler) |
| 160 | 60.0 H1000 | 2810 (Barnes) |
| 160 | 55.0 RL-19 | 2800 (Hodgdon) |
| 162 | 53.6 IMR 4350 | 2800 (Hornady) |
| 168 | 57.0 AA 3100 | 2720 (Accurate) |
| 175 | 55.0 IMR 7828 | 2700 (Nosler) |

**CASE CAPACITY**
*(grains water)*
**69**

**CASE TRIM LENGTH**
**2.53"**

**STANDARD OPERATING PRESSURE**
**60,000 PSI**

**STANDARD RIFLING TWIST**
**1-IN-9.25"**

17°30'

.473
12,01

.470
11,94

.441
11,20

.315
8,00

.2845
7,226

.341
8,65

1.999 (50,77)

2.540 (64,52)

3.330 (84,58) MAXIMUM

*Cartridge Illustrations courtesy of Wolfe Publishing Company*

been a resounding success. Initially the .280 Remington made hardly a stir at market, partly because the auto-loading 740 rifle could not demonstrate its potential. Later, Remington chambered the new round in its 760 pump and 721 and 725 bolt guns. The subsequent introduction of Remington's 700 rifle and 7mm Magnum cartridge fueled interest in the 7mm bore and expanded the selection of 7mm bullets.

In 1979, in an effort to hike sales, Remington renamed the .280 the 7mm Express. The round has become more popular recently, but under its old name. Like the .270, it is slightly longer than the .30-06. The .280 also has a longer base-to-shoulder measure than the .270 and .30-06 (the same at 1.948). The .05 disparity gives the .280 no appreciable advantage ballistically, but it does prevent the round from chambering in a .270 with a washed-out throat. Inherently accurate, the .280 is among the most versatile big game rounds available. When used with thick-jacketed 150-grain and 160-grain bullets, it has proven adequate for elk; and with 140-grain spitzers at 3000 fps it gives hunters flat trajectory, great reach and the light recoil that encourage accurate shooting.

## 7mm REMINGTON MAGNUM

Remington's 7mm Magnum may be the most successful sporting cartridge developed in this century. Remarkably, it even rivals the .30-06 in popularity among elk hunters. While the two rounds deliver about the same punch and are both widely chambered, the .30-06 had a 50-year head start. The belted 7mm was hardly the first of its breed, though, when Remington introduced it in 1963 along with its new 700 bolt rifle. Indeed, Holland & Holland had fielded its .275 Belted Rimless Magnum back in 1912. Roy Weatherby developed the first "short" 7mm magnum in the 1940s on a .300 H&H hull. Nine years later the 7x61 Sharpe & Hart appeared. Warren Page used (and wrote about) the Mashburn 7mm Super Magnum, and in 1958 Winchester brought out its .264 Magnum. Les Bowman, the Wyoming outfitter, necked the .264 up to .284. The story goes that Jack O'Connor's gift of a .275 H&H to Bowman stirred his interest in a belted 7mm. Whatever its lineage, Remington's 7mm Magnum was developed largely at the urging of Bowman and others, quickly overtaking the .264 Winchester Magnum in sales.

Hunters in those days wanted a light-recoiling rifle with magnum punch for deer and elk, not a deer rifle with magnum blast and varmint loadings. With 120- to 150-grain bullets, the 7mm Remington and .264 Winchester Magnums have nearly the same ballistic potential. That's because they have essentially the same case dimensions. But Remington's advertising divined the market more accurately. The shooting press played a hand as well, lamenting throat erosion in .264s while praising the 7mm Magnum for its effectiveness on game. A huge selection of bullets followed public acceptance of this 7mm, which truly is a versatile cartridge. Still, a .270 loaded briskly will match the performance of standard 7mm Magnum factory loads; and as for tough animals this popular belted round is no match for the .300 Winchester or .308 Norma Magnums.

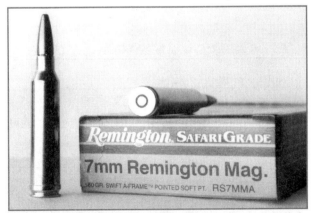

7mm Remington Magnum Safari Grade ammunition featured Swift A-Frame bullets designed for deep penetration.

Winchester's synthetic-stocked Model 70 in 7mm Remington Magnum is a popular choice among elk hunters.

| Bullet Weight (grains) | Maximum Loads (grains, type of powder) | Top Velocity (fps) And Data Source |
|---|---|---|
| 100 | 75.0 N160 | 3570 (VihtaVuori) |
| 115 | 72.5 AA 3100 | 3370 (Accurate) |
| 120 | 63.5 H414 | 3330 (Barnes) |
| 130 | 67.5 N205 | 3270 (Speer) |
| 140 | 66.0 IMR 4831 | 3220 (Nosler) |
| 140 | 70.0 RL-22 | 3180 (A-Square) |
| 150 | 67.5 IMR 7828 | 3150 (Nosler) |
| 160 | 72.5 H1000 | 3040 (Hodgdon) |
| 162 | 63.0 RL-22 | 3060 (Nosler) |
| 175 | 64.8 H450 | 2900 (Sierra) |
| 175 | 77.0 AA 8700 | 2820 (Barnes) |
| 195 | 62.0 H4831 | 2690 (Barnes) |

**Case Capacity**
(grains water)
**83**

**Case Trim Length**
**2.49"**

**Standard Operating Pressure**
**61,000 PSI**

**Standard Rifling Twist**
**1-in-9.5"**

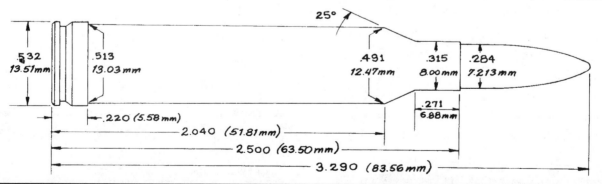

*Cartridge Illustrations courtesy of Wolfe Publishing Company*

**MODERN SPORTING RIFLE CARTRIDGES**

# 7mm WEATHERBY MAGNUM

Roy Weatherby began building his line of magnum cartridges during World War II, but they didn't appear in magazine ads until the early 1950s. When the cartridge finally did become public, few people bought it. Like other Weatherby cartridges, the 7mm Magnum was a proprietary round not chambered in standard rifles. It offers more punch than the 7x61 S&H, which was developed about the same time by the French military, but neither cartridge was selling. Weatherby's 7mm lanquished in the shadow of the firm's more popular .300. And Roy Weatherby didn't help sales much when he chose a 1-in-12 twist for early 7mm barrels.

In his exploits with the various 7mm Mashburn magnums, Warren Page had convinced hunters they needed sub-.30 big game rounds that would handle heavy bullets. The slow Weatherby twist wasn't well suited to the 160- and 175-grain bullets Page found so effective. Indeed, 7mm Weatherby factory loads featured 139- and 154-grain Hornadys only. The twist was steepened later to 1-in-10; but not until the 7mm Remington Magnum appeared in 1962 and the 7mm bore became more popular did the 7mm Weatherby begin to attract buyers. Actually, it has a lot to offer. Case capacity is about the same as the Remington, but the Weatherby 7mm has a longer neck; and like the other members of its family, it has radiused shoulder junctures. Loaded by Norma to higher pressures than U.S. production affords, the 7mm Weatherby Magnum is an undersung and versatile cartridge. It is a more efficient round than the new 7mm STW.

| Bullet Weight (grains) | Maximum Loads (grains, type of powder) | Top Velocity (fps) And Data Source |
|---|---|---|
| 100 | 79.3 RL-22 | 3650 (Sierra) |
| 120 | 78.0 IMR 7828 | 3510 (Hodgdon) |
| 140 | 74.0 RL-22 | 3350 (A-Square) |
| 140 | 71.0 H450 | 3320 (Nosler) |
| 150 | 72.0 AA 3100 | 3200 (Accurate) |
| 154 | 68.9 IMR 4350 | 3200 (Hornady) |
| 160 | 66.0 IMR 4831 | 3080 (Nosler) |
| 160 | 72.0 H4831 | 3070 (A-Square) |
| 162 | 73.0 IMR 7828 | 3040 (Nosler) |
| 175 | 69.5 RL-22 | 2970 (Barnes) |
| 175 | 75.0 H1000 | 2950 (Hodgdon) |
| 195 | 66.0 H4831 | 2720 (Barnes) |

**CASE CAPACITY**
(grains water)
**87**

**CASE TRIM LENGTH**
**2.54"**

**STANDARD OPERATING PRESSURE**
**65,000 PSI**

**STANDARD RIFLING TWIST**
**1-IN-12" (ALSO 1-IN10")**

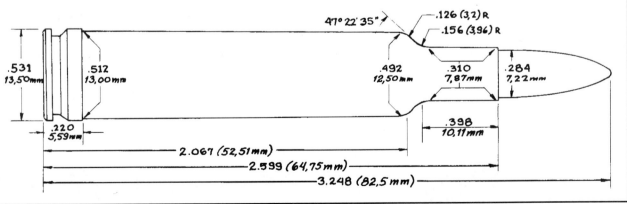

*Cartridge Illustrations courtesy of Wolfe Publishing Company*

# 7mm STW

The 7mm Shooting Times Westerner (STW), developed by gun writer Layne Simpson in 1989, began as an 8mm Remington case necked down. Like any "full-length" magnum, this cartridge needs a rifle with a long magazine. Rifles built for the short magnums and with .30-06-length boxes will not work without extensive alteration. The huge case and high expansion ratio (case volume to bore volume) also dictate long barrels for top performance.

The 7mm STW is ideally suited for dropping-block single-shot rifles--the Ruger Number One, for example. Despite its specialized nature, voracious appetite for powder and bullet-seatng constraints imposed by its great length, the 7mm STW has gained popularity. Hunters have been seduced by the 3500-fps take-off speed of its 140-grain bullet, not to mention a trajectory that's as flat at 400 yards as the flight paths produced by 30-06-class cartridges at 300. It is also an accurate round. One early 7mm STW rifle assembled on a Remington 700 action with a match-grade Schneider barrel reportedly drilled out five-shot groups as small as .300. Only the slowest of powders are suitable for this cartridge, which is best served by bullets of 140 to 175 grains in weight delivering more than a ton of energy at 500 yards.

| Bullet Weight (grains) | Maximum Loads (grains, type of powder) | Top Velocity (fps) and Data Source |
|---|---|---|
| 120 | 83.0 IMR 7828 | 3700 (Hodgdon) |
| 130 | 81.0 IMR 7828 | 3570 (Hodgdon) |
| 140 | 82.0 H1000 | 3500 (Hodgdon) |
| 140 | 79.0 RL-22 | 3480 (Hodgdon) |
| 140 | 83.0 IMR 7828 | 3410 (A-Square) |
| 150 | 81.0 H1000 | 3400 (Barnes) |
| 160 | 75.0 H4831 | 3200 (A-Square) |
| 160 | 93.0 AA 8700 | 3180 (Accurate) |
| 175 | 77.0 H1000 | 3130 (Barnes) |
| 175 | 86.0 H5010 | 3100 (Hodgdon) |
| 195 | 72.0 RL-22 | 2990 (Barnes) |

**CASE CAPACITY**
(grains water)
**98**

**CASE TRIM LENGTH**
**2.85"**

**STANDARD OPERATING PRESSURE**
**65,000 PSI**

**STANDARD RIFLING TWIST**
**1-IN-12" (ALSO 1-IN10")**

.532 13,51mm  .5126 13,02mm  .4868 12,36mm  .355 9,02mm  .354 8,99mm  .3235 8,217mm  25°  .320 8,13mm  .220 (5,59mm)  2.389 (60,68mm)  2.850 (72,39mm)  3.60 (91,44mm)

*Cartridge Illustrations courtesy of Wolfe Publishing Company*

# .30-30 WINCHESTER

ntroduced in 1895 for the Winchester Model 94 carbine, the .30-30 was so named after the fashion of black-powder rounds for its 30-caliber bullet and a propellant charge of 30 grains. But this was America's first sporting cartridge designed for *smokeless* powder, and that's what fueled the first .30-30 ammunition enough to give a 160-grain bullet a muzzle velocity of 1970 fps. Later loads included a 150-grain bullet at 2400 and a 170-grain at 2200. All bullets for the .30-30 have been designed with flat or round noses for use in carbines with tubular magazines, such as on Winchester 94 and Marlin 336. The trim lines of these carbines with their fast-shucking actions and natural pointing ability have kept the .30-30 popular. Long after its ballistic performance was eclipsed by more potent rounds in scope-sighted rifles. Box magazines in bolt guns like the

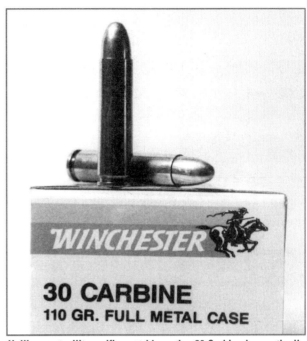

Unlike most military rifle cartridges, the .30 Carbine is practically useless for hunting.

| Bullet Weight (grains) | Maximum Loads (grains, type of powder) | Top Velocity (fps) And Data Source | | Case Capacity (grains water) 42 |
|---|---|---|---|---|
| 100 | 32.0 IMR 4198 | 2790 (Hodgdon) | | |
| 110 | 38.0 AA 2520 | 2690 (Accurate) | | Case Trim Length 2.03" |
| 125 | 32.5 H322 | 2500 (Sierra) | | |
| 130 | 32.8 N133 | 2470 (VihtaVuori) | | Standard Operating Pressure 42,000 PSI |
| 150 | 34.5 Win 748 | 2390 (Speer) | | |
| 150 | 34.0 IMR 4895 | 2380 (Hodgdon) | | Standard Rifling Twist 1-in-12" |
| 170 | 33.0 IMR 4320 | 2190 (Nosler) | | |
| 170 | 33.0 BL-C(2) | 2180 (Hodgdon) | | |
| 170 | 30.0 IMR 3031 | 2170 (Nosler) | | |

15° 39'

.506 / 12.85mm  .422 / 10.72mm  .401 / 10.18mm  .333 / 8.46mm  .330 / 8.38mm  .309 / 7.848mm

.063 (1.60mm)

1.440 (36.57mm)

.476 / 12.09mm

2.039 (51.79mm)

2.550 (64.77mm)

*Cartridge Illustrations courtesy of Wolfe Publishing Company*

Winchester 54 and Savage 340, and the spool magazine of Savage's Model 99 enable handloaders to use pointed bullets. Modern single-shot rifles and pistols, plus the Remington 788 bolt rifle, allow the .30-30 more punch because they can bottle pressures in excess of the standard 38,000 CUP ceiling. The .30-30's case has thin walls, though, so even in a stout action handloaders must be conservative.

Most hunters using .30-30s have been pleased with the dependable terminal performance of factory-loaded 170-grain bullets, which have greater sectional density and penetrate better than 150s. At normal ranges in the woods, the slightly higher velocity of the 150-grain bullet is of no account. In 1979 Remington introduced a sabot loading for the .30-30 with a 55-grain .224 soft-point in a 7-grain plastic cup. Advertised velocity for this "Accelerator" small game load is 3400 fps. The .30-30 may still have downed more deer than any other cartridge. A 1939 survey of elk hunters in Washington indicated it and the .30 Remington outnumbered every other cartridge afield. While the .30-30 hardly ever goes elk hunting these days, it remains among the most effective rounds for woodland whitetails.

## .300 SAVAGE

The designers who fashioned the .300 Savage started out around 1920 with an ambitious goal: to generate .30-06 ballistic performance in a case short enough to work in a compact action (the Savage 99). They didn't succeed; nor has anyone since then developed a cartridge this small that can match the .30-06 over the chronograph. Hunters have nonetheless found the .300 Savage a considerable improvement over the .30-30 and almost as effective on big game as the .308 Winchester. A rimless round developed for reasonably strong actions and staggered-stack or spool magazines, the .300 Savage is now commonly loaded with pointed bullets. But in the early days most factory ammunition featured round-nose bullets because that's what most people were used to. In addition, more bullet weight could be packed into a .300 cartridge without increasing overall length. Expansion might also have been a concern. The modest velocity of a heavy .300 Savage bullet had little jacket-rupturing power beyond woods ranges, and the greater lead exposure of a blunt bullet tip hastened expansion.

The author practices his offhand shooting with a favorite rifle: a .300 Savage 99 with a 3xLeupold.

Now 150-grain factory-loaded bullets are commonly spitzers. The .300 Savage gives them enough speed (2630 fps) to ensure expansion. Round-nose bullets remain the norm for 180-grain factory loads. While the .300 Savage is still popular for deer, it has earned a solid reputation on bigger game. A pre-World War II elk hunter survey placed it among the six most popular cartridges, and it was widely considered one of the most powerful hunting rounds of that day. When a shooter bragged that he had a "three hunnerd" back in the Depression, it meant he owned a .300 Savage. One old hunter told of accidentally backing a pickup over his Model 99 and bending the barrel. After surveying the damage, he put the rifle (other side up) down, and ran over it again. The next year he killed a moose with that salvaged .300. The big bull dropped to one shot.

A shooter examines a tight group from a Remington 700 in .243, a popular deer and pronghorn cartridge.

| BULLET WEIGHT (grains) | MAXIMUM LOADS (grains, type of powder) | TOP VELOCITY (fps) AND DATA SOURCE |
|---|---|---|
| 100 | 48.0 Win 748 | 3100 (Speer) |
| 110 | 41.7 IMR 3031 | 3000 (Hornady) |
| 130 | 36.0 H4198 | 2840 (Hodgdon) |
| 150 | 42.5 IMR 4064 | 2700 (Hornady) |
| 150 | 42.5 RL-12 | 2650 (Barnes) |
| 165 | 37.5 2015 BR | 2570 (Accurate) |
| 170 | 40.4 H4895 | 2500 (Hornady) |
| 180 | 38.0 AA 2460 | 2380 (Barnes) |
| 180 | 45.0 IMR 4350 | 2370 (Speer) |
| 200 | 36.0 IMR 4064 | 2280 (Barnes) |

**CASE CAPACITY** (grains water)
**51**

**CASE TRIM LENGTH**
**1.86"**

**STANDARD OPERATING PRESSURE**
**46,000 CUP**

**STANDARD RIFLING TWIST**
**1-IN-12"**

30°

.473 / 12.01mm
.471 / 11.96mm
.446 / 11.34mm
.3405 / 8.65mm
.339 / 8.61
.3085 / 7.835mm
.220 / 5.58mm

1.558 (39.59mm)
1.871 (47.52mm)
2.60 (66.04mm)

*Cartridge Illustrations courtesy of Wolfe Publishing Company*

# .30-40 KRAG

Captain Ole H.J. Krag of Norway invented the rifle that later served American troops between 1892 and 1903. Modified for adoption by the U.S. Army, it was officially known as the Krag-Jorgensen; but to the soldiers who carried it, it was simply "the Krag." The cartridge designed for this rifle replaced the .45-70, a big-bore black powder round dating to the days of the trap-door Springfield. The .30-40 Krag, like its Mauser counterparts in Europe, was fueled by smokeless powder. In those days it was considered a small-bore, high-velocity cartridge. Its 220-grain bullet left the muzzle at around 2200 fps, greatly extending effective battle range. The Krag repeater, though not strong by modern standards, was beautifully machined, quite accurate, and one of the smoothest actions ever designed. It won out in military tests over a hammerless lever-action rifle designed by Arthur Savage.

The country's first smokeless U.S. military round--the .30-40 Krag-- was soon replaced by the more potent .30-06. No commercial sporting rifles are currently chambered for the Krag.

| Bullet Weight (grains) | Maximum Loads (grains, type of powder) | Top Velocity (fps) and Data Source |
|---|---|---|
| 130 | 47.0 H4895 | 2900 (Hodgdon) |
| 150 | 44.8 IMR 4320 | 2500 (Sierra) |
| 150 | 50.0 H380 | 2810 (Hodgdon) |
| 165 | 49.0 IMR 4831 | 2430 (Nosler) |
| 180 | 46.0 4350 | 2360 (Accurate) |
| 180 | 48.0 H414 | 2520 (Hodgdon) |
| 200 | 47.0 H4350 | 2340 (Hodgdon) |
| 220 | 48.0 AA 3100 | 2170 (Accurate) |

**Case Capacity** (grains water)
**53**

**Case Trim Length**
**2.30"**

**Standard Operating Pressure**
**40,000 CUP**

**Standard Rifling Twist**
**1-in-10" (also 1-in-12)**

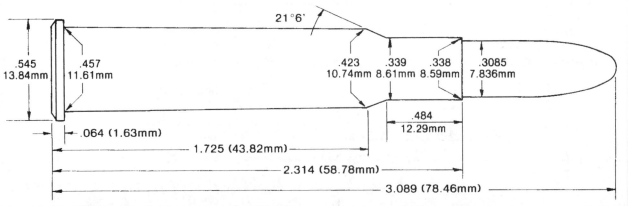

*Cartridge Illustrations courtesy of Wolfe Publishing Company*

When the .30-06 replaced the .30-40 soon after the turn of the century, Krag rifles flooded the surplus market at $1.50 apiece. Winchester chambered the .30-40 cartridge in its High Wall and Model 95 lever rifles. The .30-40 also turned up in Remington-Lee bolt guns and Remington Rolling Blocks. By the start of World War II it had been dropped by all major gunmakers. Between 1973 and 1977 Ruger resurrected the round in its Number 3 Single-Shot, where it was loaded to much higher pressures than in

the Krag. It has been necked down by wildcatters (the .25 Krag was at one time a popular number) but remains most effective on big game in its original form. Still factory loaded with 180-grain bullets, the 30-40 Krag is slightly more potent than the .300 Savage but cannot match the .308 Winchester. Moreover, its case length (2.314 inches) precludes its use in short-action rifles; and the large (.545) rimmed head makes this cartridge an unlikely alternative in any rifle built around the .30-06.

# .307 WINCHESTER

For decades after its debut near the turn of the century Winchester's Model 94 carbine in .30-30 was known simply as a deer rifle. Even loyal 94 fans became aware of the .30-30's limitations once cartridges like the .300 Savage, .257 Roberts and .270 Winchester came along. Alas, in pre-war whitetail coverts, hunters who wanted to carry Winchester carbines had to accept .30-30 performance. Winchester changed all that in 1982 when it

announced a new 94 chambered for two new and potent rounds: the .307 and .356 Winchester. The right side of the receiver on the Model 94XTR Angle Eject was cut away, allowing spent cases to fly off at an angle and enabling a scope to be mounted on top. The .307 and .356 cartridges had the same case head diameter as the .30-30 but much thicker walls. With the beefed-up action they could now be loaded to 52,000 CUP, compared to 38,000 for the .30-30.

| Bullet Weight (grains) | Maximum Loads (grains, type of powder) | Top Velocity (fps) And Data Source | Case Capacity (grains water) |
|---|---|---|---|
| 110 | 49.0 BL-C(2) | 2950 (Hodgdon) | **52** |
| 130 | 43.0 H4895 | 2760 (Hodgdon) | |
| 150 | 39.0 2015 BR | 2640 (Accurate) | **Case Trim Length** |
| 170 | 42.5 AA 2520 | 2570 (Accurate) | **2.01"** |
| 170 | 41.5 2495 BR | 2520 (Accurate) | |
| 180 | 46.0 Win 760 | 2460 (Hodgdon) | **Standard Operating Pressure** |
| 180 | 45.0 H380 | 2440 (Hodgdon) | **52,000 CUP** |
| 200 | 45.0 H414 | 2370 (Hodgdon) | **Standard Rifling Twist** |
| | | | **1-in-10** |

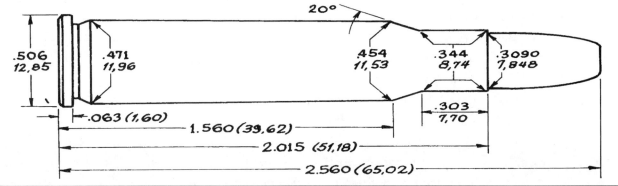

*Cartridge Illustrations courtesy of Wolfe Publishing Company*

Had the .307 arrived decades earlier it would have been a whitetail hunter's dream come true. But by the 1980s even woodland deer hunters had been seduced by scope-sighted bolt guns. Neither the .307 nor its companion .356 has flourished. Marlin announced that it would chamber the .307 in a Model 336 lever rifle but never followed through. The .307 remains a fine choice for deer and black bear at woods ranges, where its blunt bullets are no handicap. Though it has been hailed in print as a semi-rimmed .308, hunters will have to be content with slightly less velocity than from the .308. The .307's case walls are heavier, for one thing, reducing powder capacity by about 6 percent. Also .307 bullets must be seated a tad deeper to keep overall length within the limits imposed by the Model 94 action.

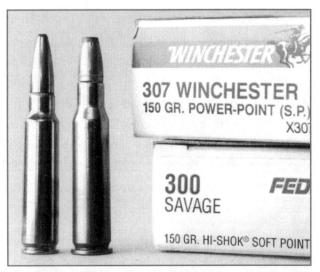

The .307 Winchester--a rimmed version of the .308 for use in beefy Winchester 94 rifles--does not quite match the .308 ballistically. Its slight edge over the .300 Savage is offset by the blunt bullets required in Model 94 magazines. The Savage 99 permits use of pointed bullets for the .300.

# .308 WINCHESTER

The .308 Winchester, as with many modern cartridges, began life as a military project. During the late 1940s, efforts to develop a compact machine gun cartridge that would also serve in a new infantry rifle resulted in the T65 experimental round. It was half an inch shorter than the .30-06, which had weathered two world wars in the 1903 Springfield, 1917 Enfield, M1 Garand and Browning Automatic Rifle. The compact T65 approached the performance of its predecessor because it was loaded to higher pressures with newly developed ball powders. Before the U.S. convinced other NATO nations to adopt the T65, Winchester obtained permission to introduce it as a sporting round; and by 1952 it had become the .308 Winchester. It was offered by Winchester in its Featherweight Model 70 and the new Models 88 and 100 lever-action and self-loading rifles.

Other gunmakers were quick to snap up the cartridge, and it has since been chambered in more domestic centerfire rifles than any other cartridge (even more than the .30-06 because it fits short actions). The .308 Winchester drives bullets 200 fps faster than the .300 Savage and comes within 100 fps of matching the .30-06. Federal and Hornady load hyper-speed .308 ammunition equaling the ballistic performance of standard '06 rounds. Some .308s have been built with 1-in-12 twists, but they will not stabilize heavy bullets as well as the standard 1-in-10. Capped with 150-grain bullets, the .308 is a top-rung deer round. It is also suitable for elk when loaded with stout 165- and 180-grain bullets. Heavier bullets work best in larger cases, mainly because to clear short magazines they must be seated deep in the .308's limited powder space. This accurate cartridge is a favorite of metallic silhouette shooters as well as National Match competitors, many of whom choose the 168-grain Sierra Match bullet.

The .308 cartridge with 150-grain SilverTip boat-tail bullet is a great choice for all-around deer hunting.

| Bullet Weight (grains) | Maximum Loads (grains, type of powder) | Top Velocity (fps) And Data Source | Case Capacity (grains water) 54 |
|---|---|---|---|
| 110 | 45.0 2015 BR | 3190 (Accurate) | |
| 125 | 53.6 H380 | 3100 (Sierra) | Case Trim Length 2.01" |
| 150 | 46.0 RL-15 | 2960 (Nosler) | |
| 150 | 47.0 IMR 4320 | 2960 (Barnes) | Standard Operating Pressure 52,000 CUP |
| 165 | 46.0 BL-C(2) | 2700 (Hodgdon) | |
| 168 | 44.0 AA 2520 | 2680 (Nosler) | |
| 180 | 45.0 IMR 4064 | 2650 (A-Square) | |
| 180 | 43.0 IMR 4895 | 2620 (Nosler) | Standard Rifling Twist |
| 200 | 47.0 AA 2700 | 2430 (Barnes) | 1-in-10" (also 1-in-12) |
| 200 | 47.0 IMR 4350 | 2400 (Speer) | |

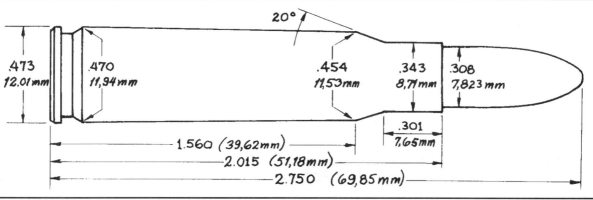

*Cartridge Illustrations courtesy of Wolfe Publishing Company*

# .30-06 SPRINGFIELD

ailed for decades as the most versatile big game cartridge ever, the .30-06 started out as a military round for the 1903 Springfield (the original chambering for this rifle, however, was the .30-03). The first sporting rifle chambered for the .30-06 may have been the Model 1895 Winchester lever rifle, which was also offered in .30-03. In 1906 the U.S. ordnance people shortened the case .07 inch and replaced the 220-grain round-nose bullet with a 150-grain spitzer, boosting velocity from 2300 to 2700 fps. A new "M1" load with a 172-grain boattail bullet at 2640 fps was replaced in 1940 with the "M2" 150-grain flatbase bullet at 2700 fps. This ammunition served U.S. troops in the M1 Garand rifle well during World War II; but in the 1950s the .30-06 was superseded by the 7.62 NATO (or .308 cartridge in the M14).

For hunting the world's deer and antelope, the .30-06 has few equals; and out to 300 yards it will easily drop elk and moose. A huge selection of commercial hunting loads (including, for a time, a 55-grain sabot offering by Remington) makes handloading unnecessary, although the .30-06 is

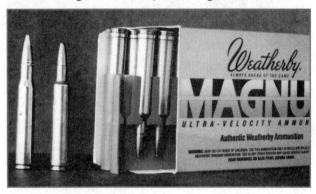

The .240 Weatherby Magnum (right) has about the same case capacity as the .30-06 (left). Unlike most Weatherby big game cartridges, the belted .240 is not based on the .300 H&H case.

| Bullet Weight (grains) | Maximum Loads (grains, type of powder) | Top Velocity (fps) and Data Source | Case Capacity (grains water) |
|---|---|---|---|
| 110 | 60.2 Win 748 | 3400 (Hornady | **68** |
| 125 | 53.0 H4895 | 3220 (Barnes) | |
| 130 | 53.0 2495 BR | 3170 (Accurate) | **Case Trim Length** |
| 150 | 59.7 N550 | 3010 (VihtaVuori) | **2.48"** |
| 150 | 54.0 RL-15 | 2980 (A-Square) | |
| 165 | 56.0 H414 | 2900 (Hodgdon) | **Standard** |
| 180 | 58.5 AA 3100 | 2780 (Nosler) | **Operating Pressure** |
| 180 | 58.0 IMR 4350 | 2750 (A-Square) | **60,000 PSI** |
| 190 | 54.6 RL-19 | 2700 (Sierra) | |
| 200 | 57.0 IMR 4831 | 2660 (Speer) | **Standard Rifling Twist** |
| 200 | 51.0 AA 2700 | 2630 (Barnes) | **1-in-10"** |
| 220 | 57.6 Norma MRP | 2500 (Hornady) | |

.473 / 12.01mm    .470 / 11.94 mm    17°28'    .436 / 11.07mm    .3397 / 8.63 mm    .3085 / 7.835mm    .388 / 9.85mm

1.948 (49.48mm)

2.494 (63.34 mm)

3.340 (84.83mm)

*Cartridge Illustrations courtesy of Wolfe Publishing Company*

easy to handload and gives long case life. Federal and Hornady both market super-velocity '06 ammunition that challenges the .300 H&H ballistically. The .30-06 shines with a wide range of bullet weights, though most hunters favor spitzers of 150 to 200 grains. On the target range Sierra's 168- and 190-grain Match bullets have contributed to this round's popularity and helped establish its reputation for fine accuracy. Among powders, IMR 4895, 4320 and 4064 excel for the light- to mid-weight bullets, while H414 and IMR and Hodgdon 4350 remain popular for 180- to 200-grain bullets. While autoloaders, pumps and Browning's lever-action have featured the .30-06 in the past, its potential is best tapped in bolt rifles and dropping-block single-shots.

# .300 HOLLAND & HOLLAND MAGNUM

The .300 H&H Magnum, known early on as the "Super .30," became a factory load in 1925, after Western Cartridge Company had adopted it from the British .375 H&H around 1912. The first commercial U.S. rifle to chamber this belted round--the Model 70 Winchester--didn't come along until 1937. Remington chambered its 721 for the .300 H&H in 1948, along with Browning's Belgian-built High Power rifles. By the end of World War II, Roy Weatherby had developed his more powerful .300 by blowing out the Holland case. Finally, in 1963, Winchester unveiled a short .30 magnum offering .300 H&H performance in .30-06-length actions. In the

| Bullet Weight (grains) | Maximum Loads (grains, type of powder) | Top Velocity (fps) and Data Source |
|---|---|---|
| 125 | 67.7 IMR 4320 | 3500 (Sierra) |
| 150 | 72.0 RL-19 | 3320 (Barnes) |
| 150 | 76.3 H450 | 3300 (Hornady) |
| 165 | 74.0 N205 | 3210 (Speer) |
| 165 | 75.0 IMR 4350 | 3190 (A-Square) |
| 168 | 70.5 AA 3100 | 3170 (Nosler) |
| 180 | 68.0 IMR 4350 | 3090 (Speer) |
| 180 | 78.0 RL-19 | 3080 (A-Square) |
| 190 | 68.4 Win 760 | 3000 (Hornady) |
| 200 | 72.0 H4831 | 2930 (Hodgdon) |
| 220 | 73.0 AA 3100 | 2790 (Accurate) |
| 250 | 62.0 IMR 4831 | 2600 (Barnes) |

**Case Capacity**
(grains water)
**89**

**Case Trim Length**
**2.84"**

**Standard Operating Pressure**
**54,000 CUP**

**Standard Rifling Twist**
**1-in-10"**

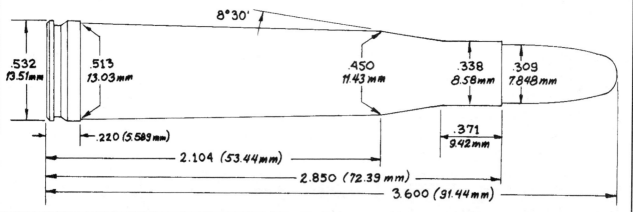

*Cartridge Illustrations courtesy of Wolfe Publishing Company*

interim, the .308 Norma (see following entry) and wildcat .30-338 made the field even more competitive.

During the past 30 years the .300 Winchester has smashed its rivals in the marketplace and all but made the .300 H&H obsolete, outperforming the old British round by about 150 fps. Some claim the .300 Holland's long, sloping shoulder can result in premature case stretching and brass flow forward; actually, such problems occur only when the .300

H&H is overloaded. A wide range of bullet weights and types makes the .300 H&H an excellent choice for all-around big game hunting. Currently it is available in factory form only with a 180-grain bullet at 2880 fps. But even conservative handloaders can better that performance, especially in the 26-inch barrels found on early Model 70 and 721 rifles. Short throats on some .300 H&H rifles mandate deep bullet seating, but there's plenty of neck for that.

# .308 NORMA MAGNUM

Norma Projektilfabrik of Sweden began courting American shooters with the .308 Norma Magnum in 1961. Shortly after the .338 Winchester made its debut in 1958, shooters necked it down to form the .30-338. But Norma's

was the first commercial short-belted .300. (The .308 Norma case is slightly longer than that of a .30-338 so cannot be interchanged with it.) Rather than import ammunition for which no U.S. factory rifles were chambered, Norma initially

| Bullet Weight (grains) | Maximum Loads (grains, type of powder) | Top Velocity (fps) and Data Source |
|---|---|---|
| 10 | 74.0 H414 | 3690 (Hodgdon) |
| 130 | 76.0 N204 | 3410 (Speer) |
| 150 | 71.5 4350 | 3200 (Accurate) |
| 165 | 76.0 RL-19 | 3160 (A-Square) |
| 165 | 74.8 H450 | 3100 (Hornady) |
| 180 | 70.7 N160 | 3050 (VihtaVuori) |
| 180 | 76.0 H4831 | 3050 (A-Square) |
| 190 | 72.3 AA 3100 | 3010 (Accurate) |
| 200 | 69.0 IMR 4350 | 2920 (Speer) |
| 220 | 68.4 IMR 4350 | 2800 (Hornady) |

**Case Capacity** (grains water)
**89**

**Case Trim Length**
**2.55"**

**Standard Operating Pressure**
**65,000 PSI**

**Standard Rifling Twist**
**1-in-10" (also 1-in-12")**

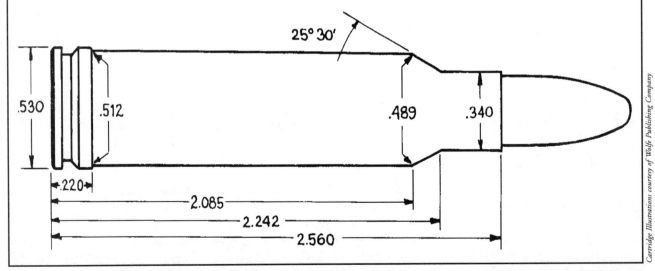

25° 30'

.530  .512  .489  .340

.220

2.085

2.242

2.560

*Cartridge Illustrations courtesy of Wolfe Publishing Company*

offered brass only and loaned chambering reamers to gunsmiths for converting surplus Springfields and Enfields. Merely by opening the bolt face and chamber of his .30-06 a rifleman could have a .308 Norma magnum, an option that proved popular.

A year and a half after introducing its cases, Norma began sending loaded ammunition to the U.S. The "re" on the headstamp signified use of Boxer primers, which made the hulls reloadable (many European cartridges have been Berdan-primed, with double flash-holes). A number of European rifles have been chambered for the .308 Norma, but among well-known American gun firms only Browning has offered the cartridge (for its Belgium-built High Power rifle). When Winchester announced its .300 magnum in 1963,

the .308 Norma lost its foothold in the U.S. The Winchester case, which is longer than the Norma's, has greater powder capacity but a .278 neck. To handloaders who think a neck should be at least one caliber long (in this case .308), the Winchester design appears flawed. The longer case is of marginal value in .30-06-length actions because bullets must be seated so far into the powder chamber. In any event, the .300 Winchester has stolen the stage. From either round, 180-grain bullets deliver nearly a ton of energy to 400 yards on a path as taut as a .270's, and with notably less recoil than .338. Like their predecessor, the .300 H&H Magnum, the .300 Winchester and .308 Norma handle heavier bullets than the .30-06 and thus excel as far-reaching elk cartridges.

## .300 WINCHESTER MAGNUM

Among the first 30-caliber cartridges to challenge the 3000-fps mark with 180-grain bullets were the .300 Holland & Holland and .30 Newton. Roy Weatherby crossed that line in the early 1940s with a blown-out .300 H&H. During the 1950s Mashburn, Ackley and other wildcatters shortened the Holland case, reduced its taper and steepened the shoulder. The result was a hull that matched the original belted .300 in capacity but fit in a .30-06-length action. Norma announced its "short" .308 Magnum in 1961, three years after Winchester introduced the .264 and .338 Magnums, leaving shooters to wonder why Winchester hadn't given them a .30. New Haven followed in 1963 with the .300 Winchester Magnum. Instead of duplicating the .30-338 wildcat as expected, Winchester fashioned a longer case (2.620 vs. 2.500) with a short, .278 neck. Usable capacity was

about the same with the heavy bullets because they must be seated deep to clear magazine boxes.

The .300 Winchester Magnum has since become one of the best-selling belted sporting cartridges in the U.S., ranking consistently among the four most popular elk rounds in hunter surveys. It has an edge of about 100 fps over the parent .300 H&H and even more than the Federal and Hornady super-performance loads. The .300 Winchester Mag. delivers as much energy to 400 yards as a .30-06 brings to 300, and it shoots as flat with a 180-grain bullet as a 7mm Remington Magnum does with a 150. Loaded with 165-grain Sierra hollowpoints, it can kill deer like lightning, while stout 180- and 200-grain bullets-- including the Swift, Nosler Partition, Winchester Fail Safe and Trophy Bonded Bear Claw--equip it for moose, elk and big bears.

A Ruger bolt rifle in .300 Winchester Magnum brought down this tough, elk-size nilgai bull on the King Ranch in Texas.

| Bullet Weight (grains) | Maximum Loads (grains, type of powder) | Top Velocity (fps) And Data Source |
|---|---|---|
| 125 | 79.0 IMR 4350 | 3440 (Speer) |
| 150 | 76.0 IMR 4831 | 3300 (Hornady) |
| 150 | 81.0 RL-22 | 3250 (Nosler) |
| 165 | 80.0 N205 | 3150 (A-Square) |
| 168 | 78.0 RL-22 | 3150 (Speer) |
| 180 | 78.6 Norma MRP | 3080 (Barnes) |
| 180 | 72.0 IMR 4831 | 3050 (Hodgdon) |
| 190 | 77.3 IMR 7828 | 2990 (A-Square) |
| 200 | 70.5 H4831 | 2950 (VihtaVuori) |
| 200 | 73.0 H450 | 2800 (Hornady) |
| 220 | 77.0 H1000 | 2690 (Barnes) |

**Case Capacity**
(grains water)
**90**

**Case Trim Length**
**2.61"**

**Standard Operating Pressure**
**64,000 PSI**

**Standard Rifling Twist**
**1-in-10"**

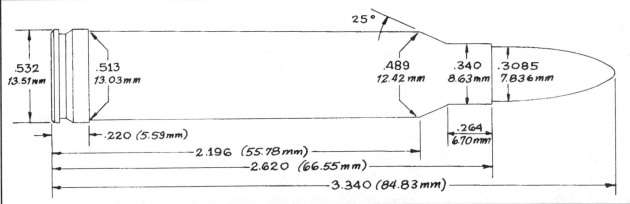

*Cartridge Illustrations courtesy of Wolfe Publishing Company*

# .300 WEATHERBY MAGNUM

The development of magnum cartridges predates World War I, when British firms matched big cases with slender bullets to boost velocities and flatten trajectories. In the U.S., Charles Newton had developed powerful high-velocity cartridges that were handicapped by a dearth of slow powders and appropriate bullets. After World War II, Bruce Hodgdon began marketing surplus military powder--called H4831--which proved to be the right fuel for a line of magnum cartridges developed by an insurance salesman in California named Roy Weatherby. His first belted round, the high-performance .257, .270 and 7mm Magnums, were based on .300 H&H cases shortened and blown out at the shoulder. The .300 Weatherby, which soon joined them, featured a case that was not shortened but merely given minimum body taper and a radiused shoulder. With 150-grain

Both the .300 (left) and .340 Weatherby Magnums require magnum-length actions. The .300 dates to the mid-1940s, the .340 to the early 1960s.

| BULLET WEIGHT (grains, powder) | MAXIMUM LOADS | TOP VELOCITY (fps) AND DATA SOURCE | |
|---|---|---|---|
| 150 | 84.0 IMR 4831 | 3500 (Sierra) | |
| 165 | 85.1 H450 | 3390 (Nosler) | |
| 168 | 82.5 RL-22 | 3330 (A-Square) | |
| 180 | 81.0 H4831 | 3270 (Speer) | |
| 180 | 82.0 N205 | 3260 (Nosler) | |
| 180 | 81.0 IMR 7828 | 3100 (Hornady) | |
| 190 | 86.0 H1000 | 3060 (Barnes) | |
| 200 | 80.0 H4831 | 3000 (Sierra) | |
| 200 | 83.1 N165 | 2910 (Nosler) | |
| 220 | 76.9 Norma MRP | 2900 (Barnes) | |
| 250 | 92.0 AA 8700 | 2880 (Hodgdon) | |

**CASE CAPACITY**
(grains water)
**100**

**CASE TRIM LENGTH**
**2.82"**

**STANDARD OPERATING PRESSURE**
**65,000 PSI**

**STANDARD RIFLING TWIST**
**1-IN-10"**

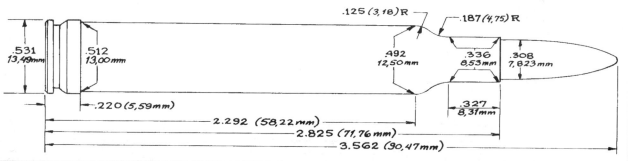

*Cartridge Illustrations courtesy of Wolfe Publishing Company*

.531 13,49mm  .512 13,00mm  .220 (5,59mm)  .125 (3,18)R  .187 (4,75) R  .492 12,50mm  .336 8,53mm  .308 7,823mm  .327 8,31mm  2.292 (58,22mm)  2.825 (71,76mm)  3.562 (90,47mm)

bullets at 3545 fps and 180s at 3245, it remained the most potent commercial .300 until 1997, when Weatherby eclipsed it with the .30-378.

The .300 Weatherby quickly established a solid record in Africa, where wealthy industrialists and movie stars on safari gave it exposure. Once Remington and Winchester began chambering the round, it drew increasing favor among America's blue-collar hunters, especially in elk camps. The .300 Weatherby is also a fine target round for

1000-yard shooting. Although Norma was for many years the only source of ammunition, Remington now loads it as well (though to lower velocity levels). The free-bored throats of Weatherby rifles enable bullets to get a running start into the rifling and flatten the pressure curve a bit. The most popular home for the .300 Weatherby Magnum remains the Mark V rifle designed by Roy Weatherby and Fred Jenny in 1958.

# .30-378 WEATHERBY MAGNUM

Though the .30-378 Weatherby Magnum was released as a commercial cartridge in 1997, its development actually began back in 1953, soon after Roy Weatherby had announced the monstrous .378. Redstone Arsenal had asked Weatherby for a military round that would send bullets whistling downrange at 5000 fps. With a special bullet designed by Ray Speer, the new

cartridge was said to deliver a velocity of 6000 fps. Most shooters agreed that a bullet designed for that speed would probably not serve well. Still, many custom .30-.378s appeared, commonly with 40-degree Ackley shoulders instead of radiused Weatherby junctures. Interest in those early days came from 1000-yard target shooters, many of whom used the wildcat 6.5/.300 Weatherby

| Bullet Weight (grains) | Maximum Loads (grains, type of powder) | Top Velocity (fps) And Data Source |
|---|---|---|
| 180 | 102.0 H870 | 3300 (B.Hutton, WC, p.421) |
| 180 | 118.0 AA 8700 | 3280 (Accurate) |
| 190 | 109.0 5010 | 3300 (B.Hutton, WC, p. 421) |
| 200 | 117.0 AA 8700 | 3210 (Accurate) |
| 220 | 115.0 AA 8700 | 3050 (Accurate) |
| 250 | 111.0 AA 8700 | 2950 (Accurate) |

**Case Capacity** (grains water): **136**

**Case Trim Length: 2.90"**

**Standard Operating Pressure Not Available**

**Standard Rifling Twist 1-in-12"**

.603 15.24mm  .582 14.73mm  .582 14.73mm  .560 14.22mm  .399 9.92mm  .375 9.40mm

.250 6.35mm

2.340 – 59.43 mm

2.537 – 64.27mm

2.908 – 73.68 m

3.562 – 90.42mm

*Cartridge Illustrations courtesy of Wolfe Publishing Company*

Wright-Hoyer (developed on the .300 Weatherby case by shooter Paul Wright and gunsmith Al Hoyer), which could drive a 140-grain bullet 3400 fps. The .30-378 offered more wind-bucking ability with a 200-grain bullet at 3300 fps, but its heavy recoil impaired shooter performance. Few target shooters have since

chosen the .30-378; in fact, many have moved down in velocity with the 6.5/.284. The .30-378 used in Weatherby's Mark V is a hunting round, and hunters aren't as concerned with recoil. Overall, the .30-378 is slightly more potent and, for many hunters, less practical than a .300 Weatherby.

# .303 BRITISH

One of many "small-bore" cartridges designed for military use shortly before the turn of the century, the .303 British was initially loaded with 70 grains of black powder and a 215-grain .311 bullet. In 1892, four years after its introduction, smokeless cordite became the propellant. During World War I the .303 got a new bullet--a 174-grain spitzer at 2400 fps. It stayed in the British arsenal until being supplanted

in the early 1950s by the 7.62x51mm NATO (.308) in the early 1950s.

The original Lee-Metford Mark I rifle gave way to a series of Short Magazine Lee-Enfields that were widely hailed as fine battle rifles. True, they featured two-piece stocks, single locking lugs and creepy triggers; but their detachable box magazines gave soldiers 10 shots between loadings, and the cock-on-closing bolt was fast to manipulate. While

| BULLET WEIGHT (grains) | MAXIMUM LOADS (grains, type of powder) | TOP VELOCITY (fps) AND DATA SOURCE |
|---|---|---|
| 125 | 46.0 2015 BR | 3080 (Accurate) |
| 125 | 47.5 AA 2520 | 3020 (Accurate) |
| 130 | 50.0 BL-C(2) | 2890 (Hodgdon) |
| 150 | 42.0 IMR 303 | 2700 (Hornady) |
| 150 | 46.0 2495 BR | 2730 (Accurate) |
| 180 | 40.0 AA 2230 | 2470 (Accurate) |
| 180 | 50.0 H450 | 2450 (Speer) |
| 215 | 43.0 H414 | 2110 (Hodgdon) |

**CASE CAPACITY** (grains water)
**51**

**CASE TRIM LENGTH**
**2.21"**

**STANDARD OPERATING PRESSURE**
**45,000 CUP**

**STANDARD RIFLING TWIST**
**1-IN-8"**

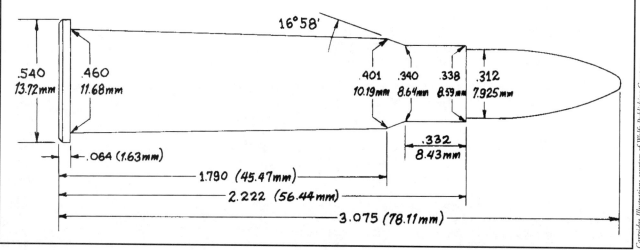

*Cartridge Illustrations courtesy of Wolfe Publishing Company*

lacking the fine machining and solid feel of the Springfield and the Mauser, these rifles proved durable and dependable under combat conditions. Many SMLEs will feed empty cases from magazine into chamber, whether the shooter nudges the bolt forward slowly or slams it shut. Without a bullet to guide the case, few other bolt-action rifles will feed so dependably. The only caveat when loading a .303 is to keep the rimmed cases stacked, with the top rims forward of those below.

The only commercial U.S. sporting rifle chambered for the .303 British was the Winchester 1895 lever-action, which was also bored for its ballistic twin, the .30-40 Krag. Commercial loadings were originally limited to a 180-grain bullet at 2460 fps, but Hornady now markets a "Light Magnum" .303 British with a 150-grain Spire Point. The cartridge has been widely used in Africa on game as big as elephants. The long, blunt 215-grain full-jacket military bullet gave adequate penetration for early ivory hunters, though the .303 is by no means a stopping cartridge. It is found throughout Canada, where it may well have taken more moose than any other round.

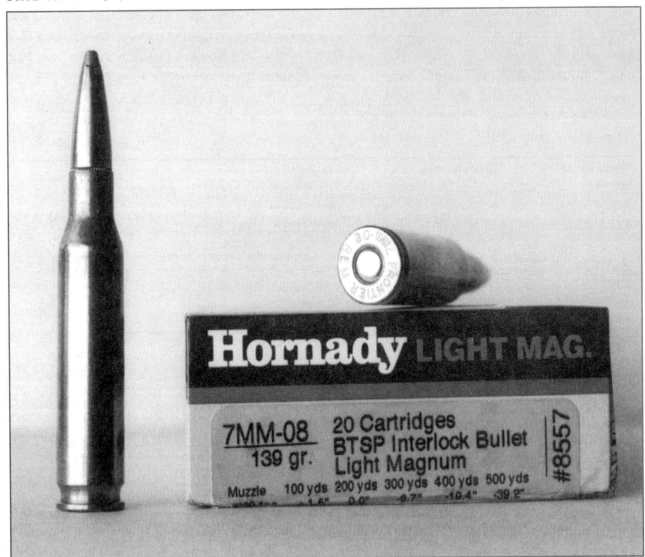

A two-step loading procedure and special powders enable Hornady to increase velocity by 100 to 150 fps in its "Light Magnum" ammunition.

# 8X57 MAUSER

he first smokeless powder cartridge adopted for military use by any major power was the 8x57 (or 7.92x57) Mauser. It was not designed by Peter Paul Mauser, however, but by a group of German ordnance engineers. The initial version appeared in 1888 in what came to be known as the "Commission rifle," featuring a 227-grain .318 round-nose bullet. The German army adopted in 1905 a high-velocity "JS" 8x57 with a 150-grain .323 spitzer. Meanwhile, Mauser had improved on several actions, including the Model 98, whose strength proved more than adequate for the high operating pressure of the new round. Eventually the .323 ammunition became standard for all commercial 8x57 cartridges.

The 8x57 Mauser, which served German troops through both world wars, is a fine cartridge for deer-size game and, with heavy bullets, for animals the size of elk at modest ranges. It has seen considerable use in Africa but received almost no attention in the U.S., partly because the more powerful .30-06 is its chief competitor and partly because the selection of 8mm bullets has always been limitedin America. Many Model 98 Mausers liberated during World War II were rechambered in the U.S. to the wildcat 8mm/.30-06. Head size of the two cartridges is the same, but the .30-06 has a larger powder chamber and thus offers more ballistic potential. American factory ammunition for the 8x57 has traditionally been underloaded as a safeguard for people with Model 1888 rifles. The 8x57 can be handloaded to exceed the performance of the .308 Winchester.

| Bullet Weight (grains) | Maximum Loads (grains, type of powder) | Top Velocity (fps) and Data Source |
|---|---|---|
| 125 | 55.1 N135 | 3200 (VihtaVuori) |
| 125 | 53.0 IMR 4064 | 3130 (Speer) |
| 150 | 51.0 IMR 4064 | 2920 (Speer) |
| 150 | 51.6 Win 748 | 2900 (Hornady) |
| 170 | 53.7 N150 | 2800 (VihtaVuori) |
| 170 | 52.5 IMR 4320 | 2800 (Hornady) |
| 180 | 50.0 RL-15 | 2800 (Barnes) |
| 200 | 52.0 IMR 4350 | 2700 (Nosler) |
| 220 | 43.0 H4895 | 2410 (Barnes) |
| 225 | 53.0 N205 | 2380 (Speer) |
| 250 | 43.0 AA 2520 | 2290 (Barnes) |

**CASE CAPACITY** (grains water)
**63**

**CASE TRIM LENGTH**
**2.23"**

**STANDARD OPERATING PRESSURE**
**35,000 PSI**

**STANDARD RIFLING TWIST**
**1-IN-9.5"**

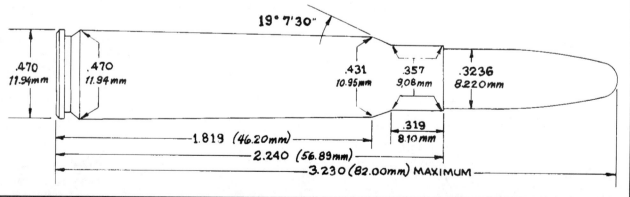

19° 7'30"

.470 / 11.94mm
.470 / 11.94mm
.431 / 10.95mm
.357 / 9.08mm
.3236 / 8.220mm
.319 / 8.10mm
1.819 (46.20mm)
2.240 (56.89mm)
3.230 (82.00mm) MAXIMUM

# 8mm REMINGTON MAGNUM

After its introduction in 1978, the 8mm Remington Magnum lived a short and marginally productive life. Having been dropped from the list of Model 700 chamberings in 1985, it was reinstated as an option in custom shop rifles two years later. It never became popular, however, and is no longer offered by Remington. Perhaps the company planned to duplicate the success it enjoyed with its 7mm Magnum by marketing an even more potent big game cartridge with a metric designation. But the 8mm had endemic flaws. Its full-length (.300 H&H-length) case was ill-suited to .30-06 actions, and it lacked the 7mm's versatility and wide spectrum of bullet choices. It also targeted a market niche that would always be smaller than the 7mm's, simply because hunters seeking a deer or elk rifle far outnumber those who lust after an elk/moose/big bear rifle. The 8mm also competed directly with Winchester's

.338 Magnum, which had a 20-year head start, offered a wider range of bullet choices, and fit nicely in the "short magnum" actions that had become popular. The need for a high-octane 8mm may be past.

With the proliferation of belted .30s and .33s, Germany's 8x68 (a beltless round that almost matches the 8mm Magnum ballistically) has not suffered the tepid reception accorded the 8mm Remington. Since its debut in the 1940s it has become well established among the European sporting community. But it is still not a hot seller. And stateside Wildcats like the 8x62 Durham and the .323 Hollis have never generated as much shooter interest as the .25-06 and .35 Whelen (which Remington eventually legitimized to its profit). Most hunters who have used the 8mm Remington Magnum praise it; but its assets are matched by other big game cartridges with bigger followings and more bullet choices.

| BULLET WEIGHT (grains) | MAXIMUM LOADS (grains, type of powder) | TOP VELOCITY (fps) AND DATA SOURCE |
|---|---|---|
| 125 | 76.4 IMR 4064 | 3600 (Hornady) |
| 150 | 91.4 RL-22 | 3450 (Sierra) |
| 175 | 87.5 AA 3100 | 3260 (Accurate) |
| 175 | 80.3 IMR 4350 | 3200 (Sierra) |
| 180 | 76.0 H414 | 3110 (Barnes) |
| 200 | 78.0 IMR 4831 | 3050 (Nosler) |
| 200 | 74.0 IMR 4350 | 3030 (Nosler) |
| 220 | 82.1 H450 | 2900 (Hornady) |
| 220 | 83.2 IMR 7828 | 2900 (Sierra) |
| 220 | 77.0 RL-19 | 2870 (A-Square) |
| 250 | 78.0 H4831 | 2790 (Barnes) |
| 250 | 80.0 H1000 | 740 (Barnes) |

**CASE CAPACITY**
(grains water)
**99**

**CASE TRIM LENGTH**
**2.84"**

**STANDARD OPERATING PRESSURE**
**65,000 PSI**

**STANDARD RIFLING TWIST**
**1-IN-10"**

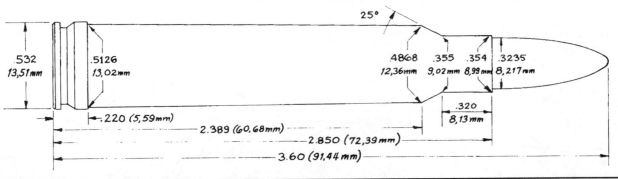

Cartridge Illustrations courtesy of Wolfe Publishing Company

# .338-06 A-SQUARE

The .338-06, long popular among hand-loaders but unavailable in factory form, is a necked-up .30-06. It is now loaded by A-Square, but its traceable roots go back to 1945, when Charles O'Neil, Elmer Keith and Don Hopkins necked the .30-06 to accept .333 bullets designed for the British .333 Jeffery. They called the new cartridge the .333 OKH, and it became reasonably popular among rifle-men who wanted something exotic; i.e., a round that was easy to make from available brass and could prove itself useful on the kind of game most hunters hunted. The .333 OKH fit that description, but its appeal was somewhat limited by the small selection of .333 bullets. When Winchester brought out its .338 Magnum in 1958, the logical response was to neck up the OKH to take .338 bullets.

Since then wildcatters have grown increasingly fond of this versatile round. It handles bullet weights of 200 to 225 grains with ease and velocities approaching those of the .338 Magnum. Even a 250-grain bullet can be started at nearly 2600 fps from a .338-06. With a sectional density of .313, a deep-driving 250 is ideal for hunting elk in timber. A 200-grain bullet can be kicked out the muzzle as fast as a 180-grain bullet from a .30-06. Recent strong demand for the .338 Winchester magnum has resulted in a broad array of .338 bullets from established bullet-makers as well as small custom shops. They make the .338-06 one of the most useful big game cartridges, wildcat or commercial, ever chambered.

| Bullet Weight (grains) | Maximum Loads (grains, type of powder) | Top Velocity (fps) and Data Source |
|---|---|---|
| 200 | 58.0 IMR 4895 | 2820 |
| 200 | 63.0 H414 | 2800 (Hodgdon) |
| 200 | 50.0 2495BR | 2720 (Accurate) |
| 210 | 60.0 AA 4350 | 2700 (Accurate) |
| 225 | 56.0 IMR 4320 | 2690 |
| 250 | 60.0 IMR 4350 | 2540 |
| 250 | 63.0 N205 | 2480 |
| 275 | 59.0 N205 | 2330 (W.Corson, WC, p.447) |

**Case Capacity** (grains water)
**70**

**Case Trim Length**
**2.48"**

**Standard Operating Pressure**
**60,000 PSI**

**Standard Rifling Twist**
**1-in-10" (also 1-in-12")**

Cartridge Illustrations courtesy of Wolfe Publishing Company

# .338 WINCHESTER MAGNUM

The .300 Holland & Holland Magnum had been around for 30 years before Winchester decided that what hunters needed was a shortened version for use in .30-06-length actions. In 1956, the company announced the .458 Winchester Magnum, the first of what would become a line of short magnum cartridges. Winchester's choice of the elephant-bashing .458 astonished many shooters, especially those who had expected a more versatile round. They were soon to get two--the .338 and .264 Winchester Magnums--both announced in 1958 and chambered in the Model 70 "Alaskan" and "Westerner" rifles respectively. The .264 took a dive in 1962 with the advent of the 7mm Remington Magnum, while the .338 has gained steadily in popularity. An efficient big game cartridge that can deliver two tons of muzzle energy, it still has half that punch at 400 yards, at which point its 225-grain bullet has dropped only two inches lower than a 175-grain bullet from a 7mm Remington Magnum.

The proliferation of stout .338 bullets--from 200 to 275 grains--has made this cartridge a top pick among brown bear guides as well as elk hunters. Winchester's choice of a .338 over a .308 bore in 1958 seemed odd at the time. After the rimmed .33 Winchester became obsolete in 1936, the future seemed bleak for 33-caliber cartridges. But Elmer Keith's promotion of the .333 OKH helped establish a spot for the .338 Winchester and fueled interest in the .338-06. In 1962 Weatherby announced competition for the .338 Magnum in the form of its potent .340. But .340 cartridges cost a lot, require a magnum-length action and have so far been chambered only in Weatherby rifles. Winchester's .338 is almost as widely chambered as Remington's 7mm Magnum, and Browning even offers it in its BAR self-loader. While recoil is stiff, and though it lacks the versatility of the belted .30s, the .338 excels for elk, moose and dangerous thin-skinned game.

| BULLET WEIGHT (grains) | MAXIMUM LOADS (grains, type of powder) | TOP VELOCITY (fps) AND DATA SOURCE |
|---|---|---|
| 175 | 73.0 H414 | 3140 (Hodgdon) |
| 200 | 77.0 H4350 | 3050 (Hodgdon) |
| 200 | 67.0 IMR 4320 | 2990 (Barnes) |
| 210 | 76.0 RL-19 | 3020 (Nosler) |
| 225 | 74.0 H4831 | 2900 (Hornady) |
| 225 | 81.0 RL-22 | 2880 (A-Square) |
| 250 | 71.5 H4831 | 2780 (Nosler) |
| 250 | 74.0 Norma MRP | 2700 (Hornady) |
| 275 | 72.0 RL-22 | 2620 (Hodgdon) |
| 300 | 70.0 IMR 7828 | 2480 (Barnes) |
| 300 | 67.0 H450 | 2450 (Hodgdon) |

**CASE CAPACITY**
(grains water)
**86**

**CASE TRIM LENGTH**
**2.49"**

**STANDARD OPERATING PRESSURE**
**64,000 PSI**

**STANDARD RIFLING TWIST**
**1-IN-10"**

25°

.532 / 13.51mm
.513 / 13.03mm
.491 / 12.47mm
.370 / 9.39mm
.369 / 9.37mm
.339 / 8.610mm
.330 / 8.38mm
.220 (5.58mm)
2.04 (51.81mm)
2.500 (63.50mm)
3.340 (84.83mm)

*Cartridge Illustrations courtesy of Wolfe Publishing Company*

# .340 WEATHERBY MAGNUM

Depending on who is offering an opinion, the .340 Weatherby Magnum either barely edges Winchester's .338 Magnum or leaves it in the dust. The .340 came along in 1962--four years after the .338--perhaps with the idea of stealing some of the 340's market share. Whereas the .338 derives from the short magnum case pioneered by Winchester with its .458 in 1956, the .340 is a full-length magnum (a .300 Weatherby necked up). Shooters have chronographed Norma's factory-loaded 250-grain bullets at an even 3000 fps. Chart velocity for the 250-grain .338 Winchester is 2660 fps. The .340 Weatherby delivers as much muzzle energy as a .375 H&H and shoots flatter. It carries more energy to 500 yards than a .338 factory load dumps at 300.

Among factory-loaded rounds the .340 has had no peers until very recently. The .338 A-Square, based on a shortened .378 Weatherby case, and A-Square's rimless .338 Excalibur, give 33-caliber bullets higher velocity. The .330 Dakota on the .404 Jeffery is similar; so are the .33s marketed by Arnold and Lazzeroni. The wildcat .338/.378 remains the most powerful .33. While the .340 Magnum makes good use of the many different .338 bullets, it is at its best with 225- and 250-grain spitzers built to handle the violent impact that results from high-speed strikes on heavy muscle or bone.

This cartridge can produce fine accuracy; but shooters sensitive to recoil find the .340 Weatherby more than a handful. Long barrels not only help wring more velocity from this cartridge, they reduce muzzle jump and blast as well. Unlike its parent .300 and the short Weatherby's chambered originally in Mauser and other actions, the .340 first appeared in the Mark V. It remains the only commercial U.S. rifle offered for this powerful .338.

| BULLET WEIGHT (grains) | MAXIMUM LOADS (grains, type of powder) | TOP VELOCITY (fps) AND DATA SOURCE |
|---|---|---|
| 200 | 92.6 Norma MRP | 3200 (Hornady) |
| 210 | 83.5 IMR 4350 | 3210 (Nosler) |
| 225 | 86.4 H450 | 3000 (Hornady) |
| 225 | 88.0 RL-22 | 2990 (A-Square) |
| 225 | 90.0 AA 3100 | 2960 (Accurate) |
| 250 | 88.5 AA 3100 | 2880 (Accurate) |
| 250 | 84.0 H4831 | 2820 (A-Square) |
| 275 | 86.0 AA 3100 | 2710 (Accurate) |
| 275 | 78.0 IMR 4831 | 2670 (Speer) |
| 275 | 75.0 H450 | 2660 (Speer) |
| 300 | 80.0 RL-22 | 2590 (Barnes) |
| 300 | 77.5 IMR 7828 | 2560 (Barnes) |

**CASE CAPACITY**
(grains water)
**102**

**CASE TRIM LENGTH**
**2.81"**

**STANDARD OPERATING PRESSURE**
**66,000 PSI**

**STANDARD RIFLING TWIST**
**1-IN-12"**

Cartridge Illustrations courtesy of Wolfe Publishing Company

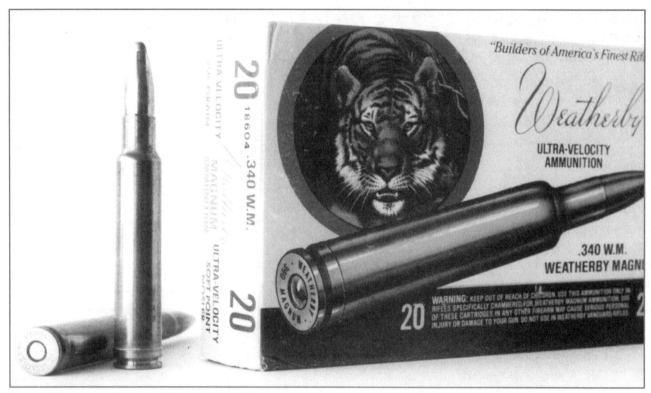

The .340 Weatherby, which arrived four years after Winchester's .338, has a bigger case and can launch 250-grain bullets at 3000 fps.

# .348 WINCHESTER

When the .348 Winchester appeared in the new Model 71 lever rifle in 1936, it replaced the .33 Winchester, which had been chambered in the earlier Model 1886. The .348 case is an original, with a wide, generously-tapered body and a rim fully .610 in diameter. Designed expressly for the tube-fed 71, it was loaded from the start with round-nose bullets. Commercial ammunition initially featured 150-, 200-, and 250-grain .348 (not .358) bullets, but only the 200-grain loading survived into the 1980s. Given the short-range shooting mandated by blunt bullets and the top ejection that precluded scope use on the Model 71, many experienced hunters felt the 250-grain bullet, with its high sectional density and 3000 foot-pounds of muzzle energy, was a better choice for the .348. But that is all academic now. Heavy by most standards, the Model 71 boasted fine workmanship and, uncannily, it seemed perfectly balanced in both

rifle and carbine forms. The action flew through its cycle with the snickety-smooth sound of a worn but well-adjusted printing press.

Predictably, a rifle like that couldn't last. It was dropped in 1958, shortly after the introduction of Winchester's hammerless, front-locking Model 88 lever gun, which was cheaper to build and featured side ejection to accommodate top-mounted scopes. It could also handle the higher breech pressures of the new rimless .243 and .308 Winchester rounds. The 71 and its beefy .348 Winchester cartridge signaled the end of a tradition. To date, this Depression-era rifle represents the last of the traditional tube-fed lever-action models designed for big game hunters in the U.S. The cartridge has been superseded by smallbore rounds with long, minimum-taper cases and pointed bullets. Still, the .348 with a 250-grain bullet remains one of the best options ever for close-cover hunting of elk, moose and big bears.

| Bullet Weight (grains) | Maximum Loads (grains, type of powder) | Top Velocity (fps) and Data Source | Case Capacity (grains water) 78 |
|---|---|---|---|
| 200 | 62.0 4350 | 2530 (Accurate) | |
| 200 | 59.1 Win 760 | 2500 (Hornady) | Case Trim Length 2.24" |
| 200 | 54.1 IMR 4320 | 2500 (Hornady) | |
| 220 | 65.0 H4831 | 2470 (Hodgdon) | Standard Operating Pressure 40,000 CUP |
| 220 | 51.0 H4895 | 2470 (Barnes) | |
| 220 | 49.0 IMR 4064 | 2390 (Barnes) | Standard Rifling Twist 1-in-12" |
| 220 | 64.0 AA 3100 | 2380 (Accurate) | |
| 250 | 50.0 H380 | 2310 (Barnes) | |
| 250 | 55.0 IMR 4350 | 2300 (Barnes) | |

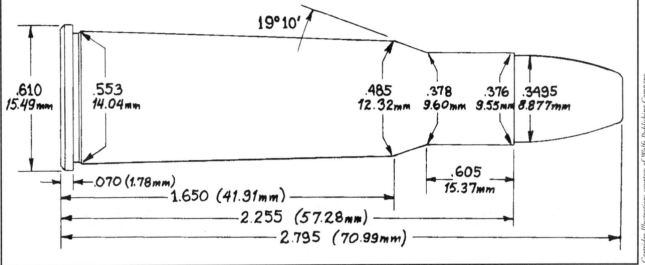

*Cartridge Illustrations courtesy of Wolfe Publishing Company*

# .35 REMINGTON

In 1906 Remington announced a series of new cartridges for its new Model 8 self-loading rifle. The .25, .30 and .32 Remingtons have faded from the shooting scene, but the .35 survives. In addition to the Model 8, it has been chambered in Remington's 81, 14, 141, 720, 600 and 760 rifles --and even in the modern Model Seven. Winchester chambered it in the Model 70 for a short time; Savage had it in a slide-action; and Mossberg offered it in the lever-action 479. While it remains a popular handgun cartridge for big game, the .35 Remington has spent most of its life in Marlin's Model 336 rifles and carbines. Oddly, this .35 has a .457-diameter head, a trifle larger than that of its three obsolete companions but .16 smaller than that of a .30-06. Factory loaded with 150- and 200-grain bullets at 2300 and 2080 fps, the .35 Remington, with its greater sectional density, is still best served by the heavier bullet. At woods ranges high velocity counts for little. On the charts the .35 Remington barely edges the 30-30 for energy; but this old rimless round has significantly greater effect, thanks to its greater bullet weight and diameter. Indeed, in one pre-war elk hunter survey, it turned up among the six most commonly-carried rounds. The .35 Remington may seem an anachronism to some hunters steeped in the post-war tradition of high velocity and long shooting, but it remains an efficient, deadly woods cartridge.

| BULLET WEIGHT (grains) | MAXIMUM LOADS (grains, type of powder) | TOP VELOCITY (fps) AND DATA SOURCE | CASE CAPACITY (grains water) 46 |
|---|---|---|---|
| 180 | 42.0 IMR 4895 | 2350 (Speer) | |
| 180 | 42.5 IMR 4064 | 2310 (Speer) | CASE TRIM LENGTH 1.91" |
| 200 | 39.0 H335 | 2060 (Hodgdon) | |
| 200 | 40.0 BL-C(2) | 2050 (Sierra) | STANDARD OPERATING PRESSURE |
| 200 | 35.0 2015 BR | 2050 (Accurate) | 33,500 PSI |
| 200 | 39.0 Win 748 | 2030 (Hodgdon) | STANDARD RIFLING TWIST |
| 220 | 35.5 IMR 3031 | 2040 (Speer) | 1-IN-16" |
| 220 | 37.0 IMR 4895 | 2010 (Speer) | |

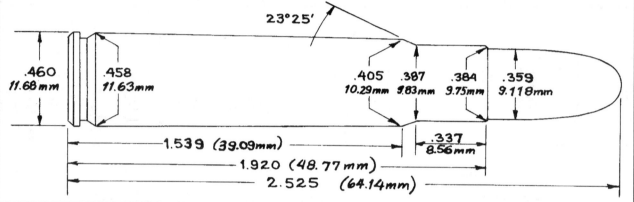

*Cartridge Illustrations courtesy of Wolfe Publishing Company*

# .356 WINCHESTER

In 1980 Winchester began developing a new version of its beloved Model 94 lever rifle. New metallurgy would make it stouter, and thicker rear receiver walls would add yet more strength. By taking a slice from the top right-hand side of the receiver and altering the ejection mechanism, spent cases would spin away from the gun at an angle, allowing a scope to be mounted on top. By 1982 Winchester was ready to introduce this rifle as its 94XTR Angle Eject. It came chambered for two new cartridges, the .307 and .356 Winchester, both with thicker case walls and more powder capacity than the .30-30. In print, the .307 was compared to the .308, but it actually duplicated the .300 Savage ballistically. The .356, essentially a rimmed .358, came within 80 fps or so of matching its predecessor. It was handicapped, however, by the heavy case walls, which kept powder capacity below that of the .358. The 94 short action created an additional drain on powder space.

The .356 is far more powerful than the .35 Remington, which had been the only .35 available in a traditional lever rifle since Winchester ditched its Model 71 .348 back in 1958. In fact, the .356 in a more compact package and a slimmer, lighter rifle challenges the .348 ballistically. Like the .348, it calls for blunt bullets because of the 94's tubular magazine (not a fatal flaw at woods ranges, however). As with other .35s designed for short shooting from carbines, the heavy 250-grain bullet makes more sense than the slightly faster 200-grain. Higher sectional density and more weight mean deeper penetration. There's no measurable difference in trajectory out to 200 yards, which is farther than most hunters expect to shoot with a Model 94. The heavier bullet also packs more energy at all ranges. Armed with a 250-grain bullet, the .356 Winchester is surely adequate for elk.

| Bullet Weight (grains) | Maximum Loads (grains, type of powder) | Top Velocity (fps) and Data Source |
|---|---|---|
| 180 | 45.0 2015 BR | 2700 (Accurate) |
| 180 | 43.0 H4198 | 2600 (Hodgdon) |
| 200 | 40.0 H4198 | 2380 (Hodgdon) |
| 200 | 44.0 H322 | 2340 (Hodgdon) |
| 220 | 39.0 2015 BR | 2320 (Accurate) |
| 220 | 45.0 2495 BR | 2290 (Accurate) |
| 250 | 48.0 BL-C(2) | 2160 (Hodgdon) |
| 250 | 48.0 Win 748 | 2160 (Hodgdon) |
| 250 | 46.0 H335 | 2150 (Hodgdon) |

**Case Capacity** (grains water)
**55**

**Case Trim Length**
**2.01"**

**Standard Operating Pressure**
**52,000 CUP**

**Standard Rifling Twist**
**1-in-12"**

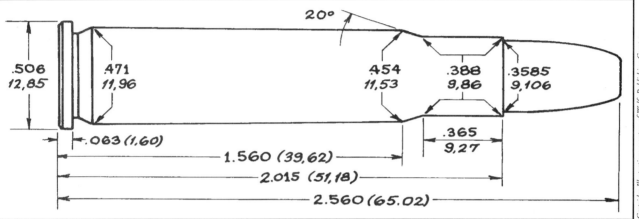

*Cartridge Illustrations courtesy of Wolfe Publishing Company*

Winchester's Angle Eject Big Bore Model 94 is chambered for the .307 Winchester (shown) as well as the .356 Winchester and .444 Marlin.

# .358 WINCHESTER

When Winchester introduced the .308 cartridge in 1952, shooters knew the case would reappear in other forms. Three years later Winchester confirmed expectations by announcing two new short rounds--the .243 and .358. Both cartridges derived from the .308 case, beginning life in the Model 70 Featherweight bolt rifle and a new hammerless lever gun: the Model 88. The .243 soon drew a crowd while the .358 languished. It didn't have the look of a powerful cartridge, plus its big, heavy bullet reminded hunters of old, stodgy deer cartridges like the .35 Remington. They wanted high velocity and greater reach. Like its parent .308, though, the .358 packed a lot of punch in a small case. The 200-grain factory load was listed at 2530 fps and the 250-grain at 2250 (a hand-loader could get 3000 foot-pounds of energy at the muzzle).

The .358 was a huge step up from the .35 Remington, matching what the much larger .348 Winchester could deliver. Only a few riflemen bought .358s, but Winchester and Savage continued to chamber it. Several European makers built rifles for it as well, calling it the 8.8x51mm. Ruger chambered the .358 in a short run of Model 77 bolt rifles, and Browning listed it, appropriately, for the BLR. All but obsolete now, the .358 Winchester remains a useful round. With 250-grain bullets it's still a natural for elk hunting in the "pole patches," and the new 225-grain spitzers should extend its reach considerably. All in all, it's the most potent .350 cartridge ever factory-loaded for lever-action rifles.

| Bullet Weight (grains) | Maximum Loads (grains, type of powder) | Top Velocity (fps) And Data Source | Case Capacity (grains water) |
|---|---|---|---|
| 180 | 43.0 H4198 | 2710 (Hodgdon) | **58** |
| 180 | 49.5 H335 | 2700 (Nosler) | |
| 200 | 46.0 IMR 3031 | 2640 (Barnes) | **Case Trim Length** |
| 200 | 46.0 H322 | 2630 (Barnes) | **2.01"** |
| 200 | 49.5 AA 2520 | 2570 (Accurate) | |
| 225 | 48.0 RL-12 | 2480 (Barnes) | **Standard Operating Pressure** |
| 225 | 48.0 AA 2520 | 2460 (Accurate) | **52,000 CUP** |
| 250 | 45.0 IMR 4895 | 2380 (Barnes) | |
| 250 | 48.0 BL-C(2) | 2370 (Hodgdon) | **Standard Rifling Twist** |
| 250 | 43.0 H335 | 2340 (Barnes) | **1-in-12"** |

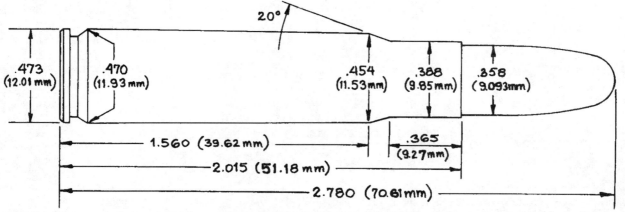

Cartridge Illustrations courtesy of Wolfe Publishing Company

**B**efore Remington began loading it commercially in 1969, the .35 Whelen had already enjoyed a long life as a wildcat cartridge. A .30-06 case necked up, the round was named after Colonel Townsend Whelen, who had allegedly developed it with gunsmith James V. Howe (of Griffin & Howe) around 1922. The modest popularity of the cartridge before 1969 was due largely to a dearth of appropriate 35-caliber bullets. Those designed for the .35 Remington would not hold up under impact at .35 Whelen velocities. Besides, they were relatively light in weight and had blunt noses to accommodate end-to-end stacking in lever-action carbines. The recent availability of 225- and 250-grain spitzers has made the .35 Whelen an extremely effective big game round. Low sectional densities limit the utility of bullets lighter than 200 grains. A 225-grain .35 spitzer from the Whelen case flies about as flat as a 180-grain .30-06 bullet over normal hunting ranges. It also carries significantly more energy. The .35 Whelen is an excellent elk and moose cartridge, with less recoil than comparable belted magnums. It's a perfect match for the first commercial rifle to chamber it: the Remington 700 Classic with 22-inch barrel. "Improving" the .35 Whelen with a 40-degree Ackley shoulder isn't worth the trouble, because there's little shoulder to "improve."

| Bullet Weight (grains) | Maximum Loads (grains, type of powder) | Top Velocity (fps) and Data Source |
|---|---|---|
| 180 | 59.5 2495 BR | 2940 (Accurate) |
| 180 | 56.5 2015 BR | 2960 (Accurate) |
| 200 | 62.0 RL-15 | 2820 (Barnes) |
| 200 | 63.0 BL-C(2) | 2810 (Hodgdon) |
| 225 | 54.0 AA 2460 | 2600 (Accurate) |
| 225 | 55.0 AA 2520 | 2600 (Accurate) |
| 250 | 55.0 IMR 4064 | 2570 (Barnes) |
| 250 | 51.3 IMR 3031 | 2500 (Hornady) |
| 250 | 59.0 BL-C(2) | 2500 (Hodgdon) |
| 300 | 49.0 AA 2015 BR | 2360 (Barnes) |
| 300 | 49.0 H322 | 2330 (Barnes) |

**Case Capacity (grains water)**
**73**

**Case Trim Length**
**2.48"**

**Standard Operating Pressure**
**52,000 CUP**

**Standard Rifling Twist**
**1-in-16"**

*Cartridge Illustrations courtesy of Wolfe Publishing Company*

# .350 REMINGTON MAGNUM

A year before the .350 Remington Magnum appeared in catalogs, it was being scrutinized in the shooting press--and for good reasons. First, it was a 35-caliber cartridge, bringing to mind the failure of the .358 Winchester during its nine-year tenure. Secondly, the case was about half an inch shorter than other magnums trimmed to fit in .30-06 actions. The .350 Remington had the head and body diameter of a magnum but was designed to fit in a .308-length magazine. (A 6.5 Magnum on the .350 case appeared a year after the .350's debut.) The rifle that chambered the .350--a carbine with an 18-inch barrel and a crooked bolt handle--was also new. The Model 600 Magnum rifle became the 660 Magnum in 1968, when Remington adopted a 20-inch barrel to reduce muzzle jump and boost velocity.

The .350 did not sell well, probably for the same reasons the .358 Winchester had struggled. It didn't look like the leggy magnums that were defining progress in modern hunting cartridges. Shooters wanted sleek bullets that raced downrange, not old carbines with stubby cartridges. Remington dropped the 600-series carbines in 1971 and, three years later, the .350 as a Model 700 chambering. The cartridge subsequently appeared in Ruger's 77 and for one year in Remington's 700 Classic. It has since made a comeback in Remington's Model Seven. The .350 Remington Magnum is an excellent cartridge, duplicating .35 Whelen velocities with bullets of up to 250 grains. It is not only a woods cartridge but, like the Whelen, adequate for game as big as elk to 250 yards. Best bullets: 220- or 225-grain spitzers at 2650 fps, 250-grain spitzers at 2450.

| Bullet Weight (grains) | Maximum Loads (grains, type of powder) | Top Velocity (fps) and Data Source |
|---|---|---|
| 180 | 62.0 H335 | 3010 (Hodgdon) |
| 200 | 59.0 AA 2230 | 2850 (Accurate) |
| 200 | 59.5 AA 2460 | 2840 (Accurate) |
| 220 | 56.0 IMR 3031 | 2650 (Speer) |
| 225 | 60.0 IMR 4320 | 2640 (Nosler) |
| 225 | 48.0 RL-7 | 2640 (Barnes) |
| 225 | 52.5 2015 BR | 2620 (Accurate) |
| 250 | 56.0 IMR 4064 | 2530 (Barnes) |
| 250 | 56.5 AA 2520 | 2520 (Accurate) |
| 250 | 54.0 H4895 | 2500 (Hodgdon) |

**CASE CAPACITY**
(grains water)
**74**

**CASE TRIM LENGTH**
**2.16"**

**STANDARD OPERATING PRESSURE**
**53,000 CUP**

**STANDARD RIFLING TWIST**
**1-in-16"**

.532 / 13,51mm · .513 / 13,03 · 25° · .495 / 12,57 · .388 / 9,86 · .359 / 9,119mm · .220 / 1,38 · .355 / 9,02 · 1.700 (43,18mm) · 2.170 (55,12mm) · 2.800 (71,12mm) MAXIMUM

*Cartridge Illustrations courtesy of Wolfe Publishing Company*

# .358 NORMA MAGNUM

The .358 Norma came to the U.S. in 1959, a year before the .308 Norma arrived. These cartridges share the same case, but at 2.520 .358 brass is .03 shorter. This big, belted .35 can, in .30-06-length actions, almost match .375 H&H performance down-range. Its 250-grain bullet exits at about 2800 fps with more than 4300 foot-pounds of energy. When Norma began marketing cases to the U.S., its .358 had not yet been chambered in any American rifle; but the Swedish company did provide reamers and chamber specifications. In 1960 Schultz & Larsen rifles (from Denmark) offered it, as did Husqvarna Mausers. But the .338 Winchester, which had gone public just prior to the .358 Norma's appearance, was already chambered in Winchester Model 70 rifles. The .358 Norma Magnum offered slightly more performance, but not enough to

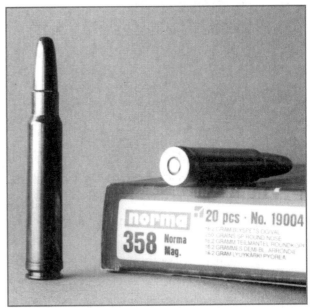

The .358 Norma Magnum is the most powerful factory-loaded .35.

| BULLET WEIGHT (grains) | MAXIMUM LOADS (grains, type of powder) | TOP VELOCITY (fps) AND DATA SOURCE |
|---|---|---|
| 180 | 69.0 IMR 4895 | 3130 (Speer) |
| 200 | 70.0 H380 | 3100 (Hodgdon) |
| 200 | 77.0 H414 | 3030 (Hodgdon) |
| 200 | 79.0 AA 2700 | 3000 (Accurate) |
| 220 | 78.0 IMR 4350 | 2850 (Speer) |
| 225 | 69.0 RL-12 | 2840 (A-Square) |
| 225 | 67.5 IMR 4895 | 2830 (Nosler) |
| 250 | 66.0 RL-15 | 2800 (Barnes) |
| 250 | 68.3 IMR 4320 | 2800 (Hornady) |
| 250 | 80.2 N160 | 2790 (VihtaVuori) |
| 275 | 82.0 RL-19 | 2750 (A-Square) |
| 300 | 72.0 H4350 | 2630 (Barnes) |

**CASE CAPACITY**
(grains water)
**88**

**CASE TRIM LENGTH**
**2.15"**

**STANDARD OPERATING PRESSURE**
**63,900 PSI**

**STANDARD RIFLING TWIST**
**1-IN-12"**

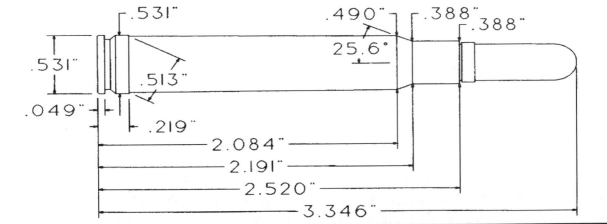

*Cartridge Illustrations courtesy of Wolfe Publishing Company*

make any practical difference on game. It lost ground quickly to the .338, and eventually .358 Norma factory loads were discontinued.

In 1989 Federal reintroduced the 250-grain Norma loading. The proliferation of stout .35 bullets for the .35 Whelen, adopted by Remington in 1988, was also good news to owners of .358 Norma rifles. One of the early drawbacks of handloading .358 ammunition was the dearth of .35 bullets that would hold together under high-velocity impact. Most were designed for the .35 Remington and .358 Winchester. Now bullets like the Nosler Partition and the Swift A-Frame ensure penetration in dense muscle and bone. The .358 Norma Magnum can deliver the bullet weight and energy to drop dangerous thin-skinned game up close. Like Winchester's .338 Magnum, it is also a fine choice for shooting elk, moose and other heavy animals at long range.

For years, only Norma loaded Weatherby cartridges commercially. Not so now, as this Remington box indicates.

## 9.3X64 BRENNEKE

Wilhelm Brenneke and Charles Newton both designed high-velocity rimless cartridges that are now considered marvels. But in the early days of the 20th century these cartridges lacked enough bullets and propellants to tap their potential. The 9.3x64 came along just before World War I. At .496, its case head was larger than the .30-06's and smaller than that of the .375 H&H. The 9.3x64 case measures 2.520, only .020 longer than that of a short magnum like the .338 Winchester. Theoretically, this round will work in a standard action. Loaded length of the 9.3x64 cartridge (as assembled by A-Square, the only U.S. firm to offer ammunition) is 3.370, not 3.340 as in the .30-06 or .338. The 9.3x64 is best served--especially with heavy bullets--in a magnum-length action. Loaded with dual-core .366 Topedo bullets designed by Brenneke, it has proved itself the ballistic equal of the .375 H&H. But having come to the States after the .375 was established, it could

not compete despite the advantages of its short rimless case. It remains a fine pick for dangerous thin-skinned game, particularly with the A-Square 286-grain Lion Load. Speer's 270-grain .366 spitzer propelled at 2700 fps gives this cartridge great reach.

The original TIG and TUG bullets, incidentally, are still loaded by RWS. The TIG (Torpedo Ideal Geschoss) features a hard rear core that slams into the softer front core on impact, ensuring quick and violent upset. The TUG hard tail incorporates a cone-shaped socket that holds the front section together for deeper penetration. Like the .30 Newton, the 9.3x64 was probably considered over-powered for all-around big game hunting in its day. Expectations among hunters are different now, and rifles with optical sights can be aimed accurately at much greater yardage. Perhaps its odd bullet and case dimensions are what keep the 9.3x64 from competing successfully with the .338 Winchester, .340 Weatherby and .375 H&H.

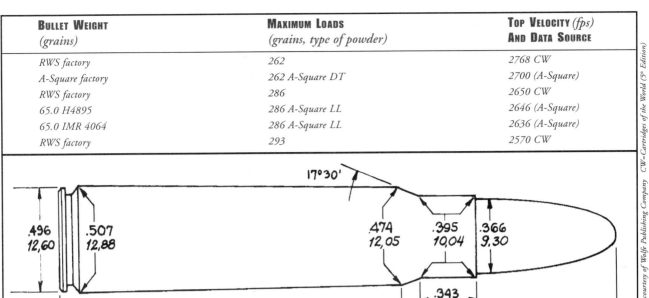

| BULLET WEIGHT (grains) | MAXIMUM LOADS (grains, type of powder) | TOP VELOCITY (fps) AND DATA SOURCE |
|---|---|---|
| RWS factory | 262 | 2768 CW |
| A-Square factory | 262 A-Square DT | 2700 (A-Square) |
| RWS factory | 286 | 2650 CW |
| 65.0 H4895 | 286 A-Square LL | 2646 (A-Square) |
| 65.0 IMR 4064 | 286 A-Square LL | 2636 (A-Square) |
| RWS factory | 293 | 2570 CW |

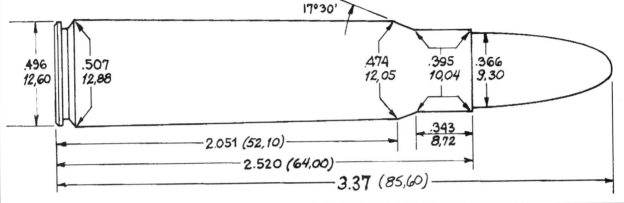

*Cartridge Illustrations courtesy of Wolfe Publishing Company  CW=Cartridges of the World (5ᵗʰ Edition)*

# .375 WINCHESTER

The .375 Winchester was introduced in 1978 with the Model 94 Big Bore, whose thick rear receiver walls distinguished it from previous renditions of the 94. The Ruger Number 3 single-shot and Marlin 336 lever rifles were also briefly chambered in this cartridge, which looks like the old .38-55 Winchester developed in 1884 mainly for use as a target cartridge. The .38-55 became popular with deer hunters when Marlin offered it in the Model 93 and Winchester in its 94 lever-action rifles. In addition, Savage chambered the round in the 99, and Colt in its slide-action Lightning. The Remington-Lee bolt action appeared in .38-55, as did single-shots by Stevens, Remington and Winchester. Winchester discontinued the .38-55 in its Model 94 just before World War II but kept on manufacturing cartridges until 1970.

With a 255-grain bullet at 1320 fps, the black-powder load had limited utility for hunting, but

The .375 Winchester with 200-grain Power-Point is essentially a modern .38-55, ideal for close-cover deer hunting.

the high-velocity load added 200 fps and proved quite effective on deer and black bears in thickets. In actions like the Ruger Number 3, the .38-55 can be handloaded to 1800 fps.

While the .375 Winchester has been described as a shortened .38-55, its case head diameter is .01 smaller and its walls are substantially thicker than those of a .38-55. Both use .375 bullets, but the .375 Winchester drives them faster: a 200-grain bullet at 2200 fps and a 250-grain at 1900, according to factory claims. These figures make it the hunting equivalent of a .35 Remington. It has proven much less popular and is no longer chambered commercially in rifles. Thompson/Center offers it in the Contender single-shot pistol, where it performs well as a big game cartridge. **Note:** Because its operating pressure exceeds 50,000 CUP, the .375 Winchester is *not* to be used in rifles bored for the .38-55, which was traditionally loaded to around 30,000.

The potent and versatile .375 H&H was introduced in 1912. It quickly became a standard for professional hunters in both Africa and Alaska.

| Bullet Weight (grains) | Maximum Loads (grains, type of powder) | Top Velocity (fps) And Data Source |
|---|---|---|
| 200 | 40.0 AA 2015 | 2250 (Accurate) |
| 200 | 33.0 H4198 | 2140 (Hodgdon) |
| 220 | 42.0 Win 748 | 1970 (Barnes) |
| 220 | 38.0 H322 | 1960 (Hodgdon) |
| 235 | 35.0 RL-7 | 1940 (Speer) |
| 235 | 32.0 N200 | 1930 (Speer) |
| 255 | 36.0 IMR 3031 | 1900 (Barnes) |
| 255 | 40.0 H4895 | 1850 (Hodgdon) |

**CASE CAPACITY** (grains water)
**49**

**CASE TRIM LENGTH**
**2.01"**

**STANDARD OPERATING PRESSURE**
**52,000 CUP**

**STANDARD RIFLING TWIST**
**1-IN-12"**

.506
12,85

.420
10,67

.400
10,16

.376
9,550

.063 (1,60)

.220
5,59

1.800 (45,72)

2.020 (51,31)

2.560 (65,02)

*Cartridge Illustrations courtesy of Wolfe Publishing Company*

# .375 H&H MAGNUM

he English gunmaking firm of Holland and Holland introduced the belted .375 H&H Magnum in 1912. It came to the U.S. in 1925, when Western Cartridge Company began loading it along with a necked down version, the .300 H&H. About that time, the New York firm of Griffin & Howe began chambering it, as had Holland and Holland, in magnum Mauser rifles. In 1937 Winchester included the .375 H&H on its charter list of Model 70 chamberings, while Remington offered it in its 725 "Kodiak." Even Weatherby took an occasional order for the .375. Now it is standard fare in nearly every bolt rifle built to accept full-length magnum cartridges. It has often been written up as the best all-around cartridge for African game.

Early factory loads featured a frangible 235-grain bullet at 2800 fps, a 270-grain at 2650 and a 300-grain at 2500. With 300-grain solids the .375 H&H has killed the biggest game (.375 is the common legal minimum bore diameter for dangerous animals). Still, many professional hunters prefer more potent rounds in their "stopping" rifles. One buffalo hunter reported that the .375 worked fine for big bovines when they were not riled up, but "they pay no attention to it when they come to give you a pounding." Early bullets for the .375 sometimes failed to stay on course in heavy game or remain in one piece. A fine selection of .375 softpoints and solids now makes this veteran round more reliable than it has been in the past. While it remains unnecessarily powerful for North American game, save for brown and polar bears, the .375 H&H remains popular with Alaskan hunting guides.

| BULLET WEIGHT (grains) | MAXIMUM LOADS (grains, type of powder) | TOP VELOCITY (fps) AND DATA SOURCE |
|---|---|---|
| 235 | 77.0 IMR 4064 | 2970 (Speer) |
| 235 | 74.0 2495 BR | 2910 (Accurate) |
| 250 | 78.0 H380 | 2840 (Barnes) |
| 250 | 80.0 AA 2700 | 2810 (Accurate) |
| 270 | 84.1 N160 | 2790 (VihtaVuori) |
| 270 | 73.3 N140 | 2760 (VihtaVuori) |
| 270 | 84.0 4350 | 2710 (Accurate) |
| 300 | 71.5 H4895 | 2660 (Nosler) |
| 300 | 78.7 IMR 4350 | 2600 (Sierra) |
| 300 | 72.0 RL-15 | 2600 (A-Square) |
| 350 | 75.0 H414 | 2420 (Barnes) |
| 350 | 66.5 RL-15 | 2410 (Barnes) |

**CASE CAPACITY** (grains water)
**96**

**CASE TRIM LENGTH**
**2.84"**

**STANDARD OPERATING PRESSURE**
**62,000 PSI**

**STANDARD RIFLING TWIST**
**1-IN-12"**

12°45'

.532 13,51mm
513 13,03mm
.448 11,38mm
.404 10,26mm
.375 9,525mm
.350 8,89mm
.220 (5,59mm)
2.402 (63,41mm)
2.850 (72,39mm)
3.515 (89,28mm)

*Cartridge Illustrations courtesy of Wolfe Publishing Company*

The 375 H&H Magnum is well served by stout, deep-penetrating bullets like the Swift A-Frame.

Zeroing a Model 70 in .257 Roberts, the author uses a sandbag to support the forend, *not* the barrel. Note placement of the left hand around the rear sandbag. Squeezing the bag lets you move the reticle vertically onto target.

# .375 WEATHERBY MAGNUM

During World War II Roy Weatherby designed a line of belted cartridges based on the .375 H&H Magnum case. The .257, .270 and 7mm were shortened versions fashioned to fit .30-06-length actions. The .300 had a full-length case that measured 2.820 and could be used only in mechanisms that would accept the original .375 or .300 Holland rounds. A logical mate to the .300 Weatherby Magnum, which appeared late in the series, was a .375. Roy Weatherby's use of minimum body taper and a radiused, blown-out shoulder provided this cartridge with more powder capacity and higher velocities than the .375 H&H. The .300 and .375 appeared about the same time, with both being loaded commercially by Weatherby. The .375 launched its 270-grain bullets at an advertised 2940 fps, while 300-grain bullets aproached at 2800. Predictably, most hunters chose the versatile .300 over the specialized, hard-kicking .375. Weatherby dropped the big-bore cartridge, only to introduce in 1953 another .375 on a larger case.

The .378 Weatherby Magnum spits 270-grain bullets out at over 3100 fps and 300-grain bullets at 2925. At nearly three tons, the muzzle energy of the .378 tops the .375 Weatherby by roughly 800 foot-pounds, or slightly more than the energy difference between the .375 Weatherby and .375 H&H. When A-Square began manufacturing its own cartridge cases, among the first rounds it resurrected was the .375 Weatherby Magnum. The trajectory of its 270-grain pointed bullets is as flat as that of a 150-grain spitzer from a .280 Remington. Because it combines great reach with 5000 foot-pounds of buffalo-stopping power, it remains a top pick for a one-rifle safari.

| Bullet Weight (grains) | Maximum Loads (grains, type of powder) | Top Velocity (fps) And Data Source |
|---|---|---|
| 235 | 81.0 H4895 | 2920 (Hodgdon) |
| 270 | Weatherby factory | 2940 CW |
| 300 | Weatherby factory | 2800 CW |
| 300 | 92.0 RL-19 | 2743 (A-Square) |
| 300 | 88.0 IMR 4831 | 2730 (A-Square) |
| 300 | 91.5 RL-22 | 2694 (A-Square) |

**Case Capacity** (grains water): **106**

**Case Trim Length: 2.830"**

**Standard Operating Pressure 60,000 PSI**

**Standard Rifling Twist 1-in-12"**

*Cartridge Illustrations courtesy of Wolfe Publishing Company   CW=Cartridges of the World (5th Edition)*

.532"   .492"   .402"   .402"
31°
.531"
.512"
.051"
.219"
2.431"
2.506"
2.860"
3.563"

Among Roy Weatherby's line of belted magnum cartridges developed in the 1940s was one that didn't survive as a commercial round. The .375 Weatherby Magnum--a .375 Holland blown out for greater powder capacity--performed well enough and offered hunters about 150 fps gain over its parent round. But not many hunters needed a cartridge bigger than a .375 H&H, and fewer still wanted to custom-chamber a rifle or to fashion their own case-- not when Winchester was selling its Model 70s in .375 H&H. In 1953 Weatherby took the idea of a super .375 a step farther with his .378 Magnum. Based on a new belted case about the size of the .416 Rigby, the .378 dwarfs Holland's .375. At .603, its belt diameter is about .07 greater; the case is .06 longer. The 378's huge powder chamber requires over 100 grains of slow powder to send 270-grain bullets downrange at 3100 fps and its 300-grain bullets at 2900.

The .378 Weatherby Magnum generates nearly three tons of muzzle energy--a 30 percent increase over that of a .375 H&H. With 270-grain spitzers it shoots as flat as the .300 Winchester Magnum with 180-grain spitzers. The .378 Weatherby is factory-chambered in the U.S. only in Weatherby Mark V rifles. Conversion of other actions is costly because the case is so large. No North American game requires the enormous striking energy of the .378, and its flat trajectory is of questionable utility in Africa, where dangerous game is generally shot at close range. The .378 Weatherby Magnum also has a brutal kick and, in ported rifles, an ear-shattering blast. But it is nonetheless an efficient cartridge and the only one that combines plains-game reach with the punch of the .500 Nitro Express and .505 Gibbs. It has recently spawned the .30-378 and .338-378 Weatherby Magnums.

| BULLET WEIGHT (grains) | MAXIMUM LOADS (grains, type of powder) | TOP VELOCITY (fps) AND DATA SOURCE |
|---|---|---|
| 235 | 109.0 H4350 | 3220 (Hodgdon) |
| 250 | 105.0 4350 | 3140 (Accurate) |
| 270 | 115.0 H4831 | 3100 (Hodgdon) |
| 270 | 108.0 N204 | 3100 (Hornady) |
| 270 | 113.2 H450 | 3100 (Hornady) |
| 300 | 114.0 IMR 7828 | 2960 (Nosler) |
| 300 | 100.0 H4350 | 2940 (Hodgon) |
| 300 | 110.0 RL-22 | 2910 (A-Square) |
| 300 | 111.4 H4831 | 2900 (Sierra) |
| 350 | 102.0 H4831 | 2650 (Barnes) |
| 350 | 103.0 RL-22 | 2630 (Barnes) |

**CASE CAPACITY**
(grains water)
**105**

**CASE TRIM LENGTH**
**2.85"**

**STANDARD OPERATING PRESSURE**
**60,000 PSI**

**STANDARD RIFLING TWIST**
**1-IN-12"**

.603 15.24mm    .582 14.73mm    .582 14.73mm    .560 14.22mm    .399 9.92mm    .375 9.40mm

.250 6.35mm

2.340 - 59.43mm
2.537 - 64.27mm
2.908 - 73.68m
3.562 - 90.42mm

*Cartridge Illustrations courtesy of Wolfe Publishing Company*

# .416 RIGBY

Developed in 1911 by the English gun firm of John Rigby & Company, the rimless .416 Rigby is quite similar to the .404 Jeffery announced a year earlier. The .416 case, however, is larger in diameter and slightly longer, giving it greater powder capacity. The .404, which was designed to duplicate the ballistic performance of Jeffery's popular .450/.400 three-inch Nitro Express. double-gun cartridge, could drive a 400-grain bullet at 2125 fps with a charge of 60 grains of Cordite. But the .416 beat them both by 200 fps, generating 5000 foot-pounds of muzzle energy. It soon established an enviable reputation among professional hunters in Africa, partly because the steel-jacketed 410-grain bullet loaded by Rigby gave dependable penetration in heavy game. The softpoint of the same weight performed well on lions and large antelope. Because Cordite was notoriously sensitive to changes in ambient temperatures, factory-loaded Kynoch .416 ammunition was held to operating pressures under 40,000 PSI. Some professionals hunters considered it too light for buffalo and elephant, but still the .416 gained in popularity. Its closest rival ballistically was the .425 Westley Richards. Introduced in 1909, it was thoroughly outclassed by the Rigby round at market (perhaps because of its rebated rim, which some shooters disliked). American hunters had little to do with the .416 Rigby until 1988, when Kimber chambered its Model 89 bolt rifle for the cartridge. A-Square had been manufacturing .416 Rigby cases and ammunition since 1987, and in 1990 Federal added the cartridge to its line.

| Bullet Weight (grains) | Maximum Loads (grains, type of powder) | Top Velocity (fps) And Data Source |
|---|---|---|
| 300 | 107.0 AA 4350 | 2900 (Barnes) |
| 350 | 102.0 AA 3100 | 2520 (Accurate) |
| 400 | 101.0 H4831 | 2450 (A-Square) |
| 400 | 100.0 RL-22 | 2400 (A-Square) |
| 400 | 97.0 IMR 4831 | 2400 (A-Square) |
| 400 | 127.5 AA 8700 | 2380 (Accurate) |

**Case Capacity** (grains water): **133**

**Case Trim Length: 2.85**

**Standard Operating Pressure 44,000 PSI**

**Standard Rifling Twist 1-in-16"**

44° 53'

.590 / 14,99 mm    .589 / 14,96 mm    .540 / 13,72 mm    .446 / 11,33 mm    .416 / 10,57 mm

.500 / 12,70 mm

2.353 (59,77 mm)

2.90 (73,66 mm)

3.720 (94,49 mm)

*Cartridge Illustrations courtesy of Wolfe Publishing Company*

When Remington introduced its 8mm Magnum in 1978, new opportunities arose for wildcatters. Though the long case offered essentially the same capacity as the decades-old .300 Weatherby, it featured standard shoulder junctures, not the radiused junctures found on the Weatherby. Any rifle that could accommodate the .375 H&H would swallow the 8mm Remington Magnum, and there were lots of those rifles around. In 1988 a necked-up 8mm Remington went commercial as the .416 Remington Magnum. Remington had apparently consulted with wildcatter and elephant hunter George Hoffman, whose own .416 magnum had become well respected. Rejecting the .416 Taylor, which was based on the shorter .338 Winchester case, Remington simply used its 8mm to give American shooters the first factory-loaded .416.

In doing so, Remington fashioned a round almost identical to the Hoffman magnum. Reloading data for the .416 Remington works for the .416 Hoffman and vice versa, but the Hoffman case will not quite fit in a Remington chamber. (It is .004 larger at the shoulder and differs in shoulder angle by 1 degree.) With 400-grain bullets at a listed 2400 fps, the .416 Remington Magnum matches the .416 Rigby down-range. Because its case derives directly from the .375 H&H, the Remington round is better adapted to modern American rifle actions. The .416 Rigby case is larger in diameter than most magnum actions can accommodate, and the loaded round is .15 longer than the .416 Remington. Though the 8mm Remington has always struggled and is commonly presumed dead, the .416 Remington Magnum has, considering its limited application, performed surprisingly well in the marketplace. Combining the trajectory of a .375 H&H with the energy of a .458 Winchester, it offers a package that slips readily into available rifles.

| Bullet Weight (grains) | Maximum Loads (grains, type of powder) | Top Velocity (fps) and Data Source |
|---|---|---|
| 300 | 93.0 RL-15 | 2960 (Hodgdon) |
| 300 | 81.0 AA 2015 | 2920 (Barnes) |
| 300 | 94.0 RL-12 | 2900 (Hodgdon) |
| 325 | 84.0 H4895 | 2830 (Barnes) |
| 325 | 83.0 AA 2520 | 2800 (Barnes) |
| 350 | 85.0 IMR 4064 | 2660 (Hodgdon) |
| 350 | 79.0 AA 2230 | 2650 (Accurate) |
| 350 | 85.0 BL-C(2) | 2630 (Barnes) |
| 400 | 82.0 RL-15 | 2480 (A-Square) |
| 400 | 80.0 2495 BR | 2450 (Accurate) |
| 400 | 87.0 4350 | 2450 (Accurate) |
| 400 | 76.0 H4895 | 2400 (A-Square) |

**Case Capacity** (grains water)
**108**

**Case Trim Length**
**2.84"**

**Standard Operating Pressure**
**54,000 CUP**

**Standard Rifling Twist**
**1-in-14"**

*Cartridge Illustrations courtesy of Wolfe Publishing Company*

# .416 WEATHERBY MAGNUM

When he designed the .378 Weatherby Magnum back in 1953, Roy Weatherby simply necked down the .416 Rigby and added a belt. Later, in 1989, the .378 case was opened back up to .416. As expected, the new .416 Weatherby Magnum outperformed the Rigby and its modern counterpart, the .416 Remington Magnum. Weatherby's cartridge, which made Remington's look small, operates at 60,000 PSI, much higher pressure than is tolerated by the Cordite-fueled Rigby.

This combination of high operating pressure and huge case volume gives the .416 Weatherby Magnum a substantial ballistic edge over both its .416 rivals. Factory-loaded 400-grain bullets leave the muzzle at 2700 fps, 300 fps faster than their Rigby and Remington counterparts. It can send a 350-grain bullet downrange at 2900 fps on an arc as taut as that of 150-grain bullets from a .30-06. It also delivers 20 percent more energy than a .458 Winchester Magnum, though it burns twice as much powder doing so. In its role as a specialized cartridge for thick-skinned African game, the .416 Weatherby Magnum is best used with full-jacketed bullets and only the stoutest of softpoints. As with other heavy-recoiling cartridges carried in magazine rifles, this one merits a crimp to hold bullets in place while they're under the bolt. Mark V rifles in .378 and its derivatives, the .30-378, .338-378, .416 and .460, are supplied with muzzle brakes. The .416 Weatherby has a most brutal kick!

| BULLET WEIGHT (grains) | MAXIMUM LOADS (grains, type of powder) | TOP VELOCITY (fps) AND DATA SOURCE |
|---|---|---|
| 300 | 124.0 RL-19 | 3080 (Hodgdon) |
| 300 | 116.0 IMR 4350 | 3060 (Hodgdon) |
| 325 | 116.0 H4350 | 3010 (Barnes) |
| 325 | 110.0 H414 | 2960 (Barnes) |
| 350 | 125.0 RL-22 | 2930 (Hodgdon) |
| 350 | 118.0 IMR 4831 | 2910 (Hodgdon) |
| 400 | 120.0 H4831 | 2740 (A-Square) |
| 400 | 120.0 IMR 7828 | 2720 (Hodgdon) |
| 400 | 124.0 H450 | 2710 (Hodgdon) |
| 400 | 117.0 RL-22 | 2710 (A-Square) |

**CASE CAPACITY (grains water)**
**141**

**CASE TRIM LENGTH**
**2.90"**

**STANDARD OPERATING PRESSURE**
**60,000 PSI**

**STANDARD RIFLING TWIST**
**1-IN-14"**

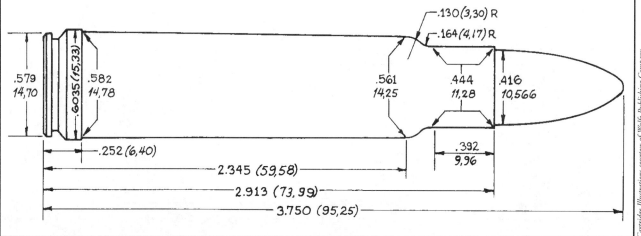

*Cartridge Illustrations courtesy of Wolfe Publishing Company*

# .444 MARLIN

Until the .444 Marlin was announced in 1964, Remington's .44 Magnum pistol cartridge--developed in 1955 and chambered in Ruger's new self-loading carbine in 1961--was the only .44 cartridge offered in rifles (the .44-40 had disappeared from long-gun lists in 1937). The .444 has the same head dimensions as the .44 Magnum but is not quite an inch longer. Both accept .429 bullets. When Remington was developing the .444 for Marlin, 240-grain pistol bullets were the heaviest commercially available. Consequently, Marlin rifled its specially-designed Model 336 with a 1-in-38 twist. Later, when 265- and 300-grain .429 bullets increased .444 horsepower, shooters questioned that twist. As with the .244 Remington and its 1-in-12 twist, apprehensions about loose groups and keyholes in the target proved largely unfounded.

When loaded to maximum safe velocities, heavy bullets can produce good accuracy in the .444. And, given their higher sectional density (.233 for the 300-grain, vs .185 for the 240-grain), they are clearly superior on game. Because the .444 is essentially a close-cover rifle, blunt bullet noses are no disadvantage; indeed, they are necessary for the tubular magazine found on the Model 336. Short bullets are a liability, however; they shed velocity faster and stop penetrating sooner than do long ones. With an action that can withstand 44,000 CUP, stubby 240-grain revolver bullets have little to recommend them. The .444 Marlin can generate as much muzzle energy as a .30-06, though it lacks the '06's downrange capabilities. With the exception of the .348 Winchester and .45-70, which deliver equivalent smash at the muzzle, the 444 is much more potent than cartridges traditionally chambered in exposed-hammer, tube-magazine lever guns.

| Bullet Weight (grains) | Maximum Loads (grains, type of powder) | Top Velocity (fps) and Data Source |
|---|---|---|
| 200 | 55.4 N120 | 2750 (VihtaVuori) |
| 200 | 57.0 1680 | 2730 (Accurate) |
| 240 | 54.4 N130 | 2470 (VihtaVuori) |
| 240 | 41.8 IMR 4227 | 2400 (Hornady) |
| 250 | 47.0 H4198 | 2320 (Hodgdon) |
| 250 | 51.0 RL-7 | 2320 (Barnes) |
| 265 | 54.0 H322 | 2250 (Hodgdon) |
| 265 | 52.0 2015 BR | 2220 (Accurate) |
| 275 | 52.0 H322 | 2200 (Barnes) |
| 275 | 44.0 IMR 4198 | 2160 (Barnes) |
| 300 | 48.0 AA 2015 | 2060 (Barnes) |
| 300 | 42.0 IMR 4198 | 2050 (Barnes) |

**CASE CAPACITY**
(grains water)
**70**

**CASE TRIM LENGTH**
**2.22"**

**STANDARD OPERATING PRESSURE**
**44,000 CUP**

**STANDARD RIFLING TWIST**
**1-IN-38"**

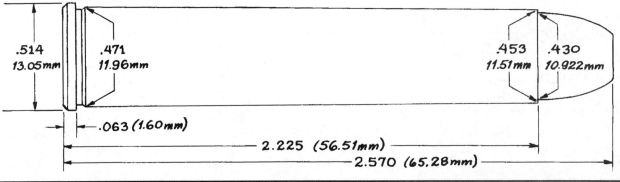

.514 13.05mm   .471 11.96mm   .453 11.51mm   .430 10.922mm

.063 (1.60mm)

2.225 (56.51mm)

2.570 (65.28mm)

Cartridge Illustrations courtesy of Wolfe Publishing Company

The .45-70 Government dates to 1873, when it was adopted as the U.S. Army service cartridge for the "trap-door" Springfield. Replaced in its military role by the .30-40 Krag in 1892, the .45-70 survived the transition from black powder to smokeless, partly because several fine rifles chambered it. This straight, rimmed round appeared in the Remington Rolling Block, the Remington-Lee, the Marlin 1881 and, perhaps most notably, the Winchester 1886. Volunteer U.S. regiments in the Spanish-American War were equipped with the obsolete Springfields in .45-70, as were many state militias well into the 1900s. The first military ammunition featured a 405-grain lead bullet in front of 70 grains of black powder, creating a muzzle velocity of around 1300 fps. When a 500-grain load was adopted later, the 405-grain bullet was retained for use in carbines.

Pressures for trap-door Springfields must be kept to around 21,000 CUP. The Winchester 86 can tolerate 28,000 CUP, as can the modern Marlin 1895 and High Wall Winchester 1885 single-shots. Ruger Number One and Browning 1885 rifles, along with the discontinued Ruger Number 3 and Siamese Mausers, can bottle the 35,000 CUP, making the .45-70 a fine short-range big game round. The most popular jacketed bullets for this cartridge--350 and 400 grains--can be driven 2100 and 2000 fps respectively, in the strongest modern rifles. While modest ballistic coefficients limit their range, they equal the chart energy of the .30-06 up close and can plow bigger wound channels. The .45-70 may seem an anemic round to modern shooters, but at one time it was considered very potent. Many bison fell to its sting. With high-pressure loads it is more than adequate for elk, moose or even big bears in the thickets. Factory loads for the .45-70 feature 300- and 405-grain bullets at 1800 and 1300 fps, throttling this round down to the power level of a .30-30, whose lighter, faster bullets produce a flatter trajectory.

| Bullet Weight (grains) | Maximum Loads (grains, type of powder) | Top Velocity (fps) and Data Source |
|---|---|---|
| 300 | 60.0 N133 | 2190 (VihtaVuori) |
| 300 | 50.0 RL-7 | 2160 (Barnes) |
| 300 | 41.4 2400 | 2150 (Sierra) |
| 350 | 58.0 H4895 | 2100 (Barnes) |
| 350 | 60.0 AA 2520 | 2090 (Accurate) |
| 350 | 61.0 2495 BR | 2060 (Accurate) |
| 400 | 64.0 IMR 4064 | 2020 (Speer) |
| 400 | 57.0 AA 2460 | 1930 (Accurate) |
| 500 | 52.0 H4895 | 1680 (Hodgdon) |
| 500 | 50.0 H322 | 1670 (Hodgdon) |

**Case Capacity (grains water)**
76

**Case Trim Length**
2.10"

**Standard Operating Pressure**
28,000 PSI

**Standard Rifling Twist**
1-in-20"

.808 / 15.44mm
.505 / 12.83mm
.480 / 12.19mm
.458 / 11.63mm
.070 (1.78mm)
2.105 (53.47mm)
2.550 (64.77mm)

*Cartridge Illustrations courtesy of Wolfe Publishing Company*

*Note: These loads are for Ruger Number One and other strong actions generating up to 50,000 CUP. Trapdoor Springfields can safely handle only about 25,000 CUP; the Marlin 1895 up to 40,000 CUP.*

# .458 WINCHESTER MAGNUM

A t its debut in 1956, Winchester's .458 became the first U.S. cartridge designed to compete with British Nitro Express cartridges on heavy African game. It was also the first commercial "short" magnum (the .375 H&H case having been trimmed to 2.500 inches in order to function in .30-06-length actions). While it's doubtful the .458 ever quite duplicated the .470 Nitro Express ballistically, it came close. Original factory listings for the 500-grain bullet claimed 2130 fps and 5040 foot-pounds for the 500-grain solid (now shaved to 2040 and 4620). Winchester's first Model 70 "African" had a 25-inch tube, but the standard length is now 22 inches. According to many professional hunters,

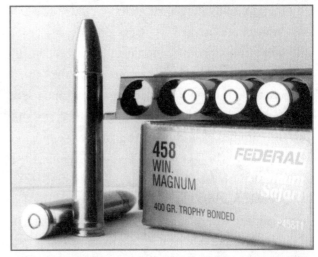

Winchester's .458 first appeared in 1956 with loads of 500- and 510-grain solids and softpoints. Even with 400-grain bullets, this is a hard-kicking cartridge.

| Bullet Weight (grains) | Maximum Loads (grains, type of powder) | Top Velocity (fps) And Data Source | Case Capacity (grains water) |
|---|---|---|---|
| 300 | 70.0 N120 | 2600 (VihtaVuori) | **93** |
| 350 | 73.7 N130 | 2520 (VihtaVuori) | **Case Trim Length** |
| 350 | 78.0 AA 2230 | 2510 (Accurate) | **2.49"** |
| 400 | 78.0 Win 748 | 2350 (Hodgdon) | **Standard Operating Pressure** |
| 400 | 72.0 IMR 3031 | 2340 (Barnes) | **53,000 CUP** |
| 465 | 77.0 H4895 | 2250 (A-Square) | |
| 465 | 81.0 RL-12 | 2250 (A-Square) | **Standard Rifling Twist** |
| 500 | 75.0 Win 748 | 2190 (Barnes) | **1-in-14"** |
| 500 | 74.0 AA 2460 | 2190 (Accurate) | **(some slower, to 1-in-18")** |
| 500 | 72.0 IMR 4895 | 2170 (Hodgdon) | |
| 500 | 72.2 IMR 3031 | 2150 (Hornady) | |
| 600 | 68.0 H335 | 1940 (Hodgdon) | |

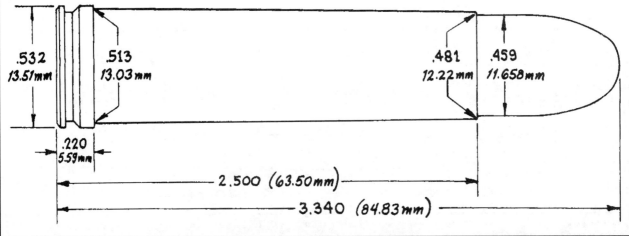

.532 / 13.51mm
.513 / 13.03mm
.481 / 12.22mm
.459 / 11.658mm
.220 / 5.59mm
2.500 (63.50mm)
3.340 (84.83mm)

*Cartridge Illustrations courtesy of Wolfe Publishing Company*

the .458 factory rounds have not lived up to their billing. In addition, the case is too small to hold more powder with the correct burning rate. Fuels faster than IMR 3031 can cause pressure problems. Ball powder has been suspected of caking in compressed loads, yielding incomplete combustion. Crimping the .458 is a good idea even if the rounds are not carried in a magazine, because heavily-compressed powder has a big bullet base to push against. Some shooters milk more performance from 458s by using 465-grain bullets with a sectional density approaching that of 500-grain bullets. They leave more room for powder and exit at higher velocity. Another solution is to handload Speer's compact 500-grain tungsten solid, which doesn't need to be seated as deeply as lead-core bullets. Among standard solid bullets, the 500-grain Hornady has a good reputation for dependability and penetration. The first 510-grain factory-loaded soft-nose bullets in the .458 opened too quickly to satisfy some hunters. The .458 Winchester Magnum remains best employed with solids as a short-range cartridge for the largest game. For many rangers culling elephants in national parks, the .458 is a top choice.

## .460 WEATHERBY MAGNUM

In 1903 the .600 Nitro Express made its appearance as an "elephant cartridge" armed with enough muzzle energy to satisfy any big game hunter. Its 900-grain bullet delivered 7600 foot pounds, and for 55 years it remained the world's most powerful sporting cartridge. In 1958, two years after Winchester challenged Britain's established double-gun firms with a belted 45-caliber round for magazine rifles, Roy Weatherby trumped the .600 N.E. with his .460 Magnum. Unlike the .458 Winchester, the .460 is not fashioned from a .375 case; rather, it derives from Weatherby's own monstrous .378 magnum, which was introduced in 1953. Factory-loaded 500-grain bullets, listed at 2700 fps, are as fast as 180-grain bullets from a .30-06. They carry nearly 8100 foot-pounds of energy, hitting the shooter with well over 100 foot-pounds of recoil.

Only the strongest solids perform well in the .460 Weatherby, which has been known to shoot lengthwise straight through Cape buffalo with A-Square's 500-grain Monolithic Solid (Hornady's .075 copper-clad steel jackets make its solids a good bet too). Softnose bullets seem out of place in this powerhouse, but some current offerings--Swift and A-Square for example--will stand up to full-throttle impact in thin-skinned game.

The Weatherby Mark V is the only commercial rifle chambered in .460 Weatherby Magnum. It comes with a muzzle brake. Although some riflemen see no practical reason for this cartridge, the biggest game may require bullets that develop several tons of energy. Hunters who want alternatives, in fact, can still get rifles in .500 Jeffery, .505 Gibbs or (for doubles) the .500 Nitro Express three-inch. The Weatherby Mark V rifle is nicely engineered and finished, and it costs much less than magazine rifles built for big British rounds, let alone double guns. If you need a .460 Weatherby, however, you probably needn't worry about rifle expense.

| BULLET WEIGHT (grains) | MAXIMUM LOADS (grains, type of powder) | TOP VELOCITY (fps) AND DATA SOURCE | CASE CAPACITY (grains water) 145 |
|---|---|---|---|
| 350 | 112.0 AA 2520 | 2960 (Accurate) | |
| 350 | 115.5 H380 | 2950 (Hornady) | **CASE TRIM LENGTH** |
| 400 | 122.0 IMR 4831 | 2750 (Barnes) | **2.90"** |
| 400 | 118.0 IMR 4350 | 2680 (Hodgdon) | |
| 500 | 124.6 N204 | 2600 (Hornady) | **STANDARD** |
| 500 | 125.0 RL-19 | 2590 (A-Square) | **OPERATING PRESSURE** |
| 500 | 128.0 H450 | 2580 (Hodgdon) | **65,000 PSI** |
| 500 | 114.0 AA 2700 | 2540 (Accurate) | |
| 600 | 115.0 H4831 | 2460 (Hodgdon) | **STANDARD RIFLING TWIST** |
| 600 | 105.0 H414 | 2420 (Hodgdon) | **1-IN-16"** |

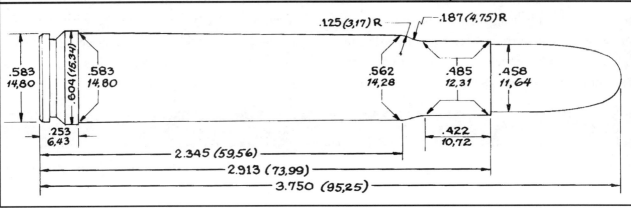

Cartridge Illustrations courtesy of Wolfe Publishing Company

# A-SQUARE CARTRIDGES

Following a distinguished career in the U.S. Army, Art Alphin started the A-Square Company in the mid-1980s. A West Point graduate (1970), he served in Germany and later in Rhodesia

Back in the States, Art shot competitively with various small arms, once qualifying as Expert firing the M-16 rifle course with a .357 revolver! He then returned to West Point to develop a new course on military weapons.

Art's experience on African game trails includes culling and licensed sport hunting. His efforts to design better bullets for heavy game led to the "Monolithic Solid", which Zimbabwe National Parks adopted in 1984. The A-Square Company later manufactured not only its own proprietary rounds for the world's largest game, but a number of popular wildcat cartridges as well. Big rifles (most on 1917 Enfields) and big cartridges have been Art's passion.

His **A-Square Handloading and Rifle Manual** contains a wealth of information for all shooters. It covers cartridges ranging in size from the .22 Hornet to Art's own .577 Tyrannosaur. For military buffs, a few pages have even been devoted to the 105x608mm tank round.

While most A-Square cartridges are bigger than most riflemen need afield, their excellence of design is worth studying. A-Square has the kind of entrepreneurial vigor that characterized the startup of America's flagship gun companies many years ago.

# .300 PEGASUS

The .300 Pegasus is an original creation of A-Square's Art Alphin, who was intent on manufacturing his own cartridge cases. The .300 is a rimless round slightly smaller in diameter than a .416 Rigby or .378 Weatherby, but significantly larger than the .375 H&H case from which most modern magnums derive. The A Square cartridge is currently the longest of the high-performance .30s, requiring a 3.75-inch magazine. Initially known as the .300 Petersen (after the publishing magnate), this cartridge was renamed after A-Square was contacted by attorneys who represented other famous Petersens.

The .300 Pegasus can launch a 180-grain bullet at 3500 fps and is among a handful of cartridges that can be zeroed at 300 yards without placing the bullet over the vitals of a small deer at midrange.

| LOADS | |
|---|---|
| 130.0 AA 8700 | 150 Nosler BalTp 3703 |
| 103.0 RL-22 | 150 Nosler BalTp 3675 |
| 106.0 IMR 7828 | 150 Nosler BalTp 3642 |
| 123.0 H 870 | 180 Nosler BalTp 3505 |
| 125.0 AA8700 | 180 Nosler BalTp 3456 |
| 106.0 IMR 7828 | 180 Nosler BalTp 3413 |

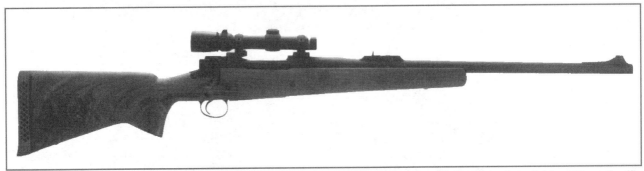

A-Square rifles built on 1917 Enfield actions are strong but have blocky lines. The steep grip, wide butt and substantial forend keep the rifle manageable under recoil.

# .338 A-SQUARE

In 1978 Art Alphin developed the .338 A-Square. Based on a shortened .378 Weatherby case, it edges out the .340 Weatherby in performance, reaching 500 yards with more energy than the .338 Winchester Magnum could deliver at 200. The base diameter of the .378 Weatherby case limits the .338 A-Square to the Weatherby Mark V rifle. A

| LOADS | |
|---|---|
| 105.0 IMR 7828 | 200 Nosler BalTp 3360 |
| 104.0 RL-22 | 200 Nosler BalTp 3355 |
| 120.0 AA 8700 | 250 Sierra SBT 3100 |
| 118.0 H 870 | 250 Sierra SBT 3094 |

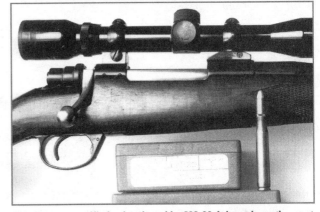

This Husqvarna rifle is chambered in .338-06. It is perhaps the most useful of common wildcat cartridges based on the .30-06 case. A-Square now manufactures the round.

superb long-distance cartridge for elk, moose and big bears, this potent round is best paired with strongly-constructed bullets to ensure against breakup on close-range hits. Its 5400 foot-pounds of muzzle energy exceeds that of most big-bore Nitro Express rounds. Recoil is substantial.

## .338 EXCALIBUR

The .338 Excalibur derives from the .300 Pegasus developed by A-Square and designed to send a 180-grain bulle over 3500 fps. The Excalibur can kiss that ceiling with a 200-grain bullet without topping 60,000 PSI breech pressure. Zeroed at 300 yards, it can keep a 200-grain spitzer within 3½ inches of point of aim to 350. Drop at 400 yards is about seven inches, or what shooters expect from a .30-06 at 300, given a 200-yard zero. It reaches that far with nearly two tons of energy, more than the .375 can claim at 100 yards. The .338 Excalibur is the most powerful factory-loaded .33 available, with only the longest rifle actions able to accept its 3.75-inch rounds.

| LOADS | |
|---|---|
| 115.0 IMR 7828 | 200 Nosler BalTp 3497 |
| 140.0 AA 8700 | 200 Nosler BalTp 3493 |
| 138.0 H 870 | 200 Nosler BalTp 3480 |
| 130.0 AA 8700 | 250 Sierra SBT 3202 |
| 128.0 H 870 | 250 Sierra SBT 3200 |
| 110.0 RL-22 | 250 Sierra SBT 3192 |

## .375 JRS MAGNUM

When the 8mm Remington Magnum was introduced in 1978, it quickly drew the attention of wildcatters. Necked up to .375, it became the .375 JRS (after gun writer Jon Sundra, who worked on the first load development). The case has about the same capacity as Weatherby's old .375 Magnum and considerably more than that of the .375 H&H. It also features traditional sharp shoulder junctures rather than the radiused Weatherby turns. With a 270-grain bullet at 2900 fps and a 300-grain at 2700, the .375 JRS is a versatile safari cartridge with the reach of a .300 magnum and the punch of a .416 Rigby. When A-Square began loading ammun tion for it in 1990, it became better known and more popular.

| LOADS | |
|---|---|
| 84.0 IMR 4350 | 300 A-Square MS 2712 |
| 88.0 RL-19 | 300 A-Square MS 2712 |
| 88.1 H 4832 | 300 A-Square MS 2712 |

## .375 A-SQUARE

The .375 A-Square was developed by Art Alphin in 1975 to match .378 Weatherby ballistics in a shorter case, one that would fit in actions designed for the .375 H&H Magnum. After trimming the .378 case from 2.913 to 2.850, Alphin lengthened the base-to-shoulder measure from 2.398 to 2.425 and changed Weatherby's radiused shoulder to a 35-degree conventional slope. The .375 A-Square now equals the punch of the .378 Weatherby. Both are loaded by A-Square, and both carry 5000 foot-pounds to 100 yards with 300-grain bullets. At 200 yards these cartridges deliver more energy than a .375 H&H Magnum at the muzzle.

| LOADS | |
|---|---|
| 113.0 RL-22 | 250 Sierra SBT 3217 |
| 114.5 H 4831 | 250 Sierra SBT 3186 |
| 106.0 IMR 4831 | 250 Sierra SBT 3184 |
| 105.0 RL-22 | 300 A-Square MS 2839 |
| 99.0 IMR 4831 | 300 A-Square MS 2837 |
| 105.0 H 4831 | 300 A-Square MS 2832 |

The A-Square Company loads solid and softnose ammunition for popular cartridges like the .375 H&H, as well as for the company's proprietary line.

# .400 PONDORO

This cartridge came about after A-Square was asked to develop a 40-caliber cartridge that could fire a 400-grain solid at velocities exceeding 2400 fps. In addition, the round had to be easily fashioned from .375 H&H brass. The result was the .400 Pondoro. Shorter than the .375 by .04, its case is about .05 larger in diameter at the shoulder. It drives the 400-grain .409 A-Frame Lion Load bullet at roughly 2400 fps, making it the equal of the .416 Rigby (or Remington). The .400 Pondoro case accepts .41 Magnum revolver bullets, which can then be loaded to 3000 fps by shooters in need of a big-bore varmint rifle.

| LOADS | |
|---|---|
| 82.0 H 4895 | 210 Nosler JHP 2965 |
| 75.0 RL-7 | 210 Nosler JHP 2939 |
| 75.1 IMR 4064 | 400 A-Square LL 2397 |
| 74.0 H 4895 | 400 A-Square LL 2393 |
| 76.5 RL-12 | 400 A-Square LL 2367 |

# .416 RIMMED

In 1991 A-Square set out to fashion a rimmed case that duplicated the performance of the .416 Rigby. The result was the .416 Rimmed, a relatively straight bottle-neck case that looked more like a round for magazine rifles. Given the cartridge's great length and powder capacity (there by reducing breech pressure), case taper was reportedly sufficient for extraction. The hefty .060 rim won't buckle, either. The .416 Rimmed can drive a 400-grain bullet over 2400 fps with about 40,000 PSI—a relatively high pressure for double-rifle cartridges

The cartridges shown are preferred by African hunters (left to right): .458 Winchester, .416 Remington and .460 Weatherby Magnums.

but comparable to what one expects from ambitious loads in the .470 and .500 Nitro Express. Factory-loaded A-Square ammunition matches the 5115 foot-pounds of the .416 Rigby and .425 Express at the muzzle.

| LOADS | |
|---|---|
| 111.0 RL-22 | 500 A-Square LL 2404 |
| 117.0 IMR 4831 | 500 A-Square LL 2378 |
| 120.0 RL-22 | 500 A-Square LL 2378 |
| 120.0 IMR 7828 | 500 A-Square LL 2323 |

# .460 SHORT A-SQUARE

Developed in 1977, the .460 A-Square is a .460 Weatherby Magnum case lopped to 2.500 inches with a .376 neck in front of a 35-degree shoulder. Thus configured, it fits a .30-06 length receiver. The wide case body of the .460 A-Square holds more powder than a .458 and it can drive a 500-grain bullet at 2400 fps--a gain of 350 fps or so. The cost involves extensive rifle alteration to ensure proper feeding of the larger case. The common compact rifle actions for which the .460 Short A-Square was intended feature bolt faces and magazine for rounds with the diameter of the .458 Winchester. Still, this A-Square cartridge is efficient and reportedly very accurate.

| LOADS | |
|---|---|
| 98.0 RL-15 | 500 A-Square LL 2475 |
| 96.0 RL-12 | 500 A-Square LL 2407 |
| 94.0 IMR 4064 | 500 A-Square LL 2389 |

# .470 CAPSTICK

Peter Hathaway Capstick, who became a literary legend with his series of books on African hunting, favored a .470 double rifle for his safaris. Thus, when Art Alphin developed a .470 cartridge on a full-length .375 Holland case in 1990, he named it after the writer. The .470 Capstick case resembles the .458 Lott's but is .050 longer. It also shares the Lott's straight-taper round with no formed shoulder. Like the .470 Nitro Express, the .470 Capstick carries a .475-diameter bullet with eight percent more frontal area than the Lott. A larger bullet base enables the Capstick to push a 500-grain bullet at 2400 fps, or as fast as the Lott can accelerate a 465-grain bullet. The .470 Capstick is the most potent round available that can fit an action designed for the .375 H&H.

| LOADS | |
|---|---|
| 89.5 RL-12 | 500 A-Square MS 2410 |
| 88.0 IMR 4064 | 500 A-Square MS 2404 |
| 85.0 H 4895 | 500 A-Square MS 2387 |
| 91.0 RL-15 | 500 A-Square MS 2385 |

# .495 A-SQUARE

In 1977 Art Alphin developed the .495 A-Square by trimming the .460 Weatherby case from 2.913 to 2.800 and necking it up to a straight case. He then formed a "ghost shoulder" .400 from the mouth so the .510 bullet was seated in a neck with parallel sides. This provided a greater, more uniform grip on the bullet. The case, moreover, doesn't have to be reduced below bullet diameter at the mouth and then belled open in a third die. As with all cartridges derived from the .460 (.378) Weatherby case, rifle actions designed for the .375 need some attention before they'll feed reliably. The .495 A-Square generates almost 7000 foot pounds at the muzzle with its 570-grain bullet.

| LOADS | |
|---|---|
| 110.0 RL-15 | 570 A-Square MS 2459 |
| 106.0 H 4895 | 570 A-Square MS 2447 |
| 102.0 IMR 4064 | 570 A-Square MS 2365 |

# .500 A-SQUARE

Similar to the .495 A-Square, the .500 A-Square, which evolved during the early 1970s as the first A-Square cartridge, is based on the .460 Weatherby case (it also uses .510-diameter bullets). Unlike the .495, however, it has a formed 35-degree shoulder and the case is .100 longer (about the same length as the .460's). The .500 A-Square generates a whopping four tons of muzzle energy, ten percent more than the .460 Weatherby, hence its crushing effectiveness on big game. The success of this cartridge is due as much to the great frontal area of the bullet as to its chart energy. In short, the .500 A-Square is easy to reload, but punishing to shoot.

| LOADS | |
|---|---|
| 117.0 IMR 4064 | 600 A-Square DT 2503 |
| 118.0 RL-12 | 600 A-Square DT 2481 |
| 115.0 H 4895 | 600 A-Square DT 2474 |
| 118.0 RL-15 | 600 A-Square DT 2467 |

# .577 TYRANNOSAUR

Even the name of this cartridge suggests power. Indeed, no other cartridge even approaches the five tons of muzzle energy delivered by the .577 Tyrannosaur at the muzzle. Its development began in 1993, when A-Square was asked to build a magazine rifle capable of launching a .585 bullet fast enough to match the performance of the .577 Nitro Express. The result was a new rimless case considerable larger in basal diameter than even the .460 Weatherby. The case is a bit longer than the Weatherby's too. A-Square's capacity to design and manufacture its own cases, and Art Alphin's fondness for big bullets, yielded what may remain for some time the most powerful sporting round ever made. The .577 is much more potent than the .600 Nitro Express. A mercury recoil reducer is a must.

The author hunts in places where rifles must be portable as well as accurate and sufficiently powerful. His favorite cartridges include the .270, which he has used often to take mule deer on this Oregon ridge.

| LOADS | |
|---|---|
| 170.0 IMR 4350 | 750 A-Square MS 2480 |
| 177.5 RL-19 | 750 A-Square MS 2473 |
| 180.0 H 4831 | 750 A-Square MS 2395 |

# NINE

# NORMA CARTRIDGES

A.B. Norma Projektilfabrik of Amotfors, Sweden, may not be the most common name exchanged over gun counters; still, it has been supplying Weatherby with ammunition almost as long as the California rifle company has been in operation. In 1960, Norma tested the readiness of the U.S. market for a new cartridge by introducing its .308 Magnum (a short, belted .30).

it only in unprimed brass. By the time Norma sent its loaded rounds to the U.S., Winchester was almost on line with its own .300 Magnum. Norma may not soon threaten established domestic ammo makers in the U.S., but it continues to produce top-quality rounds for Weatherby. They have a little more vinegar than you will find in American ammunition because Norma need not adhere to SAAMI

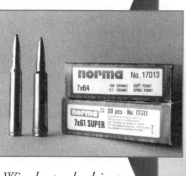

Winchester had just announced its .264 and .338 Magnums, while Remington was yet to show its 7mm Magnum. The .30-338 wildcat looked like a sure winner. Norma's version of the .30-338 did not sell well because no American rifles were chambered for it, not to mention the Swedish firm's decision to offer

specifications regarding pressures. The cartridges are safe, however, when fired in modern bolt rifles; and many hunters prefer Norma fodder because of its proven performance downrange. Norma also continues to supply foreign cartridges that are not available from American factories.

# 5.6X52R

The 5.6x52R, known in the U.S. as the .22 Savage High-Power , is a rimmed cartridge designed around 1912 by Charles Newton for the Model 99 Savage lever rifle. Essentially the .25-35 case necked down to hold a .228 bullet, this little round was nicknamed the "Imp." As a varmint cartridge in a lever-action rifle, it suffered from the same malady that befell the .219 Zipper. In tight, accurate single-shots most shooters preferred the Zipper because it fired the more common .224 bullets. The 5.6x52R has been widely chambered in European combination guns along with the BSA Martini single-shot. While no .22 High-Power rifles or cartridges have been produced commercially in the U.S. since the 1930s, Norma manufactures the 5.6x52R, with two types of 71-grain bullets.

| LOADS | | |
|---|---|---|
| 29.0 H 380 | 55 | 3200 CW |
| 290 IMR 4320 | 70 | 2820 CW |
| Savage commercial | 70 | 2800 CW |
| Norma commercial | 71 | 2789 CW |

*CW=Cartridges of the World (5ª Edition)*

# 6.5X50 JAPANESE ARISAKA

Introduced in 1897, when almost all military powers were switching to small-bore, high-velocity rifles, the 6.5mm Arisaka was chambered in a rifle subsequently found to be unsafe. It took several years to find a new home in a modified Mauser known as the Japanese Model 38. Years later, in 1939 the cartridge was officially replaced by the 7.7x58 Arisaka, which appeared in a new Model 99 bolt rifle. Both rounds were used by Japanese troops during World War II. Smallest of the military 6.5mm cartridges, the 6.5x50 found its way to the U.S. with returning GIs. The Model 38, while not a pretty action, is stout. Norma still loads Boxer-primed ammunition for this semi-rimmed round. Ballistically, it trails the 6.5x55 Swedish Mauser by about 10 percent, but it remains a useful, light-recoiling deer cartridge.

*Note: Norma's ballistic data was obtained from 24-inch barrels, Hornadys's from 32-inch barrels standard on Model 38 military rifles.*

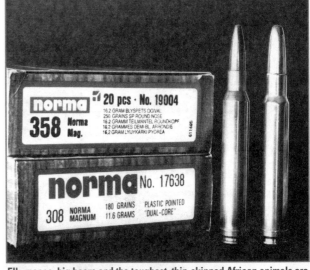

Elk, moose, big bears and the toughest, thin-skinned African animals are fair game for the .308 (left) and .358 Norma Magnums.

| LOADS | | |
|---|---|---|
| 29.0 H 380 | 55 | 3200 CW |
| 290 IMR 4320 | 70 | 2820 CW |
| Savage commercial | 70 | 2800 CW |
| Norma commercial | 71 | 2789 CW |
| Savage commercial | 70 | 2800 CW |
| Norma commercial | 71 | 2789 CW |

*CW=Cartridges of the World (5ª Edition)*

# 6.5X52 MANNLICHER-CARCANO

Few people had heard of this Italian military cartridge until 1963, when a deranged man used it to assassinate U.S. President John F. Kennedy. The 6.5x52 Mannlicher-Carcano was developed in 1891 and became one of the first small-bore, smokeless-powder rounds adopted by a European government. While the rifle itself has double Mauser-type bolt lugs, it is not particularly strong. Still, Norma's 139- and 156-grain factory loads place the 6.5x52 Mannlicher-Carcano about midway between the 6.5 Arisaka and the 6.5x55 Swedish Mauser in effectiveness. Model 91 Carcano rifles are the only military rifles produced in quantity with gain-twist rifling; that is, a pitch that becomes progressively steeper toward the muzzle. The idea was to ease entry of the bullet into the lands while imparting a fast spin upon exit at the muzzle.

*Note: Loading manuals indicate maximum Carcano velocities are approximately 10 percent lower than those claimed for Norma factory ammunition. Heed the manuals!*

## LOADS

| | | |
|---|---|---|
| **Norma commercial** | *139* | *2575 CW* |
| **Norma commercial** | *156* | *2428 CW* |
| **38.5 IMR 4350** | *160 Hornady* | *220 (Hornady)* |

*CW=Cartridges of the World (5ᵗʰ Edition)*

# 6.5X54 MANNLICHER SCHOENAUER

Though not widely used by hunters in the U.S., the 6.5x54 Mannlicher-Schoenauer has a long and solid reputation among sportsmen abroad. Following its development around 1900, it soon turned up in Africa, where ivory hunters armed with the 1903 Mannlicher used it to brain-shoot with long, blunt, full-jacketed bullets. Though hardly a "stopping" cartridge, it produced excellent penetration. Moreover, its soft report didn't stampede the herds. Light in weight and widely available, it also appealed to men headed into the bush for months at a time. American ammunition companies loaded the 6.5x54 M-S until World War II, and RWS still imports reloadable Boxer-primed cases. This cartridge is a fine choice for deer at modest ranges.

## LOADS

| | | |
|---|---|---|
| **38.5 H 380** | *100 Hornady* | *2600 (Hornady)* |
| **44.0 N 204** | *129 Hornady* | *2400 (Hornady)* |
| **36.0 IMR 4895** | *139* | *2400 CW* |
| **41.1 IMR 4350** | *140 Hornady* | *2400 CW* |
| **military** | *159* | *2223 CW* |
| **42.0 N 204** | *160 Hornady* | *2200 (Hornady)* |

*CW=Cartridges of the World (5ᵗʰ Edition)*

# 7.64 BRENNEKE

Wilhelm Brenneke, the brilliant firearms and ammunition designer, developed his 7x64 in 1917 as a big game round for Mauser rifles. A rimmed version, called the 7x65R, was later used in hinged-breech combination guns. Originally, the 7x64 was capped with a Brenneke bullet called the Torpedo. Norma now offers three softpoints, and Remington markets the 7x64 with both 140-grain and 175-grain Core-Lokts. While their case head diameter is a tad smaller than that of the .280 Remington, these cartridges are essentially identical (the .280 didn't arrive until 1957). This World War I-era Brenneke cartridge remains among the most useful ever designed for hunting antlered game throughout the world.

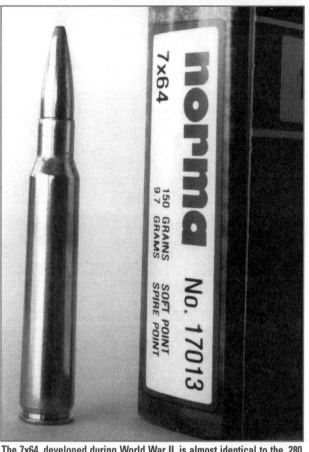

The 7x64, developed during World War II, is almost identical to the .280 Remington, which appeared 40 years later (Remington now loads both).

## LOADS

| | | |
|---|---|---|
| 53.0 IMR 4350 | 140 | 3000 CW |
| Norma commercial | 154 | 2821 |
| Norma commercial | 170 | 2756 |
| 49.0 IMR 4350 | 175 | 2680 CW |

*CW=Cartridges of the World (5th Edition)*

# 7X61 SUPER

The 7x61 Super—a derivative of the 7x61 Sharpe & Hart—was developed shortly after World War II by Americans Phil Sharpe and Richard Hart from a French experimental cartridge. The Danish firm of Schultz & Larsen chambered its bolt rifle for the new round beginning in 1953. Originally rimless, the 7x61 case was later changed to add powder capacity, whence it

## LOADS

| | | |
|---|---|---|
| 64.2 IMR 4350 | 120 Hornady | 3300 (Hornady) |
| 66.9 H 450 | 139 Hornady | 3200 (Hornady) |
| Norma commercial | 154 | 3061 CW |
| 65.2 N 205 | 154 Hornady | 3000 (Hornady) |
| 62.4 H 450 | 162 Hornady | 2900 (Hornady) |
| 58.3 IMR 4350 | 175 Hornady | 2800 (Hornady) |

*CW=Cartridges of the World (5th Edition)*

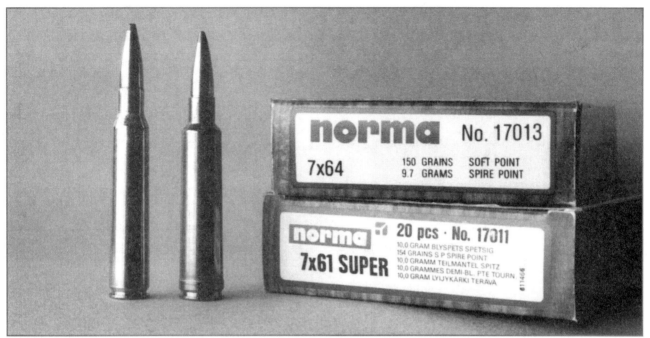

The 7x64, developed during World War I, is almost identical to the later .280 Remington. The 7x61 Super predates the similar 7mm Remington Magnum

became the belted 7x61 Super. Shorter than the 7mm Remington Magnum, this cartridge delivers about 100 fps less velocity, edging the .280 Remington by about the same margin. Norma sells loaded ammunition with a 154-grain softpoint at over 3000 fps. Although the 7x61 Super is an efficient 7mm with power aplenty for elk hunting, no U.S. rifles are currently chambered for it.

## 7.5X55 SCHMIDT-RUBIN

When it was first adopted in 1889 by the Swiss army for its straight-pull Schmidt-Rubin bolt rifle, the rimless 7.5x55 featured a paper-patched 210-grain bullet pushed at less than 2000 fps by a light charge of semi-smokeless powder. In 1911 the Swiss government issued ammunition with 174-grain spitzer boat-tails, thereby increasing bullet diameter to .308 (7.62mm). Breech pressures were also boosted from 37,000 PSI for the 190-grain bullet to 47,500 PSI for the 174. The front-locking Model 1911 (and later the 31 Schmidt-Rubin) rifles were a vast improvement over the 1889, with its long receiver, bulky magazine and rear locking lugs. Modern 7.5x55 ammunition imported by Norma is for the late actions *only* (Schmidt-Rubin bolts do not fully support the case head, so ruptures are particularly dangerous).

## LOADS

| | | |
|---|---|---|
| **46.0 IMR 4895** | *130 Hornady* | *2900 (Hornady)* |
| **46.1 IMR 4064** | *150 Hornady* | *2800 (Hornady)* |
| **46.2 IMR 4320** | *65 Hornady* | *2700 (Hornady)* |
| **Norma commercial** | *180* | *2651 CW* |
| **49 IMR 4350** | *200* | *2460 CW* |

*CW=Cartridges of the World (5ᵗʰ Edition)*

# 7.62X54R RUSSIAN

The Russian government adopted the 7.62x54R as its military cartridge in 1891 for use in the Mosin-Nagant bolt rifle of that same year. The performance of this cartridge received a boost in 1909 with the substitution of a 150-grain spitzer bullet. During World War II Winchester, Remington and New England Westinghouse all manufactured Mosin-Nagant rifles, many of which were later sold as surplus to the public. Until about 1950, Remington loaded its 7.62x54R cartridges with 150-grain Bronze Points. Though the original Russian specifications call for .310-diameter bullets, .308s generally give acceptable accuracy. In 1943 this cartridge was supplanted by the 7.62x39 M43, a rimless, compact round designed for self-loading rifles. Ballistically, the 7.62x54R ranks with the .308 Winchester, performing well for the Russians as a target cartridge.

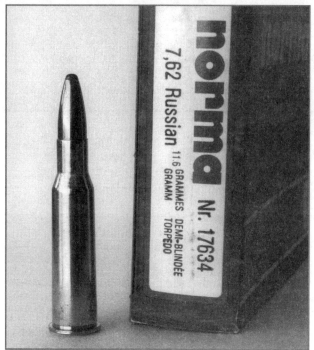

Norma's 7.62 Russian "Torpedo" is ballistic twin to the .308 Winchester.

## LOADS

| | | |
|---|---|---|
| 53.7 IMR 4320 | 130 Hornady | 3000 (Hornady) |
| Norma commercial | 150 | 2953 CW |
| 51.0 IMR 4064 | 150 Hornady | 2858 (A-Square) |
| 54.2 Win. 760 | 165 Hornady | 2700 (Hornady) |
| Norma commercial | 180 | 2575 CW |
| 45 IMR 4350 | 220 | 2350 CW |

*CW=Cartridges of the World (5ᵗʰ Edition)*

# 7.65X53 ARGENTINE MAUSER

Paul Mauser designed the 7.65x53 for the first smallbore, smokeless-powder military rifle produced by the Mauser firm: the Model 1889. Belgium bought manufacturing rights to the rifle and built improved versions into the 1930s. The 7.65x53 appeared in Models 1890 and 1891 Mausers that went to Argentina, Bolivia, Ecuador, Peru, Columbia and Turkey. Its .313 bullet diameter limited ammunition options, but Remington and Winchester both loaded the round—which became known as the 7.65 Argentine—until shortly before World War II. Remington chambered its Model 30 rifle in 7.65x53, Winchester its Model 54. Norma still imports Boxer-primed ammunition, and handloaders can use .311 bullets designed for the .303 British. Like the 7.62x54R, this cartridge is adequate for all deer-size game.

| | LOADS | |
|---|---|---|
| 44.1 IMR 4064 | 150 Hornady | 2700 (Hornady) |
| Norma commercial | 150 | 2661 CW |
| 46.9 H 380 | 174 Hornady | 2600 (Hornady) |
| 45.0 IMR 4895 | 174 | 2590 CW |
| Norma commercial | 180 | 2592 CW |

*CW=Cartridges of the World (5ᵗʰ Edition)*

# 7.7X58 JAPANESE ARISAKA

In 1939 the Japanese army replaced the 6.5x50 Arisaka cartridge and Model 38 rifle with the more potent 7.7x58 Arisaka in the new Model 99. Later, during World War II, both cartridges were pressed into service. As with the .303 British, the 7.7 Arisaka used .311-diameter bullets, and these two rounds were ballistic twins. The availability of cheap surplus rifles made this cartridge somewhat popular in the U.S. for a time, but neither the Model 38 nor the 99 could compare in looks, quality or ease of conversion with a Mauser or Springfield. No commercial American rifles have ever been chambered for the 7.7x58 Arisaka; but Norma continues to import Boxer-primed 7.7 cartridges.

| | LOADS | |
|---|---|---|
| Norma commercial | 130 | 2953 CW |
| 41.0 IMR 3031 | 150 | 2680 CW |
| 54.3 IMR 4350 | 150 Hornady | 270 (Hornady) |
| Norma commercial | 180 | 2493 CW |

*CW=Cartridges of the World (5ᵗʰ Edition)*

# 9.3X57 MAUSER

Sometime around the 1900s, the 9.3x57 Mauser began life as a sporting round. Like the 9x57 Mauser, it derives from the 8x57, which was introduced as a military round back in 1888. The 9x57 became reasonably popular even in the U.S., where Winchester chambered its Model 54 and a few (now coveted) Model 70s for the cartridge (Remington also offered it in the Model 30 bolt rifles). American ammunition companies even loaded the 9x57 until the mid-1930s. Unfortunately, the 9.3x7 has a thin history in the U.S. While it has been chambered in Mauser and Mannlicher hunting rifles, the cartridge has never been offered in a commercial American rifle. Oddly enough, Norma markets 9.3x57 ammunition —but not 9x57. The 9.3 cartridge mirrors the .358 Winchester in performance and is a fine choice for close-cover hunting of deer and elk.

| | LOADS | |
|---|---|---|
| 47.0 IMR 3031 | 232 | 2330 CW |
| Norma commercial | 232 | 2329 CW |
| 43.0 IMR 3031 | 232 | 2329 CW |
| Norma commercial | 286 | 2067 CW |

*CW=Cartridges of the World (5ᵗʰ Edition)*

# 9.3X62 MAUSER

oon after Berlin gunmaker Otto Bock designed the 9.3x62 around 1905, it was promptly chambered in sporting rifles built on the 1898 Mauser action, becoming an instant favorite with farmers and hunters in colonial Africa. It proved so popular and effective that in 1958, when Kenya mandated a .375 minimum bore for the hunting of dangerous game, it exempted the 9.3x62. The cartridge also won plaudits from European hunters who went after boars and stags. Originally loaded with solid and soft-nose 286-grain bullets (sectional density .305), the 9.3x62 was noted for deep penetration. It has the head size of the .30-06 and slightly more capacity, though its case is a millimeter shorter. Proper headspacing may require relocating the shoulder of necked-up .30-06 cases. Speer makes a fine 270-grain bullet that gives the 9.3x62 the smash of the .35 Whelen.

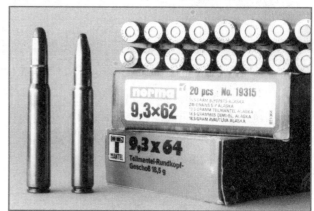

The 9.3x62 (right), which is ballisticaly close to the American .35 Whelen, is considerably less powerful than the 9.3x64 (left).

## LOADS

| | | |
|---|---|---|
| 62.0 IMR 4320 | 232 | 2640 CW |
| Norma commercial | 232 | 2625 |
| 55.5 IMR 3031 | 286 A-Square LL | 2380 (A-Square) |
| Norma commercial | 286 | 2362 |
| 59.0 RL-12 | 286 A-Square LL | 2362 (A-Square) |
| 56.0 H 4895 | 286 A-Square LL | 2356 (A-Square) |

*CW=Cartridges of the World (5ᵗʰ Edition)*

# 9.3X74R

he German 9.3x74R, while slightly longer than the British .400/.360 Westley Richards, yields about the same performance. Fashioned as a cartridge for single-shot and double rifles in the early 1900s, it was an update of the black-powder 9.3x72R. The 9.3x74R sports a slight shoulder, whereas its predecessor's case is straight-tapered. American shooters have had little exposure to the 9.3x74, though in the 1980s Valmet imported the Model 412S over/under in this chambering. It is still available in Europe, principally from Beretta, Bernardelli and Heym. Norma and A-Square supply both cases and loaded ammunition, and Speer sells an appropriate 270-grain .366 bullet. Though its case is larger, the 9.3x74R duplicates the 9.3x62 ballistically.

## LOADS

| | | |
|---|---|---|
| 58.0 IMR 4064 | 270 Speer | 2379 (Speer) |
| 61.0 RL-15 | 286 A-Square LL | 2386 (A-Square) |
| 57.0 IMR 4064 | 286 | 2360 CW |
| A-Square commercial | 286 A-Square DT | 2360 (A-Square) |

*CW=Cartridges of the World (5ᵗʰ Edition)*

# BRITISH AND AMERICAN BIG-BORE CARTRIDGES

F ew double-barrel rifles appear on deer stands come October. Of all the cartridges commonly used for North American big game, only the .444 Marlin and .45-70 qualify as big-bores. But most hunters who are enthusiastic about their sport dream of a chance to hunt dangerous game in Africa. That's where shooting bullets the size of cigar butts claim dominion, and where London-built rifles are more common than khaki bush jackets at Abercrombie and Fitch.

The term "Nitro Express" evolved from the 40- and 50- caliber "Express Train" rifles built in 1856 by James Purdey. Similar black powder Express cartridges followed. Some

made the transition from black to smokeless or "nitro" powders. A full century later, American hunters bound for the veldt had to buy a foreign-made big-bore or satisfy themselves with a .375 bolt rifle.

Then, in 1956, Winchester announced its .458, a compact round made by cutting the .300 H&H case down to fit .30-06-length actions. It was not only America's first short magnum, it had a great deal more power than was evident in comparison with the popular .470 Nitro Express. In fact, it was a ballistic twin to England's double-rifle cartridges, launching its 500-grain bullets at roughly 2100 fps with more than

5000 foot-pounds of muzzle energy.

Professional hunters fell in love with the "four-five-eight" because it was relatively cheap, and because .458 rifles (i.e.; Model 70 Winchesters) cost far less than even cheap doubles. But soon there were grumblings about its inadequate penetration due to erratic velocities. Also, the .458 case, having been stuffed full of powder, compressed mightily under the heavy bullet and proved too small for the job. Any proper solid from a .375, however, seemed to penetrate deeper. It might not strike with the stopping authority of a cast-iron skillet, but a .458 might not produce that either. In fact, it was rumored that early factory cartridges clocked only 1800 fps.

The current crop of .458 ammo is reportedly consistent and potent. In addition, Federal is loading .470 cartridges for those who can afford doubles. The .416 Remington on the 8mm Remington Magnum case, along with the .416 Weatherby on the .378 Weatherby case, have become more popular than some experts predicted. The wildcat .458 Lott—essentially a .416 Remington with no shoulder—has also turned up frequently on safari. A-Square rifles, built on 1917 Enfield actions, are bored for that company's proprietary rounds as well as for commercial numbers.

# .450/.400 NITRO EXPRESS 3" (.400 JEFFREY)

Introduced in England around 1896, the .450/.400 3" cartridge seems identical at first glance to the .450/.400 3¼" which had become reasonably well known as a black-powder round for big game in the Tropics. But the Jeffery case is much heavier, and its rim is thicker (.06 vs .04) so as to withstand the higher pressures of smokeless powder. A 60-grain charge of Cordite kicks a 400-grain .410 bullet out at 2150 fps. While many hunters used the .450/.400 in Africa, it gained fame as a tiger cartridge in the hands of men like Jim Corbett. As with many British big-bore rounds, bullet diameters can vary. A difference of more than .002 between bore and groove diameter is cause for concern. Also in accordance with British tradition, the bullet diameter appears last in the name, unlike U.S. wildcat designations that put bullet diameter first, parent case last.

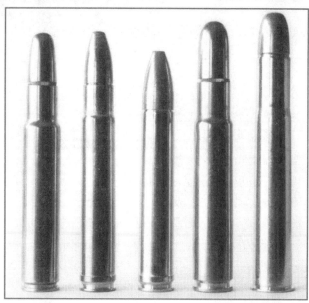

Some top choices for thick-skinned African game include (left to right): .416 Rigby, .416 Remington Magnum, .458 Winchester magnum, .450 Dakota and 470 Nitro Express.

## LOADS

| | | |
|---|---|---|
| 85.0 IMR 4831 | 400 A-Square DT | 2190 |
| 87.0 H 4831 | 400 A-Square DT | 2187 |
| 87.1 RL-22 | 400 A-Square DT | 2172 |

# .416 TAYLOR

When rifle enthusiast, hunter and writer Robert Chatfield-Taylor developed the .416 Taylor on a .458 Winchester case, he sought to generate .416 Rigby performance in a shorter package. While most appropriate powders must be compressed to accomplish this, the .416 Taylor fulfills its mission, pushing 400-grain bullets at 2350 fps. It can, moreover, be used in any action long enough to accommodate a .30-06.

Chatfield-Taylor's untimely death left the cartridge with few champions, however, and when Remington and Weatherby announced commercial .416s in the late 1980s, both had bigger cases. This short .416 is truly useful, though, as an all-around cartridge for African big game. It may lack the stopping power of the big .45s and .50s, but it hits harder than the .375 H&H and shoots almost as flat. It can also be chambered in lightweight, quick-pointing rifles.

## LOADS

| | | |
|---|---|---|
| 75.0 RL-15 | 400 A-Square DT | 2394 |
| 72.0 H 4895 | 400 A-Square DT | 2379 |

# .404 JEFFERY

nstead of being retained as a proprietary cartridge upon its release in 1910, the .404 Jeffery was made available for use by other London gunmakers and by German riflesmiths who carried Mausers. Partly for that reason, the cartridge became the choice of East African game departments for control work. In Europe this rimless round became known as the 10.75x73mm.

The .404 Jeffery offers .450/400 performance in a bolt-action rifle, with a 400-grain .423 bullet exiting the muzzle at 2125 fps. Initially this cartridge was also loaded with a 300-grain softpoint, but that was dropped after it failed on tough game. There's no question that a 400-grain bullet, with its superior sectional density, is the better choice.

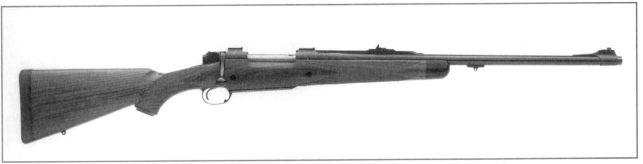

Kimber's Model 89 African-Super Grade has been made in .416 Rigby, .505 Gibbs, .404 Jeffery, and .460 Weatherby.

## LOADS

| | | |
|---|---|---|
| 86.0 H 4350 | A-Square DT | 2221 |
| 72.0 RL-15 | A-Square DT | 2210 |
| 71.0 IMR 4064 | A-Square DT | 2171 |

# .425 EXPRESS

his cartridge is a wildcat developed by Cameron Hopkins in 1986 and based on short-magnum brass. To drive a 400-grain .423 bullet as fast as practicable from a rifle with a standard-length magazine, Hopkins chose the .300 Winchester Magnum case over the slightly shorter .338 and .458. A-Square standardized the cartridge in 1991 and now offers both cases and

loaded ammunition. The 400-grain bullet, traveling just shy of 2400 fps, offers as much muzzle energy as a .300 Winchester hull can bottle. Its short (.309) neck appears long enough to keep bullets in line and seated under recoil. The .425 Express is a useful option for hunters eager to build a heavy-game rifle on a standard-length bolt action.

## LOADS

| | | |
|---|---|---|
| 76.6 RL-15 | 400 A-Square DT | 2399 |
| 73.3 H 4895 | 400 A-Square DT | 2396 |
| 72.0 IMR 4895 | 400 A-Square DT | 2342 |

# .425 WESTLEY RICHARDS MAGNUM

After its introduction in 1909, the .425 Westley Richards became a proprietary cartridge designed for use in magazine rifles. It had a rebated rim (so the head could fit a standard Mauser bolt face), which got mixed reviews from hunters. The top round in the magazine, they complained, had to pop up higher than necessary for an ordinary rimless cartridge. If it didn't, and the bolt ran forward to catch on the protruding case ahead of the extractor groove, then a jam was almost certain. That's an unsettling thought for a big-bore rifle meant for close-up shots on dangerous game. The .425 Westley Richards is a powerful round, though. It can kick a 410-grain bullet down range at 2350 fps, equaling the .416 Rigby with over 5000 foot-pounds of punch. Bullet diameter is .435. *[As of this writing, the .425 Westley Richards Magnum is not offered commercially in the U.S.]*

# .450 NITRO EXPRESS 3¼"

When John Rigby introduced the smokeless-powder .450 Nitro Express back in 1898, it was an updated version of a black-powder round; but it quickly became popular for large African game. A 480-grain bullet propelled by 70 grains of Cordite in the straight, rimmed case churned up almost 5000 foot-pounds of energy at the muzzle. Proper bullet diameter was .458, but with so many different gunmakers building .450 Nitro Express rifles, the bores varied. Another problem arose in 1905, when the British government banned .450 rifles in India and the Sudan. Insurrectionists took to stealing British Martini-Henrys, whose .577/.450 cases would accept bullets from a .450 Nitro. The solution: Ban the .450s and bleed the insurgents of ammunition. When cartridges of other diameters quickly surfaced to equip big game hunters, however, the insurgents stayed and the .45s returned.

| LOADS | | |
|---|---|---|
| 101.0 H 4831 | 465 A-Square MS | 2196 |
| 92.7 IMR 4350 | 465 A-Square MS | 2191 |
| 99.0 RL-19 | 465 A-Square MS | 2186 |

# .500/.450 MAGNUM NITRO EXPRESS 3¼"

In all likelihood, Holland & Holland fashioned this cartridge in response to the popularity of the Rigby-designed .450 Nitro Express. The H&H case was the same length—3¼ inches—but unlike the Rigby round it had a slight shoulder. Both are rimmed cases designed for smokeless-powder loads in double guns and dropping-block single-shots. The .500/.450 Magnum Nitro Express derives from a black-powder case of similar appearance (the Black Powder Express) which drove lighter bullets at lower speeds for about half the 5100 foot-pounds of energy produced by the Nitro Express version. Initially loaded with 75 grains of Cordite pushing a 480-grain bullet at 2175 fps, the .500/.450 Magnum has since faded in popularity and is not available commercially in the U.S.

# .450 #2 NITRO EXPRESS

The 3¹/₂-inch case of the .450 #2 Nitro Express (introduced by Eley in 1903) looks big enough to roll cookie dough. A mild round for its size, it nevertheless launches the same weight (480-grain) bullet as the .450 Nitro Express and the .500/.450 Magnum Nitro Express 3¹/₄". The roomy case allows it to generate the same 2150 fps at lower pressures.

Apparently the switch from black to smokeless powder caused some extraction problems. Before cartridge designers learned how to make thicker and better brass cases, the common cure was to increase case size. The minimal case taper and short, relatively sharp neck make the .450 #2 look modern next to other double-gun cartridges of the day.

## LOADS

| | | |
|---|---|---|
| 110.0 IMR 4831 | 465 A-Square MS | 2201 |
| 117.0 RL-22 | 465 A-Square MS | 2200 |
| 118.5 H 4831 | 465 A-Square MS | 2178 |

# .458 LOTT

Purportedly, the reason Jack Lott developed the .458 Lott was because he thought the .458 Winchester Magnum lacked horsepower. Necked up to take 450-caliber bullets, the new case actually has no neck but is tapered straight from belt to mouth. That may not sit will with shooters who like parallel gripping surfaces formed by the sizing die, not by a bullet seated hard in a belled mouth after the case has

been squeezed undersize. It does offer one advantage, however: you can now fire .458 Winchester cartridges in his .458 Lott. Fortunately, cases are easy to find, form and load. Any rifle action that can swallow a .375 H&H can be chambered for the .458 Lott. One custom gunmaker I know reports that the Lott is among the most called-for cartridges in his safari rifles.

## LOADS

| | | |
|---|---|---|
| 87.0 RL-12 | 465 A-Square MS | 2421 |
| 85.0 H 4895 | 465 A-Square MS | 2410 |
| 84.0 IMR 4064 | 465 A-Square MS | 2387 |

# .450 ACKLEY

When wildcatting was in its heyday, P.O. Ackley put his name on more wildcat cartridges than anyone. He had an experimenter's inquisitive mind as well as great respect

for the practical. Among his most popular wildcats was the .450 Ackley, which derives from the .375 H&H necked to .45 caliber. Ackley then added a 20-degree shoulder to ensure minimum body taper along with parallel surfaces for bullet seating. The neck remains an ample .421 in length. Bullets from the .450 Ackley travel 200 fps faster than from the .458 Winchester Magnum, mainly because there's more room for propellant. The Ackley is easy to fit to any action that can handle the .375 H&H.

## LOADS

| | | |
|---|---|---|
| 86.0 H 4895 | *465 A-Square MS* | *2422* |
| 86.0 IMR 4064 | *465 A-Square MS* | *2404* |
| 88.0 RL-12 | *465 A-Square MS* | *2395* |

# .500/.465 NITRO-EXPRESS

The British ban on all .450-bore rifles in India and Sudan in 1905 gave rise to several new cartridges designed to replace the .450 Nitro-Express 3¼". Among them was the .500/465, a rimmed bottleneck round that grew in popularity after its introduction in 1907. A 480-grain .468-diameter bullet in front of 73 grains Cordite, exited the muzzle at 2150 fps. Like the .450 Nitro Express and other big-bore cartridges of its era, the .500/465 was widely favored in India.

## LOADS

| | | |
|---|---|---|
| 106.0 IMR 4831 | *480 A-Square DT* | *2177* |
| 105.0 RL-22 | *480 A-Square DT* | *2150* |
| 105.1 H 4831 | *480 A-Square DT* | *2146* |

# .470 NITRO-EXPRESS

Probably the most popular of the British big-bores designed for Cordite powder, the .470 became a standard heavy-game cartridge following its introduction by Joseph Lang in 1907. Like the .500/465 Nitro Express, it was designed to replace the .450 Nitro Express 3¼", which was outlawed by the British government in some of its colonies. The .470 uses a 500-grain .475 bullet to generate a velocity of 2150 fps at the muzzle. At 5100 foot-pounds it offers slightly more punch than that delivered by most other rounds of its time—and more than can be expected from factory-loaded .458 Winchester Magnum cartridges. Robert Ruark carried a .470, as have many other hunters since. This rimmed double-gun round is so popular, in fact, that Federal offers it as loaded ammunition.

## LOADS

| | | |
|---|---|---|
| 109.0 R1-19 | *500 A-Square MS* | *2170* |
| 109.5 IMR 4831 | *500 A-Square MS* | *2158* |
| 112.0 IMR 7828 | *500 A-Square MS* | *2112* |
| 109.0 RL-22 | *500 A-Square MS* | *2105* |

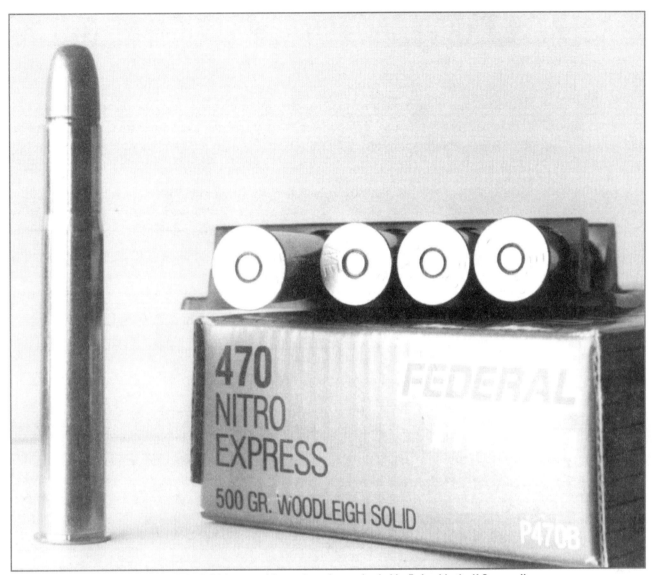

The .470 Nitro Express, once sold only by British ammunition makers, is now loaded by Federal in the U.S. as well.

## .475 NITRO EXPRESS AND .476 NITRO EXPRESS

When the .450-bore Nitro Express rounds were outlawed by British decree in India and the Sudan in 1905, the .475 Nitro Express appeared, along with a bevy of other cartridges. Its 480-grain .476-diameter bullet at 2150 fps produced just over 5000 foot-pounds of muzzle energy, matching Westley-Richards' .476 Nitro Express, which used a 520-grain bullet of the same diameter at lower velocity. Both were factory-charged with 75 grains Cordite. Like that of the .450 3¼", the .475 has a straight, rimmed case, while the Westley Richards round has a slight shoulder. Neither has fared well in competition with the .470 and .475 No. 2 in double guns, or from the .458 and other magnums in bolt rifles. *[These cartridges are not now offered commercially in the U.S.]*

# .475 NO. 2 NITRO EXPRESS AND .475 NO. 2 JEFFERY

Both the .475 No. 2 Nitro Express and .475 No. 2 Jeffery are big-bore solutions to Britain's 1905 ban on .450 cartridges (denying ammunition to colonial insurgents). But while the .475 Nitro Express uses .476-diameter bullets, the No. 2 version fires .483s. An original charge of 85 grains Cordite propels 480-grain bullets 2200 fps, slightly faster than was common for similar cartridges of the era. The .475 No. 2 was also developed by Eley and was not kept as a proprietary cartridge. It became almost as popular as its ballistic twin, the .470 Nitro Express. The .475 No. 2 Jeffery is almost identical to the .475 No. 2 Nitro Express, but it uses a 500-grain .488 bullet. The .475 No. 2 Nitro Express can be fired in a Jeffery chamber because, save for the neck, the two cases are the same right down to the heavy .080 rim. Theoretically, .475 No. 2 Jeffery ammunition will not chamber in a .475 No. 2 Nitro Express; but given a variation in chamber dimensions, such a mis-match could occur. A .488 bullet shoved down a .483 bore could produce dangrous breech pressures.

## LOADS

| .475 NO. 2 NITRO EXPRESS | | |
|---|---|---|
| 112.0 RL-22 | 480 A-Square MS | 2262 |
| 111.0 H 4831 | 480 A-Square MS | 2201 |
| 117.5 IMR | 480 A-Square MS | 2193 |
| **.475 NO. 2 NITRO JEFFERY** | | |
| 113.0 H 4831 | 500 A-Square MS | 2228 |
| 105.0 IMR 4831 | 500 A-Square MS | 2209 |
| 112.0 RL-22 | 500 A-Square MS | 2198 |

# .505 GIBBS

The .505 Gibbs—originally a proprietary cartridge designed in 1913 by George Gibbs of England for use in Mauser bolt rifles—featured a 525-grain bullet at a muzzle velocity of 2300 fps. Resulting energy: over 6000 foot-pounds! Partly because of its great power, and partly because magazine rifles have largely supplanted doubles for heavy-game hunting in Africa, this rimless bottle-neck round has survived to the present. Professional hunters note that it delivers considerably more stopping effect than the .458 Winchester and .470 Nitro Express. Its .505-diameter bullet makes the .505 Gibbs something of an anomaly among big-bore cartridges. Its length (3.850 loaded) and base diameter (.640) limit chambering to Magnum Mausers, the 1917 Enfield and the largest modern commercial actions.

## LOADS

| 133.0 RL-22 | 525 A-Square DT | 2269 |
|---|---|---|
| 132.0 H 4831 | 525 A-Square DT | 2257 |
| 140.0 IMR 7828 | 525 A-Square DT | 2238 |

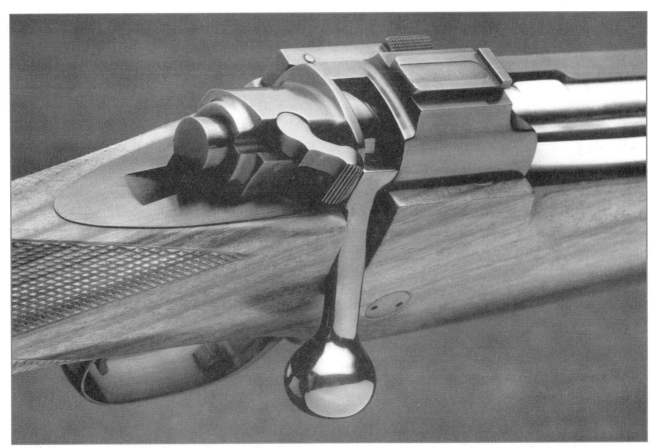

This well-designed Kimber Model 89 features a handy Model 70-style three-position safety, a Mauser-style bolt stop and an integral set of scope bases.

## .500 NITRO EXPRESS "3"

As one of the few professional hunters whose career spanned the final days of the ivory trade and the first years of commercial safari hunting, John Hunter favored the .500 Nitro Express. Its rimmed, straight-taper case evolved in the 1890s from a black powder round developed a decade earlier. A 3¼" version also exists, but most .500 Nitro Express rifles are bored for the 3-inch. Provided the barrels are proofed for high-pressure loads, the 3-inch round can be safely fired in the longer chambers. Launching a 570-grain bullet at 2150 fps with 80 grains Cordite, the .500 Nitro Express delivers 5850 foot-pounds of muzzle energy, not quite as much as the .505 Gibbs but nearly 1000 foot-pounds more than the .450 Nitro Express. The .500's limited popularity has been attributed to a shortage of ammunition and competition from the .505 and .577 Nitro Express.

| LOADS | | |
|---|---|---|
| 115.0 H 4831 | 570 A-Square DT | 2198 |
| 113.0 RL-19 | 570 A-Square DT | 2149 |
| 105.0 IMR 4350 | 570 A-Square DT | 2141 |

# .500 RIMLESS JEFFERY

**W**hile shorter than the .505 Gibbs, the .500 Rimless Jeffery was also designed for bolt-action magazine rifles. Loaded to higher pressures than the Gibbs, it delivers more velocity and energy. With 95 grains Cordite, the original ammunition drove .510-diameter 535-grain bullets 2400 fps, developing 6800 foot-pounds at the muzzle. Until the advent of Weatherby's .460, the .500 Jeffery was the world's most powerful cartridge for repeating rifles. Jeffery obtained the cartridge from a German firm, where it had been developed as the 12.7x70mm Schuler. This .500 has never been common. Jeffery reportedly chambered fewer than two dozen rifles for the .500. Its rebated rim design is shared among English big-bores by the .425 Westley Richards and, to a lesser degree, the .404 Jeffery.

## LOADS

| | | |
|---|---|---|
| 101.0 H 4895 | 570 A-Square MS | 2303 |
| 105.0 RL-15 | 570 A-Square MS | 2291 |
| 101.0 IMR 4064 | 570 A-Square MS | 2274 |

# .577 NITRO EXPRESS

**T**he three-inch .577 Nitro Express case evolved during the 1880s from a shorter hull loaded with black powder. With a charge of 100 grains Cordite, the modern version heaved 750-grain .585-diameter bullets downrange at 2050 fps. It delivers half a ton more energy at the muzzle than the .500 Nitro Express and .505 Gibbs (it even beat the mighty .500 Jeffery). A bullet 25 percent heavier suggests an even greater edge in stopping power. Given its limited versatility, the .577 was surprisingly popular at one time. It is less common in the bush now, with hunters commonly carrying their own rifles instead of depending on gunbearers. Some "light" .577s exist with short chambers intended for mild loads. These, as with rifles proofed for black powder only, do not bring the top prices commanded by heavy .577 Nitro Express doubles built to drop elephants.

## LOADS

| | | |
|---|---|---|
| 163.0 H 4831 | 750 A-Square LL | 2128 |
| 135.0 RL-15 | 750 A-Square LL | 2081 |
| 167.0 IMR 7828 | 750 A-Square LL | 2071 |

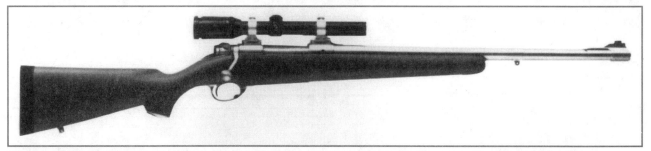

This custom-built, big-bore magazine rifle by Brown Precision has details and features that have proven useful on safari.

# .600 NITRO EXPRESS

The .600 Nitro Express first appeared in 1903 during a decade that produced many new British big-bore cartridges. Until the introduction of the .460 Weatherby Magnum in 1958, the .600 Nitro Express was the most potent commercial sporting cartridge in the world, designed to stop an elephant charge. Its straight, rimmed case bottled 110 grains of Cordite that drove a huge 900-grain bullet 1950 fps. Its muzzle energy of 7600 foot-pounds exceeded that of the more popular .577 Nitro Express (7000 foot-pounds). Unlike many cartridges of its era, the .600 did not derive from an existing round. Its .810 base is nearly twice the diameter of the .30-06's and roughly 25 percent larger than that of a .500 Nitro Express. Predictably, double guns in .600 Nitro Express weigh a lot— and kick hard!

Most game is shot close to the rifle. This mule deer doesn't require much more reach than you get with an iron-sighted .30-30.

## LOADS

| | | |
|---|---|---|
| 165.0 IMR 7828 | 900 A-Square LL | 1951 |
| 159.0 RL-22 | 900 A-Square LL | 1943 |
| 158.0 H 4831 | 900 A-Square LL | 1943 |

# THE BEST OF POPULAR WILDCAT CARTRIDGES

Independent experimenters have been responsible for much of the progress in firearms development. The father of the lever-action repeating rifle was not Oliver Winchester but an inventor named Walter Hunt who, in 1849, patented a crude repeating rifle with a tube magazine. Winchester, blessed with a good business sense, had enough money to capitalize later on the efforts of Hunt and others—notably B. Tyler Henry, Horace Smith and Dan Wesson.

So it has come to pass in the ammunition industry. Roughly half the cartridges adopted commercially since World War II were conceived as wildcats by experimenters who sought better performance—or simply something different to shoot. The .22-250

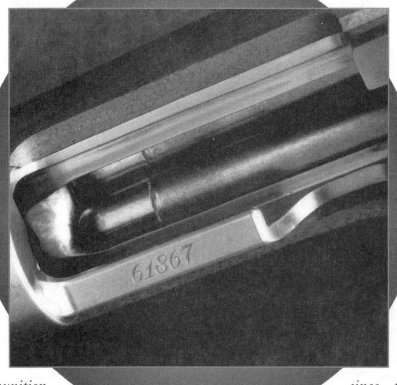

and 6mm Remington, the .25-06, .280, 7 STW .30-.378, .338-378 and .35 Whelen were all wildcats. Some of these experimental cartridges have floundered, naturally. The .270 Titus—a .300 Savage necked down—probably never will reach the length of an assembly line. For some reason, the .338-06 has been neglected as well, though its chances for adoption are considerably better.

The wildcats listed in this chapter represent only a small contingent of the myriad designs that have been chambered since the turn of the century. Charles Newton, P.O. Ackley, Rocky Gibbs and others have ably led the arms industry in its quest for more effective, more efficient cartridges.

# .22 K-HORNET

Shortly after the .22 Hornet appeared in 1930, shooters tried to turn it into something else. Sired by the black-powder .22 Winchester Center Fire, the Hornet offered limited options to wildcatters. But various improved versions popped up, the best-known being Lysle Kilbourne's "K-Hornet" in 1940. Its reduced body taper and 35-degree case neck offer enough additional powder space to boost bullet velocities by 10 percent. While velocities of over 3000 fps are possible with 40- and even 45-grain bullets, best accuracy comes typically at 2800 to 2900. The K-Hornet is efficient, economical, relatively quiet and delivers no recoil. It can also push a 50-grain bullet 2700 fps, matching the .218 Bee.

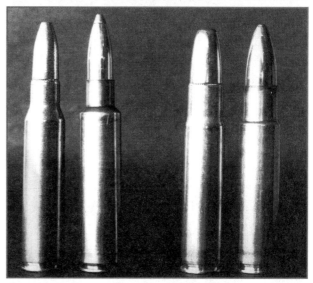

These improved cartridges and their parents include (left to right): .280 and .280 Improved, .35 Whelen and .35 Whelen improved. The increase in case capacity is greatest with the .280 Improved because it has more shoulder to stretch.

## LOADS

| | | |
|---|---|---|
| **11.0 Hercules 2400** | *40 Speer* | *2925* |
| **11.5 Hercules 2400** | *45 Hornady* | *2835* |
| **10.5 Hercules 2400** | *55 Speer* | *2625 (M. Thomas, WC, p.39)* |

# R-2 LOVELL

In 1934 Harvey Lovell developed a wildcat on the rimmed .25-20 Single-Shot case, calling it the .22-3000 Lovell. It became popular immediately. Three years later Harvey Donaldson gave it a sharper shoulder and a new name, the R-2 Lovell (the "R" is for machinist M.S. Risley, who supplied the reamer). Griffin & Howe and J.B. Smith loaded custom ammunition. Each contracted for R-2 Lovell cases with their head-stamps, and the round was chambered in a variety of bolt-action and single-shot rifles. The R-2 (sometimes called 2R) fills the velocity gap between the .218 Bee and the .222 Remington, which appeared in 1950, three years after *American Rifleman* noted that .25-20 Single Shot cases were to be discontinued. The R-2 Lovell floundered in the wake of the .222 but remains an accurate, useful wildcat.

## LOADS

| | | |
|---|---|---|
| **16.0 IMR 4198** | *50 Sierra* | *2935* |
| **19.5 N 201** | *50 Sierra* | *3042* |
| **18.0 N 201** | *55 Hornady* | *2750 (R. Avery, WC, p.94)* |

# .219 DONALDSON WASP

When Winchester introduced the .219 Zipper in 1937, it was destined for a short life. The main reason: its chambering in the Model 64, a lever-action, tube-fed rifle that was ill-suited for scope use. But the case design itself didn't make sense either. Like its parent—the .25-35—the Zipper has a long shoulder and pronounced body taper. Though it did feed smoothly through the 64, shooters wanted a cartridge for single-shots. They got it during the 1940s when Harvy Donaldson introduced the Wasp, a shortened, blown-out Zipper with a 30-degree shoulder. While not more potent than the Zipper, the Wasp is more efficient with propellants of medium burn rate (like IMR 3031 and 4320). More important, it proved accurate in the rifles chambered for it by wildcatters who didn't mind trimming and fire-forming cases.

## LOADS

| | | |
|---|---|---|
| 30.0 IMR 4320 | 45 Hornady | 3700 |
| 31.0 H 380 | 50 | 3567 CW |
| 28.3 IMR 4895 | 55 Hornady | 3400 |
| 26.6 IMR 4064 | 60 Hornady | 3200 (Hornady) |

*CW=Cartridges of the World (5th Edition)*

# .22/.243 (AND .22 CHEETAH AND .220 JAYBIRD)

This cartridge took shape in the early 1960s, when Paul Middlested developed a .22 cartridge for long shooting at slender West Coast ground squirrels. He needed one that would handle the heavy bullets needed to buck wind but still give half-minute accuracy. Accordingly, he necked down the .243 Winchester case to .224 and gave it a 30-degree shoulder to form one of the first .22/.243 wildcats. Jim Carmichel followed with the .22 Cheetah and Kenny Jarrett with the .220 Jaybird, both in the 1980s. Only slight differences exist among these three .22s, which hold slightly more powder than the .220 Swift. The high ratio of case capacity to case diameter in a .243 mandates slow powders, while heavy bullets require at least a 1-in-12 rifling pitch. For bullets heavier than 70 grains, a 1-in-10 twist works best. The .22/.243 matches the Swift for speed and can be chambered in any short-action rifle.

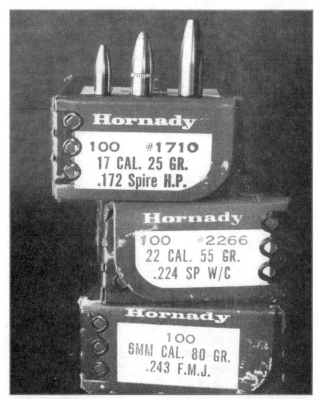

These bullets are all meant for small critters and fast cartridges.

## LOADS

| | | |
|---|---|---|
| 47.0 H 4350 | 55 | 3981 (Hodgdon for .220 Jaybird) |
| 48.0 IMR 7828 | 60 | 3811 (Hodgdon for .220 Jaybird) |
| 47.0 H 4831 | 60 | 3772 (Hodgdon for .220 Jaybird) |
| 44.0 IMR 4831 | 68 | 3602 (Hodgdon for .220 Jaybird) |
| 44.1 IMR 4350 | 72 | 3575 (J. Mason, WC, p. 145) |
| 45.0 N 205 | 76 | 3444 (J. Mason, WC, p. 145) |

# 6X47

The .222 Remington Magnum failed as a prototype military round in the 1950s because it was too long for the self-loading mechanisms army ordnance engineers wanted at the time. After its commercial release in 1958, the cartridge drew modest attention from varmint shooters; but the .222 beat it at the bench thanks to an eight-year head start. The .222 Magnum died after the Army adopted the shorter 5.56x45 M193 Ball Cartridge in 1964. Flooding civilian markets as the .223, the 5.56x45 case is 2mm shorter than the .222's. The .222 Magnum's 47mm case appealed more to wildcatters who sought a mild, efficient 6mm. The 6x74 proved an effective mid-range varmint round; indeed, until the 6mm PPC came along in the late 1970s it won steadily at benchrest matches. With Nosler's 85-grain Partition, it even served well for big game hunting. Remington chambers it in its custom shop Model 40x target rifle, and Kimber once offered a 6x47 Model 84.

## LOADS

| | | |
|---|---|---|
| 30.5 BL-C(2) | 60 | 3233 (Hodgdon) |
| 28.0 H 322 | 70 | 3116 (Hodgdon) |
| 28.1 H 335 | 75 Hornady | 2940 (C. Hunt, WC, p. 176) |
| 28.2 H 335 | 80 Speer | 2825 (C. Hunt, WC, p. 170) |

# 6mm INTERNATIONAL

Winchester's adoption of Warren Page's .243/.308 wildcat in 1955 satisfied most hunters who pined for an open-country deer cartridge that could be used in the 'chuck pasture as well. The .244 (later 6mm) Remington appeared about the same time. Seated to clear short magazines, its bullets ate up the greater powder capacity

## LOADS

| | | |
|---|---|---|
| 37.0 IMR 4064 | 70 Nosler | 3330 |
| 36.0 Win. 748 | 80 Super | 3144 |
| 35.0 Win. 748 | 87 Hornady | 2913 |
| 35.1 Win. 748 | 100 Hornady | 2839 (G. Matthews, WC, p. 200) |

of the .257 Roberts parent case. Some wild-catters, however, had no use for more case capacity than the .250 Savage offered. In its several guises as the 6mm International, the 6mm/.250 probably dates back to Charles Newton, who developed the .250 for Savage before World War II. Necking down the .250 produces an efficient short-action deer cartridge with less blast and almost as much authority down-range as the .243. Loads listed are for a slightly modified International fashioned by Australian Greg Matthews as a cartridge for culling kangaroos.

These commercial cartridges owe their origins to wildcatters (left to right): .250 Savage, .243 Winchester, .257 Roberts, 6mm Remington, .25-06 Remington

## .25-35 TOMCAT

Most wildcat cartridges are designed to improve ballistic performance, but some give much more improvement than others. The .25-35 Tomcat has much greater capacity than a .25-35 case. By blowing out the body almost straight to a 35-degree shoulder and shortening the neck to .287, wildcatter Francis Sell gave the Tomcat a case capacity of 38.5 grains (water). Chambered in a Marlin 336 lever-action, it is ideal for deer hunting in heavy cover; and cases were easy to form from .30-30 brass. When breech pressures are kept to levels suitable for rear-locking lever guns, the .25-35 Tomcat generates almost as much velocity and energy with a 117-grain bullet as do standard (not +P) factory loads for the .257 Roberts. It is a pleasant round to shoot.

### LOADS

| | | |
|---|---|---|
| 31.0 IMR 4064 | 117 Hornady | 2650 |
| 32.0 IMR 4320 | 117 Hornady | 2600 |
| 30.0 IMR 4064 | 117 Hornady | 2585 (F. Sell, WC, p. 273) |

## .25 SOUPER

Sometime in the 1950s, Warren Page and Fred Huntington, apparently thinking the 6mm was more newsworthy than a short, high-velocity .25, necked the .308 Winchester case to .243. After all, shooters already had the .257 Roberts, and wildcatters had been forming .26-06 cases since the 1920s. Besides, the smaller bore lent itself more readily to bullets for long-range varmint shooting. Ignoring the .25 bore, Winchester and Remington adopted the .243/.308 and .243/.257 wildcats as the .243 and .244 Remington. The .257/.308, or .25

Souper, remains obscure, but it's still among the most useful of small-bore wildcats and more efficient than the .243. As such, it is more effective on deer because it can handle heavier bullets. The .25 Souper is easy to form and a better fit in short actions than the .257 Roberts. Ballistically, it matches the Roberts and comes within 100 fps of the .25-06.

| LOADS | | |
|---|---|---|
| 43.0 H 4831 | 87 Hornady | 3448 |
| 42.0 IMR 3031 | 87 Hornady | 3445 |
| 44.0 RL-15 | 87 Hornady | 3399 |
| 48.0 RL-19 | 117 Sierra | 3029 |
| 40.0 RL-15 | 117 Sierra | 2929 (A-Square) |

## .257 ROBERTS IMPROVED (AND .25 KRAG IMPROVED)

In 1934 Remington adopted (with slight modifications) Ned Roberts' .25/7x57 wildcat. Until Winchester and Remington came out with flatter-shooting 6mm cartridges in 1955, the .257 Roberts held sway as an ideal big game and/or varmint round. To approach .25-06 velocities while staying with short-action rifles and the milder blast of the .257, shooters put postwar powders to use in a blown-out, sharp-shouldered Roberts. Concurrently, single-shot enthusiasts reconfigured the wildcat .25 Krag. The rimless Roberts became the most popular of the two improved cartridges because it was designed for bolt-action rifles. But powder capacities are nearly identical, and in actions of equivalent strength performance remains the same. The .257 Improved is best served in magazines built for the 7x57, where bullets needn't be seated deep. Ballistically, this cartridge almost matches the .25-06.

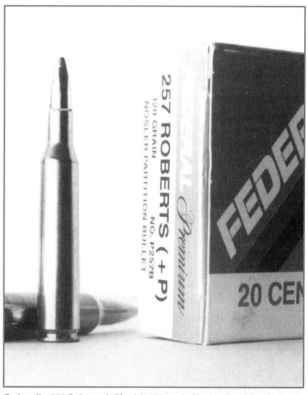

Federal's .257 Roberts (+P) with 120-grain Nosler Partition bullet.

| LOADS | | |
|---|---|---|
| 52.0 IMR 4064 | 60 Hornady | 3853 |
| 52.0 H 414 | 87 Remington | 3412 |
| 53.0 IMR 4350 | 100 Sierra | 3311 |
| 53.1 N 205 | 120 Hornady | 3087 (D. Zutz, WC, p. 285) |

# 6.5 REDDING

The .308 Winchester case offers plenty of strength for high-velocity loads and a capacity that's ideal for wildcatting to medium-bore rounds for short-action rifles. Among the most useful of the myriad wildcats derived from this case is the .264/.308 Improved or 6.5 Redding--named for the New York die and reloading tool company. Redding's Richard Beebe gave the case a 30-degree shoulder and minimum body taper. Necking down .308 brass is easy, but sometimes thick neck walls result, a problem avoided by necking up .243 cases. For open-country deer hunting, the 6.5 Redding is a shade better than the .257 Improved. It can drive 120-grain bullets as fast and can handle the heavier 140-grain spitzers with their higher ballistic coefficients. The emergence of the .260 Remington promises factory loads for shooters in search of a .264/.308. The Remington case and shoulder have more taper than the .270 Redding.

The .243 Winchester necked up to 6.5mm (left) is essentially the .260 Remington and only a fire-forming away from becoming a 6.5 Redding (right).

## LOADS

| | | |
|---|---|---|
| 44.0 H335 | 85 Sierra | 3450 |
| 42.5 AA 2230 | 100 Hornady | 3120 |
| 43.0 Win 748 | 100 Hornady | 3120 |
| 42.0 IMR 4895 | 120 Speer | 2970 |
| 40.0 H335 | 120 Sierra | 2940 |
| 46.5 IMR 4350 | 125 Nosler | 2910 |
| 48.0 H4831 | 129 Acme | 2890 |
| 46.5 RL-19 | 140 Hornady | 2740 |

# 6.5/06 (AND 6.5/284)

Few 6.5mm cartridges have originated in the U.S., though they've proliferated in other countries, notably Japan, Italy and Sweden. Favored for military rounds early in this century, 6.5mm bullets also turned up in Europe in sporting cartridges (the 6.5x68 Schuler, for example). In the U.S., Charles Newton offered the first commercial 6.5 or .264 cartridge—his .256 Newton—but World War I scuttled his plans for a .256 rifle. Half a century elapsed before

Winchester brought out its .264 Magnum. The 6.5/06 is now an old wildcat that excels as a long-range deer cartridge. Its 120-grain bullet can be driven faster than bullets of the same weight from a .25-06, and its 140-grain spitzers boast higher ballistic coefficients than the .270's. The short-action .284 case has about the same capacity as the .30-06, and when necked to .264 has become a favorite among 1000-yard target shooters and hunters alike.

| LOADS | | |
|---|---|---|
| 58.0 IMR 4350 | 87 | 3515 |
| 56.0 IMR 4350 | 100 | 3380 |
| 59.0 H 4831 | 120 | 3256 |
| 58.0 H 4831 | 129 | 3247 |
| 56.0 NMRP | 140 | 2927 |
| 63.5 H 870 | 160 | 2778 (D. Roberts, WC, p. 314) |

# .270 REDDING

When Winchester announced its .270 in 1925, it was essentially a .30-06 case necked down to accept a .277 bullet. Roy Weatherby followed nearly 20 years later with a short, belted .270 magnum, which remains the only .270 cartridge manufactured commercially. Despite a limited selection of bullets, the .270 Winchester flourished (thanks in part to Jack O'Connor's personal endorsement). A few year later, wildcatter Maynard Sorensen necked up the new .243 to .270, but little else was done with his cartridge until Richard Beebe (Redding Reloading Company) put a 30-degree shoulder on a .270/.308 case. The .270 Redding, like the factory-loaded Remington 7mm-08, is a versatile, light-recoiling big game cartridge. Ballistically, it comes quite close to duplicating the .270 Winchester in a short action. Case forming consists of a one-step neck change from the .308 or the .243, then fire-forming.

The .270 Redding with a 150-grain spitzer boattail is a ballistic match for any short-action 7mm cartridge and approaches the .270 Winchester.

## LOADS

| | | |
|---|---|---|
| 46.0 AA 22520 | *100 Hornady* | *3264* |
| 47.0 IMR 4320 | *110 Hornady* | *3185* |
| 50.5 H414 | *130 Speer* | *2977* |
| 51.5 RL-19 | *130 Speer* | *2932* |
| 50.0 Win. 760 | *130 Speer* | *2921* |
| 45.0 IMR 4064 | *140 Trophy Bonded* | *2280 (W. van Zwoll, WC, p. 798)* |

## 7mm MASHBURN SUPER MAGNUM

Perhaps no single development has driven the trend to high-velocity 7mm cartridges more than Art Mashburn's 7mm Super Magnum. While Holland & Holland's .275 magnum (circa 1912) may have sired all existing belted 7mms, American designers took up the .284 bore much later. After World War II Mashburn developed three 7mm wildcats, each from the .300 H&H case but of differing lengths. The shortest, notably the 7x61 that appeared in 1953, performed with the old .275 Holland. The longest, on a full-length case, was much like the current 7STW Mashburn's best design, which he called "Super Magnum," featured a 2.635-inch case with a 30-degree shoulder. His cartridge predated the 7mm Remington magnum and remains the more potent option. The 7mm Mashburn Super case can also be formed from .300 Winchester brass.

Remington's Safari Grade 7mm Remington Magnum with 160-grain Swift A-Frame (left) derives from early Mashburn wildcats. The .280 Remington Improved (right) is almost as potent.

## LOADS

| | | |
|---|---|---|
| 68.0 IMR 4350 | *140 Nosler* | *3314* |
| 75.0 H 4831 | *140 Nosler* | *3305* |
| 69.0 IMR 4831 | *150 Nosler* | *3252* |
| 74.0 IMR 7828 | *160 Nosler* | *3238* |
| 84.0 H 870 | *160 Nosler* | *3205* |
| 71.0 H 4831 | *175 Nosler* | *3008 (B. Hagel, WC, p. 356)* |

# .30-284

When the .284 Winchester arrived in 1963, it was meant to duplicate .270 and .280 performance in a short action. The fat case with the rebated rim held as much powder as a .30-06 and pushed its bullets fast enough to satisfy most shooters. It also provided new wildcatting material, whereupon a flurry of new .284-based cartridges ensued, with the 6mm/.284 becoming quite popular. The next-most-chambered wildcat was probably the .30/.284. Ballistically, it can match the .30-06 with light bullets, but short magazines and throats throttle heavy bullets. At 2.170, the .284 Winchester case is only .065 shorter than that of a 7x57 and .155 longer than a .308 Winchester case. A 7x57-length magazine and a long throat are needed to realize all that the .30/.284 can offer. Thus modified, a short-action rifle can deliver .30-06 performance with bullets at least as heavy as 180 grains.

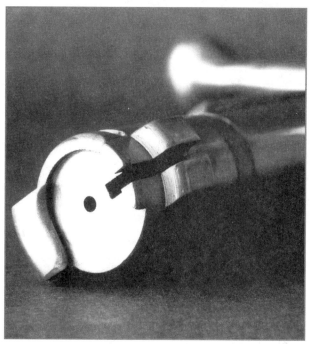

Winchester's early Model 70 bolt face reveals a Mauser extractor, ejector slot and cutaway lip so cartridges can slide up into the extractor claw. Altering .30-06 rifles to accept belted cases requires magazine work and opening up the bolt face.

| LOADS | | |
|---|---|---|
| 60.0 Win 760 | 150 Speer | 3028 |
| 59.0 Win 760 | 165 Speer | 2859 |
| 58.5 IMR 4831 | 180 Sierra | 2728 (D. Young, WC, p. 402) |

# .30 GIBBS

Rocky Gibbs (of Viola, Idaho) began developing wildcat cartridges in the early 1950s, his first success being a .270 based on the .30-06 case (with the shoulder moved forward to increase capacity). The .30 Gibbs followed and became by far the most popular of Gibbs' line, which eventually included eight rounds: .240, .25, 6.5, .270, 7mm, .30, 8mm and .338. The .30 Gibbs has minimum taper, a 35-degree shoulder and a neck barely a quarter-inch long. Cases can be fashioned by employing a false shoulder in a two-step operation. They can also be fireformed directly from .30-06 brass *as long as bullets are seated firmly against the rifling*. Maximum loads in the .30 Gibbs approach .300 H&H in performance. Designed when surplus Springfields and .30-06 cases were cheap and magnums made headlines, the .30 Gibbs offered power-hungry shooters a true bargain.

## LOADS

| | | |
|---|---|---|
| 65.0 H 414 | 150 | 3219 |
| 63.0 Win 760 | 165 | 3106 |
| 65.0 H 4350 | 180 | 3036 |
| 62.0 H 414 | 180 | 2958 |
| 62.1 IMR 4831 | 200 | 2852 |
| 64.0 IMR 7828 | 220 | 2670 (R. Stowers, WC, p. 801) |

# 8mm-06

When World War II ended, returning GIs brought back boatloads of 8x57 Mausers. U.S. cartridge production during the war had been so focused on the .30-06 and .30 Carbine rounds that stocks of other ammunition, including the 8x57JS, had dwindled. Some shooters trimmed and sized .30-06 cases to fit their Mausers, while others rechambered their rifles to the 8mm-06. Similar to the pre-war .333 OKH, the 8mm-06 uses a slightly smaller .323 bullet. Both cartridges—the 8x57 Mauser and the 8mm-06—beat the .30-06 for big game hunting at modest ranges. Although some shooters may reject the 8mm bore because of a limited bullet choice. Speer, for example, makes an excellent 200-grain whose sectional density is slightly higher than that of a 180-grain 30-caliber. From an 8mm-06 it can be driven faster than a 200-grain .30-06 bullet. The only serious fault with the 8mm-06 is that bullets seated to normal depth make the round a bit long for the 8x57 Mauser magazine.

Remington's 8mm Rem. Magnum cartridge with 185-grain Core-Lokt Pointed Soft Point bullet.

## LOADS

| | | |
|---|---|---|
| 53.0 BL-C(2) | 150 Speer | 2981 |
| 51.0 BL-C(2) | 170 Speer | 2762 |
| 53.0 IMR 4064 | 200 Speer | 2647 |
| 62.0 Win. 760 | 200 Speer | 2615 (Speer) |

# .33-308

Perhaps because powder chamber on the .308 Winchester case is relatively small, few wildcatters have bothered to neck it up. Necked-down versions of the .308— including the .22 Cheetah, .220 Jaybird, .25 Souper, 6.5 and .270 Redding—are all useful and abundant wildcats, as are such factory rounds as the .243 and 7mm-08 Remington. The newest in this line of sub-30x52 cartridges is the .260 Remington. Winchester's attempt to interest shooters in a necked-up .308-- the .358--failed. The .358 is, however, a useful round. The .33-308 produces flatter trajectory and offers greater versatility to big game hunters. A 210-grain Nosler Partition at nearly 2600 fps delivers decidedly more punch than a 180-grain factory .308 load at that speed.

## LOADS

| | | |
|---|---|---|
| 48.0 H 4895 | 10 Nosler | 2576 (R. Smith, WC, p. 436) |

# .338-.378 WEATHERBY

Winchester announced our first .33 in 1902 with its .33 Winchester in the Model 1886 rifle. While Great Britain fielded a number of 33-caliber cartridges between 1910 and 1925, bullet diameters were .333. Some English rounds, like the .333 Jeffery, earned praise for their effectiveness, but the .33 Winchester never became popular. In 1958, Winchester offered its .338 Winchester Magnum whose reach and power, coupled with the Model 70 rifle, ensured its success. A few years later, Roy Weatherby upstaged it with his full-length .340 Magnum. Weatherby's .378 Magnum was available by then, and a natural for wildcatting. The .338-.378 edges the .340 by 150 fps, with an attendant boost in recoil. It requires a bigger bolt face than the .338 and .340, which are still more practical and more efficient magnums.

## LOADS

| | | |
|---|---|---|
| 105.0 IMR 4350 | 200 Winchester | 3383 |
| 109.0 NMRP | 210 Nosler | 3330 |
| 126.0 H 870 | 225 Hornady | 3265 |
| 122.0 H 870 | 250 Nosler | 3127 |
| 114.0 H 870 | 300 Barnes | 2803 (B. Hagel, WC, p. 489) |

# .375 WHELEN IMPROVED

When L.R. "Bob" Wallack developed the .375 Whelen around 1951, he named the new round after Townsend Whelen, who had earlier necked the .30-06 to .35. While some shooters have shied away from the .375 Whelen because of its limited shoulder contact, riflemen who have used the cartridge claim there's more than enough shoulder for secure headspacing. The .375 Whelen Improved holds about five percent more powder than the standard .375 Whelen. Its sharper shoulder also provides a more definite stop for the cartridge. Neck expansion is best done in two steps: from .30 to .35 and then to .375. Expanded cases can be fire-formed. With traditional 270-grain soft points and Nosler's 250-grain Partitions, the .375 Whelen makes an excellent choice for close-cover hunting of elk, moose and big bears.

## LOADS

| | | |
|---|---|---|
| 60.0 IMR 4064 | 235 Speer | 2460 |
| 56.0 IMR 4320 | 235 Speer | 2410 |
| 57.0 IMR 4064 | 270 Hornady | 2340 |
| 53.0 IMR 4064 | 300 Hornady | 2140 |
| 52.0 IMR 4895 | 300 Hornady | 2150 (M. Thomas, WC, P. 501) |

## .375 EPSTEIN MAGNUM

The .375 Epstein made its debut at a 1972 World Series baseball game, when a rain delay prompted TV announcer Curt Gowdy to interview Mike Epstein, a member of the Oakland A's. The talk soon turned to Epstein's passion for shooting and reloading. He told about his latest wildcatting project—a .375 cartridge that equaled the punch of a Holland & Holland round but fit in standard actions. Whether or not Epstein was the first to trim a .375 case to 2.605 inches and give it a longer neck than the .375/.338 wildcat is moot; in any event, the results gave Mike what he wanted. The blown-out case has a 25-degree shoulder for easy feeding. Because they are formed from full-length brass, new cases must be turned to reduce thickness at the neck.

## LOADS

| | | |
|---|---|---|
| 70.0 IMR 4064 | 235 Speer | 2963 |
| 77.0 IMR 4350 | 270 Nosler | 2802 |
| 82.0 H 450 | 270 Nosler | 2769 |
| 78.0 IMR 4350 | 285 Speer | 2777 |
| 80.0 H 450 | 300 Honrady | 2660 (M. Epstein, WC, p. 508) |

## .411 HAWK

Bob Fulton, who designed the Hawk line of controlled-expansion bullets, also dabbled in wildcat cartridges. He and Casper, Wyoming gunsmith Fred Zeglan collaborated on several cartridges based on the .30-06 case with the shoulder blown forward. The neck is almost exactly one caliber long. The first cartridge to get any attention was a .338 used by Dave Scovill (editor of *Rifle/Handloader Magazine*), which became known as the .338 Scovill or Hawk/Scovill. The same case was subsequently necked to .411, despite warnings that the .30-06 had barely enough diameter at the shoulder to sustain a .375 neck. But the Hawk is a bit wider there than its parent; and the round headspaces securely. Velocity of 300-grain Hawk bullets fired from a Douglas-barreled Mauser approaches that of the .375 H&H Magnum with bullets of the same weight.

## LOADS

| | | |
|---|---|---|
| 61.0 H4895 | 300 Hawk | 2420 |
| 59.0 H322 | 300 Hawk | 2470 |
| 62.0 H4895 | 300 Hawk | 2480 |
| 63.0 H4895 | 300 Hawk | 2520 |

# .423 VAN HORN

While the rimless .404 Jeffery case has long had a following, it became a popular starting point for wildcat rounds when gunmaker Don Allen first based his Dakota line on the shortened .404. Among the few wildcat cartridges employing the full-length case is the .423 Van Horn, designed by veteran wildcatter Gil Van Horn. In fashioning this round, he moved the shoulder forward and steepened it to 30 degrees; leaving the case mouth unaltered. To headspace fresh cases, bullets are seated against the lands. A more economical method, however, is to substitute a paraffin plug for the bullet, then launch it with 25 grains of bullseye (firing the rifle upward to keep the powder in the case). The .423 Van Horn is an efficient big-bore cartridge for magazine rifles.

## LOADS

| | | |
|---|---|---|
| 101.0 N 204 | 400 Barnes | 2684 |
| 99.0 IMR 4350 | 400 Barnes | 2664 |
| 104.0 Win 760 | 400 Barnes | 2611 |
| 87.0 IMR 4064 | 400 Barnes | 2610 (B. Hagel, WC, p. 553) |

# .458 AMERICAN

Ever since the .375 and .300 Holland & Holland Magnums arrived in the U.S. prior to the Great Depression, shooters have been finding ways to improve them. Roy Weatherby increased their powder capacity by reducing case taper and steepening shoulder angle. When Winchester came out with its short .458 in 1856, shooters necked it down to achieve magnum velocities in .30-06-length actions. Frank Barnes broke with tradition in 1962 when he developed the .458 American by trimming the .458 Winchester case to two inches. It seemed like a throwback to the .45-70, but the .458 case added strength and fed smoothly through bolt-action rifles. Not only does it promise a knockout punch on elk, moose and big bears, it can be chambered in short-action rifles. The .458 American case can most easily be made by necking up, trimming and annealing the .350 Remington.

## LOADS

| | | |
|---|---|---|
| 60.0 N 200 | 300 Barnes | 2355 |
| 52.0 IMR 4198 | 350 Hornady | 2160 |
| 47.0 IMR 4198 | 405 Remington | 1950 (W. Hafler, WC, p. 566) |

The .458 Lott is a wildcat round based on the .375 H&H case. Most rifles require magazine work to ensure faultless feeding.

# .450 ALASKAN

In 1952 Harold Johnson was a hunting guide and gunsmith in Cooper Landing, Alaska, when he necked up the .348 Winchester case to form what he called the .450 Alaskan. Elmer Keith had encouraged Johnson in this endeavor after Johnson had given up on the .30-06 as a stopping cartridge for brown bears. Johnson preferred the .45-70, using Remington's 400-grain, tin-jacketed bullets in a cut-off Model 1886 Winchester (he was partial to lever guns because they could be reloaded while locked and ready). After Frank Barnes developed his flat-nose .45 bullets with .032 jackets for Alaska and .049 jackets for thick-skinned game, the demand for Johnson's .450 Alaskan and Model 71 Winchesters grew. The round is similar to P.O. Ackley's .450/.348 Improved. With 300-grain bullets loaded down, it serves nicely for deer as well and is a favorite among cast-bullet shooters.

## LOADS

| | | |
|---|---|---|
| 66.7 IMR 3031 | *400 Speer* | *2050* |
| 66.0 H 322 | *400 Barnes* | *2018* |
| 63.9 IMR 3031 | *465 A-Square* | *1954* |
| 67.0 Win. 748 | *465 A-Square* | *1887* |
| 63.5 IMR 3031 | *500 Hornady* | *1880 (J. Kronfeld, WC, p. 852)* |

# CHAPTER TWELVE 12

# USEFUL EARLY SMOKELESS ROUNDS THAT DIED

**S**hooters habitually change their minds about what they want from rifle cartridges. The market responds with new shapes and sizes to meet new needs. The results are powders that burn faster or slower, and bullets that open in certain ways or are shaped or jacketed the way contemporary shooters think they should be.

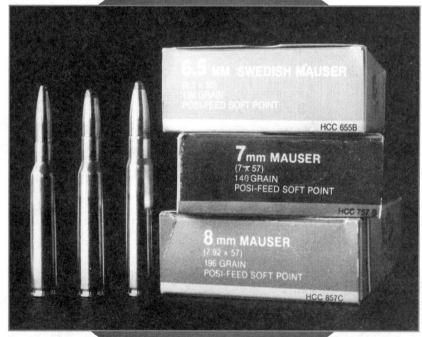

Some old cartridges withstand the pressures of modernization because of their innate utility. For example, the 90-year-old .30-06 still excels as an all-around choice for big game. The .30 Newton may never be produced as Charles Newton designed it, but ballistically it arrived in the form of short, belted .300 wildcats following World War II. Winchester and Norma emerged with their factory versions. Today's shooters want cases without belts, so even the popular .30 magnums are a step behind Newton's original round.

Sadly, many fine cartridges are dropped by arms companies and forgotten. "Death by obsolescence" may mean simply that a cartridge won't perform as well as new ones. Who would want to carry a lever-action .44 rimfire into battle? Or hunt deer with a rifle chambered for the .35 Winchester Self-Loading? At one time, such choices seemed not only reasonable but were highly recommended.

It can be argued that the nature and requirements of battle and hunting have changed. But this explanation falls short. True, the .348, .358 and .405 Winchester cartridges lack the reach of modern hunting rounds; nonetheless, they are still effective at the ranges most game is shot. Modern hunters—enamored of velocity and rimless or belted rounds with straight bodies and long, pointed bullets—simply don't want anything else.

# .219 ZIPPER

**W**inchester announced the .219 Zipper in 1937, the same year the company introduced its new Model 70 bolt rifle. But the Zipper, essentially a necked-down .25-35, had a steeply-tapered rimmed case not well suited to the Model 70. Winchester chambered it instead for the Model 64 lever-action, reserving the 70 for the flashy .220 Swift, which was only two years old at the time. (Oddly enough, the .22 Hornet found its way into the Model 70, which was extensively altered to accommodate it.). The Model 64, a proven deer rifle, was not built for precise shooting with a .22 centerfire. It gave mediocre accuracy and

could not accommodate a top-mounted scope. Marlin offered the Zipper in its solid-top Model 336 until 1961, long after Winchester had dropped the 64. But even with a scope topside, this lever action couldn't tap the Zipper's potential, partly because the tubular magazine required the use of flat-nose bullets. Single-shot rifles—the Winchester High Wall, for example—did better by it; but without a bolt-action home this fine cartridge was doomed. The Zipper was factory loaded with a 56-grain bullet at 3110 fps. In a strong bolt or dropping-block action it almost matches the .225 Winchester and handily beats the .223 Remington.

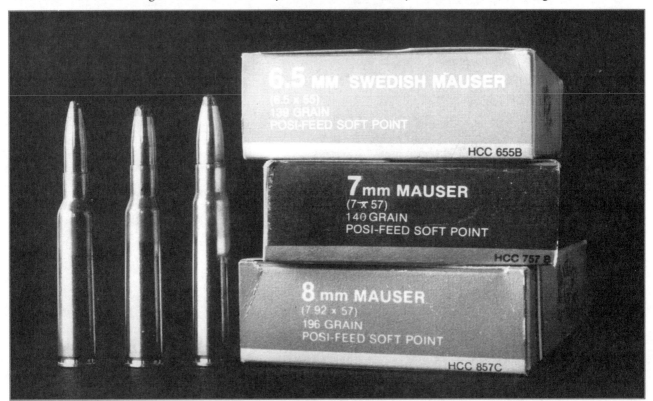

Three turn-of-the-century smokeless military cartridges, from left: 6.5x55 Swedish, 7x57 and 8x57. Bullets under .40 at that time were considered small-bores and those traveling 2500 fps were fast indeed.

# .22 SAVAGE HIGH POWER

*(See 5.6x52R, under Norma Imported Cartridges.)*

# .25-20 WINCHESTER

The .25-20 WCF was developed back in the mid-1890s by Winchester for its short-action Model 92 lever (later to become Model 65). Remington put the .25-20 on its list of chamberings for the Model 25 slide-action; and Marlin chambered it in the Model 94 lever-action and Model 27 pump. Savage also offered the small rimmed round in its bolt-action Model 23. Factory-loaded with 60- and 86-grain bullets, the .25-20 became quite popular in a day when smokeless powder was still new and high velocity meant speeds of over 2000 fps. It sold better than its parent cartridge, the .32-20, and was in fact more useful. Though both saw action as deer cartridges and were even used for elk, neither could be called a big game round—at least by modern standards. The .25-20 was more effective on small game, its bullets flying faster and flatter. Of course, both had round-nose bullets for the 92's under-barrel magazine. At short ranges the 60-grain softpoint at 2250 fps could be more destructive than the 86-grain bullet strolling out the muzzle at 1460. The .25-20 Winchester has turned in good accuracy when chambered in single-shot rifles and in Kimber's bolt-action, the only modern rifle chambered for this turn-of-the-century cartridge. The .25-20 is still commercially loaded.

.25-20 Winchester (WCF) 86-grain

# .25-35 WINCHESTER

Introduced in 1895 as a chambering for the then-new Model 94 Winchester rifle, the .25-35 has not fared nearly as well as the .30-30. To keep breech pressures below 40,000 PSI, its 117-grain round-nose bullet was factory-loaded to only 2300 fps. At that speed the bullet barely beat a 170-grain softpoint from a .30-30. The huge weight difference gave the .30-30 nearly 500 foot-pounds more muzzle energy—a whopping 30-percent advantage. The .25-35 did not shoot fast or flat enough to compete in the 'chuck pastures with centerfire .22s or, later, the .250 Savage or .257 Roberts. In the deer thickets it was handily thrashed by cartridges of approximately the same case capacity but with bigger bullets. Like the .219 Zipper, it was a small-bore round whose design and developers relegated it to iron-sighted lever-action rifles. In a scope-sighted single-shot—a Winchester High Wall, for example—the .25-35 can yield better accuracy and reach much farther with pointed bullets. The relatively weak case won't allow it to be loaded to .250 Savage performance. In Europe, where it is known as the 6.5x52R, the cartridge has been chambered in hinged-breech guns. No commercial American rifles have been offered in .25-35 for 50 years.

# .25 (AND .30 AND .32) REMINGTON

In 1906 Remington introduced a quartet of cartridges for its new Model 8 self-loading rifle. All had modern, rimless cases that subsequently found their way into Remington's slide-action Model 14 and bolt-action Model 30. The .35 Remington prospered and was chambered in many other rifles (it is still offered in Marlin's Model 336). The other members of its cohort—the .25, .30 and .32—have all withered, with only the .30 Remington still being loaded by its parent firm. These three seem to have been developed to compete with the rimmed cartridges Winchester had successfully marketed in turn-of-the-century lever-actions: the .25-35, .30-30 and .32 Special. They offered comparable ballistic performance, and in self-loaders and pumps a rimless round did make sense. But by the time lever-actions gave away any market share, most hunters were looking to more powerful rounds, such as the .270 and .30-06 in bolt-action rifles. No one has chambered a factory rifle for the .25 or .32 Remington since World War II. Interestingly, the .35 was the only member of this sedate group without a Winchester counterpart.

# .256 NEWTON

Just before the start of World War I, Charles Newton developed a series of high-velocity rimless rounds. The .256 was highly promising. A .30-06 necked down and slightly shortened, it was factory-loaded by Western Cartridge Company with a 129-grain bullet at 2760 fps. The .256 Newton used a .264 (6.5mm) bullet. Until Winchester introduced its .264 magnum in 1958, it was the only American 6.5 cartridge loaded commercially. Newton chose the .264 bore because he had planned to build his own rifle and knew the Mauser factory could supply actions with 6.5mm barrels. Alas, only 10 days after he formed Newton Arms in August of 1914, Germany went to war. Newton did, however, persuade Marlin to supply .256 barrels he could install on U.S. 1903 Springfield actions. But then the war escalated, and both the Springfields and the machinery with which to make them became unavailable. Though bad luck pursued him, Newton persevered. His brilliance as a cartridge designer remains apparent. He necked the .30-06 to .25 and called it the .25 Special before anyone even spoke of a .25-06, and his 7mm/06 preceded not only the .280 Remington but the 7x64 Brenneke as well. With Fred Adolph he also fashioned rimless .280, .300, 350 and .400 rounds that hit like magnums. The .256 and .30 are Charles Newton's best-remembered cartridges.

# .280 ROSS

The rimless, steeply-tapered .280 Ross was a high-velocity round designed in 1906 by Sir Charles Ross of Canada. Ross's military rifle featured a peculiar straight-pull bolt that allowed for fast operation but lacked the strength of a 98 Mauser. In addition, the bolt could be assembled so that the rifle fired without locking, causing serious injury or worse. Despite its weaknesses, the Ross rifle saw service in the military, and its fast-stepping cartridge soon caught the attention of hunters. With 140-grain bullets at 2900 fps and 160s at 2700, the .280 Ross seemed a hot number indeed.

Not until 1925, when the .270 Winchester appeared, did a small-bore cartridge kick big-game bullets downrange with such ferocity. As a result, both Winchester and Remington began to load it. But soft-nose bullets then had thin jackets, which meant they'd open reliably on thin-skinned game at impact velocities of 1000 fps or so. Most sporting rounds were showing less than 2200 fps at the muzzle. When the .280 Ross hit deer, it killed like lightning. But heavily-muscled and dangerous game hits at close range often blew .280 jackets on entry, causing only surface wounds. Some hunters lost their lives before their quarry expired. No commercial rifles have been chambered in the U.S. for the .280 Ross, and ammunition production has been discontinued since 1935.

## .275 HOLLAND & HOLLAND MAGNUM

With the base and belt of the .375 H&H Magnum, and a case length of 2.500 like that of the 7mm Remington and .338 Winchester Magnums, the .275 H&H Magnum was clearly ahead of its time. When it appeared in England in 1912, no one had heard of a "short" magnum, and few British cartridge designers gave a thought as to how their ammunition would feed in a l903 Springfield. In 1926 the .275 H&H Magnum finally went to America, where it was loaded by Western Cartridge Company until 1939. Following the .280 Ross, it offered slightly more potential (though 160-grain bullets were factory-loaded to only 2700 fps). The ballistic equivalent of Norma's 7x61 Sharpe & Hart (now the 7x61 Super), the .275 H&H was slightly less potent than the 7mm Remington Magnum. A rimmed or "flanged" version was loaded in England to lower pressures for double rifles, driving a 160-grain bullet at 2575 fps. Though useful (and subsequently duplicated by American wild-catters as the .276 Dubiel and 7mm Mashburn Short Magnum and others), the .275 Holland was never commercially chambered in the U.S.

## .30 NEWTON

The .30 Newton, initially called the .30 Adolph Express, was really designed by gunsmith Fred Adolph, with whom Newton also collaborated on high-velocity .280, .338, .358 and .400 cartridges. These rimless rounds roughly matched the ballistic performance of the modern 7mm Remington, .338 Winchester and .358 Norma Magnums and wildcat .416 Taylor. Balllistically, the .30 Newton, which pushed a 180-grain bullet at 2860 fps, duplicated the .300 H&H. Various parent cases have been named, including the .404 Jeffery and ll.2x72 Schuler, but the various Newtons had slightly smaller head diameters. Newton also developed (with Adolph) a rimmed version of his big .30 for use in single-shot rifles. From the .30-06 case he then formed .25 and 7mm "Specials"—dead ringers for the modern .25-06 and .280 Remington. These were later adapted to single-shots with the .405 Winchester as the parent hull (World War II scuttled Newton's plans for a rifle based on the 98 Mauser when Germany declared war the day before his first shipment of actions was due). Western Cartridge Company supplied Newton ammunition from 1921 to 1938, though not all Newton cartridges were manufactured, and some only briefly.

# .33 WINCHESTER

The Model 1886 Winchester, designed by John Browning, was an elegant but imposing rifle. Its action accepted cartridges as big as the .45-70, and though by modern standards it had only modest strength, shooters of that day considered it stout indeed. In 1902 the Model 86 received a new chambering: the .33 Winchester. This rimmed, steeply tapered round looked like a .30-30 grown up. Its case was slightly longer, but at .610 its rim was larger in diameter than even that of the more powerful .35 Winchester (which appeared at about the same time in the stronger Model 95). The .33 also found its way onto the list of Model 95 chamberings, with the .30-40 Krag, .30-06, .303 British and .405 Winchester. Next to these potent rounds the .33 seemed mild indeed, but its 200-grain bullet loaded to 2200 fps had a considerable edge over the .30-30. The .35 Remington matched it at the muzzle, but the .338 bullet offered greater sectional density. The .33 gained a reputation for sure kills on game as big as elk and was chambered for a time in Winchester's 1885 single-shot. In strong actions its performance can be boosted to equal that of the modern .356 Winchester. Introduction of the .348 Model 71 lever-rifle in 1936 signaled the end for both the .33 cartridge and 1886 rifle, whereupon ammunition companies quietly dropped the round.

# .35 WINCHESTER

Although it was introduced at nearly the same time as the .33 Winchester, the .35 Winchester sports a different case altogether. The rim is smaller, for one, and overall length is greater. It was initially chambered (in 1903) in the Model 95 Winchester lever rifle. Unlike the host of previous Winchesters, whose tubular magazines mandated use of flat- or round-nose bullets to protect against accidental detonation under recoil, the 95 featured a box magazine and vertical stacking of cartridges. The .35 Winchester could have been loaded with pointed bullets; but deferring to the custom of the day, and perhaps to pack more bullet weight into a given overall length, the standard 250-grain bullets were given round tips. Factory loads clocked 2195 at the muzzle—about equal to the speed of a 200-grain .33 Winchester bullet. Resulting energy was 2670 foot-pounds, or nearly 25 percent higher. The .35 Winchester fell well short of matching its successor, the .348 Winchester, whose 250-grain bullet exited at 2350 fps. The .348 appeared with the Model 71 (an improved Model 86) in 1936, the same year Winchester discontinued both the Models 95 and 86—and with them the .33 and .35 Winchester cartridges. The 95 had a massive receiver, but it could not bottle the pressures of Springfield bolt guns, limiting .35 Winchester handloads to 45,000 PSI.

# .35 NEWTON

The .35 Newton was formed in 1915 by necking up the .30 Newton case (introduced two years earlier). Gunsmith Fred Adolph and Charles Newton teamed up once again to develop these and several other cartridges, from .280 to .400. The rimless case, with its base diameter of .524, was about the size of a modern short magnum. Newton was reportedly inspired by the .404 Jeffery and ll.2x72 Schuler, but these rounds have larger case heads and rebated rims. Though various ballistic claims have been made for this round, it can be loaded to match the performance of the .358 Norma Magnum—i.e., a 250-grain bullet at 2800 fps. The .35 proved more popular than the 8mm, .33 and .40 Newtons on the same case, though it was probably not as widely chambered as the designer's big .30. Like the .30 and 8mm, the .35 became an "Express" round for single-shot rifles by substituting the rimmed .405 Winchester as the parent case. Lack of proper bullets and powders put the .35 Newton at a disadvantage during the inventor's lifetime, though he developed bullets that would expand reliably at high impact velocities.

## .38-55 WINCHESTER

The .38-55 began its career in 1884 as a black powder cartridge in single-shot target rifles—the kind used for Schuetzen competition. It was adopted 10 years later by Winchester as a charter chambering in the new lever-action Model 1894 rifle. This cartridge has its roots in the .38-50 Ballard, introduced in 1876, and the longer .38-55 Everlasting in 1881. But those forebears faded after the turn of the century. The .38-55 not only survived the transition to smokeless powder but prospered as a deer cartridge in the 94 carbine, Marlin's Model 93 and Savage's 99. It was also chambered in the Colt Lightning slide-action rifle and the best-known single-shots of the early 1900s. Various factory loadings for the .38-55 pushed a 255-grain bullet at advertised velocities of 1320 to over 1700 fps. In black-powder rifles velocities are best kept under 1500 fps. The .38-55's big bullet made it very effective on game in close cover, although on paper it looks less impressive than a .30-30. Winchester discontinued the .38-55 in the 94 carbine just before World War II. Factory loads were dropped in 1970 but later brought back. The .375 Winchester is a modern version, more compact but also more powerful. Meanwhile, the .38-55 continues to win Schuetzen matches.

.38-55 Winchester 255-grain Soft Points were at one time a favorite of whitetail hunters in the north woods.

# .401 WINCHESTER

In 1910 Winchester introduced its .401 for the Model 10 self-loading rifle, an updated Model 07. With a 200-grain bullet clocking 2135 fps and a 250-grain bullet at 1870, this round delivered nearly the punch of the .35 Remington, though its 200-grain bullets lacked the sectional density of the .35's. The .401 supplanted the company's less potent .351 which had, in turn, put the .35 Self-Loading out of business. The .35 SL had been the original chambering in Model 1905 Winchester autoloaders, but it proved ineffective and was abandoned in 1920—as was the .32 Winchester SL. None of these cartridges appealed much to sportsmen. In Model 07 autoloaders the .351 saw some police and military service, but like the later .30 Carbine it lacked the reach for varmint shooting and the punch for deer hunting. (The .30 Carbine is almost identical to Winchester's old .32 SL). After U.S. firms stopped loading the round in 1957, British and Canadian .351 ammunition became available. Both the Model 10 rifle and its cartridge were officially dropped in 1936, though ammunition remained available until after the war. The .401 was the only cartridge in the Winchester self-loading line that could be considered adequate for big game.

# .405 WINCHESTER

With its rimmed, straight case, the .405 Winchester looks out of place among its turn-of-the-century cohorts. Most new cartridges at that time were of bottleneck designs meant to drive small-bore bullets at high speed with smokeless powders. Winchester developed the .405 for its Model 1895 lever rifle, which also chambered the .30-40 Krag, .30-06 Springfield, .303 British and .33 and .35 Winchesters. It capped the lineup as a heavy-game cartridge, driving 300-grain bullets 2200 fps to deliver 3200 foot-pounds of muzzle energy. Professional African hunters recognized the limits imposed by the .405's low sectional density. The Model 95's low, sharp-combed stock gave the cartridge a reputation for wicked recoil. A few Remington-Lee bolt rifles and Winchester 1885 single-shots also chambered the round, which became modestly popular in England as a double-gun cartridge. In a market flooded with cartridges that duplicate other cartridges, the .405 has few competitors. Maximum-pressure .45-70 loads come close, as will the .444 Marlin with heavy bullets.

Still, the .405 Winchester has a different and appealing heritage. It was one of Teddy Roosevelt's favorite rounds. Not until 1956 did America field another "safari" cartridge.

Peppier cartridges may have upstaged the .30-30 in the field, but it's found a place in competition designed expressly for iron-sighted lever guns.

# PART 3

## EVALUATING HUNTING CARTRIDGES: THE GOOD & THE ADEQUATE

# FROM OLD THUMPERS TO ROCKET SCIENCE

In the fall of 1939 Adolf Hitler was on his way to creating World War II. But in the U.S. people knew little of the German Reich's plans and were content to discount the alarmists. In the Western states, hunters prepared for another elk season, as they still do each October. As far as sporting rifle design is concerned, little has changed since the late 1930s. In fact, modern bolt-action sporters that look and function like pre-war Model 70 Winchesters command high prices from hunters. Optics have certainly improved. Equally significant have been changes in ammunition--not just in bullets and loads, but in cartridge design as well.

During the 1930s, the .30-06 was widely regarded as the best all-around big game cartridge. The .300 Holland had appeared in 1925, but it needed a long action like the expensive square-bridged Mauser. Also known as the "Super .30," this original .300 magnum became a charter chambering for the Winchester 70, which didn't become available until 1937. Before 1939, most American bolt rifles were built around the .30-06 case. Heaps of inexpensive military ought-six ammo and serviceable surplus Springfields made this *the* logical cartridge choice for big game hunters everywhere (the .270, dating to 1925, had its supporters too, especially in the West). A survey of elk hunters conducted by the Washington Department of Game in 1939 indicated that more than 25 percent of them used a .30-30 or a .30

Remington in lever and slide-action-rifles. The '06 followed with 21 percent, and the .30-40 Krag ranked third with a 12 percent share. Only nine hunters, or less than half a percent, recorded rifles chambered for the .270.

Most of the ambiguities can be resolved, however. The .25, .32 and .35 are probably Remington's cartridges, the .33 no doubt the Winchester round chambered in the 1886. The 7mm and 8mm should read 7x57 and 8x57 (the 7.62 is almost surely the old Russian round). The 6mm is the Lee Navy cartridge; and most likely the .220 Swift, .280 Ross and .257 Roberts made the list along with the

The .356 Winchester (left) arrived three decades after the .348 Model 71 Winchester rifle was discontinued. The .348 was not commercially chambered in any other rifle. Though its successor, the rimless .358 Winchester, boasted as much power and was better designed for modern rifles, it failed to win lever-action fans to the Model 88. The .356 is essentially a semi-rimmed .358 and is still offered in Winchester's Model 94.

The .250 Savage, developed by wildcatter Charles Newton around 1912, drove an 87-grain bullet 3000 fps, hence the name .250-3000.

.375 H&H. The puzzlers are the .38-40, .38--55 and the .38-56. This survey occurred, however, before the advent of Weatherby and Winchester magnums. In factory loadings, only the .300 Savage and .300 H&H existed; nearly all the 123 rifles of this caliber were .300 Savages. The Model 99 was very popular then, and Savage's short .300 was for many years its best-selling chambering. Hunters who sought a .300 H&H in 1939 had few rifles from which to choose. Moreover, the belted ammunition was costly.

Interestingly, the top two finishers in the 1939 survey accounted for 27 percent of cartridges used, yet they were less potent than the next two. The .30-30 and .30 Remington do not match the .30-06 or .30-40 in velocity or energy.

Elk hunters surveyed for this book favored more modern cartridges. The top five were: .30-06, 7mm Remington Magnum, .300 and .338 Winchester Magnum and .270. The .30-06 and 7mm Remington finished well ahead of the others, with the .30-06 edging the belted 7mm Remington overall. On the most recent survey, Weatherby's .300 came in a distant sixth.

Do these surveys indicate the preferences of all big game hunters? Or do elk hunters choose differently? A quick survey of the companies that make most of the rifles used by hunters showed the six most popular rounds according to rifle model:

**BROWNING A-BOLT:**

*.30-06, .270, 7mm Remington Magnum, .300 Winchester Magnum, .243, .308*

**REMINGTON 700:**

*.30-06, .270, 7mm Remington Magnum, .243 (Here the .30-06 and the .270 repeat in a different version of the 700, attesting to their overwhelming popularity.)*

**RUGER 77:**

*.270, .30-06, .300 Winchester Magnum, 7mm Remington Magnum, .338 Winchester Magnum, 22-250*

**SAVAGE 110:**

*.270, .30-06, .243, .300 Winchester Magnum, .338 Winchester Magnum, 7mm Remington Magnum*

**WINCHESTER 70:**

*.30-06, .270, 7mm Remington Magnum, .300 Winchester Magnum, .243, .308*

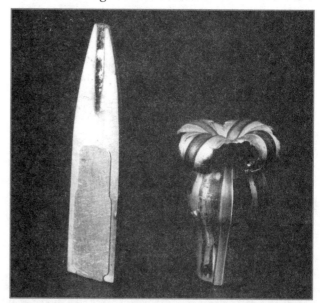

Bullets like Winchester's Fair Safe weren't necessary with black powder cartridges or early smokeless rounds that launched bullets no faster than 2300 fps.

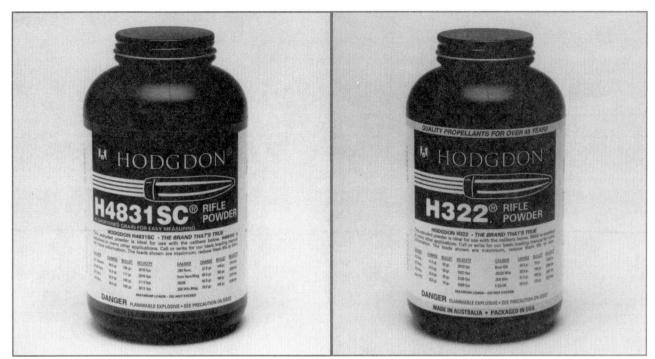

Early smokeless cartridges would have been more effective with modern powders like Hodgdon's H4832SC and H322.

Hunters in these recent surveys have a logical preference for belted magnums over the .243, which appears four times out of five in the manufacturers' "Top Six" lists. The .270, commonly considered a superb deer round (but marginal for elk), predictably finishes stronger in the factory records. The .338 Winchester Magnum, a popular elk number, nets fewer votes as an all-around cartridge; while the .308, which receives surprisingly little support, sells well overall.

In all cases, the .30-06 and .270 took first and second place. In three of the five cases, the 7mm Remington and .300 Winchester Magnums finished third and fourth, and both remaining tallies show one of these magnums paired with the .243. It may be that the most popular cartridges will always be the veterans, and that lower placings in the top five or six are "staging grounds" for the coming generation. Just as the .30-06 in bolt rifles supplanted the .30-30 in lever guns, so the friskier belted rounds are nipping at the heels of the .270 and .30-06.

Cartridge lists evolve like forests, with the dead wood making way for vigorous sprouts. But in examining that list of 1939 cartridges, one wonders why so many hunters of that day ignored the .30-06 and .270 and instead took to the woods with relatively ineffective rounds. Why would 613 riflemen be satisfied with .30-30 performance? Why would 71 hunters choose a .25-35 for elk hunting? And why were 24 hunters toting .22 High Powers, .25-20s and .32-20s? Sixteen of the favored rounds even carried black-powder designations!

Flipping the page of the 1939 report, one discovers that 276 hunters shot bull elk in Yakima County, where the survey was taken. Of the bulls killed, 55 percent were five-points, 26 percent six-points and 9 percent seven-points. In other words, 90 percent of the kill comprised five-point-or-better elk (no antler restrictions were indicated). Unfortunately, the report did not include cartridge data from successful hunters only. The curve in cartridge trends today is definitely moving up the velocity axis. Since Roy Weatherby pioneered the

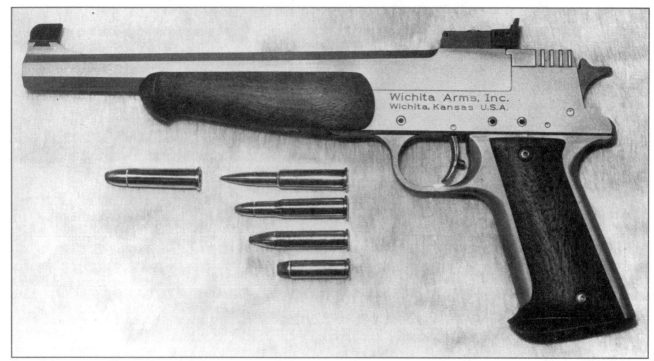

Turn-of-the-century rifle rounds and their progeny are finding a new home in high-performance handguns, such as this single-shot from Wichita Arms.

sharp-shouldered magnum in the early 40s, there has been little change in case design. Benchresters are now keen on short powder columns; but to hold enough powder to match velocities of conventional magnums, a big game cartridge shaped like a bench round would defy staggered columns in existing box magazines.

John Lazzeroni has such a cartridge in his 7.82 Patriot, a 30-caliber round with a squat body that squirts a 180-grain bullet out at over 3,000 fps. The magazine is a straight-column box made just for this cartridge. Cases designed from scratch are expensive, though. Figure at least $60 a box for loaded ammo from a maker like Lazzeroni. After their well-publicized debuts, Weatherby rifles and ammunition remained scarce in the field for some time, largely because rifles and ammo cost more than most hunters were willing to pay. Now that companies other than Norma are loading Weatherby cartridges--and Winchester, Ruger and Remington have added Weatherby Magnums to

their chamberings--these rounds have received a lift in the marketplace.

Popular too are extra-capacity cases based on available long-magnum brass. The 7mm STW and .300 Jarrett hail from the 8mm Remington Magnum hull. Dakota, like Lazzeroni and A-Square and Arnold, has its own high-performance line of big game cartridges. Eschewing the belted case, A-Square's Don Allen chose the .404 Jeffery from which to fashion most Dakota rounds. Allen's shop has also developed a .416 (essentially a .404 necked up) and a .330 Dakota necked to .338. The latter holds 15 grains more powder than the .338 Winchester and matches the .340 Weatherby in performance.

Naturally, flat flight and high retained energy downrange are of little use without accuracy. A pre-war hunter with a .30-30 would be helped only a little if by some magic he could have kicked that 170-grain softnose out the muzzle at 3300 fps. Hunting scopes from the World War II era

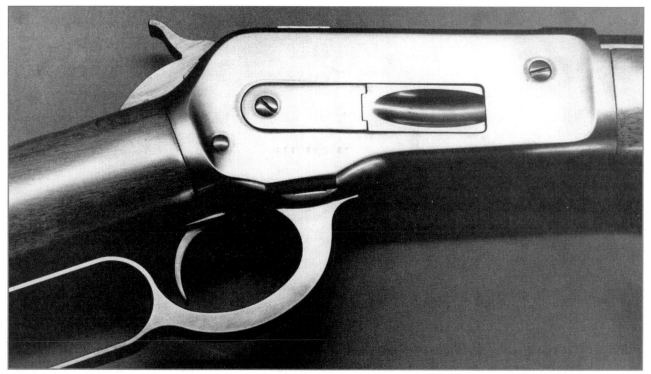
This Winchester Model 86 remains an elegant example of John Browning's genius.

typically had modest power and often fogged. In 1939 engineers at Zeiss were still a year away from their discovery of lens coatings to reduce light loss. Meanwhile, hunters put up with dim, dark images. As scopes improved, shooters chose cartridges to match their eye's extra reach. The popular 3-9x variable is even now being shouldered aside by the 3.5-10 and the 4.5-14. The 6-18x and 6-24x, which used to be relegated to the bench, have gone to the hills with hunters intent on testing the limits of their flat-shooting cartridges.

Surely modern rifles are more deadly than their forebears. But the capability to kill is not the same as success in killing. I've seen hunters cripple an elk with .300 and .338 Winchester Magnums. One hunter shot seven times with a 7mm Remington Magnum to kill one elk, while another used nine cartridges from a .340 Weatherby. In these cases, the animals were well within reach of a .30-06. Higher bullet velocity and more power, with glass that can bring distant animals up close, do not

seem to guarantee success. One reason is only peripherally linked to rifles and ammunition: Game receives more hunting pressure than it did half a century ago. Pressure--not just hunter traffic, but shots fired--teaches animals how to avoid hunters. Low hunter density and shooting limited

The author levers another round into a Winchester 94, arguably the most popular sporting rifle of all time.

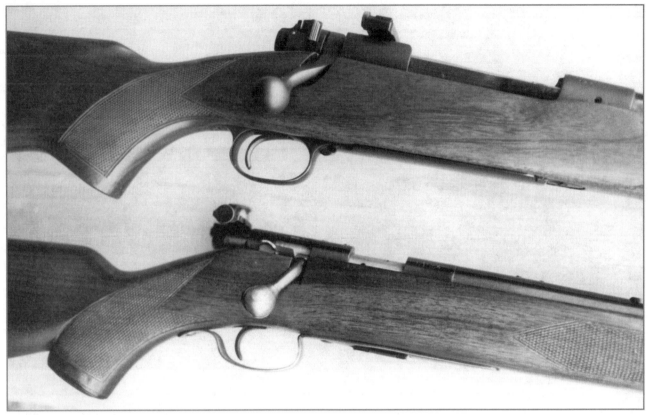

Winchester's Model 70 (top) and rimfire Model 75 marked the transition from lever-action rifle to bolt gun between World Wars I and II.

to dense timber alarms fewer animals. The shots do not echo across canyons, and there are no repeated sonic cracks. Game not downed quickly in the woods is soon out of sight, precluding cannonades that can swiftly consume a box of cartridges.

Another reason modern hunters don't always bring home more game than their forebears is that the rifles and cartridges of yesteryear were, and remain, effective. At woods ranges the .30-30 can kill deer as neatly as a .300 Winchester. Lever-actions may not be as accurate as bolt rifles on average, but for most big game shooting three minutes of angle suffices. The 94-class lever-action carbine and Remington's 141 pump are easy to carry and quick to point.

Iron sights get little praise primarily because most hunters, having grown up with scopes, never practiced with irons. The argument that modern cartridges, rifles and optics allow hits at longer

distances has merit; but open country doesn't mandate long shooting. A few years ago, another hunter and I spied a grand elk on an open hill a quarter mile away. The fellow wanted to start lobbing bullets, but I suggested we sneak. After a taxing stalk, we got within 175 yards. The bull dropped to the first shot. Now that's hunting!

Ballistic comparisons are popular hot-stove fare in hunting camps these days, and in this arena the .30-30 doesn't fare well. At a muzzle velocity of 2200 fps, its 170-grain bullet cranks up a little over 1800 foot-pounds of energy. The flat bullet nose drains energy quickly to 1000 foot-pounds or so at 200 yards. A .30 Remington won't even match that. The .30-06, however, kicks a 180-grain bullet out at 2700 fps, generating nearly 3000 foot-pounds of energy; and at 200 yards there's roughly a ton of energy left, twice the thump of the .30-30. A 180-grain .300 Winchester bullet exits at 3000 fps with 3500 foot-pounds, cruising past 200 yards with nearly 2600. At 300 yards it delivers more punch than the .30-06 at 200, and more than the .30-30 at the muzzle. Zeroed at 150 yards, the .30-30 prints five inches low at 200. Zeroed at 200 yards, a .30-06 or a .300 Winchester will keep its bullets within 5 inches of sightline to somewhere between 260 and 290 yards, depending on the load. Modern rounds surely have more reach.

But some misconceptions persist concerning the energy required to kill big game--and in the way we calculate bullet energy. Foot-pounds, the common measure, give what some would call unfair advantage to rounds that spit lightweight bullets fast, because in the arithmetic velocity is squared. A Keith-style formula yielding pounds-feet does not square the bullet speed. Bullets at modest velocities score better; bullet weight becomes more important. Thus the notion of minimum terminal energy levels bears scrutiny. For deer, 1000 foot-pounds seems about right. For elk, make that 1500. But such thresholds hinge on several assumptions: that all target animals are of the same size and physical condition; that they're struck in the same spot; that they're either pumping adrenaline or placidly chewing their cud or at some physical state in between. It must be assumed, meanwhile that the bullets upset in predictable fashion, and that bullet energy is an adequate measure of killing power.

The fact is, the moment of truth in hunting comprises too many variables that can't be neatly quantified. While the .22 High Power hardly makes the grade as an elk round, elk have no doubt been killed with it. We consider the .458 Winchester Magnum an acceptable cartridge for elephants, yet the ratio of bullet energy to body

The .30-30 (right) first appeared in 1895 as a smokeless powder round in the Winchester Model 94 rifle. The modern .307 (left) and .356 Winchester cartridges are more powerful but still not as popular.

Winchester's .32-20 has been chambered in both rifle and handgun.

weight doesn't match the ratio of .22 Long Rifle energy to the weight of a big whitetail. Bullet enthusiasm absorbed in thick shoulder muscle can't be used to destroy vitals. Energy spent beyond the off-side ribs in a pass-through is wasted. A bullet that shatters, or one that doesn't open, squanders energy.

The .30-30 and its kin use bullet energy efficiently. Modest velocity, combined with flat or round bullet tips, yields predictable expansion. The bullets typically dump all or most of their kinetic energy deep inside. Their black powder predecessors proved deadly, despite even lower velocities, partly because their fat bullets plowed a wide path without perfect expansion. Heavy as well, these bullets had plenty of inertia left over to aid penetration.

The main reason pre-war cartridges filled freezers probably had nothing to do with those cartridges directly. It may be that the riflemen who used them were simply better hunters. They surely did not rely on their equipment to the extent that modern hunters do. Their rifles did not wear tripods and scopes with bullet-drop compensators. They had no laser rangefinders. Limited to shots within 200 yards, they hunted as

if more distant game was safe. When they spotted an animal far away, they got closer. Often they were able to close to within effective range. These days, shooting is long even when it doesn't have to be, simply because the equipment has more perceived capabilities.

A hunter aiming at a buck 150 yards away with a .30-30 may be more apt to kill that deer than another hunter firing a flat-shooting bullet from 300 steps. Human variables, not the innate properties of rifle and cartridge, determine the results of almost every shot taken at big game. An accomplished marksman, restricted by certain limits imposed by his equipment and ability, can kill no matter what his choice of cartridge.

In the Canadian North, Inuit hunters still depend on iron-sighted .30-30s to shoot caribou on treeless tundra. I saw one Inuit kill six caribou in only a few hours with a .22 rimfire rusted from canoe spray and wearing crude open sights. True, the same task could have been accomplished more efficiently with a scope-sighted centerfire. but this hunter's skill in finding and stalking game, plus close familiarity with his rifle, kept the family in meat.

Post-war developments in sporting rifles, optics and ammunition have given hunters more than they need to succeed. But just as the automobile keeps us from walking our legs into shape, so far-reaching rifles can cause still-hunting, stalking and gun-handling skills to atrophy. The fellow who uncased his .30-30 at trailhead in the blush of an October dawn back in 1939 may have wished for a .30-06. But as he slipped those rimmed cartridges into the loading gate, he may also have thanked his lucky bunions that he carried a modern carbine chambered for a high-velocity round with nearly six times the muzzle energy of his partner's .32-20.

# THE .30-06: STILL UNBEATABLE?

We snaked along the coulee bottom, out of sight of the elk on the hillside. We saw at least two, but the brush was thick enough to have hidden others. We owned the wind, but a low red sun bored through our binoculars. We would judge the bull up close. Just before we eased around the coulee's last fold, I signaled Jack to check his chamber. A seasoned hunter, he didn't have to be told. The bolt closed noiselessly.

But suddenly, above us, branches popped. We gaped as a small entourage of mule deer bounced toward the rim. How could I have missed that gang in my reconnaissance? Worried that their commotion had spooked the elk, Jack and I scrambled up a rise until we could see the distant slope. Still there—but three bulls now. The top one was just what we'd hoped for.

Jack took his time, wrapping up in his sling, balling up in a sitting position best described as a between-the-rock-and-cactus-on-a-pebbly-side-hill-pointing-up-at-a-browbanging-angle pose. Then his Browning went to sleep. I held my glasses still with one hand, covering my rifle-side ear with the other. The .30-06 still made my head ring. It is, I was reminded, a powerful cartridge.

As expected, a solid "thwuck" bounced back. The two lower elk froze, the bull upslope staggered. Then the stricken animal backed downhill, tottering. It lunged to keep its footing, reared, then fell over backward into a serviceberry bush and died.

Jack pocketed the empty, grinned and shook my hand. We each took a guess at the range, then started pacing as the two remaining elk made dust down-canyon. I counted 210 steps. We talked "hunter-talk" all during the post-mortem: sun in the eyes, an imminent thermal switch, the deer, the uphill shot. It was not all as hard as we made it out to be, but I find that dead bulls elicit justifica-

The author shot this mule deer in eastern Washington with a .30-06 Model 70 Winchester.

Winchester's Model 95 was for a long time the only lever-action rifle chambered for the powerful .30-06. Its vertical magazine allowed the use of pointed bullets to tap the round's long-range potential.

tion. I flatly told Jack that I like people who can assassinate elk. "Not everybody makes the grade," I reminded him. "Lots of hunters think shooting should be sport too. Uh-uh. You hunt tough country, like we just did. You set a standard and stick to it. You glass and hike when neither is fun anymore, and when you find a big bull you do all the right things getting close it. Then you kill it."

Some hunters say the .30-06 is marginal for elk, that it lacks the muscle for tough angles and long yardage. Jack and I disagree. The .30-06 is not only a versatile round, it still goes elk hunting more often than any other cartridge. Some years ago, as I lay down on a cold rock high on a mountain, I tried to steady the crosswire of my scope on a deer standing in the canyon shadows far below. It was a long shot. I held off a bit for the soft north breeze. When the .30-06 bucked, the deer raced into the timber. Some

minutes later I was on its track, and in short order I found it dead. I've managed other good shots with the .30-06, along with many poor ones. The biggest elk I've killed fell to an '06, as did a pair of bucks at 20 steps. My rifle rack holds five .30-06s now, and I only wish I could buy back several others I've sold over the years.

The .30-06 was conceived in 1900, when U.S. Ordnance engineers at Springfield Armory began work on it. The .30-40 Krag was then our official military round, having served capably in the Spanish-American War. But Paul Mauser's new rifle was upstaging the Krag-Jorgensen, which was costly to build; moreover, rimless cartridges were proving superior to the rimmed .30-40. A prototype rifle emerged at Springfield Armory in 1901. Two years later the Model 1903 Springfield was in production. Like the 8x57 Mauser, its 30-caliber rimless cartridge headspaced on the shoulder. Longer than both the German round and the Krag, its 220-grain bullet cruised at 2300 fps, the ballistic equivalent of an 8x57's 236-grain bullet at 2125.

About a year after the .30-03 appeared, German 8mm ammunition got a new bullet: a 154-grain spitzer clocking a remarkable 2800 fps. The Americans, obliged to catch up quickly, introduced the "Ball Cartridge, Caliber .30, Model 1906." It launched a 150-grain bullet at 2700 fps, increasing probable-hit range. The case could have been left as it was, but someone decided to shorten it to .494, causing all .30-03 chambers to be a tad long. Soon all .30-03 rifles were recalled and rechambered.

Bullets for the .30-06 were initially jacketed with an alloy of 85 percent copper, 15 percent nickel. While satisfactory in the Krag, this mixture did not hold up at .30-06 velocities. Bore-fouling rendered the rifles inaccurate and tin plating proved ineffective. But an alloy of zinc and copper in 5-95 or 10-90 proportions—which became known as gilding metal—reduced fouling substantially.

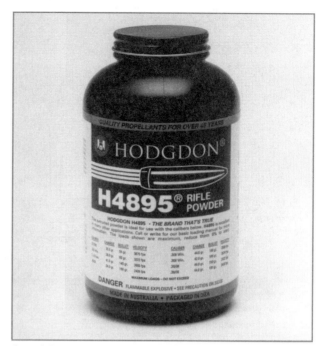

One of the early powders that's still hard to beat in a .30-06 case: Hodgdon's 4895.

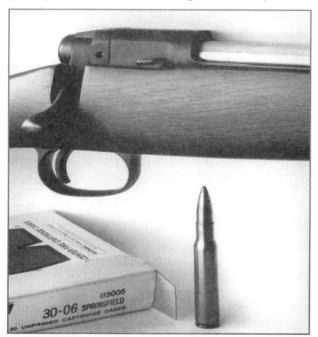

For hunters on a budget, the Savage 110 in .30-06 makes a fine one-rifle arsenal.

The great speed of the 150-grain bullet was supposed to give it a maximum range of 4700 yards, but troops in World War I found the real limit was about 3400. To increase reach, the Army again changed the bullet, this time to a sleek 173-grain spitzer with a 7-caliber ogive and 9-degree boattail. Velocity was trimmed to 2647 fps, a minor concession given the substantial boosts in sectional density and ballistic coefficient. Introduced in 1925, the new "M-1" round extended maximum range to 5500 yards. Oddly enough, the Army saw fit in 1939 to change bullets once more. Apparently the 173-grain bullet gave soldiers a bit too much recoil, so it yielded to a 152-grain replacement at 2805 fps.

Years ago, old military '06 ammo could be bought by the bucket. Indeed, every shooting column in the outdoors magazines (which then cost 35 cents) warned against using it. The reason: Corrosive primers deposited salts in the bore. Though Remington developed non-corrosive "Kleanbore" priming in 1927 (and commercial

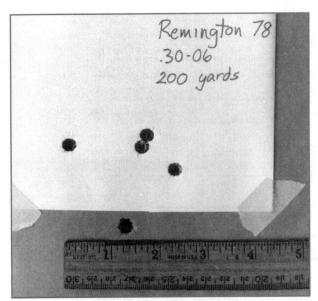

A 2.5-inch group at 200 yards is considered acceptable for an off-the-shelf hunting-weight .30-06.

rounds featured non-corrosive priming exclusively from about 1930), military cartridges were fitted with the corrosive FA 70 primers as late as 1952. Corrosive priming, incidentally, does not weaken the case, as does mercuric priming (which the Army was quick to abandon at the turn of the century). Conversely, mercuric priming does not damage bores. Since the Korean War, the only domestic .30-06 ammunition to leave harmful residue was a run of Western Match cartridges with Western "8 1/2 G" primers, both of which were corrosive and mercuric.

It's certainly not necessary to handload for the .30-06. Factory loads are available with bullets weighing from 125 to 220 grains. Remington has offered .30-06 owners a novel option with its sabot-style "Accelerator" -- a 55-grain .224 bullet in a plastic sleeve, clocking over 4,000 fps from the .30-06 case. Federal, Remington and Winchester all market premier-class bullets. Hornady offers "Light Magnum" loads with 150- and 180-grain bullets that (by Hornady tables) generate 180 fps more muzzle velocity than standard ammo without exceeding allowable pressures.

The .30-06's reputation as an all-around cartridge derives in part from its range of factory-loaded bullet weights, and in part from its field service early in this century, when no other rifle round was as widely used for all types of game. Hunters whose luggage has roamed mindlessly for weeks among the oily shadows of foreign airports can appreciate its ubiquity. You can buy .30-06 ammo in more out-of-the-way places, world-wide, than perhaps any other kind of rifle ammunition. The competition is much stiffer now, though, and magnum cartridges have taken some of the shine off this veteran. But hunters who look to belted cases for versatility are wise to give the '06 a second stare.

Today, versatility in its pure form is not what most shooters want. They don't lean on one rifle for cottontails, prairie dogs, rockchucks, pronghorns, whitetails, elk, moose, brown bears and Africa's big five. With proper loads, the .30-06 and a few magnum cartridges may stretch this far. But all-around use more commonly means killing deer and elk, perhaps pronghorns and an unlucky black bear, dusting the odd coyote and spending an occasional Saturday at a metallic silhouette match. A versatile cartridge is one that recoils gently enough to shoot comfortably in a light-weight woods rifle, offers fine long-range accuracy and puts elk down with authority at any reasonable yardage.

The chambering of Winchester's Model 70 for the .300 H&H in 1937 did not pull many hunters away from the .30-06, and Roy Weatherby's reshaping of the Holland case during World War II didn't swing the public to magnums either. But the development during the 1950s of Winchester short magnums, and the debut in 1962 of Remington's belted 7mm, convinced many hunters they could kill more game with cartridges bigger than the '06.

Scopes were partly responsible for this. By the 1950s glass sights had earned common acceptance, and they were good enough that shooters could aim with precision farther than they thought they could kill with a .30-06. Magnum cartridges seemed a logical next step. During the 1950s handloading became popular and wildcatting grew into something of a subculture. Shooters learned about ballistics, and no longer were all "shells" at the hardware store the same. High-velocity bullets, minute-of-angle accuracy and quarter-mile kills dominated the headlines in gun and hunting magazines. Suddenly, the .30-06 looked stodgy. It couldn't reach as far as magnums, nor could it kill as authoritatively. At least, that's what many hunters thought.

Here is a table comparing the .30-06 with two highly touted magnum cartridges in terms of factory-listed velocity (fps) and energy (ft-lbs). Data used are for Winchester's 160- and 165-grain Silvertip Boattails and 180-grain Fail-Safes.

| Range/Yards | Muzzle | 100 | 200 | 300 | 400 |
|---|---|---|---|---|---|
| .30-06/165 | v. 2800 | 2597 | 2402 | 2216 | 2038 |
| | e. 2873 | 2421 | 2114 | 1719 | 1522 |
| 7mm Rem Mag/160 | v. 2950 | 2745 | 2550 | 2363 | 2184 |
| | e. 3093 | 2697 | 2311 | 1984 | 1694 |
| .30-06/180 | v. 2700 | 2486 | 2283 | 2089 | 1904 |
| | e. 2914 | 2472 | 2083 | 1744 | 1450 |
| .300 Win Mag/180 | v. 2960 | 2732 | 2514 | 2307 | 2110 |
| | e. 3503 | 2983 | 2528 | 2129 | 1780 |

Thirty-caliber magnums reach farther than the .30-06 (left), but they kick harder too. The author has had good results with the .308 Norma (second from left), .300 Winchester and .300 Weatherby Magnums on elk, but he maintains the .30-06 is all you need for hunting North American game.

For any given level of velocity or energy, the 7mm Remington Magnum has roughly a 75-yard edge on the .30-06. Winchester's .300 delivers at 400 yards the same energy carried by an '06 out to only about 290. Differences in drop are less substantial, however: The 7mm bullet dives 7.2 and 20.6 inches at 300 and 400 steps, compared to 8.2 and 23.4 inches for the 165-grain .30-06 bullet. At 300 yards the 180-grain bullet from the .300 Magnum dips 7.1 inches while the same bullet from a .30-06 falls 8.7 inches. At 400 paces the .300 dominates, registering 20.7 to 25.5 inches of drop. To at least 300 yards, a .30-06 will hold the same, enough to make a kill.

Note that the .300 Winchester with a 180-grain bullet performs about the same as a 7mm Remington does with a 160. There's a much wider performance gap between this .300 and the .30-06 than between the 7mm Remington Magnum and the .30-06. With a 175-grain bullet, the factory-loaded 7mm actually generates less velocity and energy than Hornady's new Light Magnum 180-grain .30-06. There is nothing in the hunting field the 7mm Remington Magnum can do that can't be done just as well with a .30-06. The truth is, the .30-06 delivers between 1700 and 1800 ft-lbs of energy to 300 yards, enough for elk, moose or bears at that range, which is considerably farther than most big animals are killed. At half that range, which is probably close to average for elk

Today, few sportsmen would go after big bears with a .30-06; but not long ago the '06 was considered a very powerful cartridge. Inuits kill polar bears routinely with .30-30s.

and mule deer--and still long for moose and bears --a standard .30-06 load dumps about 2200 ft-lbs, more than the 7mm Remington Magnum at 250 yards or the .300 Winchester at .300.

To get "more whump" from the .30-06, many shooters do their own handloading. The .30-06 is commercially loaded to function safely in all rifles for which it is commonly chambered. These include autoloaders, lever-actions and Remington's 760-series pump. A stout bolt rifle or dropping-block single-shot will handle slightly higher pressures. But before boosting those powder charges, it's a good idea to think about the ultimate goal. Is it worth inching toward those maximum safe pressures? It's really not necessary to freeze that bolt shut, give primers the bug-eye, and polish case heads with an ejector hole to find an effective load.

One veteran hunter I know owned a battered 1917 Enfield that had never digested a .30-06 handload. He insisted on factory ammo, main-taining that cartridges originating from a nice new box couldn't fail. He was probably right. Deer and elk crumpled like empty puppets when he fired. But the secret wasn't in the ammo; it was his hunting style. He didn't try to make unreasonably long shots, and he found the zest of hunting in the

stalk. The alpine crags where he killed his biggest bucks offered many shots over 200 yards, but he took them only when a sneak seemed untenable. His factory-loaded Core-Lokts and Power Points had all the reach he needed.

While this particular hunter insisted on 180-grain bullets in his .30-06, that doesn't mean other weights can't be equally useful from time to time. You can buy 30-caliber bullets as light as 100 grains from Hornady and Speer, or as heavy as 250 grains from Barnes. A 150-grain bullet also boasts some utility, but it's over-rated. Let's consider a .30-06 rifle with a low-mounted scope zeroed at 200 yards. A factory-loaded 180-grain Remington Core-Lokt will strike an inch above sight-line at 50 yards, 2.4 inches high at 100 yards and 2 inches high at 150. At 250, it drops 3.7 inches, 9.3 inches at 300 and 27 inches at 400 yards. Now compare those figures with those from a factory-loaded 150-grain Core-Lokt: +.8 at 50, +2.1 at 100, +1.8 at 150, -3.3 at 250, -8.5 at 300 and -25 at 400. Essentially, there's no difference, even though the 150-grain bullet leaves the muzzle at 2910 fps, rather than 2700. At 300 yards the 180-grain hits an inch lower, and at 400 it's only 2 inches. At all yardages, however, the 180-grain bullet packs a 20 percent weight advantage.

A Husqvarna in .30-06 accounted for this Wyoming pronghorn.

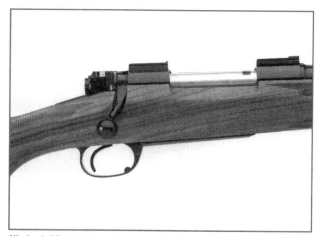
Kimber's Model 89 has the clean, trim lines one expects of a .30-06. There's no more versatile cartridge.

A minute-of-angle rifle spreads its bullets across 3 inches of target face at 300 yards, and 4 inches at 400. So differences in point of impact between 150- and 180-grain .30-06 bullets at the longest practical hunting ranges--and with very accurate rifles--lie within half the extreme spread of a machine-rest group. Add wind, shooter wobbles and aiming error, and groups emerge big enough to all but obliterate any difference in bullet performance due to weight.

When nose shape is changed, down-range differences can grow in a hurry. Because of their blunt noses, 220-grain 30-caliber Core-Lokts (and similar bullets) generate less velocity and energy at all ranges--and drop like cantaloupes beyond 250 yards. At 300 yards they plummet about twice as far as a 180-grain spitzer. But ballistics tables don't give them enough credit. Up close--say, to 150 yards--the 220 is superior for heavy game because it wields greater sectional density than lighter bullets; and, assuming proper construction, it can drive deeper. Also, the calculation of ft-lbs of energy includes the velocity *squared*, which many riflemen claim skews comparisons in favor of fast, light bullets that don't kill as well.

An often-overlooked advantage of any round-nose bullet is its shortness. Thus, for a given overall cartridge length there's more room for powder because the bullet doesn't have to be seated as deep as a spitzer. In cases of modest capacity, this consideration is important. If shooting distance is anticipated under 200 yards, increased speed may more than counter the effect of wind and gravity on a blunt nose.

For some applications light-weight bullets are best. One fellow, who some years back promoted himself as an expert deer hunter, wrote that, in order to shoot bucks so they stayed down, he used 220-grain bullets in his .30-06. The implication: Lighter bullets don't put deer down for keeps. Actually, speedy 150- and 165-grain bullets often kill deer quicker than 220s. They open more violently, which is what you want on thin-skinned game. Usually they'll expend most of their energy in the vitals. In contrast, 220-grain bullets squander a good deal of their energy after exit.

Another reason for choosing a relatively light bullet is its ability to tighten groups. Standard rifling twist for the .30-06 is one turn in 10 inches, which is sharp enough to stabilize standard bullets

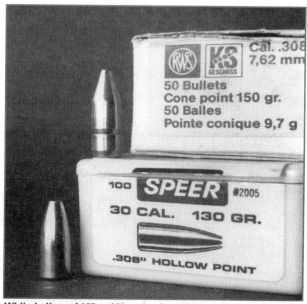
While bullets of 165 to 200 grains in weight are best for big game in the .30-06, lighter missiles can also be used for smaller game and to take recoil.

up to 220 grains. But rifles can demonstrate individual tastes in bullets and loads. While the broad choice of 30-caliber factory loads all but ensures that **one** load within each weight class will shoot acceptably, the preferred bullet style may produce smaller clusters on target when the hunter drops a step in weight.

Handloaders have so many bullet options in 30 caliber that to try them all is to wear out the barrel. Speer, Hornady, Sierra and Nosler are as far as you need to look for a match bullet or a softpoint for any North American game. I get good results from 165-grain Sierras on deer-size game; and Hornady's 180-grain Spire Point ranks as an all-around favorite. For elk, the 200-grain Speer Grand Slam and Nosler Partition are hard to beat.

With a ballistic coefficient of .481, the 200-grain Partition, which can be driven at 2650 fps from the .30-06, wastes little energy en route. Given that velocity, it crosses the 200-yard line at nearly 2300 fps and reaches 300 yards still clocking over 2100. With 2330 ft-lbs of energy at 200 steps and an even ton at 300, it's a first-round draft pick among elk bullets for the .30-06 and the .30 magnums. Swift, Hawk, Jensen, Blue Mountain, Trophy-Bonded, Elkhorn and other custom bullets enable handloaders to get more killing power from the .30-06. Because they hold together in tough game like elk and moose, these bullets penetrate deeper, open wider channels, and are less apt to alter course than are less cohesive bullets.

When handloading heavy bullets, you'll find the .30-06 case is too small for some slow powders that seem suited to the job. Just 62.5 grains of H483l can fill a Winchester case to the mouth. Slightly faster powders--IMR or Hodgdon 4350, Scot 4351, Winchester 760, Hodgdon 414 or Hercules RL-19-- all work fine with 180- and 200-grain bullets. On the other hand, Accurate Arms 3100, a good propellant for heavy bullets, must be compressed in ambitious loads. For 150- to 165-grain bullets, IMR's 4320, 4064 and 4895 give excellent results, as does Winchester 748, Hercules RL-15 and Scot 4065. Because of the .30-06's modest case capacity, it is a good idea to boost charges gradually when developing loads. Performance and pressure can change quickly.

Big game hunters bring all manner of rifles into the hills. Those who bring .30-06s on hunts seem, on average, to fare better than those who bring magnums. That's partly because they aren't afraid to shoot .30-06 rifles. They've practiced with them. They aim the rifle the way they might the family .22, not like some prototype rocket-launcher. They also harbor no grand expectations, no illusions about shooting at extreme range. There's nothing to prove--because the .30-06 has been so well proven! They have all the whump they need for an assassination. All they have to do is steady the rifle and squeeze. ●

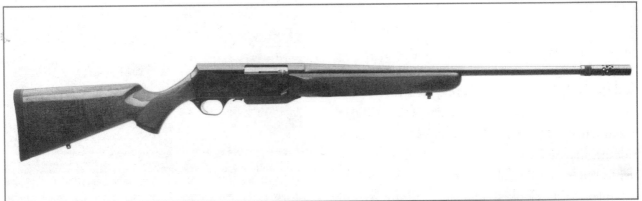

This Browning BAR, equipped with a BOSS brake and barrel-tuning device, is chambered in .30-06.

# THE .22: NONE SMALLER, STILL NONE BETTER!

**K**illing big game is like shooting rats in a barnyard. You look hard, listen closely, sneak quietly and aim carefully. About the only difference is the scenery. The best hunting rifles are oviously those we can hit with. But most hunters hit best with guns not used on big game. Kids who are serious about shooting do remarkable things with air guns because they use them so often. When BBs cost a nickel a tube and some youngster squandered their weekly allowances on ice cream. I fed my Daisy. Despite its short stock, crude sights, abysmal accuracy and a trigger that moved like the handle on a bumper jack, I somehow learned to hit with that anemic gun. You could follow with your eye every BB launched, then make the correction for the next shot. Those lessons in trajectory stuck!

Except for the visible projectile, a good .22 is like that. Modern rifles shoot big game tighter at 250 yards than that Daisy could at 25. They boast good sights and triggers, stocks that fit, and enough horsepower to drop a dinosaur. Trouble is, they don't feel "homey." Shooting should be like pushing the right buttons on the keyboard without ever having to watch your fingers. If I could have but one hunting rifle, it would be a .308 or .30-06; but given a quota of two, one would surely be a .22 rimfire. Long before Holland and Holland wrapped a belt around a cigar-like cartridge and called it a .375, shooters worked magic with .22 rifles. Trick shooters, they were called, but no trickery could rival their unerring aim. Bang-bang-

bang! And all sorts of tiny targets, tossed aloft, shattered or caromed off into the blue.

Around the turn of the century, Ad Topperwein, "Doc" Carver and B.A. Bartlett staged marathon shoots to show off their talents. Firing Model 1890 Winchester slide-action .22s at 60,000 thrown glass balls, Carver broke 59,350 of them. Bartlett answered with 59,720. And in 1907 Topperwein pulled into San Antonio's fairgrounds with an armload of Model 1903 Winchester auto-loading rifles, crates of

Because of its low recoil and light report, the .22 Long Rifle is a perfect cartridge for beginners.

The .22 Long Rifle is truly an international round (this rifle and ammo turned up in Zimbabwe.)

ammunition and a great bin full of 2 1/4 x 2 1/4-inch wood blocks. The wiry Texan shot at 72,500 hand-thrown blocks, missing only nine. Wood blocks left no carpet of shards and were lighter to toss than glass balls. They may have been cheaper and easier to hit, too. Whatever the reason, Remington exhibition shooter Tom Frye used them in an attempt to break Topperwein's record. Firing Model 66 autoloaders at 100,010 targets, Frye missed six.

Hitting was only part of the challenge for these men. Just holding the gun became work. Bartlett shot fast, but his 60,000 targets kept him on the line for 144 hours. Ad Topperwein needed help after each performance simply to lower his arms! Yet his reflexes remained sharp. In later exhibitions, he would shoot ejected .22 cases out of the air as they flew from his gun!

Phoebe Ann Moses, a young girl from Ohio, had set standards for rimfire marksmanship before Custer's battle at the Little Bighorn. By the time she was 15, she'd become bored shotgunning quail and switched to the .22 rifle. One day she entered a local match against renowned shooter Frank Butler and beat him. She later married Butler and joined his theatrical group under the stage name of Annie Oakley. As part of her act, she would shoot glass balls

by sighting through a mirror, the rifle held over her shoulder. Victim of a train wreck and subsequent car crash, Annie Oakley was left with permanent injuries, but she never lost her touch. At age 62 she used a .22 rifle to hit all 25 consecutive pennies tossed in the air.

Shooting like that should humble all shooters who beam over a minute-of-angle group shot on stationary paper from a bench with a scope strong enough to watch ticks cavort on the target frame. No product—be it rifle, race car or tennis racquet--can make you a marksman. Practice does.

## ENTER SMITH & WESSON

The .22 story started long ago with Horace W. Smith and Daniel B. Wesson, who found themselves together, quite by chance, at the tool-making firm of Allen, Brown & Luther near Worcester, Massachusetts. Smith had worked 18 years at Springfield Armory before taking a job building pepperbox pistols at the Allen & Thurber plant in Norwich, Connecticut. He had also worked for Robbins & Lawrence of Windsor,

Compared to the .308 Winchester (far right), the .22 rimfires look tiny. The .22 CB and Short (left) have the same 29-grain bullet as the .22 Long (center). The Long Rifle cartridge combines a 40-grain bullet with the Long's case. Other bullet weights are now available for the .22 Long Rifle.

To prepare for hunting season, the author shoots a Winchester 75 target rifle.

Vermont, a firm that built guns on contract. Smith had even opened his own shop.

Dan Wesson had been apprenticed as a boy to his older brother and rifle-maker, Edwin. The pair went into partnership with a Thomas Smith (no relation to Horace) in 1848 after a move to Hartford, Connecticut. The new business was called Wesson & Smith. A year earlier, Texas Ranger Captain Samuel Walker, while on a visit to Samuel Colt, examined a Wesson rifle and promised an order of 1,000. This government contract was what Edwin had been hoping for. But the contract never came; and two years later Edwin died suddenly. In August of 1849, after creditors had seized all his gunshop property. Dan Wesson returned home to Worcester and got a job at the Leonard Pistol Works making pepperbox guns for Robbins & Lawrence. It was there that Wesson probably met Horace Smith for the first time.

In 1852 the two gunsmiths talked about the Hunt-Jennings repeater, a troublesome rifle that New York financier Courtlandt Palmer had hired them to fix. Palmer had just paid $100,000 for patent rights to the mechanism, which had

been designed in 1848 by inventor Walter Hunt, then modified by Lewis Jennings. Walter Hunt's recalcitrant repeater later became the Henry rifle, grandfather of all Winchester lever-actions. By 1851 Smith had improved the breech pin and lifter, but Dan Wesson thought ammunition was the problem. Hunt's rifle fired "Rocket Balls"—hollow-based conical bullets with the propellant and primer inside. Wesson favored the French Flobert cartridge--a ball seated atop a primer—so in 1853 the two men filed for a patent covering a disc that held the priming compound in the Flobert round.

Courtlandt Palmer and his gunsmiths reasoned that even if they could make the rifle function, its ammunition doomed it. The trio gave up that project, moving to Norwich, where they manufactured parts for 250 pistols chambered for their new cartridge. The enterprise eventually failed, but in 1854 Palmer gamely shelled out $10,000 for new tooling to anchor a partnership known as "Smith & Wesson." By late summer of 1856, Wesson had completed a wooden model of a revolver that fired a rimfire cartridge (later to become the .22 Short). Upon learning that Rollin White, a former Colt employee, held the patent for a revolver cylinder bored end to end, Wesson called on White one day and came away with the exclusive manufacturing rights to cartridge revolvers. Legend has it that Rollin White had earlier approached Colt with the idea of bored-through cylinders but had been given a cool reception. By the time Sam Colt died in 1862, Smith & Wesson had already produced more than 22,000 cartridge revolvers.

For the first couple of years, ammunition receipts matched gun revenues at Smith & Wesson. In 1862 the company shipped 6.4 million rimfire cartridges—about 3 million each of .22 and .32 revolver rounds and just over 400,000 .44 cartridges for the Frank Wesson rifle. A year later production totaled 7.7 million. Enough .22 (Short)

Pat McGuire fires a modified Remington 37 offhand. Receiver-mounted scopes like his Leupold have supplanted the barrel-mounted scopes common on early .22 match rifles.

ammunition was manufactured to provide every owner of a Smith & Wesson revolver with 115 rounds.

Flobert's work in 1845 had effectively produced the .22 BB (bulleted breech) cap. When U.S. cartridge firms later started making the round, they substitued an 18-grain conical bullet for the ball and added a pinch of powder to generate 780 fps and 24 foot-pounds at the muzzle. The CB (conical bullet) cap appeared in catalogs in 1888, but it was probably developed earlier. It featured the case of a BB cap and the 29-grain bullet of the .22 Short.

The original load of 1.5 grains of black powder kicked that bullet out at 720 fps, producing 33 foot-pounds. Later, smokeless powder was used. American companies discontinued BB and CB caps in the 1940s, but Germany's RWS still makes them.

The .22 Short was first charged with 4 grains of black powder. In 1887 a semi-smokeless propellant was introduced, with smokeless arriving shortly after that. The little round has been widely used (with frangible bullets) for gallery shooting and is chambered in International-style match pistols.

A Marlin autoloading .22, one of many thousands still in circulation from America's premier maker of .22s.

Mostly, it's a pest cartridge. As a lad creeping along rail fences outside old sheep barns, I used it on rats that made their homes in tunnels in the packed sheep dung. The .22 Short was just right for that job because it was the cheapest way to boot a bullet along at a lethal 1,100 fps.

It's possible to get 100 fps more from a .22 Long, which looks like a .22 Long Rifle wearing a Short bullet. The Long, introduced around 1870, predates the Long Rifle by over 16 years. Originally loaded with 5 grains of black powder, the Long fell out of favor after the Long Rifle became established. Indeed, the .22 Long Rifle has to be one of the most useful cartridges of all. Developed by the J. Stevens Arms and Tool Company in 1887, it used the same case and powder charge as the Long but offered a 40-grain bullet that delivered more energy. Like its shorter cousins, this round features a "heeled" bullet--i.e., one with a small base (crimped in since 1900) and case-diameter mid-section.

The workhorse .22 Long Rifle high-speed round pushes its 40-grain solid bullet at 1,330 fps. A 37-grain hollowpoint ekes out an additional 30 fps. Slower match bullets have less lag (the difference

Ruger's Bearcat single-action revolver features two cylinders, one in .22 LR and the other in .22 WMR.

between muzzle and target velocities). Bullets started below 1,100 fps also avoid violence at the sound barrier. The best .22 Long Rifle ammunition is extremely accurate. While shooting in prone matches, I've tested ammo by lot with an Anschutz 1413 and McMillan-barreled Remington 37, drilling out eigth-inch 5-round groups at 50 yards and 1-inch 10-shot groups at 100. But match fodder costs more than it's worth for informal practice with ordinary rifles.

Among other .22 rimfire rounds that went public are the .22 Remington Automatic, developed in 1914 for that company's Model 16 autoloading rifle and discontinued in 1928. Like the similar .22 Winchester Automatic, it had a 45-grain, inside-lubricated bullet. Since both cases had to be substantially bigger in diameter than their .222 bullets, they couldn't be chambered in guns bored for the Short, Long or Long Rifle, with case mouth diameters of only .224. Why bother with these oddballs? Rimfire cartridges at the time were loaded with black, semi-smokeless and smokeless powders. By making new smokeless cartridges for autoloaders, armsmakers ensured that shooters wouldn't gum up those guns with blackpowder ammo.

Whereas the .22 Automatic was a milquetoast round, clocking only 1,000 fps, the Winchester .22 WRF fired its 45-grain solid and 40-grain hollow-point bullets at 1,450! Case length was .960, half again that of the Automatics and the .22 Long Rifle. An inside-lubricated bullet produced a fat case and

Winchester's Super-X 22 Magnum is the most potent .22 rimfire, but it won't match the performance of centerfires like the .223.

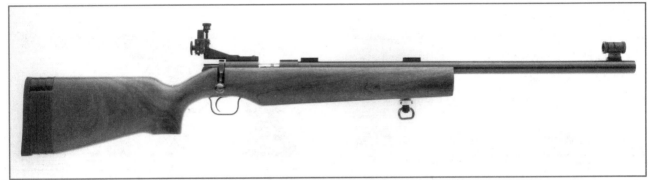

Kimber's Model 82 target rifle is one of few high-quality .22 match guns still made in the U.S.

a chamber too big for other .22 ammunition. Shooters who used Shorts, Longs and Long Rifles in WRF guns experienced split cases and spotty extraction. Remington made an interchangeable cartridge and called it the .22 Remington Special.

Between 1880 and 1935 some ammunition firms offered the .22 Extra Long, a round with the Long Rifle's 40-grain bullet in a slightly longer case. Initially, it held 6 grains of black powder and was hawked as a 200-yard target cartridge. But blunt 40-grain bullets don't do well at 200 yards, especially when launched at 1,050 fps. As the .22 Short, Long and Long Rifle established themselves in the post-World War I marketplace, gunmakers fashioned mechanisms that handled all three and even functioned with mixed magazine loads. Because .22 Short bullets shoot best in barrels rifled one turn in 24 inches, they didn't perform well in guns chambered and rifled 1-in-16 for the Long Rifle. A

Short bullet also had to jump some distance into the rifling of one of these barrels. Rumor had it that the jumps deposited enough lead on the land corners to cause eventual problems.

Winchester's .22 Magnum Rimfire, introduced in 1959, offered significantly more power than earlier .22s. Essentially a .22 WRF case stretched to 1.052 inches, with a 40-grain jacketed bullet at 2,000 fps, the WMR was first chambered in pistols. Ruger and Smith & Wesson sold Magnum revolvers right away, while Winchester was slow in bringing out its first WMR rifle (the Model 61 pump). Since then the cartridge has trundled along steadily but has never threatened the .22 Long Rifle. In 1977 CCI had a better idea. Its Stinger had the overall length of a Long Rifle cartridge; but its hollowpoint bullet, about 6 grains lighter and backed by a stiffer charge of powder, reached 1,680 fps. Winchester soon brought out the Expediter and Remington

CCI's 22 LR is an inexpensive alternative tom competition-grade ammo like Western's Super Match Mark III .22 LR

The .22 Long Rifle (right) is far more useful for hunting and target shooting than the Long, Short or CB ("conical bullet") parlor round.

introduced its Yellow Jacket. These super Long Rifle rounds and their clones have since become quite popular. The selection and quality of .22 ammunition have improved over the past 25 years while prices have stayed low. Only match-grade and high-performance cartridges cost more than a few dollars per box. Compare that with the cost of centerfire ammo—or even bullets!

Any big game hunter who doesn't shoot a .22 during the off-season is missing a chance to shoot better. Practicing with a rimfire makes sense not only because it saves money, but because the gentle bounce of a .22 will neither encourage nor hide a flinch. A .22 makes little noise, so it can be used near suburbia, where centerfire guns bring complaints. You learn most when working on the fundamentals, using paper targets. Want more interesting targets to finish off a box of ammo? Try empty plastic film cans, or ping-pong balls, offhand at 50 yards.

Unlike many centerfire cartridges, the .22 doesn't need a long barrel to gain its highest velocity. Long

Rifle ammunition is quickest from 16- to 18-inch barrels. And heavy rifles won't necessarily offer better accuracy. Anschutz and other target guns drill out one-hole groups because their bores and chambers are finely finished and held to close tolerances, and because the people who buy them quickly learn that match-grade ammunition is essential for top scores.

Most .22 rifles go to youngsters who use them for plinking and small game hunting. Serious big game hunters know the value of an understudy rifle, and they recognize in the .22 rimfire the perfect practice round. To bring lightweight .22s up to the proper weight, they add tire weights under the barrel channel, or they drill stock cavities to fill with shot. Because heavy accurate .22s are hard to find these days, the people who want them poke around hock shops and gun shows for used smoke poles. The Remington 513 T or Winchester 75 Target were made in sporter versions but the target configurations weigh about the same as a centerfire bolt-action rifle. So does Winchester's early 52A with medium-weight barrel and grooved forend. Another option is the 1922 Springfield. All these rifles stake out a middle ground between sporters and rifles for serious target shooters. They're ideal picks for understudy rifles.

Not everyone uses a bolt gun., however. For slide-action people a second-hand Remington 121 or Winchester 61 is a hard .22 to beat. Winchester's 9422 is almost unchallenged among rimfire lever guns. It's so well made, in fact, that U.S. Repeating Arms claims it barely shows a profit. The Browning BL-22 is nicely finished, but at 5 pounds it seems light for an understudy gun. Autoloaders also abound, with the best being Remington's 550 and Winchester's 74.

Back in the days when I was still shooting rats, my Remington pump gun wore a scope as skinny as a cheap hot dog. It seemed sophisticated at the time because few shooters were using scopes on big-game rifles, let alone .22s. Now there's no excuse for not using a good scope on a .22. Most 1-inch models can be mounted on .22s; Leupold even makes a 4x Compact for rimfires, parallax-corrected to 75 yards instead of 150.

Early on, I learned how to hold a gun so its jiggles kept the crosswire near the target, how much breath to lock in my lungs, and when to start over because I'd used too much. I learned how to mash a trigger gently, and how to keep my eye in the scope. I still have too much pulse, and I run out of breath and jerk triggers far too often. No matter the game, my heart still pounds when the crosswire settles in. But whenever a bullet lands in the right place, memories of my days with the .22 rimfire come flooding back. No other cartridge still in use can claim its longevity. None comes close to matching it for number of shots fired, matches won or animals bagged. It has been chambered in guns used in hunting, target shooting, survival and self defense. It is, in its various forms, clearly the most enduring, most useful cartridge ever designed. ●

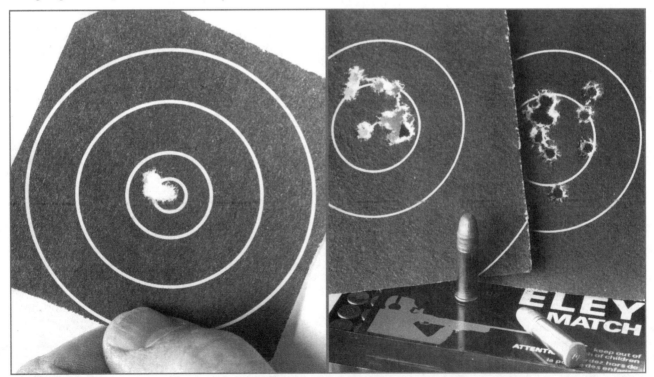

The author fired this 5-shot group (left) in prone competition at 50 yards with a 37 Remington rebarreled with a McMillan tube. A couple of 10-shot groups (right) with the same rifle shows the advantage of a Redfield 20x scope at 100 yards.

# THE THRIFTY THIRTY-FIVES

It's not easy to find a 35-caliber rifle these days. They're not listed in catalogs from Savage or Browning, though both once offered lever rifles for the .358 Winchester. Nor is there a .35 to be found in the Weatherby lineup. Remington lists only the 7600 pump in .35 Whelen, and Winchester sells a few Big Bore Model 94s in .356. Neither company manufactures a bolt rifle reamed for a .35; nor does Ruger. Marlin continues to chamber its 336 in .35 Remington, and Thompson-Center offers that round in some of its Contender handguns.

Compared to big game rifles bored to .277, .284, .308 and .338, there's no selection to speak of for .35 fans. The truth is, modern .35s deliver much greater punch than their forebears; and contrary to popular wisdom, they shoot almost as flat as their 30-caliber counterparts. Thirty-fives make big, deep holes, too, and even when they shed a third of their weight in bone and beef these bullets weigh as much as *unfired* 7mm missiles. Besides, relatively fast powders can be used in most .35 cases, which means extra-long barrels aren't needed to get bullets up to speed or to keep muzzle blast out of harm's way.

The oldest .35s aren't made any more. Unless you wax nostalgic over flatnose bullets that develop less than 1000 foot-pounds at the muzzle, you won't miss these early marvels. The .35-30 Maynard, introduced with the 1882 Maynard single-shot rifle, gave a 250-grain bullet just over 1200 fps. The .35-40, a more powerful variant, offered about 1350 for an even half

ton of muzzle energy. Winchester introduced its semi-rimmed .35 Self-Loading model in 1905, but it lasted only until 1920, probably because no one had any use for a 180-grain flatnose bullet at 1452 fps. After all, it carried less than half the energy of a .30-30! It was, one might say, the .30 Carbine of its time--more popular with law enforcement people than with hunters.

Two years before Winchester's autoloader arrived, however, New Haven came up with a much better cartridge: the .35 Winchester. Developed for the 1895 lever-action rifle (also chambered in .30-40 Krag, .303 British, .30-06 and .405 Winchester), this .35 kicked a 250-grain bullet out at nearly 2200 fps. Its muzzle energy of 2670 foot-pounds was ample even for elk at woods ranges. This rimmed round lasted until

The .358 Winchester (right), a necked-up .308, appeared in 1955 to replace the equally potent .348 Winchester. Chambered in Model 70 and 88 rifles, it failed at market and was eventually dropped. The .35 Remington showed up in 1908 and has been a steady seller in Marlin's lever-action carbines.

The .35 Whelen (left) began life in 1922 as a wildcat development of James V. Howe and Colonel Townsend Whelen. The .358 Norma Magnum is on a shortened .300 H&H case; essentially, it's a .338 Winchester necked to 35 caliber. It appeared in 1959, a year before rifles were chambered for it Stateside.

1936, when it was supplanted by the more potent .348.

In 1907 Winchester trotted out an improved autoloading rifle, the Model '07, including a new cartridge to replace the .35 Self-Loading. Like its predecessor, the straight-cased .351 Winchester used a 180-grain .351 bullet, not a .358 bullet like the powerful bottle-necked .35 Winchester in the Model 1895. Generating 1370 foot pounds, it was a substantial improvement over the old S-L, but hardly enough to give deer nightmares. Once again, the police kept it alive, and some Model '07s were even used by French forces during World Wars I and II. Winchester dropped the .351 in 1957.

Remington must have been watching Winchester's experiments with its mild-mannered .35s and decided that a more useful round was possible. So, in 1906 it unveiled the .35 Remington--and it's still with us. Designed for the Model 8 autoloader, it also found a home in the later Model

81 as well as Remington's 14, 141 and 760 pumps. With a muzzle velocity of 2210 fps, Remington's 200-grain roundnose soft-point generates over a ton of muzzle energy with foot-pounds to spare. It is easily a 150-yard deer cartridge and adequate for use on elk at more modest ranges.

Marlin's decision to keep the .35 Remington among its Model 336 chamberings must have been driven in part by hunter demand. A mild rifle round, it proved effective on deer at the ranges most deer are shot. In a handgun, however, it is a veritable tornado, efficient in short barrels because of its big bore and compact case, with a reach equal to its substantial recoil. Remington's Model 8 rifle is long obsolete, and few hunters mourn it. Remington still loads a 150-grain pointed Core-Lokt and a 200-grain roundnose Core-Lokt in this old .35. The heavy bullet's higher

The author shot this mule deer in British Columbia with a 250-grain Remington factory load from his Model 700 rifle in .35 Whelen.

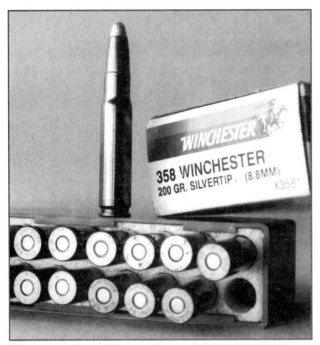

The .358 Winchester may look anemic, but it's actually a very potent cartridge, effective on game as big as elk at modest ranges.

sectional density offsets the light bullet's sleeker form, but not enough to even the velocity spread at practical ranges. Still, the roundnose has the edge in energy all the way out on the deer trail.

The most powerful .35 in pre-Depression days was fashioned by Charles Newton in 1915. This rimless round could drive a 250-grain bullet at 2800 fps, matching the .338 Winchester. The .35 and other Newton cartridges were decades ahead of their time. They used magnum cases without belts, generating ballistic performances requiring modern scopes and modern bullets to prove themselves. Loaded to unleash two tons of muzzle energy, the .35 Newton was--and remains--a top choice for elk, moose and big bears.

The .35 Whelen in wildcat form appeared around 1922. It may have come from Colonel Townsend Whelen's own reloading room, or possibly James Howe (of Griffin and Howe) necked up the .30-06 and named it after his good friend. At that time, Whelen was the commanding officer at Frankfort Arsenal, where Howe worked as a toolmaker. For

certain, both men contributed to the project. The new cartridge, like the .400 Whelen which followed, enabled owners of surplus Springfields to rebarrel (or rebore) their '06's to a more powerful round. Case forming was simply a matter of neck expansion, because headspacing stayed at the same point on the shoulder. Mausers as well as Springfields proved ripe for conversion. Bores pitted by potassium chlorate primers cleaned up nicely around a .35 reamer. Surprisingly, the .35 Whelen found no commercial home in the bolt guns of the 1920s and '30s. It first appeared in a factory rifle in 1988, when Remington so chambered its 700 Classic and began loading Whelen ammunition. Remington currently offers a 200-grain bullet at 2675 fps and a 250-grain bullet at 2400. Both now are pointed Core-Lokts.

The biggest mule deer I ever shot fell to a .35 Whelen, one of Remington's Classics. I'd spotted the deer from a distance, bungled the stalk, retraced my

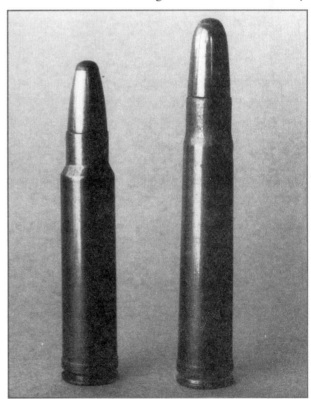

The .358 Norma (left) is substantially smaller than its grandparent, the .375 H&H, but there's not much difference ballistically.

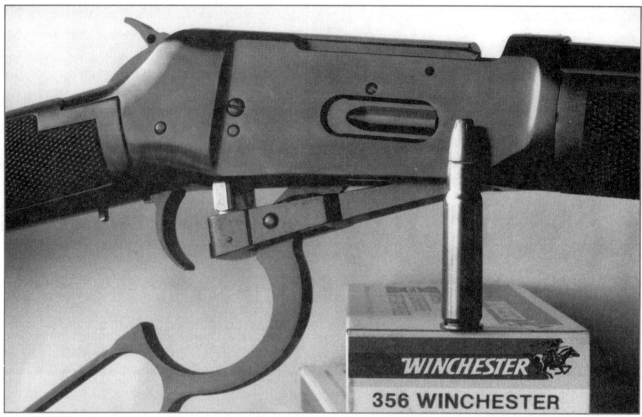

The .356 Winchester is a semi-rimmed version of the rimless .358. It was developed in the 1980s for Winchester's beefed-up Model 94.

steps and cleared ridgetop just in time to spy the buck hoofing it to safety across an opposite face. The range was only a couple hundred yards, if that. But I was winded, and the mountain seemed to be heaving too. Had I not been confident in the great penetrating power of that 250-grain Core-Lokt, I'd not have taken the quick shot. As it happened, my bullet went in behind the last rib on the left side, angled up between the shoulders, exiting to knock a huge chip out of the base of one antler. The buck turned downhill, plowing snow toward a gaping chute, then piled into a deadfall.

The ballistic advantage of pointed bullets is clear, but until World War II hunters saw no reason to shoot farther than iron sights allowed them to aim. Tube magazines and blunt bullets, therefore, seemed to make as much sense as they had back in the 1880s. The Model 71 Winchester, essentially a revamped 1886, appeared in 1935, firing a .348 cartridge with

a flatnose bullet. At first, 150-, 200- and 250-grain bullets were cataloged. Then, for several years, Winchester offered only the 200-grain. At present no .348 ammunition is listed. The Model 71, in both rifle and carbine form, is truly an elegant rifle--collectors have boosted their value into four figures on the gun-show circuit. While not a true .35, the .348 bridged the eras of the .35 and .358 Winchesters.

The .358, a derivative of the .308 Winchester (military 7.62 NATO) first appeared in 1955. Chambered in Winchester's lever-action Model 88 and the Featherweight 70, this stubby cartridge caught on slowly with the public. The ballistic equal of the larger .348, its 200-grain bullet leaves at about 2500 fps, generating over 2750 foot-pounds. Because it was designed for stack-magazine rifles, the .358 can be loaded with spitzer bullets for improved down-range performance. Winchester offers only one factory load: a 200-grain Silvertip semi-spitzer (a 250-grain roundnose loading was available but has been discontinued). As one might expect, the .358 compares to the .35 Whelen as the .308 Winchester does to the .30-06. Savage had the .358 in its list of Model 99 chamberings for some time, then reintroduced it in 1976 for a brief run. Ruger also built some .358 Model 77s, and Browning offered the round in its BLR. Mannlicher-Schoenauer even chambered a few of its carbines in .358 during the late 1950s.

The 1950s were the decade of the short magnum. Roy Weatherby had popularized high velocity and belted cases in the 1940s, but only a few hunters bought his rifles and proprietary cartridges. In 1956 Winchester announced its .458 Magnum, following quickly with a .264 and a .338. Remington's 7mm came along in 1962, followed a year later by Winchester's .300. But nobody on this side of the ocean launched a belted .35. That job was left to Norma of Sweden when, in 1959, it made a .358 Magnum available to U.S. hunters. Slightly longer than the .338 Winchester Magnum, it has essentially the same case (a cut-down .300 Holland) and pounds a 250-grain bullet down the bore at 2800 fps, delivering well over two tons of energy--slightly less potent than the .375 H&H with a 270-grain bullet.

Still, the .358 Norma did not sell well initially, mainly because only the Schultz & Larsen 65 and Husqvarna's Mausers were chambered for it. Besides, Norma ammunition was expensive, and the round had more power than anyone needed. Indeed, even the .338 Winchester Magnum was making poor headway at market. There was, moreover, little hope in the 1960s for a costlier cartridge chambered in fewer rifles, especially with a foreign name and enough power to lift the roof at the range whenever it spoke from the bench.

I'll concede to a fondness for Norma's big .35. I can think of no better rifle for big bull elk and moose, and for the bears that bite back. It would also be a fine choice for African lions and the larger antelopes. It is not necessary, however, for any hoofed game save the big bovines (the .308 Norma does just fine with less recoil). But it is an efficient, flat-shooting round that will stop with authority any thin-skinned game at any hunting yardage

The next .35 rifle round to appear commercially after Norma's belted snorter was the .350 Remington Magnum, which made its debut in the firm's Model 600 carbine. The 18-inch barrel gave way in 1968 to a 20-inch. Despite an attractive laminated stock, the 660 (as the later .350 was called), suffered from a dog-leg bolt and other non-traditional lines. The carbine was discontinued in 1971, but the cartridge made its way into the Model 700 line. Ruger also chambered it in its Model 77. With a 200-grain bullet exiting at 2710 fps, this .35 duplicates the ballistic performance of the .35 Whelen and is an excellent round, offering the most muscle possible for a short rifle action.

The .35 Whelen Improved case (right) has a sharper shoulder but not much more case capacity than the standard hull.

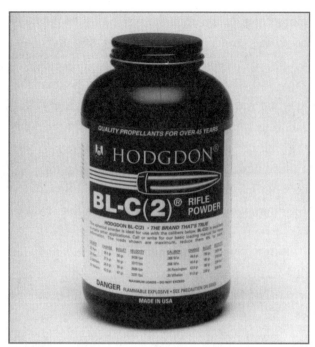

BL-C(2) is a veteran powder that's still useful in medium-capacity cases like the .300 Savage and .358 Winchester. It's also a good performer in the .35 Whelen.

In 1980 Winchester bravely tested the .35 waters with a new rimmed round developed to complement a redesigned Model 94. The .356 Winchester is essentially a rimmed .358, though the case is thicker and the bullet is factory-seated deeper. That means less case capacity and a bit less velocity. But with a 200-grain bullet at 2460 fps, the .356 is no flyweight. Winchester's 94 Big Bore Angle Eject allows low-over-center scope use. The receiver walls are thicker at the back to take extra pounding.

Since Remington brought the .35 Whelen to commercial life a few years ago, .35 bullets have proliferated. For years, shooters whined that they'd buy a .35 if only someone would offer an alternative to 200-grain roundnoses built to open at .35 Remington velocities. Now Nosler has a 225-grain Partition spitzer that seems ideal for the Whelen and the .350 Remington. Speer offers a 250-grain Grand Slam, plus lighter bullets. Sierra lists a 250-grain Game King in boattail configuration. Hornady has both roundnose and spitzer bullets in the 250-grain weight, as well as a

200-grain spitzer (a fine missile for whitetails). Blue Mountain Bullets (John Day, Oregon) specializes in .358 bullets for tough game, with lots of testing on elk locally. Jack Carter's Trophy Bonded 225-grain .35 is also a first-round pick for those who have a .350 Remington, a Whelen or a .358 Norma.

For hunters who don't handload, Federal offers a .35 Whelen load in its Premium line -- a 225-grain Trophy Bonded Bear Claw at 2500 fps. Other .35s based on belted cases include the .350 Griffin & Howe Magnum, one of the first Magnum wildcats. As the story goes, it was commissioned shortly after World War II by Leslie Simpson, a widely-traveled hunter, who suggested an American version of the British rounds he'd used so successfully on the African veldt; namely, a 275-grain bullet at 2500 fps. Griffin & Howe necked down a full-length .375 H&H case to give 275-grain bullets 2440, and 220-grain bullets 2790. The substantial killing energy was often lost to fragmentation, however, because the light bullet jackets of the day came apart at high impact speeds.

A few years ago, I decided to build a .35 Whelen Improved, keeping the datum line on the shoulder unchanged to simplify case forming. Intermountain Arms (Boise, Idaho) chambered a #4 Douglas barrel and screwed it onto my Remington 78 action. I scoped the rifle with an old Lyman All-American--a 6x with a post reticule--and settled on 53 grains H335 behind a 250-grain Speer Grand Slam bullet for an elk hunt. The Improved Whelen bullet plowed through both lungs of a mature bull at 220 yards in Washington's Blue Mountains. The elk died in two jumps. Though pleased with this sharp-shouldered .35, I'll not soon build another rifle for it. There's too little shoulder to "improve." I gained at most five percent in case capacity, or roughly 100 fps in a long barrel. The standard Whelen is fine. P. O. Ackley's *Handbook for Shooters and Reloaders* (Volume 1) dedicates 13 pages to the .35s. Most are wildcats, and many are so similar as to be all but interchangeable.

Iron sights and blunt bullets limit the reach of the .356 Winchester. It's a fine close-cover round for deer, however, and well suited to the Model 94 carbine.

The .35 Ackley Improved Magnum is a straighter, sharp-shouldered .350 G&H. So is the .350 Mashburn Super Magnum and the .358 Barnes Supreme. The .35 Ackley Magnum, the .350 Williams, the .350 Mashburn Short Magnum, the .35 Apex and the .35 Belted Newton are all very close to the .358 Norma in appearance and performance. The .358 Lee Magnum, with its reformed .425 Westley Richards case, offers a slight edge. A good project for lever-action fans is the .35/.348, with its sharp shoulder and minimum body taper. The .35 Lever Power (on a shortened Krag case) was designed by Fred Wade to add steam to rifles built for the .30-30.

A lot of shooters think the .35s are all short-range rounds. The bullets, after all, are fat -- not long and sleek like those you'd stuff in a .270 case, or a 7mm Magnum or a belted .30. But 225- or 250-grain .35 spitzers driven 2500 fps or faster shoot about as flat to 300 yards as 180-grain .30-06 bullets. Federal's new .35 Whelen load, with a 225-grain Trophy Bonded at 2500, for example, gives 10.2 inches of drop at 300 yards with a 200-yard zero. A 180-grain Trophy Bonded started at 2700 fps from a .30-06 drops 9.2 inches. And the .35 bullet delivers 260 foot-pounds more energy. Even a roundnose Core-Lokts launched from a Whelen (before Remington replaced them with pointed 250-grain bullets) did not sag appreciably more than the pointed .30-06 bullets out to 200 yards. Most game is shot closer than that.

While there's no magic in a number, the wide range of .35-bore cartridges includes some exceedingly useful rounds. For whitetails close up and quick, you can't do much better than the .35 Remington or the .356 Winchester. And while the .30-06 is tough to unseat as an all-around cartridge, the .350 Remington and .35 Whelen will perform better on all but the ground squirrels. For bruisers in Alaska's brush, and to clobber big elk at a distance, the .358 Norma has few rivals. In fact, without a .35, some hunters may accuse you of not having much in the way of hunting rifles at all!

# FAST, FLAT AND FORGOTTEN

A friend of mine has built several rifles and sold them all. "One of these days," he told me, "I'm going to put one together for myself." Meanwhile, he's been using a borrowed Model 70 Winchester made in the early 1960s and chambered in a .264 Winchester Magnum. Saddled alternately with 4x Zeiss and 6.5-20x Leupold scopes, it has delivered many a lethal sting on the plains, in the mountains and at the northern fringe of Canadian bush.

My friend has spent considerable time cooking up loads and has a great supply of new .264 cases, each one selected by weight, flash-hole uniformity and case neck concentricity. The rifle will keep its bullets in a bottle cap at 100 yards. But when he talks about a rifle for himself, he never mentions the .264, despite having shot several big deer with his Model 70 loaner. Indeed, this belted 6.5mm greyhound is well along the tail of the popularity curve and remains one of the last cartridges many hunters consider when buying or chambering a rifle.

When Winchester introduced the .264 in 1958, expectations were high. A "short" magnum with a case length of 2.500 inches, it could be chambered in any bolt-action rifle designed for the .30-06 (case length: 2.494). The .264 followed close on the heels of the .338 Winchester Magnum. Both were necked-down versions of the .458 Winchester, announced in 1965. Winchester magazine ads at the time showed a .264 muzzle, end-on, with this caption: "It makes a helluva noise and packs a helluva wallop."

Despite velocity claims of 3200 and 3700 fps for factory-loaded 140- and 100-grain bullets, sales were disappointing. One problem was that the .264 was chambered for Winchester's Model 70 only. By the time hunters had given the .264 its first trials, Remington was developing its own short magnum-- the 7mm--based on the same case. It was not about to market a round for its competition. Winchester dubbed its new rifle the "Westerner," complementing the .338 "Alaskan" introduced about the same time. Designed for long shooting at plains and mountain game, the Westerner wore a 26-inch barrel, though a Featherweight version with a 22-inch barrel appeared later. Winchester's 1-in-9 twist proved adequate for the speedy 140-grain bullets hunters favored for mule deer and sheep. Some hunters snapped up the rifles and hurried off to the hinterlands with great enthusiasm.

Sage flats and pronghorns prompted Winchester to dub its first .264 rifle the "Westerner."

The .264 Winchester Magnum (left), introduced in 1959, was poorly marketed and never became as popular as the 7mm Remington Magnum (right), which made its debut with the Model 700 rifle in 1962.

Reports varied, but the consensus of gun gurus was that the .264 offered little more than a .270, while consuming a lot more powder. Recoil and muzzle blast were substantial, and it took a long barrel to get all that slow powder burned up in such a tiny hole. The .264 was criticized for being "over bore capacity," which means it had too big a case and too skinny a bullet. "Inefficient and abusive," agreed the scribes. The folks at Winchester were understandably dismayed--especially since its .338 Magnum was slow getting started. If the .264 was abusive to the ears and shoulder, the belted .33 was downright brutal. Moreover, the .338's narrow range of application (elk, moose, big bears) guaranteed a smaller market. The .264 should have appealed to the multitudes of western deer and pronghorn hunters, as well as to whitetail enthusiasts who shot bucks across acres of corn stubble, soy beans and alfalfa. The 100-grain bullet seemed ideal for coyotes as well. Elk hunters were not courted.

But here Winchester miscalculated. Deer hunters had plenty of range with their .270s and .30-06s; and coyote hunters favored the .243 over the .264. Remington, in its wisdom, decided that a dual-purpose magnum would sell best if it were designed to bracket deer and elk, not coyotes and deer. The 7mm Remington Magnum was subsequently loaded

at the factory with 150- and 175-grain bullets. Its case was essentially the same, only its mouth was .020 bigger than that of the .264. Sales of the belted 7 zoomed, spurred by ads hawking a big-game cartridge with the punch of a .300 magnum and the mild recoil of a .30-06. Paired with the new Model 700 Remington rifle, the 7mm soon threatened the predominance of the .30-06 as the all-around cartridge of choice among western hunters.

Failure of the .264 to displace the .270, along with its poor showing against the 7mm Remington Magnum after that cartridge appeared in 1963, left it badly positioned for Winchester's ill-fated remake of the Model 70 in 1964. As "Pre-64" 70s shot up in value, the redesigned 70 took a beating at market not only from the Remingtons and Rugers but from its own predecessor. Sadly, the .264 Winchester Magnum shared its fate; but this was not without precedent. Back in 1913, Charles Newton had fashioned America's first 6.5mm cartridge: the .256 Newton. Its case was slightly smaller than that of the .30-06, but 140-grain bullets could be handloaded to nearly 2900 fps, a gain of about 10 percent over the most ambitious 6.5 military cartridges made abroad. Like the .264 Winchester and its overseas cousins, this round used .264-inch bullets. It was offered in Newton

The author hunts in country that stretches a cartridge.

rifles, which failed at market. The last Newton rifle firm folded in the early 1920s, and Winchester stopped loading the .256 just before World War II. Though the 6.5 bore remained hugely popular in other countries, it survived in the U.S. only in wildcat form until the .264 Magnum made its debut. The 6.5/06 was probably the most popular round during this interim, pushing 140-grain bullets at almost 3000 fps.

I bought my first .264 soon after the cartridge was introduced. I couldn't afford a Model 70 (a new Westerner cost $154 at the time), so I bought an imported Mauser barreled action and stocked the rifle with a piece of Claro walnut. Shaping and inletting the stock took an awfully long time, as I had only the crudest tools. But eventually I trotted out to a nearby farm with a completed rifle and a handful of Winchester cartridges given to me by my father, who owned no guns and considered ammunition an extravagance. On that sharp, windy spring evening, I carefully closed the bolt, sighted through the K4 and pressed the trigger. As the sharp report echoed from the hills, I was exhilarated--until I saw that the recoil had split the stock's wrist. I hadn't bedded the rifle properly and was now forced to start over.

By November's deer season, the new rifle was zeroed. I'd also managed to save enough money for a whole box of 140-grain Winchester Power Points. One cold day, while trudging over a hill separating swamp from cornfield, I startled three deer. As they bounded off toward the cattails, I managed one shot as my crosswire flew by the buck's ribcage. To my astonishment, he slid on his nose. Working the bolt with stiff hands, I foolishly started down toward the tall grass where he'd fallen. Suddenly he was up and off, tail down. As he dashed into a stand of hardwoods I fired twice more; then he was gone. There was little blood and only patchy snow. Frosted leaves revealed his path for perhaps 100 yards, but eventually I lost the trail. I never did retrieve that deer, and I had no idea where my bullet had struck. It was easy to blame the .264, though of course the fault was mine. Had I readied myself fast enough for a second shot and waited on the hill, the buck would have either died where he lay or struggled to his feet and given me a second chance. Later that season, I dropped a buck standing in wheat stubble. He went down so fast he vanished during recoil. Again I charged forward, failing to mark the spot. I spent a quarter hour ranging up and down the knee-high stubble field looking for that deer. The .264, I learned, could kill like lightning or cripple like a .25-20, depending on where the bullet went. That rifle accounted for a few other animals but was never a favorite. It shot 140-grain factory loads quite well-- just over an inch consistently--but it sprayed 100-grain spitzers like a fire hose. I traded it for a .270, which proved a more pleasing rifle. Later, in a rash moment, I sold it, but not before I was convinced that the .270 was all the deer cartridge I'd ever need.

Other hunters had apparently reached the same conclusion about Roy Weatherby's .270 Magnum. Developed in 1943, it was his first successful big game round and followed Roy's experiments with an improved .220 Swift, which he called the .220 Rocket. Weatherby didn't incorporate his business until 1945, but field experience with the belted .270 revealed that high velocity was both useful and marketable to big game hunters. From this rootstock would spring, in 1944, the .257, 7mm and .300 Weatherby Magnums (the .240 and .340 were added during the 1960s).

Like Winchester's .264, the .270 Weatherby derives from a shortened, blown-out .300 Holland case. It is factory loaded with 100-, 130- and 150-grain bullets, each .277 in diameter. The success of Winchester's .270, launched in 1925, no doubt influenced Weatherby's choice of bores. Fueled by praise from Jack O'Connor and other writers, the popularity of the Winchester round soared. By the early 1940s, this offspring of the .30-06 had become the deer cartridge against which all other open-country deer cartridges were judged.

The .270 Weatherby got tepid reviews, however, not that it lacked sizzle. In 26-inch barrels with generous free-bore, the results showed 3760, 3375 and 3245 fps for the three bullet weights -- better than a 10-percent boost in muzzle velocities over the Winchester cartridge. The case holds substantially

The .250 Savage was a hot number before World War II; but Weatherby's .257 Magnum, developed in the early 1940s, made the .250 seem sedate.

more powder, of course, and the free-boring helps. Any comparisons between the .270 Weatherby and .264 Winchester, incidentally, must also be made with throating in mind. Giving the bullet room to accelerate before the lands bite into it relieves pressure, so a brawnier load can be used. The cost is in accuracy, though Weatherby rifles with long .375 throats typically shoot well. The super-charged performance of Weatherby's .270 didn't trigger stampedes of shooters at gun counters, mainly because the cartridge was chambered only in expensive Weatherby rifles. In addition, hunters were killing deer, pronghorns, sheep and elk handily with .270s and .30-06s. The .300 Holland & Holland had become more popular in 1937 when Winchester offered it as a charter chambering in its Model 70 (Remington later offered its Model 721 for this round). Ammunition for the .300 H&H was better distributed and less costly than that for a .270 Weatherby, mainly because Weatherby--the only source for its cartridges--imported them from Sweden. The same problems hamstrung the 7mm Weatherby Magnum after its debut in 1944.

Like the .264 Winchester, the .270 Weatherby remains well behind the 7mm Remington Magnum in sales. Factory-loaded, the belted Remington falls well short of both the .270 and 7mm Weatherby in performance, but it has become available in every domestic bolt rifle made for magnum cases. It has also been offered in autoloading and even lever-action guns. In most places that peddle centerfire rounds, cartridges are available for the 7mm Remington Magnum, whereas .270 Weatherby ammo can be exceedingly hard to find.

The same can be said for the .257 Weatherby Magnum, whose case capacity is essentially the same as that of the .270 Weatherby and .264 Winchester. Its bullets mike just .007 smaller in diameter than the .264's. But differences in bullet weights are significant; 25-caliber rounds are stuck with bullets

These belted cartridges work fine for long shooting in open country. From left: .264 Winchester, .270 Weatherby, 7mm Remington and 7mm Weatherby Magnums.

of 75 to 120 grains. The Weatherby .257 case is the same as that of Weatherby's .270 and 7mm Magnums, with the distinctive round ("venturi") shoulder angles. Only the neck diameter differs. Factory loads spit 87-grain bullets out at 3825 fps, while 100-grain softpoints reach 3600 and 120-grain Partitions leave the muzzle at 3300. This racehorse beats the .25-06 Remington as handily as the .270 Weatherby outpaces the .270 Winchester. The drawbacks are the same as well, including noise, recoil and ammo expense. Like all big cartridges launching little bullets, the .257 Weatherby benefits from long barrels. It has traditionally been chambered only in Weatherby rifles.

The strange twists of cartridge evolution have left a plethora of 7mm bullets in weights of 100 to 175 grains. This vast assortment of weights and styles appealed to handloaders during the adolescence of Remington's 7mm Magnum. The .257, .264 and .270 bores have been blessed with fewer bullet choices and narrower weight ranges, which still influences some shooters in their choice of cartridges. While bullet lists have expanded considerably since the 1960s, the selection of 7mm spitzers was quite good during the 20 years Weatherby's 7mm Magnum was drawing little fanfare. The contrast in market histories of the Weatherby and Remington 7mm

rounds was probably due mainly to disparities in the cost and availability of rifle and ammunition. Advertising played a role, too. Roy Weatherby may have been a master marketer, but he did not target blue-collar hunters as effectively as did Remington or Winchester. Apparently he preferred to cultivate the image of a superlative rifle to be used by elite hunters.

The success of Remington's 7mm Magnum has prompted the development of other high-performance 7mms; namely, the 7mm Imperial, 7mm Dakota and 7mm STW. Oddly enough, Weatherby's 7mm has received only modest attention in this renaissance. The .264 Winchester and the .270 and .257 Weatherbys remain in the popularity cellar, as it were. To ensure that the .264 never climbs out, Winchester has all but dropped the cartridge from its list of Model 70 chamberings (only the Classic Sporter and rifles from the custom shop offer the cartridge). There is no longer a 100-grain .264 load, and in factory charts 140-grain bullets clock 3030 instead of the original 3200 fps. That's slower than factory-loaded 130-grain bullets from a .270 Winchester. Strangely, Winchester has added the .270 Weatherby Magnum to the Classic Sporter chamberings, while Ruger offers it in the company's Number One single-shots. Remington, meanwhile, manufactures 140-grain .264 Magnum cartridges and 150-, 165- and 175-grain loads for the 7mm Weatherby, even though its 700 rifles include neither chambering. Sako rifles were once built for the .264 Winchester, too, but that no longer applies.

Lately, American ammunition firms have shown some interest in Weatherby cartridges under 30-bore. Hornady assembles ammo for Weatherby's 7mm, with 154- and 175-grain bullets. Federal loads 130-grain Nosler Partitions and 150-grain Trophy Bonded Bear Claws for the .270 Weatherby, and 160-grain bullets of both these types for the

7mm Weatherby. Ammo for the .257 Magnum is still available only from Weatherby and custom loading shops.

Unquestionably, the 7mm magnums are more versatile than the .264 Winchester and the .257 and .270 Weatherbys. But their differences aren't as great as sales records suggest. First, the wide range of 7mm bullet weights is useful only if applications demand it. Few hunters who shoot belted 7mm cartridges load 100-grain bullets for them. These lightweights can provide diversion to experimenters, but they're a much better match for rimless cases of modest capacity. Most shooters who use 7mm magnum rifles carry them for game at least the size of pronghorns. The gap between a 100-pound prairie goat and an 800-pound bull elk can be handled by a bullet weight ranging from 140 to 175 grains. By settling on one accurate load tossing a 160-grain bullet at around 3050 fps, or a 150-grain at 3150, most hunters won't need anything else.

That kind of performance can result from the use of a 7mm Remington or Weatherby without a free-bore assist--but it can be matched with a .270 Weatherby. Comparing 150-grain loads, higher sectional density and ballistic coefficient are obtainable with the .270. Not many elk will keel over when smacked with a 160-grain bullet at 3050, but they'll run off after absorbing a 150-grain at 3150. Bullet construction matters more than slight differences in velocity, weight and diameter.

If a 150-grain bullet crumples a big bull elk, what about the 140 from Winchester's .264? Obviously, there's a point at which effectiveness diminishes as bullet weight is dumped. Elk hunter surveys show the .270 Winchester is still among the five most popular elk rounds, with many of its fans prefering 130-grain bullets. Those who use 140-grain loads must be content with velocities of around 3000 fps, with 150s pulling it back another 100 fps. Despite what the catalogs claim, a 140-grain bullet from a .264 is not limited to .270-level performance. Even the factory loads I've chronographed exceed the manufacturer's dismal predictions. Moreover, the right handloads from long barrels can really scoot (I've consistently milked over 3300 fps from a 140-grain bullet out of a Model 70 with no signs of excessive pressure). The high ballistic coefficient and sectional density of that 140-grain spitzer ensure its potency to great distances.

The drop from 140 to 120 grains is, in my mind, significant. No matter that the case of a .257 Weatherby holds as much fuel as that of a .270 Weatherby or .264 Winchester. No matter that the bullet skates across three football fields faster than you can wink. Speed can compensate for bullet weight to some degree, and in light-boned animals it's much more effective than added weight in producing the lightning-quick kills Roy Weatherby promoted so successfully as the mark of accomplished hunters. But with elk--their leg bones as thick as automobile axles, scapulas like plowshares, and joints that turn bullets to pulp--the more lead that can be delivered, the better. In fact, speed can work against hunters when a bullet strikes bone or even hard muscle, because speed ruptures the bullet. The faster the bullet, the higher the energy--but also the more violent the rupture.

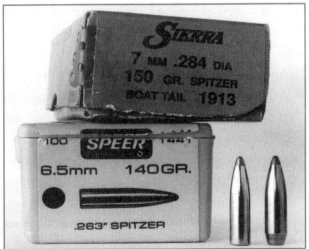

When driven at the same speed, there's not much difference ballistically between 140-grain .264 bullets and 150-grain 7mm bullets.

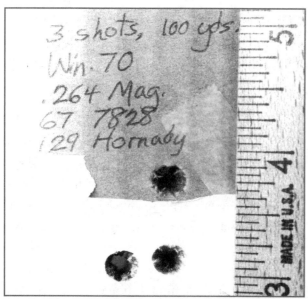

With 140-grain bullets, the .264 Winchester Magnum is deadly on game as big as elk. While accuracy depends on many things, groups like this are possible.

So-called "controlled expansion" design has helped make light bullets more deadly on tough game; but they cannot duplicate the bigger wound channel that's possible with a heavier bullet.

Why not give the .25 a longer bullet? Surely enough custom bullet-makers are around now so that a 130-grain bullet--or even a 140--can be ordered up for the .257 Weatherby. After all, many 6.5mm military rounds were capped with 156-grain bullets, and these were a mere snakeskin fatter than a .25. The problem, of course, is pressure. As weight increases, pressure climbs. A heavier bullet also means a longer one, which, unless its shape is drastically changed, increases bearing surface and friction. One way to reduce friction is to use two-diameter bullets, which feature a groove-diameter band at the base. The front is turned to bore diameter so it rides on the lands. Some bullets for the .264 Winchester Magnum have been made this way.

Heavier bullets have higher sectional density, which not only improves penetration but also boosts ballistic coefficient (as long as nose profile isn't compromised). High ballistic coefficient helps the bullet retain velocity and energy, keeps drop to a minimum, and acts as a hedge against wind. At some point, though, velocity loss becomes critical. Taking this to an extreme, consider a rocket-shaped bullet that's six inches long. Its sectional density and ballistic coefficient are off the charts, but to stay under pressure ceilings, its speed may have to be limited to that of a horse-drawn milk wagon. The laws of physics demand that we pay for weight in acceleration.

Increasing bore diameter reduces the effect of any given weight increase. Adding 30 grains to an 87-grain .25 caliber bullet robs more than 500 fps. Compare that with what happens when bullet weight in a .300 Weatherby Magnum is boosted 30 grains, from 150 to 180. The sacrifice is only 300 fps--another reason why small bores mandate a narrow range of bullets. If more bullet weight is needed, it's a good idea to move up in diameter before reaching the heaviest available bullet.

In my view, the best bullets for the .257 Weatherby weigh from 115 to 120 grains. Their huge cases, along with the ability of modern powders to drive such bullets at 3300 fps, justify use of the heaviest bullets commonly available in this diameter. The .257 Roberts--even the .25-06--seem better served with 100-grain bullets. Given the slender range of weights for .25s, it's a wonder that no bullet maker has come out with a 110-grain spitzer. This would be an ideal top-end weight for both the Roberts and the .25-06, as well as the .257 Weatherby. The magnum could easily kick a 110-grain bullet out at 3400, a deadly combination indeed for long shooting at whitetails or pronghorns. Nosler's 115-grain Ballistic Tip should fill that mid-weight slot nicely.

For hunting tough game like elk with the .264 Winchester, the 140-grain bullet has an edge over the

120-, 125- and 129-grain bullets that can summarily flatten deer-size animals at any reasonable range. Bullets lighter than 120 grains are, to my mind, useless in a .264 Winchester Magnum. When shooting small animals, a .243 or its equivalent is a better choice. Muzzle blast, recoil and powder consumption are all higher than most shooters are willing to tolerate when going after animals that can be dispatched with 100-grain bullets.

Like its counterparts, the .270 Weatherby performs best when loaded with bullets heavy for its bore. There's so much fuel, one might as well put it to work behind a 150-grain bullet, or at least a 140. In the .270 Winchester, 150s trundle along at 2900 or so; in the Weatherby they rocket out of the muzzle above 3200. Besides, the 150-grain bullet is much better suited for elk. If deer are the only game around, a .270 Winchester, .280 Remington or .25-06 with lighter bullets work fine. All of these rimless rounds give deer-weight bullets plenty of speed for shooting at extreme range. They kick less, behave in a civil manner in 24-inch barrels and are cheaper to shoot.

Powder selection for small-bore magnums is either limited or easy, depending on how you want to look at it. Slow fuels are best. I use mostly IMR

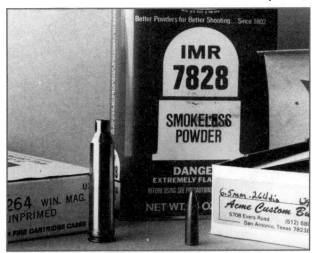

IMR's 7828 powder is for the .264 Win. Mag. and other small bore magnums--especially with heavy bullets.

7828, Hodgdon H4831, H570 and H1000, Hercules RL-19 and RL-22 and Accurate Arms 3100. While these powders are only a bit less sluggish than charcoal, serious trouble can ensue when reaching too quickly for velocity ceilings. This is especially true in custom rifles chambered for Weatherby magnums. The SAAMI chamber has a generous throat, but shooters who don't like free-bore have used reamers to build rifles with short throats. These can be dangerous with Weatherby's factory-loaded ammunition--one reason perhaps why Remington and Federal give their Weatherby rounds substantially lower starting velocities. Rifling twist and land configuration also affect pressure. Our litigious times have made company engineers wary of discussing internal ballistics outside the ammo plant, but one highly respected gunmaker builds a .300 Weatherby with short throats. He pulls the bullets on Weatherby factory ammunition and dumps measured amounts of powder in various increments while he bores out a throat in stages. A .100 throat--.030 longer than SAAMI specs for a .300 Winchester-- generates excess pressure from Weatherby loads after bleeding six grains of powder. Not until he reaches a throat length of .315 is he able to use unaltered factory ammunition.

To sum up, Weatherby's .257 and .270 magnums, along with the .264 Winchester, comprise a small cadre of flat-shooting cartridges that have never received their due at market. For deer-size game at long range, there's nothing better. With heavy bullets, the .264 and .270 magnums deliver far more energy than either the .270 Winchester or .30-06. Given proper bullet construction, they are a match for any elk. It's hard to argue that either should supplant the belted 7mms, or that a .25-06 should be traded for a .257 Weatherby. But to write these belted speedsters off as examples of excess is to underestimate their versatility.

# MY FAVORITE CARTRIDGES

When I was a kid ogling Winchester catalogs and saving hay money for .303 ammo, I resented gun writers who airily promoted their favorites as if every hunter cared--or could afford more than one $30 surplus SMLE. Those fellows weren't arrogant; they were just having fun; and, as I later conceded, they wrote well enough to keep me reading. The world is full of useful cartridges and even more so of opinions about them. Regardless, I'll announce here my picks for six eminently useful hunting cartridges--and the reasons why I think they are.

## 1. THE 22-250

For small game at a distance, the .22-250 Remington has no peer. Beginning in 1915, its parent case, the .250 Savage (developed by Charles Newton) was loaded commercially. During the 1930s, several noted experimenters necked the .250 Savage to 22 caliber. Grosvenor Wotkyns developed a round that almost went commercial just before Winchester replaced its Model 54 rifle with the Model 70. But in 1935 Winchester chose instead a .22 centerfire based on the 6mm Lee Navy case: the .220 Swift, which became reasonably popular in the Model 70.

Not until 1965 did factory loads appear. That year, Remington adopted the cartridge and chambered it in its Model 700 hunting rifles as well as in the Model 40XB match rifles. Since then it has gained broad acceptance by American, British and European firearms firms and has become one of the most popular smallbore centerfire cartridges ever (it's still known by some old-timers as the "Varminter"). Commercial loads feature a narrow range of bullet weights. The heavy 55-grain bullet clocks 3680 fps.

The .22-250 is a hotshot round, capable of pushing 50-grain bullets at 3850 fps--roughly 150 fps shy of the Swift. But its smaller, rimless case is more efficient than the Swift's, and it can be loaded down to .222 velocities with ease. The .22-250 seems an inherently accurate cartridge, one that is not too fussy about fuel or bullets. At full throttle, its trajectory lies as flat as a Nevada highway, with 50-grain bullets striking only 5 inches low at 300 yards, and 16 inches low at 400. That's less drop than a 7mm Remington Magnum can produce with a 150-grain bullet stoked to redline. The comparison is moot, of course, because the belted seven is a big-

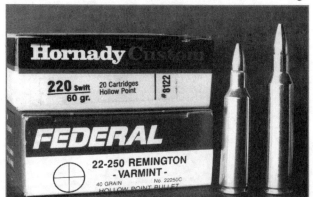

As soon as Winchester brought it to market in the 1930s, the .220 Swift was hailed for its great speed. The more efficient .22-250 languished as a wildcat until 1964, when Remington adopted it. Only about 100 fps differ between the two with bullets of equal weight.

The .22-250 Remington and .225 Winchester are comparable in performance, but the .22-250 "Varminter" is far more popular. The .225 case is best suited to single-shot rifles.

game cartridge, while the .22-250 is a small-game round. With correct bullets and shot placement, the Varminter (with a few other .22 centerfires) has proven deadly on deer-size game. Kills have not only been certain but sudden. Still, few states now allow use of 22-caliber rifles for any hoofed game, and the .22-250 appears mostly in 'chuck pasture and prairie dog towns. It's also a superb cartridge for coyotes, causing less pelt damage than the larger 6mms. As with any .22, wind drift can be significant -- nearly a foot at 300 yards in a gentle 10-mph breeze, or half again as much as the give of a hard-charging 100-grain spitzer from a 6mm.

My own .22-250 is an early Remington 700 purchased from a friend and fellow smallbore competitor. It has a 24-inch sporting-weight barrel that sucks groups tight and a T-16 Weaver scope that offers precise aim at little things far away. When the trigger breaks according to script, my bullets hit where the dot paused. For powders, IMR 3031, 4895 and 4320 are hard to beat, as are Accurate 2230, BL-C(2) and Hodgdon H380.

## 2. THE .270 WINCHESTER

Another veteran round worth its keep is the .270 Winchester. Introduced in 1925, it was chambered originally in Winchester's Model 54 and became a charter offering in the Model 70, ranking second to

the .30-06 in sales of that rifle. The high velocity of its 130-grain bullet ensured flat flight and violent expansion with standard softnose bullets. In fact, hunters used to the performance of the .30-30 complained early on that the new round was too destructive. Eager to please its customers, Winchester down-loaded a 150-grain bullet to 2675 fps; but nobody bought the ammo and it was soon discontinued. Now all .270 cartridges get a full tank of fuel with bullets from 100 to 150 grains in weight. "Light Magnum" ammunition from Hornady has boosted the already ambitious velocity levels of the .270, its cartridges matching claims while punching out groups with unprecedented accuracy.

Jack O'Connor's praise of the .270 certainly helped it along, as did the lack of any real competition during those formative pre-war years. When the .280 Remington appeared in 1957, it made nary a blip in the .270's soaring sales curve. Following its introduction in 1963, even the 7mm Remington Magnum failed to shake hunter support for the .270. Addition of 140-grain bullets in factory loads upped the .270's utility and appeal, if only incrementally. In my view, no finer all-around deer cartridge exists, although the argument can be made that the .280 offers the same modest recoil, taut

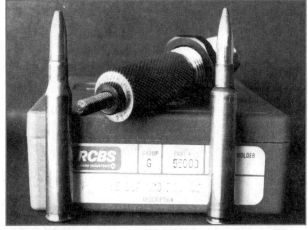

The .280 Remington Improved (right) has more powder capacity than the parent .280 (left). It can be loaded to perform almost on a par with the 7mm Remington Magnum.

The .270 Winchester is still popular and remains a top choice for long shots at deer-size game. Bullets like Winchester's Fail Safe improve its performance on elk.

bullet path and downrange smash, plus a larger assortment of bullets. Of course, the .30-06 handles heavier bullets; but for deer they're not needed. The .270's 130-grain bullets match 150-grain .30s in sectional density and boast an edge in velocity of around 150 fps, given standard factory loads in the .270 and .30-06.

As an elk cartridge, the .270 is by most accounts marginal. The .30-06 and 7mm Remington Magnum, with their heavier bullets offer more punch. Advances in bullet design, however, have helped the .270. Predictable, controlled expansion and 90-percent weight retention from custom bullets by Hawk, Swift, Jensen, Blue Mountain, Armfield, Trophy Bonded, Elkhorn and others have added depth and diameter to .270 wound channels and ensured adequate penetration in elk-size game. Nosler's well-proven Partition is offered in ammunition by Federal, which also loads Trophy Bonded bullets in its Premium line. Winchester markets its superlative Fail Safe bullet in both component and loaded form. Remington's Safari big game ammunition features Swift bullets.

Why do I like the .270? Probably because I've clobbered more deer with it than with any other cartridge, plus elk and sheep. I've always liked the

.270 rifles I've owned, too, mostly for their gentle recoil. The cartridge seems to accept most slow powders without complaint and has thrown most bullets where I wanted them. To approach 3100 fps, I mainly use 59 grains of H4831 behind a 130-grain bullet. The old Model 70 I often hunt with, however, doesn't quibble about its diet. Almost any potent .270 big game load nips out a tight cluster of holes in the middle at 200 yards. Minute-of-angle accuracy is routine.

## 3. THE .308

The .308 Winchester is another fine cartridge. First appearing in 1952, it was the sporting version of the U.S. T-65 or NATO 7.62x51 military round. Oddly, commercial manufacture predated its acceptance as the official U.S. Army cartridge (1954) and its chambering in the M14 rifle (1957). As a battle round, the .308 (or 7.62) has two important advantages over the .30-06 that it replaced. The case is smaller (lighter), enabling soldiers to boost firepower without increasing pack weight or bulk. That short case also permits the use of shorter rifle and machine gun actions. While some might argue that efficiency hardly matters in a hunting

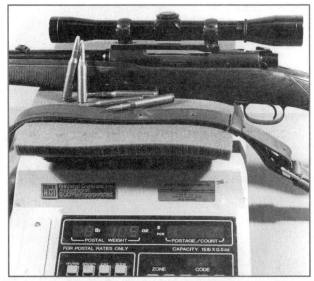

Even a Model 70 Featherweight can weigh over 8.5 pounds trailside. Scope and mount, sling and ammunition add ounces. The .270 is the author's all-time favorite deer cartridge, while this 4x Leupold is one of his favorite scopes.

The .308 Winchester (right) isn't much bigger than the .30-30, but it drives a bullet 400 fps faster. The vertical magazines in .308 rifles don't mandate the blunt bullet noses required in tube magazines.

round, the compact .308 case certainly does generate lots of energy for its size, and it uses less powder per unit of velocity or energy than does the .30-06. The .308 is also a favorite of metallic silhouette shooters.

Of the three .308s I now own, one is an old Model 70 target rifle that began life as a .30-06 National Match gun, then was rebarreled and altered to .308. It is wonderfully accurate and has outperformed more powerful 30-caliber rifles at the 600-yard line. Loaded ambitiously with 168-grain Sierra match bullets, the .308 still has manageable recoil, even in lighter rifles. Bullet drop at 300 yards is only 9 inches, given a 200-yard zero. I've clocked 180-grain handloads from this Winchester's 24-inch barrel at 2700 fps (factory-listed velocity for 180-grain .30-06 loads) The Hornady Light Magnum and new Federal High Energy .308 ammunition will duplicate velocities of standard .30-06 rounds. With a significant difference in case capacity, the .308 won't equal the .30-06 ballistically when both are loaded to maximum safe pressure with carefully matched powders. According to the books, 100 fps less can be expected with the .308; and there's not a lot of room in which to maneuver, because the .308 (like the .22-250 and .270) is factory-loaded to relatively high pressures.

The same bullets that make the .30-06 so versatile are available for the .308. While 180-grain spitzers perform well in the .308, I prefer 165s and slightly faster fuel than one finds acceptable in the '06. IMR and Hodgdon 4350, along with Scot 4351, are winners for both these bullet weights in the .308. The same applies to Hodgdon H414 and H380, Vihtavuori N135 and N140, The 165-grain bullets also do well with faster powders, namely: IMR 4895, 4064 and 4320, RL-15, BL-C(2), H335 and Accurate 2520. Those powders excel with 150-grain loads.

The other .308s in my rack are a 1950's-vintage Model 70 Featherweight and an Ultra Light Model 20. Among the endearing qualities of this cartridge is its squat profile. It fits nicely in short actions, which are lighter than long ones and more rigid as well. Because it has a fairly small powder capacity in relation to case mouth diameter the .308 performs well in short barrels. The result is lots of muscle in a compact rifle with tolerable recoil. While the .308 is for some reason hardly ever listed in the company of the .270 and 7x57 as a "classic" cartridge for mountain game, it is certainly one of the best rounds a hunter could chamber in a lightweight rifle for sheep or mule deer.

This Model 70 target rifle, originally a .30-06, is now chambered in .308 Winchester. A magazine block adapts it to the shorter round.

The .35 Whelen (right) and .35 Whelen Improved are efficient killers but lack the speed that attracts today's shooters.

## 4. THE .35 WHELEN

For heavier animals, I'm partial to efficient cartridges that don't burn out barrels or bloody my nose. Among the top performers is the .35 Whelen, a necked-up .30-06 circa 1922. Some claim that James V. Howe of Griffin and Howe was responsible, naming the new case after Colonel Townsend Whelen, a noted rifleman and gun writer of his day. Another view is that Whelen requested reamers of his own specifications from Howe. At the time, Whelen was the commanding officer at Frankfort Arsenal, where Howe worked as a toolmaker. No doubt both men contributed greatly to this .35, thus filling the need for a potent big game cartridge, one that shot flatter than Winchester's .405 and worked satisfactorily in any rifle built for the .30-06.

The .35 Whelen plodded along as a wildcat with a loyal but modest following until 1988, when Remington chambered its Model 700 Classic for the round and offered two factory loads: a 200-grain bullet at 2675 fps and a 250-grain bullet at 2400. Though the heavier of these had a blunt nose, its higher sectional density made it the best choice for hunters who bought .35 rifles. The advantages of this round over its parent .30-06 are bullet weight and diameter for large animals at modest range. If a 200-grain

bullet will do, the 30-caliber wins with superior sectional density -- as does the wildcat .338-06. For the .35 bore, nothing lighter than a 225-grain bullet makes sense. Remington's 250-grain factory round has since been improved with the substitution of a pointed Core-Lokt bullet. Federal loads the Whelen with a 225-grain Trophy Bonded payload that offers great penetration and weight retention in tough game.

Although the .35 Whelen is generally considered useful up close in timber only, it shoots almost as flat as a .30-06. Federal's 225-grain .35 load, for example, prints 10 inches low at 300 yards with a 200-yard zero, and a 180-grain .30-06 bullet strikes 9 inches low. At that range, the .35 Whelen delivers 1870 foot-pounds of energy compared to 1605 for the '06. The .30-06 may be more versatile--because it accommodates lighter bullets that move faster for long shooting at deer-size game--but the Whelen gets all the marbles for bigger animals at any reasonable yardage.

My three .35 Whelens are Remington 700 Classics, whose 22-inch barrels are sufficient for the wide-mouthed case best fueled with the medium-rate 4895-class of powders. IMR 4320 and 4064, H335, H380 and H414, Winchester 748, RL-15, Accurate 2520 and Scot 4065 also work well for most bullets. As bullet weights climb, IMR 4350, Scot 4351 and Winchester 760 become more useful. The selection of .358 bullets has, incidentally, broadened considerably in the last decade. Nosler offers a fine 225-grain Partition, and Speer has a 250-grain Grand Slam. The 225 Trophy Bonded loaded by Federal and custom-contoured .358s by Blue Mountain give elk hunters even more choice. Other small bullet shops have come up with additional fare.

I like my .35 Whelens so much I once decided to build a .35 Whelen Improved. To simplify case forming, I chose the Ackley version, which boosts shoulder angle from 17.5 to 40 degrees without changing headspace measurement. (The Brown-Whelen wildcat has a shorter neck and more capacity, but its shoulder has to be moved forward, which means new cases must be fashioned.) My .35 Whelen Improved features a 26-inch #4 Douglas barrel on a Remington Model 78 action and the original Remington stock. My elk-hunting load of 53 grains H335 sends a 250-grain Grand Slam bullet out the muzzle at 2600 fps. Still, I'm not sold on the Improved Whelen case. There's not much shoulder to blow out, and the velocity increase is probably due in part to those four additional inches of barrel. In sum, the .35 Whelen is an accurate, potent, efficient, manageable cartridge, one that is surely adequate for elk to 300 yards.

## 5. THE .308 NORMA

These days, thanks to improved optics and far-reaching cartridges, hunters routinely shoot beyond 300 yards. The most popular long-range multi-purpose rounds are the 7mm Remington Magnum and Winchester's belted .300. But I'll

Stuart Maitland guides big game hunters in British Columbia. The author shot a fine mule deer here with a Remington rifle in .35 Whelen, one of his favorite cartridges.

The .308 Norma, introduced to American shooters in the early 1960s, faded fast when no commercial rifles appeared (and Winchester brought out its .300 Magnum). The .308 Norma is identical to the .30-338 in performance, and almost identical in dimensions.

take the .308 Norma Magnum over both.

Like all popular short magnums, Norma's obscure .30 derives from the .300 Holland and Holland, which appeared in 1925. This long, Coke-bottle cartridge was itself an offspring of the .375 H&H. Later in the early 1940s, Roy Weatherby developed the first commercial line of belted magnum rounds for the U.S. market. His .300 was a full-length .300 H&H case blown out at the shoulder. The .257, .270 and 7mm Weatherbys were shorter and made to work in .30-06-length actions. Then, in 1956, Winchester initiated its short-magnum line with the .458, followed quickly by the .264 and .338. Remington's 7mm arrived in 1962, with the .300 Winchester following a year later. By this time, Norma's .308 Magnum was three years old--and going nowhere. Not that the design was flawed. The Norma is essentially a .30-338, with a 2.549-inch case. The Winchester Magnum has more capacity than the .308 Norma, but with a shorter neck. And except in long actions and long-throated barrels, bullets must be seated very deep in the Winchester case. As for performance, there's essentially no difference between the two, both falling squarely between the .300 H&H and the .300 Weatherby. The 26-inch Douglas barrel on my

Remington 78, given a charge of 74 grains H4831, launches a 180-grain Speer bullet at just over 3100 fps, not much faster than Norma's factory load (Norma also loads a 200-grain spitzer at 2900).

I like the .308 Norma because it kills elk as far away as I care to shoot. At 400 yards the 180-grain bullet delivers nearly 1800 ft-lbs of energy, close to what a 225-grain .35 Whelen bullet dumps at 300. A 200-grain spitzer boosts that punch to over 2100 ft-lbs. A 200-yard zero with the 180-grain bullet yields a drop at 300 of about 6 inches, while at 400 steps it drops 19 inches, which is roughly equivalent to the trajectory of a frisky 130-grain .270 load. While any medium-bore magnum delivers substantial recoil, the .308 Norma's manageable. It does what you might expect from a rocket that lands a ton of energy some 400 yards distant. It is, in my experience, noticeably less severe than the bounce of a .338 Magnum with heavy-bullet loads.

I'll admit that the reason I prefer the .308 Norma over the .300 Winchester has more to do with case design than with practicality. For the hunter who must content himself with a single big game rifle, either round will do the job. I use a lot of H4831 and Accurate 3100, but IMR 7828, H1000 and RL-22

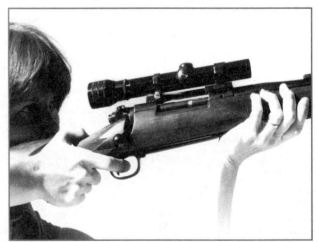

Despite the rifle's 9.5 pounds of heft, recoil on this .375 is substantial. Some professional hunters prefer the .375; others say it is more than is needed for plains game and not big enough for buffalo and elephant

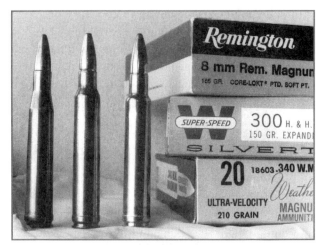

The .300 H&H Magnum (left) spawned the Weatherby line of cartridges in the 1940s, which later included the .340 Weatherby (right). The 8mm Remington Magnum has not fared well, but its offspring, the 7 STW, has become quite popular

are also acceptable. For long-reaching deer loads, I'm partial to 165-grain Sierra hollow-points driven by IMR 4350 or RL-19. There's no animal in North America that can't be taken handily with a .308 Norma rifle and any one of the many excellent 30-caliber bullets from Hornady, Speer, Sierra and Nosler, not to mention the small shops that are kept in business by hunters who seek more reliability and weight retention. If Africa is in your plans, though, you'll need a bigger rifle, partly because for dangerous game a bore diameter of .375 is the commonly legal minimum. But even if the law didn't dictate more bullet weight for buffalo, common sense would.

## 6. THE .458

The .458 is a child of the mid-50s and about as specialized as a cartridge can get. Its 510-grain soft-point lumbers out of the muzzle at around 2000 fps. Old Winchester lists give it 2130, while Federal shows 2090. In addition, Federal loads a standard 350-grain softnose to 2470, a 400-grain Trophy Bonded to 2370, and a 500-grain Trophy Bonded to 2090. The 450-grain Swift in Remington's lineup leaves the muzzle at 2150. The dismal sectional density of bullets lighter than 400 grains, and the

steep trajectory of blunt heavyweights, make this magnum a poor choice for thin-skinned game (save, perhaps, for lions). For the armor-plated denizens of Africa, you'd best load solids.

Remington and Federal both list solids in loaded .458 ammo: 500-grain payloads that hit with nearly $2\frac{1}{2}$ tons of punch. The .458's enthusiasm wanes quickly to 3690 ft-lbs at 100 yards. But that's acceptable, because this cartridge is used up close and traditionally with iron sights. Professional hunters have praised the .458 with handloaded Hornady solids (mainly to boost velocities, but also because of the Hornady's great reputation on elephants). Early factory ammo did not produce consistent velocities, according to some professional hunters.

My .458 is a commercial Mauser that weighs nine pounds. It has a plain original stock and a Lyman receiver sight with the aperture disk removed. The barrel is 23 inches long and slender enough to make it lively, but not so light that it won't settle quickly on target. Its an excellent rifle for its narrow application. As for the cartridge, I can't think of a better one for the big game of Africa. The .416 Rigby and Remington offer flatter trajectory, but at the expense of bullet weight. British Nitro Express rounds like the .470 may look more impressive, but the majority only equal the .458

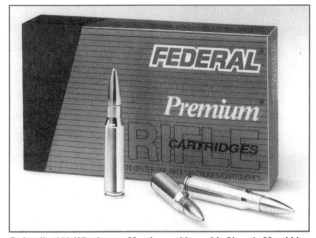

Federal's .308 Winchester Match cartridge with Sierra's Matchking 168-grain hollow point Boattail bullet is part of the company's Premium line, which includes deep-penetrating bullets for big game.

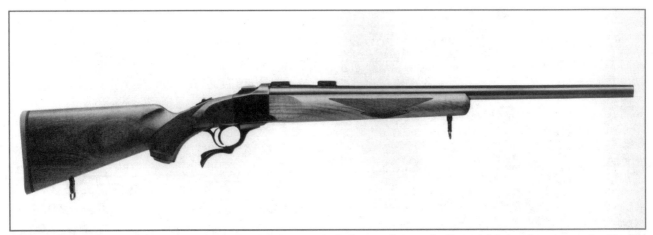

Ruger's Number One accommodates rimmed, belted and rimless rounds. Bullets can be seated without giving thought to a magazine. The rifle is short for its barrel length because there's no bolt.

ballistically. Besides, rimmed rounds are not suited to bolt-action rifles (which are more accurate than doubles as a rule), but eminently more affordable.

The handful of magazine-rifle cartridges that make the .458 seem wimpy in comparison-- Weatherby's .416 and .460, the .500 Jeffery and .505 Gibbs come to mind--mandate larger magazine boxes and rail spacing than the .458, which fits comfortably into any ordinary rifle designed for short magnums. Though ammunition cost is of little consequence compared to the price of a modern safari, the .458 Winchester Magnum is the least expensive cartridge of any round meant for dangerous game. It is no less punishing to shoot than the popular .470.

This short list of my favorite hunting cartridges is, of course, too short. And so, to appease any irate readers who may be growling out there, herewith an explanation as to why other cartridges have been omitted. The .280 Remington and .30-06 offer great versatility but are no better as deer cartridges than the .270 or, for most hunting, the .308. They surely can't match the .308 Norma Magnum for elk. The .300 H&H is another pet round, pleasant to shoot, accurate and useful. The .375 Holland, with its fine track record, was dismissed because of its narrow range of application in North America. Except perhaps in an

alder patch facing an angry brown bear, it is hardly an ideal cartridge for the task. Weatherby's powerful .340 Magnum and the .358 Norma are of the same cloth. The .416 Remington Magnum and the Rigby have the practical profile of a .30-06, but neither sees much use in North America.

The proprietary cartridges offered by custom-rifle firms--Dakota and A-Square, for example--didn't make the list because their distribution is too limited, not that some don't merit chambering in common bolt rifles. I especially like the .300 and .330 Dakota, based on the .404 Jeffery case. Wildcats have not been included, mainly because few shooters go to the trouble of having rifles built for them, and also because there are too many good ones to consider. The .338-06 is my pick among wildcats. It's among the most versatile of all cartridges for North American hunting.

Long ago I bought a couple of boxes of .300 short Mashburn cases, convincing myself that was probably reason enough to build a rifle for this round. But that still hasn't happened, so for the indefinite future my needs will be met with the .22-250 Remington, .270 Winchester, .308 Winchester, .35 Whelen, .308 Norma Magnum and .458 Winchester Magnum. They span a variety of uses and have all endeared themselves to me for one reason or another. ●

# CHAPTER 19 NINETEEN

# LAST THOUGHTS ON LONG SHOTS

The hunter spotted him first, below us and facing away, his wide antlers almost wrapped around the black ooze that made his feet a target in the gloaming. I yanked the legs of the tripod all the way out to put the Big Eye above the alders crowded close on the north slope. A deep canyon, purple now, sagged between us and the bull.

"Is it him?" The animal hadn't moved. "Can't say," I replied. We stared, hoping. It had been three long days since the shot. The antlers looked tall enough.

Then the bull took a step. "It's him!"

We said it together, but our actions were quite different. I jerked the scope down, folding the tripod legs and sliding them short. My companion raised his rifle. "How far?" he asked.

It took a moment to register. This bull was nearly half a mile distant! Range estimation isn't my long suit, but game beyond 400 yards is just too far. Stars that catch my eye at night are light years away. I can't comprehend the distance even one light year represents, but that's OK--I can simply marvel that a star whose light I see may have burned out long since. To *reach* a star, though, I'd first have to figure out what was practical. It would do me little good to travel in a spacecraft at the speed of sound toward a star 100 light years away. Many hunters who shoot at long range don't think about what's practical, so they miss. A long shot is any shot that's almost too far to make every time under existing conditions. This hunter was understandably keen to kill; but wanting

to is only part of the job. Yonder elk, I brusquely told my hunting companion, was twice as far as most hunters should consider shooting--and about six times as far as it had been three days ago when he bungled the two shots that had crippled this bull.

The author shot this caribou at roughly 200 yards with a 165-grain Sierra from a Winchester Model 70 in .300 Winchester Magnum. Hunters who shoot beyond 200 yards are as apt to cripple or miss game as they are to kill it.

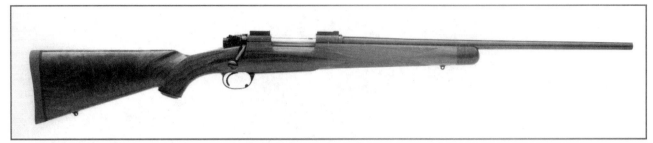
The Model 89 Big Game Rifle (Super Grade) is based on Winchester's pre-64 M70 action. This featherweight is chambered in .270.

Sleek bullets, powerful cartridges and high-magnification scopes have conspired to focus hunter attention on "The Long Shot." Killing game far from the rifle has too often become the object of the hunt, replacing the traditional challenge of getting close. Both tasks require skill. The long-range rifleman depends more on superior equipment, less on physical prowess. While the stalker need not shoot so precisely, he must also have a woodsman's bag of tricks. Long shooting has ethical implications, too, but those become a nuisance only after a rifleman has cleared more pragmatic hurdles, chiefly: hitting and delivering a killing blow.

Delivering lethal energy is not the problem it's often made out to be. Hunters between the two world wars shot elk with .25-20s, and where I grew up legal whitetail cartridges included .22 rimfires. A 100-grain bullet in the mild-mannered .25-06 can reach 500 yards with 1000 foot-pounds--certainly enough energy to kill a deer. Some 30-caliber magnums double that. Scores of big game animals have fallen to cartridges that don't generate 1000 foot-pounds *at the muzzle*. Also, modern rifles with vertical magazines allow hunters to use pointed bullets. These sleek projectiles retain their speed and energy more efficiently than did the blunt bullets of yesteryear's tube-fed lever guns.

Launch speed combines with ballistic coefficient to determine energy and flight path. A bullet's ballistic coefficient describes mathematically its ability to cleave air. The shape of a bullet also figures into ballistic coefficient. Streamlined spitzer bullets slip through the air easily because they minimize nose friction. The other part of ballistic coefficient--sectional density--most commonly shows up in text as a three-digit decimal number: bullet weight in pounds (w) divided by the square of bullet diameter (d2). The higher the sectional density, the greater the momentum. Thus, a long bullet resists the decelerating force of air friction more successfully than does a short bullet. Think of it as inertia, or resistance to change (in speed). More energy is needed to thrust a long bullet down the barrel because it is heavier (for the bore diameter) than a short bullet and generates more friction. But once it gets going it doesn't slow down as quickly. That's because the hole it bores through the air is no larger than that drilled by the short bullet, so nose friction is--given the same nose shape and velocity--essentially the same. Side friction, which is incrementally greater, is offset by extra mass. Like the weight of a pendulum, it acts to battle deceleration.

Big cases with heavy 25- to 30-caliber bullets call for slow powders like these.

Air exerts a huge pull on any bullet. In a vacuum, a 150-grain .30-06 bullet launched at a 45-degree angle at the modest velocity of 2700 fps can travel nearly *43 miles*. The same bullet shot at the same angle and velocity through earth's atmosphere exhausts itself in less than two miles. Retardation caused by air resistance is roughly 56 times as strong as the force of gravity on that particular bullet. The higher the velocity, the stronger the drag--as all children learn when they stick their hands out car windows to feel the rush of wind on a hot day. In a car moving at highway speed, they can hardly keep their arms from being flung back.

Isaac Newton thought about this after dropping glass spheres filled with air, water and mercury from the dome of St. Paul's Cathedral. He concluded that drag was proportional to the square of a ball's velocity, something later experimenters found true for other projectiles, but only at low speeds. In 1881 a Russian named Mayevski determined that drag was proportional to some power of the velocity within a range of velocities. He based his conclusion on firings done by Krupp in Germany with a projectile three calibers long and an ogival nose of two-caliber radius. In France, the Gavre Commission's similar experimentation generated velocities up to 6000 fps. The Commission discovered a sharp rise in bullet retardation occurring around the speed of sound. In 1909 and 1929 the British came up with ballistic tables, with each entry specific to only one projectile. Using a bullet shaped much like Britain's one-inch experimental projectile with a two-caliber ogive, U.S. Army Colonel James Ingalls later developed ballistics tables that still work for most hunting bullets up to velocities of 3600 fps.

While ballistic coefficient is most accurately measured experimentally because it changes with velocity, an approximation can be made with this formula: $C=w/id^2$, where $C$ is the ballistic coefficient,

Groups like this from a sporting-weight rifle are unnecessary even for long shots at big game. After estimating range, hold the rifle still and execute the shot flawlessly. A group double this size will be small enough.

$w$ is weight in pounds, $i$ is a form factor derived from bullet shape, and $d$ is caliber. Fortunately, modern loading manuals published by Hodgdon, Hornaday, Nosler, Sierra and Speer save you the trouble. Incidentally, high $C$ values (long-nosed, boattail bullets) have little effect on trajectory at normal hunting ranges. They matter most at extreme range. At some point increasing $C$ won't work even far away, because the bullet must by definition be too long to seat or too heavy to drive fast.

Energy deficiencies at long yardage may have less to do with kinetic force than with its transfer. Bullets are designed to open within a range of impact speeds. High velocity puts bullets to the test because it demands that they hold together under the jacket-shredding impact of close-range hits, yet still expand when they strike game at great distance. Contrary to what some hunters think, high-speed bullets do not zip through animals so fast that they don't have a chance to open. Indeed, most expansion occurs during the first inch of penetration. Fast bullets sustain more nose damage, just as automobiles colliding at high speed destroy themselves. Similarly, bullets meeting flesh at low speed are like cars meeting in a fender-bender.

Long shooting isn't just for rifles. This scoped Thompson-Center Contender weights almost as much and, given a skilled shooter on the trigger, is effective on big game to 200 yards.

It's useful to think of a game animal as a hammer hitting a bullet nose--it doesn't really matter which object is the stationary one. The damage to each results from the *combined velocity*. If the hammer strikes the bullet nose sharply, the bullet will open more violently than if the hammer is swung gently into contact. At long range, after the bullet has been slowed down by air resistance, a hit between the ribs of a deer exerts little pressure on the bullet nose. Mushrooming may not occur, and the bullet will dump little of its remaining energy. Penetration of bullets that don't open is typically greater than that of bullets whose noses rupture at impact, even when the upset bullets were moving faster on impact. Pass-throughs at extended range are common when bullets retain pre-impact shape. Bones and muscle help bullets open by providing solid resistance. Driving a car through a picket fence damages the car less than driving it at the same speed into a steel guard rail.

Energy transfer depends on deceleration within the animal. A solid bullet that whizzes through will destroy tissue in its path--but the path is not very broad. The bullet's kinetic energy remains *with the bullet* to the extent that the bullet retains velocity. A bullet exiting the muzzle carries a finite level of energy that is, during its travel, reduced by air resistance. When it enters an animal and expands, the bullet sheds energy more quickly because its deceleration rate has increased sharply. Animal tissue offers more resistance than air, causing the mushroomed bullet nose to act like a parachute as it opens up a wide channel. A bullet that stops inside the animal has expended all its energy upon entry; whereas full penetration means some energy is carried beyond with the bullet.

The point is: to become lethal, kinetic energy must be transferred. At normal hunting yardage, modern

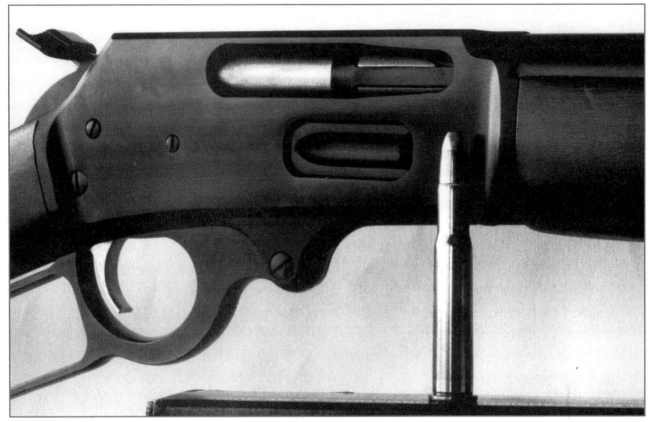

The .30-30 is effective well beyond the 100-yard range, often touted as its limit. Shooters who aim iron-sighted carbines, however, aren't very precise beyond 100 steps.

softnose bullets transfer their energy very effectively; but at extreme range, low impact forces impair expansion. Exactly where one wants the highest percentage of energy delivered is where one derives the lowest percentage. Bullets designed for conservative expansion in tough game predictably produce the smallest wound channels far away. That doesn't mean high-velocity, controlled-expansion bullets are useless at long range. Indeed, the faster the bullet leaves the muzzle, the faster it will travel to the point where it strikes flesh (all other factors being equal). Also, the greater will be the internal damage, despite the fact that high initial speed is taxed more heavily by air friction, and that a stout bullet will open more reluctantly than ordinary bullets at magnum yardages.

A 180-grain bullet from a .300 Weatherby reaches 500 yards with more punch than a 170-grain .30 Remington can offer at the muzzle.

But there's more to killing game than unleashing a battering ram at 3300 fps. All that energy must still be directed. Notwithstanding the flat trajectory of Weatherby's belted magnum, it's easier to hit at point-blank range with a .30 Remington than at 500 steps with a .300. At extreme range, hitting the target is a much bigger problem than delivering or converting energy. A rifle and ammo must be suited for the task at hand. Unfortunately, few hunters can blame shoddy long-range shooting on their equipment. Barrels, bullets and bedding techniques are now so sophisticated that 1000-yard benchrest shooters can punch groups that measure less than half a minute of angle! While hunting rifles and ammunition can't be expected to perform that well, most can be tuned to yield minute-and-a-half clusters at 250 yards and 2-minute spreads at 500. Thus, if all human error could be removed, modern equipment could corral all bullet holes in a 4-inch circle at 250, or a 10-inch circle at 500.

Some rifles will do much better, witness a friend's purchase of a Remington 700 in .308, which he intended to rebarrel. When his first group nipped a nickel-size group at 100 yards, he changed his mind. He couldn't have done that shooting with iron sights or the scopes popular with prewar hunters. Modern optics eliminate another excuse for long-range misses by giving us bright, flat, sharp sight pictures with all the magnification needed. Scopes on many big game rifles now are as powerful as yesteryear's target scopes. They're optically superior and less fragile, too.

Tight groups from the bench instill confidence in the rifle, the load and the shooter's own ability. But long shots on the mountain or across sage flats require more than a stellar bench record. Hitting is almost entirely a human challenge. Beyond point-blank range, the shooter's first job is estimating yardage. As the naturalist, W.T. Hornaday, wrote around the turn of the century, "Last fall [I shot] two bull moose..... I hurriedly estimated the distance to be between 300 and 400 yards, and we afterwards found it to be 280.... In November [my guide] killed a very fine large mountain sheep [with] the first shot 237 yards off and in a very strong wind."

Hornaday's error in range estimation remains a common one. Animals often appear farther away than they really are, especially in broken terrain or woods. His blunt .303 Savage bullet would have dropped significantly between 280 and, say, 350 yards, so holding for 350 would have resulted in a high hit. Luckily for Mr. Hornaday, moose are very deep through the chest.

The most popular bullets in Hornaday's era had reasonably high sectional densities but, because of their round noses, relatively low ballistic coefficients. They flew at modest velocities. Aiming to kill a deer at 300 yards could send the bullet over the spine if the actual range was really 225. The high speed and sleek form of modern spitzers compress bullet arc, so that holding for 300 puts the shooter only 5 inches high at 225, rather than 18. At extreme range, however, the trajectory steepens and presents the problem faced by prewar hunters at shorter yardage. Even the flat-shooting .300 Weatherby drops about 18 inches between 400 and 500 yards. An error of just 50 yards in range estimation at 450 will plant a bullet roughly 8 inches high or 10 low. That's either a miss or, on a big animal, a poor hit.

Another gremlin encountered by Hornaday and his guide was *wind*. One advantage the Savage rifle

This Ruger Deerstalker in .44 Magnum with a 2.5x Leupold scope has adequate range for whitetail shooting in timber.

Careful zeroing is essential for long shooting.

held over traditional lever guns at the time was its rotary magazine. Not only did it allow the use of pointed bullets with high ballistic coefficients; it didn't act like a sail rigged to the barrel. "He says he likes the Savage to shoot in the wind as the barrel is small and [has] no long magazine to catch the wind and blow your rifle off to one side," wrote Hornaday.

A small barrel may not catch much wind, but the less weight to the tube, the less firmly it stays anchored on target during a blow. Modern bolt rifles built for long-range shooting typically have medium-weight or heavy barrels that resist the push of the wind, plus the warping effects of a barrel heating up from repeated firings. Still, most of the damage done by wind is to the bullet. As smallbore competitors

know, it doesn't take much of a breeze to move a .22 bullet a few scoring rings from center. You can no more fight the wind than you can gravity. High ballistic coefficient and velocity can reduce its effects, but ignoring wind will guarantee poor shooting.

Not long ago I was lobbing .22 bullets into a BR-50 card, sticking most within a pencil's width of center. A lazy breeze fishtailed from 4 to 7 o'clock on the line; but my spotting scope, focused just shy of the target frame, indicated a steady 3 to 4 o'clock current. I clicked into it and, after several nervous shots to the sighter bull, decided that was the prevailing condition. About halfway through the match, I got careless and stopped checking mirage. Smugly watching holes pop up in the middle of the

This Savage 110 in "tactical" form is an affordable rifle, yet accurate and dependable for long-range shooting.

tiny green circle, I missed a let-up. Then, as the breeze suddenly died and mirage boiled, I sent a bullet across two green lines at 4 o'clock.

Hunters are quick to point out that their 7mm STWs and .30-378 Weatherbys move lead a lot faster than my old Remington 37. True enough. And big game bullets built for long-distance shooting are more streamlined than a .22 match bullet. But what a rimfire bullet does in wind at 50 yards mirrors the behavior of that boulder-splitting Canyon Thunder farther out. A 200-grain .30 magnum boattail bullet launched at 3000 fps drifts 6 inches at 300 yards in a 10-mile-per-hour wind, which isn't much wind at all. Double wind speed and you double drift. Increase the range by only 50 percent to 450 yards and you *more than double* drift. That's because the bullet is decelerating. Wind produces a sideways trajectory, taking the bullet on a curving path farther and farther from sightline. At 500 yards a 20-mile-per-hour wind, which is only strong enough to lift kites, can move a 200-grain 3$\frac{1}{2}$ feet. Reducing velocity or ballistic coefficient also increases drift. Raising both at once becomes progressively harder as you seek efficient loads. The only way to learn how to shoot in the wind is to practice it. Knowing drift values isn't enough--you have to know what a 17-mile-per-hour wind looks and feels like. Wind is different than gravity, because the latter is a constant force, whereas doping wind is like estimating distance.

Crimes of the atmosphere, however, pale in comparison to what our own twitchy, loose-limbed bodies do to the path of a bullet. The human shooting platform wasn't built to keep bullets in tight groups. No matter how still the wind, the big game hunter of average ability does well to keep his shots inside a pie tin at 100 yards without artificial support. Even an improvised rest seldom brings groups under 3 minutes of angle. Of course, practiced shooters can do better, but the notion that for long shooting everyone needs half-minute equipment is absurd. Only on a target range, from prone or off the bench, can most shooters tell whether they're firing a half-minute rifle or one that's sprinkling bullets across two minutes of angle.

This is not to denigrate shooters or suggest that accurate rifles are worthless. But on a hunt, the short barrel stave is typically the human frame. Couple that rickety launchpad with emotions the brain can't control, a heart that won't stop thumping, lungs that need regular inflation, and it's like trying to do a crossword puzzle on the back of a trotting horse. That's why the old buffalo hunters used crossed sticks to support their rifles. It also explains why three-position target shooters use slings with shooting loops, and why bipods have become popular among long-range enthusiasts. A tree limb can take the wobble out of a rifle, but it'll never be found growing in just the right place at just the right angle. Packing your own support makes sense if you expect long shots. I prefer a sling, because it's more versatile than a bipod and doesn't add extra weight. Actually, practice is like a rest because it can trim the amplitude of muzzle swing. It also teaches mind, eye and muscles to work together. Beyond reducing muzzle movement, body functions must be coordinated to deliver accurate shots at any range. As with riding a bicycle, we learn best by bungling, then correcting. Bullet holes well out from center are the skinned knees of beginners.

In his novel, *A Story like the Wind*, Laurens van der Post tells of a professional hunter, Mopani Theron, who has become disgusted by the bunglings of unskilled hunters. The novel's central character, Francois, recounts a shooting lesson from Theron, who taught that "Shooting was not a matter of the will but a kind of two-way traffic between target and rifleman, and that if one wanted to shoot accurately without hurt or unnecessary pain to animals, one must never force one's shot by pulling the trigger with one's finger. Instead one had to keep the gun aimed truly at the target, until the target filled not only all one's eyes but activated one's imagination, until one's finger gradually tightened on the trigger, releasing the shot only when target and rifleman were one."

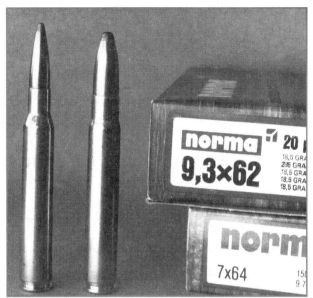

The 7x64 (left) and 9.3x62, which correspond to the .280 Remington and .35 Whelen, are popular European big game rounds. Standard bullet weight for the 9.3 (.366 diameter) is 286 grains.

That may sound uncomfortably mystical to riflemen who use a ball micrometer on case mouths and a dial caliper to gauge head expansion. Decimals measure success on the range, and most hunters assume they apply as directly to the hunt. Not so. At least, the record doesn't bear that out. Even accomplished target shooters commonly fail to make what should be easy shots at game. The reason: They haven't trained under hunting conditions. It's like an aspiring basketball star who eats properly, exercises regularly and religiously visits the basketball court-- but who never plays on a team. His body may be wonderfully sculpted and well-conditioned, and his shooting form flawless; but he will be useless until he learns how to move the ball in traffic and shoot under pressure.

The fellow who hurried after me down that brushy slope after a crippled elk lacked practice under pressure. Like most of us, he was too busy to practice, and for that he can be excused. But he could have substituted a few short afternoons climbing in steep country with a .22 and shooting at small targets to test his marksmanship. Simply mastering some

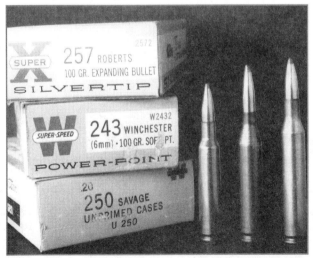

The cartridges shown (left to right: the .250 Savage, .243 Winchester and .257 Roberts) all work fine for open-country deer.

Offhand practice at metallic silhouettes is a great way to learn about range estimation, bullet drop and proper shooting technique.

It's not necessary to shoot at game from where it's spotted. The best part of the hunt is the final yards of the stalk.

shooting fundamentals would have enabled him to make a 120-yard shot on a broadside bull from the sit. Knowing and heeding his limitations, he would have declined a followup shot when the elk ran off into the brush and prevented the animal's suffering.

We made better time down the shadowed north slope than I'd thought, perhaps because it was so steep we skidded between steps, making too much noise. But time was more precious than silence. I stopped once and spied the bull again through a hole in the foliage. I pointed.

"Where?" the hunter gasped, peering through the leaves. He was looking too close, assuming that since we'd come so far the bull must be right there in front of us. The notion that this elk was still a small speck of tan on the far hillside was hardly credible.

Halfway to the canyon floor, I slid to a halt beside a stout aspen. This looked like the best shot alley we could get, but still nearly 400 yards. "Figure twenty inches," I told him.

The Ruger steadied against an aspen limb. Squinting through the spotting scope, I hoped the elk would stand and that the hunter would not force the shot by pulling the trigger. The longer the silence, the better I felt. Finally, the rifle boomed, the aspen shook, and hair winked on the quartering bull's flank. Another shot, this one a miss. The last bullet hit the elk through the chest as it turned. The great animal sank into the aspen suckers fringing the seep.

"Good shooting!" I exclaimed, and meant it. Four hundred yards, after all, is a long shot. ⬤

# PART 4

## BALLISTICS TABLES, FORMULAS AND LISTS FOR SHOOTERS

# SECTION 1 ONE

# MANUFACTURING LISTS OF HUNTING BULLETS

## HORNADY RIFLE BULLETS

## Rifle Bullets

### 17 CALIBER (.172)

 25 gr. HP #1710

### 22 CALIBER (.222)

 40 gr. Jet #2210

### 22 CALIBER (.223)

 45 gr. Hornet #2220

### 22 CALIBER (.224)

 45 gr. BEE #2229

 45 gr. Hornet #2230

 50 gr. SXSP #2240

 50 gr. SP #2245

### 22 CALIBER MATCH

 52 gr. BTHP #2249

### 22 CALIBER MATCH

 53 gr. HP #2250

 55 gr. SXSP #2260

 55 gr. SP #2265

 55 gr. SP w c #2266

 55 gr. FMJ-BT w c #2267

 60 gr. SP #2270

 60 gr. HP #2275

### 22 CALIBER MATCH

 68 gr. BTHP #2278

### 22 CALIBER (.227)

 70 gr. SP #2280

### 6MM CALIBER (.243)

 70 gr. SP #2410

 70 gr. SXSP #2415

 75 gr. HP #2420

 80 gr. FMJ #2430

 80 gr. SP Single Shot Pistol #2435

 87 gr. SP #2440

 87 gr. BTHP #2442

 100 gr. SP #2450 InterLock

 100 gr. BTSP #2453 InterLock

 100 gr. RN #2455 InterLock

# HORNADY RIFLE BULLETS

## 25 CALIBER (.257)

60 gr. FP
#2510

75 gr. HP
#2520

87 gr. SP
#2530

100 gr. SP
#2540
InterLock

117 gr. RN
#2550
InterLock

117 gr. BTSP
#2552
InterLock

120 gr. HP
#2560
InterLock

## 6.5MM CALIBER (.264)

100 gr. SP
#2610

129 gr. SP
#2620
InterLock

140 gr. SP
#2630
InterLock

### 6.5MM CALIBER MATCH

140 gr. BTHP
#2633

160 gr. RN
#2640
InterLock

## 270 CALIBER (.277)

100 gr. SP
#2710

110 gr. HP
#2720

130 gr. SP
#2730
InterLock

140 gr. BTSP
#2735
InterLock

150 gr. SP
#2740
InterLock

150 gr. RN
#2745
InterLock

## 7MM CALIBER (.284)

100 gr. HP
#2800

120 gr. SP
#2810

120 gr. SP
Single Shot Pistol
#2811

120 gr. HP
#2815

## 139 gr. SP

139 gr. SP
#2820
InterLock

139 gr. FP
#2822
InterLock

139 gr. BTSP
#2825
InterLock

154 gr. SP
#2830
InterLock

154 gr. RN
#2835
InterLock

### 7MM MATCH

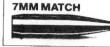
162 gr. BTHP
#2840

162 gr. BTSP
#2845
InterLock

175 gr. SP
#2850
InterLock

175 gr. RN
#2855
InterLock

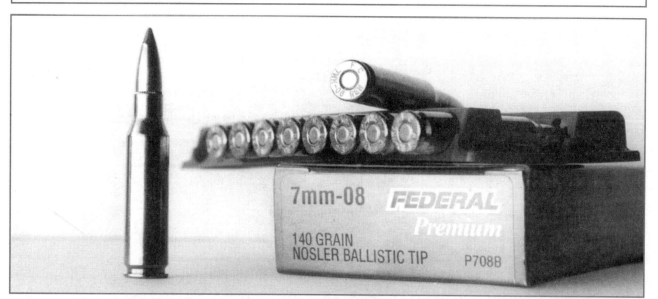

Remington's 7mm-08, a necked-down .308, is a close relative of the new .260 Remington. Both are excellent short-action deer cartridges.

# HORNADY RIFLE BULLETS

## 30 CALIBER (.308)

**100 gr. SJ**
#3005

**110 gr. SP**
#3010

**110 gr. RN**
#3015

**110 gr. FMJ**
#3017

**130 gr. SP**
#3020

**130 gr. SP**
Single Shot Pistol
#3021

**150 gr. SP**
#3031
InterLock

**150 gr. BTSP**
#3033
InterLock

**150 gr. RN (30-30)**
#3035
InterLock

**150 gr. FMJ-BT**
#3037

**165 gr. SP**
#3040
InterLock

**165 gr. BTSP**
#3045
InterLock

### 30 CALIBER NATIONAL MATCH

**168 gr. BTHP**
#30501

**170 gr. FP (30-30)**
#3060
InterLock

**180 gr. SP**
#3070
InterLock

**180 gr. BTSP**
#3072
InterLock

**180 gr. RN**
#3075
InterLock

### 30 CALIBER MATCH

**190 gr. BTHP**
#3080

**190 gr. BTSP**
#3085
InterLock

**220 gr. RN**
#3090
InterLock

## 7.62 x 39 (.311)

**123 gr. SP**
#3140

**123 gr. FMJ**
#3147

## 303 CAL. and 7.7 JAP (.312)

**150 gr. SP**
#3120
InterLock

**174 gr. RN**
#3130
InterLock

## 32 SPECIAL (.321)

**170 gr. FP**
#3210
InterLock

## 8MM CALIBER (.323)

**125 gr. SP**
#3230

**150 gr. SP**
#3232
InterLock

**170 gr. RN**
#3235
InterLock

**220 gr. SP**
#3238
InterLock

## 338 CALIBER (.338)

**200 gr. SP**
#3310
InterLock

**200 gr. FP**
(33 Win.)
#3315
InterLock

**225 gr. SP**
#3320
InterLock

**250 gr. RN**
#3330
InterLock

**250 gr. SP**
#3335
Interlock

## 348 CALIBER (.348)

**200 gr. FP**
#3410
InterLock

## 35 CALIBER (.358)

**180 gr. SP**
Single Shot Pistol
#3505

**200 gr. SP**
#3510
InterLock

**200 gr. RN**
#3515
InterLock

**250 gr. SP**
#3520
Interlock

**250 gr. RN**
#3525
InterLock

## 375 CALIBER (.375)

**220 gr. FP**
(375 Win.)
#3705
InterLock

***270 gr. SP**
#3710
InterLock

***270 gr. RN**
#3715
InterLock

***300 gr. RN**
#3720
InterLock

**300 gr. BTSP**
#3725
Interlock

***300 gr. FMJ-RN**
#3727

## 416 CALIBER (.416)

**340 gr. BTSP**
#4163

**400 gr. FMJ**
#4167

**400 gr. RN**
#4165
Interlock

## 44 CALIBER (.430)

***265 gr. FP**
#4300
InterLock

# HORNADY RIFLE BULLETS

## 45 CALIBER (.458)

*300 gr. HP
#4500

*350 gr. RN
#4502
InterLock

*500 gr. RN
#4504
InterLock

*500 gr. FMJ-RN
#4507

750 gr. AMAX
#5165

## Pistol Bullets

### 25 CALIBER (.251)

35 gr. HPXTP
#35450

50 gr. FMJ-RN
#3545

### 32 CALIBER (.311)

71 gr. FMJ-RN
#3200

### 32 CALIBER (.312)

85 gr. HP/XTP
#32050

100 gr. HP/XTP
#32070

### 9MM CALIBER (.355)

90 gr. HP/XTP
#35500

100 gr. FMJ
#3552

115 gr. HP/XTP
#35540

115 gr. FMJ-RN
#3555

124 gr. FMJ-FP
#3556

124 gr. FMJ-RN
#3557

124 gr. HP XTP
#35571

147 gr. HP/XTP
#35580

147 gr. FMJ
#3559

### 38 CALIBER (.357)

110 gr. HP/XTP
#35700

125 gr. HP/XTP
#35710

125 gr. FP/XTP
#35730

140 gr. HP/XTP
#35740

158 gr. HP/XTP
#35750

158 gr. FP/XTP
#35780

NEW
160 gr. CL-SIL
#3572

NEW
180 gr. CL-SIL
#3577

180 gr. JHP/XTP
#35771

### 9x18 MAKAROV

NEW
95 gr. HP/XTP
#36500

### 10MM CALIBER (.400)

155 gr. HP/XTP
#40000

180 gr. HP/XTP
#40040

180 gr. FMJ-FP
#40041

200 gr. FMJ-FP
#4007

200 gr. HP/XTP
#40060

### 41 CALIBER (.410)

210 gr. HP/XTP
#41000

210 gr. CL-SIL
#4105

## 44 CALIBER (.430)

180 gr. HP/XTP
#44050

200 gr. HP/XTP
#44100

240 gr. HP/XTP
#44200

NEW
240 gr. CL-SIL
#4425

300 gr. HP/XTP
#44280

## 45 CALIBER (.451)

185 gr. HP/XTP
#45100

### 45 CALIBER MATCH

185 gr. SWC
#4513

200 gr. HP/XTP
#45140

### 45 CALIBER MATCH

200 gr. FMJ-C/T
#4515

230 gr. JHP/XTP
#45160

230 gr. FMJ-RN
#4517

230 gr. FMJ-FP
#4518

## 45 CALIBER (.452)

250 gr. Long
Colt HP/XTP
#45200

300 gr. HP/XTP
#45230

264

MODERN SPORTING RIFLE CARTRIDGES

## RIFLE CARTRIDGES

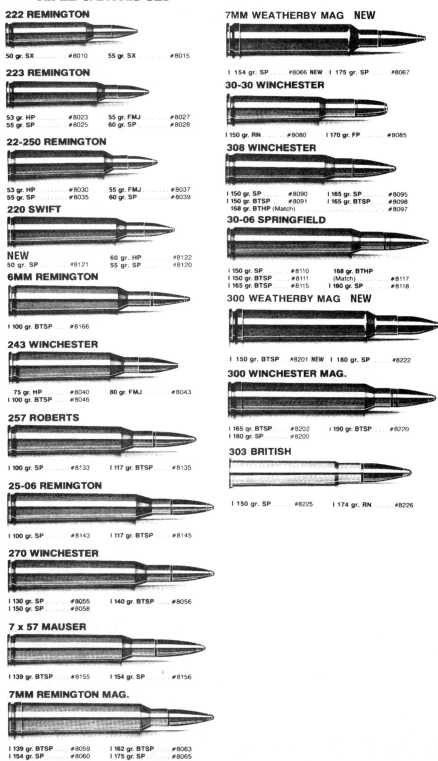

### 222 REMINGTON

| | | | |
|---|---|---|---|
| 50 gr. SX | #8010 | 55 gr. SX | #8015 |

### 223 REMINGTON

| | | | |
|---|---|---|---|
| 53 gr. HP | #8023 | 55 gr. FMJ | #8027 |
| 55 gr. SP | #8025 | 60 gr. SP | #8028 |

### 22-250 REMINGTON

| | | | |
|---|---|---|---|
| 53 gr. HP | #8030 | 55 gr. FMJ | #8037 |
| 55 gr. SP | #8035 | 60 gr. SP | #8039 |

### 220 SWIFT

**NEW**

| | | | |
|---|---|---|---|
| 50 gr. SP | #8121 | 60 gr. HP | #8122 |
| | | 55 gr. SP | #8120 |

### 6MM REMINGTON

| | |
|---|---|
| I 100 gr. BTSP | #8166 |

### 243 WINCHESTER

| | | | |
|---|---|---|---|
| 75 gr. HP | #8040 | 80 gr. FMJ | #8043 |
| I 100 gr. BTSP | #8046 | | |

### 257 ROBERTS

| | | | |
|---|---|---|---|
| I 100 gr. SP | #8133 | I 117 gr. BTSP | #8135 |

### 25-06 REMINGTON

| | | | |
|---|---|---|---|
| I 100 gr. SP | #8143 | I 117 gr. BTSP | #8145 |

### 270 WINCHESTER

| | | | |
|---|---|---|---|
| I 130 gr. SP | #8055 | I 140 gr. BTSP | #8056 |
| I 150 gr. SP | #8058 | | |

### 7 x 57 MAUSER

| | | | |
|---|---|---|---|
| I 139 gr. BTSP | #8155 | I 154 gr. SP | #8156 |

### 7MM REMINGTON MAG.

| | | | |
|---|---|---|---|
| I 139 gr. BTSP | #8059 | I 162 gr. BTSP | #8063 |
| I 154 gr. SP | #8060 | I 175 gr. SP | #8065 |

### 7MM WEATHERBY MAG   NEW

| | | | |
|---|---|---|---|
| I 154 gr. SP | #8066 NEW | I 175 gr. SP | #8067 |

### 30-30 WINCHESTER

| | | | |
|---|---|---|---|
| I 150 gr. RN | #8080 | I 170 gr. FP | #8085 |

### 308 WINCHESTER

| | | | |
|---|---|---|---|
| I 150 gr. SP | #8090 | I 165 gr. SP | #8095 |
| I 150 gr. BTSP | #8091 | I 165 gr. BTSP | #8098 |
| 168 gr. BTHP (Match) | | | #8097 |

### 30-06 SPRINGFIELD

| | | | |
|---|---|---|---|
| I 150 gr. SP | #8110 | 168 gr. BTHP | |
| I 150 gr. BTSP | #8111 | (Match) | #8117 |
| I 165 gr. BTSP | #8115 | I 180 gr. SP | #8118 |

### 300 WEATHERBY MAG   NEW

| | | | |
|---|---|---|---|
| I 150 gr. BTSP | #8201 NEW | I 180 gr. SP | #8222 |

### 300 WINCHESTER MAG.

| | | | |
|---|---|---|---|
| I 165 gr. BTSP | #8202 | I 190 gr. BTSP | #8220 |
| I 180 gr. SP | #8200 | | |

### 303 BRITISH

| | | | |
|---|---|---|---|
| I 150 gr. SP | #8225 | I 174 gr. RN | #8226 |

# NOSLER RIFLE BULLETS

| Cal. Dia. | PARTITION® | BULLET WEIGHT AND STYLE | SECT. DENS. | BAL. COEF. | PART# |
|---|---|---|---|---|---|
| **6mm .243"** | | 85 GR. SPITZER | .206 | .315 | 16314 |
| | | 95 GR. SPITZER | .230 | .365 | 16315 |
| | | 100 GR. SPITZER | .242 | .384 | 35642 |
| **25 .257"** | | 100 GR. SPITZER | .216 | .377 | 16317 |
| | | 115 GR. SPITZER | .249 | .389 | 16318 |
| | | 120 GR. SPITZER | .260 | .391 | 35643 |
| **6.5mm .264"** | | 125 GR. SPITZER | .256 | .449 | 16320 |
| | | 140 GR. SPITZER | .287 | .490 | 16321 |
| **270 .277"** | | 130 GR. SPITZER | .242 | .416 | 16322 |
| | | 150 GR. SPITZER | .279 | .465 | 16323 |
| | | 160 GR. SEMI SPITZER | .298 | .434 | 16324 |
| **7mm .284"** | | 140 GR. SPITZER | .248 | .434 | 16325 |
| | | 150 GR. SPITZER | .266 | .456 | 16326 |
| | | 160 GR. SPITZER | .283 | .475 | 16327 |
| | | 175 GR. SPITZER | .310 | .519 | 35645 |
| **30 .308"** | | 150 GR. SPITZER | .226 | .387 | 16329 |
| | | 165 GR. SPITZER | .248 | .410 | 16330 |
| | | 170 GR. ROUND NOSE | .256 | .252 | 16333 |
| | | 180 GR. PROTECTED POINT | .271 | .361 | 25396 |
| | | 180 GR. SPITZER | .271 | .474 | 16331 |
| | | 200 GR. SPITZER | .301 | .481 | 35626 |
| | | 220 GR. SEMI SPITZER | .331 | .351 | 16332 |

| Cal. Dia. | PARTITION® | BULLET WEIGHT AND STYLE | SECT. DENS. | BAL. COEF. | PART# |
|---|---|---|---|---|---|
| **8mm .323"** | | 200 GR. SPITZER | .274 | .426 | 35277 |
| **338 .338"** | | 210 GR. SPITZER | .263 | .400 | 16337 |
| | | 225 GR. SPITZER | .281 | .454 | 16336 |
| | | 250 GR. SPITZER | .313 | .473 | 35644 |
| **35 .358"** | | 225 GR. SPITZER | .251 | .430 | 44800 |
| | | 250 GR. SPITZER | .279 | .446 | 44801 |
| **375 .375"** | | 260 GR. SPITZER | .264 | .314 | 44850 |
| | | 300 GR. SPITZER | .305 | .398 | 44845 |

# NOSLER BULLETS

| Cal. Dia. | SOLID BASE® BALLISTIC TIP® *Hunting* | BULLET WEIGHT AND STYLE | SECT. DENS. | BAL. COEF. | PART# |
|---|---|---|---|---|---|
| 6mm .243" | | 95 GR. SPITZER (PURPLE TIP) | .230 | .379 | 24095 |
| 25 .257" | | 100 GR. SPITZER (BLUE TIP) | .216 | .393 | 25100 |
| | | 115 GR. SPITZER (BLUE TIP) | .249 | .453 | 25115 |
| 6.5mm .264" | | 100 GR. SPITZER (BROWN TIP) | .205 | .350 | 26100 |
| | | 120 GR. SPITZER (BROWN TIP) | .246 | .458 | 26120 |
| 270 .277" | | 130 GR. SPITZER (YELLOW TIP) | .242 | .433 | 27130 |
| | | 140 GR. SPITZER (YELLOW TIP) | .261 | .456 | 27140 |
| | | 150 GR. SPITZER (YELLOW TIP) | .279 | .496 | 27150 |
| 7mm .284" | | 120 GR. FLAT POINT (SOFT LEAD TIP) | .213 | .195 | 28121 |
| | | 120 GR. SPITZER (RED TIP) | .213 | .417 | 28120 |
| | | 140 GR. SPITZER (RED TIP) | .248 | .485 | 28140 |
| | | 150 GR. SPITZER (RED TIP) | .266 | .493 | 28150 |
| 30 .308" | | 125 GR. SPITZER (GREEN TIP) | .188 | .366 | 30125 |
| | | 150 GR. SPITZER (GREEN TIP) | .226 | .435 | 30150 |
| | | 165 GR. SPITZER (GREEN TIP) | .248 | .475 | 30165 |
| | | 180 GR. SPITZER (GREEN TIP) | .271 | .507 | 30180 |
| 338 .338" | | 180 GR. SPITZER (MAROON TIP) | .225 | .372 | 33180 |
| | | 200 GR. SPITZER (MAROON TIP) | .250 | .414 | 33200 |
| 35 .358" | | 225 GR. WHELEN (BUCKSKIN TIP) | .251 | .421 | 35225 |

# SIERRA RIFLE BULLETS

## .22 Caliber Hornet (.223/5.66MM Diameter)

40 gr. Hornet
Varminter #1100

45 gr. Hornet
Varminter #1110

## .22 Caliber Hornet (.224/5.69MM Diameter)

40 gr. Hornet
Varminter #1200

45 gr. Hornet
Varminter #1210

## .22 Caliber (.224/5.69MM Diameter)

40 gr. HP
Varminter #1385

45 gr. SMP
Varminter #1300

45 gr. SPT
Varminter #1310

50 gr. SMP
Varminter #1320

50 gr. SPT
Varminter #1330

50 gr. Blitz
Varminter #1340

52 gr. HPBT
MatchKing #1410

53 gr. HP
MatchKing #1400

55 gr. Blitz
Varminter #1345

55 gr. SMP
Varminter #1350

55 gr. FMJBT
GameKing #1355

55 gr. SPT
Varminter #1360

55 gr. SBT
GameKing #1365

55 gr. HPBT
GameKing #1390

60 gr. HP
Varminter #1375

63 gr. SMP
Varminter #1370

69 gr. HPBT
MatchKing #1380

*7"-10" TWST BBLS*

## 6MM .243 Caliber (.243/6.17MM Diameter)

60 gr. HP
Varminter #1500

## 6MM .243 Caliber (.243/6.17MM Diameter)

70 gr. HPBT
MatchKing #1505

75 gr. HP
Varminter #1510

80 gr. Blitz
Varminter #1515

85 gr. SPT
Varminter #1520

85 gr. HPBT
GameKing #1530

90 gr. FMJBT
GameKing #1535

100 gr. SPT
Pro-Hunter #1540

100 gr. SMP
Pro-Hunter #1550

100 gr. SBT
GameKing #1560

107 gr. HPBT
MatchKing #1570

*7"-8" TWST BBLS*

## .25 Caliber (.257/6.53MM Diameter)

75 gr. HP
Varminter #1600

87 gr. SPT
Varminter #1610

90 gr. HPBT
GameKing #1615

100 gr. SPT
Pro-Hunter #1620

100 gr. SBT
GameKing #1625

**100 gr. HPBT
MatchKing #1628**

117 gr. SBT
GameKing #1630

117 gr. SPT
Pro-Hunter #1640

120 gr. HPBT
GameKing #1650

## 6.5MM .264 Caliber (.264/6.71MM Diameter)

85 gr. HP
Varminter #1700

100 gr. HP
Varminter #1710

107 gr. HPBT
MatchKing #1715

120 gr. SPT
Pro-Hunter #1720

120 gr. HPBT
MatchKing #1725

140 gr. SBT
GameKing #1730

## 6.5MM .264 Caliber (cont.)
### (.264/6.71MM Diameter)

140 gr. HPBT
MatchKing #1740

142 gr. HPBT
MatchKing #1742

160 gr. SMP
Pro-Hunter #1750

## .270 Caliber (.277/7.04MM Diameter)

90 gr. HP
Varminter #1800

110 gr. SPT
Pro-Hunter #1810

130 gr. SBT
GameKing #1820

130 gr. SPT
Pro-Hunter #1830

135 gr. HPBT
MatchKing #1833

140 gr. HPBT
GameKing #1835

140 gr. SBT
GameKing #1845

150 gr. SBT
GameKing #1840

150 gr. RN
Pro-Hunter #1850

## 7MM .284 Caliber (.284/7.21MM Diameter)

100 gr. HP
Varminter #1895

120 gr. SPT
Pro-Hunter #1900

130 gr. HPBT
MatchKing #1903

140 gr. SBT
GameKing #1905

140 gr. SPT
Pro-Hunter #1910

150 gr. SBT
GameKing #1913

150 gr. HPBT
MatchKing #1915

160 gr. SBT
GameKing #1920

160 gr. HPBT
GameKing #1925

168 gr. HPBT
MatchKing #1930

170 gr. RN
Pro-Hunter #1950

175 gr. SBT
GameKing #1940

# SIERRA RIFLE BULLETS

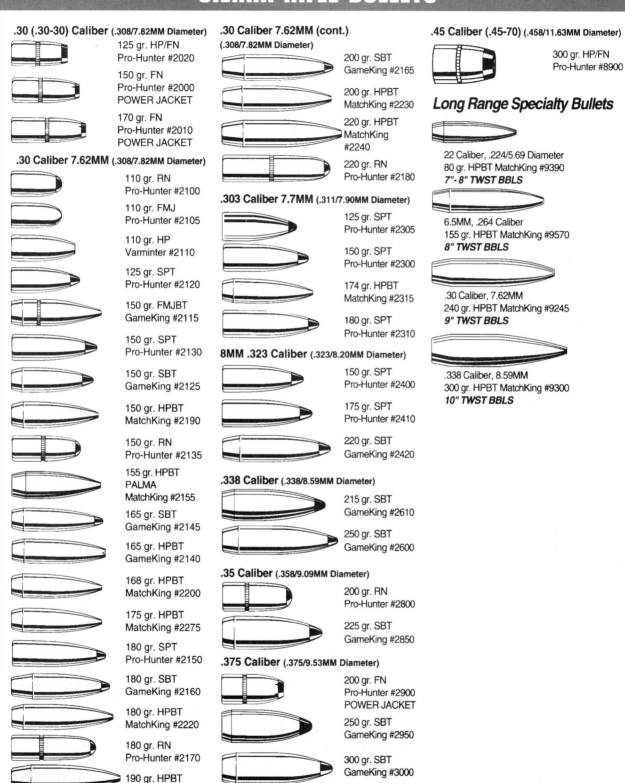

### .30 (.30-30) Caliber (.308/7.82MM Diameter)

125 gr. HP/FN
Pro-Hunter #2020

150 gr. FN
Pro-Hunter #2000
POWER JACKET

170 gr. FN
Pro-Hunter #2010
POWER JACKET

### .30 Caliber 7.62MM (.308/7.82MM Diameter)

110 gr. RN
Pro-Hunter #2100

110 gr. FMJ
Pro-Hunter #2105

110 gr. HP
Varminter #2110

125 gr. SPT
Pro-Hunter #2120

150 gr. FMJBT
GameKing #2115

150 gr. SPT
Pro-Hunter #2130

150 gr. SBT
GameKing #2125

150 gr. HPBT
MatchKing #2190

150 gr. RN
Pro-Hunter #2135

155 gr. HPBT
PALMA
MatchKing #2155

165 gr. SBT
GameKing #2145

165 gr. HPBT
GameKing #2140

168 gr. HPBT
MatchKing #2200

175 gr. HPBT
MatchKing #2275

180 gr. SPT
Pro-Hunter #2150

180 gr. SBT
GameKing #2160

180 gr. HPBT
MatchKing #2220

180 gr. RN
Pro-Hunter #2170

190 gr. HPBT
MatchKing #2210

### .30 Caliber 7.62MM (cont.)
**(.308/7.82MM Diameter)**

200 gr. SBT
GameKing #2165

200 gr. HPBT
MatchKing #2230

220 gr. HPBT
MatchKing
#2240

220 gr. RN
Pro-Hunter #2180

### .303 Caliber 7.7MM (.311/7.90MM Diameter)

125 gr. SPT
Pro-Hunter #2305

150 gr. SPT
Pro-Hunter #2300

174 gr. HPBT
MatchKing #2315

180 gr. SPT
Pro-Hunter #2310

### 8MM .323 Caliber (.323/8.20MM Diameter)

150 gr. SPT
Pro-Hunter #2400

175 gr. SPT
Pro-Hunter #2410

220 gr. SBT
GameKing #2420

### .338 Caliber (.338/8.59MM Diameter)

215 gr. SBT
GameKing #2610

250 gr. SBT
GameKing #2600

### .35 Caliber (.358/9.09MM Diameter)

200 gr. RN
Pro-Hunter #2800

225 gr. SBT
GameKing #2850

### .375 Caliber (.375/9.53MM Diameter)

200 gr. FN
Pro-Hunter #2900
POWER JACKET

250 gr. SBT
GameKing #2950

300 gr. SBT
GameKing #3000

### .45 Caliber (.45-70) (.458/11.63MM Diameter)

300 gr. HP/FN
Pro-Hunter #8900

## Long Range Specialty Bullets

22 Caliber, .224/5.69 Diameter
80 gr. HPBT MatchKing #9390
*7"- 8" TWST BBLS*

6.5MM, .264 Caliber
155 gr. HPBT MatchKing #9570
*8" TWST BBLS*

.30 Caliber, 7.62MM
240 gr. HPBT MatchKing #9245
*9" TWST BBLS*

.338 Caliber, 8.59MM
300 gr. HPBT MatchKing #9300
*10" TWST BBLS*

# SPEER RIFLE BULLETS

**SPEER Rifle Bullets**

| Bullet Caliber & Type | 22 Spitzer Soft Point | 22 Spire Soft Point | 22 Spitzer Soft Point | 22 218 Bee Flat Soft Point w/Cann. | 22 Spitzer Soft Point | 22 "TNT" Hollow Point | 22 Hollow Point | 22 Hollow Point B.T. Match | 22 FMJ B.T. w/Cann. | 22 Spitzer Soft Point | 22 Spitzer S.P. w/Cann. | 22 FMJ B.T. w/Cann. | 22 Semi-Spitzer Soft Point | 6mm "TNT" Hollow Point | 6mm Hollow Point |
|---|---|---|---|---|---|---|---|---|---|---|---|---|---|---|---|
| Diameter | .223" | .224" | .224" | .224" | .224" | .224" | .224" | .224" | .224" | .224" | .224" | .224" | .224" | .243" | .243" |
| Weight (grs.) | 45 | 40 | 45 | 46 | 50 | 50 | 52 | 52 | 55 | 55 | 55 | 62 | 70 | 70 | 75 |
| Ballist. Coef. | 0.166 | 0.144 | 0.167 | 0.094 | 0.231 | 0.223 | 0.225 | 0.253 | 0.269 | 0.255 | 0.241 | 0.307 | 0.214 | 0.282 | 0.234 |
| Part Number | 1011 | 1017 | 1023 | 1024 | 1029 | 1030 | 1035 | 1036 | 1044 | 1047 | 1049 | 1050 | 1053 | 1206 | 1205 |
| Box Count | 100 | 100 | 100 | 100 | 100 | 100 | 100 | 100 | 100 | 100 | 100 | 100 | 100 | 100 | 100 |

**SPEER Rifle Bullets**

| Bullet Caliber & Type | 270 Hollow Point | 270 Spitzer Soft Point B.T. | 270 Spitzer Soft Point | 270 Spitzer Soft Point B.T. | 270 Spitzer Soft Point | 7mm "TNT" Hollow Point | 7mm Hollow Point | 7mm Spitzer Soft Point | 7mm Spitzer Soft Point | 7mm Spitzer Soft Point B.T. | 7mm Spitzer Soft Point B.T. | 7mm Spitzer Soft Point B.T. | 7mm Match Hollow Point B.T. | 7mm Spitzer Soft Point B.T. | 7mm Spitzer Soft Point |
|---|---|---|---|---|---|---|---|---|---|---|---|---|---|---|---|
| Diameter | .277" | .277" | .277" | .277" | .277" | .284" | .284" | .284" | .284" | .284" | .284" | .284" | .284" | .284" | .284" |
| Weight (grs.) | 100 | 130 | 130 | 150 | 150 | 110 | 115 | 120 | 130 | 130 | 145 | 145 | 145 | 160 | 160 |
| Ballist. Coef. | 0.225 | 0.449 | 0.408 | 0.496 | 0.481 | 0.338 | 0.257 | 0.386 | 0.394 | 0.411 | 0.502 | 0.457 | 0.465 | 0.556 | 0.502 |
| Part Number | 1447 | 1458 | 1459 | 1604 | 1605 | 1616 | 1617 | 1620 | 1623 | 1624 | 1628 | 1629 | 1631 | 1634 | 1635 |
| Box Count | 100 | 100 | 100 | 100 | 100 | 100 | 100 | 100 | 100 | 100 | 100 | 100 | 100 | 100 | 100 |

**SPEER Rifle Bullets**

| Bullet Caliber & Type | 30 Spitzer Soft Point B.T. | 30 Spitzer Soft Point | 30 Match Hollow Point B.T. | 30 Flat Soft Point | 30 Round Soft Point | 30 Spitzer Soft Point B.T. | 30 Spitzer Soft Point | 30 Mag-Tip Soft Point | 30 Spitzer Soft Point | 303 Spitzer Soft Point w/Cann. | 303 Spitzer Soft Point | 303 Round Soft Point | 32 Flat Soft Point | 8mm Spitzer Soft Point |
|---|---|---|---|---|---|---|---|---|---|---|---|---|---|---|
| Diameter | .308" | .308" | .308" | .308" | .308" | .308" | .308" | .308" | .308" | .311" | .311" | .311" | .321" | .323" |
| Weight (grs.) | 165 | 165 | 168 | 170 | 180 | 180 | 180 | 180 | 200 | 125 | 150 | 180 | 170 | 150 |
| Ballist. Coef. | 0.477 | 0.433 | 0.480 | 0.304 | 0.304 | 0.540 | 0.483 | 0.352 | 0.556 | 0.292 | 0.411 | 0.328 | 0.297 | 0.369 |
| Part Number | 2034 | 2035 | 2040 | 2041 | 2047 | 2052 | 2053 | 2059 | 2211 | 2213 | 2217 | 2223 | 2259 | 2277 |
| Box Count | 100 | 100 | 100 | 100 | 100 | 100 | 100 | 100 | 50 | 100 | 100 | 100 | 100 | 100 |

**SPEER Grand Slam**

| Bullet Caliber & Type | 6mm GS Soft Point | 25 GS Soft Point | 6.5mm GS Soft Point | 270 GS Soft Point | 270 GS Soft Point | 7mm GS Soft Point | 7mm GS Soft Point | 7mm GS Soft Point | 30 GS Soft Point | 30 GS Soft Point | 30 GS Soft Point | 30 GS Soft Point | 338 GS Soft Point | 35 GS Soft Point | 375 GS Soft Point |
|---|---|---|---|---|---|---|---|---|---|---|---|---|---|---|---|
| Diameter | .243" | .257" | .264" | .277" | .277" | .284" | .284" | .284" | .308" | .308" | .308" | .308" | .338" | .358" | .375" |
| Weight (grs.) | 100 | 120 | 140 | 130 | 150 | 145 | 160 | 175 | 150 | 165 | 180 | 200 | 250 | 250 | 285 |
| Ballist. Coef. | 0.351 | 0.328 | 0.385 | 0.345 | 0.385 | 0.327 | 0.387 | 0.465 | 0.305 | 0.393 | 0.416 | 0.448 | 0.431 | 0.335 | 0.354 |
| Part Number | 1222 | 1415 | 1444 | 1465 | 1608 | 1632 | 1638 | 1643 | 2026 | 2038 | 2063 | 2212 | 2408 | 2455 | 2473 |
| Box Count | 50 | 50 | 50 | 50 | 50 | 50 | 50 | 50 | 50 | 50 | 50 | 50 | 50 | 50 | 50 |

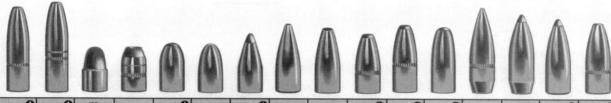

| | 7mm Mag.Tip Soft Point | 7mm Mag.Tip Soft Point | 30 Round Soft Point Plinker | 30 Hollow Point | 30 Round Soft Point | 30 Carbine Round FMJ | 30 Spire Soft Point | 30 "TNT" Hollow Point | 30 Hollow Point | 30 Flat Soft Point | 30 Flat Soft Point | 30 Round Soft Point | 30 FMJ B.T. w/Cann. | 30 Spitzer Soft Point B.T. | 30 Spitzer Soft Point | 30 Mag-Tip Soft Point |
|---|---|---|---|---|---|---|---|---|---|---|---|---|---|---|---|---|
| | .284" | .284" | .308" | .308" | .308" | .308" | .308" | .308" | .308" | .308" | .308" | .308" | .308" | .308" | .308" | .308" |
| | 160 | 175 | 100 | 110 | 110 | 110 | 110 | 125 | 130 | 130 | 150 | 150 | 150 | 150 | 150 | 150 |
| | 0.354 | 0.385 | 0.124 | 0.136 | 0.144 | 0.179 | 0.273 | 0.326 | 0.263 | 0.248 | 0.268 | 0.266 | 0.425 | 0.423 | 0.389 | 0.301 |
| | 1637 | 1641 | 1805 | 1835 | 1845 | 1846 | 1855 | 1986 | 2005 | 2007 | 2011 | 2017 | 2018 | 2022 | 2023 | 2025 |
| | 100 | 100 | 100 | 100 | 100 | 100 | 100 | 100 | 100 | 100 | 100 | 100 | 100 | 100 | 100 | 100 |

| | 8mm Semi-Spitzer Soft Point | 8mm Spitzer Soft Point | 338 Spitzer Soft Point | 338 Spitzer Soft Point B.T. | 35 Flat Soft Point | 35 Flat Soft Point | 35 Spitzer Soft Point | 9.3mm Semi-Spitzer Soft Point | 375 Semi-Spitzer Soft Point | 375 Spitzer Soft Point B.T. | 416 Mag Tip | 45 Flat Soft Point | 45 Flat Soft Point |
|---|---|---|---|---|---|---|---|---|---|---|---|---|---|
| | .323" | .323" | .338" | .338" | .358" | .358" | .358" | .366" | .375" | .375" | .416" | .458" | .458" |
| | 170 | 200 | 200 | 225 | 180 | 220 | 250 | 270 | 235 | 270 | 350 | 350 | 400 |
| | 0.354 | 0.411 | 0.448 | 0.484 | 0.245 | 0.316 | 0.446 | 0.361 | 0.317 | 0.429 | 0.332 | 0.232 | 0.214 |
| | 2283 | 2285 | 2405 | 2406 | 2435 | 2439 | 2453 | 2459 | 2471 | 2472 | 2477 | 2478 | 2479 |
| | 100 | 50 | 50 | 50 | 100 | 50 | 50 | 50 | 50 | 50 | 50 | 50 | 50 |

**SPEER. African Grand Slam**

| Bullet Caliber & Type | 375 AGS Tungsten Solid | 416 AGS Soft Point | 416 AGS Tungsten Solid | 45 AGS Soft Point | 45 AGS Tungsten Solid |
|---|---|---|---|---|---|
| Diameter | .375" | .416" | .416" | .458" | .458" |
| Weight (grs.) | 300 | 400 | 400 | 500 | 500 |
| Ballist. Coef. | 0.258 | 0.318 | 0.262 | 0.285 | 0.277 |
| Part Number | 2474 | 2475 | 2476 | 2485 | 2486 |
| Box Count | 25 | 25 | 25 | 25 | 25 |

# FORMULAS FOR BALLISTICIANS

## BALLISTIC COEFFICIENT

C = W / id

C = ballistic coefficient

W = bullet weight *(pounds)*

i = form factor

d = bullet diameter *(inches)*

## SECTIONAL DENSITY

SD = W / d2

SD = sectional density

W = bullet weight *(pounds)*

d = bullet diameter *(inches)*

## SPIN RATE

RPS = V (12 / barrel twist rate)

RPS = spin rate at the muzzle in
revolutions per second

V = bullet velocity *(feet per second)*

## ENERGY

E = V2 (W) / 450,240

E = energy *(foot-pounds)*

V = bullet velocity *(feet per second)*

W = bullet weight *(grains)*

## ENERGY

E = VW / 7,000

E = energy *(pounds-feet)*

V = bullet velocity *(feet per second)*

W = bullet weight *(grains)*

## TIME OF FLIGHT

T = R / (Vm + Vt / 2)

T = time of flight *(seconds)*

R = range *(feet)*

Vm = muzzle velocity *(feet per second)*

Vt = terminal velocity *(feet per second)*

## TARGET MOVEMENT
## DURING BULLET FLIGHT (LEAD)

Td = Ts x T

Td = target displacement *(feet)*

Ts = target speed *(feet per second)*

T = time of flight *(seconds)*

## WIND DEFLECTION

Dw = Vw (T - R / Vm)

Dw = wind deflection *(inches)*

Vw = wind speed--or 90-degree
component *(inches per second)*

T = time of flight *(seconds)*

R = range *(feet)*

Vm = muzzle velocity *(feet per second)*

# EXTERIOR BALLISTICS FOR BIG GAME BULLETS
## with ballistic coefficients of .300 to .500, at velocities of 2,400 to 3,200 fps

*Note: To find the ballistic coefficient of any bullet, refer to section 1 of this chapter. Use published or chronographed velocity. Actual C and V for a given cartridge will probably fall between listed values—but those values are close enough that extrapolation will provide valid figures. Wind drift is figured with a 10-mph wind at right angles to the shot. Oblique angles reduce drift in direct proportion to the angle—i.e., a 45-degree wind has half the effect of a 90-degree wind. Doubling wind speed doubles bullet displacement. Doubling range more than doubles displacement because of bullet deceleration.*

| C=.300 | Muzzle | RANGE IN YARDS 100 | 200 | 300 | 400 | 500 |
|---|---|---|---|---|---|---|
| velocity, fps | 2,400 | 2,122 | 1,863 | 1,627 | 1,418 | 1,142 |
| energy, ft-lb/gr. | 12.79 | 10.00 | 7.71 | 5.88 | 4.46 | 3.42 |
| flight time, sec. | 0 | .1330 | .2839 | .4563 | .6540 | .8805 |
| trajectory, in. | -1.5 | 3.1 | 0 | -13.2 | -39.6 | -83.5 |
| wind drift, in. | 0 | 1.3 | 5.9 | 14.1 | 26.5 | 43.9 |
| velocity, fps | 2,600 | 2,309 | 2,037 | 1,785 | 1,557 | 1,357 |
| energy, ft-lb/gr. | 15.01 | 11.84 | 9.21 | 7.07 | 5.38 | 4.09 |
| flight time, sec. | 0 | .1224 | .2608 | .4183 | .5983 | .8049 |
| trajectory, in. | -1.5 | 2.5 | 0 | -11.0 | -32.9 | -69.3 |
| wind drift, in. | 0 | 1.2 | 5.3 | 12.6 | 23.9 | 39.6 |
| velocity, fps | 2,800 | 2,496 | 2,212 | 1,946 | 1,702 | 1,483 |
| energy, ft-lb/gr. | 17.41 | 13.83 | 10.86 | 8.41 | 6.43 | 4.88 |
| flight time, sec. | 0 | .1135 | .2412 | .3858 | .5507 | .7396 |
| trajectory, in. | -1.5 | 2.1 | 0 | -9.2 | -27.6 | -58.2 |
| wind drift, in. | 0 | 1.1 | 4.8 | 11.5 | 21.6 | 35.9 |
| velocity, fps | 3,000 | 2,682 | 2,386 | 2,109 | 1,851 | 1,616 |
| energy, ft-lb/gr. | 19.98 | 15.97 | 12.64 | 9.87 | 7.61 | 5.80 |
| flight time, sec. | 0 | .1058 | .2244 | .3581 | .5100 | .6835 |
| trajectory, in. | -1.5 | 1.7 | 0 | -7.8 | -23.5 | -49.4 |
| wind drift, in. | 0 | 1.0 | 4.3 | 10.4 | 19.5 | 32.6 |
| velocity, fps | 3,200 | 2,868 | 2,559 | 2,271 | 2,001 | 1,752 |
| energy, ft-lb/gr. | 22.73 | 18.26 | 14.54 | 11.45 | 8.89 | 6.81 |
| flight time, sec.. | 0 | .0991 | .2098 | .3342 | .4750 | .6352 |
| trajectory, in. | -1.5 | 1.4 | 0 | -6.7 | -20.2 | -42.4 |
| wind drift, in. | 0 | .9 | 3.9 | 9.4 | 17.8 | 29.5 |

| C=.350 | Muzzle | RANGE IN YARDS 100 | 200 | 300 | 400 | 500 |
|---|---|---|---|---|---|---|
| velocity, fps | 2,400 | 2,160 | 1,935 | 1,725 | 1,534 | 1,364 |
| energy, ft-lb/gr. | 12.79 | 10.36 | 8.31 | 6.61 | 5.22 | 4.13 |
| flight time, sec. | 0 | .1318 | .2785 | .4428 | .6273 | .8349 |
| trajectory, in. | -1.5 | 3.0 | 0 | -12.3 | -36.4 | -75.3 |
| wind drift, in. | 0 | 1.1 | 4.9 | 11.6 | 22.2 | 36.2 |
| velocity, fps | 2,600 | 2,349 | 2,113 | 1,890 | 1,684 | 1,497 |
| energy, ft-lb/gr. | 15.01 | 12.25 | 9.91 | 7.93 | 6.30 | 4.98 |
| flight time, sec. | 0 | .1214 | .2561 | .4062 | .5744 | .7635 |
| trajectory, in. | -1.5 | 2.4 | 0 | -10.2 | -30.2 | -62.6 |
| wind drift, in. | 0 | 1.0 | 4.4 | 10.5 | 19.8 | 32.7 |
| velocity, fps | 2,800 | 2,538 | 2,291 | 2,058 | 1,839 | 1,637 |
| energy, ft-lb/gr. | 17.41 | 14.30 | 11.65 | 9.40 | 7.51 | 5.95 |
| flight time, sec. | 0 | .1125 | .2370 | .3751 | .5294 | .7024 |
| trajectory, in. | -1.5 | 2.0 | 0 | -8.6 | -25.5 | -52.6 |
| wind drift, in. | 0 | .9 | 4.0 | 9.6 | 17.9 | 29.5 |
| velocity, fps | 3,000 | 2,726 | 2,469 | 2,225 | 1,996 | 1,781 |
| energy, ft-lb/gr. | 19.98 | 16.50 | 13.53 | 10.99 | 8.84 | 7.04 |
| flight time, sec. | 0 | .1049 | .2205 | .3485 | .4909 | .6500 |
| trajectory, in. | -1.5 | 1.6 | 0 | -7.3 | -21.7 | -44.8 |
| wind drift, in | 0 | .8 | 3.7 | 8.7 | 16.3 | 26.7 |
| velocity, fps | 3,200 | 2,914 | 2,645 | 2,392 | 2,153 | 1,928 |
| energy, ft-lb/sec. | 22.73 | 18.85 | 15.53 | 12.70 | 10.29 | 8.25 |
| flight time, sec. | 0 | .0983 | .2063 | .3256 | .4578 | .6051 |
| trajectory, in. | -1.5 | 1.3 | 0 | -6.3 | -18.7 | -38.6 |
| wind drift, in. | 0 | .7 | 3.3 | 7.9 | 14.8 | 24.3 |

## C=.400

| C=.400 | Muzzle | 100 | 200 | 300 | 400 | 500 |
|---|---|---|---|---|---|---|
| velocity, fps | 2,400 | 2,190 | 1,990 | 1,802 | 1,627 | 1,467 |
| energy, ft-lb/gr. | 12.79 | 10.65 | 8.79 | 7.21 | 5.88 | 4.78 |
| flight time, sec. | 0 | .1309 | .2746 | .4331 | .6083 | .8026 |
| trajectory, in. | -1.5 | 2.9 | 0 | -11.7 | -34.1 | -69.8 |
| wind drift, in. | 0 | 1.0 | 4.2 | 10.1 | 18.9 | 30.7 |
| | | | | | | |
| velocity, fps | 2,600 | 2,380 | 2,171 | 1,972 | 1,785 | 1,611 |
| energy, ft-lb/gr. | 15.01 | 12.58 | 10.46 | 8.63 | 7.07 | 5.76 |
| flight time, sec. | 0 | .1206 | .2526 | .3976 | .5576 | .7345 |
| trajectory, in. | -1.5 | 2.3 | 0 | -9.7 | -28.4 | -58.1 |
| wind drift, in. | 0 | .8 | 3.9 | 9.1 | 16.9 | 27.6 |
| | | | | | | |
| velocity, fps | 2,800 | 2,570 | 2,352 | 2,143 | 1,946 | 1,761 |
| energy, ft-lb/gr. | 17.41 | 14.66 | 12.28 | 10.20 | 8.41 | 6.88 |
| flight time, sec. | 0 | .1118 | .2339 | .3675 | .5144 | .6765 |
| trajectory, in. | -1.5 | 1.9 | 0 | -8.2 | -24.0 | -49.0 |
| wind drift, in. | 0 | .8 | 3.5 | 8.2 | 15.3 | 25.0 |
| | | | | | | |
| velocity, fps | 3,000 | 2,760 | 2,532 | 2,315 | 2,109 | 1,914 |
| energy, ft-lb/gr. | 19.98 | 16.91 | 14.23 | 11.90 | 9.87 | 8.13 |
| flight time, sec. | 0 | .1043 | .2178 | .3417 | .4775 | .6268 |
| trajectory, in. | -1.5 | 1.5 | 0 | -7.0 | -20.5 | -41.8 |
| wind drift, in. | 0 | .7 | 3.1 | 7.4 | 13.9 | 22.6 |
| | | | | | | |
| velocity, fps | 3,200 | 2,948 | 2,711 | 2,485 | 2,271 | 2,067 |
| energy, ft-lb/gr. | 22.73 | 19.29 | 16.32 | 13.71 | 11.45 | 9.49 |
| flight time, sec. | 0 | .0977 | .2038 | .3194 | .4457 | .5841 |
| trajectory, in. | -1.5 | 1.3 | 0 | -6.0 | -17.6 | -36.0 |
| wind drift, in. | 0 | .7 | 2.8 | 6.7 | 12.5 | 20.5 |

## C=.450

| C=.450 | Muzzle | 100 | 200 | 300 | 400 | 500 |
|---|---|---|---|---|---|---|
| velocity, fps | 2,400 | 2,212 | 2,033 | 1,863 | 1,703 | 1,554 |
| energy, ft-lb/gr. | 12.79 | 10.86 | 9.18 | 7.71 | 6.44 | 5.36 |
| flight time, sec. | 0 | .1302 | .2716 | .4258 | .5943 | .7787 |
| trajectory, in. | -1.5 | 2.8 | 0 | -11.2 | -32.5 | -65.8 |
| wind drift, in. | 0 | 1.0 | 3.8 | 8.6 | 16.3 | 26.6 |
| | | | | | | |
| velocity, fps | 2,600 | 2,404 | 2,216 | 2,037 | 1,866 | 1,706 |
| energy, ft-lb/gr. | 15.01 | 12.83 | 10.90 | 9.21 | 7.73 | 6.46 |
| flight time, sec. | 0 | .1200 | .2500 | .3912 | .5451 | .7132 |
| trajectory, in. | -1.5 | 2.3 | 0 | -9.4 | -27.1 | -54.9 |
| wind drift, in. | 0 | .9 | 3.3 | 7.7 | 14.2 | 23.4 |
| | | | | | | |
| velocity, fps | 2,800 | 2,595 | 2,399 | 2,212 | 2,033 | 1,862 |
| energy, ft-lb/gr. | 17.41 | 14.95 | 12.78 | 10.86 | 9.18 | 7.70 |
| flight time, sec. | 0 | .1113 | .2315 | .3518 | .5033 | .6575 |
| trajectory, in. | -1.5 | 1.8 | 0 | -7.9 | -22.9 | -46.3 |
| wind drift, in. | 0 | .8 | 3.0 | 6.9 | 12.9 | 20.8 |
| | | | | | | |
| velocity, fps | 3,000 | 2,789 | 2,587 | 2,394 | 2,209 | 2,033 |
| energy, ft-lb/gr. | 19.98 | 17.26 | 14.86 | 12.72 | 10.84 | 9.18 |
| flight time, sec. | 0 | .1038 | .2157 | .3366 | .4675 | .6099 |
| trajectory, in. | -1.5 | 1.5 | 0 | -6.6 | -19.5 | -39.3 |
| wind drift, in. | 0 | .7 | 2.8 | 6.2 | 11.6 | 18.8 |
| | | | | | | |
| velocity, fps | 3,200 | 2,979 | 2,768 | 2,568 | 2,375 | 2,192 |
| energy, ft-lb/gr. | 22.74 | 19.70 | 17.02 | 14.63 | 12.53 | 10.66 |
| flight time, sec. | 0 | .0973 | .2019 | .3147 | 4368 | .5691 |
| trajectory, in. | -1.5 | 1.2 | 0 | -5.8 | -16.7 | -34.0 |
| wind drift, in. | 0 | .6 | 2.5 | 5.8 | 10.6 | 17.3 |

## C=.500

| C=.500 | Muzzle | 100 | 200 | 300 | 400 | 500 |
|---|---|---|---|---|---|---|
| velocity, fps | 2,400 | 2,231 | 2,068 | 1,913 | 1,766 | 1,627 |
| energy, ft-lb/gr. | 12.79 | 11.05 | 9.49 | 8.12 | 6.92 | 5.88 |
| flight time, sec. | 0 | .1297 | .2693 | .4201 | .5834 | .7604 |
| trajectory, in. | -1.5 | 2.7 | 0 | -10.9 | -31.3 | -62.9 |
| wind drift, in. | 0 | .8 | 3.3 | 7.9 | 14.6 | 23.5 |
| | | | | | | |
| velocity, fps | 2,600 | 2,423 | 2,253 | 2,090 | 1,933 | 1,785 |
| energy, ft-lb/gr. | 15.01 | 13.03 | 11.27 | 9.70 | 8.30 | 7.07 |
| flight time, sec. | 0 | .1195 | .2479 | .3862 | .5354 | .6970 |
| trajectory, in. | -1.5 | 2.2 | 0 | -9.1 | -26.1 | -52.5 |
| wind drift, in. | 0 | .6 | 3.0 | 7.0 | 13.1 | 21.2 |
| | | | | | | |
| velocity, fps | 2,800 | 2,615 | 2,438 | 2,267 | 2,103 | 1,946 |
| energy, ft-lb/gr. | 17.41 | 15.18 | 13.20 | 11.41 | 9.82 | 8.41 |
| flight time, sec. | 0 | .1109 | .2297 | .3573 | .4947 | .6430 |
| trajectory, in. | -1.5 | 1.8 | 0 | -7.7 | -22.1 | -44.4 |
| wind drift, in. | 0 | .6 | 2.7 | 6.4 | 11.8 | 19.1 |
| | | | | | | |
| velocity, fps | 3,000 | 2,807 | 2,622 | 2,444 | 2,273 | 2,109 |
| energy, ft-lb/gr. | 19.98 | 17.49 | 15.26 | 13.26 | 11.47 | 9.87 |
| flight time, sec. | 0 | .1034 | .2140 | .3325 | .4598 | .5968 |
| trajectory, in. | -1.5 | 1.5 | 0 | -6.5 | -18.9 | -38.0 |
| wind drift, in. | 0 | .5 | 2.4 | 5.8 | 10.7 | 17.3 |
| | | | | | | |
| velocity, fps | 3,200 | 2,998 | 2,804 | 2,619 | 2,442 | 2,271 |
| energy, ft-lb/gr. | 22.73 | 19.95 | 17.46 | 15.23 | 13.24 | 11.45 |
| flight time, sec. | 0 | .0969 | .2004 | .3110 | .4297 | .5571 |
| trajectory, in. | -1.5 | 1.2 | 0 | -5.6 | -16.3 | -32.8 |
| wind drift, in. | 0 | .5 | 2.2 | 5.2 | 9.7 | 15.7 |

# RECOIL ENERGIES OF BIG GAME RIFLES

| CARTRIDGE | BULLET WEIGHT (GR.) | POWDER WEIGHT (GR.) | BULLET VELOCITY (FPS) | RIFLE WEIGHT (FT-LBS) | RECOIL ENERGY | CARTRIDGE | BULLET WEIGHT (GR.) | POWDER WEIGHT (GR.) | BULLET VELOCITY (FPS) | RIFLE WEIGHT (FT-LBS) | RECOIL ENERGY |
|---|---|---|---|---|---|---|---|---|---|---|---|
| .243 Win. | 100 | 39.5 | 2,950 | 7.0 | 11.2 | .300 Win. Mag. | 150 | 66.5 | 3,230 | 9.0 | 26.0 |
| .243 Win. | 100 | 39.5 | 2,950 | 9.0 | 8.7 | .300 Win. Mag. | 220 | 66.0 | 2,690 | 7.0 | 36.8 |
| .257 Robts. | 100 | 44.5 | 2,930 | 7.0 | 12.2 | .300 Win. Mag. | 220 | 66.0 | 2,690 | 9.0 | 28.6 |
| .257 Robts. | 100 | 44.5 | 2,930 | 9.0 | 9.5 | .300 Wby. Mag. | 150 | 80.0 | 3,340 | 7.0 | 42.5 |
| .257 Robts. | 120 | 41.5 | 2,780 | 7.0 | 12.9 | .300 Wby. Mag. | 150 | 80.0 | 3,340 | 9.0 | 33.0 |
| .257 Robts. | 120 | 41.5 | 2,780 | 9.0 | 10.0 | .300 Wby. Mag. | 220 | 73.0 | 2,880 | 7.0 | 45.3 |
| .25-06 Rem. | 120 | 50.0 | 2,950 | 7.0 | 16.9 | .300 Wby. Mag. | 220 | 73.0 | 2,880 | 9.0 | 35.2 |
| .25-06 Rem. | 120 | 50.0 | 2,950 | 9.0 | 13.1 | 8mm Rem. Mag. | 200 | 74.0 | 3,000 | 7.0 | 44.0 |
| .270 Win. | 150 | 47.5 | 2,830 | 7.0 | 19.7 | 8mm Rem. Mag. | 200 | 74.0 | 3,000 | 9.0 | 34.3 |
| .270 Win. | 150 | 47.5 | 2,830 | 9.0 | 15.3 | .338 Win. Mag. | 200 | 76.0 | 3,020 | 7.0 | 45.7 |
| .280 Rem. | 160 | 53.0 | 2,800 | 7.0 | 22.5 | .338 Win. Mag. | 200 | 76.0 | 3,020 | 9.0 | 35.6 |
| .280 Rem. | 160 | 53.0 | 2,800 | 9.0 | 17.5 | .338 Win. Mag. | 300 | 64.5 | 2,410 | 7.0 | 44.8 |
| 7mm Wby. Mag. | 139 | 69.0 | 3,310 | 7.0 | 33.4 | .338 Win. Mag. | 300 | 64.5 | 2,410 | 9.0 | 34.8 |
| 7mm Wby. Mag. | 139 | 69.0 | 3,310 | 9.0 | 25.9 | .375 H&H Mag. | 270 | 82.5 | 2,690 | 7.0 | 56.2 |
| 7mm Wby. Mag. | 175 | 65.0 | 2,950 | 7.0 | 32.7 | .375 H&H Mag. | 270 | 82.5 | 2,690 | 9.0 | 43.7 |
| 7mm Wby. Mag. | 175 | 65.0 | 2,950 | 9.0 | 25.4 | .378 Wby. Mag. | 270 | 117.0 | 3,100 | 7.0 | 98.1 |
| .308 Win. | 150 | 46.0 | 2,800 | 7.0 | 18.8 | .378 Wby. Mag. | 270 | 117.0 | 3,100 | 9.0 | 76.3 |
| .308 Win. | 150 | 46.0 | 2,800 | 9.0 | 14.6 | .378 Wby. Mag. | 300 | 103.0 | 2,920 | 7.0 | 89.1 |
| .30-06 Sprg. | 180 | 57.0 | 2,700 | 7.0 | 25.0 | .378 Wby Mag. | 300 | 103.0 | 2,920 | 9.0 | 69.3 |
| .30-06 Sprg. | 180 | 57.0 | 2,700 | 9.0 | 19.0 | .45-70 Govt. | 405 | 52.5 | 1,780 | 7.0 | 35.6 |
| .300 Win. Mag. | 150 | 66.5 | 3,230 | 7.0 | 33.5 | .45-70 Govt. | 405 | 52.5 | 1,780 | 9.0 | 27.6 |

*(most data courtesy of Answer Products Co., 1519 Westbury Dr., Davison MI 48423)*

# BALLISTICS TABLES FOR U.S. AMMUNITION

## FEDERAL BALLISTICS – PREMIUM CENTERFIRE RIFLE

| USAGE | FEDERAL LOAD NO. | CALIBER | BULLET WGT. GRAINS | WGT. IN GRAMS | BULLET STYLE* | FACTORY PRIMER NO. | VELOCITY IN FEET PER SECOND (TO NEAREST 10 FPS) MUZZLE | 100 YDS. | 200 YDS. | 300 YDS. | 400 YDS. | 500 YDS. | ENERGY IN FOOT-POUNDS (TO NEAREST 5 FOOT-POUNDS) MUZZLE | 100 YDS. | 200 YDS. | 300 YDS. | 400 YDS. | 500 YDS. |
|---|---|---|---|---|---|---|---|---|---|---|---|---|---|---|---|---|---|---|
| 1 | P223E | 223 Rem. (5.56x45mm) | 55 | 3.56 | Sierra GameKing BTHP | 205 | 3240 | 2770 | 2340 | 1950 | 1610 | 1330 | 1280 | 935 | 670 | 465 | 315 | 215 |
| 1 | P22250B | 22-250 Rem. | 55 | 3.56 | Sierra GameKing BTHP | 210 | 3680 | 3280 | 2920 | 2590 | 2280 | 1990 | 1655 | 1315 | 1040 | 815 | 630 | 480 |
| 2 | P243C | 243 Win. (6.16x51mm) | 100 | 6.48 | Sierra GameKing BTSP | 210 | 2960 | 2760 | 2570 | 2380 | 2210 | 2040 | 1950 | 1690 | 1460 | 1260 | 1080 | 925 |
| 2 | P243D | 243 Win. (6.16x51mm) | 85 | 5.50 | Sierra GameKing BTHP | 210 | 3320 | 3070 | 2830 | 2600 | 2380 | 2180 | 2080 | 1770 | 1510 | 1280 | 1070 | 890 |
| 1 | P243F | 243 Win. (6.16x51mm) | 70 | 4.54 | Nosler Ballistic Tip | 210 | 3400 | 3070 | 2760 | 2470 | 2200 | 1950 | 1795 | 1465 | 1185 | 950 | 755 | 590 |
| 2 | P6C | 6mm Rem. | 100 | 6.48 | Nosler Partition | 210 | 3100 | 2860 | 2640 | 2420 | 2220 | 2020 | 2135 | 1820 | 1545 | 1300 | 1090 | 910 |
| 2 | P257B | 257 Roberts (High-Velocity + P) | 120 | 7.77 | Nosler Partition | 210 | 2780 | 2560 | 2360 | 2160 | 1970 | 1790 | 2060 | 1750 | 1480 | 1240 | 1030 | 855 |
| 2 | P257WBA | 257 Weatherby Magnum | 115 | 7.45 | Nosler Partition | 210 | 3150 | 2900 | 2660 | 2440 | 2220 | 2020 | 2535 | 2145 | 1810 | 1515 | 1260 | 1040 |
| 2 | P257WBT1 | 257 Weatherby Magnum | 115 | 7.45 | Trophy Bonded Bear Claw | 210 | 3150 | 2890 | 2640 | 2400 | 2180 | 1970 | 2535 | 2125 | 1775 | 1470 | 1210 | 990 |
| 2 | P2506C | 25-06 Rem. | 117 | 7.58 | Sierra GameKing BTSP | 210 | 2990 | 2770 | 2570 | 2370 | 2190 | 2000 | 2320 | 2000 | 1715 | 1465 | 1240 | 1045 |
| 2 | P2506D | 25-06 Rem. | 100 | 6.48 | Nosler Ballistic Tip | 210 | 3210 | 2960 | 2720 | 2490 | 2280 | 2070 | 2290 | 1940 | 1640 | 1380 | 1150 | 955 |
| 2 | P2506E | 25-06 Rem. | 115 | 7.45 | Nosler Partition | 210 | 2990 | 2750 | 2520 | 2300 | 2100 | 1900 | 2285 | 1930 | 1620 | 1350 | 1120 | 915 |
| 2 | P2506T1 | 25-06 Rem. | 115 | 7.45 | Trophy Bonded Bear Claw | 210 | 2990 | 2740 | 2500 | 2270 | 2050 | 1850 | 2285 | 1910 | 1590 | 1310 | 1075 | 870 |
| 2 | P270C | 270 Win. | 150 | 9.72 | Sierra GameKing BTSP | 210 | 2850 | 2660 | 2480 | 2300 | 2130 | 1970 | 2705 | 2355 | 2040 | 1760 | 1510 | 1290 |
| 2 | P270D | 270 Win. | 130 | 8.42 | Sierra GameKing BTSP | 210 | 3060 | 2830 | 2620 | 2410 | 2220 | 2030 | 2700 | 2320 | 1980 | 1680 | 1420 | 1190 |
| 2 | P270E | 270 Win. | 150 | 9.72 | Nosler Partition | 210 | 2850 | 2590 | 2340 | 2100 | 1880 | 1670 | 2705 | 2225 | 1815 | 1470 | 1175 | 930 |
| 2 | P270F | 270 Win. | 130 | 8.42 | Nosler Ballistic Tip | 210 | 3060 | 2840 | 2630 | 2430 | 2230 | 2050 | 2700 | 2325 | 1990 | 1700 | 1440 | 1210 |
| 2 | P270T1 | 270 Win. | 140 | 9.07 | Trophy Bonded Bear Claw | 210 | 2940 | 2700 | 2480 | 2260 | 2060 | 1860 | 2685 | 2270 | 1905 | 1590 | 1315 | 1080 |
| 2 | P270T2 | 270 Win. | 130 | 8.42 | Trophy Bonded Bear Claw | 210 | 3060 | 2810 | 2570 | 2340 | 2130 | 1930 | 2705 | 2275 | 1905 | 1585 | 1310 | 1070 |
| 2 | P270WBA | 270 Weatherby Magnum | 130 | 8.42 | Nosler Partition | 210 | 3200 | 2960 | 2740 | 2520 | 2320 | 2120 | 2955 | 2530 | 2160 | 1835 | 1550 | 1300 |
| 2 | P270WBT1 | 270 Weatherby Magnum | 140 | 9.07 | Trophy Bonded Bear Claw | 210 | 3100 | 2840 | 2600 | 2370 | 2150 | 1950 | 2990 | 2510 | 2100 | 1745 | 1440 | 1175 |
| 2 | P730A | 7-30 Waters | 120 | 7.77 | BTSP | 210 | 2700 | 2300 | 1930 | 1600 | 1330 | 1140 | 1940 | 1405 | 990 | 685 | 470 | 345 |
| 2 | P7C | 7mm Mauser (7x57mm Mauser) | 140 | 9.07 | Nosler Partition | 210 | 2660 | 2450 | 2260 | 2070 | 1890 | 1730 | 2200 | 1865 | 1585 | 1330 | 1110 | 930 |
| 2 | P708A | 7mm-08 Rem. | 140 | 9.07 | Nosler Partition | 210 | 2800 | 2590 | 2390 | 2200 | 2020 | 1840 | 2435 | 2085 | 1775 | 1500 | 1265 | 1060 |
| 2 | P708B | 7mm-08 Rem. | 140 | 9.07 | Nosler Ballistic Tip | 210 | 2800 | 2610 | 2430 | 2260 | 2100 | 1940 | 2440 | 2135 | 1840 | 1590 | 1360 | 1165 |
| 2 | P764A | 7x64 Brenneke | 160 | 10.37 | Nosler Partition | 210 | 2650 | 2480 | 2310 | 2150 | 2000 | 1850 | 2495 | 2180 | 1895 | 1640 | 1415 | 1215 |
| 2 | P280A | 280 Rem. | 150 | 9.72 | Nosler Partition | 210 | 2890 | 2620 | 2370 | 2140 | 1910 | 1710 | 2780 | 2295 | 1875 | 1520 | 1215 | 970 |
| 2 | P280T1 | 280 Rem. | 140 | 9.07 | Trophy Bonded Bear Claw | 210 | 2990 | 2630 | 2310 | 2040 | 1730 | 1480 | 2770 | 2155 | 1655 | 1250 | 925 | 680 |
| 2 | P7RD | 7mm Rem. Magnum | 150 | 9.72 | Sierra GameKing BTSP | 215 | 3110 | 2920 | 2750 | 2580 | 2410 | 2250 | 3220 | 2850 | 2510 | 2210 | 1930 | 1690 |
| 3 | P7RE | 7mm Rem. Magnum | 165 | 10.69 | Sierra GameKing BTSP | 215 | 2950 | 2800 | 2650 | 2510 | 2370 | 2230 | 3190 | 2865 | 2570 | 2300 | 2050 | 1825 |
| 3 | P7RF | 7mm Rem. Magnum | 160 | 10.37 | Nosler Partition | 215 | 2950 | 2770 | 2590 | 2420 | 2250 | 2090 | 3090 | 2715 | 2375 | 2075 | 1800 | 1555 |
| 2 | P7RG | 7mm Rem. Magnum | 140 | 9.07 | Nosler Partition | 215 | 3150 | 2930 | 2710 | 2510 | 2320 | 2130 | 3085 | 2660 | 2290 | 1960 | 1670 | 1415 |
| 2 | P7RH | 7mm Rem. Magnum | 150 | 9.72 | Nosler Ballistic Tip | 215 | 3110 | 2910 | 2720 | 2540 | 2370 | 2200 | 3220 | 2825 | 2470 | 2150 | 1865 | 1610 |
| 3 | P7RT1 | 7mm Rem. Magnum | 175 | 11.34 | Trophy Bonded Bear Claw | 215 | 2860 | 2600 | 2350 | 2120 | 1900 | 1700 | 3180 | 2625 | 2150 | 1745 | 1400 | 1120 |
| 3 | P7RT2 | 7mm Rem. Magnum | 160 | 10.37 | Trophy Bonded Bear Claw | 215 | 2940 | 2660 | 2390 | 2140 | 1900 | 1680 | 3070 | 2505 | 2025 | 1620 | 1280 | 1005 |
| 3 | P7WBA | 7mm Weatherby Magnum | 160 | 10.37 | Nosler Partition | 215 | 3050 | 2850 | 2650 | 2470 | 2290 | 2120 | 3305 | 2880 | 2505 | 2165 | 1865 | 1600 |
| 3 | P7WBT1 | 7mm Weatherby Magnum | 160 | 10.37 | Trophy Bonded Bear Claw | 215 | 3050 | 2730 | 2420 | 2140 | 1880 | 1640 | 3305 | 2640 | 2085 | 1630 | 1255 | 955 |
| 2 | P3030D | 30-30 Win. | 170 | 11.01 | Nosler Partition | 210 | 2200 | 1900 | 1620 | 1380 | 1190 | 1060 | 1830 | 1355 | 990 | 720 | 535 | 425 |
| 2 | P308C | 308 Win. (7.62x51mm) | 165 | 10.69 | Sierra GameKing BTSP | 210 | 2700 | 2520 | 2330 | 2160 | 1990 | 1830 | 2670 | 2310 | 1990 | 1700 | 1450 | 1230 |
| 3 | P308E | 308 Win. (7.62x51mm) | 180 | 11.66 | Nosler Partition | 210 | 2620 | 2430 | 2240 | 2060 | 1890 | 1730 | 2745 | 2355 | 2005 | 1700 | 1430 | 1200 |
| 2 | P308F | 308 Win. (7.62x51mm) | 150 | 9.72 | Nosler Ballistic Tip | 210 | 2820 | 2610 | 2410 | 2220 | 2040 | 1860 | 2650 | 2270 | 1935 | 1640 | 1380 | 1155 |
| 3 | P308T1 | 308 Win. (7.62x51mm) | 165 | 10.69 | Trophy Bonded Bear Claw | 210 | 2700 | 2440 | 2200 | 1970 | 1760 | 1570 | 2670 | 2185 | 1775 | 1425 | 1135 | 900 |
| 2 | P3006D | 30-06 Spring. (7.62x63mm) | 165 | 10.69 | Sierra GameKing BTSP | 210 | 2800 | 2610 | 2420 | 2240 | 2070 | 1910 | 2870 | 2490 | 2150 | 1840 | 1580 | 1340 |
| 3 | P3006F | 30-06 Spring. (7.62x63mm) | 180 | 11.66 | Nosler Partition | 210 | 2700 | 2500 | 2320 | 2140 | 1970 | 1810 | 2915 | 2510 | 2150 | 1830 | 1550 | 1350 |
| 2 | P3006G | 30-06 Spring. (7.62x63mm) | 150 | 9.72 | Sierra GameKing BTSP | 210 | 2910 | 2690 | 2480 | 2270 | 2070 | 1880 | 2820 | 2420 | 2040 | 1710 | 1430 | 1180 |
| 3 | P3006L | 30-06 Spring. (7.62x63mm) | 180 | 11.66 | Sierra GameKing BTSP | 210 | 2700 | 2540 | 2380 | 2220 | 2080 | 1930 | 2915 | 2570 | 2260 | 1975 | 1720 | 1495 |
| 2 | P3006P | 30-06 Spring. (7.62x63mm) | 150 | 9.72 | Nosler Ballistic Tip | 210 | 2910 | 2700 | 2490 | 2300 | 2110 | 1940 | 2820 | 2420 | 2070 | 1760 | 1485 | 1245 |
| 2 | P3006Q | 30-06 Spring. (7.62x63mm) | 165 | 10.69 | Nosler Ballistic Tip | 210 | 2800 | 2610 | 2430 | 2250 | 2080 | 1920 | 2870 | 2495 | 2155 | 1855 | 1585 | 1350 |
| 3 | P3006T1 | 30-06 Spring. (7.62x63mm) | 165 | 10.69 | Trophy Bonded Bear Claw | 210 | 2800 | 2540 | 2290 | 2050 | 1830 | 1630 | 2870 | 2360 | 1915 | 1545 | 1230 | 975 |
| 3 | P3006T2 | 30-06 Spring. (7.62x63mm) | 180 | 11.66 | Trophy Bonded Bear Claw | 210 | 2700 | 2460 | 2220 | 2000 | 1800 | 1610 | 2915 | 2410 | 1975 | 1605 | 1290 | 1035 |
| 3 | P300WC | 300 Win. Magnum | 200 | 12.96 | Sierra GameKing BTSP | 215 | 2830 | 2680 | 2530 | 2380 | 2240 | 2110 | 3560 | 3180 | 2830 | 2520 | 2230 | 1970 |
| 3 | P300WT4 | 300 Win. Magnum | 150 | 9.72 | Trophy Bonded Bear Claw | 215 | 3280 | 2980 | 2700 | 2430 | 2190 | 1950 | 3570 | 2450 | 2420 | 1970 | 1590 | 1270 |
| 3 | P35WT1 | 35 Whelen | 225 | 14.58 | Trophy Bonded Bear Claw | 210 | 2500 | 2300 | 2110 | 1930 | 1770 | 1610 | 3120 | 2650 | 2235 | 1870 | 1560 | 1290 |

Usage Key: 1 = Varmints, predators, small game   2 = Medium game   3 = Large, heavy game   4 = Dangerous game   5 = Target shooting, training, practice
+P ammunition is loaded to a higher pressure. Use only in firearms so recommended by the gun manufacturer.   *BTHP = Boat-Tail Hollow Point   BTSP = Boat-Tail Soft Point
Partition and Ballistic Tip are registered trademarks of Nosler Bullets, Inc. Weatherby is a registered trademark of Weatherby, Inc. GameKing is a registered trademark of Sierra Bullets. Bear Claw is a registered trademark of Trophy Bonded Bullets, Inc. Trophy Bonded Bear Claw is manufactured by Federal under U.S. Patent numbers 4,750,427; 4,793,037; 4,879,953, and patents pending.

MODERN SPORTING RIFLE CARTRIDGES

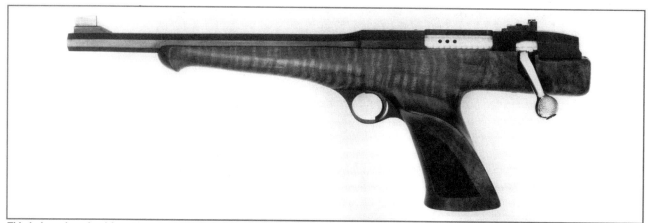

This bolt-action pistol from Wichita Arms is as accurate as most hunting rifles. Its barrel is stiff, which translates into tighter groups.

# FEDERAL BALLISTICS – PREMIUM CENTERFIRE RIFLE

| WIND DRIFT IN INCHES 10 MPH CROSSWIND | | | | | HEIGHT OF BULLET TRAJECTORY IN INCHES ABOVE OR BELOW LINE OF SIGHT IF ZEROED AT ⊕ YARDS. SIGHTS 1.5 INCHES ABOVE BORE LINE | | | | | | | | | | TEST BARREL LENGTH INCHES | FEDERAL LOAD NO. |
|---|---|---|---|---|---|---|---|---|---|---|---|---|---|---|---|---|
| | | | | | AVERAGE RANGE | | | | LONG RANGE | | | | | | | |
| 100 YDS. | 200 YDS. | 300 YDS. | 400 YDS. | 500 YDS. | 50 YDS. | 100 YDS. | 200 YDS. | 300 YDS. | 50 YDS. | 100 YDS. | 200 YDS. | 300 YDS. | 400 YDS. | 500 YDS. | | |
| 1.3 | 5.8 | 14.2 | 27.7 | 47.6 | -0.3 | ⊕ | -2.7 | -10.8 | +0.4 | +1.4 | ⊕ | -6.7 | -20.5 | -43.4 | 24 | P223E |
| 0.8 | 3.6 | 8.4 | 15.8 | 26.3 | -0.4 | ⊕ | -1.7 | -7.6 | 0.0 | +0.9 | ⊕ | -5.0 | -15.1 | -32.0 | 24 | P22250B |
| 0.6 | 2.6 | 6.1 | 11.3 | 18.4 | -0.2 | ⊕ | -3.1 | -11.4 | +0.6 | +1.5 | ⊕ | -6.8 | -19.8 | -39.9 | 24 | P243C |
| 0.7 | 2.7 | 6.3 | 11.6 | 18.8 | -0.3 | ⊕ | -2.2 | -8.8 | +0.2 | +1.1 | ⊕ | -5.5 | -16.1 | -32.8 | 24 | P243D |
| 0.8 | 3.4 | 8.1 | 15.2 | 25.1 | -0.3 | ⊕ | -2.2 | -9.0 | +0.2 | +1.1 | ⊕ | -5.7 | -17.1 | -35.7 | 24 | P243F |
| 0.7 | 2.9 | 6.7 | 12.5 | 20.4 | -0.3 | ⊕ | -2.8 | -10.5 | +0.4 | +1.4 | ⊕ | -6.3 | -18.7 | -38.1 | 24 | P6C |
| 0.8 | 3.3 | 7.7 | 14.3 | 23.5 | -0.1 | ⊕ | -3.8 | -14.0 | +0.8 | +1.9 | ⊕ | -8.2 | -24.0 | -48.9 | 24 | P257B |
| 0.7 | 3.0 | 6.9 | 12.9 | 21.1 | -0.3 | ⊕ | -2.7 | -10.2 | +0.4 | +1.3 | ⊕ | -6.2 | -18.4 | -37.5 | 24 | P257WBA |
| 0.7 | 3.1 | 7.3 | 13.7 | 22.4 | -0.3 | ⊕ | -2.7 | -10.4 | +0.4 | +1.4 | ⊕ | -6.3 | -18.8 | -38.5 | 24 | P257WBT1 |
| 0.7 | 2.8 | 6.5 | 12.0 | 19.6 | -0.2 | ⊕ | -3.0 | -11.4 | +0.5 | +1.5 | ⊕ | -6.8 | -19.9 | -40.4 | 24 | P2506C |
| 0.7 | 2.9 | 6.7 | 12.4 | 20.2 | -0.3 | ⊕ | -2.5 | -9.7 | +0.3 | +1.2 | ⊕ | -6.0 | -17.5 | -35.8 | 24 | P2506D |
| 0.8 | 3.2 | 7.4 | 13.9 | 22.6 | -0.2 | ⊕ | -3.1 | -11.7 | +0.6 | +1.6 | ⊕ | -7.0 | -20.8 | -42.2 | 24 | P2506E |
| 0.8 | 3.4 | 7.9 | 14.8 | 21.4 | -0.2 | ⊕ | -3.2 | -11.9 | +0.6 | +1.6 | ⊕ | -7.2 | -21.1 | -43.2 | 24 | P2506T1 |
| 0.7 | 2.7 | 6.3 | 11.6 | 18.9 | -0.2 | ⊕ | -3.4 | -12.5 | +0.7 | +1.7 | ⊕ | -7.4 | -21.4 | -43.0 | 24 | P270C |
| 0.7 | 2.8 | 6.5 | 12.1 | 19.7 | -0.2 | ⊕ | -2.8 | -10.7 | +0.5 | +1.4 | ⊕ | -6.5 | -19.0 | -38.5 | 24 | P270D |
| 0.9 | 3.9 | 9.2 | 17.3 | 28.5 | -0.2 | ⊕ | -3.7 | -13.8 | +0.8 | +1.9 | ⊕ | -8.3 | -24.4 | -50.5 | 24 | P270E |
| 0.7 | 2.7 | 6.4 | 11.9 | 19.3 | -0.2 | ⊕ | -2.8 | -10.7 | +0.5 | +1.4 | ⊕ | -6.5 | -18.8 | -38.2 | 24 | P270F |
| 0.8 | 3.2 | 7.6 | 14.2 | 23.0 | -0.2 | ⊕ | -3.3 | -12.2 | +0.6 | +1.6 | ⊕ | -7.3 | -21.5 | -43.7 | 24 | P270T1 |
| 0.7 | 3.2 | 7.4 | 13.9 | 22.5 | -0.2 | ⊕ | -2.9 | -11.1 | +0.5 | +1.5 | ⊕ | -6.7 | -19.8 | -40.5 | 24 | P270T2 |
| 0.7 | 2.7 | 6.3 | 11.7 | 19.0 | -0.3 | ⊕ | -2.5 | -9.6 | +0.3 | +1.2 | ⊕ | -5.9 | -17.3 | -35.1 | 24 | P270WBA |
| 0.8 | 3.1 | 7.4 | 13.7 | 22.5 | -0.3 | ⊕ | -2.8 | -10.8 | +0.4 | +1.4 | ⊕ | -6.6 | -19.3 | -39.6 | 24 | P270WBT1 |
| 1.6 | 7.2 | 17.7 | 34.5 | 58.1 | 0.0 | ⊕ | -5.2 | -19.8 | +1.2 | +2.6 | ⊕ | -12.0 | -37.6 | -81.7 | 24 | P730A |
| 1.3 | 3.2 | 8.2 | 15.4 | 23.4 | -0.1 | ⊕ | -4.3 | -15.4 | +1.0 | +2.1 | ⊕ | -9.0 | -26.1 | -52.9 | 24 | P7C |
| 0.8 | 3.1 | 7.3 | 13.5 | 21.8 | -0.2 | ⊕ | -3.7 | -13.5 | +0.8 | +1.8 | ⊕ | -8.0 | -23.1 | -46.6 | 24 | P708A |
| 0.7 | 2.7 | 6.4 | 11.9 | 19.1 | -0.2 | ⊕ | -3.6 | -13.1 | +0.7 | +1.8 | ⊕ | -7.7 | -14.1 | -44.5 | 24 | P708B |
| 0.7 | 2.8 | 6.6 | 12.3 | 19.5 | -0.1 | ⊕ | -4.2 | -14.9 | +0.9 | +2.1 | ⊕ | -8.7 | -24.9 | -49.4 | 24 | P764A |
| 0.9 | 3.8 | 9.0 | 16.8 | 27.8 | -0.2 | ⊕ | -3.6 | -13.4 | +0.7 | +1.8 | ⊕ | -8.0 | -23.8 | -49.2 | 24 | P280A |
| 1.2 | 4.9 | 11.8 | 22.5 | 37.8 | -0.2 | ⊕ | -3.5 | -13.7 | +0.7 | +1.6 | ⊕ | -8.4 | -25.4 | -54.3 | 24 | P280T1 |
| 0.5 | 2.2 | 5.1 | 9.3 | 15.0 | -0.3 | ⊕ | -2.6 | -9.8 | +0.4 | +1.3 | ⊕ | -5.9 | -17.0 | -34.2 | 24 | P7RD |
| 0.5 | 2.0 | 4.6 | 8.4 | 13.5 | -0.2 | ⊕ | -3.0 | -10.9 | +0.5 | +1.5 | ⊕ | -6.4 | -18.4 | -36.6 | 24 | P7RE |
| 0.6 | 2.5 | 5.6 | 10.4 | 16.9 | -0.2 | ⊕ | -3.1 | -11.3 | +0.6 | +1.5 | ⊕ | -6.7 | -19.4 | -39.0 | 24 | P7RF |
| 0.6 | 2.6 | 6.0 | 11.1 | 18.2 | -0.3 | ⊕ | -2.6 | -9.9 | +0.4 | +1.3 | ⊕ | -6.0 | -17.5 | -35.6 | 24 | P7RG |
| 0.5 | 2.3 | 5.4 | 9.9 | 16.2 | -0.3 | ⊕ | -2.6 | -9.9 | +0.4 | +1.3 | ⊕ | -6.0 | -17.4 | -35.0 | 24 | P7RH |
| 1.0 | 3.8 | 9.1 | 16.7 | 27.9 | -0.2 | ⊕ | -3.6 | -13.6 | +0.7 | +1.8 | ⊕ | -8.2 | -24.0 | -49.8 | 24 | P7RT1 |
| 1.0 | 3.9 | 9.4 | 17.5 | 29.3 | -0.2 | ⊕ | -3.4 | -13.0 | +0.7 | +1.7 | ⊕ | -7.9 | -23.3 | -48.7 | 24 | P7RT2 |
| 0.6 | 2.5 | 5.8 | 10.7 | 17.3 | -0.2 | ⊕ | -2.8 | -10.5 | +0.4 | +1.4 | ⊕ | -6.3 | -18.4 | -37.1 | 24 | P7WBA |
| 1.0 | 4.2 | 10.1 | 19.1 | 31.9 | -0.2 | ⊕ | -3.2 | -12.4 | +0.6 | +1.6 | ⊕ | -7.6 | -22.7 | -47.8 | 24 | P7WBT1 |
| 0.9 | 8.0 | 19.4 | 36.7 | 59.8 | -0.3 | ⊕ | -8.3 | -29.8 | +2.4 | +4.1 | ⊕ | -17.4 | -52.4 | -109.4 | 24 | P3030D |
| 0.7 | 3.0 | 7.0 | 13.0 | 21.1 | -0.1 | ⊕ | -4.0 | -14.4 | +0.9 | +2.0 | ⊕ | -8.4 | -24.3 | -49.0 | 24 | P308C |
| 0.8 | 3.3 | 7.7 | 14.3 | 23.3 | -0.1 | ⊕ | -4.4 | -15.8 | +1.0 | +2.2 | ⊕ | -9.2 | -26.5 | -53.6 | 24 | P308E |
| 0.7 | 3.1 | 7.2 | 13.3 | 21.7 | -0.2 | ⊕ | -3.6 | -13.2 | +0.7 | +1.8 | ⊕ | -7.8 | -22.7 | -46.0 | 24 | P308F |
| 1.0 | 4.2 | 10.0 | 18.7 | 31.1 | -0.1 | ⊕ | -4.4 | -15.9 | +1.0 | +2.2 | ⊕ | -9.4 | -27.7 | -57.5 | 24 | P308T1 |
| 0.7 | 2.8 | 6.6 | 12.3 | 19.9 | -0.2 | ⊕ | -3.6 | -13.2 | +0.8 | +1.8 | ⊕ | -7.8 | -22.4 | -45.2 | 24 | P3006D |
| 0.7 | 3.0 | 7.3 | 13.4 | 27.7 | -0.1 | ⊕ | -4.0 | -14.6 | +0.9 | +2.0 | ⊕ | -8.6 | -24.6 | -49.6 | 24 | P3006F |
| 0.7 | 3.0 | 7.1 | 13.4 | 22.0 | -0.2 | ⊕ | -3.3 | -12.4 | +0.6 | +1.7 | ⊕ | -7.4 | -21.5 | -43.7 | 24 | P3006G |
| 0.6 | 2.6 | 6.0 | 11.0 | 17.8 | -0.1 | ⊕ | -3.9 | -13.9 | +0.9 | +1.9 | ⊕ | -8.1 | -23.1 | -46.1 | 24 | P3006L |
| 0.7 | 2.9 | 6.8 | 12.7 | 20.7 | -0.2 | ⊕ | -3.3 | -12.2 | +0.6 | +1.6 | ⊕ | -7.3 | -21.1 | -42.8 | 24 | P3006P |
| 0.7 | 2.8 | 6.6 | 12.1 | 19.7 | -0.2 | ⊕ | -3.6 | -13.2 | +0.7 | +1.8 | ⊕ | -7.7 | -22.3 | -45.0 | 24 | P3006Q |
| 1.0 | 4.0 | 9.6 | 17.8 | 29.7 | -0.1 | ⊕ | -3.9 | -14.5 | +0.8 | +2.0 | ⊕ | -8.7 | -25.4 | -53.1 | 24 | P3006T1 |
| 0.9 | 4.0 | 9.4 | 17.7 | 29.4 | -0.1 | ⊕ | -4.3 | -15.6 | +1.0 | +2.2 | ⊕ | -9.2 | -27.0 | -56.1 | 24 | P3006T2 |
| 0.5 | 2.2 | 5.0 | 9.2 | 14.9 | -0.2 | ⊕ | -3.4 | -12.2 | +0.7 | +1.7 | ⊕ | -7.1 | -20.4 | -40.5 | 24 | P300WC |
| 0.8 | 3.3 | 7.8 | 14.6 | 24.0 | -0.3 | ⊕ | -2.4 | -9.6 | +0.3 | +1.2 | ⊕ | -6.0 | -17.9 | -37.1 | 24 | P300WT4 |
| 0.9 | 3.8 | 8.6 | 16.1 | 26.6 | 0.0 | ⊕ | -5.1 | -17.9 | +1.3 | +2.6 | ⊕ | -10.2 | -29.9 | -61.0 | 24 | P35WT1 |

These trajectory tables were calculated by computer using the best available data for each load. Trajectories are representative of the nominal behavior of each load at standard conditions (59°F temperature; barometric pressure of 29.53 inches; altitude at sea level). Shooters are cautioned that actual trajectories may differ due to variations in altitude, atmospheric conditions, guns, sights, and ammunition.

| USAGE | FEDERAL LOAD NO. | CALIBER | BULLET GRAINS | WGT. IN GRAMS | BULLET STYLE** | FACTORY PRIMER NO. | VELOCITY IN FEET PER SECOND (TO NEAREST 10 FPS) | | | | | | ENERGY IN FOOT-POUNDS (TO NEAREST 5 FOOT-POUNDS) | | | | | |
|---|---|---|---|---|---|---|---|---|---|---|---|---|---|---|---|---|---|---|
| | | | | | | | MUZZLE | 100 YDS. | 200 YDS. | 300 YDS. | 400 YDS. | 500 YDS. | MUZZLE | 100 YDS. | 200 YDS. | 300 YDS. | 400 YDS. | 500 YDS. |
| 1 | 222A | 222 Rem. (5.56x43mm) | 50 | 3.24 | Hi-Shok Soft Point | 205 | 3140 | 2600 | 2120 | 1700 | 1350 | 1110 | 1095 | 750 | 500 | 320 | 200 | 135 |
| 5 | 222B | 222 Rem. (5.56x43mm) | 55 | 3.56 | Hi-Shok FMJ Boat-Tail | 205 | 3020 | 2740 | 2480 | 2230 | 1990 | 1780 | 1115 | 915 | 750 | 610 | 485 | 385 |
| 1 | 223A | 223 Rem. (5.56x45mm) | 55 | 3.56 | Hi-Shok Soft Point | 205 | 3240 | 2750 | 2300 | 1910 | 1550 | 1270 | 1280 | 920 | 650 | 445 | 295 | 195 |
| 5 | 223B | 223 Rem. (5.56x45mm) | 55 | 3.56 | Hi-Shok FMJ Boat-Tail | 205 | 3240 | 2950 | 2670 | 2410 | 2170 | 1940 | 1280 | 1060 | 875 | 710 | 575 | 460 |
| 1 | 22250A | 22-250 Rem. | 55 | 3.56 | Hi-Shok Soft Point | 210 | 3680 | 3140 | 2660 | 2220 | 1830 | 1490 | 1655 | 1200 | 860 | 605 | 410 | 270 |
| 1 | 243AS | 243 Win. (6.16x51mm) | 80 | 5.18 | Sierra Pro-Hunter SP | 210 | 3350 | 2960 | 2590 | 2260 | 1950 | 1670 | 1995 | 1550 | 1195 | 905 | 675 | 495 |
| 2 | 243B | 243 Win. (6.16x51mm) | 100 | 6.48 | Hi-Shok Soft Point | 210 | 2960 | 2700 | 2450 | 2220 | 1990 | 1790 | 1945 | 1615 | 1330 | 1090 | 880 | 710 |
| 1 | 6AS | 6mm Rem. | 80 | 5.18 | Sierra Pro-Hunter SP | 210 | 3470 | 3060 | 2690 | 2350 | 2040 | 1750 | 2140 | 1665 | 1290 | 980 | 735 | 540 |
| 2 | 6B | 6mm Rem. | 100 | 6.48 | Hi-Shok Soft Point | 210 | 3100 | 2830 | 2570 | 2330 | 2100 | 1890 | 2135 | 1775 | 1470 | 1205 | 985 | 790 |
| 2 | 2506BS | 25-06 Rem. | 117 | 7.58 | Sierra Pro-Hunter SP | 210 | 2990 | 2730 | 2480 | 2250 | 2030 | 1830 | 2320 | 1985 | 1645 | 1350 | 1100 | 885 |
| 2 | 270A | 270 Win. | 130 | 8.42 | Hi-Shok Soft Point | 210 | 3060 | 2800 | 2560 | 2330 | 2110 | 1900 | 2700 | 2265 | 1890 | 1565 | 1285 | 1045 |
| 2 | 270B | 270 Win. | 150 | 9.72 | Hi-Shok Soft Point RN | 210 | 2850 | 2500 | 2180 | 1890 | 1620 | 1390 | 2705 | 2085 | 1585 | 1185 | 870 | 640 |
| 2 NEW | 270GS | 270 Win. | 130 | 8.42 | Sierra Pro-Hunter SP | 210 | 3060 | 2830 | 2600 | 2390 | 2190 | 2000 | 2705 | 2305 | 1960 | 1655 | 1390 | 1155 |
| 2 | 7A | 7mm Mauser (7x57mm Mauser) | 175 | 11.34 | Hi-Shok Soft Point RN | 210 | 2440 | 2140 | 1860 | 1600 | 1380 | 1200 | 2315 | 1775 | 1340 | 1000 | 740 | 565 |
| 2 | 7B | 7mm Mauser (7x57mm Mauser) | 140 | 9.07 | Hi-Shok Soft Point | 210 | 2660 | 2450 | 2260 | 2070 | 1890 | 1730 | 2200 | 1865 | 1585 | 1330 | 1110 | 930 |
| 2 NEW | 708CS | 7mm-08 Rem. | 150 | 9.72 | Sierra Pro-Hunter SP | 210 | 2650 | 2440 | 2230 | 2040 | 1860 | 1690 | 2340 | 1980 | 1660 | 1390 | 1150 | 950 |
| 2 | 280B | 280 Rem. | 150 | 9.72 | Hi-Shok Soft Point | 210 | 2890 | 2670 | 2460 | 2260 | 2060 | 1880 | 2780 | 2370 | 2015 | 1695 | 1420 | 1180 |
| 2 NEW | 280CS | 280 Rem. | 140 | 9.07 | Sierra Pro-Hunter SP | 210 | 2990 | 2740 | 2500 | 2270 | 2060 | 1860 | 2770 | 2325 | 1940 | 1605 | 1320 | 1070 |
| 2 | 7RA | 7mm Rem. Magnum | 150 | 9.72 | Hi-Shok Soft Point | 215 | 3110 | 2830 | 2570 | 2320 | 2090 | 1870 | 3220 | 2670 | 2200 | 1790 | 1450 | 1160 · |
| 3 | 7RB | 7mm Rem. Magnum | 175 | 11.34 | Hi-Shok Soft Point | 215 | 2860 | 2650 | 2440 | 2240 | 2060 | 1880 | 3180 | 2720 | 2310 | 1960 | 1640 | 1370 |
| 3 NEW | 7RJS | 7mm Rem. Magnum | 160 | 10.37 | SierraPro-Hunter SP | 215 | 2940 | 2730 | 2520 | 2320 | 2140 | 1960 | 3070 | 2640 | 2260 | 1920 | 1620 | 1360 |
| 1 | 30CA | 30 Carbine (7.62x33mm) | 110 | 7.13 | Hi-Shok Soft Point RN | 205 | 1990 | 1570 | 1240 | 1040 | 920 | 840 | 965 | 600 | 375 | 260 | 210 | 175 |
| 2 | 76239B | 7.62x39mm Soviet | 123 | 7.97 | Hi-Shok Soft Point FN | 210 | 2300 | 2030 | 1780 | 1550 | 1350 | 1200 | 1445 | 1125 | 860 | 655 | 500 | 395 |
| 2 | 3030A | 30-30 Win. | 150 | 9.72 | Hi-Shok Soft Point FN | 210 | 2390 | 2020 | 1680 | 1400 | 1180 | 1040 | 1900 | 1355 | 945 | 650 | 460 | 355 |
| 2 | 3030B | 30-30 Win. | 170 | 11.01 | Hi-Shok Soft Point RN | 210 | 2200 | 1900 | 1620 | 1380 | 1190 | 1060 | 1830 | 1355 | 990 | 720 | 535 | 425 |
| 1 | 3030C | 30-30 Win. | 125 | 8.10 | Hi-Shok Hollow Point | 210 | 2570 | 2090 | 1660 | 1320 | 1080 | 960 | 1830 | 1210 | 770 | 480 | 320 | 260 |
| 2 NEW | 3030FS | 30-30 Win. | 170 | 11.01 | Sierra Pro-Hunter SP | 210 | 2200 | 1820 | 1500 | 1240 | 1060 | 960 | 1830 | 1255 | 845 | 575 | 425 | 345 |
| 2 | 300A | 300 Savage | 150 | 9.72 | Hi-Shok Soft Point | 210 | 2630 | 2350 | 2100 | 1850 | 1630 | 1430 | 2305 | 1845 | 1460 | 1145 | 885 | 685 |
| 2 | 300B | 300 Savage | 180 | 11.66 | Hi-Shok Soft Point | 210 | 2350 | 2140 | 1940 | 1750 | 1570 | 1410 | 2205 | 1825 | 1495 | 1215 | 985 | 800 |
| 2 | 308A | 308 Win. (7.62x51mm) | 150 | 9.72 | Hi-Shok Soft Point | 210 | 2820 | 2530 | 2260 | 2010 | 1770 | 1560 | 2650 | 2140 | 1705 | 1345 | 1050 | 810 |
| 2 | 308BB | 308 Win. (7.62x51mm) | 180 | 11.66 | Hi-Shok Soft Point | 210 | 2620 | 2390 | 2180 | 1970 | 1780 | 1600 | 2745 | 2290 | 1895 | 1555 | 1270 | 1030 |
| 2 NEW | 308HS | 308Win. (7.62x51mm) | 180 | 11.66 | Sierra Pro-Hunter SP | 210 | 2620 | 2410 | 2200 | 2010 | 1820 | 1650 | 2745 | 2315 | 1940 | 1610 | 1330 | 1090 |
| 2 | 3006A | 30-06 Springfield (7.62x63mm) | 150 | 9.72 | Hi-Shok Soft Point | 210 | 2910 | 2620 | 2340 | 2080 | 1840 | 1620 | 2820 | 2280 | 1825 | 1445 | 1130 | 875 |
| 3 | 3006B | 30-06 Springfield (7.62x63mm) | 180 | 11.66 | Hi-Shok Soft Point | 210 | 2700 | 2470 | 2250 | 2040 | 1850 | 1660 | 2915 | 2435 | 2025 | 1665 | 1360 | 1105 |
| 1 | 3006CS | 30-06 Springfield (7.62x63mm) | 125 | 8.10 | Sierra Pro-Hunter SP | 210 | 3140 | 2780 | 2450 | 2140 | 1850 | 1600 | 2735 | 2145 | 1660 | 1270 | 955 | 705 |
| 3 | 3006HS | 30-06 Springfield (7.62x63mm) | 220 | 14.25 | Sierra Pro-Hunter SP RN | 210 | 2410 | 2130 | 1870 | 1630 | 1420 | 1250 | 2835 | 2215 | 1705 | 1300 | 985 | 760 |
| 3 | 3006JS | 30-06 Springfield (7.62x63mm) | 180 | 11.66 | Sierra Pro-Hunter SP RN | 210 | 2700 | 2350 | 2020 | 1730 | 1470 | 1250 | 2915 | 2200 | 1630 | 1190 | 860 | 620 |
| 2 NEW | 3006SS | 30-06 Springfield (7.62x63mm) | 150 | 9.72 | Sierra Pro-Hunter SP | 210 | 2910 | 2640 | 2380 | 2130 | 1900 | 1690 | 2820 | 2315 | 1880 | 1515 | 1205 | 950 |
| 2 NEW | 3006TS | 30-06 Springfield (7.62x63mm) | 165 | 10.69 | Sierra Pro-Hunter SP | 210 | 2800 | 2560 | 2340 | 2130 | 1920 | 1730 | 2875 | 2410 | 2005 | 1655 | 1360 | 1100 |
| 3 | 300WBS | 300 Win. Magnum | 180 | 11.66 | Sierra Pro-Hunter SP | 215 | 2960 | 2750 | 2540 | 2340 | 2160 | 1980 | 3500 | 3010 | 2580 | 2195 | 1860 | 1565 |
| 2 | 300WGS | 300 Win. Magnum | 150 | 9.72 | Sierra Pro-Hunter SP | 215 | 3280 | 3030 | 2800 | 2570 | 2360 | 2160 | 3570 | 3055 | 2600 | 2205 | 1860 | 1560 |
| 2 | 303AS | 303 British | 180 | 11.66 | Sierra Pro-Hunter SP | 210 | 2460 | 2230 | 2020 | 1820 | 1630 | 1460 | 2420 | 1995 | 1625 | 1315 | 1060 | 850 |
| 2 | 303B | 303 British | 150 | 9.72 | Hi-Shok Soft Point | 210 | 2690 | 2440 | 2210 | 1980 | 1780 | 1590 | 2400 | 1980 | 1620 | 1310 | 1055 | 840 |
| 2 | 32A | 32 Win. Special | 170 | 11.01 | Hi-Shok Soft Point | 210 | 2250 | 1920 | 1630 | 1370 | 1180 | 1040 | 1910 | 1395 | 1000 | 710 | 520 | 410 |
| 2 | *8A | 8mm Mauser (8x57mm JS Mauser) | 170 | 11.01 | Hi-Shok Soft Point | 210 | 2360 | 1970 | 1620 | 1330 | 1120 | 1000 | 2100 | 1465 | 995 | 670 | 475 | 375 |
| 3 NEW | 338ES | 338 Win.Magnum | 225 | 14.58 | Sierra Pro-Hunter SP | 215 | 2780 | 2570 | 2360 | 2170 | 1980 | 1800 | 3860 | 3290 | 2780 | 2340 | 1960 | 1630 |
| 2 | 357G | 357 Magnum | 180 | 11.66 | Hi-Shok Hollow Point | 100 | 1550 | 1160 | 980 | 860 | 770 | 680 | 960 | 535 | 385 | 295 | 235 | 185 |
| 2 | 35A | 35 Rem. | 200 | 12.96 | Hi-Shok Soft Point | 210 | 2080 | 1700 | 1380 | 1140 | 1000 | 910 | 1920 | 1280 | 840 | 575 | 445 | 370 |
| 3 | 375A | 375 H&H Magnum | 270 | 17.50 | Hi-Shok Soft Point | 215 | 2690 | 2420 | 2170 | 1920 | 1700 | 1500 | 4340 | 3510 | 2810 | 2220 | 1740 | 1355 |
| 4 | 375B | 375 H&H Magnum | 300 | 19.44 | Hi-Shok Soft Point | 215 | 2530 | 2270 | 2020 | 1790 | 1580 | 1400 | 4265 | 3425 | 2720 | 2135 | 1665 | 1295 |
| 2 | 44A | 44 Rem. Magnum | 240 | 15.55 | Hi-Shok Hollow Point | 150 | 1760 | 1380 | 1090 | 950 | 860 | 790 | 1650 | 1015 | 640 | 485 | 395 | 330 |
| 2 | 4570AS | 45-70 Government | 300 | 19.44 | Sierra Pro-Hunter HP FN | 210 | 1880 | 1650 | 1430 | 1240 | 1110 | 1010 | 2355 | 1815 | 1355 | 1015 | 810 | 680 |

Usage Key: 1 = Varmints, predators, small game   2 = Medium game   3 = Large, heavy game   4 = Dangerous game   5 = Target shooting, training, practice

* Only for use in barrels intended for .323 inch diameter bullets. Do not use in 8x57mm J Commission Rifles (M1888) or in sporting or other military arms of .318 inch bore diameter.   **RN = Round Nose   SP = Soft Point   FN = Flat Nose   FMJ = Full Metal Jacket   HP = Hollow Point

# FEDERAL BALLISTICS – Classic® Centerfire Rifle

| WIND DRIFT IN INCHES 10 MPH CROSSWIND | | | | | HEIGHT OF BULLET TRAJECTORY IN INCHES ABOVE OR BELOW LINE OF SIGHT IF ZEROED AT ⊕ YARDS. SIGHTS 1.5 INCHES ABOVE BORE LINE | | | | | | | | | | TEST BARREL LENGTH INCHES | FEDERAL LOAD NO. |
| | | | | | AVERAGE RANGE | | | | LONG RANGE | | | | | | | |
| 100 YDS. | 200 YDS. | 300 YDS. | 400 YDS. | 500 YDS. | 50 YDS. | 100 YDS. | 200 YDS. | 300 YDS. | 50 YDS. | 100 YDS. | 200 YDS. | 300 YDS. | 400 YDS. | 500 YDS. | | |
|---|---|---|---|---|---|---|---|---|---|---|---|---|---|---|---|---|
| 1.7 | 7.3 | 18.3 | 36.4 | 63.1 | -0.2 | ⊕ | -3.7 | -15.3 | +0.7 | +1.9 | ⊕ | -9.7 | -31.6 | -71.3 | 24 | 222A |
| 0.9 | 3.4 | 8.5 | 16.8 | 26.3 | -0.2 | ⊕ | -3.1 | -12.0 | +0.6 | +1.6 | ⊕ | -7.3 | -21.5 | -44.6 | 24 | 222B |
| 1.4 | 6.1 | 15.0 | 29.4 | 50.8 | -0.3 | ⊕ | -3.2 | -12.9 | +0.5 | +1.6 | ⊕ | -8.2 | -26.1 | -58.3 | 24 | 223A |
| 0.8 | 3.3 | 7.8 | 14.5 | 24.0 | -0.3 | ⊕ | -2.5 | -9.9 | +0.3 | +1.3 | ⊕ | -6.1 | -18.3 | -37.8 | 24 | 223B |
| 1.2 | 5.2 | 12.5 | 24.4 | 42.0 | -0.4 | ⊕ | -2.1 | -9.1 | +0.1 | +1.0 | ⊕ | -6.0 | -19.1 | -42.6 | 24 | 22250A |
| 1.0 | 4.3 | 10.4 | 19.8 | 33.3 | -0.3 | ⊕ | -2.5 | -10.2 | +0.3 | +1.3 | ⊕ | -6.4 | -19.7 | -42.2 | 24 | 243AS |
| 0.9 | 3.6 | 8.4 | 15.7 | 25.8 | -0.2 | ⊕ | -3.3 | -12.4 | +0.6 | +1.6 | ⊕ | -7.5 | -22.0 | -45.4 | 24 | 243B |
| 1.0 | 4.1 | 9.9 | 18.8 | 31.6 | -0.3 | ⊕ | -2.2 | -9.3 | +0.2 | +1.1 | ⊕ | -5.9 | -18.2 | -39.0 | 24 | 6AS |
| 0.8 | 3.3 | 7.9 | 14.7 | 24.1 | -0.3 | ⊕ | -2.9 | -11.0 | +0.5 | +1.4 | ⊕ | -6.7 | -19.8 | -40.6 | 24 | 6B |
| 0.8 | 3.4 | 8.1 | 15.1 | 24.9 | -0.2 | ⊕ | -3.2 | -12.0 | +0.6 | +1.6 | ⊕ | -7.2 | -21.4 | -44.0 | 24 | 2506BS |
| 0.8 | 3.2 | 7.6 | 14.2 | 23.3 | -0.2 | ⊕ | -2.9 | -11.2 | +0.5 | +1.5 | ⊕ | -6.8 | -20.0 | -41.1 | 24 | 270A |
| 1.2 | 5.3 | 12.8 | 24.5 | 41.3 | -0.1 | ⊕ | -4.1 | -15.5 | +0.9 | +2.0 | ⊕ | -9.4 | -28.6 | -61.0 | 24 | 270B |
| 0.8 | 3.0 | 6.9 | 12.8 | 20.7 | +0.3 | ⊕ | -2.8 | -10.7 | +0.5 | +1.4 | ⊕ | -6.4 | -19.0 | -38.5 | 24 | 270GS |
| 1.5 | 6.2 | 15.0 | 28.7 | 47.8 | -0.1 | ⊕ | -6.2 | -22.6 | +1.6 | +3.1 | ⊕ | -13.3 | -40.1 | -84.6 | 24 | 7A |
| 1.3 | 3.2 | 8.2 | 15.4 | 23.4 | -0.1 | ⊕ | -4.3 | -15.4 | +1.0 | +2.1 | ⊕ | -9.0 | -26.1 | -52.9 | 24 | 7B |
| 0.9 | 3.6 | 8.4 | 15.6 | 25.5 | -0.1 | ⊕ | -4.4 | -15.7 | +1.0 | +2.2 | ⊕ | -9.2 | -26.7 | -54.4 | 24 | 708CS |
| 0.7 | 3.1 | 7.2 | 13.4 | 21.9 | -0.2 | ⊕ | -3.4 | -12.6 | +0.7 | +1.7 | ⊕ | -7.5 | -21.8 | -44.3 | 24 | 280B |
| 0.9 | 3.4 | 7.9 | 14.7 | 23.9 | -0.2 | ⊕ | -3.1 | -11.7 | +0.6 | +1.6 | ⊕ | -7.0 | 20.8 | -42.6 | 24 | 280CS |
| 0.8 | 3.4 | 8.1 | 15.1 | 24.9 | -0.3 | ⊕ | -2.9 | -11.0 | +0.5 | +1.4 | ⊕ | -6.7 | -19.9 | -41.0 | 24 | 7RA |
| 0.7 | 3.1 | 7.2 | 13.3 | 21.7 | -0.2 | ⊕ | -3.5 | -12.8 | +0.7 | +1.7 | ⊕ | -7.6 | -22.1 | -44.9 | 24 | 7RB |
| 0.7 | 2.9 | 6.8 | 12.5 | 20.4 | -0.2 | ⊕ | -3.2 | -11.9 | +0.6 | +1.6 | ⊕ | -7.1 | -20.6 | -42.2 | 24 | 7RJS |
| 3.4 | 15.0 | 35.5 | 63.2 | 96.7 | +0.6 | ⊕ | -12.8 | -46.9 | +3.9 | +6.4 | ⊕ | -27.7 | -81.8 | -167.8 | 18 | 30CA |
| 1.5 | 6.4 | 15.2 | 28.7 | 47.3 | +0.2 | ⊕ | -7.0 | -25.1 | +1.9 | +3.5 | ⊕ | -14.5 | -43.4 | -90.6 | 20 | 76239B |
| 2.0 | 8.5 | 20.9 | 40.1 | 66.1 | +0.2 | ⊕ | -7.2 | -26.7 | +1.9 | +3.6 | ⊕ | -15.9 | 49.1 | -104.5 | 24 | 3030A |
| 1.9 | 8.0 | 19.4 | 36.7 | 59.8 | +0.3 | ⊕ | -8.3 | -29.8 | +2.4 | +4.1 | ⊕ | -17.4 | -52.4 | -109.4 | 24 | 3030B |
| 2.2 | 10.1 | 25.4 | 49.4 | 81.6 | +0.1 | ⊕ | -6.6 | -26.0 | +1.7 | +3.3 | ⊕ | -16.0 | -50.9 | -109.5 | 24 | 3030C |
| 2.7 | 10.9 | 25.9 | 48.3 | 76.5 | +0.3 | ⊕ | -9.1 | -33.6 | +2.6 | +4.5 | ⊕ | -20.0 | -63.5 | -137.4 | 24 | 3030FS |
| 1.1 | 4.8 | 11.6 | 21.9 | 36.3 | 0.0 | ⊕ | -4.8 | -17.6 | +1.2 | +2.4 | ⊕ | -10.4 | -30.9 | -64.4 | 24 | 300A |
| 1.1 | 4.6 | 10.9 | 20.3 | 33.3 | +0.1 | ⊕ | -6.1 | -21.6 | +1.7 | +3.1 | ⊕ | -12.4 | -36.1 | -73.8 | 24 | 300B |
| 1.0 | 4.4 | 10.4 | 19.7 | 32.7 | -0.1 | ⊕ | -3.9 | -14.7 | +0.8 | +2.0 | ⊕ | -8.8 | -26.3 | -54.8 | 24 | 308A |
| 0.9 | 3.9 | 9.2 | 17.2 | 28.3 | -0.1 | ⊕ | -4.6 | -16.5 | +1.1 | +2.3 | ⊕ | -9.7 | -28.3 | -57.8 | 24 | 308B |
| 1.0 | 3.9 | 8.9 | 16.4 | 26.8 | -0.1 | ⊕ | -4.5 | -16.0 | +1.1 | +2.3 | ⊕ | -9.3 | -27.1 | -55.8 | 24 | 308HS |
| 1.0 | 4.2 | 9.9 | 18.7 | 31.2 | -0.2 | ⊕ | -3.6 | -13.6 | +0.7 | +1.8 | ⊕ | -8.2 | -24.4 | -50.9 | 24 | 3006A |
| 0.9 | 3.7 | 8.8 | 16.5 | 27.1 | -0.1 | ⊕ | -4.2 | -15.3 | +1.0 | +2.1 | ⊕ | -9.0 | -26.4 | -54.0 | 24 | 3006B |
| 1.1 | 4.5 | 10.8 | 20.5 | 34.4 | -0.3 | ⊕ | -3.0 | -11.9 | +0.5 | +1.5 | ⊕ | -7.3 | -22.3 | 47.5 | 24 | 3006CS |
| 1.4 | 6.0 | 14.3 | 27.2 | 45.0 | -0.1 | ⊕ | -6.2 | -22.4 | +1.7 | +3.1 | ⊕ | -13.1 | -39.3 | -82.2 | 24 | 3006HS |
| 1.5 | 6.4 | 15.7 | 30.4 | 51.2 | -0.1 | ⊕ | -4.9 | -18.3 | +1.1 | +2.4 | ⊕ | -11.0 | -33.6 | -71.9 | 24 | 3006JS |
| 1.1 | 4.0 | 9.5 | 17.5 | 29.0 | -0.2 | ⊕ | -3.4 | -13.1 | +0.7 | +1.7 | ⊕ | -7.9 | -23.3 | -48.7 | 24 | 3006SS |
| 0.9 | 3.6 | 8.4 | 15.7 | 25.7 | -0.1 | ⊕ | -3.8 | -14.0 | +0.8 | +1.9 | ⊕ | -8.3 | -24.3 | -49.8 | 24 | 3006TS |
| 0.7 | 2.8 | 6.6 | 12.3 | 20.0 | -0.2 | ⊕ | -3.1 | -11.7 | +0.6 | +1.6 | ⊕ | -7.0 | -20.3 | -41.1 | 24 | 300WBS |
| 0.7 | 2.7 | 6.3 | 11.5 | 18.8 | -0.3 | ⊕ | -2.3 | -9.1 | +0.3 | +1.1 | ⊕ | -5.6 | -16.4 | -33.6 | 24 | 300WGS |
| 1.1 | 4.5 | 10.6 | 19.9 | 32.7 | 0.0 | ⊕ | -5.5 | -19.6 | +1.4 | +2.8 | ⊕ | -11.3 | -33.2 | -68.1 | 24 | 303AS |
| 1.0 | 4.1 | 9.6 | 18.1 | 29.9 | -0.1 | ⊕ | -4.4 | -15.9 | +1.0 | +2.2 | ⊕ | -9.4 | -27.6 | -56.8 | 24 | 303B |
| 1.9 | 8.4 | 20.3 | 38.6 | 63.0 | +0.3 | ⊕ | -8.0 | -29.2 | +2.3 | +4.0 | ⊕ | -17.2 | -52.3 | -109.8 | 24 | 32A |
| 2.1 | 9.3 | 22.9 | 43.9 | 71.7 | +0.2 | ⊕ | -7.6 | -28.5 | +2.1 | +3.8 | ⊕ | -17.1 | -52.9 | -111.9 | 24 | *8A |
| 0.8 | 3.3 | 7.6 | 14.1 | 23.1 | -0.1 | ⊕ | -3.8 | -13.8 | +0.8 | +1.9 | ⊕ | -8.2 | -23.7 | -48.2 | 24 | 338ES |
| 5.8 | 21.7 | 45.2 | 76.1 | NA | ⊕ | -3.4 | -29.7 | -88.2 | +1.7 | ⊕ | -22.8 | -77.9 | -173.8 | -321.4 | 18 | 357G |
| 2.7 | 12.0 | 29.0 | 53.3 | 83.3 | +0.5 | ⊕ | -10.7 | -39.3 | +3.2 | +5.4 | ⊕ | -23.3 | -70.0 | -144.0 | 24 | 35A |
| 1.1 | 4.5 | 10.8 | 20.3 | 33.7 | -0.4 | ⊕ | -5.5 | -18.4 | +1.0 | +2.4 | ⊕ | -10.9 | -33.3 | -71.2 | 24 | 375A |
| 1.2 | 5.0 | 11.9 | 22.4 | 37.1 | +0.5 | ⊕ | -6.3 | -21.2 | +1.3 | +2.6 | ⊕ | -11.2 | -33.3 | -69.1 | 24 | 375B |
| 4.2 | 17.8 | 39.8 | 68.3 | 102.5 | ⊕ | -2.2 | -21.7 | -67.2 | +1.1 | ⊕ | -17.4 | -60.7 | -136.0 | -250.2 | 20 | 44A |
| 1.7 | 7.6 | 18.6 | 35.7 | NA | ⊕ | -1.3 | -14.1 | -43.7 | +0.7 | ⊕ | -11.5 | -39.7 | -89.1 | -163.1 | 24 | 4570AS |

These trajectory tables were calculated by computer using the best available data for each load. Trajectories are representative of the nominal behavior of each load at standard conditions (59°F temperature; barometric pressure of 29.53 inches; altitude at sea level). Shooters are cautioned that actual trajectories may differ due to variations in altitude, atmospheric conditions, guns, sights, and ammunition.

| USAGE | | FEDERAL LOAD NO. | CALIBER | BULLET WGT. IN GRAINS | WGT. IN GRAMS | BULLET STYLE | FACTORY PRIMER NO. | VELOCITY IN FEET PER SECOND (TO NEAREST 10 FPS) | | | | | | ENERGY IN FOOT-POUNDS (TO NEAREST 5 FOOT-POUNDS) | | | | | |
|---|---|---|---|---|---|---|---|---|---|---|---|---|---|---|---|---|---|---|---|
| | | | | | | | | MUZZLE | 100 YDS. | 200 YDS. | 300 YDS. | 400 YDS. | 500 YDS. | MUZZLE | 100 YDS. | 200 YDS. | 300 YDS. | 400 YDS. | 500 YDS. |
| 2 | NEW | P270T3 | 270 Win. | 140 | 9.07 | Trophy Bonded Bear Claw | 210 | 3100 | 2860 | 2620 | 2400 | 2200 | 2000 | 2990 | 2535 | 2140 | 1795 | 1500 | 1240 |
| 3 | | P308T2 | 308 Win. (7.62x51mm) | 165 | 10.69 | Trophy Bonded Bear Claw | 210 | 2870 | 2600 | 2350 | 2120 | 1890 | 1690 | 3020 | 2485 | 2030 | 1640 | 1310 | 1040 |
| 3 | | P308G | 308 Win. (7.62x51mm) | 180 | 11.66 | Nosler Partition | 210 | 2740 | 2550 | 2370 | 2200 | 2030 | 1870 | 3000 | 2600 | 2245 | 1925 | 1645 | 1395 |
| 3 | | P3006T3 | 30-06 Spring (7.62x63mm) | 180 | 11.66 | Trophy Bonded Bear Claw | 210 | 2880 | 2630 | 2380 | 2160 | 1940 | 1740 | 3315 | 2755 | 2270 | 1855 | 1505 | 1210 |
| 3 | | P3006R | 30-06 Spring (7.62x63mm) | 180 | 11.66 | Nosler Partition | 210 | 2880 | 2690 | 2500 | 2320 | 2150 | 1980 | 3315 | 2880 | 2495 | 2150 | 1845 | 1570 |
| 3 | | P300WT3 | 300 Win. Mag. | 180 | 11.66 | Trophy Bonded Bear Claw | 215 | 3100 | 2830 | 2580 | 2340 | 2110 | 1900 | 3840 | 3205 | 2660 | 2190 | 1790 | 1445 |
| 3 | | P300WE | 300 Win. Mag. | 200 | 12.96 | Nosler Partition | 215 | 2930 | 2740 | 2550 | 2370 | 2200 | 2030 | 3810 | 3325 | 2885 | 2495 | 2145 | 1840 |
| 3 | NEW | P300WBT3 | 300 Weatherby Magnum | 180 | 11.66 | Trophy Bonded Bear Claw | 215 | 3330 | 3080 | 2850 | 2750 | 2410 | 2210 | 4430 | 3795 | 3235 | 2750 | 2320 | 1950 |
| 3 | NEW | P300WBB | 300 Weatherby Magnum | 180 | 11.66 | Nosler Partition | 215 | 3330 | 3110 | 2910 | 2710 | 2520 | 2340 | 4430 | 3875 | 3375 | 2935 | 2540 | 2190 |
| 3 | | P338T2 | 338 Win. Mag | 225 | 14.58 | Trophy Bonded Bear Claw | 215 | 2940 | 2690 | 2450 | 2230 | 2010 | 1810 | 4320 | 3610 | 3000 | 2475 | 2025 | 1640 |
| 3 | | P338D | 338 Win. Mag | 250 | 16.20 | Nosler Partition | 215 | 2800 | 2610 | 2420 | 2250 | 2080 | 1920 | 4350 | 3775 | 3260 | 2805 | 2395 | 2035 |

**Usage Key:** ① = Varmints, predators, small game   ② = Medium game   ③ = Large, heavy game   ④ = Dangerous game   ⑤ = Target shooting, training, practice

| USAGE | FEDERAL LOAD NO. | CALIBER | BULLET WGT. IN GRAINS | WGT. IN GRAMS | BULLET STYLE* | FACTORY PRIMER NO. | VELOCITY IN FEET PER SECOND (TO NEAREST 10 FPS) | | | | | | ENERGY IN FOOT-POUNDS (TO NEAREST 5 FOOT-POUNDS) | | | | | |
|---|---|---|---|---|---|---|---|---|---|---|---|---|---|---|---|---|---|---|
| | | | | | | | MUZZLE | 100 YDS. | 200 YDS. | 300 YDS. | 400 YDS. | 500 YDS. | MUZZLE | 100 YDS. | 200 YDS. | 300 YDS. | 400 YDS. | 500 YDS. |
| 3 | P300HA | 300 H&H Magnum | 180 | 11.66 | | 215 | 2880 | 2620 | 2380 | 2150 | 1930 | 1730 | 3315 | 2750 | 2260 | 1840 | 1480 | 1190 |
| 3 | P300WD2 | 300 Win. Magnum | 180 | 11.66 | Nosler Partition | 215 | 2960 | 2700 | 2450 | 2210 | 1990 | 1780 | 3500 | 2905 | 2395 | 1955 | 1585 | 1270 |
| 3 | P300WT1 | 300 Win. Magnum | 200 | 12.96 | Trophy Bonded Bear Claw | 215 | 2800 | 2570 | 2350 | 2150 | 1950 | 1770 | 3480 | 2935 | 2460 | 2050 | 1590 | 1385 |
| 3 | P300WT2 | 300 Win. Magnum | 180 | 11.66 | Trophy Bonded Bear Claw | 215 | 2960 | 2700 | 2460 | 2220 | 2000 | 1800 | 3500 | 2915 | 2410 | 1975 | 1605 | 1290 |
| 3 | P300WBA | 300 Weatherby Magnum | 180 | 11.66 | Nosler Partition | 215 | 3190 | 2980 | 2780 | 2590 | 2400 | 2230 | 4055 | 3540 | 3080 | 2670 | 2305 | 1985 |
| 3 | P300WBT1 | 300 Weatherby Magnum | 180 | 11.66 | Trophy Bonded Bear Claw | 215 | 3190 | 2950 | 2720 | 2500 | 2290 | 2100 | 4065 | 3475 | 2955 | 2500 | 2105 | 1760 |
| 3 | P300WBT2 | 300 Weatherby Magnum | 200 | 12.96 | Trophy Bonded Bear Claw | 215 | 2900 | 2670 | 2440 | 2230 | 2030 | 1830 | 3735 | 3150 | 2645 | 2200 | 1820 | 1490 |
| 3 | P338A2 | 338 Win. Magnum | 210 | 13.60 | Nosler Partition | 215 | 2830 | 2590 | 2370 | 2160 | 1960 | 1770 | 3735 | 3140 | 2620 | 2170 | 1785 | 1455 |
| 3 | P338B2 | 338 Win. Magnum | 250 | 16.20 | Nosler Partition | 215 | 2660 | 2400 | 2150 | 1910 | 1690 | 1500 | 3925 | 3185 | 2555 | 2055 | 1590 | 1245 |
| 3 | P338T1 | 338 Win. Magnum | 225 | 14.58 | Trophy Bonded Bear Claw | 215 | 2800 | 2560 | 2330 | 2110 | 1900 | 1710 | 3915 | 3265 | 2700 | 2220 | 1800 | 1455 |
| 4 | P375F | 375 H&H Magnum | 300 | 19.44 | Nosler Partition | 215 | 2530 | 2320 | 2120 | 1930 | 1750 | 1590 | 4265 | 3585 | 2995 | 2475 | 2040 | 1675 |
| 4 | P375T1 | 375 H&H Magnum | 300 | 19.44 | Trophy Bonded Bear Claw | 215 | 2530 | 2280 | 2040 | 1810 | 1610 | 1425 | 4265 | 3450 | 2765 | 2190 | 1725 | 1350 |
| 4 | P375T2 | 375 H&H Magnum | 300 | 19.44 | Trophy Bonded Sledgehammer | 215 | 2530 | 2160 | 1820 | 1520 | 1280 | 1100 | 4265 | 3105 | 2210 | 1550 | 1090 | 810 |
| 2 | P458A | 458 Win. Magnum | 350 | 22.68 | Soft Point | 215 | 2470 | 1990 | 1570 | 1250 | 1060 | 950 | 4740 | 3065 | 1915 | 1205 | 870 | 705 |
| 4 | P458B | 458 Win. Magnum | 510 | 33.04 | Soft Point | 215 | 2090 | 1820 | 1570 | 1360 | 1190 | 1080 | 4945 | 3730 | 2790 | 2080 | 1605 | 1320 |
| 4 | P458C | 458 Win. Magnum | 500 | 32.40 | Solid | 215 | 2090 | 1870 | 1670 | 1480 | 1320 | 1190 | 4850 | 3880 | 3085 | 2440 | 1945 | 1585 |
| 4 | P458T1 | 458 Win. Magnum | 400 | 25.92 | Trophy Bonded Bear Claw | 215 | 2380 | 2170 | 1960 | 1770 | 1590 | 1430 | 5030 | 4165 | 3415 | 2785 | 2255 | 1825 |
| 4 | P458T2 | 458 Win. Magnum | 500 | 32.40 | Trophy Bonded Bear Claw | 215 | 2090 | 1870 | 1660 | 1480 | 1310 | 1180 | 4850 | 3870 | 3065 | 2420 | 1915 | 1550 |
| 4 | P458T3 | 458 Win. Magnum | 500 | 32.40 | Trophy Bonded Sledgehammer | 215 | 2090 | 1860 | 1650 | 1460 | 1300 | 1170 | 4850 | 3845 | 3025 | 2365 | 1865 | 1505 |
| 4 | P416A | 416 Rigby | 410 | 26.57 | Woodleigh Weldcore SP | 216 | 2370 | 2110 | 1870 | 1640 | 1440 | 1280 | 5115 | 4050 | 3165 | 2455 | 1895 | 1485 |
| 4 | P416B | 416 Rigby | 410 | 26.57 | Solid | 216 | 2370 | 2110 | 1870 | 1640 | 1440 | 1280 | 5115 | 4050 | 3165 | 2455 | 1895 | 1485 |
| 4 | P416T1 | 416 Rigby | 400 | 25.92 | Trophy Bonded Bear Claw | 216 | 2370 | 2210 | 2050 | 1900 | 1750 | 1620 | 4990 | 4315 | 3720 | 3185 | 2720 | 2315 |
| 4 | P416T2 | 416 Rigby | 400 | 25.92 | Trophy Bonded Sledgehammer | 216 | 2370 | 2120 | 1890 | 1660 | 1460 | 1290 | 4990 | 3975 | 3130 | 2440 | 1895 | 1480 |
| 4 | P416RT1 | 416 Rem. Magnum | 400 | 25.92 | Trophy Bonded Bear Claw | 216 | 2400 | 2180 | 1970 | 1770 | 1590 | 1420 | 5115 | 4215 | 3440 | 2785 | 2245 | 1800 |
| 4 | P470A | 470 Nitro Express | 500 | 32.40 | Woodleigh Weldcore SP | 216 | 2150 | 1890 | 1650 | 1440 | 1270 | 1140 | 5130 | 3965 | 3040 | 2310 | 1790 | 1435 |
| 4 | P470B | 470 Nitro Express | 500 | 32.40 | Woodleigh Weldcore Solid | 216 | 2150 | 1890 | 1650 | 1440 | 1270 | 1140 | 5130 | 3965 | 3040 | 2310 | 1790 | 1435 |
| 4 | P470T1 | 470 Nitro Express | 500 | 32.40 | Trophy Bonded Bear Claw | 216 | 2150 | 1940 | 1740 | 1560 | 1400 | 1260 | 5130 | 4170 | 3360 | 2695 | 2160 | 1750 |
| 4 | P470T2 | 470 Nitro Express | 500 | 32.40 | Trophy Bonded Sledgehammer | 216 | 2150 | 1940 | 1740 | 1560 | 1400 | 1260 | 5130 | 4170 | 3360 | 2695 | 2160 | 1750 |

**Usage Key:** ① = Varmints, predators, small game   ② = Medium game   ③ = Large, heavy game   ④ = Dangerous game   ⑤ = Target shooting, training, practice
SP = Soft Point   Sledgehammer = Sledgehammer Solid   Trophy Bonded Sledgehammer is a registered trademark of Trophy Bonded Bullets, Inc. Woodleigh Weldcore is a registered trademark of Woodleigh Corporation.

| WIND DRIFT IN INCHES 10 MPH CROSSWIND | | | | | HEIGHT OF BULLET TRAJECTORY IN INCHES ABOVE OR BELOW LINE OF SIGHT IF ZEROED AT ⊕ YARDS. SIGHTS 1.5 INCHES ABOVE BORE LINE | | | | | | | | | | TEST BARREL LENGTH INCHES | FEDERAL LOAD NO. |
| | | | | | AVERAGE RANGE | | | | LONG RANGE | | | | | | | |
| 100 YDS. | 200 YDS. | 300 YDS. | 400 YDS. | 500 YDS. | 50 YDS. | 100 YDS. | 200 YDS. | 300 YDS. | 50 YDS. | 100 YDS. | 200 YDS. | 300 YDS. | 400 YDS. | 500 YDS. | | |
| 0.7 | 3.0 | 6.9 | 12.9 | 21.2 | -0.3 | ⊕ | -2.8 | -10.6 | +0.4 | +1.4 | ⊕ | -6.4 | -18.9 | -38.7 | 24 | P270T3 |
| 1.0 | 3.8 | 9.2 | 17.0 | 28.4 | -0.2 | ⊕ | -3.6 | -13.6 | +0.7 | +1.8 | ⊕ | -8.2 | -24.0 | -49.9 | 24 | P308T2 |
| 0.7 | 2.9 | 6.8 | 12.6 | 20.2 | -0.1 | ⊕ | -3.8 | -13.9 | +0.8 | +1.9 | ⊕ | -8.2 | -23.5 | -47.1 | 24 | P308G |
| 0.9 | 3.6 | 8.7 | 16.1 | 26.6 | -0.2 | ⊕ | -3.5 | -13.3 | +0.7 | +1.8 | ⊕ | -8.0 | -23.3 | -48.2 | 24 | P3006T3 |
| 0.7 | 2.8 | 6.3 | 11.7 | 19.0 | -0.2 | ⊕ | -3.3 | -12.2 | +0.7 | +1.7 | ⊕ | -7.2 | -21.0 | -42.2 | 24 | P3006R |
| 0.8 | 3.3 | 7.7 | 14.5 | 23.6 | -0.3 | ⊕ | -2.9 | -10.9 | +0.5 | +1.4 | ⊕ | -6.6 | -19.7 | -40.4 | 24 | P300WT3 |
| 0.7 | 2.6 | 6.0 | 11.2 | 18.2 | -0.2 | ⊕ | -3.2 | -11.6 | +0.6 | +1.6 | ⊕ | -6.9 | -20.1 | -40.4 | 24 | P300WE |
| 0.7 | 2.6 | 6.1 | 11.2 | 18.3 | -0.3 | ⊕ | -2.2 | -8.6 | +0.2 | +1.1 | ⊕ | -5.4 | -15.8 | -32.3 | 24 | P300WBT3 |
| 0.6 | 2.2 | 5.2 | 9.6 | 15.4 | -0.3 | ⊕ | -2.1 | -8.3 | +0.2 | +1.0 | ⊕ | -5.2 | -15.1 | -30.4 | 24 | P300WBB |
| 0.9 | 3.4 | 8.1 | 15.1 | 24.7 | -0.2 | ⊕ | -3.3 | -12.4 | +0.6 | +1.7 | ⊕ | -7.5 | -22.0 | -45.0 | 24 | P338T2 |
| 0.7 | 2.8 | 6.6 | 12.3 | 19.7 | -0.2 | ⊕ | -3.6 | -13.1 | +0.7 | +1.8 | ⊕ | -7.8 | -22.5 | -44.9 | 24 | P338D |

| WIND DRIFT IN INCHES 10 MPH CROSSWIND | | | | | HEIGHT OF BULLET TRAJECTORY IN INCHES ABOVE OR BELOW LINE OF SIGHT IF ZEROED AT ⊕ YARDS. SIGHTS 1.5 INCHES ABOVE BORE LINE | | | | | | | | | | TEST BARREL LENGTH INCHES | FEDERAL LOAD NO. |
| | | | | | AVERAGE RANGE | | | | LONG RANGE | | | | | | | |
| 100 YDS. | 200 YDS. | 300 YDS. | 400 YDS. | 500 YDS. | 50 YDS. | 100 YDS. | 200 YDS. | 300 YDS. | 50 YDS. | 100 YDS. | 200 YDS. | 300 YDS. | 400 YDS. | 500 YDS. | | |
| 0.9 | 3.7 | 8.8 | 16.3 | 27.1 | -0.3 | ⊕ | -3.5 | -13.3 | +0.7 | +1.8 | ⊕ | -8.0 | -23.4 | -48.6 | 24 | P300HA |
| 0.9 | 3.5 | 8.4 | 15.8 | 25.9 | -0.2 | ⊕ | -3.3 | -12.4 | +0.6 | +1.6 | ⊕ | -7.5 | -22.1 | -45.4 | 24 | P300WD2 |
| 0.9 | 3.4 | 8.1 | 14.9 | 24.5 | -0.1 | ⊕ | -3.7 | -13.8 | +0.8 | +1.9 | ⊕ | -8.2 | -23.9 | -48.8 | 24 | P300WT1 |
| 0.9 | 3.5 | 8.3 | 15.4 | 25.4 | -0.2 | ⊕ | -3.3 | -12.3 | +0.6 | +1.6 | ⊕ | -7.4 | -21.9 | -45.0 | 24 | P300WT2 |
| 0.6 | 2.4 | 5.5 | 10.1 | 16.3 | -0.3 | ⊕ | -2.4 | -9.4 | +0.3 | +1.2 | ⊕ | -5.7 | -16.7 | -33.6 | 24 | P300WBA |
| 0.6 | 2.7 | 6.4 | 11.9 | 19.5 | -0.3 | ⊕ | -2.5 | -9.7 | +0.3 | +1.3 | ⊕ | -5.9 | -17.5 | -35.7 | 24 | P300WBT1 |
| 0.8 | 3.3 | 7.8 | 14.4 | 23.5 | -0.2 | ⊕ | -3.4 | -12.7 | +0.7 | +1.7 | ⊕ | -7.6 | -22.2 | -45.1 | 24 | P300WBT2 |
| 0.9 | 3.4 | 8.2 | 15.2 | 24.9 | -0.2 | ⊕ | -3.6 | -13.6 | +0.8 | +1.8 | ⊕ | -8.1 | -23.6 | -48.3 | 24 | P338A2 |
| 1.1 | 4.5 | 10.8 | 20.3 | 33.6 | -0.1 | ⊕ | -4.6 | -16.7 | +1.1 | +2.3 | ⊕ | -9.8 | -29.1 | -60.2 | 24 | P338B2 |
| 0.9 | 3.7 | 8.7 | 16.1 | 26.7 | -0.2 | ⊕ | -3.8 | -14.1 | +0.8 | +1.9 | ⊕ | -8.4 | -24.5 | -50.6 | 24 | P338T1 |
| 0.9 | 3.9 | 9.1 | 17.0 | 27.8 | 0.0 | ⊕ | -5.0 | -17.7 | +1.2 | +2.5 | ⊕ | -10.3 | -29.9 | -60.8 | 24 | P375F |
| 1.1 | 4.8 | 11.3 | 21.5 | 35.4 | -0.1 | ⊕ | -5.3 | -18.8 | +1.3 | +2.6 | ⊕ | -10.9 | -32.8 | -67.8 | 24 | P375T1 |
| 1.7 | 7.4 | 18.3 | 35.4 | 59.1 | ⊕ | -0.1 | -6.2 | -23.0 | +0.1 | ⊕ | -6.0 | -22.7 | -54.6 | -108.4 | 24 | P375T2 |
| 2.5 | 11.0 | 27.6 | 52.6 | 83.9 | ⊕ | -1.5 | -11.0 | -34.9 | +0.1 | ⊕ | -7.5 | -29.1 | -71.1 | -138.0 | 24 | P458A |
| 1.9 | 7.9 | 18.9 | 35.3 | 56.8 | ⊕ | -1.8 | -13.7 | -39.7 | +0.4 | ⊕ | -9.1 | -32.3 | -73.9 | -138.0 | 24 | P458B |
| 1.5 | 6.1 | 14.5 | 26.9 | 43.7 | ⊕ | -1.7 | -12.9 | -36.7 | +0.4 | ⊕ | -8.5 | -29.5 | -66.2 | -122.0 | 24 | P458C |
| 1.1 | 4.5 | 10.7 | 19.9 | 32.7 | ⊕ | -0.2 | -6.3 | -21.5 | +0.1 | ⊕ | -5.9 | -20.9 | -47.1 | -87.0 | 24 | P458T1 |
| 1.5 | 6.2 | 14.6 | 27.3 | 44.5 | ⊕ | -0.7 | -10.0 | -31.8 | +0.4 | ⊕ | -8.5 | -29.7 | -66.8 | -124.2 | 24 | P458T2 |
| 1.5 | 6.4 | 15.2 | 28.3 | 46.1 | ⊕ | -0.7 | -10.1 | -32.2 | +0.4 | ⊕ | -8.6 | -30.0 | -67.8 | -126.3 | 24 | P458T3 |
| 1.3 | 5.7 | 13.6 | 25.6 | 42.3 | ⊕ | -1.2 | -9.8 | -28.5 | +0.6 | ⊕ | -7.4 | -24.8 | -55.0 | -101.6 | 24 | P416A |
| 1.3 | 5.7 | 13.6 | 25.6 | 42.3 | ⊕ | -1.2 | -9.8 | -28.5 | +0.6 | ⊕ | -7.4 | -24.8 | -55.0 | -101.6 | 24 | P416B |
| 0.8 | 3.4 | 7.9 | 14.7 | 23.8 | ⊕ | -0.2 | -6.0 | -20.1 | +0.1 | ⊕ | -5.7 | -19.6 | -43.3 | -78.4 | 24 | P416T1 |
| 1.3 | 5.5 | 13.2 | 24.8 | 41.0 | ⊕ | -0.2 | -6.8 | -23.2 | +0.1 | ⊕ | -6.3 | -22.5 | -51.5 | -96.7 | 24 | P416T2 |
| 1.2 | 4.6 | 10.9 | 20.6 | 33.5 | ⊕ | -0.2 | -6.2 | -21.2 | +0.1 | ⊕ | -5.8 | -20.6 | -46.9 | -86.5 | 24 | P416RT1 |
| 1.6 | 7.0 | 16.6 | 31.1 | 50.6 | ⊕ | -1.6 | -12.6 | -36.2 | +0.8 | ⊕ | -9.3 | -31.3 | -69.7 | -128.6 | 24 | P470A |
| 1.6 | 7.0 | 16.6 | 31.1 | 50.6 | ⊕ | -1.6 | -12.6 | -36.2 | +0.8 | ⊕ | -9.3 | -31.3 | -69.7 | -128.6 | 24 | P470B |
| 1.3 | 5.5 | 13.0 | 24.3 | 39.7 | ⊕ | -0.6 | -9.0 | -28.9 | +0.3 | ⊕ | -7.8 | -27.1 | -60.8 | -112.4 | 24 | P470T1 |
| 1.3 | 5.5 | 13.0 | 24.3 | 39.7 | ⊕ | -0.6 | -9.0 | -28.9 | +0.3 | ⊕ | -7.8 | -27.1 | -60.8 | -112.4 | 24 | P470T2 |

These trajectory tables were calculated by computer using the best available data for each load. Trajectories are representative of the nominal behavior of each load at standard conditions (59°F temperature; barometric pressure of 29.53 inches; altitude at sea level). Shooters are cautioned that actual trajectories may differ due to variations in altitude, atmospheric conditions, guns, sights, and ammunition.

| USAGE | TYPE | FEDERAL LOAD NO. | CARTRIDGE PER BOX | CALIBER | BULLET WGT. IN GRAINS | BULLET STYLE | VELOCITY IN FEET PER SECOND (TO NEAREST 10 FPS) | | | | | ENERGY IN FOOT-POUNDS (TO NEAREST 5 FOOT-POUNDS) | | | | | WIND DRIFT IN INCHES 10 MPH CROSSWIND | | | | HEIGHT OF BULLET TRAJECTORY IN INCHES ABOVE OR BELOW LINE OF SIGHT IF ZEROED AT ⊕ YARDS. SIGHTS 1.5 INCHES ABOVE BORE LINE. | | | |
|---|---|---|---|---|---|---|---|---|---|---|---|---|---|---|---|---|---|---|---|---|---|---|---|---|---|
| | | | | | | | MUZZLE | 25 YDS. | 50 YDS. | 75 YDS. | 100 YDS. | MUZZLE | 25 YDS. | 50 YDS. | 75 YDS. | 100 YDS. | 25 YDS. | 50 YDS. | 75 YDS. | 100 YDS. | 25 YDS. | 50 YDS. | 75 YDS. | 100 YDS. |
| 4 | UltraMatch | 1000A | 50 | 22 Long Rifle | 40 | Solid | 1140 | 1090 | 1040 | 1000 | 970 | 115 | 105 | 95 | 90 | 80 | 0.3 | 1.2 | 2.6 | 4.5 | 0.2 | ⊕ | -2.2 | -6.6 |
| 4 NEW | UltraMatch | 1000B | 50 | 22 Long Rifle | 40 | Solid | 1080 | 1030 | 1000 | 960 | 930 | 105 | 95 | 90 | 80 | 75 | 0.3 | 1.1 | 2.3 | 4.1 | 0.3 | ⊕ | -2.4 | -7.2 |
| 4 | Match | 900A* | 50 | 22 Long Rifle | 40 | Solid | 1140 | 1090 | 1040 | 1000 | 970 | 115 | 105 | 95 | 90 | 80 | 0.3 | 1.2 | 2.6 | 4.5 | 0.2 | ⊕ | -2.2 | -6.6 |
| 4 NEW | Match | 900B | 50 | 22 Long Rifle | 40 | Solid | 1080 | 1030 | 1000 | 960 | 930 | 105 | 95 | 90 | 80 | 75 | 0.3 | 1.1 | 2.3 | 4.1 | 0.3 | ⊕ | -2.4 | -7.2 |
| 4 | Target | 711 | 50 | 22 Long Rifle | 40 | Solid | 1150 | 1090 | 1045 | 1005 | 970 | 115 | 105 | 95 | 90 | 80 | 0.3 | 1.2 | 2.6 | 4.5 | 0.2 | ⊕ | -2.2 | -6.4 |

Usage Key: 1 = Varmints, predators, small game   2 = Medium game   3 = Self-defense   4 = Target shooting, training, practice
*Formerly 900  These ballistic specifications were derived from test barrels 24 inches in length.

| USAGE | FEDERAL LOAD NO. | CALIBER | BULLET WGT. IN GRAINS | GRAMS | BULLET STYLE* | FACTORY PRIMER NO. | VELOCITY IN FEET PER SECOND (TO NEAREST 10 FPS) | | | | | | | | | | |
|---|---|---|---|---|---|---|---|---|---|---|---|---|---|---|---|---|---|
| | | | | | | | MUZZLE | 100 YDS. | 200 YDS. | 300 YDS. | 400 YDS. | 500 YDS. | 600 YDS. | 700 YDS. | 800 YDS. | 900 YDS. | 1000 YDS. |
| 5 | GM223M | 223 Rem. (5.56x45mm) | 69 | 4.47 | Sierra MatchKing BTHP | GM205M | 3000 | 2720 | 2460 | 2210 | 1980 | 1760 | 1560 | 1390 | 1240 | 1130 | 1060 |
| 5 | GM308M | 308 Win. (7.62x51mm) | 168 | 10.88 | Sierra MatchKing BTHP | GM210M | 2600 | 2410 | 2230 | 2060 | 1890 | 1740 | 1590 | 1460 | 1340 | 1230 | 1150 |
| 5 NEW | GM308M2 | 308 Win. (7.62x51mm) | 175 | 11.34 | Sierra MatchKing BTHP | GM210M | 2600 | 2420 | 2260 | 2090 | 1940 | 1790 | 1650 | 1520 | 1400 | 1300 | 1200 |
| 5 | GM3006M | 30-06 Springfield (7.62x63mm) | 168 | 10.88 | Sierra MatchKing BTHP | GM210M | 2700 | 2510 | 2330 | 2150 | 1990 | 1830 | 1680 | 1540 | 1410 | 1300 | 1210 |
| 5 NEW | GM300WM | 300 Win. Magnum | 190 | 12.31 | Sierra MatchKing BTHP | GM215M | 2900 | 2730 | 2560 | 2400 | 2240 | 2090 | 1940 | 1810 | 1680 | 1550 | 1440 |

Usage Key: 1 = Varmints, predators, small game   2 = Medium game   3 = Large, heavy game   4 = Dangerous game   5 = Target shooting, training, practice
*BTHP = Boat-Tail Hollow Point

## LIGHTNING™ .22

| TYPE | FEDERAL LOAD NO. | CARTRIDGES PER BOX | CALIBER | BULLET WGT. IN GRAINS | BULLET STYLE | VELOCITY IN FEET PER SECOND (TO NEAREST 10 FPS) | | | | ENERGY IN FOOT-POUNDS (TO NEAREST 5 FOOT-POUNDS) | | | | WIND DRIFT IN INCHES 10 MPH CROSSWIND | | | HEIGHT OF BULLET TRAJECTORY IN INCHES ABOVE OR BELOW LINE OF SIGHT IF ZEROED AT ⊕ YDS. SIGHTS 1.5 INCHES ABOVE BORE LINE | | | | | |
|---|---|---|---|---|---|---|---|---|---|---|---|---|---|---|---|---|---|---|---|---|---|---|
| | | | | | | MUZZLE | 50 YDS. | 100 YDS. | 150 YDS. | MUZZLE | 50 YDS. | 100 YDS. | 150 YDS. | 50 YDS. | 100 YDS. | 150 YDS. | 50 YDS. | 100 YDS. | 150 YDS. | 50 YDS. | 100 YDS. | 150 YDS. |
| High Velocity | 510 | 50 | 22 Long Rifle HV | 40 | Solid | 1260 | 1100 | 1020 | 940 | 140 | 110 | 90 | 80 | 1.5 | 5.5 | 11.4 | ⊕ | -6.5 | -21.0 | +2.7 | ⊕ | -10.8 |

## AMERICAN EAGLE® CENTERFIRE RIFLE

| USAGE | FEDERAL LOAD NO. | CALIBER | BULLET WGT. IN GRAINS | GRAMS | BULLET STYLE | FACTORY PRIMER NO. | VELOCITY IN FEET PER SECOND (TO NEAREST 10 FPS) | | | | | | ENERGY IN FOOT-POUNDS (TO NEAREST 5 FOOT-POUNDS) | | | | | |
|---|---|---|---|---|---|---|---|---|---|---|---|---|---|---|---|---|---|---|
| | | | | | | | MUZZLE | 100 YDS. | 200 YDS. | 300 YDS. | 400 YDS. | 500 YDS. | MUZZLE | 100 YDS. | 200 YDS. | 300 YDS. | 400 YDS. | 500 YDS. |
| 5 | AE223 | 223 Rem. (5.56x45mm) | 55 | 3.56 | Full Metal Jacket Boat-Tail | 205 | 3240 | 2950 | 2670 | 2410 | 2170 | 1940 | 1280 | 1060 | 875 | 710 | 575 | 460 |
| 5 | AE223G | 223 Rem. (5.56x45mm) | 50 | 3.24 | Jacketed Hollow Point | 205 | 3400 | 2910 | 2460 | 2060 | 1700 | 1390 | 1285 | 940 | 675 | 470 | 320 | 215 |
| 5 | AE30CB | 30 Carbine | 110 | 7.13 | Full Metal Jacket | 205 | 1990 | 1570 | 1240 | 1040 | 920 | 840 | 965 | 600 | 375 | 260 | 210 | 175 |
| 5 | AE76239A | 7.62x39mm Soviet | 124 | 8.03 | Full Metal Jacket | 210 | 2300 | 2030 | 1780 | 1560 | 1360 | 1200 | 1455 | 1135 | 875 | 670 | 510 | 400 |
| 5 | AE308D | 308 Win. | 150 | 9.72 | Full Metal Jacket Boat-Tail | 210 | 2820 | 2620 | 2430 | 2250 | 2070 | 1900 | 2650 | 2285 | 1965 | 1680 | 1430 | 1205 |
| 5 | AE3006N | 30-06 Spring | 150 | 9.72 | Full Metal Jacket Boat-Tail | 210 | 2910 | 2710 | 2510 | 2320 | 2150 | 1970 | 2820 | 2440 | 2100 | 1800 | 1535 | 1300 |

Usage Key: 1 = Varmints, predators, small game   2 = Medium game   3 = Large, heavy game   4 = Dangerous game   5 = Target shooting, training, practice

| USAGE | FEDERAL LOAD NO. | CALIBER | BULLET WGT. IN GRAINS | GRAMS | BULLET STYLE* | FACTORY PRIMER NO. | VELOCITY IN FEET PER SECOND (TO NEAREST 10 FPS) | | | | | ENERGY IN FOOT-POUNDS (TO NEAREST 5 FOOT-POUNDS) | | | | | MID-RANGE TRAJECTORY | | | | TEST BARREL LENGTH INCHES |
|---|---|---|---|---|---|---|---|---|---|---|---|---|---|---|---|---|---|---|---|---|---|
| | | | | | | | MUZZLE | 25 YDS. | 50 YDS. | 75 YDS. | 100 YDS. | MUZZLE | 25 YDS. | 50 YDS. | 75 YDS. | 100 YDS. | 25 YDS. | 50 YDS. | 75 YDS. | 100 YDS. | |
| 4 | GM9MP | 9mm Luger (9x19mm Parabellum) | 124 | 8.03 | Truncated FMJ Match | GM100M | 1120 | 1070 | 1030 | 990 | 960 | 345 | 315 | 290 | 270 | 255 | 0.2 | 0.9 | 2.2 | 4.1 | 4 |
| 4 | GM38A | 38 Special | 148 | 9.59 | Lead Wadcutter Match | GM100M | 710 | 670 | 630 | 600 | 560 | 165 | 150 | 130 | 115 | 105 | 0.6 | 2.4 | 5.7 | 10.8 | 4-V |
| 4 | GM356SW | 356 TSW | 147 | 9.52 | Truncated FMJ Match | GM100M | 1220 | 1170 | 1120 | 1080 | 1040 | 485 | 445 | 410 | 380 | 355 | 0.2 | 0.8 | 1.9 | 3.5 | 5 |
| 4 | GM44D | 44 Rem. Magnum | 250 | 16.20 | MC Profile Match | GM150M | 1180 | 1140 | 1100 | 1070 | 1040 | 775 | 715 | 670 | 630 | 600 | 0.2 | 0.8 | 1.9 | 3.6 | 6½-V |
| 4 | GM45B | 45 Auto | 185 | 11.99 | FMJ-SWC Match | GM150M | 780 | 730 | 700 | 660 | 620 | 245 | 220 | 200 | 175 | 160 | 0.5 | 2.0 | 4.8 | 9.0 | 5 |

Usage Key: 1 = Varmints, predators, small game   2 = Medium game   3 = Self-defense   4 = Target shooting, training, practice
*MC Profile Match = Metal Case Profile Match   FMJ = Full Metal Jacket   SWC = Semi-Wadcutter
"V" indicates vented barrel to simulate service conditions.

| ENERGY IN FOOT-POUNDS (TO NEAREST 5 FOOT-POUNDS) | | | | | | | | | | WIND DRIFT IN INCHES 10 MPH CROSSWIND | | | | | | | | | | HEIGHT OF BULLET TRAJECTORY IN INCHES ABOVE OR BELOW LINE OF SIGHT IF ZEROED AT ⊕ YARDS. SIGHTS 1.5 INCHES ABOVE BORE LINE. | | | | | | | | | | FEDERAL LOAD NO. |
|---|---|---|---|---|---|---|---|---|---|---|---|---|---|---|---|---|---|---|---|---|---|---|---|---|---|---|---|---|---|---|
| MUZZLE | 100 YDS. | 200 YDS. | 300 YDS. | 400 YDS. | 500 YDS. | 600 YDS. | 700 YDS. | 800 YDS. | 900 YDS. | 1000 YDS. | 100 YDS. | 200 YDS. | 300 YDS. | 400 YDS. | 500 YDS. | 600 YDS. | 700 YDS. | 800 YDS. | 900 YDS. | 1000 YDS. | 100 YDS. | 200 YDS. | 300 YDS. | 400 YDS. | 500 YDS. | 600 YDS. | 700 YDS. | 800 YDS. | 900 YDS. | 1000 YDS. | |
| 1380 | 1135 | 925 | 750 | 600 | 475 | 375 | 295 | 235 | 195 | 170 | 0.9 | 3.7 | 8.7 | 16.3 | 27.0 | 41.3 | 59.5 | 82.2 | 109.2 | 140.0 | +1.6 | ⊕ | -7.4 | -21.9 | -45.3 | -79.8 | -128.7 | -194.1 | -280.2 | -388.7 | GM223M |
| 2520 | 2170 | 1855 | 1580 | 1340 | 1130 | 970 | 795 | 670 | 565 | 490 | 0.7 | 3.2 | 7.6 | 13.8 | 22.8 | 34.3 | 48.4 | 66.1 | 86.9 | 111.0 | +17.7 | +31.0 | +37.2 | +35.4 | +23.5 | ⊕ | -36.7 | -90.8 | -164.3 | -261.7 | GM308M |
| 2625 | 2285 | 1975 | 1705 | 1460 | 1245 | 1060 | 900 | 765 | 650 | 560 | 0.6 | 2.95 | 7.0 | 12.7 | 20.8 | 31.4 | 44.3 | 60.1 | 79.1 | 101.0 | +17.2 | +29.9 | +35.8 | +33.9 | +22.6 | ⊕ | -34.8 | -84.9 | -153.7 | -243.1 | GM308M2 |
| 2720 | 2350 | 2025 | 1730 | 1470 | 1245 | 1050 | 880 | 740 | 630 | 540 | 0.7 | 3.0 | 7.0 | 13.0 | 21.2 | 31.8 | 45.1 | 61.5 | 81.0 | 103.6 | +16.1 | +28.1 | +33.8 | +31.9 | +21.1 | ⊕ | -33.4 | -81.3 | -146.0 | -230.1 | GM3006M |
| 3550 | 3135 | 2760 | 2420 | 2115 | 1840 | 1595 | 1375 | 1185 | 1015 | 870 | 0.6 | 2.4 | 5.5 | 10.1 | 16.4 | 24.2 | 34.2 | 46.6 | 61.1 | 78.0 | +12.9 | +22.5 | +26.9 | +25.1 | +16.4 | ⊕ | -25.8 | -63.0 | -112.2 | -175.6 | GM300WM |

These trajectory tables were calculated by computer using the best available data for each load. Trajectories are representative of the nominal behavior of each load at standard conditions (59°F temperature; barometric pressure of 29.53 inches; altitude at sea level). Shooters are cautioned that actual trajectories may differ due to variations in altitude, atmospheric conditions, guns, sights, and ammunition.

## AMERICAN EAGLE® RIMFIRE

| USAGE | FEDERAL LOAD NO. | CARTRIDGES PER BOX | CALIBER | BULLET WGT. IN GRAINS | BULLET STYLE* | VELOCITY IN FEET PER SECOND (TO NEAREST 10 FPS) | | | | ENERGY IN FOOT-POUNDS (TO NEAREST 5 FOOT-POUNDS) | | | | WIND DRIFT IN INCHES 10 MPH CROSSWIND | | | HEIGHT OF BULLET TRAJECTORY IN INCHES ABOVE OR BELOW LINE OF SIGHT IF ZEROED AT ⊕ YARDS. SIGHTS 1.5 INCHES ABOVE BORE LINE. | | | | | |
|---|---|---|---|---|---|---|---|---|---|---|---|---|---|---|---|---|---|---|---|---|---|---|
| | | | | | | MUZZLE | 50 YDS. | 100 YDS. | 150 YDS. | MUZZLE | 50 YDS. | 100 YDS. | 150 YDS. | 50 YDS. | 100 YDS. | 150 YDS. | 50 YDS. | 100 YDS. | 150 YDS. | 50 YDS. | 100 YDS. | 150 YDS. |
| 1,4 | AE22 | 40 | 22 Long Rifle High Velocity | 38 | HP Copper-Plated | 1280 | 1120 | 1020 | 950 | 140 | 105 | 90 | 75 | 1.6 | 5.8 | 12.1 | ⊕ | -6.3 | -20.6 | +2.7 | ⊕ | -10.6 |
| 1,4 | AE5022 | 50 | 22 Long Rifle High Velocity | 40 | Solid | 1260 | 1100 | 1020 | 940 | 140 | 110 | 90 | 80 | 1.5 | 5.5 | 11.4 | ⊕ | -6.5 | -21.0 | +2.7 | ⊕ | -10.8 |

Usage Key: 1 = Varmints, predators, small game   2 = Medium game   3 = Self-defense   4 = Target shooting, training, practice
*HP = Hollow Point

| | Bullet | | | Velocity(fps) | | | | | | Energy (ft. lbs.) | | | | | | Bullet Path | | | | | |
|---|---|---|---|---|---|---|---|---|---|---|---|---|---|---|---|---|---|---|---|---|---|
| Cartridge | Weight | Type | Mzl. | 100 | 200 | 300 | 400 | 500 | Mzl. | 100 | 200 | 300 | 400 | 500 | Mzl. | 100 | 200 | 300 | 400 | 500 |
| .22 PPC | 52 | BERGER | 3300 | 2952 | 2629 | 2329 | 2049 | | 1257 | 1006 | 798 | 626 | 485 | | -1.50 | +1.26 | ZERO | -6.27 | -19.06 | |
| 6mm PPC | 68 | BERGER | 3100 | 2751 | 2428 | 2128 | 1850 | | 1451 | 1143 | 890 | 684 | 516 | | -1.50 | +1.55 | ZERO | -7.52 | -22.64 | |
| 7mm REM | 175 | MONO | 2860 | 2557 | 2273 | 2008 | 1771 | | 3178 | 2540 | 2008 | 1567 | 1219 | | -1.50 | +1.92 | ZERO | -8.68 | -25.89 | |
| 7mm STW | 140 | NOS B-TIP | 3450 | 3254 | 3067 | 2888 | 2715 | 2550 | 3700 | 3291 | 2924 | 2592 | 2292 | 2021 | -1.50 | +2.42 | +3.04 | ZERO | -7.27 | -19.23 |
| 7mm STW | 160 | NOS PAR | 3250 | 3071 | 2900 | 2735 | 2576 | 2422 | 3752 | 3351 | 2987 | 2657 | 2357 | 2084 | -1.50 | +2.83 | +3.50 | ZERO | -8.16 | -21.45 |
| 7mm STW | 160 | SBT | 3250 | 3087 | 2930 | 2778 | 2631 | 2490 | 3752 | 3385 | 3049 | 2741 | 2460 | 2202 | -1.50 | +2.78 | +3.42 | ZERO | -7.97 | -20.92 |
| .30-06 | 180 | M & D-T | 2700 | 2365 | 2054 | 1769 | 1524 | | 2913 | 2235 | 1687 | 1251 | 928 | | -1.50 | +2.39 | ZERO | -10.64 | -32.41 | |
| .30-06 | 220 | MONO | 2380 | 2108 | 1854 | 1623 | 1424 | | 2767 | 2171 | 1679 | 1287 | 990 | | -1.50 | +3.14 | ZERO | -13.56 | -39.90 | |
| .300 WIN | 180 | M & D-T | 3120 | 2756 | 2420 | 2108 | 1820 | | 3890 | 3035 | 2340 | 1776 | 1324 | | -1.50 | +1.55 | ZERO | -7.57 | -22.90 | |
| .300 WBY | 180 | M & D-T | 3180 | 2811 | 2471 | 2155 | 1863 | | 4041 | 3158 | 2440 | 1856 | 1387 | | -1.50 | +1.46 | ZERO | -7.21 | -21.85 | |
| .300 WBY | 220 | MONO | 2700 | 2407 | 2133 | 1877 | 1653 | | 3561 | 2830 | 2223 | 1721 | 1334 | | -1.50 | +2.28 | ZERO | -9.82 | -29.75 | |
| .300 PEG | 180 | SBT | 3500 | 3319 | 3145 | 2978 | 2817 | 2663 | 4896 | 4401 | 3953 | 3544 | 3172 | 2833 | -1.50 | +2.28 | +2.89 | ZERO | -6.79 | -18.04 |
| .300 PEG | 180 | NOS PAR | 3500 | 3295 | 3100 | 2913 | 2734 | 2563 | 4896 | 4339 | 3840 | 3392 | 2988 | 2624 | -1.50 | +2.34 | +2.96 | ZERO | -7.10 | -18.86 |
| .300 PEG | 180 | M & D-T | 3500 | 3103 | 2740 | 2405 | 2095 | | 4896 | 3848 | 3001 | 2312 | 1753 | | -1.50 | +1.06 | ZERO | -5.70 | -17.51 | |
| 8mm REM | 220 | MONO | 2800 | 2501 | 2221 | 1959 | 1718 | | 3829 | 3055 | 2409 | 1875 | 1442 | | -1.50 | +2.05 | ZERO | -9.10 | -27.56 | |
| .338-06 | 200 | NOS B-TIP | 2750 | 2553 | 2364 | 2184 | 2011 | | 3358 | 2894 | 2482 | 2118 | 1796 | | -1.50 | +1.90 | ZERO | -8.22 | -23.63 | |
| .338-06 | 250 | SBT | 2500 | 2374 | 2252 | 2134 | 2019 | | 3496 | 3129 | 2816 | 2528 | 2263 | | -1.50 | +2.36 | ZERO | -9.27 | -26.01 | |
| .338-06 | 250 | DT | 2500 | 2222 | 1963 | 1724 | 1507 | | 3496 | 2742 | 2139 | 1649 | 1261 | | -1.50 | +2.78 | ZERO | -11.90 | -35.51 | |
| .338 WIN | 250 | SBT | 2700 | 2568 | 2439 | 2314 | 2193 | 2075 | 4046 | 3659 | 3302 | 2972 | 2669 | 2390 | -1.50 | +4.44 | +5.15 | ZERO | -11.73 | -30.62 |
| .338 WIN | 250 | TRIAD | 2700 | 2407 | 2133 | 1877 | 1653 | | 4046 | 3216 | 2526 | 1956 | 1516 | | -1.50 | +2.28 | ZERO | -9.82 | -29.75 | |
| .340 WBY | 250 | SBT | 2820 | 2684 | 2552 | 2424 | 2299 | 2179 | 4414 | 3999 | 3615 | 3261 | 2935 | 2635 | -1.50 | +3.98 | +4.63 | ZERO | -10.57 | -27.82 |
| .340 WBY | 250 | TRIAD | 2820 | 2520 | 2238 | 1976 | 1741 | | 4414 | 3524 | 2781 | 2166 | 1683 | | -1.50 | +2.00 | ZERO | -8.98 | -26.79 | |
| .338 A-SQ | 200 | NOS B-TIP | 3500 | 3266 | 3045 | 2835 | 2634 | 2442 | 5440 | 4737 | 4117 | 3568 | 3081 | 2648 | -1.50 | +2.42 | +3.08 | ZERO | -7.46 | |
| .338 A-SQ | 250 | SBT | 3120 | 2974 | 2834 | 2697 | 2565 | 2436 | 5403 | 4911 | 4457 | 4038 | 3652 | 3295 | -1.50 | +3.07 | +3.72 | ZERO | -8.47 | -22.10 |
| .338 A-SQ | 250 | TRIAD | 3120 | 2799 | 2500 | 2220 | 1958 | | 5403 | 4348 | 3469 | 2736 | 2128 | | -1.50 | +1.49 | ZERO | -7.05 | -20.37 | |
| .338 EXCALBR | 200 | NOS B-TIP | 3600 | 3361 | 3134 | 2920 | 2715 | 2520 | 5755 | 5015 | 4363 | 3785 | 3274 | 2820 | -1.50 | +2.23 | 2.87 | ZERO | -6.99 | -18.67 |
| .338 EXCALBR | 250 | SBT | 3250 | 3101 | 2958 | 2819 | 2684 | 2553 | 5863 | 5339 | 4855 | 4410 | 3998 | 3618 | -1.50 | +2.72 | 3.35 | ZERO | -7.78 | -20.35 |
| .338 EXCALBR | 250 | TRIAD | 3250 | 2922 | 2618 | 2333 | 2066 | 1818 | 5863 | 4740 | 3804 | 3021 | 2370 | 1834 | -1.50 | +1.30 | ZERO | -6.35 | -19.20 | -40.10 |
| .358 NORMA | 275 | TRIAD | 2700 | 2394 | 2108 | 1842 | 1653 | | 4451 | 3498 | 2713 | 2072 | 1668 | | -1.50 | +2.32 | ZERO | -10.06 | -29.75 | |
| .358 STA | 275 | TRIAD | 2850 | 2562 | 2292 | 2039 | 1764 | | 4959 | 4009 | 3208 | 2539 | 1899 | | -1.50 | +1.90 | ZERO | -8.58 | -26.11 | |
| 9.3x62 | 286 | TRIAD | 2360 | 2089 | 1844 | 1623 | 1369 | | 3538 | 2771 | 2157 | 1670 | 1189 | | -1.50 | +3.04 | ZERO | -13.12 | -42.16 | |
| 9.3x64 | 286 | TRIAD | 2700 | 2391 | 2103 | 1835 | 1602 | | 4629 | 3630 | 2808 | 2139 | 1631 | | -1.50 | +2.33 | ZERO | -10.11 | -30.77 | |
| 9.3x74R | 286 | TRIAD | 2360 | 2089 | 1844 | 1623 | | | 3538 | 2771 | 2157 | 1670 | | | -.90 | +3.61 | ZERO | -14.02 | | |
| .375 H&H | 300 | SBT | 2550 | 2415 | 2284 | 2157 | 2034 | 1914 | 4331 | 3884 | 3474 | 3098 | 2755 | 2441 | -1.50 | +5.24 | +5.99 | ZERO | -13.33 | -34.26 |
| .375 H&H | 300 | TRIAD | 2550 | 2251 | 1973 | 1717 | 1496 | | 4331 | 3375 | 2592 | 1964 | 1491 | | -1.50 | +2.70 | ZERO | -11.72 | -35.13 | |
| .375 WBY | 300 | SBT | 2700 | 2560 | 2425 | 2293 | 2166 | 2043 | 4856 | 4366 | 3916 | 3503 | 3125 | 2779 | -1.50 | +4.49 | +5.22 | ZERO | -11.91 | -31.08 |
| .375 WBY | 300 | TRIAD | 2700 | 2391 | 2103 | 1835 | 1602 | | 4856 | 3808 | 2946 | 2243 | 1710 | | -1.50 | +2.33 | ZERO | -10.11 | -30.77 | |
| .375 JRS | 300 | SBT | 2700 | 2560 | 2425 | 2293 | 2166 | 2043 | 4856 | 4366 | 3916 | 3503 | 3125 | 2779 | -1.50 | +4.49 | +5.22 | ZERO | -11.91 | -31.08 |
| .375 JRS | 300 | TRIAD | 2700 | 2391 | 2103 | 1835 | 1602 | | 4856 | 3808 | 2946 | 2243 | 1710 | | -1.50 | +2.33 | ZERO | -10.11 | -30.77 | |
| .375 A-SQ | 300 | SBT | 2920 | 2773 | 2631 | 2494 | 2360 | 2231 | 5679 | 5123 | 4611 | 4142 | 3710 | 3314 | -1.50 | +3.70 | +4.36 | ZERO | -9.80 | -26.01 |
| .375 A-SQ | 300 | TRIAD | 2920 | 2596 | 2294 | 2012 | 1762 | | 5679 | 4488 | 3505 | 2698 | 2068 | | -1.50 | +1.83 | ZERO | -8.49 | -25.49 | |
| .378 WBY | 300 | SBT | 2900 | 2754 | 2612 | 2475 | 2342 | 2214 | 5602 | 5051 | 4546 | 4081 | 3655 | 3264 | -1.50 | +3.76 | +4.41 | ZERO | -9.99 | -26.47 |
| .378 WBY | 300 | TRIAD | 2900 | 2577 | 2276 | 1997 | 1747 | | 5602 | 4423 | 3452 | 2656 | 2034 | | -1.50 | +1.87 | ZERO | -8.69 | -25.92 | |
| .450/.400 (3") | 400 | TRIAD | 2150 | 1910 | 1690 | 1490 | | | 4105 | 3241 | 2537 | 1972 | | | -.90 | +4.39 | ZERO | -16.52 | | |
| .450/.400 (3¼") | 400 | TRIAD | 2150 | 1910 | 1690 | 1490 | | | 4105 | 3241 | 2537 | 1972 | | | -.90 | +4.39 | ZERO | -16.52 | | |
| .416 TAYLOR | 400 | TRIAD | 2350 | 2093 | 1853 | 1634 | 1443 | | 4905 | 3892 | 3049 | 2371 | 1849 | | -1.50 | +3.19 | ZERO | -13.62 | -39.83 | |
| .416 REM | 400 | TRIAD | 2380 | 2122 | 1879 | 1658 | 1464 | | 5031 | 3998 | 3136 | 2440 | 1903 | | -1.50 | +3.08 | ZERO | -13.22 | -38.71 | |
| .416 HOFF | 400 | TRIAD | 2380 | 2122 | 1879 | 1658 | 1464 | | 5031 | 3998 | 3136 | 2440 | 1903 | | -1.50 | +3.08 | ZERO | -13.22 | -38.71 | |
| .416 RIMMED | 400 | TRIAD | 2400 | 2140 | 1897 | 1673 | | | 5115 | 4069 | 3194 | 2487 | | | -.90 | +3.31 | ZERO | -13.19 | | |
| .416 RIGBY | 400 | TRIAD | 2400 | 2140 | 1897 | 1673 | 1478 | | 5115 | 4069 | 3194 | 2487 | 1940 | | -1.50 | +3.02 | ZERO | -12.95 | -37.99 | |
| .416 WBY | 400 | TRIAD | 2600 | 2328 | 2073 | 1834 | 1624 | | 6004 | 4813 | 3816 | 2986 | 2343 | | -1.50 | +2.49 | ZERO | -10.49 | -31.56 | |
| .404 JEFFERY | 400 | TRIAD | 2150 | 1901 | 1674 | 1468 | 1299 | | 4105 | 3211 | 2489 | 1915 | 1499 | | -1.50 | +4.14 | ZERO | -16.45 | -49.10 | |
| .425 EXPRESS | 400 | TRIAD | 2400 | 2136 | 1888 | 1662 | 1465 | | 5115 | 4052 | 3167 | 2454 | 1906 | | -1.50 | +3.04 | ZERO | -13.07 | -38.34 | |
| .458 WIN | 465 | TRIAD | 2220 | 1999 | 1791 | 1601 | 1433 | | 5088 | 4127 | 3312 | 2646 | 2121 | | -1.50 | +3.57 | ZERO | -14.69 | -42.46 | |
| .450 N.E. (3¼") | 465 | TRIAD | 2190 | 1970 | 1765 | 1577 | | | 4952 | 4009 | 3216 | 2567 | | | -.90 | +4.33 | ZERO | -15.40 | | |
| .450 #2 | 465 | TRIAD | 2190 | 1970 | 1765 | 1577 | | | 4952 | 4009 | 3216 | 2567 | | | -.90 | +4.33 | ZERO | -15.40 | | |
| .458 LOTT | 465 | TRIAD | 2380 | 2150 | 1932 | 1730 | 1551 | | 5848 | 4773 | 3855 | 3091 | 2485 | | -1.50 | +2.99 | ZERO | -12.46 | -36.45 | |
| .450 ACKLEY | 465 | TRIAD | 2400 | 2169 | 1950 | 1747 | 1567 | | 5947 | 4857 | 3927 | 3150 | 2534 | | -1.50 | +2.93 | ZERO | -12.17 | -35.75 | |
| .460 SH. A-SQ. | 500 | TRIAD | 2420 | 2198 | 1987 | 1789 | 1613 | | 6501 | 5362 | 4385 | 3553 | 2890 | | -1.50 | +2.87 | ZERO | -11.59 | -34.25 | |
| .460 WBY | 500 | TRIAD | 2580 | 2349 | 2131 | 1923 | 1737 | | 7389 | 6126 | 5040 | 4107 | 3351 | | -1.50 | +2.43 | ZERO | -9.96 | -29.45 | |
| .500/.465 N.E. | 480 | TRIAD | 2150 | 1928 | 1722 | 1533 | | | 4926 | 3960 | 3160 | 2505 | | | -.90 | +4.28 | ZERO | -16.03 | | |
| .470 N.E. | 500 | TRIAD | 2150 | 1912 | 1693 | 1494 | | | 5132 | 4058 | 3182 | 2478 | | | -.90 | +4.38 | ZERO | -16.48 | | |
| .470 CAP | 500 | TRIAD | 2400 | 2172 | 1958 | 1761 | 1553 | | 6394 | 5236 | 4255 | 3445 | 2678 | | -1.50 | +2.91 | ZERO | -11.88 | -36.06 | |
| .475 #2 N.E. | 480 | TRIAD | 2200 | 1964 | 1744 | 1544 | | | 5158 | 4109 | 3240 | 2539 | | | -.90 | +4.09 | ZERO | -15.63 | | |
| .475 #2 JEFF | 500 | TRIAD | 2200 | 1966 | 1748 | 1550 | | | 5373 | 4291 | 3392 | 2666 | | | -.90 | +4.07 | ZERO | -15.58 | | |
| .505 GIBBS | 525 | TRIAD | 2300 | 2063 | 1840 | 1637 | | | 6166 | 4962 | 3948 | 3122 | | | -.90 | +3.61 | ZERO | -14.18 | | |
| .500 N.E. (3") | 570 | TRIAD | 2150 | 1928 | 1722 | 1533 | | | 5850 | 4703 | 3752 | 2975 | | | -.90 | +4.28 | ZERO | -16.03 | | |
| .495 A-SQ | 570 | TRIAD | 2350 | 2117 | 1896 | 1693 | 1513 | | 6989 | 5671 | 4552 | 3629 | 2899 | | -1.50 | +3.10 | ZERO | -13.02 | -37.83 | |
| .500 A-SQ | 600 | TRIAD | 2470 | 2235 | 2013 | 1804 | 1620 | | 8127 | 6654 | 5397 | 4336 | 3495 | | -1.50 | +2.74 | ZERO | -11.29 | -33.47 | |
| .577 N.E. | 750 | TRIAD | 2050 | 1811 | 1595 | 1401 | | | 6998 | 5463 | 4234 | 3267 | | | -.90 | +4.94 | ZERO | -18.48 | | |
| .577 TYRNSR | 750 | TRIAD | 2460 | 2197 | 1950 | 1723 | 1516 | | 10077 | 8039 | 6335 | 4941 | 3825 | | -1.50 | +2.85 | ZERO | -12.12 | -35.95 | |
| .600 N.E. | 900 | TRIAD | 1950 | 1680 | 1452 | 1336 | | | 7596 | 5634 | 4212 | 3564 | | | -.90 | +5.61 | ZERO | -20.74 | | |
| .700 N.E. | 1000 | MONO | 1900 | 1669 | 1461 | 1288 | | | 8015 | 6188 | 4740 | 3685 | | | -.90 | +5.78 | ZERO | -22.22 | | |

# DAKOTA ARMS AMMUNITIONS

*Rifle- Barrel: Dakota*
*Barrel Length: 26"*
*Barrel Twist: 1-9*
*Trim Cases to: 2.490"*

*Case: Dakota*
*Primer: CCI 250*
*Velocity Change for each 1"*
*Change in Barrel Length = 30 FPS*

## CALIBER: 7mm Dakota — BULLET: 100 Gr. XFB, Solid

| POWDER | START WEIGHT | VELOCITY | MAX WEIGHT | VELOCITY | ACCURACY |
|---|---|---|---|---|---|
| H 4831 | 77.0 | 3596 | 82.0 | 3856 | |
| H 1000 | 80.0 | 3461 | 85.0 | 3672 | |
| IMR 7828 | 78.0 | 3652 | 83.0 | 3901 | |
| WIN WMR | 80.0 | 3663 | 85.0 | 3843 | |
| VIT N 170 | 80.0 | 3361 | 85.0 | 3610 | |
| VIT 24 N 41 | 81.0 | 3202 | 86.0 | 3329 | |
| RL 22 | 78.0 | 3628 | 83.0 | 3865 | |
| AA 3100 | 76.0 | 3566 | 81.0 | 3789 | |
| AA 8700 | 88.0 | 3251 | 93.0 | 3374 | |

# Accuracy Loads

## CALIBER: 7mm Dakota — BULLET: 120 Gr. XFB, XBT, SOLID

| POWDER | START WEIGHT | VELOCITY | MAX WEIGHT | VELOCITY | ACCURACY |
|---|---|---|---|---|---|
| H 4831 | 72.0 | 3430 | 77.0 | 3570 | |
| H 1000 | 79.0 | 3399 | 84.0 | 3584 | |
| IMR 7828 | 73.5 | 3366 | 78.5 | 3605 | |
| WIN WMR | 78.0 | 3411 | 83.0 | 3641 | * |
| VIT N 170 | 80.0 | 3374 | 85.0 | 3536 | * |
| VIT 24 N 41 | 81.0 | 3006 | 86.0 | 3223 | |
| RL 22 | 74.5 | 3403 | 79.5 | 3613 | |
| AA 3100 | 73.0 | 3309 | 78.0 | 3534 | * |
| AA 8700 | 88.0 | 3213 | 93.0 | 3395 | * |

# Accuracy Loads

## CALIBER: 7mm Dakota — BULLET: 130 Gr. XBT

| POWDER | START WEIGHT | VELOCITY | MAX WEIGHT | VELOCITY | ACCURACY |
|---|---|---|---|---|---|
| H 4831 | 71.0 | 3350 | 76.0 | 3481 | * |
| H 1000 | 77.0 | 3308 | 82.0 | 3461 | * |
| IMR 7828 | 72.0 | 3363 | 77.0 | 3507 | * |
| WIN WMR | 75.0 | 3302 | 80.0 | 3509 | |
| VIT N 170 | 78.0 | 3245 | 83.0 | 3448 | * |
| VIT 24 N 41 | 81.0 | 3110 | 86.0 | 3273 | |
| RL 22 | 73.0 | 3112 | 78.0 | 3523 | * |
| AA 3100 | 71.0 | 3204 | 76.0 | 3418 | |
| AA 8700 | 88.0 | 3215 | 93.0 | 3411 | |

# Accuracy Loads

*Reloading information courtesy of Barnes Bullets*

# DAKOTA ARMS AMMUNITIONS

## CALIBER: 7mm Dakota — BULLET: 140 Gr. XFB, XBT

| POWDER | START WEIGHT | VELOCITY | MAX WEIGHT | VELOCITY | ACCURACY |
|---|---|---|---|---|---|
| H 4831 | 68.0 | 3107 | 73.0 | 3301 | |
| H 1000 | 75.0 | 3161 | 80.0 | 3317 | |
| IMR 7828 | 70.5 | 3099 | 75.5 | 3333 | |
| WIN WMR | 73.0 | 3118 | 78.0 | 3356 | |
| VIT N 170 | 76.5 | 3111 | 81.5 | 3298 | |
| VIT 24 N 41 | 81.0 | 3029 | 86.0 | 3221 | |
| RL 22 | 71.5 | 3149 | 76.5 | 3375 | |
| AA 3100 | 69.5 | 2999 | 74.5 | 3252 | |
| AA 8700 | 87.0 | 3128 | 92.0 | 3316 | * |

# Accuracy Loads

## CALIBER: 7mm Dakota — BULLET: 150 Gr. XFB, XBT

| POWDER | START WEIGHT | VELOCITY | MAX WEIGHT | VELOCITY | ACCURACY |
|---|---|---|---|---|---|
| H 4831 | 66.0 | 2977 | 71.0 | 3162 | |
| H 1000 | 74.0 | 3039 | 79.0 | 3209 | |
| IMR 7828 | 69.0 | 2984 | 74.0 | 3216 | |
| WIN WMR | 71.5 | 2993 | 76.5 | 3239 | |
| VIT N 170 | 74.5 | 2965 | 79.5 | 3162 | |
| VIT 24 N 41 | 81.0 | 3006 | 86.0 | 3188 | |
| RL 22 | 69.5 | 3013 | 74.5 | 3244 | |
| AA 3100 | 68.5 | 2923 | 73.5 | 3146 | |
| AA 8700 | 87.0 | 3136 | 92.0 | 3284 | |

# Accuracy Loads

## CALIBER: 7mm Dakota — BULLET: 160 Gr. XFB, SOLID

| POWDER | START WEIGHT | VELOCITY | MAX WEIGHT | VELOCITY | ACCURACY |
|---|---|---|---|---|---|
| H 4831 | 65.0 | 2864 | 70.0 | 3049 | |
| H 1000 | 72.0 | 2834 | 77.0 | 3042 | |
| IMR 7828 | 68.0 | 2910 | 73.0 | 3101 | |
| WIN WMR | 69.0 | 2881 | 74.0 | 3054 | |
| VIT N 170 | 72.5 | 2823 | 77.5 | 3014 | |
| VIT 24 N 41 | 81.0 | 2966 | 86.0 | 3127 | |
| RL 22 | 67.5 | 2874 | 72.5 | 3103 | |
| AA 3100 | 66.5 | 2791 | 71.5 | 3007 | |
| AA 8700 | 84.0 | 2985 | 89.0 | 3183 | |

# Accuracy Loads

## CALIBER: 7mm Dakota — BULLET: 175 Gr. XFB, SOLID

| POWDER | START WEIGHT | VELOCITY | MAX WEIGHT | VELOCITY | ACCURACY |
|---|---|---|---|---|---|
| H 4831 | 63.0 | 2672 | 68.0 | 2843 | |
| H 1000 | 70.0 | 2685 | 75.0 | 2876 | |
| IMR 7828 | 66.5 | 2701 | 71.5 | 2938 | |
| WIN WMR | 68.0 | 2728 | 73.0 | 2937 | |
| VIT N 170 | 70.0 | 2628 | 75.0 | 2834 | |
| VIT 24 N 41 | 79.0 | 2810 | 84.0 | 2979 | |
| RL 22 | 66.0 | 2682 | 71.0 | 2933 | |
| AA 3100 | 65.0 | 2615 | 70.0 | 2842 | |
| AA 8700 | 82.0 | 2872 | 87.0 | 2996 | |

# Accuracy Loads

*Courtesy of: Barnes Bullets*

# DAKOTA ARMS AMMUNITIONS

## CALIBER: 300 Dakota     BULLET: 110 Gr. XFB, Solid

| POWDER | START WEIGHT | VELOCITY | MAX WEIGHT | VELOCITY | ACCURACY |
|--------|-------------|----------|------------|----------|----------|
| H414 | 80.0 | 3720 | 86.0 | 3969 | * |
| H 4350 | 82.0 | 3691 | 88.0 | 3983 | |
| H 4831 | 82.0 | 3518 | 88.0 | 3755 | |
| H 1000 | 84.0 | 3287 | 90.0 | 3460 | * |
| IMR 4350 | 80.0 | 3759 | 86.0 | 4020 | |
| IMR 4831 | 81.0 | 3665 | 87.0 | 3952 | |
| IMR 7828 | 82.0 | 3442 | 88.0 | 3725 | * |
| WIN 760 | 80.0 | 3740 | 86.0 | 4002 | * |
| WIN WMR | 82.0 | 3363 | 88.0 | 3623 | * |
| RL 15 | 72.0 | 3751 | 78.0 | 3999 | |
| RL 19 | 84.0 | 3535 | 90.0 | 3870 | * |
| AA 4350 | 80.0 | 3578 | 86.0 | 3884 | * |
| AA 3100 | 82.0 | 3503 | 88.0 | 3754 | |
| VIT N 160 | 83.0 | 3724 | 89.0 | 3960 | |
| VIT N 170 | 84.0 | 3297 | 90.0 | 3509 | |

# Accuracy Loads

## CALIBER: 300 Dakota     BULLET: 125 Gr. XFB, Solid/130 gr. XBT

| POWDER | START WEIGHT | VELOCITY | MAX WEIGHT | VELOCITY | ACCURACY |
|--------|-------------|----------|------------|----------|----------|
| H414 | 76.0 | 3450 | 82.0 | 3939 | |
| H 4350 | 78.0 | 3500 | 84.0 | 3772 | * |
| H 4831 | 82.0 | 3477 | 88.0 | 3708 | |
| H 1000 | 84.0 | 3293 | 90.0 | 3458 | * |
| IMR 4350 | 76.0 | 3466 | 82.0 | 3784 | |
| IMR 4831 | 77.5 | 3493 | 83.0 | 3769 | * |
| IMR 7828 | 81.0 | 3406 | 87.0 | 3682 | |
| WIN 760 | 76.0 | 3564 | 82.0 | 3735 | |
| WIN WMR | 82.0 | 3427 | 88.0 | 3672 | |
| RL 15 | 66.0 | 3449 | 72.0 | 3682 | |
| RL 19 | 82.0 | 3538 | 88.0 | 3824 | |
| AA 4350 | 78.0 | 3542 | 84.0 | 3788 | |
| AA 3100 | 80.0 | 3381 | 86.0 | 3675 | * |
| VIT N 160 | 78.0 | 3516 | 84.0 | 3747 | |
| VIT N 170 | 84.0 | 3360 | 90.0 | 3570 | * |

# Accuracy Loads

*Courtesy of: Barnes Bullets*

# DAKOTA ARMS AMMUNITIONS

## CALIBER: 300 Dakota                          BULLET: 140 Gr. XBT

| POWDER | START WEIGHT | VELOCITY | MAX WEIGHT | VELOCITY | ACCURACY |
|--------|--------------|----------|------------|----------|----------|
| H414 | 72.0 | 3398 | 78.0 | 3544 | |
| H 4350 | 74.0 | 3452 | 80.0 | 3589 | |
| H 4831 | 79.0 | 3476 | 85.0 | 3608 | |
| H 1000 | 84.0 | 3259 | 90.0 | 3512 | |
| IMR 4350 | 72.0 | 3411 | 78.0 | 3580 | * |
| IMR 4831 | 74.0 | 3364 | 80.0 | 3590 | * |
| IMR 7828 | 80.0 | 3369 | 86.0 | 3645 | |
| WIN 760 | 73.0 | 3369 | 79.0 | 3581 | |
| WIN WMR | 82.0 | 3371 | 88.0 | 3608 | * |
| RL 15 | 65.0 | 3285 | 71.0 | 3507 | |
| RL 19 | 79.0 | 3375 | 85.0 | 3650 | |
| AA 4350 | 75.0 | 3345 | 81.0 | 3636 | |
| AA 3100 | 78.0 | 3284 | 84.0 | 3554 | |
| VIT N 160 | 75.5 | 3327 | 81.5 | 3566 | * |
| VIT N 170 | 84.0 | 3299 | 90.0 | 3563 | |

# Accuracy Loads

## CALIBER: 300 Dakota                          BULLET: 150 Gr. XFB, XBT

| POWDER | START WEIGHT | VELOCITY | MAX WEIGHT | VELOCITY | ACCURACY |
|--------|--------------|----------|------------|----------|----------|
| H414 | 71.0 | 3221 | 76.0 | 3417 | |
| H 4350 | 72.0 | 3253 | 78.0 | 3467 | * |
| H 4831 | 77.0 | 3324 | 83.0 | 3482 | * |
| H 1000 | 83.0 | 3199 | 89.0 | 3429 | * |
| IMR 4350 | 70.5 | 3267 | 76.5 | 3455 | * |
| IMR 4831 | 72.0 | 3253 | 78.0 | 3453 | * |
| IMR 7828 | 77.0 | 3216 | 83.0 | 3482 | * |
| WIN 760 | 70.0 | 3216 | 76.0 | 3419 | * |
| WIN WMR | 80.0 | 3249 | 86.0 | 3513 | |
| RL 19 | 77.0 | 3309 | 83.0 | 3523 | * |
| RL 22 | 78.0 | 3243 | 84.0 | 3489 | * |
| AA 4350 | 72.0 | 3235 | 78.0 | 3468 | |
| AA 3100 | 74.0 | 3118 | 80.0 | 3360 | |
| VIT N 160 | 70.0 | 3120 | 76.0 | 3353 | |
| VIT N 170 | 82.0 | 3249 | 88.0 | 3424 | |

# Accuracy Loads

*Courtesy of: Barnes Bullets*

# DAKOTA ARMS AMMUNITIONS

## CALIBER: 300 Dakota        BULLET: 165 Gr. XFB, XBT

| POWDER | START WEIGHT | VELOCITY | MAX WEIGHT | VELOCITY | ACCURACY |
|---|---|---|---|---|---|
| H414 | 67.5 | 2959 | 73.5 | 3230 | |
| H 4350 | 71.0 | 3129 | 77.0 | 3295 | * |
| H 4831 | 75.0 | 3157 | 81.0 | 3314 | |
| H 1000 | 82.0 | 3098 | 88.0 | 3319 | |
| IMR 4350 | 69.0 | 3086 | 75.0 | 3312 | |
| IMR 4831 | 71.0 | 3110 | 77.0 | 3314 | |
| IMR 7828 | 75.0 | 3047 | 81.0 | 3324 | |
| WIN 760 | 69.0 | 3079 | 75.0 | 3262 | |
| WIN WMR | 78.0 | 3075 | 84.0 | 3341 | |
| RL 15 | 76.0 | 3155 | 82.0 | 3385 | * |
| RL 19 | 78.0 | 3170 | 84.0 | 3413 | |
| AA 4350 | 71.5 | 3075 | 77.5 | 3347 | |
| AA 3100 | 74.0 | 3003 | 80.0 | 3234 | * |
| VIT N 160 | 69.5 | 3013 | 75.5 | 3198 | |
| VIT N 170 | 80.0 | 3054 | 86.0 | 3264 | |

# Accuracy Loads

## CALIBER: 300 Dakota        BULLET: 180 Gr. XFB, XBT
## CASE: DAKOTA        PRIMER: CCI 250

| POWDER | START WEIGHT | VELOCITY | MAX WEIGHT | VELOCITY | ACCURACY |
|---|---|---|---|---|---|
| H414 | 64.0 | 2847 | 70.0 | 3038 | * |
| H 4350 | 66.0 | 2908 | 72.0 | 3106 | * |
| H 4831 | 69.0 | 2968 | 75.0 | 3113 | * |
| H 1000 | 78.0 | 3021 | 84.0 | 3185 | * |
| IMR 4350 | 66.0 | 2901 | 72.0 | 3135 | |
| IMR 4831 | 68.0 | 2914 | 74.0 | 3142 | |
| IMR 7828 | 72.0 | 2894 | 78.0 | 3166 | |
| WIN 760 | 65.0 | 2803 | 71.0 | 3069 | |
| WIN WMR | 75.0 | 2953 | 81.0 | 3194 | |
| RL 15 | 74.0 | 3010 | 80.0 | 3253 | |
| RL 19 | 75.0 | 3020 | 81.0 | 3252 | |
| AA 4350 | 68.0 | 2899 | 74.0 | 3161 | |
| AA 3100 | 71.0 | 2863 | 77.0 | 3100 | |
| VIT N 160 | 68.0 | 2861 | 74.0 | 3083 | |
| VIT N 170 | 78.0 | 2971 | 84.0 | 3151 | |

# Accuracy Loads

*Courtesy of: Barnes Bullets*

# DAKOTA ARMS AMMUNITIONS

## CALIBER: 300 Dakota      BULLET: 200 Gr. XFB

| POWDER | START WEIGHT | VELOCITY | MAX WEIGHT | VELOCITY | ACCURACY |
|---|---|---|---|---|---|
| H 4350 | 62.0 | 2706 | 68.0 | 2881 | |
| H 4831 | 64.0 | 2730 | 70.0 | 2895 | * |
| H 1000 | 74.0 | 2795 | 80.0 | 2990 | * |
| H 870 | 86.0 | 2809 | 92.0 | 2968 | * |
| IMR 4350 | 62.0 | 2668 | 68.0 | 2910 | * |
| IMR 4831 | 64.0 | 2743 | 70.0 | 2932 | * |
| IMR 7828 | 68.0 | 2745 | 74.0 | 2969 | |
| WIN WMR | 72.0 | 2743 | 78.0 | 3008 | |
| RL 19 | 70.0 | 2863 | 76.0 | 3034 | |
| RL 22 | 71.0 | 2872 | 77.0 | 3050 | * |
| AA 4350 | 65.0 | 2724 | 71.0 | 2935 | |
| AA 3100 | 68.0 | 2737 | 74.0 | 2924 | * |
| AA 8700 | 87.0 | 2797 | 93.0 | 2965 | |
| VIT N 170 | 73.0 | 2759 | 79.0 | 2971 | |
| VIT 24 N 41 | 80.0 | 2751 | 86.0 | 3018 | * |

# Accuracy Loads

## CALIBER: 300 Dakota      BULLET: 250 Gr. ORIGINAL
## CASE: DAKOTA      PRIMER: CCI 250

| POWDER | START WEIGHT | VELOCITY | MAX WEIGHT | VELOCITY | ACCURACY |
|---|---|---|---|---|---|
| H 4831 | 63.0 | 2466 | 69.0 | 2614 | * |
| H 1000 | 71.0 | 2548 | 77.0 | 2706 | |
| H 870 | 84.0 | 2618 | 90.0 | 2783 | * |
| IMR 4831 | 62.0 | 2444 | 68.0 | 2649 | * |
| IMR 7828 | 67.0 | 2483 | 73.0 | 2694 | * |
| WIN WMR | 68.0 | 2492 | 74.0 | 2734 | |
| RL19 | 67.0 | 2526 | 73.0 | 2749 | |
| RL 22 | 67.5 | 2560 | 73.5 | 2737 | |
| AA 3100 | 66.0 | 2452 | 72.0 | 2659 | |
| AA 8700 | 84.0 | 2590 | 90.0 | 2775 | * |
| VIT N 170 | 70.0 | 2507 | 76.0 | 2668 | |
| VIT 24 N 41 | 78.0 | 2538 | 84.0 | 2733 | |

# Accuracy Loads

*Courtesy of: Barnes Bullets*

# DAKOTA ARMS AMMUNITIONS

*Rifle- Barrel: Dakota*
*Barrel Length: 26"*
*Barrel Twist: 1-10*
*Trim Cases to: 2.530"*

*Case: Dakota*
*Primer: CCI 250*
*Velocity Change for each 1"*
*Change in Barrel Length = 22 FPS*

## CALIBER: 330 Dakota — BULLET: 160 Gr. XFB

| POWDER | START WEIGHT | VELOCITY | MAX WEIGHT | VELOCITY | ACCURACY |
|--------|--------------|----------|------------|----------|----------|
| BLC 2 | 77.0 | 3286 | 82.0 | 3499 | |
| H4895 | 72.0 | 3250 | 77.0 | 3476 | |
| VARG | 75.0 | 3297 | 80.0 | 3517 | |
| H414 | 82.0 | 3267 | 87.0 | 3466 | |
| IMR4320 | 73.5 | 3209 | 78.5 | 3427 | |
| IMR4350 | 82.0 | 3275 | 87.0 | 3475 | |
| IMR4831 | 82.0 | 3161 | 87.0 | 3354 | |
| WIN760 | 83.0 | 3271 | 88.0 | 3468 | |
| AA2700 | 82.0 | 3223 | 87.0 | 3419 | |
| AA4350 | 82.0 | 3185 | 87.0 | 3379 | |
| N204 | 82 | 3155 | 87.0 | 3347 | |
| VIT N 150 | 74.0 | 3182 | 79.0 | 3397 | |
| VIT N 160 | 82.0 | 3120 | 87.0 | 3310 | |

\# Accuracy Loads

## CALIBER: 330 Dakota — BULLET: 175 Gr. XFB

| POWDER | START WEIGHT | VELOCITY | MAX WEIGHT | VELOCITY | ACCURACY |
|--------|--------------|----------|------------|----------|----------|
| BLC | 73.5 | 3047 | 78.5 | 3254 | |
| H4895 | 70.0 | 3037 | 75.0 | 3254 | |
| VARG | 73.0 | 3109 | 78.0 | 3322 | |
| H414 | 79.0 | 3085 | 84.0 | 3280 | |
| H4831 | 85.0 | 3024 | 90.0 | 3202 | |
| IMR4320 | 71.5 | 3035 | 76.5 | 3247 | |
| IMR4350 | 79.0 | 3122 | 84.0 | 3320 | |
| IMR4831 | 82.0 | 3115 | 87.0 | 3305 | |
| WIN760 | 81.0 | 3145 | 86.0 | 3339 | |
| AA2700 | 79.0 | 3029 | 84.0 | 3221 | |
| AA4350 | 81.0 | 3110 | 86.0 | 3292 | |
| N204 | 81.0 | 3101 | 86.0 | 3292 | |
| VIT N 150 | 72.0 | 3014 | 77.0 | 3223 | |
| VIT N 160 | 82.0 | 3075 | 87.0 | 3262 | |
| RL19 | 85.0 | 3050 | 90.0 | 3229 | |

\# Accuracy Loads

*Courtesy of: Barnes Bullets*

# DAKOTA ARMS AMMUNITIONS

*Rifle- Barrel: Dakota*
*Barrel Length: 26"*
*Barrel Twist: 1-10*
*Trim Cases to: 2.530"*

*Case: Dakota*
*Primer: CCI 250*
*Velocity Change for each 1"*
*Change in Barrel Length = 22 FPS*

## CALIBER: 330 Dakota        BULLET: 185 Gr. XBT

| POWDER | START WEIGHT | VELOCITY | MAX WEIGHT | VELOCITY | ACCURACY |
|---|---|---|---|---|---|
| BLC 2 | 71.5 | 2959 | 76.5 | 3166 | |
| H4895 | 68.0 | 2927 | 73.0 | 3142 | |
| VARG | 71.0 | 3017 | 76.0 | 3229 | |
| H414 | 77.0 | 3000 | 82.0 | 3195 | |
| H4831 | 84.0 | 2978 | 89.0 | 3155 | |
| IMR4320 | 69.0 | 2913 | 74.0 | 3124 | |
| IMR4350 | 76.0 | 2999 | 81.0 | 3196 | |
| IMR4831 | 79.0 | 3025 | 84.0 | 3216 | |
| WIN760 | 77.0 | 3015 | 82.0 | 3211 | |
| AA2700 | 76.0 | 2929 | 81.0 | 3122 | |
| AA4350 | 78.0 | 3002 | 83.0 | 3194 | |
| N204 | 78.0 | 2978 | 83.0 | 3169 | |
| VIT N 150 | 69.0 | 2874 | 74.0 | 3082 | |
| VIT N 160 | 79.0 | 2964 | 84.0 | 3152 | |
| RL19 | 84.0 | 3054 | 89.0 | 3236 | |

# Accuracy Loads

## CALIBER: 330 Dakota        BULLET: 200 Gr. XFB

| POWDER | START WEIGHT | VELOCITY | MAX WEIGHT | VELOCITY | ACCURACY |
|---|---|---|---|---|---|
| BLC 2 | 69.5 | 2772 | 74.5 | 2971 | |
| H4895 | 66.0 | 2775 | 71.0 | 2985 | |
| VARG | 69.0 | 2837 | 74.0 | 3043 | |
| H414 | 75.0 | 2853 | 80.0 | 3043 | |
| H4831 | 83.0 | 2897 | 88.0 | 3072 | |
| IMR4320 | 68.0 | 2782 | 73.0 | 2987 | |
| IMR4350 | 74.0 | 2878 | 79.0 | 3072 | |
| IMR4831 | 77.0 | 2886 | 82.0 | 3073 | |
| WIN760 | 75.0 | 2892 | 80.0 | 3085 | |
| AA2700 | 74.0 | 2794 | 79.0 | 2983 | |
| AA4350 | 76.0 | 2869 | 81.0 | 3058 | |
| N204 | 76.0 | 2853 | 81.0 | 3041 | |
| VIT N 150 | 67.0 | 2735 | 72.0 | 2939 | |
| VIT N 160 | 78.0 | 2846 | 83.0 | 3028 | |
| RL19 | 82.0 | 2937 | 87.0 | 3116 | |

# Accuracy Loads

*Courtesy of: Barnes Bullets*

# DAKOTA ARMS AMMUNITIONS

## CALIBER: 330 Dakota                                      BULLET: 210 Gr. XBT

| POWDER | START WEIGHT | VELOCITY | MAX WEIGHT | VELOCITY | ACCURACY |
|--------|--------------|----------|------------|----------|----------|
| BLC 2 | 67.5 | 2675 | 72.5 | 2873 | |
| H4895 | 65.5 | 2710 | 70.0 | 2918 | |
| VARG | 67.0 | 2779 | 72.0 | 2986 | |
| H414 | 74.0 | 2805 | 79.0 | 2995 | |
| H4831 | 81.0 | 2834 | 86.0 | 3009 | |
| IMR4320 | 67.0 | 2749 | 72.0 | 2954 | |
| IMR4350 | 73.0 | 2817 | 78.0 | 3010 | |
| IMR4831 | 76.0 | 2824 | 81.0 | 3010 | |
| WIN760 | 73.0 | 2798 | 78.0 | 2990 | |
| AA2700 | 71.0 | 2705 | 76.0 | 2895 | |
| AA4350 | 75.0 | 2817 | 80.0 | 3005 | |
| N204 | 74.5 | 2794 | 79.5 | 2981 | |
| VIT N 150 | 66.5 | 2699 | 71.5 | 2902 | |
| VIT N 160 | 77.0 | 2816 | 82.0 | 2999 | |
| RL19 | 81.0 | 2897 | 86.0 | 3076 | |

# Accuracy Loads

## CALIBER: 330 Dakota                                      BULLET: 225 Gr. XFB

| POWDER | START WEIGHT | VELOCITY | MAX WEIGHT | VELOCITY | ACCURACY |
|--------|--------------|----------|------------|----------|----------|
| BLC | 65.0 | 2523 | 70.0 | 2717 | |
| VARG | 65.0 | 2560 | 70.0 | 2757 | |
| H414 | 71.0 | 2622 | 76.0 | 2807 | |
| H4350 | 72.0 | 2719 | 77.0 | 2908 | |
| H4831 | 80.0 | 2745 | 85.0 | 2917 | |
| IMR4320 | 65.0 | 2598 | 70.0 | 2798 | |
| IMR4350 | 71.0 | 2673 | 76.0 | 2861 | |
| IMR4831 | 74.0 | 2662 | 79.0 | 2842 | |
| WIN760 | 70.0 | 2619 | 75.0 | 2806 | |
| AA2700 | 70.0 | 2578 | 75.0 | 2762 | |
| AA4350 | 73.5 | 2690 | 78.5 | 2873 | |
| N204 | 73.0 | 2663 | 78.0 | 2845 | |
| VIT N 150 | 64.0 | 2515 | 69.0 | 2712 | |
| VIT N 160 | 74.0 | 2635 | 79.0 | 2813 | |
| RL | 80.0 | 2800 | 85.0 | 2975 | |

# Accuracy Loads

## CALIBER: 330 Dakota                                      BULLET: 250 Gr. XFB

| POWDER | START WEIGHT | VELOCITY | MAX WEIGHT | VELOCITY | ACCURACY |
|--------|--------------|----------|------------|----------|----------|
| H414 | 68.0 | 2454 | 73.0 | 2634 | |
| H4350 | 70.0 | 2529 | 75.0 | 2710 | |
| H4831 | 78.0 | 2607 | 83.0 | 2774 | |
| IMR4350 | 70.0 | 2539 | 75.0 | 2720 | |
| IMR4831 | 72.0 | 2553 | 77.0 | 2730 | |
| IMR7828 | 79.0 | 2568 | 84.0 | 2730 | |
| WIN760 | 67.0 | 2439 | 72.0 | 2621 | |
| WIN WMR | 81.0 | 2626 | 86.0 | 2788 | |
| AA4350 | 71.0 | 2522 | 76.0 | 2700 | |
| AA3100 | 77.00 | 2547 | 82.0 | 2712 | |
| N204 | 70.0 | 2472 | 75.0 | 2649 | |
| VIT N 160 | 71.5 | 2477 | 76.5 | 2650 | |
| VIT N 170 | 80.0 | 2478 | 85.0 | 2633 | |
| RL19 | 77.0 | 2622 | 82.0 | 2792 | |

# Accuracy Loads

*Courtesy of: Barnes Bullets*

# DAKOTA ARMS AMMUNITIONS

*Rifle- Barrel: Dakota*
*Barrel Length: 26"*
*Barrel Twist: 1-12*
*Trim Cases to: 2.560"*

*Case: Dakota*
*Primer: CCI 250*
*Velocity Change for each 1"*
*Change in Barrel Length = 20 FPS*

## CALIBER: 375 Dakota      BULLET: 270 Gr.

| POWDER | START WEIGHT | VELOCITY | MAX WEIGHT | VELOCITY |
|---|---|---|---|---|
| IMR 4350 | 80.0 | 2706 | 85 | 2895 |
| H 4350 | 80.0 | 2696 | 85 | 2883 |
| RL 15 | 71 | 2705 | 75 | 2829 |

## CALIBER: 375 Dakota      BULLET: 300 Gr.

| POWDER | START WEIGHT | VELOCITY | MAX WEIGHT | VELOCITY |
|---|---|---|---|---|
| IMR 4350 | 73.0 | 2448 | 78.0 | 2660 |
| H 4350 | 75.0 | 2539 | 78.0 | 2648 |
| IMR 4831 | 75.0 | 2488 | 79.0 | 2641 |
| RL 19 | 81.0 | 2579 | 835 | 2662 |

*Rifle- Barrel: Dakota*
*Barrel Length: 26"*
*Barrel Twist: 1-12*
*Trim Cases to: 2.840"*

*Case: Dakota*
*Primer: CCI 250*
*Velocity Change for each 1"*
*Change in Barrel Length = 15 FPS*

## CALIBER: 416 Dakota      BULLET: 400 Gr.

| POWDER | START WEIGHT | VELOCITY | MAX WEIGHT | VELOCITY |
|---|---|---|---|---|
| IMR4350 | 82.0 | 2274 | 90.0 | 2489 |
| IMR4831 | 85.0 | 2282 | 95.0 | 2527 |
| RL19 | 90.0 | 2310 | 100 | 2558 |
| H4831 | 89.0 | 2333 | 100 | 2556 |

*Rifle- Barrel: Dakota*
*Barrel Length: 26"*
*Barrel Twist: 1-14*
*Trim Cases to: 2.890"*

*Case: Dakota*
*Primer: CCI 250*
*Velocity Change for each 1"*
*Change in Barrel Length = 15 FPS*

## CALIBER: 450 Dakota      BULLET: 400 Gr.

| POWDER | START WEIGHT | VELOCITY | MAX WEIGHT | VELOCITY |
|---|---|---|---|---|
| RL 15 | | | 105 | 2732 |
| IMR4064 | | | 105 | 2763 |
| IMR4350 | 108 | 2479 | 115 | 2650 |

## CALIBER: 450 Dakota      BULLET: 500 Gr.

| POWDER | START WEIGHT | VELOCITY | MAX WEIGHT | VELOCITY |
|---|---|---|---|---|
| H4350 | 105 | 2342 | 110 | 2460 |
| IMR4350 | 104 | 2315 | 110 | 2470 |
| IMR4831 | 110 | 2395 | 112 | 2444 |

# DAKOTA ARMS AMMUNITIONS
## BALLISTIC COMPARISONS

| 7mm Dakota | 140 Gr. | 160 Gr. | |
|---|---|---|---|
| 7mm Dakota | 3400 | 3200 | |
| 280 Rem | 3000 | 2840 | |
| 7 Rem Mag | 3150 | 2950 | |
| 7MM Wea | 3225 | 3100 | |

| 300 Dakota | 165 Gr. | 180 Gr. | 200 Gr. |
|---|---|---|---|
| 300 Dakota | 3250 | 3200 | 3050 |
| 30-06 | 2800 | 2700 | 2600 |
| 300 Win | 3100 | 2960 | 2825 |
| 300 Wea | 3200 | 3120 | 2950 |

| 330 Dakota | 225 Gr. | 250Gr. |
|---|---|---|
| 330 Dakota | 3000 | 2900 |
| 338 Win | 2785 | 2660 |
| 340 Wea | 2950 | 2850 |

| 375 Dakota | 270 Gr. | 300 Gr. |
|---|---|---|
| 375 Dakota | 2850 | 2650 |
| 375 HH | 2690 | 2530 |

| 416 Dakota | 400 Gr. |
|---|---|
| 416 Dakota | 2550 |
| 416 Rig | 2370 |
| 416 Rem | 2400 |

| 450 Dakota | 500 Gr. |
|---|---|
| 450 Dakota | 2550 |
| 458 Win | 2040 |
| 458 Lott | 2300 |

# LAZZERONI BALLISTICS

| CARTRIDGE | BULLET | | VELOCITY in Feet per Second | | | | | | ENERGY In Foot-Pounds | | | | | | PATH OF BULLET Above or below line-of-sight of riflescopes mounted 1.5" above bore | | | | |
|---|---|---|---|---|---|---|---|---|---|---|---|---|---|---|---|---|---|---|---|
| Cartridge | Weight Grains | Bullet Type | Muzzle | 100 Yards | 200 Yards | 300 Yards | 400 Yards | 500 Yards | Muzzle | 100 Yards | 200 Yards | 300 Yards | 400 Yards | 500 Yards | 100 Yards | 200 Yards | 300 Yards | 400 Yards | 500 Yards |
| 6.53 (.257) SCRAMJET™ | 85 | B/T | 3960 | 3652 | 3365 | 3096 | 2844 | 2605 | 2961 | 2517 | 2137 | 1810 | 1526 | 1281 | 1.7 | 2.4 | 0.0 | −6.0 | −16.4 |
| | 100 | PART | 3740 | 3465 | 3208 | 2965 | 2735 | 2516 | 3106 | 2667 | 2285 | 1953 | 1661 | 1406 | 2.1 | 2.7 | 0.0 | −6.7 | −17.9 |
| 7.21 (7mm/.284) FIREHAWK™ | 140 | PART | 3580 | 3349 | 3130 | 2923 | 2724 | 2534 | 3985 | 3488 | 3048 | 2656 | 2308 | 1997 | 2.2 | 2.9 | 0.0 | −7.0 | −18.6 |
| | 160 | A/FR | 3385 | 3167 | 2961 | 2763 | 2574 | 2393 | 4072 | 3565 | 3115 | 2713 | 2354 | 2034 | 2.6 | 3.3 | 0.0 | −7.8 | −20.9 |
| 7.82 (.308) WARBIRD™ | 150 | PART | 3680 | 3432 | 3197 | 2975 | 2764 | 2563 | 4512 | 3923 | 3406 | 2949 | 2546 | 2188 | 2.1 | 2.7 | 0.0 | −6.6 | −17.9 |
| | 180 | PART | 3425 | 3220 | 3026 | 2839 | 2661 | 2489 | 4689 | 4147 | 3661 | 3224 | 2831 | 2477 | 2.5 | 3.2 | 0.0 | −7.5 | −19.8 |
| | 200 | A/FR | 3290 | 3105 | 2928 | 2758 | 2594 | 2435 | 4808 | 4283 | 3808 | 3378 | 2988 | 2635 | 2.7 | 3.4 | 0.0 | −7.9 | −21.1 |
| 8.59 (.338) TITAN™ | 200 | B/T | 3430 | 3211 | 3002 | 2803 | 2613 | 2430 | 5226 | 4579 | 4004 | 3491 | 3033 | 2624 | 2.5 | 3.2 | 0.0 | −7.6 | −20.3 |
| | 225 | PART | 3235 | 3031 | 2836 | 2650 | 2471 | 2299 | 5229 | 4591 | 4021 | 3510 | 3052 | 2642 | 3.0 | 3.6 | 0.0 | −8.6 | −22.9 |
| | 250 | A/FR | 3100 | 2908 | 2725 | 2549 | 2379 | 2216 | 5336 | 4697 | 4123 | 3607 | 3143 | 2726 | 3.3 | 4.0 | 0.0 | −9.3 | −24.8 |
| 10.57 (.416) METEOR™ | 400 | A/FR | 2730 | 2532 | 2342 | 2161 | 1987 | 1823 | 6621 | 5695 | 4874 | 4147 | 3508 | 2951 | 1.9 | 0.0 | −8.3 | −24.0 | −48.7 |

PART = Partition™        A/FR = Swift A-Frame        B/T = Ballistic Tip®

*Note:* This table was calculated by computer using a standard modern technique to predict trajectories and recoil energies from the best available cartridge data. Figures shown are expected to be reasonably accurate; however, the shooter is cautioned that performance will vary because of variations in rifles, ammunition, atmospheric conditions and altitude. Velocities were determined using 27-inch barrels; shorter barrels will reduce velocity by 30 to 85 fps per inch of barrel removed. Trajectories were computed with the line-of-sight 1.5 inches above the bore centerline. *B.C.:* Ballistic Coefficient supplied by the bullet manufacturers. Partition and Ballistic Tip are registered trademarks of Nosler, Inc.

# BALLISTICS INFORMATION

| STANDARD AMMO | MUZZLE VELOCITY | VELOCITY FEET PER SECOND | | | | | ENERGY FOOT - POUNDS | | | | | | TRAJECTORY TABLES | | | | |
|---|---|---|---|---|---|---|---|---|---|---|---|---|---|---|---|---|---|
| RIFLE CALIBER | Muzzle | 100 yds. | 200 yds. | 300 yds. | 400 yds. | 500 yds. | Muzzle | 100 yds. | 200 yds. | 300 yds. | 400 yds. | 500 yds. | 100 yds. | 200 yds. | 300 yds. | 400 yds. | 500 yds. |
| 223 Rem., 53 gr. HP | 3330 | 2882 | 2477 | 2106 | 1710 | 1475 | 1305 | 978 | 722 | 522 | 369 | 356 | +1.7 | -0- | -7.4 | -22.7 | -49.1 |
| 223 Rem., 60 gr. SP | 3150 | 2782 | 2442 | 2127 | 1837 | 1575 | 1322 | 1031 | 795 | 603 | 450 | 331 | +1.6 | -0- | -7.5 | -22.5 | -48.1 |
| 223 Rem., 75 gr. BTHP MATCH | 2790 | 2554 | 2330 | 2119 | 1926 | 1744 | 1296 | 1086 | 904 | 747 | 617 | 506 | 2.37 | -0- | -8.75 | -25.06 | -50.80 |
| 22-250 Rem., 53 gr. HP | 3680 | 3185 | 2743 | 2341 | 1974 | 1646 | 1594 | 1194 | 886 | 645 | 459 | 319 | +1.0 | -0- | -5.7 | -17.8 | -38.8 |
| 22-250 Rem., 60 gr. SP | 3600 | 3195 | 2826 | 2485 | 2169 | 1878 | 1727 | 1360 | 1064 | 823 | 627 | 470 | +1.0 | -0- | -5.4 | -16.3 | -34.8 |
| 220 Swift, 50 gr. SP | 3850 | 3327 | 2862 | 2442 | 2060 | 1716 | 1645 | 1228 | 909 | 662 | 471 | 327 | +0.8 | -0- | -5.1 | -16.1 | -35.3 |
| 220 Swift, 60 gr. HP | 3600 | 3199 | 2824 | 2475 | 2156 | 1868 | 1727 | 1364 | 1063 | 816 | 619 | 465 | +1.0 | -0- | -5.4 | -16.3 | -34.8 |
| 243 Win., 75 gr. HP | 3400 | 2970 | 2578 | 2219 | 1890 | 1595 | 1926 | 1469 | 1107 | 820 | 595 | 425 | +1.2 | -0- | -6.5 | -20.3 | -43.8 |
| 243 Win., 100 gr. BTSP | 2960 | 2728 | 2508 | 2299 | 2099 | 1910 | 1945 | 1653 | 1397 | 1174 | 979 | 810 | +1.6 | -0- | -7.2 | -21.0 | -42.8 |
| 6MM Rem., 100 gr. BTSP | 3100 | 2861 | 2634 | 2419 | 2231 | 2018 | 2134 | 1818 | 1541 | 1300 | 1088 | 904 | +1.3 | -0- | -6.5 | -18.9 | -38.5 |
| 257 Roberts, 117 gr. BTSP | 2780 | 2550 | 2331 | 2122 | 1925 | 1740 | 2007 | 1689 | 1411 | 1170 | 963 | 787 | +1.9 | -0- | -8.3 | -24.4 | -49.9 |
| 25-06 117 gr. BTSP | 2990 | 2749 | 2520 | 2302 | 2096 | 1900 | 2322 | 1962 | 1649 | 1377 | 1141 | 938 | +1.6 | -0- | -7.0 | -20.7 | -42.2 |
| 270 Win, 130 gr. SP | 3060 | 2800 | 2560 | 2330 | 2110 | 1900 | 2700 | 2265 | 1890 | 1565 | 1285 | 1045 | +1.8 | -0- | -7.1 | -20.6 | -42.0 |
| 270 Win, 140 gr. BTSP | 2940 | 2747 | 2562 | 2385 | 2214 | 2050 | 2688 | 2346 | 2041 | 1769 | 1524 | 1307 | +1.6 | -0- | -7.0 | -20.2 | -40.3 |
| 270 Win, 150 gr. SP | 2800 | 2684 | 2478 | 2284 | 2100 | 1927 | 2802 | 2400 | 2046 | 1737 | 1469 | 1237 | +1.7 | -0- | -7.4 | -21.6 | -43.9 |
| 7 x 57 Mau, 139 gr. BTSP | 2700 | 2504 | 2316 | 2137 | 1965 | 1802 | 2251 | 1936 | 1656 | 1410 | 1192 | 1002 | +2.0 | -0- | -8.5 | -24.9 | -50.3 |
| 7MM Rem. Mag., 139 gr. BTSP | 3150 | 2933 | 2727 | 2530 | 2341 | 2160 | 3063 | 2656 | 2296 | 1976 | 1692 | 1440 | +1.2 | -0- | -6.1 | -17.7 | -35.5 |
| 7MM Rem. Mag., 154 gr. SP | 3035 | 2814 | 2604 | 2404 | 2212 | 2029 | 3151 | 2708 | 2319 | 1977 | 1674 | 1408 | +1.3 | -0- | -6.7 | -19.3 | -39.3 |
| 7MM Rem. Mag., 162 gr. BTSP | 2940 | 2757 | 2582 | 2413 | 2251 | 2094 | 3110 | 2735 | 2399 | 2095 | 1823 | 1578 | +1.6 | -0- | -6.7 | -19.7 | -39.3 |
| 7MM Rem. Mag., 175 gr. SP | 2860 | 2650 | 2440 | 2240 | 2060 | 1880 | 3180 | 2720 | 2310 | 1960 | 1640 | 1370 | +2.0 | -0- | -7.9 | -22.7 | -45.8 |
| 7MM Wby. Mag., 154 gr. SP | 3200 | 2971 | 2753 | 2546 | 2348 | 2159 | 3501 | 3017 | 2592 | 2216 | 1885 | 1593 | +1.2 | -0- | -5.8 | -17.0 | -34.5 |
| 7MM Wby. Mag., 175 gr. SP | 2910 | 2709 | 2516 | 2331 | 2154 | 1985 | 3290 | 2850 | 2459 | 2111 | 1803 | 1531 | +1.6 | -0- | -7.1 | -20.6 | -41.7 |
| 30-30 Win., 150 gr. RN | 2390 | 1973 | 1605 | 1303 | 1095 | 974 | 1902 | 1296 | 858 | 565 | 399 | 316 | -0- | -8.2 | -30.0 | | |
| 30-30 Win., 170 gr. FP | 2200 | 1895 | 1619 | 1381 | 1191 | 1064 | 1827 | 1355 | 989 | 720 | 535 | 425 | -0- | -8.9 | -31.1 | | |
| 308 Win., 150 gr. BTSP | 2820 | 2560 | 2315 | 2084 | 1866 | 1644 | 2648 | 2183 | 1785 | 1447 | 1160 | 922 | +2.0 | -0- | -8.5 | -25.2 | -51.8 |
| 308 Win., 165 gr. BTSP | 2700 | 2496 | 2301 | 2115 | 1937 | 1770 | 2670 | 2283 | 1940 | 1639 | 1375 | 1148 | +2.0 | -0- | -8.7 | -25.2 | -51.0 |
| 308 Win., 168 gr. BTHP MATCH | 2700 | 2524 | 2354 | 2191 | 2035 | 1885 | 2720 | 2377 | 2068 | 1791 | 1545 | 1326 | +2.0 | -0- | -8.4 | -23.9 | -48.0 |
| 308 Win., 168 gr. A-MAX MATCH | 2620 | 2446 | 2280 | 2120 | 1972 | 1831 | 2560 | 2232 | 1939 | 1677 | 1450 | 1251 | 2.60 | -0- | -9.23 | -25.65 | -51.92 |
| 308 Win., 180 gr. A-MAX MATCH | 2550 | 2397 | 2249 | 2106 | 1974 | 1848 | 2598 | 2295 | 2021 | 1773 | 1557 | 1364 | 2.71 | -0- | -9.49 | -26.22 | -52.95 |
| 30-06 150 gr. SP | 2910 | 2617 | 2342 | 2083 | 1843 | 1622 | 2820 | 2281 | 1827 | 1445 | 1131 | 876 | +2.1 | -0- | -8.5 | -25.0 | -51.8 |
| 30-06 150 gr. BTSP | 2910 | 2683 | 2467 | 2262 | 2066 | 1880 | 2820 | 2397 | 2027 | 1706 | 1421 | 1177 | +2.0 | -0- | -7.7 | -22.2 | -44.9 |
| 30-06 165 gr. BTSP | 2800 | 2591 | 2392 | 2202 | 2020 | 1848 | 2873 | 2460 | 2097 | 1777 | 1495 | 1252 | +1.8 | -0- | -8.0 | -23.3 | -47.0 |
| 30-06 168 gr. BTHP MATCH | 2790 | 2620 | 2447 | 2280 | 2120 | 1966 | 2925 | 2561 | 2234 | 1940 | 1677 | 1442 | +1.7 | -0- | -7.7 | -22.2 | -44.3 |
| 30-06 180 gr. SP | 2700 | 2469 | 2258 | 2042 | 1846 | 1663 | 2913 | 2436 | 2023 | 1666 | 1362 | 1105 | +2.4 | -0- | -9.3 | -27.0 | -54.9 |
| 300 Wby. Mag., 180 gr. SP | 3120 | 2891 | 2673 | 2466 | 2268 | 2079 | 3890 | 3340 | 2856 | 2430 | 2055 | 1727 | +1.3 | -0- | -6.2 | -18.1 | -36.8 |
| 300 Win. Mag., 150 gr. BTSP | 3275 | 2988 | 2718 | 2464 | 2224 | 1998 | 3573 | 2974 | 2461 | 2023 | 1648 | 1330 | +1.2 | -0- | -6.0 | -17.8 | -36.5 |
| 300 Win. Mag., 165 gr. BTSP | 3100 | 2877 | 2665 | 2462 | 2269 | 2084 | 3522 | 3033 | 2603 | 2221 | 1887 | 1592 | +1.3 | -0- | -6.5 | -18.5 | -37.3 |
| 300 Win. Mag., 180 gr. SP | 2960 | 2745 | 2540 | 2344 | 2157 | 1979 | 3501 | 3011 | 2578 | 2196 | 1859 | 1565 | +1.9 | -0- | -7.3 | -20.9 | -41.9 |
| 300 Win. Mag., 190 gr. BTSP | 2900 | 2711 | 2529 | 2355 | 2187 | 2026 | 3549 | 3101 | 2699 | 2340 | 2018 | 1732 | +1.6 | -0- | -7.1 | -20.4 | -41.0 |
| 303 British, 150 gr. SP | 2685 | 2441 | 2210 | 1992 | 1787 | 1598 | 2401 | 1984 | 1627 | 1321 | 1064 | 500 | +2.2 | -0- | -9.3 | -27.4 | -56.5 |
| 303 British, 174 gr. RN | 2500 | 2181 | 1886 | 1669 | 1387 | 1201 | 2414 | 1837 | 1374 | 1012 | 743 | 557 | +2.9 | -0- | -12.8 | -39.0 | -83.4 |

Barrel length is 24" except for 30-30 Win., which is 20."

| LIGHT MAGNUM | MUZZLE VELOCITY | VELOCITY FEET PER SECOND | | | | | ENERGY FOOT - POUNDS | | | | | | TRAJECTORY TABLES | | | | |
|---|---|---|---|---|---|---|---|---|---|---|---|---|---|---|---|---|---|
| RIFLE CALIBER | Muzzle | 100 yds. | 200 yds. | 300 yds. | 400 yds. | 500 yds. | Muzzle | 100 yds. | 200 yds. | 300 yds. | 400 yds. | 500 yds. | 100 yds. | 200 yds. | 300 yds. | 400 yds. | 500 yds. |
| 6MM Rem., 100 gr. BTSP LM | 3250 | 2997 | 2756 | 2528 | 2311 | 2105 | 2345 | 1995 | 1687 | 1418 | 1186 | 984 | 1.59 | -0- | -6.33 | -18.25 | -36.51 |
| 243 Win., 100 gr. BTSP LM | 3100 | 2839 | 2592 | 2358 | 2138 | 1936 | 2133 | 1790 | 1491 | 1235 | 1014 | 832 | +1.5 | -0- | -6.81 | -19.8 | -40.2 |
| 257 Roberts, 117 gr. BTSP LM | 2940 | 2694 | 2460 | 2240 | 2031 | 1844 | 2245 | 1885 | 1572 | 1303 | 1071 | 883 | +1.7 | -0- | -7.6 | -21.8 | -44.7 |
| 25-06, 117 gr. BTSP LM | 3110 | 2855 | 2613 | 2384 | 2168 | 1968 | 2512 | 2117 | 1774 | 1476 | 1220 | 1006 | 1.81 | -0- | -7.08 | -20.28 | -40.35 |
| 7 x 57 Mau, 139 gr. BTSP LM | 2830 | 2620 | 2450 | 2250 | 2070 | 1910 | 2475 | 2135 | 1835 | 1565 | 1330 | 1115 | +1.8 | -0- | -7.6 | -22.1 | -45.0 |
| 7 x 57MM, 139 gr. SP LM-E | 2950 | 2736 | 2532 | 2337 | 2152 | 1979 | 2686 | 2310 | 1978 | 1686 | 1429 | 1209 | 2.02 | -0- | -7.60 | -21.51 | -42.25 |
| 7MM-08, 139 gr. BTSP LM | 3000 | 2790 | 2590 | 2399 | 2216 | 2041 | 2777 | 2403 | 2071 | 1776 | 1515 | 1285 | +1.5 | -0- | -6.7 | -19.4 | -39.2 |
| 308 Win., 150 gr. SP LM | 2980 | 2703 | 2442 | 2195 | 1964 | 1748 | 2959 | 2433 | 1986 | 1606 | 1285 | 1018 | +1.6 | -0- | -7.5 | -22.2 | -46.0 |
| 308 Win., 165 gr. BTSP LM | 2870 | 2658 | 2456 | 2283 | 2078 | 1903 | 3019 | 2589 | 2211 | 1877 | 1583 | 1327 | +1.7 | -0- | -7.5 | -21.8 | -44.1 |
| 308 Win., 168 gr. BTHP LM MATCH | 2640 | 2630 | 2429 | 2238 | 2056 | 1892 | 3008 | 2579 | 2201 | 1868 | 1577 | 1335 | 1.84 | -0- | -7.83 | -22.38 | -45.23 |
| 30-06 150 gr. SP LM | 3100 | 2815 | 2548 | 2295 | 2058 | 1835 | 3200 | 2639 | 2161 | 1755 | 1410 | 1121 | +1.4 | -0- | -6.8 | -20.3 | -42.0 |
| 30-06 165 gr. BTSP LM | 3015 | 2790 | 2575 | 2370 | 2176 | 1994 | 3330 | 2850 | 2428 | 2058 | 1734 | 1496 | 1.55 | -0- | -6.96 | -20.11 | -39.77 |
| 30-06 180 gr. BTSP LM | 2880 | 2676 | 2480 | 2293 | 2114 | 1943 | 3316 | 2862 | 2459 | 2102 | 1786 | 1509 | +1.7 | -0- | -7.3 | -21.3 | -43.1 |
| 303 British, 150 gr. SP LM | 2830 | 2570 | 2325 | 2094 | 1884 | 1690 | 2667 | 2199 | 1800 | 1461 | 1185 | 952 | +2.0 | -0- | -8.4 | -24.6 | -50.3 |
| 6.5 x 55MM, 129 gr. SP LM | 2770 | 2561 | 2361 | 2171 | 1994 | 1830 | 2197 | 1878 | 1597 | 1350 | 1138 | 959 | 1.98 | -0- | -8.25 | -23.16 | -47.95 |
| 6.5 x 55, 140 gr. SP LM-E | 2740 | 2541 | 2351 | 2169 | 1999 | 1842 | 2333 | 2006 | 1717 | 1463 | 1242 | 1054 | 2.40 | -0- | -8.71 | -24.02 | -49.33 |
| 270 Win., 140 gr. BTSP LM | 3100 | 2894 | 2697 | 2508 | 2327 | 2155 | 2987 | 2604 | 2261 | 1955 | 1684 | 1443 | 1.37 | -0- | -6.32 | -18.30 | -36.61 |
| 300 Win. Mag., 180 gr. BTSP HM | 3100 | 2879 | 2668 | 2467 | 2275 | 2092 | 3840 | 3313 | 2845 | 2431 | 2068 | 1749 | 1.39 | -0- | -6.45 | -18.72 | -37.51 |
| 338 Win. Mag., 225 gr. SP HM | 2920 | 2678 | 2449 | 2232 | 2027 | 1843 | 4259 | 3583 | 2996 | 2489 | 2053 | 1697 | 1.75 | -0- | -7.65 | -22.01 | -45.05 |
| 375 H&H, 270 gr. SP HM | 2870 | 2620 | 2385 | 2162 | 1957 | 1767 | 4937 | 4116 | 3408 | 2802 | 2296 | 1871 | 2.24 | -0- | -8.39 | -23.87 | -48.79 |
| 375 H&H, 300 gr. FMJ-RN HM | 2705 | 2376 | 2072 | 1804 | 1560 | 1355 | 4873 | 3760 | 2861 | 2167 | 1621 | 1222 | 2.73 | -0- | -10.81 | -32.13 | -68.38 |

Barrel length is 24" except for 30-30 Win., which is 20."

| VARMINT EXPRESS™ | MUZZLE VELOCITY | VELOCITY FEET PER SECOND | | | | | ENERGY FOOT - POUNDS | | | | | | TRAJECTORY TABLES | | | | |
|---|---|---|---|---|---|---|---|---|---|---|---|---|---|---|---|---|---|
| RIFLE CALIBER | Muzzle | 100 yds. | 200 yds. | 300 yds. | 400 yds. | 500 yds. | Muzzle | 100 yds. | 200 yds. | 300 yds. | 400 yds. | 500 yds. | 100 yds. | 200 yds. | 300 yds. | 400 yds. | 500 yds. |
| 222 Rem., 40 gr. V-MAX | 3600 | 3117 | 2673 | 2269 | 1911 | 1596 | 1151 | 863 | 634 | 457 | 324 | 226 | 1.07 | -0- | -6.13 | -18.92 | -41.15 |
| 222 Rem., 50 gr. V-MAX | 3140 | 2729 | 2352 | 2008 | 1710 | 1450 | 1094 | 827 | 614 | 448 | 325 | 233 | 1.67 | -0- | -7.88 | -24.39 | 52.94 |
| 223 Rem., 40 gr. V-MAX | 3800 | 3305 | 2845 | 2424 | 2044 | 1715 | 1282 | 970 | 719 | 522 | 371 | 261 | 0.84 | -0- | -5.34 | -16.57 | -36.06 |
| 223 Rem., 55 gr. V-MAX | 3240 | 2859 | 2507 | 2181 | 1891 | 1628 | 1282 | 998 | 767 | 581 | 437 | 324 | 1.44 | -0- | -7.10 | -21.38 | -45.22 |
| 22-250 Rem., 40 gr. V-MAX | 4150 | 3631 | 3147 | 2699 | 2293 | 1932 | 1529 | 1171 | 879 | 647 | 467 | 331 | 0.54 | -0- | -4.15 | -13.30 | -28.90 |
| 22-250 Rem., 50 gr. V-MAX | 3800 | 3349 | 2925 | 2535 | 2178 | 1862 | 1603 | 1245 | 950 | 713 | 527 | 385 | 0.79 | -0- | -5.02 | -15.58 | -33.34 |
| 22-250 Rem., 55 gr. V-MAX | 3680 | 3265 | 2876 | 2517 | 2183 | 1887 | 1654 | 1302 | 1010 | 772 | 582 | 435 | 0.88 | -0- | -5.26 | -16.12 | -34.13 |
| 220 Swift, 40 gr. V-MAX | 4200 | 3678 | 3190 | 2739 | 2329 | 1962 | 1566 | 1201 | 904 | 666 | 482 | 342 | 0.51 | -0- | -4.00 | -12.88 | -27.94 |
| 220 Swift, 50 gr. V-MAX | 3850 | 3396 | 2970 | 2576 | 2215 | 1894 | 1645 | 1280 | 979 | 736 | 545 | 398 | 0.74 | -0- | -4.84 | -15.08 | -32.25 |
| 220 Swift, 55 gr. V-MAX | 3680 | 3265 | 2876 | 2517 | 2183 | 1887 | 1654 | 1302 | 1010 | 772 | 582 | 435 | 0.88 | -0- | -5.26 | -16.12 | -34.13 |
| 243, 58 gr. V-MAX | 3750 | 3319 | 2913 | 2539 | 2195 | 1889 | 1811 | 1418 | 1093 | 830 | 620 | 459 | 1.19 | -0- | -5.46 | -16.44 | -34.49 |

Barrel length is 24."

# PMC – CENTERFIRE RIFLE BALLISTICS

| CALIBER | ITEM NO. | BULLET TYPE | WEIGHT (Grain) | VELOCITY (feet/second) | | | | | |
|---|---|---|---|---|---|---|---|---|---|
| | | | | Muzzle | 100 Yds. | 200 Yds. | 300 Yds. | 400 Yds. | 500 Yds. |
| 222 Rem | 222B | PSP | 50 | 3044 | 2727 | 2354 | 2012 | 1651 | 1269 |
| NEW! 223 Rem | 223VB | HPBT | 55 | 3240 | 2717 | 2250 | 1832 | 1473 | 1196 |
| 223 Rem | 223A | FMJ-BT | 55 | 3195 | 2882 | 2525 | 2169 | 1843 | 1432 |
| 223 Rem | 223B | PSP | 55 | 3112 | 2767 | 2421 | 2100 | 1806 | 1516 |
| 223 Rem | 223C | PSP | 64 | 2775 | 2511 | 2261 | 2026 | 1806 | 1604 |
| NEW! 22-250 Rem | 22-250VB | HPBT | 55 | 3680 | 3104 | 2596 | 2141 | 1737 | 1395 |
| 22-250 Rem | 22-250B | PSP | 55 | 3586 | 3203 | 2852 | 2505 | 2178 | 1877 |
| NEW! 243 Win | 243VA | HPBT | 85 | 3275 | 2922 | 2596 | 2292 | 2009 | 1748 |
| NEW! 243 Win | 243HB | SPBT | 100 | 2960 | 2742 | 2534 | 2335 | 2144 | 1964 |
| 243 Win | 243A | PSP | 80 | 2940 | 2684 | 2444 | 2215 | 1999 | 1796 |
| 243 Win | 243B | PSP | 100 | 2743 | 2507 | 2283 | 2070 | 1869 | 1680 |
| NEW! 6.5 x 55 Swed | 6.5SMA | HPBT | 140 | 2560 | 2398 | 2243 | 2093 | 1949 | 1811 |
| NEW! 6.5 x 55 Swed | 6.5HB | SPBT | 140 | 2560 | 2386 | 2218 | 2057 | 1903 | 1757 |
| 6.5 x 55 Swedish | 6.5MA | FMJ | 144 | 2650 | 2370 | 2110 | 1870 | 1650 | 1450 |
| 6.5 x 55 Swedish | 6.5MB | PSP | 139 | 2850 | 2560 | 2290 | 2030 | 1790 | 1570 |
| 270 Win | 270XA | X | 130 | 2910 | 2717 | 2533 | 2356 | 2186 | 2023 |
| 270 Win | 270XB | X | 150 | 2700 | 2541 | 2387 | 2238 | 2095 | 1957 |
| NEW! 270 Win | 270HA | SPBT | 130 | 3050 | 2830 | 2620 | 2421 | 2229 | 2047 |
| NEW! 270 Win | 270HB | SPBT | 150 | 2850 | 2660 | 2477 | 2302 | 2134 | 1973 |
| 270 Win | 270A | PSP | 130 | 2816 | 2593 | 2381 | 2179 | 1987 | 1805 |
| 270 Win | 270B | PSP | 150 | 2547 | 2368 | 2197 | 2032 | 1875 | 1727 |
| 7mm Mauser | 7MA | PSP | 140 | 2660 | 2450 | 2260 | 2070 | 1890 | 1730 |
| 7mm Mauser | 7MB | SP | 175 | 2440 | 2140 | 1860 | 1600 | 1380 | 1200 |
| 7mm Rem Mag | 7XA | X | 140 | 3000 | 2808 | 2624 | 2448 | 2279 | 2116 |
| 7mm Rem Mag | 7XB | X | 160 | 2800 | 2639 | 2484 | 2334 | 2189 | 2049 |
| NEW! 7mm Rem Mag | 7HA | SPBT | 140 | 3125 | 2891 | 2669 | 2457 | 2255 | 2063 |
| NEW! 7mm Rem Mag | 7HB | SPBT | 160 | 2900 | 2696 | 2501 | 2314 | 2135 | 1965 |
| 7mm Rem Mag | 7A | PSP | 140 | 3099 | 2878 | 2668 | 2469 | 2279 | 2097 |
| 7mm Rem Mag | 7B | PSP | 160 | 2914 | 2748 | 2586 | 2428 | 2276 | 2130 |
| 7mm Rem Mag | 7C | PSP | 175 | 2860 | 2645 | 2442 | 2244 | 2057 | 1879 |
| 7.62 x 39 | 7.62A | FMJ | 123 | 2350 | 2072 | 1817 | 1583 | 1368 | 1171 |
| 7.62 x 39 | 7.62B | PSP | 125 | 2320 | 2046 | 1794 | 1563 | 1350 | 1156 |

**ABBREVIATIONS:** **X–** X-Bullet    **SFHP–** Starfire Hollow Point    **SP–** Soft Point    **PSP–** Pointed Soft Point    **FNSP–** Flat Nose Soft Point    **FMJ–** Full Metal Jacket

This Ballistics Table was calculated by using current data for each load. Velocity figures are from test barrels; user velocities may vary from those listed. The data in the table represents the approximate behavior of each loading under the following conditions: 59°F., barometric pressure of 29.52 inches, sea level altitude.

| ENERGY (foot/pounds) | | | | | | Bullet Path (inches) | | | | | |
|---|---|---|---|---|---|---|---|---|---|---|---|
| Muzzle | 100 Yds. | 200 Yds. | 300 Yds. | 400 Yds. | 500 Yds. | Muzzle | 100 Yds. | 200 Yds. | 300 Yds. | 400 Yds. | 500 Yds. |
| 1131 | 908 | 677 | 494 | 333 | 197 | -1.50 | +1.62 | 0.00 | -7.93 | -24.54 | -54.33 |
| 1282 | 901 | 618 | 410 | 265 | 175 | -1.50 | +1.65 | 0.00 | -8.61 | -27.67 | -62.20 |
| 1246 | 1014 | 779 | 574 | 415 | 250 | -1.50 | +1.36 | 0.00 | -6.85 | -21.13 | -46.03 |
| 1182 | 935 | 715 | 539 | 398 | 281 | -1.50 | +1.54 | 0.00 | -7.49 | -22.91 | -49.12 |
| 1094 | 896 | 726 | 583 | 464 | 366 | -1.50 | +2.01 | 0.00 | -8.82 | -26.11 | -54.08 |
| 1654 | 1176 | 823 | 560 | 368 | 238 | -1.50 | +1.08 | 0.00 | -6.30 | -20.20 | -45.76 |
| 1570 | 1253 | 993 | 766 | 579 | 430 | -1.50 | +0.95 | 0.00 | -5.24 | -16.05 | -34.21 |
| 2024 | 1611 | 1272 | 991 | 761 | 577 | -1.50 | +1.31 | 0.00 | -6.51 | -19.66 | -41.41 |
| 1945 | 1669 | 1425 | 1210 | 1021 | 856 | -1.50 | +1.61 | 0.00 | -7.03 | -20.46 | -41.42 |
| 1535 | 1280 | 1060 | 871 | 709 | 573 | -1.50 | +1.66 | 0.00 | -7.48 | -22.06 | -45.34 |
| 1670 | 1395 | 1157 | 951 | 776 | 626 | -1.50 | +2.02 | 0.00 | -8.69 | -25.50 | -52.26 |
| 2037 | 1788 | 1563 | 1361 | 1181 | 1020 | -1.50 | +2.29 | 0.00 | -9.19 | -26.35 | -52.74 |
| 2037 | 1769 | 1529 | 1315 | 1126 | 960 | -1.50 | +2.31 | 0.00 | -9.42 | -27.09 | -54.25 |
| 2425 | 1950 | 1550 | 1215 | 945 | 730 | -1.50 | +2.70 | 0.00 | -10.50 | -30.90 | -64.00 |
| 2515 | 2025 | 1615 | 1270 | 985 | 760 | -1.50 | +2.20 | 0.00 | -8.90 | -26.30 | -54.50 |
| 2444 | 2131 | 1852 | 1602 | 1379 | 1181 | -1.50 | +1.64 | 0.00 | -7.08 | -20.40 | -41.06 |
| 2428 | 2150 | 1897 | 1668 | 1461 | 1275 | -1.50 | +1.97 | 0.00 | -8.07 | -23.08 | -46.04 |
| 2685 | 2312 | 1982 | 1691 | 1435 | 1209 | -1.50 | +1.46 | 0.00 | -6.54 | -19.02 | -38.52 |
| 2705 | 2355 | 2043 | 1765 | 1516 | 1296 | -1.50 | +1.74 | 0.00 | -7.40 | -21.41 | -43.02 |
| 2288 | 1941 | 1636 | 1370 | 1139 | 941 | -1.50 | +1.83 | 0.00 | -7.96 | -23.24 | -47.33 |
| 2160 | 1868 | 1607 | 1375 | 1171 | 993 | -1.50 | +2.35 | 0.00 | -9.54 | -27.49 | -55.32 |
| 2200 | 1865 | 1585 | 1330 | 1110 | 930 | -1.50 | +2.40 | 0.00 | -9.60 | -27.30 | -53.50 |
| 2315 | 1775 | 1340 | 1000 | 740 | 565 | -1.50 | +1.50 | -3.60 | -18.60 | -46.80 | -92.80 |
| 2797 | 2451 | 2141 | 1863 | 1614 | 1391 | -1.50 | +1.49 | 0.00 | -6.56 | -18.93 | -37.99 |
| 2785 | 2474 | 2192 | 1935 | 1703 | 1492 | -1.50 | +1.78 | 0.00 | -7.41 | -21.20 | -42.33 |
| 3035 | 2597 | 2213 | 1877 | 1580 | 1322 | -1.50 | +1.35 | 0.00 | -6.29 | -18.35 | -37.23 |
| 2987 | 2582 | 2222 | 1903 | 1620 | 1371 | -1.50 | +1.68 | 0.00 | -7.22 | -20.98 | -42.33 |
| 2984 | 2574 | 2212 | 1895 | 1614 | 1366 | -1.50 | +1.35 | 0.00 | -6.22 | -18.14 | -36.75 |
| 3016 | 2682 | 2375 | 2095 | 1840 | 1611 | -1.50 | +1.55 | 0.00 | -6.74 | -19.35 | -38.67 |
| 3178 | 2718 | 2313 | 1956 | 1644 | 1372 | -1.50 | +2.00 | 0.00 | -7.90 | -22.70 | -45.80 |
| 1495 | 1162 | 894 | 678 | 507 | 371 | +0.60 | 0.00 | -5.00 | -26.40 | -67.80 | -135.00 |
| 1493 | 1161 | 893 | 678 | 505 | 371 | +0.70 | 0.00 | -5.20 | -27.50 | -70.60 | -140.00 |

**FMJ-BT**– Full Metal Jacket - Boat Tail

# PMC – CENTERFIRE RIFLE BALLISTICS

| CALIBER | ITEM NO. | BULLET TYPE | WEIGHT (Grain) | VELOCITY (feet/second) | | | | |
|---|---|---|---|---|---|---|---|---|
| | | | | Muzzle | 50 Yds. | 100 Yds. | 150 Yds. | 200 Yds. |
| 30-30 Win | C3030SFA | SFHP | 150 | 2100 | 1930 | 1769 | 1618 | 1478 |
| 30-30 Win | 3030A | FNSP | 150 | 2159 | 1984 | 1819 | 1669 | 1554 |
| 30-30 Win | 3030B | FNSP | 170 | 1965 | 1817 | 1680 | 1577 | 1480 |
| 30 Carbine | 30A | FMJ | 110 | 1927 | 1730 | 1548 | 1386 | 1248 |

| CALIBER | ITEM NO. | BULLET TYPE | WEIGHT (Grain) | VELOCITY (feet/second) | | | | |
|---|---|---|---|---|---|---|---|---|
| | | | | Muzzle | 100 Yds. | 200 Yds. | 300 Yds. | 400 Yds. | 500 Yds. |
| 308 Win | 308XA | X | 150 | 2700 | 2504 | 2316 | 2135 | 1964 | 1801 |
| 308 Win | 308XB | X | 165 | 2600 | 2425 | 2256 | 2095 | 1940 | 1793 |
| NEW! 308 Win | 308HA | SPBT | 150 | 2820 | 2581 | 2354 | 2139 | 1935 | 1744 |
| NEW! 308 Win | 308HC | SPBT | 180 | 2620 | 2446 | 2278 | 2117 | 1962 | 1815 |
| NEW! 308 Win | 308SMB | HPBT | 168 | 2650 | 2460 | 2278 | 2103 | 1936 | 1778 |
| 308 Win (7.62 NATO) | 308B | FMJ-BT | 147 | 2751 | 2473 | 2257 | 2052 | 1859 | 1664 |
| 308 Win | 308A | PSP | 150 | 2643 | 2417 | 2203 | 1999 | 1807 | 1632 |
| 308 Win | 308C | PSP | 180 | 2410 | 2223 | 2044 | 1874 | 1714 | 1561 |
| 30-06 Sprg | 3006XA | X | 150 | 2750 | 2552 | 2361 | 2179 | 2005 | 1840 |
| 30-06 Sprg | 3006XB | X | 165 | 2750 | 2569 | 2395 | 2228 | 2067 | 1914 |
| 30-06 Sprg | 3006XC | X | 180 | 2650 | 2487 | 2331 | 2179 | 2034 | 1894 |
| NEW! 30-06 Sprg | 3006HA | SPBT | 150 | 2900 | 2657 | 2427 | 2208 | 2000 | 1805 |
| NEW! 30-06 Sprg | 306HC | SPBT | 180 | 2700 | 2523 | 2352 | 2188 | 2030 | 1879 |
| 30-06 Sprg | 3006A | PSP | 150 | 2773 | 2542 | 2322 | 2113 | 1916 | 1730 |
| 30-06 Sprg | 3006B | PSP | 180 | 2550 | 2357 | 2172 | 1996 | 1829 | 1671 |
| 30 M2 | 3006C | FMJ | 150 | 2773 | 2542 | 2322 | 2113 | 1916 | 1730 |
| 300 Win Mag | 300XA | X | 150 | 3135 | 2918 | 2712 | 2515 | 2327 | 2146 |
| 300 Win Mag | 300XC | X | 180 | 2910 | 2738 | 2572 | 2412 | 2258 | 2109 |
| NEW! 300 Win Mag | 300HA | SPBT | 150 | 3250 | 2987 | 2739 | 2504 | 2281 | 2070 |
| NEW! 300 Win Mag | 300HC | SPBT | 180 | 2900 | 2714 | 2536 | 2365 | 2200 | 2042 |
| 300 Win Mag | 300A | PSP | 150 | 3150 | 2902 | 2665 | 2438 | 2222 | 2017 |
| 300 Win Mag | 300B | PSP | 180 | 2853 | 2643 | 2446 | 2258 | 2077 | 1906 |
| NEW! 303 British | 303HB | SPBT | 180 | 2450 | 2276 | 2110 | 1951 | 1799 | 1656 |
| 8mm Mauser | 8MA | PSP | 170 | 2360 | 1969 | 1622 | 1333 | 1123 | 997 |
| 338 Win Mag | 338XA | X | 225 | 2780 | 2619 | 2464 | 2313 | 2168 | 2028 |
| 375 H&H Mag | 375XA | X | 270 | 2690 | 2528 | 2372 | 2221 | 2076 | 1936 |
| 375 H&H Mag | 375XB | X | 300 | 2530 | 2389 | 2252 | 2120 | 1993 | 1870 |

**ABBREVIATIONS:** **X**– X-Bullet    **SFHP–** Starfire Hollow Point    **SP–** Soft Point    **PSP–** Pointed Soft Point    **FNSP–** Flat Nose Soft Point    **FMJ–** Full Metal Jacket

This Ballistics Table was calculated by using current data for each load. Velocity figures are from test barrels; user velocities may vary from those listed. The data in the table represents the approximate behavior of each loading under the following conditions: 59°F., barometric pressure of 29.52 inches, sea level altitude.

# PMC – CENTERFIRE RIFLE BALLISTICS

| ENERGY (foot/pounds) | | | | | Bullet Path (inches) | | | | |
|---|---|---|---|---|---|---|---|---|---|
| Muzzle | 50 Yds. | 100 Yds. | 150 Yds. | 200 Yds. | Muzzle | 50 Yds. | 100 Yds. | 150 Yds. | 200 Yds. |
| 1469 | 1240 | 1042 | 871 | 728 | -0.50 | +0.92 | 0.00 | -3.67 | -10.75 |
| 1552 | 1311 | 1102 | 928 | 804 | -1.50 | +0.35 | 0.00 | -2.97 | -9.04 |
| 1457 | 1246 | 1065 | 939 | 827 | -1.50 | +0.56 | 0.00 | -3.60 | -10.69 |
| 906 | 731 | 585 | 469 | 380 | -0.50 | +1.20 | 0.00 | -4.85 | -14.24 |

| ENERGY (foot/pounds) | | | | | | Bullet Path (inches) | | | | | |
|---|---|---|---|---|---|---|---|---|---|---|---|
| Muzzle | 100 Yds. | 200 Yds. | 300 Yds. | 400 Yds. | 500 Yds. | Muzzle | 100 Yds. | 200 Yds. | 300 Yds. | 400 Yds. | 500 Yds. |
| 2428 | 2087 | 1786 | 1518 | 1284 | 1080 | -1.50 | +2.03 | 0.00 | -8.56 | -24.73 | -49.99 |
| 2476 | 2154 | 1865 | 1608 | 1379 | 1177 | -1.50 | +2.23 | 0.00 | -9.04 | -26.04 | -52.38 |
| 2648 | 2218 | 1846 | 1523 | 1247 | 1013 | -1.50 | +1.89 | 0.00 | -8.18 | -23.96 | -49.00 |
| 2743 | 2391 | 2074 | 1790 | 1538 | 1316 | -1.50 | +2.17 | 0.00 | -8.89 | -25.54 | -51.32 |
| 2619 | 2257 | 1935 | 1649 | 1399 | 1179 | -1.50 | +2.14 | 0.00 | -8.85 | -25.59 | -51.64 |
| 2428 | 2037 | 1697 | 1403 | 1150 | 922 | -1.50 | +2.30 | 0.00 | -9.30 | -27.30 | -57.90 |
| 2326 | 1946 | 1615 | 1331 | 1088 | 887 | -1.50 | +2.23 | 0.00 | -9.39 | -27.49 | -56.22 |
| 2320 | 1975 | 1670 | 1404 | 1174 | 973 | -1.50 | +2.77 | 0.00 | -11.08 | -32.04 | -64.84 |
| 2518 | 2168 | 1857 | 1582 | 1339 | 1127 | -1.50 | +1.95 | 0.00 | -8.17 | -23.73 | -47.95 |
| 2770 | 2418 | 2101 | 1818 | 1565 | 1342 | -1.50 | +1.91 | 0.00 | -7.97 | -22.98 | -46.14 |
| 2806 | 2472 | 2171 | 1898 | 1652 | 1433 | -1.50 | +2.07 | 0.00 | -8.48 | -24.34 | -48.62 |
| 2801 | 2351 | 1961 | 1623 | 1332 | 1085 | -1.50 | +1.74 | 0.00 | -7.66 | -22.51 | -46.04 |
| 2913 | 2543 | 2210 | 1913 | 1646 | 1411 | -1.50 | +2.00 | 0.00 | -8.28 | -23.89 | -47.94 |
| 2560 | 2152 | 1796 | 1487 | 1222 | 997 | -1.50 | +1.94 | 0.00 | -8.39 | -24.56 | -50.21 |
| 2598 | 2220 | 1886 | 1592 | 1336 | 1115 | -1.50 | +2.38 | 0.00 | -9.74 | 28.20 | -57.05 |
| 2560 | 2152 | 1796 | 1487 | 1222 | 997 | -1.50 | +1.94 | 0.00 | -8.39 | -24.56 | -50.21 |
| 3273 | 2836 | 2449 | 2107 | 1803 | 1534 | -1.50 | +1.30 | 0.00 | -6.13 | -17.71 | -35.74 |
| 3384 | 2995 | 2644 | 2325 | 2037 | 1778 | -1.50 | +1.61 | 0.00 | -6.89 | -19.77 | -39.43 |
| 3517 | 2970 | 2498 | 2088 | 1733 | 1426 | -1.50 | +1.20 | 0.00 | -5.96 | -17.41 | -35.55 |
| 3361 | 2944 | 2571 | 2235 | 1935 | 1666 | -1.50 | +1.65 | 0.00 | -7.08 | -20.34 | -40.85 |
| 3304 | 2804 | 2364 | 1979 | 1644 | 1355 | -1.50 | +1.31 | 0.00 | -6.21 | -18.26 | -37.36 |
| 3252 | 2792 | 2391 | 2037 | 1724 | 1451 | -1.50 | +1.73 | 0.00 | -7.53 | -21.89 | -44.29 |
| 2399 | 2071 | 1779 | 1521 | 1294 | 1096 | -1.50 | +2.61 | 0.00 | -10.44 | -30.14 | -60.15 |
| 2102 | 1463 | 993 | 671 | 476 | 375 | -1.50 | +1.80 | -4.50 | -24.30 | -63.80 | -130.70 |
| 3860 | 3426 | 3032 | 2673 | 2348 | 2054 | -1.50 | +1.81 | 0.00 | -7.55 | -21.61 | -43.11 |
| 4337 | 3831 | 3371 | 2957 | 2582 | 2247 | -1.50 | +1.99 | 0.00 | -8.15 | -23.39 | -46.70 |
| 4263 | 3801 | 3378 | 2994 | 2644 | 2329 | -1.50 | +2.31 | 0.00 | -9.15 | -26.09 | -51.79 |

**FMJ-BT**– Full Metal Jacket - Boat Tail

These tables were calculated by computer. A standard scientific technique was used to predict trajectories from the best available data for each round. Trajectories shown typify the ammunition's performance at sea level, but note that they may vary due to atmospheric conditions and the equipment.

All velocity and energy figures in these charts have been derived by using test barrels of indicated lengths.

Ballistics shown are for 24" barrels, except those for .30 carbine and .44 Remington Magnum, which are for 20" barrels. These barrel lengths were chosen as representative, as it's impractical to show performance figures for all barrel lengths.

The muzzle velocities, muzzle energies and trajectory data in these tables represent the approximate performance expected of each specified loading. Differences in barrel lengths, internal firearm dimensions, temperature, and test procedure can produce actual velocities that vary from those given here.

### Centerfire Rifle Velocity vs. Barrel Length

| Muzzle Velocity Range (ft./sec.) | Approx. Change in Muzzle Velocity per 1" Change in Barrel Length (ft./sec.) |
|---|---|
| 2000-2500 | 10 |
| 2500-3000 | 20 |
| 3000-3500 | 30 |
| 3500-4000 | 40 |

1. Determine how much shorter, or longer, your barrel is than the test barrel.
2. In the left column of the above table, select the muzzle-velocity class of your cartridge.
3. To the right of that class, read the approximate change in velocity per inch of barrel length.
4. Multiply this number by the difference in the length of your barrel from that of the test barrel.
5. If your barrel is shorter than the test barrel, subtract this figure from the muzzle velocity shown for your cartridge.
6. If your barrel is longer, add this figure to the muzzle velocity shown.

The trajectory figures shown in these ballistic tables are the rise or drop, in inches, of the bullet from a direct line of sight at selected yardage. Sighting-in distances have been set at 100 to 250 yards.

The line of sight used is 1½" above the axis of the bore. Since the rise or drop figures shown at the stated yardage are points of impact, you must hold low for positive figures, high for negative figures.

Many shooters who use the same cartridge often find it helpful to commit the rise and drop figures for that cartridge to memory, or tape them to their rifle stock. That way, they know instantly the right "hold" as soon as they estimate the target's range.

Specifications are nominal. Ballistics figures established in test barrels. Individual rifles may vary from test-barrel specifications.

\* Inches above or below line of sight. Hold low for positive numbers, high for negative numbers.

† 280 Rem. and 7mm Express® Rem. are interchangeable.

‡ Interchangeable in 244 Rem.

[1] Bullet does not rise more than 1" above line of sight from muzzle to sighting-in range.

[2] Bullet does not rise more than 3" above line of sight from muzzle to sighting-in range.

NOTE: "zero" indicates yardage at which rifle was sighted in.

## Centerfire Rifle Ballistics Tables

| Caliber | Index/EDI Number | Wt. (grs.) | Bullet Style | Primer No. | Muzzle | 100 yds. | 200 yds. | 300 yds. | 400 yds. | 500 yds. |
|---|---|---|---|---|---|---|---|---|---|---|
| .17 Remington | R17REM | 25 | Hollow Point Power-Lokt* | 7½ | 4040 | 3284 | 2644 | 2086 | 1606 | 1235 |
| .22 Hornet | R22HN1 | 45 | Pointed Soft Point | 6½ | 2690 | 2042 | 1502 | 1128 | 948 | 840 |
| | R22HN2 | 45 | Hollow Point | 6½ | 2690 | 2042 | 1502 | 1128 | 948 | 840 |
| .220 Swift | R220S1 | 50 | Pointed Soft Point | 9½ | 3780 | 3158 | 2617 | 2135 | 1710 | 1357 |
| | PRV220SA | 50 | V-Max™, Boat Tail | 9½ | 3780 | 3321 | 2908 | 2532 | 2185 | 1866 |
| .222 Remington | R222R1 | 50 | Pointed Soft Point | 7½ | 3140 | 2602 | 2123 | 1700 | 1350 | 1107 |
| | R222R3 | 50 | Hollow Point Power-Lokt* | 7½ | 3140 | 2635 | 2182 | 1777 | 1432 | 1172 |
| | PRV222RA | 50 | V-Max™, Boat Tail | 7½ | 3140 | 2744 | 2380 | 2045 | 1740 | 1471 |
| .223 Remington | PRV223RA | 50 | V-Max™, Boat Tail | 7½ | 3300 | 2889 | 2514 | 2168 | 1851 | 1568 |
| | R223R1 | 55 | Pointed Soft Point | 7½ | 3240 | 2747 | 2304 | 1905 | 1554 | 1270 |
| | R223R2 | 55 | Hollow Point Power-Lokt* | 7½ | 3240 | 2773 | 2352 | 1969 | 1627 | 1341 |
| | R223R3 | 55 | Metal Case | 7½ | 3240 | 2759 | 2326 | 1933 | 1587 | 1301 |
| | R223R6 | 62 | Hollow Point Match | 7½ | 3025 | 2572 | 2162 | 1792 | 1471 | 1217 |
| .22-250 Remington | R22501 | 55 | Pointed Soft Point | 9½ | 3680 | 3137 | 2656 | 2222 | 1832 | 1493 |
| | R22502 | 55 | Hollow Point Power-Lokt* | 9½ | 3680 | 3209 | 2785 | 2400 | 2046 | 1725 |
| | PRV2250A | 50 | V-Max™, Boat Tail | 9½ | 3725 | 3272 | 2864 | 2491 | 2147 | 1832 |
| .243 Win. | R243W1 | 80 | Pointed Soft Point | 9½ | 3350 | 2955 | 2593 | 2259 | 1951 | 1670 |
| | R243W2 | 80 | Hollow Point Power-Lokt* | 9½ | 3350 | 2955 | 2593 | 2259 | 1951 | 1670 |
| | R243W3 | 100 | Pointed Soft Point Core-Lokt* | 9½ | 2960 | 2697 | 2449 | 2215 | 1993 | 1786 |
| | PRV243WC ★ | 75 | V-Max™, Boat Tail | 9½ | 3375 | 3065 | 2775 | 2504 | 2248 | 2008 |
| | PRB243WA ★ | 100 | Pointed Soft Point, Boat Tail | 9½ | 2960 | 2720 | 2492 | 2275 | 2069 | 1875 |
| | PRT243WC ★ | 90 | Pointed Soft Point, Ballistic Tip* | 9½ | 3120 | 2871 | 2635 | 2411 | 2199 | 1997 |
| 6mm Remington | R6MM4 | 100 | Pointed Soft Point Core-Lokt* | 9½ | 3100 | 2829 | 2573 | 2332 | 2104 | 1889 |
| | PRV6MMRC ★ | 75 | V-Max™, Boat Tail | 9½ | 3400 | 3088 | 2797 | 2524 | 2267 | 2026 |
| | PRB6MMRA ★ | 100 | Pointed Soft Point, Boat Tail | 9½ | 3100 | 2852 | 2617 | 2394 | 2183 | 1982 |
| .25-20 Win. | R25202 | 86 | Soft Point | 6½ | 1460 | 1194 | 1030 | 931 | 858 | 797 |
| .250 Savage | R250SV | 100 | Pointed Soft Point | 9½ | 2820 | 2504 | 2210 | 1936 | 1684 | 1461 |
| .257 Roberts | R257 | 117 | Soft Point Core-Lokt* | 9½ | 2650 | 2291 | 1961 | 1663 | 1404 | 1199 |
| .25-06 Remington | R25062 | 100 | Pointed Soft Point Core-Lokt* | 9½ | 3230 | 2893 | 2580 | 2287 | 2014 | 1762 |
| | R25063 | 120 | Pointed Soft Point Core-Lokt* | 9½ | 2990 | 2730 | 2484 | 2252 | 2032 | 1825 |
| 6.5x55 Swedish | R65SWE1 | 140 | Pointed Soft Point Core-Lokt* | 9½ | 2550 | 2353 | 2164 | 1984 | 1814 | 1654 |
| .260 Remington | R260R1 | 140 | Pointed Soft Point Core-Lokt* | 9½ | 2750 | 2544 | 2347 | 2158 | 1979 | 1812 |
| | PRT260RC ★ | 140 | Pointed Soft Point, Ballistic Tip | 9½ | 2890 | 2688 | 2494 | 2309 | 2131 | 1962 |
| .264 Win. Mag. | R264W2 | 140 | Pointed Soft Point Core-Lokt* | 9½ M | 3030 | 2782 | 2548 | 2326 | 2114 | 1914 |
| .270 Win. | R270W1 | 100 | Pointed Soft Point | 9½ | 3320 | 2924 | 2561 | 2225 | 1916 | 1636 |
| | R270W2 | 130 | Pointed Soft Point Core-Lokt* | 9½ | 3060 | 2776 | 2510 | 2259 | 2022 | 1801 |
| | R270W3 | 130 | Bronze Point™ | 9½ | 3060 | 2802 | 2559 | 2329 | 2110 | 1904 |
| | R270W4 | 150 | Soft Point Core-Lokt* | 9½ | 2850 | 2504 | 2183 | 1886 | 1618 | 1385 |
| | RS270WA | 140 | Swift A-Frame™ PSP | 9½ | 2925 | 2652 | 2394 | 2152 | 1923 | 1711 |
| | PRB270WA ★ | 140 | Pointed Soft Point, Boat Tail | 9½ | 2960 | 2749 | 2548 | 2355 | 2171 | 1995 |
| | PRT270WB ★ | 140 | Pointed Soft Point, Ballistic Tip | 9½ | 2960 | 2754 | 2557 | 2366 | 2187 | 2014 |
| 7mm Mauser (7 x 57) | R7MSR1 | 140 | Pointed Soft Point Core-Lokt* | 9½ | 2660 | 2435 | 2221 | 2018 | 1827 | 1648 |
| 7mm-08 Remington | R7M081 | 140 | Pointed Soft Point Core-Lokt* | 9½ | 2860 | 2625 | 2402 | 2189 | 1988 | 1798 |
| | R7M083 | 120 | Hollow Point | 9½ | 3000 | 2725 | 2467 | 2223 | 1992 | 1778 |
| | PRB7M08RA ★ | 140 | Pointed Soft Point, Boat Tail | 9½ | 2860 | 2656 | 2460 | 2273 | 2094 | 1923 |
| | PRT7M08RA ★ | 140 | Pointed Soft Point, Ballistic Tip | 9½ | 2860 | 2670 | 2488 | 2313 | 2145 | 1984 |
| .280 Remington | R280R3 † | 140 | Pointed Soft Point Core-Lokt* | 9½ | 3000 | 2758 | 2528 | 2309 | 2102 | 1905 |
| | R280R1 † | 150 | Pointed Soft Point Core-Lokt* | 9½ | 2890 | 2624 | 2373 | 2135 | 1912 | 1705 |
| | R280R2 † | 165 | Soft Point Core-Lokt* | 9½ | 2820 | 2510 | 2220 | 1950 | 1701 | 1479 |
| | PRB280RA ★ | 140 | Pointed Soft Point, Boat Tail | 9½ | 3000 | 2789 | 2588 | 2395 | 2211 | 2035 |
| | PRT280RA ★ | 140 | Pointed Soft Point, Ballistic Tip | 9½ | 3000 | 2804 | 2616 | 2436 | 2263 | 2097 |
| 7mm Remington Mag. | R7MM2 | 150 | Pointed Soft Point Core-Lokt* | 9½ M | 3110 | 2830 | 2568 | 2320 | 2085 | 1866 |
| | R7MM3 | 175 | Pointed Soft Point Core-Lokt* | 9½ M | 2860 | 2645 | 2440 | 2244 | 2057 | 1879 |
| | R7MM4 | 140 | Pointed Soft Point Core-Lokt* | 9½ M | 3175 | 2923 | 2684 | 2458 | 2243 | 2039 |
| | RS7MMA | 160 | Swift A-Frame™ PSP | 9½ M | 2900 | 2659 | 2430 | 2212 | 2008 | 1812 |
| | PRB7MMRA ★ | 140 | Pointed Soft Point, Boat Tail | 9½ M | 3175 | 2956 | 2747 | 2547 | 2356 | 2174 |
| | PRT7MMC ★ | 150 | Pointed Soft Point, Ballistic Tip | 9½ M | 3110 | 2912 | 2723 | 2542 | 2367 | 2200 |
| 7mm STW | R7MSTW1 | 140 | Pointed Soft Point Core-Lokt* | 9½ M | 3325 | 3064 | 2818 | 2585 | 2364 | 2153 |
| | RS7MSTWA ★ | 140 | Swift A-Frame™ PSP | 9½ M | 3325 | 3020 | 2735 | 2467 | 2215 | 1978 |
| .30 Carbine | R30CAR | 110 | Soft Point | 6½ | 1990 | 1567 | 1236 | 1035 | 923 | 842 |
| .30-30 Win. Accelerator® | R3030A | 55 | Soft Point | 9½ | 3400 | 2693 | 2085 | 1570 | 1187 | 986 |
| .30-30 Win. | R30301 | 150 | Soft Point Core-Lokt* | 9½ | 2390 | 1973 | 1605 | 1303 | 1095 | 974 |
| | R30302 | 170 | Soft Point Core-Lokt* | 9½ | 2200 | 1895 | 1619 | 1381 | 1191 | 1061 |
| | R30303 | 170 | Hollow Point Core-Lokt* | 9½ | 2200 | 1895 | 1619 | 1381 | 1191 | 1061 |
| .300 Savage | R30SV3 | 180 | Soft Point Core-Lokt* | 9½ | 2350 | 2025 | 1728 | 1467 | 1252 | 1098 |
| | R30SV2 | 150 | Pointed Soft Point Core-Lokt* | 9½ | 2630 | 2354 | 2095 | 1853 | 1631 | 1432 |

★ NEW FOR 1998

# REMINGTON BALLISTICS

■ = Premier® Safari Grade   ■ = Premier® Varmint   □ = Premier® Ballistic Tip®   □ = Premier® Boat Tail

| Muzzle | Energy (ft.-lbs.) 100 yds. | 200 yds. | 300 yds. | 400 yds. | 500 yds. | Short-range[1] Trajectory* 50 yds. | 100 yds. | 150 yds. | 200 yds. | 250 yds. | 300 yds. | Long-range[2] Trajectory* 100 yds. | 150 yds. | 200 yds. | 250 yds. | 300 yds. | 400 yds. | 500 yds. | Barrel Length |
|---|---|---|---|---|---|---|---|---|---|---|---|---|---|---|---|---|---|---|---|
| 906 | 599 | 388 | 242 | 143 | 85 | -0.3 | 0.3 | zero | -1.3 | -3.8 | -7.8 | 1.8 | 2.3 | 1.8 | zero | -3.3 | -16.6 | -43.6 | 24" |
| 723 | 417 | 225 | 127 | 90 | 70 | -0.1 | zero | -2.1 | -7.1 | -16.0 | -30.0 | 1.4 | zero | -4.3 | -12.4 | -25.8 | -74.2 | -162.0 | |
| 723 | 417 | 225 | 127 | 90 | 70 | -0.1 | zero | -2.1 | -7.1 | -16.0 | -30.0 | 1.4 | zero | -4.3 | -12.4 | -25.8 | -74.2 | -162.0 | |
| 1586 | 1107 | 760 | 506 | 325 | 204 | -0.2 | 0.3 | zero | -1.4 | -4.0 | -8.2 | 0.4 | 1.0 | zero | -2.3 | -6.2 | -20.1 | -46.1 | 24" |
| 1586 | 1224 | 939 | 711 | 530 | 387 | -0.3 | 0.3 | zero | -1.2 | -3.3 | -6.7 | 0.8 | 0.9 | zero | -1.9 | -5.0 | -15.4 | -33.2 | 24" |
| 1094 | 752 | 500 | 321 | 202 | 136 | 0.1 | 0.7 | zero | -2.3 | -6.5 | -13.1 | 1.9 | 1.7 | zero | -3.6 | -9.7 | -31.7 | -72.8 | 24" |
| 1094 | 771 | 529 | 351 | 228 | 152 | 0.1 | 0.7 | zero | -2.2 | -6.2 | -12.5 | 1.8 | 1.6 | zero | -3.5 | -9.2 | -29.6 | -67.1 | |
| 1094 | 836 | 629 | 464 | 336 | 240 | 0.1 | 0.6 | zero | -1.9 | -5.4 | -10.7 | 1.6 | 1.5 | zero | -3.0 | -7.8 | -23.9 | -51.7 | 24" |
| 1209 | 927 | 701 | 522 | 380 | 273 | -0.1 | 0.5 | zero | -1.7 | -4.8 | -9.4 | -0.1 | 1.3 | zero | -2.6 | -6.9 | -21.2 | -45.8 | 24" |
| 1282 | 921 | 648 | 443 | 295 | 197 | -0.1 | 0.6 | zero | -2.0 | -5.6 | -11.2 | 1.6 | 1.5 | zero | -3.1 | -8.2 | -26.2 | -58.6 | |
| 1282 | 939 | 675 | 473 | 323 | 220 | -0.1 | 0.6 | zero | -1.9 | -5.4 | -10.7 | 1.5 | 1.4 | zero | -3.0 | -7.9 | -24.8 | -55.1 | 24" |
| 1282 | 929 | 660 | 456 | 307 | 207 | -0.1 | 0.6 | zero | -1.9 | -5.5 | -11.0 | 1.6 | 1.5 | zero | -3.1 | -8.1 | -25.5 | -57.0 | |
| 1260 | 911 | 643 | 442 | 298 | 204 | 0.2 | 0.7 | zero | -2.3 | -6.5 | -12.9 | 1.9 | 1.7 | zero | -3.6 | -9.4 | -29.9 | -66.4 | 24" |
| 1654 | 1201 | 861 | 603 | 410 | 272 | -0.2 | 0.3 | zero | -1.4 | -4.0 | -8.1 | 1.9 | 2.4 | 1.8 | zero | -3.3 | -15.5 | -38.3 | |
| 1654 | 1257 | 947 | 703 | 511 | 363 | -0.2 | 0.3 | zero | -1.3 | -3.7 | -7.4 | 1.8 | 2.2 | 1.7 | zero | -3.0 | -13.7 | -32.8 | 24" |
| 1540 | 1188 | 910 | 689 | 512 | 372 | -0.3 | 0.3 | zero | -1.2 | -3.5 | -7.0 | 1.7 | 2.1 | 1.6 | zero | -2.8 | -12.8 | -30.4 | |
| 1993 | 1551 | 1194 | 906 | 676 | 495 | -0.1 | 0.5 | zero | -1.6 | -4.5 | -8.8 | 2.2 | 2.7 | 2.0 | zero | -3.5 | -15.8 | -37.3 | |
| 1993 | 1551 | 1194 | 906 | 676 | 495 | -0.1 | 0.5 | zero | -1.6 | -4.5 | -8.8 | 2.2 | 2.7 | 2.0 | zero | -3.5 | -15.8 | -37.3 | |
| 1945 | 1615 | 1332 | 1089 | 882 | 708 | 0.1 | 0.7 | zero | -2.0 | -5.4 | -10.4 | 1.6 | 1.5 | zero | -2.9 | -7.5 | -22.1 | -45.4 | 24" |
| 1897 | 1564 | 1282 | 1044 | 842 | 671 | -0.1 | 0.4 | zero | -1.4 | -4.0 | -7.8 | 2.0 | 2.4 | 1.8 | zero | -3.0 | -13.3 | -30.6 | |
| 1945 | 1642 | 1378 | 1149 | 950 | 780 | 0.1 | 0.7 | zero | -1.9 | -5.3 | -10.1 | 2.8 | 3.2 | 2.3 | zero | -3.8 | -16.6 | -37.6 | |
| 1946 | 1647 | 1388 | 1162 | 966 | 797 | -0.1 | 0.5 | zero | -1.7 | -4.5 | -8.9 | 1.4 | 1.3 | zero | -2.5 | -6.4 | -18.8 | -38.3 | |
| 2133 | 1777 | 1470 | 1207 | 983 | 792 | -0.1 | 0.6 | zero | -1.8 | -4.8 | -9.3 | 1.4 | 1.3 | zero | -2.6 | -6.7 | -19.8 | -40.8 | |
| 1925 | 1587 | 1303 | 1061 | 856 | 683 | -0.1 | 0.4 | zero | -1.4 | -3.9 | -7.6 | 1.9 | 2.3 | 1.7 | zero | -3.0 | -13.1 | -30.1 | 24" |
| 2134 | 1806 | 1521 | 1273 | 1058 | 872 | -0.1 | 0.5 | zero | -1.7 | -4.7 | -9.0 | 1.4 | 1.3 | zero | -2.6 | -6.5 | -19.1 | -38.9 | |
| 407 | 272 | 203 | 165 | 141 | 121 | zero | -3.5 | -13.2 | -30.0 | -54.7 | -89.1 | zero | -7.9 | -22.9 | -45.8 | -78.5 | -173.0 | -315.5 | |
| 1765 | 1392 | 1084 | 832 | 630 | 474 | -0.1 | zero | -1.3 | -4.1 | -8.7 | -15.3 | 2.0 | 1.8 | zero | -3.6 | -9.2 | -27.7 | -58.6 | 24" |
| 1824 | 1363 | 999 | 718 | 512 | 373 | -0.1 | zero | -1.6 | -5.2 | -10.5 | -19.5 | 2.6 | 2.3 | zero | -4.1 | -11.7 | -36.1 | -78.2 | 24" |
| 2316 | 1858 | 1478 | 1161 | 901 | 689 | -0.1 | 0.5 | zero | -1.7 | -4.6 | -9.1 | 1.3 | 1.3 | zero | -2.6 | -6.6 | -19.8 | -41.7 | |
| 2382 | 1985 | 1644 | 1351 | 1100 | 887 | 0.1 | 0.6 | zero | -1.9 | -5.2 | -10.1 | 1.6 | 1.4 | zero | -2.8 | -7.2 | -21.4 | -44.1 | 24" |
| 2021 | 1720 | 1456 | 1224 | 1023 | 850 | -0.1 | zero | -1.5 | -4.8 | -9.9 | -17.0 | 2.4 | 2.1 | zero | -3.9 | -9.8 | -27.0 | -57.8 | 24" |
| 2351 | 2011 | 1712 | 1448 | 1217 | 1021 | 0.3 | 0.8 | zero | -2.3 | -6.1 | -11.7 | 1.9 | 1.7 | zero | -3.3 | -8.3 | -24.0 | -47.2 | 24" |
| 2226 | 1924 | 1657 | 1420 | 1210 | 1025 | 0.2 | 0.7 | zero | -2.0 | -5.4 | -10.2 | 1.7 | 1.5 | zero | -2.9 | -7.3 | -21.1 | -42.5 | |
| 2854 | 2406 | 2018 | 1682 | 1389 | 1139 | 0.1 | 0.6 | zero | -1.8 | -5.0 | -9.6 | 1.5 | 1.4 | zero | -2.7 | -6.9 | -20.2 | -41.3 | 24" |
| 2448 | 1898 | 1456 | 1099 | 815 | 594 | -0.1 | 0.5 | zero | -1.6 | -4.6 | -9.1 | 2.3 | 2.8 | 2.0 | zero | -3.6 | -16.2 | -38.5 | |
| 2702 | 2225 | 1818 | 1472 | 1180 | 936 | 0.1 | 0.6 | zero | -1.8 | -5.1 | -9.8 | 1.5 | 1.4 | zero | -2.8 | -7.0 | -20.9 | -43.3 | |
| 2702 | 2267 | 1890 | 1565 | 1285 | 1046 | -0.1 | 0.6 | zero | -1.8 | -4.9 | -9.5 | 1.5 | 1.3 | zero | -2.7 | -6.8 | -20.0 | -41.1 | |
| 2705 | 2087 | 1587 | 1185 | 872 | 639 | 0.3 | 0.8 | zero | -2.4 | -6.7 | -13.0 | 2.0 | 1.8 | zero | -3.6 | -9.4 | -28.6 | -61.2 | 24" |
| 2659 | 2186 | 1782 | 1439 | 1150 | 910 | 0.2 | 0.7 | zero | -2.1 | -5.6 | -10.9 | 1.7 | 1.5 | zero | -3.1 | -7.8 | -23.2 | -48.0 | |
| 2723 | 2349 | 2018 | 1724 | 1465 | 1237 | 0.1 | 0.6 | zero | -1.9 | -5.1 | -9.7 | 1.6 | 1.4 | zero | -2.7 | -6.9 | -20.1 | -40.7 | |
| 2724 | 2358 | 2032 | 1743 | 1487 | 1262 | 0.1 | 0.6 | zero | -1.9 | -5.0 | -9.7 | 1.6 | 1.4 | zero | -2.7 | -6.9 | -20.0 | -40.3 | |
| 2199 | 1843 | 1533 | 1266 | 1037 | 844 | -0.1 | zero | -1.4 | -4.4 | -9.1 | -15.8 | 2.2 | 1.9 | zero | -3.6 | -9.2 | -27.4 | -55.3 | 24" |
| 2542 | 2142 | 1793 | 1490 | 1228 | 1005 | 0.2 | 0.7 | zero | -2.1 | -5.7 | -11.0 | 1.8 | 1.6 | zero | -3.1 | -7.8 | -22.9 | -46.8 | |
| 2398 | 1979 | 1621 | 1316 | 1058 | 842 | 0.1 | 0.6 | zero | -1.9 | -5.3 | -10.2 | 1.6 | 1.4 | zero | -2.9 | -7.3 | -21.7 | -44.9 | 24" |
| 2542 | 2192 | 1881 | 1606 | 1363 | 1150 | 0.2 | 0.7 | zero | -2.0 | -5.5 | -10.5 | 1.7 | 1.5 | zero | -3.0 | -7.5 | -21.7 | -43.9 | |
| 2543 | 2217 | 1925 | 1663 | 1431 | 1224 | 0.2 | 0.7 | zero | -2.0 | -5.4 | -10.3 | 1.7 | 1.6 | zero | -2.9 | -7.3 | -21.2 | -42.6 | |
| 2797 | 2363 | 1986 | 1657 | 1373 | 1128 | 0.1 | 0.6 | zero | -1.9 | -5.1 | -9.8 | 1.5 | 1.4 | zero | -2.8 | -7.0 | -20.5 | -42.0 | |
| 2781 | 2293 | 1875 | 1518 | 1217 | 968 | 0.2 | 0.7 | zero | -2.1 | -5.8 | -11.2 | 1.8 | 1.6 | zero | -3.1 | -8.0 | -23.6 | -48.8 | |
| 2913 | 2308 | 1805 | 1393 | 1060 | 801 | -0.1 | zero | -1.3 | -4.1 | -8.6 | -15.2 | 2.0 | 1.8 | zero | -3.6 | -9.1 | -27.4 | -57.8 | 24" |
| 2797 | 2418 | 2081 | 1783 | 1519 | 1287 | 0.1 | 0.6 | zero | -1.8 | -4.9 | -9.3 | 1.5 | 1.4 | zero | -2.7 | -6.7 | -19.5 | -39.4 | |
| 2799 | 2445 | 2128 | 1848 | 1593 | 1368 | 0.1 | 0.6 | zero | -1.8 | -4.8 | -9.2 | 1.5 | 1.3 | zero | -2.6 | -6.8 | -19.0 | -38.2 | |
| 3221 | 2667 | 2196 | 1792 | 1448 | 1160 | -0.1 | 0.5 | zero | -1.6 | -4.6 | -9.0 | 1.3 | 1.2 | zero | -2.5 | -6.6 | -20.2 | -43.4 | |
| 3178 | 2718 | 2313 | 1956 | 1644 | 1372 | 0.2 | 0.7 | zero | -2.1 | -5.6 | -10.7 | 1.7 | 1.5 | zero | -3.0 | -7.6 | -22.1 | -44.8 | |
| 3133 | 2655 | 2240 | 1878 | 1564 | 1292 | -0.1 | 0.5 | zero | -1.6 | -4.4 | -8.5 | 2.2 | 2.6 | 1.9 | zero | -3.2 | -14.2 | -32.0 | 24" |
| 2987 | 2511 | 2097 | 1739 | 1430 | 1166 | 0.2 | 0.7 | zero | -2.0 | -5.5 | -10.7 | 1.7 | 1.5 | zero | -3.0 | -7.6 | -22.4 | -44.7 | |
| 3133 | 2715 | 2345 | 2017 | 1726 | 1469 | -0.1 | 0.5 | zero | -1.6 | -4.2 | -8.2 | 2.2 | 2.6 | 1.6 | zero | -3.1 | -13.4 | -30.0 | |
| 3222 | 2825 | 2470 | 2152 | 1867 | 1612 | -0.1 | 0.5 | zero | -1.6 | -4.3 | -8.3 | 1.2 | 1.2 | zero | -2.3 | -5.9 | -17.3 | -34.8 | |
| 3436 | 2918 | 2468 | 2077 | 1737 | 1441 | -0.1 | 0.4 | zero | -1.4 | -3.9 | -7.6 | 2.0 | 2.4 | 1.7 | zero | -2.9 | -12.8 | -28.8 | 24" |
| 3436 | 2934 | 2324 | 1892 | 1525 | 1215 | -0.1 | 0.4 | zero | -1.5 | -4.1 | -8.0 | 2.1 | 2.5 | 1.8 | zero | -3.1 | -13.8 | -31.5 | |
| 967 | 600 | 373 | 262 | 208 | 173 | 0.6 | zero | -4.2 | -12.9 | -27.2 | -48.6 | zero | -4.2 | -12.9 | -27.2 | -48.6 | -116.6 | -225.5 | 20" |
| 1412 | 886 | 521 | 301 | 172 | 119 | -0.1 | 0.6 | zero | -2.2 | -6.2 | -13.2 | 1.7 | 1.6 | zero | -3.5 | -9.9 | -34.3 | -83.3 | 24" |
| 1902 | 1296 | 858 | 565 | 399 | 316 | 0.2 | zero | -2.4 | -7.6 | -16.1 | -28.8 | 1.6 | zero | -4.3 | -12.1 | -24.0 | -64.2 | -133.2 | |
| 1827 | 1355 | 989 | 720 | 535 | 425 | 0.3 | zero | -2.7 | -8.3 | -17.1 | -29.9 | 1.8 | zero | -4.6 | -12.6 | -24.5 | -62.6 | -125.3 | 24" |
| 1827 | 1355 | 989 | 720 | 535 | 425 | 0.3 | zero | -2.7 | -8.3 | -17.1 | -29.9 | 1.8 | zero | -4.6 | -12.6 | -24.5 | -62.6 | -125.3 | |
| 2207 | 1639 | 1193 | 860 | 626 | 482 | 0.2 | zero | -2.3 | -7.1 | -14.7 | -25.9 | 1.5 | zero | -4.0 | -10.9 | -21.3 | -54.8 | -110.3 | 24" |
| 2303 | 1845 | 1462 | 1143 | 806 | 685 | -0.1 | zero | -1.5 | -4.8 | -10.1 | -17.6 | 2.4 | 2.1 | zero | -4.1 | -10.4 | -30.9 | -64.6 | |

## Vented Test-Barrel Ballistics

This Remington® patented, industry-accepted method provides data that more precisely reflect actual use of revolver ammunition. It considers cylinder gap, barrel length, powder position, and production tolerances. Although our final values differ from conventional figures, the ammunition is unchanged. Key elements of our patented procedure include: (a) horizontal powder orientation; (b) cylinder gap: .008"; (c) barrel length: 4".

## Interchangeability Chart

Cartridges within groups shown are interchangeable. Other substitutions should not be made without specific recommendation of the firearms manufacturer since improper combinations could result in firearm damage or personal injury.

### Rimfire
.22 W.R.F.
.22 Remington Special
.22 Win. Model 1890 in a .22 Win. Mag. Rimfire but
  not conversely

### Centerfire
.25-20 Remington
.25-20 W.C.F.
.25-20 Win.
.25-20 Win. High Speed
.25-20 Marlin
.25 W.C.F.

6mm Rem. (80 & 90 grain)
.244 Remington

.25 Automatic
.25 Auto. Colt Pistol (ACP)
.25 (6.35mm) Automatic Pistol
6.35mm Browning

7mm Express® Remington
.280 Remington

.30-30 Sav.
.30-30 Win.
.30-30 Win. Accelerator* (SEE NOTE A)
.30-30 Marlin
.30-30 Win. High Speed
.30 W.C.F.

.32 Colt Automatic
.32 Auto. Colt Pistol (ACP)
.32 (7.65mm) Automatic Pistol
7.65mm Automatic Pistol
7.65mm Browning (not interchangeable with 7.65mm
  Luger)

.32 Short Colt in .32 Long Colt but not conversely
                                    (SEE NOTE C)

.32 S&W in .32 S.& W. Long but not conversely

.32 S&W Long
.32 Colt New Police
.32 Colt Police Positive

.32 W.C.F.* (SEE NOTE A)
.32 Win.* (SEE NOTE A)
.32-20 Win. High Speed* (SEE NOTE A)

.32-20 Colt L.M.R
.32-20 W.C.F (SEE NOTE G)
.32-20 Win. and Marlin

.38 S.&W.
.38 Colt New Police
.380 Webley

.38 Colt Special
.38 S&W Special
.38 Special Targetmaster®
.38 S&W Special Mid-Range (SEE NOTE D)
.38 Special (+P) (SEE NOTE B)
.38-44 Special (+P) (SEE NOTE B)
.38 Special
.38 Special Flat Point

.38 Short Colt in .38 Long Colt but not conversely.
  Both can be used in .38 Special

.38 Marlin
.38 Win.* (SEE NOTE A)
.38-40 Win.
.38 W.C.F.* (SEE NOTE A)

.38 Remington* (SEE NOTE A)

.38 Automatic in .38 Super (+P)
  but not conversely

.380 Automatic
9mm Browning Short (Corto Kurz)

9mm Luger (SEE NOTE E)
9mm Parabellum

.44 S&W Special (SEE NOTE F)

.44 Marlin
.44 Win.
.44 Remington
.44-40 Win.
.44 W.C.F.

.45-70 Government
.45-70 Marlin, Win.
.45-70-405

# Centerfire Rifle Ballistics Tables

| Caliber | Index/EDI Number | Wt. (grs.) | Bullet Style | Primer No. | Muzzle | 100 yds. | 200 yds. | 300 yds. | 400 yds. | 500 yds. |
|---|---|---|---|---|---|---|---|---|---|---|
| .308 Win. | R308W1 | 150 | Pointed Soft Point Core-Lokt® | 9½ | 2820 | 2533 | 2263 | 2009 | 1774 | 1560 |
| | R308W2 | 180 | Soft Point Core-Lokt® | 9½ | 2620 | 2274 | 1955 | 1666 | 1414 | 1212 |
| | R308W3 | 180 | Pointed Soft Point Core-Lokt® | 9½ | 2620 | 2393 | 2178 | 1974 | 1782 | 1604 |
| | R308W7 | 168 | Boat Tail HP Match | 9½ | 2680 | 2493 | 2314 | 2143 | 1979 | 1823 |
| | PRB308WA ★ | 165 | Pointed Soft Point, Boat Tail | 9½ | 2700 | 2497 | 2303 | 2117 | 1941 | 1773 |
| | PRT308WT ★ | 165 | Pointed Soft Point, Ballistic Tip | 9½ | 2700 | 2613 | 2333 | 2161 | 1996 | 1838 |
| .30-06 Springfield | R30061 | 125 | Pointed Soft Point | 9½ | 3140 | 2780 | 2447 | 2138 | 1853 | 1595 |
| | R30062 | 150 | Pointed Soft Point Core-Lokt® | 9½ | 2910 | 2617 | 2342 | 2083 | 1843 | 1622 |
| | R30063 | 150 | Bronze Point™ | 9½ | 2910 | 2656 | 2416 | 2189 | 1974 | 1773 |
| | R3006B | 165 | Pointed Soft Point Core-Lokt® | 9½ | 2800 | 2534 | 2283 | 2047 | 1825 | 1621 |
| | R30064 | 180 | Soft Point Core-Lokt® | 9½ | 2700 | 2348 | 2023 | 1727 | 1466 | 1251 |
| | R30065 | 180 | Pointed Soft Point Core-Lokt® | 9½ | 2700 | 2469 | 2250 | 2042 | 1846 | 1663 |
| | R30067 | 220 | Soft Point Core-Lokt® | 9½ | 2410 | 2130 | 1870 | 1632 | 1422 | 1246 |
| | RS3006A | 180 | Swift A-Frame™ PSP | 9½ | 2700 | 2465 | 2243 | 2032 | 1833 | 1648 |
| | PRB3006SA ★ | 165 | Pointed Soft Point, Boat Tail | 9½ | 2800 | 2592 | 2394 | 2204 | 2023 | 1852 |
| | PRT3006A ★ | 150 | Pointed Soft Point, Ballistic Tip* | 9½ | 2910 | 2696 | 2492 | 2298 | 2112 | 1934 |
| | PRT3006B ★ | 165 | Pointed Soft Point, Ballistic Tip* | 9½ | 2800 | 2609 | 2426 | 2249 | 2080 | 1919 |
| .300 Win. Mag. | R300W1 | 150 | Pointed Soft Point Core-Lokt® | 9½M | 3290 | 2951 | 2636 | 2342 | 2068 | 1813 |
| | R300W2 | 180 | Pointed Soft Point Core-Lokt® | 9½M | 2960 | 2745 | 2540 | 2344 | 2157 | 1979 |
| | RS300WA | 200 | Swift A-Frame™ PSP | 9½M | 2825 | 2595 | 2376 | 2167 | 1970 | 1783 |
| | PRB300WA ★ | 190 | Pointed Soft Point, Boat Tail | 9½M | 2885 | 2691 | 2506 | 2327 | 2156 | 1993 |
| .300 Wby. Mag. | R300WB1 | 180 | Pointed Soft Point Core-Lokt® | 9½M | 3120 | 2866 | 2627 | 2400 | 2184 | 1979 |
| | RS300WBB | 200 | Swift A-Frame™ PSP | 9½M | 2925 | 2690 | 2467 | 2254 | 2052 | 1861 |
| | PRB300WBA★ | 190 | Pointed Soft Point, Boat Tail | 9½M | 3030 | 2830 | 2638 | 2455 | 2279 | 2110 |
| .303 British | R303B1 | 180 | Soft Point Core-Lokt® | 9½ | 2460 | 2124 | 1817 | 1542 | 1311 | 1137 |
| 7.62 x 39mm | R762391 | 125 | Pointed Soft Point | 7½ | 2365 | 2062 | 1783 | 1533 | 1320 | 1154 |
| .32-20 Win. | R32201 | 100 | Lead | 6½ | 1210 | 1021 | 913 | 834 | 769 | 712 |
| .32 Win. Special | R32WS2 | 170 | Soft Point Core-Lokt® | 9½ | 2250 | 1921 | 1626 | 1372 | 1175 | 1044 |
| 8mm Remington Mag. | RS8MMRA ★ | 200 | Swift A-Frame™ PSP | 9½M | 2900 | 2623 | 2361 | 2115 | 1885 | 1672 |
| 8mm Mauser | R8MSR | 170 | Soft Point Core-Lokt® | 9½ | 2360 | 1969 | 1622 | 1333 | 1123 | 997 |
| .338 Win. Mag. | R338W1 | 225 | Pointed Soft Point Core-Lokt® | 9½M | 2780 | 2572 | 2374 | 2184 | 2003 | 1832 |
| | R338W2 | 250 | Pointed Soft Point Core-Lokt® | 9½M | 2660 | 2456 | 2261 | 2075 | 1898 | 1731 |
| | RS338WA | 225 | Swift A-Frame™ PSP | 9½M | 2785 | 2517 | 2266 | 2029 | 1808 | 1605 |
| | PRT338WB ★ | 200 | Pointed Soft Point, Ballistic Tip | 9½M | 2950 | 2724 | 2509 | 2303 | 2108 | 1922 |
| .35 Remington | R35R1 | 150 | Pointed Soft Point Core-Lokt® | 9½ | 2300 | 1874 | 1506 | 1218 | 1039 | 934 |
| | R35R2 | 200 | Soft Point Core-Lokt® | 9½ | 2080 | 1698 | 1376 | 1140 | 1001 | 911 |
| .35 Whelen | R35WH1 | 200 | Pointed Soft Point | 9½M | 2675 | 2378 | 2100 | 1842 | 1606 | 1399 |
| | R35WH3 | 250 | Pointed Soft Point | 9½M | 2400 | 2197 | 2005 | 1823 | 1652 | 1496 |
| .375 H&H Mag. | R375M1 | 270 | Soft Point | 9½M | 2690 | 2420 | 2166 | 1928 | 1707 | 1507 |
| | RS375MA | 300 | Swift A-Frame™ PSP | 9½M | 2530 | 2245 | 1979 | 1733 | 1512 | 1321 |
| .416 Remington Mag. | R416R2 | 400 | Swift A-Frame™ PSP | 9½M | 2400 | 2175 | 1962 | 1763 | 1579 | 1414 |
| .44-40 Win. | R4440W | 200 | Soft Point | 2½ | 1190 | 1006 | 900 | 822 | 756 | 699 |
| .44 Remington Mag. | R44MG2 | 240 | Soft Point | 2½ | 1760 | 1380 | 1114 | 970 | 878 | 806 |
| | R44MG3 | 240 | Semi-Jacketed Hollow Point | 2½ | 1760 | 1380 | 1114 | 970 | 878 | 806 |
| | R44MG6 | 210 | Semi-Jacketed Hollow Point | 2½ | 1920 | 1477 | 1155 | 982 | 880 | 802 |
| | RH44MGA | 275 | JHP Core-Lokt® | 2½ | 1580 | 1293 | 1093 | 976 | 896 | 832 |
| .444 Mar. | R444M | 240 | Soft Point | 9½ | 2350 | 1815 | 1377 | 1087 | 941 | 846 |
| .45-70 Government | R4570G | 405 | Soft Point | 9½ | 1330 | 1168 | 1055 | 977 | 918 | 869 |
| | R4570L | 300 | Jacketed Hollow Point | 9½ | 1810 | 1497 | 1244 | 1073 | 969 | 895 |
| .458 Win. Mag. | RS458WA | 450 | Swift A-Frame™ PSP | 9½M | 2150 | 1901 | 1671 | 1465 | 1289 | 1150 |

★ New For 1998

NOTE A: *High-speed cartridges must not be used in revolvers. They should be used only in rifles made especially for them.
NOTE B: Ammunition with (+P) on the case headstamp is loaded to higher pressure. Use only in firearms designated for this cartridge and so recommended by the gun manufacturer.
NOTE C: Not for use in revolvers chambered for .32 S&W or .32 S&W Long.
NOTE D: All .38 Special cartridges can be used in .357 Magnum revolvers but not conversely.
NOTE E: 9mm sub-machine gun cartridges should not be used in handguns.
NOTE F: .44 Russian and .44 S&W Special can be used in .44 Remington Magnum revolvers but not conversely.
NOTE G: Not to be used in Win. M-66 and M-73.

## (continued)

▮ = Premier® Safari Grade  ▯ = Premier® Ballistic Tip®  ▯ = Premier® Boat Tail

| Muzzle | Energy (ft.-lbs.) 100 yds. | 200 yds. | 300 yds. | 400 yds. | 500 yds. | Short-range¹ Trajectory* 50 yds. | 100 yds. | 150 yds. | 200 yds. | 250 yds. | 300 yds. | Long-range² Trajectory* 100 yds. | 150 yds. | 200 yds. | 250 yds. | 300 yds. | 400 yds. | 500 yds. | Barrel Length |
|---|---|---|---|---|---|---|---|---|---|---|---|---|---|---|---|---|---|---|---|
| 2648 | 2137 | 1705 | 1344 | 1048 | 810 | -0.1 | zero | -1.2 | -3.9 | -8.4 | -14.7 | 2.0 | 1.7 | zero | -3.4 | -8.8 | -26.2 | -54.8 | |
| 2743 | 2066 | 1527 | 1109 | 799 | 587 | -0.1 | zero | -1.7 | -5.3 | -10.7 | -19.7 | 2.6 | 2.3 | zero | -4.1 | -11.8 | -36.3 | -78.2 | |
| 2743 | 2288 | 1896 | 1557 | 1269 | 1028 | -0.1 | zero | -1.5 | -4.6 | -9.5 | -16.5 | 2.3 | 2.0 | zero | -3.8 | -9.7 | -28.3 | -57.8 | 24" |
| 2678 | 2318 | 1998 | 1713 | 1460 | 1239 | -0.1 | zero | -1.3 | -4.1 | -8.5 | -14.7 | 2.1 | 1.8 | zero | -3.4 | -8.6 | -24.7 | -49.9 | |
| 2670 | 2284 | 1942 | 1642 | 1379 | 1152 | -0.1 | zero | -1.3 | -4.1 | -8.5 | -14.8 | 2.0 | 1.8 | zero | -3.4 | -8.6 | -25.0 | -50.6 | |
| 2672 | 2314 | 1995 | 1711 | 1460 | 1239 | 0.1 | zero | -1.3 | -4.0 | -6.4 | -14.4 | 2.0 | 1.7 | zero | -3.3 | -8.4 | -24.3 | -48.9 | |
| 2736 | 2145 | 1662 | 1269 | 953 | 706 | -0.1 | 0.6 | zero | -1.9 | -5.2 | -10.1 | 1.5 | 1.4 | zero | -2.8 | -7.4 | -22.4 | -47.6 | |
| 2820 | 2281 | 1827 | 1445 | 1131 | 876 | 0.2 | 0.7 | zero | -2.2 | -5.9 | -11.4 | 1.8 | 1.6 | zero | -3.2 | -8.2 | -24.4 | -50.9 | |
| 2820 | 2349 | 1944 | 1596 | 1298 | 1047 | 0.2 | 0.7 | zero | -2.0 | -5.6 | -10.8 | 1.7 | 1.5 | zero | -3.0 | -7.7 | -22.7 | -46.6 | |
| 2872 | 2352 | 1909 | 1534 | 1220 | 963 | 0.3 | 0.8 | zero | -2.3 | -6.3 | -12.1 | 2.0 | 1.7 | zero | -3.4 | -8.7 | -25.9 | -53.2 | |
| 2913 | 2203 | 1635 | 1192 | 859 | 625 | -0.1 | zero | -1.5 | -4.9 | -10.3 | -18.3 | 2.4 | 2.1 | zero | -4.3 | -11.0 | -33.8 | -72.8 | |
| 2913 | 2436 | 2023 | 1666 | 1362 | 1105 | -0.1 | zero | -1.3 | -4.2 | -8.8 | -15.4 | 2.1 | 1.8 | zero | -3.5 | -9.0 | -26.3 | -54.0 | |
| 2837 | 2216 | 1708 | 1301 | 988 | 758 | 0.1 | zero | -2.0 | -6.2 | -12.9 | -22.4 | 1.3 | zero | -3.5 | -9.5 | -18.4 | -46.4 | -91.6 | |
| 2913 | 2429 | 2010 | 1650 | 1343 | 1085 | -0.1 | zero | -1.3 | -4.2 | -8.9 | -15.4 | 2.1 | 1.8 | zero | -3.6 | -9.1 | -26.6 | -54.4 | |
| 2872 | 2462 | 2100 | 1780 | 1500 | 1256 | 0.2 | 0.8 | zero | -2.2 | -5.8 | -11.2 | 1.8 | 1.6 | zero | -3.1 | -7.9 | -23.0 | -46.6 | |
| 2821 | 2422 | 2070 | 1769 | 1485 | 1247 | 0.1 | 0.7 | zero | -2.0 | -5.3 | -10.2 | 1.6 | 1.5 | zero | -2.9 | -7.3 | -21.1 | -42.8 | |
| 2873 | 2494 | 2155 | 1854 | 1588 | 1350 | 0.2 | 0.8 | zero | -2.1 | -5.7 | -10.9 | 1.8 | 1.6 | zero | -3.1 | -7.7 | -22.3 | -45.0 | 24" |
| 3605 | 2900 | 2314 | 1827 | 1424 | 1095 | -0.1 | 0.5 | zero | -1.6 | -4.4 | -8.7 | 2.2 | 2.6 | 1.9 | zero | -3.4 | -15.0 | -34.4 | |
| 3501 | 3011 | 2578 | 2196 | 1859 | 1565 | 0.1 | 0.6 | zero | -1.9 | -5.1 | -9.8 | 1.6 | 1.4 | zero | -2.8 | -7.0 | -20.2 | -41.0 | 24" |
| 3544 | 2989 | 2506 | 2086 | 1722 | 1412 | 0.2 | 0.8 | zero | -2.2 | -5.9 | -11.3 | 1.8 | 1.6 | zero | -3.2 | -8.0 | -23.5 | -47.9 | |
| 3511 | 3055 | 2648 | 2285 | 1961 | 1675 | 0.1 | 0.7 | zero | -2.0 | -5.3 | -10.1 | 1.6 | 1.5 | zero | -2.9 | -7.2 | -20.8 | -41.9 | |
| 3890 | 3284 | 2758 | 2301 | 1905 | 1565 | -0.1 | 0.5 | zero | -1.7 | -4.6 | -8.9 | 2.4 | 2.8 | 2.0 | zero | -3.4 | -14.9 | -33.6 | |
| 3799 | 3213 | 2701 | 2256 | 1870 | 1538 | 0.1 | 0.7 | zero | -2.0 | -5.4 | -10.4 | 2.8 | 3.2 | 2.3 | zero | -3.9 | -17.0 | -38.3 | 24" |
| 3873 | 3378 | 2936 | 2542 | 2190 | 1878 | -0.1 | 0.6 | zero | -1.7 | -4.7 | -9.0 | 1.4 | 1.3 | zero | -2.6 | -6.4 | -18.6 | -37.6 | |
| 2418 | 1803 | 1319 | 950 | 687 | 517 | 0.1 | zero | -2.0 | -5.8 | -13.2 | -23.3 | 1.3 | zero | -3.1 | -9.9 | -19.3 | -49.9 | -100.8 | 24" |
| 1552 | 1180 | 882 | 652 | 483 | 370 | 0.1 | zero | -2.2 | -6.7 | -14.0 | -24.5 | 1.5 | zero | -3.8 | -10.4 | -20.1 | -51.3 | -102.5 | 24" |
| 325 | 231 | 185 | 154 | 131 | 113 | zero | -5.9 | -20.0 | -43.3 | -77.4 | -122.4 | zero | -11.1 | -31.6 | -62.6 | -104.7 | -226.7 | -410.6 | 24" |
| 1911 | 1393 | 998 | 710 | 521 | 411 | 0.3 | zero | -2.6 | -8.0 | -16.7 | -29.3 | 1.7 | zero | -4.5 | -12.4 | -24.1 | -62.1 | -125.3 | 24" |
| 3734 | 3054 | 2476 | 1987 | 1577 | 1241 | 0.2 | 0.7 | zero | -2.1 | -5.8 | -11.2 | 1.3 | 1.6 | zero | -3.1 | -8.0 | -23.9 | -49.6 | 24" |
| 2102 | 1463 | 993 | 671 | 476 | 375 | 0.2 | zero | -2.4 | -7.6 | -16.1 | -28.6 | 1.6 | zero | -4.4 | -12.0 | -23.7 | -62.8 | -128.9 | 24" |
| 3860 | 3305 | 2815 | 2383 | 2004 | 1676 | -0.3 | 0.8 | zero | -2.2 | -5.9 | -11.4 | 1.9 | 1.7 | zero | -3.2 | -8.1 | -23.4 | -47.5 | |
| 3927 | 3348 | 2837 | 2389 | 1999 | 1663 | -0.1 | zero | -1.4 | -4.3 | -8.9 | -15.4 | 2.1 | 1.9 | zero | -3.5 | -8.9 | -26.0 | -52.7 | 24" |
| 3871 | 3165 | 2565 | 2057 | 1633 | 1286 | -0.1 | zero | -1.2 | -4.0 | -8.5 | -14.8 | 2.0 | 1.8 | zero | -3.5 | -8.8 | -25.2 | -54.1 | |
| 3866 | 3295 | 2795 | 2357 | 1973 | 1641 | 0.1 | 0.6 | zero | -1.9 | -5.2 | -10.0 | 1.6 | 1.4 | zero | -2.8 | -7.1 | -20.8 | -42.4 | |
| 1762 | 1169 | 755 | 494 | 359 | 291 | 0.3 | zero | -2.7 | -8.6 | -18.2 | -32.6 | 1.8 | zero | -4.9 | -13.7 | -27.1 | -72.5 | -150.4 | 24" |
| 1921 | 1280 | 841 | 577 | 445 | 369 | 0.5 | zero | -3.5 | -10.7 | -22.6 | -40.1 | 2.3 | zero | -6.1 | -16.7 | -33.0 | -86.6 | -174.8 | |
| 3177 | 2510 | 1958 | 1506 | 1145 | 869 | -0.1 | zero | -1.5 | -4.7 | -9.9 | -17.3 | 2.3 | 2.0 | zero | -4.0 | -10.3 | -30.8 | -64.9 | 24" |
| 3197 | 2680 | 2230 | 1844 | 1515 | 1242 | 0.1 | zero | -1.9 | -5.7 | -11.8 | -20.4 | 1.3 | zero | -3.2 | -8.6 | -16.6 | -40.0 | -76.3 | |
| 4337 | 3510 | 2812 | 2228 | 1747 | 1361 | -0.1 | zero | -1.4 | -4.5 | -9.4 | -16.4 | 2.2 | 1.9 | zero | -3.8 | -9.7 | -28.7 | -59.8 | 24" |
| 4282 | 3357 | 2608 | 2001 | 1523 | 1163 | -0.1 | zero | -1.7 | -5.4 | -11.4 | -19.8 | 2.7 | 2.3 | zero | -4.6 | -11.7 | -35.0 | -73.6 | |
| 5115 | 4201 | 3419 | 2760 | 2214 | 1775 | 0.1 | zero | -1.9 | -5.9 | -12.1 | -20.8 | 1.3 | zero | -3.3 | -8.9 | -17.0 | -41.9 | -80.8 | 24" |
| 629 | 449 | 360 | 300 | 254 | 217 | zero | -5.8 | -20.0 | -44.6 | -78.6 | -126.1 | zero | -11.3 | -33.1 | -64.1 | -108.7 | -235.2 | -422.3 | 24" |
| 1650 | 1015 | 661 | 501 | 411 | 346 | zero | -2.1 | -8.7 | -21.2 | -40.6 | -67.7 | zero | -5.6 | -17.0 | -35.4 | -61.4 | -143.0 | -269.9 | |
| 1650 | 1015 | 661 | 501 | 411 | 346 | zero | -2.1 | -8.7 | -21.2 | -40.6 | -67.7 | zero | -5.6 | -17.0 | -35.4 | -61.4 | -143.0 | -269.9 | 20" |
| 1719 | 1017 | 622 | 450 | 361 | 300 | zero | -1.6 | -7.1 | -17.9 | -35.1 | -60.2 | zero | -4.8 | -14.7 | -31.2 | -55.5 | -131.3 | -253.7 | |
| 1524 | 1020 | 730 | 582 | 490 | 422 | 1.4 | zero | -6.6 | -19.4 | -39.2 | -67.5 | zero | -6.6 | -19.4 | -39.2 | -67.5 | -210.8 | -280.8 | |
| 2942 | 1755 | 1010 | 630 | 472 | 381 | 0.2 | zero | -3.2 | -9.7 | -20.8 | -37.8 | 2.2 | zero | -5.4 | -15.4 | -31.4 | -86.7 | -180.0 | 24" |
| 1590 | 1227 | 1001 | 858 | 758 | 679 | zero | -4.0 | -14.5 | -32.0 | -57.5 | -90.6 | zero | -8.5 | -24.0 | -47.4 | -78.6 | -169.4 | -301.3 | 24" |
| 2182 | 1492 | 1031 | 767 | 625 | 533 | zero | -1.3 | -6.6 | -16.5 | -32.0 | -54.1 | zero | -4.6 | -13.8 | -28.6 | -50.1 | -115.7 | -219.1 | |
| 4510 | 3609 | 2789 | 2144 | 1659 | 1321 | 0.3 | zero | -2.7 | -8.2 | -16.7 | -28.9 | 1.8 | zero | -4.6 | -12.2 | -23.4 | -58.5 | -114.7 | 24" |

Specifications are nominal. Ballistics figures established in test barrels.
Individual rifles may vary from test-barrel specifications.
*Inches above or below line of sight. Hold low for positive numbers, high for negative numbers.
¹ Bullet does not rise more than 1" above line of sight from muzzle to sighting-in range.
² Bullet does not rise more than 3" above line of sight from muzzle to sighting-in range.
NOTE: "zero" indicates yardage at which rifle was sighted in.

# WEATHERBY BALLISTICS

| SUGGESTED USAGE | CARTRIDGE | Weight Grains | Bullet Type | B/C | VELOCITY in Feet per Second | | | | | | ENERGY in Foot-Pounds | | | | | | PATH OF BULLET (Above or below line-of-sight of riflescopes mounted 1.5" above bore) | | | | |
|---|---|---|---|---|---|---|---|---|---|---|---|---|---|---|---|---|---|---|---|---|---|
| | | | | | Muzzle | 100 Yards | 200 Yards | 300 Yards | 400 Yards | 500 Yards | Muzzle | 100 Yards | 200 Yards | 300 Yards | 400 Yards | 500 Yards | 100 Yards | 200 Yards | 300 Yards | 400 Yards | 500 Yards |
| V | .224 Wby. | 55 | Pt-Ex | .235 | 3650 | 3192 | 2780 | 2403 | 2056 | 1741 | 1627 | 1244 | 944 | 705 | 516 | 370 | 2.8 | 3.7 | 0.0 | -9.8 | -27.9 |
| V | .240 Wby. | 87 | Pt-Ex | .327 | 3523 | 3199 | 2898 | 2617 | 2352 | 2103 | 2397 | 1977 | 1622 | 1323 | 1069 | 855 | 2.7 | 3.4 | 0.0 | -8.4 | -23.3 |
| | | 90 | Barnes-X | .382 | 3500 | 3222 | 2962 | 2717 | 2484 | 2264 | 2448 | 2075 | 1753 | 1475 | 1233 | 1024 | 2.6 | 3.3 | 0.0 | -8.0 | -21.6 |
| | | 95 | Bst | .379 | 3420 | 3146 | 2888 | 2645 | 2414 | 2195 | 2467 | 2087 | 1759 | 1475 | 1229 | 1017 | 2.7 | 3.5 | 0.0 | -8.4 | -22.9 |
| M | | 100 | Pt-Ex | .381 | 3406 | 3134 | 2878 | 2637 | 2408 | 2190 | 2576 | 2180 | 1839 | 1544 | 1287 | 1065 | 2.8 | 3.5 | 0.0 | -8.4 | -23.0 |
| | | 100 | Partition | .384 | 3406 | 3136 | 2882 | 2642 | 2415 | 2199 | 2576 | 2181 | 1844 | 1550 | 1294 | 1073 | 2.8 | 3.5 | 0.0 | -8.4 | -22.9 |
| V | .257 Wby. | 87 | Pt-Ex | .322 | 3825 | 3472 | 3147 | 2845 | 2563 | 2297 | 2826 | 2328 | 1913 | 1563 | 1269 | 1019 | 2.1 | 2.8 | 0.0 | -7.1 | -19.5 |
| M | | 100 | Pt-Ex | .357 | 3602 | 3298 | 3016 | 2750 | 2500 | 2264 | 2881 | 2416 | 2019 | 1680 | 1388 | 1138 | 2.4 | 3.1 | 0.0 | -7.7 | -21.0 |
| | | 100 | Bst | .393 | 3602 | 3325 | 3066 | 2822 | 2590 | 2370 | 2881 | 2455 | 2087 | 1768 | 1490 | 1247 | 2.3 | 3.0 | 0.0 | -7.4 | -19.9 |
| | | 115 | Barnes-X | .429 | 3400 | 3158 | 2929 | 2711 | 2504 | 2306 | 2952 | 2546 | 2190 | 1877 | 1601 | 1358 | 2.7 | 3.4 | 0.0 | -8.1 | -21.7 |
| | | 117 | Rn-Ex | .243 | 3402 | 2984 | 2595 | 2240 | 1921 | 1639 | 3007 | 2320 | 1742 | 1302 | 956 | 690 | 3.4 | 4.3 | 0.0 | -11.1 | -31.9 |
| | | 120 | Partition | .391 | 3305 | 3046 | 2801 | 2570 | 2350 | 2141 | 2910 | 2472 | 2091 | 1760 | 1471 | 1221 | 3.0 | 3.7 | 0.0 | -8.9 | -24.3 |
| V | .270 Wby. | 100 | Pt-Ex | .307 | 3760 | 3396 | 3061 | 2751 | 2462 | 2190 | 3139 | 2560 | 2081 | 1681 | 1346 | 1065 | 2.3 | 3.0 | 0.0 | -7.6 | -19.0 |
| M | | 130 | Pt-Ex | .409 | 3375 | 3123 | 2885 | 2659 | 2444 | 2240 | 3288 | 2815 | 2402 | 2041 | 1724 | 1448 | 2.8 | 3.5 | 0.0 | -8.4 | -22.6 |
| | | 130 | Partition | .416 | 3375 | 3127 | 2892 | 2670 | 2458 | 2256 | 3288 | 2822 | 2415 | 2058 | 1744 | 1470 | 2.8 | 3.5 | 0.0 | -8.3 | -22.4 |
| | | 140 | Bst | .456 | 3300 | 3077 | 2865 | 2663 | 2470 | 2285 | 3385 | 2943 | 2551 | 2204 | 1896 | 1622 | 2.9 | 3.6 | 0.0 | -8.4 | -22.6 |
| | | 140 | Barnes-X | .462 | 3250 | 3032 | 2825 | 2628 | 2438 | 2257 | 3283 | 2858 | 2481 | 2146 | 1848 | 1583 | 3.0 | 3.7 | 0.0 | -8.7 | -23.2 |
| | | 150 | Pt-Ex | .462 | 3245 | 3028 | 2821 | 2623 | 2434 | 2253 | 3507 | 3053 | 2650 | 2292 | 1973 | 1690 | 3.0 | 3.7 | 0.0 | -8.7 | -23.3 |
| | | 150 | Partition | .465 | 3245 | 3029 | 2823 | 2627 | 2439 | 2259 | 3507 | 3055 | 2655 | 2298 | 1981 | 1699 | 3.0 | 3.7 | 0.0 | -8.7 | -23.2 |
| M | 7MM Wby. | 139 | Pt-Ex | .392 | 3340 | 3079 | 2834 | 2601 | 2380 | 2170 | 3443 | 2926 | 2478 | 2088 | 1748 | 1453 | 2.9 | 3.6 | 0.0 | -8.7 | -23.7 |
| | | 140 | Partition | .434 | 3303 | 3069 | 2847 | 2636 | 2434 | 2241 | 3391 | 2927 | 2519 | 2159 | 1841 | 1562 | 2.9 | 3.6 | 0.0 | -8.5 | -23.1 |
| | | 140 | Bst | .485 | 3302 | 3092 | 2892 | 2700 | 2517 | 2341 | 3389 | 2972 | 2599 | 2267 | 1969 | 1703 | 2.8 | 3.5 | 0.0 | -8.2 | -21.9 |
| | | 150 | Barnes-X | .488 | 3100 | 2901 | 2710 | 2527 | 2352 | 2183 | 3200 | 2802 | 2446 | 2127 | 1842 | 1588 | 3.3 | 4.0 | 0.0 | -9.4 | -25.3 |
| | | 154 | Pt-Ex | .433 | 3260 | 3028 | 2807 | 2597 | 2397 | 2206 | 3634 | 3134 | 2694 | 2307 | 1964 | 1663 | 3.0 | 3.7 | 0.0 | -8.8 | -23.8 |
| | | 160 | Partition | .475 | 3200 | 2991 | 2791 | 2600 | 2417 | 2241 | 3638 | 3177 | 2767 | 2401 | 2075 | 1784 | 3.1 | 3.8 | 0.0 | -8.9 | -23.8 |
| B | | 175 | Pt-Ex | .462 | 3070 | 2861 | 2662 | 2471 | 2288 | 2113 | 3662 | 3181 | 2753 | 2373 | 2034 | 1735 | 3.5 | 4.2 | 0.0 | -9.9 | -26.5 |
| M | .300 Wby. | 150 | Pt-Ex | .338 | 3540 | 3225 | 2932 | 2657 | 2399 | 2155 | 4173 | 3462 | 2862 | 2351 | 1916 | 1547 | 2.6 | 3.3 | 0.0 | -8.2 | -22.6 |
| | | 150 | Partition | .387 | 3540 | 3263 | 3004 | 2759 | 2528 | 2307 | 4173 | 3547 | 3005 | 2536 | 2128 | 1773 | 2.5 | 3.2 | 0.0 | -7.7 | -20.9 |
| | | 165 | Pt-Ex | .387 | 3390 | 3123 | 2872 | 2634 | 2409 | 2195 | 4210 | 3573 | 3021 | 2542 | 2126 | 1765 | 2.8 | 3.5 | 0.0 | -8.5 | -23.1 |
| | | 165 | Bst | .475 | 3350 | 3133 | 2927 | 2730 | 2542 | 2361 | 4111 | 3596 | 3138 | 2730 | 2367 | 2042 | 2.7 | 3.4 | 0.0 | -8.1 | -21.4 |
| B | | 180 | Pt-Ex | .425 | 3240 | 3004 | 2781 | 2569 | 2366 | 2173 | 4195 | 3607 | 3091 | 2637 | 2237 | 1886 | 3.1 | 3.8 | 0.0 | -9.0 | -24.4 |
| | | 180 | Barnes-X | .511 | 3190 | 2995 | 2809 | 2631 | 2459 | 2294 | 4067 | 3586 | 3154 | 2766 | 2417 | 2103 | 3.1 | 3.8 | 0.0 | -8.7 | -23.2 |
| | | 180 | Partition | .474 | 3240 | 3028 | 2826 | 2634 | 2449 | 2271 | 4195 | 3665 | 3193 | 2772 | 2396 | 2062 | 3.0 | 3.7 | 0.0 | -8.6 | -23.1 |
| | | 200 | Partition | .461 | 3060 | 2860 | 2668 | 2485 | 2308 | 2139 | 4158 | 3631 | 3161 | 2741 | 2366 | 2032 | 3.5 | 4.2 | 0.0 | -9.8 | -26.2 |
| | | 220 | Rn-Ex | .300 | 2845 | 2543 | 2260 | 1996 | 1751 | 1530 | 3954 | 3158 | 2495 | 1946 | 1497 | 1143 | 4.9 | 5.9 | 0.0 | -14.6 | -40.8 |
| B | .340 Wby. | 200 | Pt-Ex | .361 | 3221 | 2946 | 2688 | 2444 | 2213 | 1995 | 4607 | 3854 | 3208 | 2652 | 2174 | 1767 | 3.3 | 4.0 | 0.0 | -9.9 | -27.0 |
| | | 200 | Bst | .502 | 3221 | 3022 | 2831 | 2649 | 2473 | 2305 | 4607 | 4054 | 3559 | 3115 | 2716 | 2358 | 3.0 | 3.7 | 0.0 | -8.6 | -22.9 |
| | | 210 | Partition | .400 | 3211 | 2963 | 2728 | 2505 | 2293 | 2092 | 4807 | 4093 | 3470 | 2927 | 2452 | 2040 | 3.2 | 3.9 | 0.0 | -9.5 | -25.7 |
| | | 225 | Pt-Ex | .397 | 3066 | 2824 | 2595 | 2377 | 2170 | 1973 | 4696 | 3984 | 3364 | 2822 | 2352 | 1944 | 3.6 | 4.4 | 0.0 | -10.7 | -28.6 |
| | | 225 | Barnes-X | .482 | 3001 | 2804 | 2615 | 2434 | 2260 | 2093 | 4499 | 3927 | 3416 | 2959 | 2551 | 2189 | 3.6 | 4.3 | 0.0 | -10.3 | -27.4 |
| | | 250 | Pt-Ex | .431 | 2963 | 2745 | 2537 | 2338 | 2149 | 1968 | 4873 | 4182 | 3572 | 3035 | 2563 | 2150 | 3.9 | 4.6 | 0.0 | -11.1 | -29.6 |
| | | 250 | Partition | .473 | 2941 | 2743 | 2553 | 2371 | 2197 | 2029 | 4801 | 4176 | 3618 | 3120 | 2678 | 2286 | 3.9 | 4.6 | 0.0 | -10.9 | -28.9 |
| MB | .30-378 Wby. | 165 | Bst | .475 | 3500 | 3275 | 3062 | 2859 | 2665 | 2480 | 4488 | 3930 | 3435 | 2995 | 2603 | 2253 | 2.4 | 3.0 | 0.0 | -7.4 | -19.5 |
| | | 180 | Barnes-X | .511 | 3450 | 3243 | 3046 | 2858 | 2678 | 2504 | 4757 | 4204 | 3709 | 3264 | 2865 | 2506 | 2.4 | 3.1 | 0.0 | -7.4 | -19.6 |
| | | 200 | Partition | .481 | 3160 | 2955 | 2759 | 2572 | 2392 | 2220 | 4434 | 3877 | 3381 | 2938 | 2541 | 2188 | 3.2 | 3.9 | 0.0 | -9.1 | -24.3 |
| MB | .338-378 Wby. | 200 | Bst | .502 | 3350 | 3145 | 2949 | 2761 | 2582 | 2409 | 4983 | 4391 | 3861 | 3386 | 2959 | 2576 | 2.7 | 3.3 | 0.0 | -7.9 | -21.0 |
| | | 225 | Barnes-X | .482 | 3180 | 2974 | 2778 | 2591 | 2410 | 2238 | 5052 | 4420 | 3856 | 3353 | 2902 | 2501 | 3.1 | 3.8 | 0.0 | -8.9 | -24.0 |
| | | 250 | Partition | .473 | 3060 | 2856 | 2662 | 2475 | 2297 | 2125 | 5197 | 4528 | 3933 | 3401 | 2927 | 2507 | 3.5 | 4.2 | 0.0 | -9.8 | -26.4 |
| B | .378 Wby. | 270 | Pt-Ex | .380 | 3180 | 2921 | 2677 | 2445 | 2225 | 2017 | 6062 | 5115 | 4295 | 3583 | 2968 | 2438 | 1.3 | 0.0 | -6.1 | -18.1 | -37.1 |
| | | 270 | Barnes-X | .503 | 3150 | 2954 | 2767 | 2587 | 2415 | 2249 | 5948 | 5232 | 4589 | 4013 | 3495 | 3031 | 1.2 | 0.0 | -5.8 | -16.7 | -33.7 |
| | | 300 | Rn-Ex | .250 | 2925 | 2558 | 2220 | 1908 | 1627 | 1383 | 5699 | 4360 | 3283 | 2424 | 1764 | 1274 | 1.9 | 0.0 | -9.0 | -27.8 | -60.0 |
| | | 300 | FMJ | .275 | 2925 | 2591 | 2280 | 1991 | 1725 | 1489 | 5699 | 4470 | 3461 | 2640 | 1983 | 1476 | 1.8 | 0.0 | -8.6 | -26.1 | -55.4 |
| A | .416 Wby. | 350 | Barnes-X | .521 | 2850 | 2673 | 2503 | 2340 | 2182 | 2031 | 6312 | 5553 | 4870 | 4253 | 3700 | 3204 | 1.7 | 0.0 | -7.2 | -20.9 | -41.8 |
| | | 400 | Swift A | .391 | 2650 | 2426 | 2213 | 2011 | 1820 | 1644 | 6237 | 5227 | 4350 | 3592 | 2941 | 2399 | 2.2 | 0.0 | -9.3 | -27.1 | -56.0 |
| | | 400 | Rn-Ex | .311 | 2700 | 2417 | 2152 | 1903 | 1676 | 1470 | 6474 | 5189 | 4113 | 3216 | 2493 | 1918 | 2.3 | 0.0 | -9.7 | -29.3 | -61.2 |
| | | 400 | **Mono | .304 | 2700 | 2411 | 2140 | 1887 | 1656 | 1448 | 6474 | 5162 | 4068 | 3161 | 2435 | 1861 | 2.3 | 0.0 | -9.8 | -29.7 | -62.1 |
| A | .460 Wby. | 450 | Barnes-X | .488 | 2700 | 2518 | 2343 | 2175 | 2013 | 1859 | 7284 | 6333 | 5482 | 4725 | 4050 | 3452 | 2.0 | 0.0 | -8.4 | -24.1 | -48.2 |
| | | 500 | Rn-Ex | .287 | 2600 | 2301 | 2022 | 1764 | 1533 | 1333 | 7504 | 5877 | 4539 | 3456 | 2608 | 1972 | 2.6 | 0.0 | -11.1 | -33.5 | -71.1 |
| | | 500 | FMJ | .295 | 2600 | 2309 | 2037 | 1784 | 1557 | 1357 | 7504 | 5917 | 4605 | 3534 | 2690 | 2046 | 2.6 | 0.0 | -10.9 | -33.0 | -69.6 |

**LEGEND:** Pt-Ex = Pointed Expanding    Rn-Ex = Round Nose-Expanding    FMJ = Full Metal Jacket    Swift A = Divided Lead Cavity or "H" Type    Barnes-X = Barnes "X" Flat Base    Bst = Nosler Ballistic Tip

**NOTE:** These tables were calculated by computer using a standard modern scientific technique to predict trajectories and recoil energies from the best available data for each cartridge. The figures shown are expected to be reasonably accurate of ammunition behavior under standard conditions. However, the shooter is cautioned that performance will vary because of variations in rifles, ammunition, atmospheric conditions and the bullet's manufacturers. Listed velocities were determined using 26-inch barrels. Velocities from shorter barrels will be reduced by 30 to 65 feet per second per inch of barrel removed. • B.C.: Ballistic Coefficients used for these tables were supplied by the ammunition manufacturers. • Trajectories were computed with the line-of-sight 1.5 inches above the bore centerline.

*Partition is a registered trademark of Nosler, Inc.   **Monolithic Solid is a registered trademark of A-Square, Inc.   • Barnes X-Bullet™ is a registered trademark of Barnes Bullets.

**USAGE:** V-Varmint    M-Medium Game (Deer, Sheep, Pronghorn, Black Bear)    B-Big Game (Elk, Moose, Grizzly)    A-African Big Game (Elephant, Cape Buffalo, Rhino, Lion)

SUPER-X® CENTERFIRE RIFLE BALLISTICS

| Cartridge | Symbol | Bullet Wt. Grs. | Bullet Type | Game Selector Guide | C/P Guide Number | Barrel Length (in.) | Velocity Muzzle | 100 | 200 | 300 | 400 | 500 | Energy Muzzle | 100 | 200 | 300 | 400 | 500 | SR 50 | SR 100 | SR 150 | SR 200 | SR 250 | SR 300 | LR 100 | LR 150 | LR 200 | LR 250 | LR 300 | LR 400 | LR 500 |
|---|---|---|---|---|---|---|---|---|---|---|---|---|---|---|---|---|---|---|---|---|---|---|---|---|---|---|---|---|---|---|---|
| 218 Bee | X218B | 46 | Hollow Point | V | 1 | 24 | 2760 | 2102 | 1550 | 1155 | 961 | 830 | 778 | 451 | 245 | 136 | 94 | 70 | 0.3 | 0 | -2.3 | -7.7 | -16.9 | -29.4 | 1.5 | 0 | -4.5 | -12.0 | -24.8 | -71.4 | -155.6 |
| 22 Hornet | X22H1 | 45 | Soft Point | V | 1 | 24 | 2690 | 2042 | 1502 | 1128 | 961 | 840 | 723 | 417 | 226 | 127 | 92 | 72 | 0.3 | 0 | -2.4 | -7.7 | -16.9 | -31.3 | 1.6 | 0 | -4.5 | -12.8 | -26.4 | -75.6 | -163.3 |
| 22 Hornet | X22H2 | 46 | Hollow Point | V | 1 | 24 | 2690 | 2042 | 1502 | 1128 | 948 | 840 | 739 | 426 | 230 | 130 | 92 | 72 | 0.2 | 0 | -2.4 | -7.7 | -16.9 | -31.3 | 1.6 | 0 | -4.5 | -12.8 | -26.4 | -75.5 | -163.3 |
| 22-250 Remington | X222501 | 55 | Pointed Soft Point | V | 1 | 24 | 3680 | 3137 | 2656 | 2222 | 1832 | 1493 | 1654 | 1201 | 861 | 603 | 410 | 277 | 0.2 | 0.5 | 0 | -1.6 | -4.4 | -8.7 | 2.3 | 2.6 | 1.9 | 0 | -3.4 | -15.9 | -38.9 |
| 220 Swift | X220S | 50 | Pointed Soft Point | V | 1 | 24 | 3870 | 3310 | 2816 | 2373 | 1977 | 1637 | 1663 | 1226 | 881 | 625 | 432 | 290 | -0.4 | 0.5 | 0 | -1.6 | -4.1 | -7.8 | 1.9 | 2.2 | 1.6 | 0 | -3.2 | -16.7 | -37.1 |
| 223 Remington | X223R | 55 | Pointed Soft Point | V | 1 | 24 | 3240 | 2747 | 2304 | 1905 | 1554 | 1270 | 1282 | 921 | 648 | 443 | 295 | 197 | 0.3 | 0.8 | 0 | -2.2 | -6.0 | -11.4 | 1.7 | 2.0 | 0 | -4.1... | | | |
| 243 Winchester | X243W2 | 100 | Power-Point | D/O/P | 2 | 24 | 2960 | 2697 | 2449 | 2215 | 1993 | 1786 | 1945 | 1615 | 1332 | 1089 | 882 | 708 | 0.3 | 0.9 | 1.6 | 0 | -3.1 | -7.8 | 2.9 | 2.9 | 2.1 | 0 | -3.6 | -16.2 | -37.9 |
| 25-06 Remington | X25061 | 90 | Positive Expanding Point | D/O/P | 2 | 24 | 3440 | 3043 | 2680 | 2344 | 2034 | 1749 | 2364 | 1850 | 1435 | 1098 | 837 | 611 | 0.3 | 0.6 | 2.4 | 0 | -4.5 | -8.8 | 2.4 | 2.7 | 2.0 | 0 | -3.4 | -15.0 | -35.2 |
| 25-06 Remington | X25062 | 120 | Positive Expanding Point | D/O/P | 2 | 24 | 2990 | 2730 | 2484 | 2252 | 2032 | 1825 | 2382 | 1985 | 1644 | 1351 | 1100 | 887 | 0.8 | 0 | -2.1 | -5.6 | -10.7 | 1.9 | 2.1 | 1.4 | 0 | -3.0 | -7.5 | -22.0 | -44.8 |
| 25-35 Winchester | X2535 | 117 | Soft Point | D | 2 | 24 | 2230 | 1866 | 1545 | 1282 | 1097 | 984 | 1292 | 904 | 620 | 427 | 313 | 252 | 0.6 | 0 | -3.1 | -9.2 | -19.0 | -33.1 | 2.1 | 0 | -5.1 | -13.8 | -27.0 | -70.1 | -142.0 |
| 6.5 x 55 Swedish | X6555 | 140 | Soft Point | D/O/P | 3 | 24 | 2550 | 2359 | 2176 | 2002 | 1836 | 1680 | 2022 | 1731 | 1473 | 1244 | 1048 | 878 | 0.4 | 0 | -1.5 | -4.8 | -9.8 | -16.9 | 2.4 | 2.3 | 0 | -3.9 | -9.7 | -28.1 | -56.8 |
| 270 Winchester | X2705 | 130 | Power-Point | D/O/P | 3 | 24 | 3060 | 2802 | 2559 | 2329 | 2110 | 1904 | 2702 | 2267 | 1890 | 1565 | 1285 | 1046 | 0.4 | 0.8 | 0 | -2.0 | -5.5 | -10.1 | 1.8 | 2.4 | 0 | -2.8 | -7.1 | -21.6 | -42.0 |
| 270 Winchester | X2703 | 130 | Silvertip | D/O/P | 3 | 24 | 3060 | 2776 | 2510 | 2259 | 2022 | 1801 | 2702 | 2225 | 1818 | 1472 | 1180 | 936 | 0.5 | 0.8 | 0 | -2.0 | -5.5 | -10.4 | 1.8 | 2.3 | 0 | -2.9 | -7.4 | -21.6 | -44.3 |
| 270 Winchester | X2704 | 150 | Power-Point | D/O/P/PA | 3 | 24 | 2850 | 2585 | 2336 | 2100 | 1879 | 1673 | 2705 | 2226 | 1817 | 1468 | 1175 | 932 | 0.6 | 1.0 | 0 | -2.4 | -6.4 | -12.2 | 2.2 | 1.8 | 0 | -3.4 | -8.6 | -25.0 | -51.4 |
| 284 Winchester | X2842 | 150 | Power-Point | D/O/P/PA | 3 | 24 | 2860 | 2595 | 2344 | 2108 | 1886 | 1680 | 2724 | 2243 | 1830 | 1480 | 1185 | 940 | 0.6 | 1.0 | 0 | -2.4 | -6.4 | -12.1 | 2.1 | 1.8 | 0 | -3.5 | -8.8 | -24.8 | -51.0 |
| 7mm-08 Remington (NEW) | X708 | 140 | Power-Point | D/O/P | 2 | 24 | 2800 | 2523 | 2268 | 2027 | 1802 | 1596 | 2429 | 1980 | 1599 | 1280 | 1010 | 797 | -0.1 | 0 | -1.2 | -4.0 | -8.4 | -14.7 | 2.0 | 1.8 | 0 | -3.4 | -8.8 | -26.0 | -54.0 |
| 7mm Remington Mag. | X7MMR1 | 150 | Power-Point | D/O/P/PA | 3 | 24 | 3110 | 2830 | 2568 | 2320 | 2085 | 1866 | 3221 | 2667 | 2196 | 1792 | 1448 | 1160 | 0.4 | 0.8 | 0 | -1.9 | -5.2 | -9.9 | 1.7 | 2.0 | 0 | -2.8 | -7.0 | -20.5 | -42.1 |
| 7mm Remington Mag. | X7MMR2 | 175 | Power-Point | D/O/P/PA | 3 | 24 | 2860 | 2645 | 2440 | 2244 | 2057 | 1879 | 3178 | 2718 | 2313 | 1956 | 1644 | 1371 | 0.6 | 0.9 | 0 | -2.3 | -6.0 | -11.3 | 2.0 | 1.7 | 0 | -3.2 | -7.9 | -22.7 | -45.8 |
| 7.62 x 39mm Russian | X76239 | 123 | Soft Point | D,V | 2 | 20 | 1990 | 1567 | 1236 | 1035 | 923 | 842 | 1527 | 1129 | 818 | 586 | 425 | 327 | 0.3 | 0 | -2.6 | -7.6 | -15.4 | -26.7 | 3.8 | 3.1 | 0 | -6.0 | -15.4 | -44.3 | -90.4 |
| 30 Carbine # | X30M1 | 110 | Hollow Soft Point | D | 2 | 20 | 1990 | 1567 | 1236 | 1035 | 923 | 842 | 967 | 600 | 373 | 260 | 208 | 173 | 0.9 | 0 | -4.5 | -13.5 | -28.3 | -49.9 | 4.5 | 0 | -13.5 | -28.3 | -118.6 | -228.2 |
| 30-30 Winchester | X30301 | 150 | Hollow Point | D | 2 | 24 | 2390 | 2018 | 1684 | 1398 | 1177 | 1036 | 1902 | 1356 | 944 | 651 | 461 | 357 | 0.4 | 0 | -2.6 | -7.7 | -16.0 | -27.9 | 1.7 | 0 | -4.3 | -11.6 | -23.7 | -59.1 | -120.5 |
| 30-30 Winchester | X30306 | 150 | Power-Point | D | 2 | 24 | 2390 | 2018 | 1684 | 1398 | 1177 | 1036 | 1902 | 1356 | 944 | 651 | 461 | 357 | 0.4 | 0 | -2.6 | -7.7 | -16.0 | -27.9 | 1.7 | 0 | -4.3 | -11.6 | -23.7 | -59.1 | -120.5 |
| 30-30 Winchester | X30303 | 150 | Silvertip | D | 2 | 24 | 2390 | 2018 | 1684 | 1398 | 1177 | 1036 | 1902 | 1356 | 944 | 651 | 461 | 357 | 0.4 | 0 | -2.6 | -7.7 | -16.0 | -27.9 | 1.7 | 0 | -4.3 | -11.6 | -23.7 | -59.1 | -120.5 |
| 30-30 Winchester | X30304 | 170 | Power-Point | D/O/P/PA | 3 | 24 | 2200 | 1895 | 1619 | 1381 | 1191 | 1061 | 1827 | 1355 | 989 | 720 | 535 | 425 | 0.8 | 0 | -2.9 | -8.9 | -18.0 | -31.1 | 2.0 | 0 | -4.8 | -13.0 | -25.1 | -63.6 | -126.7 |
| 30-30 Winchester | X30062 | 125 | Pointed Soft Point | V | 1 | 24 | 3140 | 2780 | 2447 | 2138 | 1853 | 1595 | 2736 | 2145 | 1662 | 1269 | 953 | 706 | 0.8 | 0 | -2.4 | -6.6 | -12.7 | 1.8 | 2.0 | 0 | -3.0 | -7.7 | -23.0 | -48.5 |
| 30-06 Springfield | X30061 | 150 | Power-Point | D/O/P | 2 | 24 | 2920 | 2580 | 2265 | 1972 | 1704 | 1466 | 2839 | 2217 | 1708 | 1301 | 967 | 716 | 1.0 | 0 | -2.4 | -6.3 | -12.0 | 1.8 | 2.1 | 0 | -3.5 | -9.0 | -27.0 | -57.1 |
| 30-06 Springfield | X30063 | 165 | Pointed Soft Point | D/O/P/PA | 3 | 24 | 2910 | 2617 | 2342 | 2083 | 1843 | 1622 | 2820 | 2281 | 1827 | 1445 | 1131 | 876 | 1.0 | 0 | -2.3 | -6.3 | -12.0 | 2.1 | 1.8 | 0 | -3.4 | -8.5 | -25.0 | -51.8 |
| 30-06 Springfield | X30064 | 180 | Power-Point | D/O/P/PA | 3 | 24 | 2700 | 2348 | 2023 | 1727 | 1466 | 1251 | 2913 | 2203 | 1635 | 1192 | 859 | 625 | 0.2 | 0 | -3.5 | -9.3 | -18.3 | 2.3 | 1.9 | 0 | -4.4 | -11.3 | -34.4 | -73.7 |
| 30-06 Springfield | X30066 | 180 | Silvertip | D/O/P/ALL | 3 | 24 | 2700 | 2469 | 2250 | 2042 | 1846 | 1663 | 2913 | 2436 | 2023 | 1666 | 1362 | 1105 | 0.2 | 0 | -2.1 | -5.7 | -11.0 | 2.4 | 2.0 | 0 | -3.7 | -9.3 | -27.0 | -54.9 |
| 300 Winchester Mag. | X30WM1 | 180 | Power-Point | D/O/P | 3 | 24 | 3070 | 2951 | 2636 | 2342 | 2068 | 1813 | 3605 | 3011 | 2578 | 2196 | 1859 | 1565 | 0.7 | 0 | -1.8 | -4.8 | -9.6 | 2.6 | 2.4 | 0 | -3.2 | -8.8 | -16.6 | -35.5 |
| 300 Winchester Mag. | X30WM2 | 190 | Silvertip | D/O/P/ALL | 3 | 24 | 2885 | 2691 | 2506 | 2327 | 2156 | 1979 | 3511 | 3055 | 2648 | 2285 | 1961 | 1674 | 0.4 | 0 | -2.1 | -5.5 | -11.0 | 2.3 | 2.0 | 0 | -3.5 | -10.4 | -15.4 | -41.9 |
| 303 British | X303B1 | 180 | Power-Point | D | 2 | 24 | 2460 | 2124 | 1817 | 1542 | 1311 | 1137 | 2418 | 1803 | 1319 | 950 | 687 | 516 | 1.4 | 0 | -3.3 | -9.2 | -18.0 | -29.9 | 2.6 | 0 | -5.1 | -13.8 | -27.4 | -77.4 |
| 307 Winchester | X3076 | 180 | Power-Point | D/M | 2 | 20 | 2510 | 2179 | 1874 | 1599 | 1362 | 1177 | 2519 | 1898 | 1404 | 1022 | 742 | 554 | 1.4 | 0 | -3.6 | -10.2 | -20.8 | -33.2 | 2.8 | 0 | -5.6 | -15.4 | -31.8 | -93.7 |
| 308 Winchester | X3085 | 150 | Power-Point | D/O/P | 2 | 24 | 2820 | 2488 | 2179 | 1893 | 1633 | 1405 | 2648 | 2061 | 1581 | 1193 | 888 | 657 | 1.0 | 0 | -2.6 | -6.9 | -13.5 | 2.0 | 2.3 | 0 | -3.8 | -9.8 | -29.3 | -62.0 |
| 308 Winchester | X3086 | 180 | Power-Point | D/O/P/PA | 3 | 24 | 2620 | 2274 | 1955 | 1666 | 1414 | 1212 | 2743 | 2066 | 1527 | 1109 | 799 | 587 | 0.2 | 0 | -3.6 | -9.5 | -18.2 | 2.9 | 2.6 | 0 | -4.7 | -12.1 | -36.9 | -79.1 |
| 308 Winchester | X3083 | 180 | Silvertip | ALL | 3 | 24 | 2620 | 2393 | 2178 | 1974 | 1782 | 1604 | 2743 | 2288 | 1896 | 1557 | 1269 | 1028 | 0.2 | 0 | -3.2 | -6.4 | -10.4 | -17.7 | 2.6 | 2.1 | 0 | -4.9 | -12.1 | -38.9 | -58.8 |
| 32 Win Special | X32WS2 | 170 | Power-Point | D | 2 | 20 | 2250 | 1870 | 1537 | 1267 | 1082 | 971 | 1911 | 1320 | 892 | 606 | 442 | 356 | 0.6 | 0 | -3.1 | -9.2 | -19.0 | -33.2 | 2.0 | 0 | -5.1 | -13.8 | -27.1 | -70.9 | -144.3 |
| 32-20 Winchester # | X32201 | 100 | Lead | D | 2 | 24 | 1210 | 1021 | 913 | 834 | 769 | 712 | 325 | 231 | 185 | 154 | 131 | 113 | -4.3 | -20.9 | -44.9 | 0 | -11.5 | -32.3 | -63.6 | 106.3 | -220.3 | -413.3 |
| 8mm Mauser (8 x 57) | X8MM | 170 | Power-Point | D | 2 | 24 | 2360 | 1969 | 1622 | 1333 | 1123 | 997 | 2102 | 1463 | 993 | 671 | 476 | 375 | 0.5 | 0 | -2.7 | -8.2 | -17.0 | -29.8 | 1.8 | 0 | -4.5 | -12.4 | -24.3 | -63.8 | -130.7 |
| 338 Winchester Mag. | X3381 | 200 | Power-Point | D/O/P/ALL | 3 | 24 | 2960 | 2658 | 2375 | 2110 | 1862 | 1635 | 3890 | 3137 | 2505 | 1977 | 1539 | 1187 | 1.7 | 0 | -3.2 | -8.2 | -24.3 | 1.7 | 2.0 | 0 | -6.7 | -23.4 | -50.4 |
| 35 Remington | X35R1 | 200 | Power-Point | D/M | 2 | 24 | 2020 | 1646 | 1335 | 1114 | 985 | 901 | 1812 | 1216 | 791 | 551 | 431 | 360 | 2.7 | 0 | -7.0 | -12.1 | -43.9 | -5.5 | -16.2 | -33.8 | -185.5 |
| 356 Winchester | X3561 | 200 | Power-Point | D/M | 2 | 20 | 2460 | 2114 | 1797 | 1517 | 1284 | 1113 | 2688 | 1985 | 1434 | 1022 | 732 | 550 | 1.6 | 0 | -4.3 | -2.3 | -24.7 | -6.2 | -10.4 | -51.2 | -102.3 |
| 357 Magnum # | X3575P | 158 | Jacketed Soft Point | VD | 2 | 20 | 1830 | 1427 | 1138 | 980 | 883 | 809 | 1175 | 715 | 399 | 337 | 274 | 229 | -2.4 | 0 | -9.1 | -21.0 | -44.3 | -13.1 | -57.0 | -128.3 | -258.8 |
| 375 Winchester | X375W | 200 | Silvertip Hollow Point | VD | 3 | 20 | 2150 | 1841 | 1564 | 1288 | 1089 | 980 | 2150 | 1506 | 1088 | 714 | 525 | 427 | 2.1 | 0 | -3.2 | -9.5 | -33.8 | -7.7 | -27.4 | -76.1 | -138.1 |
| 38-40 Winchester # | X3840 | 180 | Hollow Soft Point | D | 2 | 20 | 538 | 399 | 324 | 714 | | | | | | | | | | | | | | | | | | | | |
| 38-55 Winchester | X3855 | 255 | Soft Point | D | 2 | 24 | 1160 | 999 | 901 | 827 | 764 | 710 | 987 | 802 | 638 | 460 | 324 | 201 | 0.6 | 0 | -23.4 | -47.3 | -83.2 | -41.6 | -110.6 | -238.3 | -425.6 |
| 44 Remington Magnum # | X44MHSP | 210 | Silvertip Hollow Point | VD | 2 | 20 | 1320 | 1190 | 1091 | 1018 | 953 | 901 | 1164 | 660 | 494 | 394 | 300 | 332 | -2.7 | 0 | -10.8 | -22.2 | -150.3 | -66.4 | -238.3 | -305.8 |
| 44 Remington Magnum # | X44MHSP2 | 240 | Hollow Soft Point | D | 2 | 20 | 1760 | 1362 | 1094 | 953 | 861 | 789 | 1650 | 988 | 638 | 481 | 395 | 332 | -6.5 | 0 | -6.1 | -18.1 | -44.2 | -65.1 | -181.0 | -282.5 |
| 44-40 Winchester # | X4440 | 200 | Soft Point | D | 2 | 24 | 629 | 449 | 360 | 254 | 217 | | | | | | | | | | | | | | | | | | | |
| 45-70 Government | X4570H | 300 | Jacketed Hollow Point | D/M | 2 | 24 | 2335 | 1650 | 1425 | 1235 | 1105 | 1010 | 2355 | 1815 | 1355 | 1015 | 810 | 680 | -2.4 | 0 | -12.8 | -33.3 | -51.5 | -4.6 | -25.4 | -95.3 | -426.2 |

## AMMUNITION

A-Square Company, Inc. (also rifles)
One Industrial Park
Bedford KY 40006

Black Hills Ammunition, Inc.
P.O. Box 3090
Rapid City SD 57709

Dynamit Nobel-RWS.Inc. (Norma)
81 Ruckman Road
Closter NJ 07624

Federal Cartridge Company
900 Ehlen Drive
Anoka MN 55303

Hansen Cartridge Company
244-246 Old Post Road
Southport CT 06490

Old Western Scrounger, Inc.
(Norma, RWS, Kynoch, obsolete ctgs.)
12924 Highway A-12
Montague CA 96064

PMC Ammunition
12801 US Highway 95 South
Boulder City NV 89005

Remington Arms Company, Inc.
870 Remington Drive
Madison NC 27025

Superior Ammunition
1320 Cedar St.
Sturgis SD 57785

Weatherby, Inc.
3100 El Camino Real
Atascadero CA 93422

Winchester Ammunition
Olin Corp.
427 North Shamrock St.
East Alton IL 62024

## BULLETS

A-Square Company, Inc.
One Industrial Park
Bedford KY 40006

Barnes Bullets, Inc.
P.O. Box 215
American Fork UT 84003

Berger Bullets, Ltd.
5342 West Camelback, Suite 200
Glendale AZ 85301

Blue Mountain Bullets
HCR 77 Box 231
John Day OR 97845

Cor-Bon Bullet Co.
1311 Industry Rd.
Sturgis SD 57785

Hawk Laboratories, Inc.
Box 112, Station 27
Lakewood CO 80215

Hornady Manufacturing Company
P.O. Box 1848
Grand Island NE 68802

Jensen Bullets
86 N. 400 W.
Blackfoot ID 83221

Northern Precision
337 S. James St.
Carthage NY 13619

Nosler, Inc.
P.O. Box 671
Bend OR 97709

Sierra Bullets
1400 West Henry St.
Sedalia MO 65301

Speer-Blount, Inc.
Omark Industries
2299 Snake River Ave., P.O. Box 856
Lewiston ID 83501

Swift Bullet Company
201 Main St., P.O. Box 27
Quinter KS 67752

Western Nevada West Coast Bullet Co.
2307 West Washington St.
Carson City NV 89703

## POWDERS

Accurate Arms Company, Inc.
5891 Highway 230 West, P.O. Box 167
McEwen TN 37101

Hercules Incorporated
Hercules Plaza
Wilmington DE 19894

Hodgdon Powder Company, Inc.
6231 Robinson, P.O. Box 2932
Shawnee Mission KS 66201

IMR Powder Company
Dept. R
RD #5, Box 247A
Plattsburgh NY 12901

Scot Powder Company of Ohio, Inc.
430 Powder Plant Road
McArthur OH 45651

Vihtavuori Oy
Kaltron-Pettibone
1241 Ellis St.
Bensenville IL 60106

Winchester
Olin Corp.
427 North Shamrock St.
East Alton IL 62024

## RELOADING EQUIPMENT

Brass Extrusion Labs Ltd.
4350 South Arville, Suite 3
Las Vegas NV 89103

Dillon Precision Products Inc.
8009 East Dillon's Way
Scottsdale AZ 85260

Forster Products, Inc. (Bonanza)
82 East Lanark Avenue
Lanark IL 61046

Hornady Manufacturing Company
P.O. Box 1848
Grand Island NE 68802

Huntington Die Specialties
601 Oro Dam Boulevard, P.O. Box 991
Oroville CA 95965

Lyman Products Corporation
475 Smith St.
Middlefield CT 06457

RCBS-Blount, Inc.
605 Oro Dam Blvd.
Oroville CA 95965

Redding Reloading Equipment
1089 Starr Road
Cortland NY 13045

Sinclair International, Inc.
2330 Wayne Haven St.
Fort Wayne IN 46803

Stoney Point Products, Inc.
1815 North Spring St.
New Ulm MN 56073-0234

Pro-Hunter, 55
Simpson, Layne, 106
Simpson, Leslie, 230
Sizing, 44-45
Smith, Bushnell, 79
Smith, Gilbert, 8
Smith, Horace W., 13, 14, 176, 218-219
Smith, Thomas, 219
Smith & Wesson, 219-220, 222
Smokeless powder, evolution of, 10-11,
    17-20, 51
Smoothbores, 23, 32
Snider coiled cartridge, 14
Sorensen, Maynard, 183
Souper .25, 180-181, 187
Speer, 57, 136, 164, 186, 216, 270-271
    .22 bullets, 77
    centerfire bullets, 21
    Grand Slam, 28, 55-57, 216, 230, 244
Speer, Dick, 16
Speer, Ray, 120
Spitzer bullet, 26, 53
Springfield, 38, 147
    .30-06, 17, 18, 114-115, 198
    1903 rifle, 35, 36, 112, 210-211
Stainless steel, 35
Star gauging, 38
Staynless primer, 15
Stekl, Jim, 81
Steyr-Mannlicher, 72
Subrero, Ascanio, 9
Sulfur, 3, 10, 18
Sundra, Jon, 153
Swift A-Frame, 136
Swift bullet, 55, 57, 117, 149
Swift .220 (the Rocket), 35, 76, 78-80, 96,
    192, 234, 240
Swiggett, Hal, 12

**T**

Taylor .416, 166
Taylor, Stephen, 13
Theiss breechloader, 8
Thompson/Center, 4, 10, 138
    Contender, 12, 252
Tomcat .25-35, 180
Topperwein, Ad, 217, 218
Trophy Bonded, 30, 53, 58, 230, 231,
    242, 244
Trophy Bonded Bear Claw, 56, 117, 230, 236

**U**

Ultra Light Arms Model 20, 102
United States Powder Company, 17
United States Repeating Arms
    Company, 97, 224

**V**

Van Horn .423, 189
Van Horn, Gil, 189
Varminter (see Remington .22-250)
Varmintmaster, 76
Vauquelin, Nicolas Louis, 5
Velocity, 59-60, 62
Vibra-Tek, 41
Vickers .242 Belted Rimless Nitro Express, 83
Vielle, Paul, 10

Volitional Repeater, 7
Volkmann, Frederick, 11
von Dreyse, Johann Nikolaus, 8

**W**

Walker, Samuel, 219
Wallack, L.R. "Bob," 187
Waters 7-30, 97-98
Waters, Ken, 97
Weatherby
    .30-378, 65
    .30-378 Magnum, 120-121
    .224 Magnum, 76-78, 79
    .228 Magnum, 76
    .240 Magnum, 85, 114
    .257 Magnum, 90, 96, 235-239, 246
    .270 Magnum, 96-97, 234-239, 246
    .300 Magnum, 15, 119-120, 213,
        238, 246, 253
    .338-.378, 187
    .340 Magnum, 126-128, 136, 248
    .375 Magnum, 141, 142, 153
    .378 Magnum, 142, 152, 153
    .416 Magnum, 145, 248
    .460 Magnum, 67, 149-150, 155, 175, 248
    7mm Magnum, 96, 102, 105, 236, 237, 246
    ballistics tables, 304
    Mark V, 33, 38, 85, 120, 127,
        142, 145, 149, 152
    Swift .220 (the Rocket), 35, 76,
        78-80, 96, 192, 234, 240
    Vanguard, 33
    Wright-Hoyer, 120-121
Weatherby, Roy, 16, 38, 76, 85, 90, 96, 103,
    105, 115, 117, 119, 120, 141, 142, 145,
    149, 183, 189, 203, 212, 229, 234, 236,
    237, 246
Wesson, Daniel B., 13, 14, 176, 218-219
Wesson, Edwin, 219
Western Cartridge Company, 27, 52,
    115, 139, 194, 195
Western Tool and Copper Works, 54
Westley Richards Company, 6, 9, 171
    .425, 143, 168, 231
Wheel locks, 4-5, 8
Whelen
    .35, 55, 101, 124, 133, 134, 164, 225-227,
        229, 230, 231, 244-245, 248, 257
    .375 Improved, 187-188
    .400, 227
Whelen, Townsend, 67, 87, 133, 227, 244
White, Rollin, 219
White powder, 10
Whitworth, Joseph, 25-26, 33
Wichita Arms, 39
Williams .350, 231
Winchester, 36
    .25.20, 20, 193
    .25.35, 193
    .30-06, 83, 101, 241
    .30-30, 107-108
    .33, 196, 198
    .35, 196, 198, 225, 226
    .38-55, 137, 138, 197
    .44-40, 14
    .225, 68, 76, 78, 79
    .243, 68, 78, 83, 84, 86, 89,

        100, 128, 182, 257
    .270, 95-96, 101, 111, 183, 195,
        235, 236, 239, 241-242, 248
    .284, 101-102, 185
    .307, 111-112
    .308, 23, 76, 83, 100, 101, 108, 111-113,
        123, 128, 132, 162, 182, 187, 228, 229,
        242-243, 247, 248
    .348, 128-129, 146, 191, 228
    .356, 130-131, 196, 201, 228, 231
    .358, 100, 132, 134, 136, 187,
        191, 225, 227-230
    .375, 137-138, 197
    .401, 198
    .405, 191, 195-198, 244
    .485, 28
    ballistics tables, 305
    Fail Safe, 28, 56-59, 117, 202, 242
    Hornet .22, 20
    Magnum .264, 94-95, 96, 103, 126,
        157, 182, 229, 232-239, 246
    Magnum .300, 15, 65, 94, 117-118, 157,
        203, 205-207, 213, 214, 229, 245, 246
    Magnum .338, 94, 124-128, 135, 136, 157,
        187, 203, 205, 227, 229, 232, 233, 246
    Magnum .458, 126, 145, 148-149, 165, 169,
        170, 172, 189, 207, 229, 232, 246-248
    Magnum Rimfire .22, 222
    Model 07, 198, 226
    Model 10, 198
    Model 54, 80, 98, 162, 240, 241
    Model 64, 71, 192
    Model 66, 13
    Model 70, 35, 69, 78, 80, 83, 84, 87, 94,
        96, 98, 104, 112, 115, 126, 129, 165, 187,
        192, 201, 202, 206, 209, 212, 233, 235,
        240, 243
        Featherweight, 94, 132, 228, 242
    Model 71, 128, 228
    Model 74, 224
    Model 86, 205
    Model 88, 101, 112, 128, 132, 228
    Model 89, 250
    Model 94, 107, 108, 111, 112, 130, 131,
        137, 193, 201, 205, 207, 228, 230
        Angle Eject, 97, 111, 130, 131, 230
        Big Bore, 137, 225
    Model 95, 111, 196, 210
    Model 100, 101
    Model 336, 111, 112
    Model 1885, 5, 18, 111, 147, 193
    Model 1886, 147, 187, 196
    Model 1895, 198
    Power Point, 41, 57, 58
    Precision Point, 54
    Silvertip, 54, 58
    Staynless primer, 15
Winchester, Oliver, 176
Wind, 60, 62, 254-256
Wiseman, Bill, 37, 38
Wotkyns, Grosvenor, 67, 80, 240
Wright, Paul, 121

**Z**

Zeglan, Fred, 188
Zipper .219, 69-71, 78, 158, 178, 192, 193